Lyric Poetry by Women of
the Italian Renaissance

Lyric Poetry by Women of the Italian Renaissance

Virginia Cox

THE JOHNS HOPKINS UNIVERSITY PRESS
Baltimore

© 2013 The Johns Hopkins University Press
All rights reserved. Published 2013
Printed in the United States of America on acid-free paper
2 4 6 8 9 7 5 3 1

The Johns Hopkins University Press
2715 North Charles Street
Baltimore, Maryland 21218-4363
www.press.jhu.edu

Library of Congress Cataloging-in-Publication Data

Cox, Virginia.
Lyric poetry by women of the Italian Renaissance / Virginia Cox.
p. cm.
Includes bibliographical references and index.
ISBN 978-1-4214-0887-3 (hardcover : acid-free paper) — ISBN 978-1-4214-0888-0 (pbk. : acid-free
paper) — ISBN 978-1-4214-0950-4 (electronic) — ISBN 1-4214-0887-2 (hardcover : acid-free paper)
— ISBN 1-4214-0888-0 (pbk. : acid-free paper) — ISBN 1-4214-0950-X (electronic)
1. Italian poetry—Women authors.   2. Italian poetry—15th century—Translations into English.
3. Italian poetry—16th century—Translations into English.   4. Women and literature—Italy—
History—15th century.   5. Women and literature—Italy—History—16th century.   I. Title.
PQ4209.C69 2013
851'.2099287—dc21   2012036067

A catalog record for this book is available from the British Library.

*Special discounts are available for bulk purchases of this book. For more information, please contact
Special Sales at 410-516-6936 or specialsales@press.jhu.edu.*

The Johns Hopkins University Press uses environmentally friendly book materials,
including recycled text paper that is composed of at least 30 percent post-consumer
waste, whenever possible.

Contents

Amorous Verse

In vita

In morte

Ventriloquized Love Poetry

Religious Verse

Correspondence Verse

Encomia of Rulers and Patrons

Political Verse

Polemical and Manifesto Verse

Verse of Friendship and Family Love

In vita

Other in morte *Verse*

Verse of Place and Selfhood

Comic and Dialect Verse

Acknowledgments

My first acknowledgment for this anthology must go to my former editor at the Johns Hopkins University Press, the late Henry Tom, whose idea it originally was. It is a sad thought indeed, given his exemplary supportiveness as an editor, that Henry is no longer here to see the result of his suggestion. I can only hope that he would have been pleased to see his legacy as editor continuing in this way.

Over this project's long period of gestation, I had the pleasure of working through portions of its material with several talented groups of graduate students, most notably during the course "Lyric Poetry from Petrarch to Marino," which I taught at New York University in spring 2011. I owe special thanks to Bryan Brazeau and Valerie Hoagland for bringing a poem of Lucia Colao's to my attention that now finds a place in this anthology (no. 100), and to Erika Mazzer and Joe Perna for critical insights on individual poems. My discussions of Vittoria Colonna's love lyrics with Shannon McHugh were useful in encouraging me to return to this body of verse and to expand my selection from it, while my work on Isabella Cervoni with Anna Wainwright prompted me to revisit her verse and to include extracts from no. 165, which I had not previously planned. I would also like to thank Danielle Callegari, Shannon McHugh, Melissa Swain, and Paola Ugolini for research assistance at various points in the course of the preparation of the manuscript; Paolo Bà for supplying me with transcriptions of nos. 129 and 211, from manuscript sources; Brett Wisniewski for checking my translations of the Latin verse included in the anthology; and Benjamin Sammons for checking the Greek text of 170. My major debt in the final stages of preparation of the manuscript was to Anna Wainwright, who worked with great dedication checking the text and appendixes and saved me numerous errors along the way.

My other principal debts are to colleagues and friends who have edited some of the poets included in this anthology for the series The Other Voice in Early Modern Europe, published originally by the University of Chicago

Press and now by the Centre for Reformation and Renaissance Studies, Toronto. These scholars generously reviewed my draft selections from "their" poets and made comments and suggestions. Julia Hairston looked over the Tullia d'Aragona section; Victoria Kirkham the selections from Laura Battiferri; and Jane Tylus those from Gaspara Stampa. I would also like to thank Gerry Milligan for reading and commenting on my selection of political verse, and Alison Smith for her comments on my notes on Ersilia Spolverini's no. 154. Several poems included in the anthology owe their place to these consultations, notably nos. 92, 161, 163, and 198.

Toward the end of the time of my work on the anthology, I had the great pleasure of discussing some of the portrait and image-related poems in the anthology with Lina Bolzoni in the context of a graduate course on poetry and portraiture she gave in my department. A legacy of these conversations was my late decision to include Lucrezia Marinella's delightfully eccentric no. 117. Other late debts are to Konrad Eisenbichler, who kindly let me have access to files of his edition of Virginia Salvi and his book *The Sword and the Pen* (both listed in the bibliography) prior to their publication, and to Philippa Jackson, who generously shared with me findings from her archival research on Siena relevant to the biographies of the Sienese poets included here.

Despite all this invaluable help and input, all editorial choices, translation from Italian and Latin texts, and commentary in this volume are entirely my responsibility, so that remaining errors must be laid at my door. The translation of Olimpia Morata, "οὔποτε μὲν ξυμπᾶσιν ἐνὶ φρεσὶν ἥνδανε ταὐτὸ" (no. 170), is by Holt Parker, from *The Complete Writings of an Italian Heretic*, published by University of Chicago Press, ©2003 The University of Chicago, used with permission.

INTRODUCTION

The "splendor and marvel of our age"

In a lecture on the modern Italian literary tradition delivered before a prestigious Roman academy in 1563, the Mantuan poet Curzio Gonzaga (1536–99) identified as one of that tradition's great claims to distinction the presence of women as writers within its ranks. If antiquity gloried so greatly in the single figure of Sappho, how much more so should present-day Italy, equipped with a plethora of female literary luminaries, "the splendor and marvel of the age"?[1] Gonzaga was not alone in this perception. A letter of 1546 by an admirer of the Neapolitan poet Laura Terracina (1519–c. 1577) lists the emergence of intellectual women as one of the glories of the modern age, along with the revival of letters, military discipline, sculpture, and architecture: all arts that had flourished in classical antiquity, but which had since been "long buried by the barbarian assaults."[2] By the second half of the sixteenth century, the production of women of intellectual distinction had become an important source of cultural boasting rights for Italian cities, along with existing topoi of civic pride such as the splendors of their artistic tradition and the prowess of their male citizens in letters and arms. An oration of 1597 on the glories of Verona fulsomely congratulates the city on its tradition of "women excellent in the most superlative grade, who have filled the world with wonderment, and shown that the female sex is as capable of learning any difficult and obscure doctrine as the male."[3]

Although we would be less inclined today to dismiss the Middle Ages as a period of "barbarism," in which icons of civilization such as the literate woman had no opportunity to flourish, this contemporary perception of sixteenth-century Italy as a golden age of female intellectual attainment still commands much credibility. Despite the impressive legacy of female intellectual and literary activity scholars have reconstructed within the convents and courts of medieval Europe, there is nothing in that period that can compete, in terms of chronological and geographic concentration, with the extraordinary tradition of female writing that grew up in Italy from the fifteenth century, reaching its peak in the sixteenth and the first decades of the seventeenth. It was during these centuries in Italy that the figure of the secular female writer, in particular, emerged into the mainstream of European culture, and that women writers went from the status of rare and miraculous, "phoenix-like" exceptions to an accepted and expected social subset of literary practitioners—tiny, of course, in terms of numbers, by comparison with men, but punching well above their weight in terms of cultural visibility, precisely on account of their novelty. The rhetoric of exceptionalism lingered long, and it is not hard to find female writers lauded as sex-transcending "monsters of Nature" well into the seventeenth century. At the same time, it is not difficult to point to gestures indicating a consciousness of women's writing as a quantitatively significant phenomenon. The first anthology of female-authored verse appeared in Italy in 1559, the first biographical dictionary of female writers in 1620.[4]

While the emergence of women as writers in the early modern period was to some extent a pan-European phenomenon, Italy may nonetheless be seen as exceptional in the richness of its tradition of women's writing, at least down to around 1650. Some indication of Italy's dominance in this field may be seen in Axel Erdmann's 1999 study, *My Gracious Silence*, which contains a geographical breakdown of female writers whose works appeared in print between 1500 and 1600. Italy heads the list with around two hundred named writers, some figuring with a single poem or a handful of poems in an anthology, but others authoring entire verse collections or letter collections, treatises, dialogues, and works of narrative fiction and drama.[5] By comparison, for the same period, Erdmann lists thirty published women writers for France, twenty names for Germany, seventeen for England, thirteen for Spain and Portugal, and three for the Netherlands.[6]

Some caution needs to be applied when assessing these striking statistics, which include only printed works, not ones that circulated exclusively in manuscript. Printing was far more widely diffused in Italy than elsewhere, with presses operating even in quite small towns. This made print publication a viable option for far greater numbers of women than was the case elsewhere in Europe, so that it may be fairly assumed that printed works constitute a higher percentage of women's total output in Italy than elsewhere.[7] Even with this caveat, however, it seems safe to assert that women's writing was a far more salient phenomenon in Italy than it was elsewhere in Europe. An idea of the extent of the phenomenon may be had from the appendix to my 2008 study, *Women's Writing in Italy, 1400–1650*, listing single-authored printed works by Italian women published in the sixteenth and seventeenth centuries. This has seventy-nine entries for the period 1540–99 and an additional seventy-one for 1600–1659.[8]

The intention of the present anthology is to make accessible to both an Italian-reading and a non-Italian-reading public one important segment of Italian women's literary production in this period: secular and religious lyric poetry. Although women wrote in a wide range of literary genres, especially in the late sixteenth and early seventeenth centuries, lyric poetry has a good claim to be regarded as the core genre of early modern Italian women's writing. It was virtually the sole genre of writing to which women dedicated themselves until around 1580, and even after that it remained an important part of their activity. Even writers better known for their narrative or dramatic works, such as Moderata Fonte (1555–92), Lucrezia Marinella (1579–1653) and Maddalena Campiglia (1553–95), left a sufficient quantity of high-quality lyric verse to merit inclusion in an anthology of this kind. As a result, although it is dedicated to a single genre of writing, this anthology may serve more broadly as an introduction to Italian women's writing of the sixteenth and seventeenth centuries, giving a sense both of the broad outlines of its development over this period, and of the outstanding figures of the tradition. Only a handful of the most significant female writers of this era are missing from this anthology, principally Giulia Bigolina (c. 1518–69), Barbara Torelli Benedetti (1546–post 1603), Margherita Sarrocchi (c. 1560–1617), and Arcangela Tarabotti (1604–52), all of whom left little or no lyric verse.[9]

Before proceeding to a fuller description of the tradition of Italian women's writing in this period, it may be useful to say something further of the position female writers occupied within Italian literary culture at this time. A first point that needs to be emphasized, since modern scholarship has often presented early modern women writers as beleaguered and isolated figures, struggling against societal prescriptions that sought to silence them, is that, for most of the sixteenth century, Italian women writers enjoyed a remarkably supportive and appreciative environment, at least by the standards of the day. This is not to say that they enjoyed a position of equality with male writers, which would have been unthinkable in the period. Women were excluded from university education and received advanced instruction only in exceptional circumstances. They were also largely excluded from the literary academies that sprang up in every Italian town and city over the course of the sixteenth century and played a key role in the informal cultural education of the male social elite. Women's literary works won extravagant praise from their male peers, but this did not necessarily equate to their being taken seriously as intellectual equals. It could, in some cases, mean exactly the opposite, as the Lucchese poet Chiara Matraini (1515–1604) comments bitterly in a letter of the 1560s in which she begs a male correspondent to set aside his reflex reaction of praise in reading her work and to give her instead the benefit of a properly critical response, such as he might be prepared to accord to a man.[10]

Despite all these caveats, however, by premodern standards, sixteenth-century Italy may still be described as a remarkably favorable environment for women's intellectual activity, comparable in many respects to the better-known example of seventeenth-century France. As in seventeenth-century France, an affirmative attitude to women was a touchstone of civility, and gallantry was a defining element in male elite identity. Praise of exceptional women was an established discourse of the period, and praise of women writers an established subdiscourse. Poets such as Laura Terracina and Tullia d'Aragona could fill volumes, quite literally, with the outpourings of their male literary admirers. Maddalena Campiglia published a work in 1588 with an appendix of poems by twenty-seven male *letterati* in its praise.[11] However patronizing and superficial some of this adulation may seem to us today, it helped foster an environment in which women were inspired to write and publish, parents to educate their daughters to bring honor on the family, and literary academies to encourage local women writers in their activities in order to bring glory on their cities and towns. Some academies even offered formal membership to women, more than is generally acknowledged in the secondary literature. Keeping solely to women represented in this anthology, there is good evidence of academy membership for Terracina, Laura Battiferri (1523–89), Virginia Salvi (fl. 1551–75), Isabella Cervoni (1576–post 1600), Isabella Andreini (1562–1604), and Francesca Turina (1553–1641).[12] Tarquinia Molza (1542–1617) was awarded honorary citizenship of Rome. To have a sense of quite how exceptional the Italian sixteenth century was in this regard, we need only look forward to the seventeenth century, when, for reasons I have examined elsewhere, gender attitudes changed quite sharply, and a reborn misogyny reigned. The figure of the secular female writer, so familiar in the sixteenth century, disappeared from Italy for almost half a century after 1650, returning to vogue only with the Arcadian movement of the very late seventeenth century and the early eighteenth.[13]

Although the focus of this volume is women's contribution to literature, it may be useful to note that the favorable cultural conditions that allowed such a strong tradition of women's writing to emerge in sixteenth-century Italy also proved conducive to women's participation in other creative fields. This is especially true of music, where, building on earlier practices of female music-making in the courts and among courtesans, a strong tradition of female virtuoso vocal performance emerged in the later sixteenth and seventeenth centuries. To a lesser extent, women were also active in this same period as composers, some, like Francesca Caccini (1587–post 1641), attaining a considerable degree of fame. Meanwhile, women's place within the visual arts was established by the mid-sixteenth century by Sofonisba Anguissola (c. 1532–1625) and consolidated by later figures such as Lavinia Fontana (1552–1614) and Artemisia Gentileschi (1593–1653). Giorgio Vasari names thirteen female artists in the 1568 edition of his *Lives*. Women's presence was especially strong in the newer profession of acting, where they emerged from around the 1560s in the guise of both performers and managers. Acting and virtuoso singing in the late sixteenth and early seventeenth centuries in Italy represent rare cases of early modern artistic fields in which women were at least as prominent and celebrated as men.[14]

This broader creative context deserves to be recalled in an anthology of female poetry such as the present one. Of the poets presented in this volume, quite a number were noted singers or actresses, of various degrees of professionalism: most famously Gaspara Stampa (c. 1525–54) and Isabella Andreini, but also Barbara Salutati (fl. 1520s), Vincenza Armani (pre-1569), Leonora Bernardi (1559–1616), and Sarra Copio (c. 1600–41). Contacts between female poets and other virtuose are also well attested: Andreini's verse includes a poem to the Milanese nun singer-composer Claudia Sessa, while Francesca Turina addressed poems to the painter Lavinia Fontana and the singer Ippolita Recupito, and Moderata Fonte and Orsina Cavaletti (d. 1592) to another famous singer, Laura Peverara (c. 1550–1601).[15] In general, the emergence of women in diverse creative fields had a mutually reinforcing effect by the end of the sixteenth century, cumulatively piling up evidence of women's ability to "transcend the limitations of their sex." Women's achievements within these various creative fields were comprehensively documented in Cristoforo Bronzini's remarkable, multivolume *Dialogo della dignità e nobiltà delle donne* (Dialogue on the Dignity and Nobility of Women; 1624–32): a kind of summa of arguments and evidence for women's intellectual and moral excellence, and their capacity for government, rather poignantly published as this great season of female creativity in Italy was drawing to a close.[16]

Contexts: Political and Religious History

During the period covered by this volume, Italy as a unified political entity did not exist, nor is it historically accurate to speak of an Italian language, rather than a series of dialects and regional koinés. For most of the later Middle Ages, southern Italy had been governed as a unified monarchy, incorporating also Sicily down to the late thirteenth century and again from the mid-fifteenth century. Central and northern Italy, meanwhile, consisted of a constellation of small autonomous states, governed either as *comuni* or city-republics, or—as became progressively more common from the thirteenth century onward—principalities or *signorie*, ruled by a single family.

By the early fifteenth century, a process of consolidation had taken place, as the larger states absorbed the smaller, establishing significant territorial empires. By 1450, the main Italian powers were the duchy of Milan and the republic of Venice in the north, the kingdom of Naples in the south, and the republic of Florence in the center. Between Florence and Naples stood Rome, ruled by the papacy in uneasy alliance with a fractious cohort of powerful barons. Besides these five great blocks, numerous smaller states survived, retaining their autonomy through military strength and careful alliances with the major powers. Culturally, the most important of these smaller states were the principalities of Ferrara, Mantua, and Urbino, and the Tuscan republic of Siena.

This mosaic of power, the product of centuries of history, was smashed apart quite dramatically in the last decade of the fifteenth century, when Italy became a battleground in the protracted struggle between the two emerging great powers of France and Spain. Interspersed with brief periods of truce, the resulting wars, known as the Wars of Italy, continued for more than half a century, from 1494 to 1559. During most of this time, large portions of the Italian peninsula were under French or Spanish rule, sometimes alternating in rapid succession. The two largest and most powerful states in Italy, Milan and Naples, had succumbed to foreign dominance by 1501. After 1559, having defeated France, Spain remained the dominant power in Italy, with only Venice remaining entirely outside its sphere of influence. Even states that remained nominally autonomous, such as the Florence-based duchy of Tuscany, which had absorbed a war-ravaged Siena into its territories in 1559, relied on Spanish power to the extent that they have sometimes been described as virtual client states.[17]

The shattering impact on the peninsula of the Italian Wars can be traced in this anthology, where many poems attest to it, from Girolama Corsi's and Camilla Scarampa's shocked responses to the original French invasions of the 1490s (nos. 156–57) to Vittoria Colonna's lament on the capture of her father and husband following the Battle of Ravenna in 1512 (no. 7) to Claudia della Rovere's pro-French account of the wars in her native Piedmont in the 1550s (no. 163). The tensions arising from local nobilities' adjustment to a new state of subordination to foreign powers are interestingly documented in a poem by Laura Terracina (no. 162) addressed to the Spanish viceroy of Naples in the wake of an uprising in 1547.

Also dating from this later period of wars is a poem by Veronica Gambara (1485–1550), regent of the tiny northern state of Correggio (no. 158). Generally an imperial partisan, Gambara takes a more neutral stance in this sonnet, urging peace between the Hapsburg emperor and Spanish king, Charles V (1500–58), and his French archrival, Francis I (1494–1547), and appealing to them to expend their military energies in a crusade against the Ottoman Empire, whose incursions into Christian territory formed a threatening backdrop to the European conflicts of the age.[18] The same theme is found in a much later canzone, from the 1590s, by Isabella Cervoni (no. 165), writing after the much-trumpeted yet ephemeral Christian victory at Lepanto in 1571 had lent new impetus to dreams of a crusade.

Especially poignant as a reflection of the turmoil of the first half of the sixteenth century is the political output of poets from Siena, where the Franco-Imperial conflict intersected with internal civic tensions to toxic effect in the 1530s–50s.[19] Prior to Siena's annexation by the Duchy of Tuscany in the 1550s, we can see Aurelia Petrucci (no. 161) warning of the disastrous effects of civil strife and Laodomia Forteguerri (no. 147) flaunting her imperial sympathies in a sonnet in praise of Charles V's daughter, Margaret of Austria (1522–86). After Siena's demise as an independent republic, the pro-French Virginia Salvi (no. 164) writes of the despair of Siena's exiles in Rome and calls on the Florentine-born queen of France Caterina de' Medici (1519–89) to urge her husband, Henri II, to "liberate" the city from the rule of Caterina's distant cousin Duke Cosimo de' Medici (1519–74). Meanwhile, within Cosimo's Florence, a more detached perspective on the Sienese conflict was possible: a sonnet (no. 148) by Laura Battiferri addressed to Cosimo's wife, Duchess Eleonora de Toledo (1522–62), portrays her serenely as "queen" of Siena, receiving deserved tribute from her new land.

The other major event shaping Italian culture in the sixteenth century was the great religious crisis of the Reformation, which split northern from southern Europe and put an end to the pan-European spiritual and temporal power the medieval popes had wielded. The spiritual ferments that led to the northern Reformation were also operative in Italy, as was the fierce outrage at ecclesiastical corruption that was such a feature of the movement, and the first half of the century saw a religious movement in Italy, often labeled the Catholic Reform movement, comparable in many ways intellectually to the Protestant Reformation, though without the latter's political effects.

In the face of the threat from the north, and in response to domestic criticism, the Catholic Church regrouped at the Council of Trent (1545–63), where leaders forged a new and more rigorous and evangelical model of Catholicism. Much of the remainder of the century was occupied in implementing the council's recommendations, using new instruments such as systematic parish and monastic visitations, improved education for priests, and press censorship of "heretical" works. Especially within the Italian critical tradition, the Counter-Reformation has often been presented in entirely negative terms, as a reactionary and repressive movement, responsible for choking off the creativity and freedom of thought that had characterized the earlier Italian Renaissance. More recently, there has been a trend toward a more balanced picture, less polarized between a "progressive," Protestant north and a "retrogressive," Catholic south. Reformation and Counter-Reformation tend to be seen now as parallel movements of religious reform, differing in their theological emphases but sharing a concern with reinvigorating the faith.[20]

The religious movements of the Italian sixteenth century—Catholic Reform and Counter-Reformation, to use the conventional labels—left a profound imprint on the literature of the era, one reflected in the present anthology. Vittoria Colonna (c. 1490–1547), the most influential female poet of this period, was a leading figure in the Catholic Reform movement of the 1530s and 1540s, close to iconic leaders of the movement such as Bernardino Ochino (no. 168) and Reginald Pole (no. 175), as well as to reform sympathizers such as the great artist Michelangelo Buonarroti (1475–1564), with whom she exchanged verse. Famed until around 1530 for her amorous verse (nos. 7 and 41–50), after this time Colonna devoted herself progressively to religious subject matter, forging a new model of religious poetry, drawing on the modes of contemporary love lyric to express a passionate yearning for God (nos. 74–84). Although Colonna's verse rarely touches explicitly on questions of dogma, it is not difficult to detect the imprint of reform theology in her religious poetry, especially in regard to its emphasis on the powerlessness of the human soul to attain salvation except through the action of grace (no. 75).[21] In other respects, however, especially in the theological centrality she accords to the Virgin Mary (nos. 80, 82–83), she is closer to the Catholic than to the Protestant reform tradition. Colonna's religious verse continued to circulate in the period following the Council of Trent and was reprinted in 1586.[22]

The later, Counter-Reformation tradition of religious verse, barely studied by critics to date, is amply exemplified in the present anthology (nos. 92–129), with selections from around a dozen poets, including some, like Laura Battiferri and Chiara Matraini, who had been close to Catholic Reform circles in their youth.[23] Although some of this later verse is distinctly "post-Tridentine" in its emphases—Laura Battiferri's hymn to the evangelizing work of the Jesuits (no. 96) or Lucrezia Marinella's lush, triumphal encomia of virgin martyrs (nos. 115–16)—more introspective models of lyric are also found in this period, such as Moderata Fonte's penitential meditation on Christ's passion (no. 98) or Francesca Turina's rapt reflection on solitude in nature as conducive to visionary prayer (no. 126). Although a distinction often made between Protestant and Catholic culture is that the former privileged a direct and unmediated relationship between the worshipper and God while the latter insisted on the mediation of the institutional

Church, the tradition of Counter-Reformation religious lyric in Italy offers evidence that this distinction should not be made absolutely. Lyric lent itself by tradition to intimacy and passion, and the Counter-Reformation did not alter this.

The richness of the post-Tridentine tradition of religious verse by women (as, generally, of religious writings in all genres) calls into question traditional views of the Counter-Reformation as programmatically misogynistic and silencing of women. It is true that some policies promoted by the Council of Trent were detrimental to women, notably the strict enforcement of claustration in convents, which was often justified by patronizing arguments concerning women's alleged weakness and incapacity for moral self-discipline. It is an unwarranted generalization, however, to speak of the post–Tridentine Church as systematically and universally misogynistic. On the contrary, it is not difficult to find instances of clerics in this period proposing women, lay and religious, as beacons of good conduct, whose piety, charity, modesty, and obedience serve as a living reproach to their more wayward male counterparts. Strikingly, it is during this period of Italian cultural history that we first find treatises on women's "nobility and excellence" being published by clerics rather than laymen. Nor is it unusual to find a high degree of supportiveness of women's literary and intellectual activity on the part of clerical writers. Indeed, it was a priest, Francesco Agostino Della Chiesa (1593–1662), who published the first biographical dictionary of female writers, the well-researched *Theatro delle donne letterate* (1620), published with a vehement prefatory essay denouncing male "tyranny" over women that owes much to Lucrezia Marinella's *Della nobiltà et l'eccellenza delle donne* (On the Nobility and Excellence of Women, 1600).[24]

An interesting feature of the sixteenth-century Catholic tradition of religious lyric, from a gender perspective, is the extraordinary prominence it gives to the Virgin Mary.[25] Catholicism accorded Mary a role of enormous dignity, seeing her as chosen by God from beginning of time as coprotagonist in the spiritual redemption of humanity. Though they were not made dogma until much later, the doctrines of Mary's Assumption and Immaculate Conception were widely believed throughout Catholic Europe. The first held that Mary was "assumed" bodily into Heaven at the end of her life; the second that, alone of all human beings subsequent to the Fall, she was conceived without original sin. Protestants frequently accused Catholicism of effectively deifying Mary and making her the object of an independent, "idolatrous" cult.

The Marian poems in this anthology (nos. 82–83, 85–86, 101, 103, 110–12, 114, 124, 129) attest powerfully both to the general importance the Virgin enjoyed in Catholic culture and to the special importance she assumed for women. Perhaps the most striking of these poems in theological terms is a sonnet by Francesca Turina (no. 129), in which the poet has a personified female sex recount its spiritual trajectory from the Creation to the Incarnation of Christ. Originally created superior to man, woman lost her status after the Fall, which Eve was generally seen as precipitating, only to be gloriously redeemed by Mary, whose role in the Incarnation compensated for and nullified Eve's sin. Although Turina is unusually explicit in her feminist reading of Mary, this vision of Mary as ennobling of the female sex generally is also present in a canzone by Leonora Bernardi (no. 111) and may perhaps also be detected more implicitly in a sonnet by Battista Vernazza (no. 101), which trespasses across the boundaries of orthodoxy in speaking of Mary as to be worshipped, where worship was a prerogative of God. Like Vernazza's, sonnets by Colonna (no. 82) and Gambara (no. 85) allude to the implicitly deifying doctrine of the Immaculate Conception, while Lucrezia Marinella (no. 114) hymns Mary's Assumption into Heaven, another doctrine that assimilates Mary to her divine son.

Another female figure to be accorded great salience within Catholic culture in this period was Mary Magdalene, revered as the archetype of the penitent sinner and as the first witness to Christ's resurrection, deserving of this honor through the strength of her faith.[26] More accessible than the Virgin as a figure for self-identification, Mary Magdalene features prominently in religious lyric in this period, as several poems in this anthology attest (nos. 84, 105–6, 120, 122).[27] Although these poems differ in their emphases, they offer powerful evidence of the strength of women's imaginative engagement with this complex and ambiguous figure, identified within medieval tradition as a courtesan and seductress prior to her conversion. Within a culture that socialized elite women to prize chastity above all virtues, Mary Magdalene presented a rare and interesting example of the redeemed "fallen woman." It is possible that women's sympathy for her contained an element of implicit social critique of the kind we find explicitly in Moderata Fonte's dialogue *Il merito delle donne* (*The Worth of Women*), where the speakers attack the hypocritical double standard that saw women vilified for sexual transgressions that would be regarded as trivial lapses in a man.[28]

Contexts: Social History

In this period in Italy, as in Europe generally, women were substantially disadvantaged in relation to men. Political power resided almost exclusively in the hands of men, especially in republican contexts. Women of a social rank above that of artisans and servants were also largely excluded from the world of paid work: the professions were closed to them, as they were effectively debarred from university education, and they had little opportunity to participate in trade other than indirectly, as investors. Even within the family, where most of women's limited power was exercised, they were legally and economically subordinated to men, first their fathers, and subsequently their husbands. Women's inheritance classically took the form of a dowry paid by their natal kin to their husbands, and controlled by their husbands during their lifetimes. Only after widowhood did they attain a degree of financial independence, as their dowries then came into their hands.[29]

The marked inequality between the sexes that was such a defining feature of Italian society in this period was rationalized by a gender ideology that regarded women as men's natural inferiors. The Aristotelian thinking that constituted scientific orthodoxy at this time taught that the female sex was a form of natural deformity. Nature strove at the moment of conception to create a male, the perfect form of humanity, but frequently failed through a lack of vital heat, producing the inferior, female model instead, characterized by less physical strength and a weaker intellect. Women's political and social subordination could be justified in this manner as a logical consequence of their natural inferiority: nature fitted men to be rulers and women to be ruled.[30]

Nevertheless, there were important exceptions to the norm of female subordination within Italy. Elite young women who chose (or were pressured into choosing) a religious life had the opportunity to attain positions of considerable authority within their convents, as abbesses or prioresses. Even after the Council of Trent, when the role of male clerics in convent governance increased and that of nuns diminished, religious life remained a sphere in which women could exert a degree of authority unusual in the secular world. Convents, especially wealthy, elite, urban ones, were also important sites for women's intellectual development and creative self-expression.[31] This anthology includes works by five cloistered women, between canonesses and nuns.[32]

Where the secular world was concerned, the prime exception to the general rule of women's subordination was the princely courts, where women of the ruling dynasties enjoyed an exceptional degree of financial power and political influence. Rulers' wives often acted as regents after widowhood and deputized for their husbands during their lifetimes when they were absent or ill. To prepare them for these contingencies, girls of the ruling families of Italy were routinely educated to a high standard, often sharing a tutor with their brothers, a practice almost unheard of in other social contexts. Gender ideology reflected these elite social realities. It is in court circles in Italy in the fifteenth and early sixteenth centuries that we first begin to see pro-feminist theoretical discourses on sex and gender emerging as an alternative to the Aristotelian model. Countering Aristotelian essentialism, court intellectuals argued that women were men's equals by nature, and that their subordination to men had no justification in biological difference.[33] These ideas were later popularized in vernacular works such as Baldassare Castiglione's much-republished *Libro del cortegiano* (*Book of the Courtier*, 1528).

Unsurprisingly, given the cultural exceptionality of the princely courts, this context was key to the emergence of women as secular writers and intellectuals in Italy. Women of the smaller courts of central Italy were the leaders of this trend. Battista da Montefeltro (1384–1450), of the ruling family of Urbino, was the first secular Italian woman to gain national fame for her learning, and her granddaughter Costanza Varano (1426–47) and great-granddaughter Battista Sforza (1446–72), duchess of Urbino, were also erudites of note. Other fifteenth-century courtly women of intellectual distinction were Cecilia Gonzaga (1426–51), of the ruling family of Mantua, and Ippolita Sforza (1446–84), daughter of Francesco Sforza, duke of Milan. Not until the end of the fifteenth century do we begin to see the first signs of female learning beginning to migrate down the Italian social hierarchy. Laura Cereta of Brescia (1469–99), author of a volume of Latin letters, was the daughter of a lawyer and married a merchant, while Cassandra Fedele of Venice (?1465–1558), famed for her oratory, was the daughter of a humanist scholar and married a physician.

Similar patterns are seen in the social distribution of female vernacular poets in the late fifteenth and sixteenth centuries, with the aristocracy continuing as an important recruiting ground for female poets. The two most celebrated vernacular poets of the early sixteenth century, Vittoria Colonna and Veronica Gambara, were both noble by birth—Colonna, a member of the very highest aristocracy. Both Gambara and Colonna quite literally represent a line of descent from the aristocratic world of fifteenth-century female learning. Colonna was descended through her mother from the great line of female erudites stretching back through Battista Sforza and Costanza Varano to Battista da Montefeltro, while Gambara's father was a nephew of the greatest secular female intellectual of the fifteenth century, Isotta Nogarola of Verona (c. 1418–66), represented in this anthology with an eminently aristocratic elegy in praise of the family's country estate (no. 192). Although few subsequent female poets came from quite such exalted backgrounds as Gambara and Colonna, many may be described as noble in the broad sense in which the term was used in sixteenth-century Italy, embracing untitled members of urban patriciates, as well as ancient feudal families with hereditary titles and vast holdings of land. Around thirty of the fifty or so poets in this collection whose backgrounds can be identified were noble in this broad definition, including all five of the canonesses and nuns.[34]

Although women's engagement with lyric was initially confined almost exclusively to aristocratic and courtly circles, it gradually became more common outside them, especially from the mid-sixteenth century, when the democratizing effects of print technology began to be apparent. Gaspara Stampa and Chiara Matraini, two of the finest female lyricists of the mid-century, were, respectively, the daughter of a jeweler and a descendent of a family of dyers—both from financially comfortable families, but not among the uppermost elites of their cities. Later in the century, Valeria Miani (?1570s–post 1620) and Issicratea Monte (1564–84/85) were daughters of lawyers in Padua and Rovigo respectively. Monte was so impecunious that a marriage planned for her fell through because of a shortfall in her dowry.[35] Moderata Fonte, also the daughter of a lawyer, came from the Venetian class of "original citizens" (cittadini originari), an elite group, but ranked below the patriciate in Venice and excluded from participation in government.[36] Lucrezia Marinella was the daughter of a doctor, again a cittadina by rank.

Although poetry as an activity was not limited to women of noble rank in Italy, it did not filter especially far down the social hierarchy: there is no Italian equivalent to a figure like Isabella Whitney, who worked as a servant in London in the 1560s–70s and published several literary works. Although there is evidence that Laura Terracina sought income from her verse and not merely recognition, she was a financially embarrassed noblewoman rather than a woman of the people, while Isabella Cervoni, whose courting of patronage has a similarly urgent tone sometimes, was the daughter of a lawyer and occasional poet.[37] Where we find women of obscurer birth participating in literary culture in Italy, they tend to be courtesans or actresses, two distinctly Italian social cohorts in this period: generally women of modest birth but often enriched by their professions and adopting a lifestyle not notably different in material respects from women of more elite social ranks.[38]

Cortigiane oneste (decent courtesans) emerged as a distinct social group in the late fifteenth and early sixteenth century, originally in the circles of the papal court (cortigiana literally means "woman of the court" or "female courtier," the equivalent of the male cortigiano). The phenomenon reflects humanist intellectuals' fascination with ancient Athens, where cultured courtesans known as hetaerae provided refined female companionship within a culture in which "respectable" women rarely mixed socially with men. Like Greek hetaerae, Renaissance courtesans were expected to be educated, especially in music, and to supplement their physical charms with the attractions of conversation, wit, and culture. In some ways, they may be seen as a sexualized version of the type of the elegant and cultivated court lady that Castiglione crafts in his *Book of the Courtier*, embodying it in the figure of Emilia Pio, Veronica Gambara's aunt.

True to their status as counterparts of aristocratic court ladies, there is evidence of courtesans engaging precociously with the practice of poetry. The novella writer Matteo Bandello records poetry as one of the accomplishments of the legendary Imperia Cognati (d. 1512), one of the first documented Roman courtesans.[39] The two most significant courtesan poets of the sixteenth century, both represented in this volume, are Tullia d'Aragona and Veronica Franco (1546–91), the latter active in Venice in the 1570s and 1580s, the former, more peripatetic, in Rome, Venice, Ferrara, Siena, and Florence in the 1530s and 1540s. The difference between these two poets' careers is indicative of the trajectory of courtesans' fortunes across the course of the century, as Counter-Reformation moralism took hold. While d'Aragona was nationally feted and suffered relatively little from her courtesan status, Franco, half a century later, was a far more marginal figure, despite the acceptance she enjoyed within her own libertine circles in Venice. The publication history of their verse is revealing in this regard: while d'Aragona's verse was published by the leading firm of Giolito and was reprinted twice after its initial appearance in 1547, Franco's appeared once, without publisher's details, having clearly been published clandestinely to avoid the prepublication censorship introduced after Trent.[40]

About the time when courtesans were declining as a cultural force in Italy, we begin to register the first mentions of actresses, who, from the 1560s onward, became an ever more significant feature of the Italian cultural scene.[41] It is tempting to hypothesize that the figure of the actress was initially a rebranding of the figure of the courtesan: certainly, the beauty, grace, literacy, and music and performance skills that were the stock-in-trade of the courtesan would have served a woman equally well on the stage. While the earliest documentation of an actress in an Italian theatrical troupe dates to 1548, actresses began to figure prominently in Italian culture from around the 1560s. This collection features a poem by one of the earliest Italian actresses, Vincenza Armani (no. 61), and several by the most famous, Isabella Andreini, co-manager with her husband of the Gelosi, the most famous theatrical troupe of its day (nos. 65–70, 145). Other poets in this volume who may be compared with these figures are the musical virtuose Barbara Salutati and Gaspara Stampa. Stampa was a solo singer who performed privately for elite audiences, while Salutati, from what we can gather, was both a musical performer and something of a musical entrepreneur. Salutati is frequently described as a courtesan, while Stampa has also sometimes been identified as one.[42] Rather than pursuing such questions of definition, however, it seems more useful to call attention to the social and cultural factors that assimilate actresses and musical virtuose to courtesans. All were women who stood somewhat apart from the norms of elite society and enjoyed a degree of freedom from the strict laws of honor that constrained their "respectable" sisters. This exceptional status is reflected in their poetry, to a greater or lesser degree.

A final distinctive social group of women writers who might be considered here are Jewish writers, represented in this anthology by a sonnet by the Venetian Sarra Copio (no. 174).[43] Italy had a tradition in the sixteenth century of relative tolerance toward Jews, though the picture was regionally differentiated: some noble families, like the Este in Ferrara and the Medici in Tuscany, encouraged Jewish communities in their territories for economic reasons, while Jews were expelled from Spanish-ruled Naples in 1510 and 1541 and from the papal states, excluding Ancona and Rome, in 1569. In general, the condition of Jewish communities deteriorated after the mid-sixteenth century under the influence of Counter-Reformation evangelizing tendencies, but Italian Jews continued to be culturally active in this period, especially in the fields of drama and music.[44] Besides Copio, who came from a wealthy Venetian-Jewish family, verse survives by two women of Jewish origin: the Roman Debora Ascarelli (fl. ?1560s), a translator from Hebrew as well as a poet, and the Venetian Rosa Levi, who converted to Christianity in 1565 but whom we still find being published under her pre-conversion name in an anthology of 1571.[45]

Contexts: Literary History

The discussion that follows locates Italian women's lyric production within the history of vernacular lyric from the late fifteenth to the early seventeenth century. Poetry in the classical languages is discussed in a separate section at the end, as is poetry written in regional variants of Italian other than the dominant literary vernacular, Tuscan.

The Age of Court Poetry

Two great phases may be identified in the history of vernacular lyric poetry in Italy in the medieval and early modern period: one starting in the early thirteenth century and continuing to the later fourteenth, the other starting around a hundred years later, in the last quarter of the fifteenth. Although vernacular poetry continued to be written in the intervening period, the principal energies of Italian elite literary culture were directed elsewhere, toward the study and imitation of classical literature, especially Latin, with a bias toward prose writings such as orations, letters, dialogues, and histories. This classicizing trend in Italian culture, customarily referred to as "humanism," was already gaining momentum in the late fourteenth century but triumphed in the fifteenth, when a mastery of classical Latin became a core skill for any educated man.

In the later fifteenth century, after its century in the relative wilderness, vernacular lyric made a strong return, thriving within the princely courts of northern Italy, in the kingdom of Naples, and in Florence, where the Medici family under Lorenzo il Magnifico (1449–92)—himself a fine vernacular lyricist—was tightening its political grip on what was still nominally a republic. The dominant role of the princely courts as a habitat for lyric is reflected in the term *poesia cortigiana* (court poetry), sometimes applied to late-fifteenth- and early-sixteenth-century lyric. The poetry of this period tends to be characterized contrastively with the stricter and more codified Petrarchist tradition that followed it. Although it took its cue from the great medieval tradition of Italian lyric, which reached its peak in the work of Dante Alighieri (1265–1321) and Francesco Petrarca (1304–74), the poetry of the late fifteenth century was not limited to the metrical and thematic repertoire established by these masters. Rather, poets of this time invented freely, borrowing from the classical Latin lyric, as well as the vernacular legacy, and evolving new meters, often with a view to musical setting. This was a poetic tradition that developed in close conjunction with performance contexts, and some of its most fashionable exponents, such as Serafino Aquilano (1466–1500), were famed for their improvised verse.

Where thematics were concerned, love was the great focus of fifteenth-century *poesia cortigiana*, as it had been in the earlier, medieval tradition. Rather than the etherealized and spiritualized love narratives of Dante and Petrarch, however, in which the lady's unearthly beauty and supreme virtue are seen as a message from God, luring the dazzled poet back to her heavenly Creator, the courtly poets of the late fifteenth century are often more realist and secularizing in their treatment of love. The greatest lyric collection of the age, Matteo Maria Boiardo's *Amorum libri* (1469–71), tells the tale of a rapturous reciprocated love, followed by misery as the poet is abandoned by his lady. Boiardo's influences include classical Roman love elegy, as the title, echoing Ovid's *Amores*, suggests. Ovid also influenced Italian lyric in this period through his *Heroides*, a collection of verse epistles in the voice of mythological and literary heroines, most typically abandoned women lamenting the perfidy of their lovers. Female-voiced fictional letters of this kind, typically composed in terza rima, became a short-lived lyric subgenre in the later fifteenth century, preparing the ground for the emergence of actual women's voices on the Italian poetic scene.[46]

This anthology contains selections from the only two female lyricists of the late fifteenth century whose work survives in any quantity, Girolama Corsi (fl. 1494–1509) and Camilla Scarampa (1476–1520) (nos. 2–3, 156–57, 166–

67, 208), and also from two poets of a younger generation, Veronica Gambara and Vittoria Colonna, who were destined to become famous through their later, Petrarchist production but who started their careers well before the advent of Petrarchism (nos. 4 and 7). A fifth poet whose work demands to be seen within the context of *poesia cortigiana* is Barbara Salutati, represented here by her sole surviving poem (no. 8). Although she was writing some decades later than Scarampa and Corsi, in the 1520s, Salutati fits well with the *poesia cortigiana* paradigm, not least in her metrical preferences: like the young Colonna, she uses the form of the terza rima lyric *capitolo*, enormously popular in the late fifteenth century but virtually eliminated with the rise of Petrarchism. Also metrically anomalous by later-sixteenth-century standards is Girolama Corsi, who employs forms such as the *barzelletta* and the *sonetto caudato*, both little used after the advent of Petrarchism.

In addition to these metrical idiosyncrasies, the examples of *poesia cortigiana* in this anthology are characterized by their linguistic eclecticism. This was a school of verse formed before any clear consensus had emerged about the "correct" version of the literary vernacular, and both in terms of phonology and morphology and of register, we find usages in Italian poetry prior to the 1520s that we would be hard put to find later, at least outside the comic tradition. Barbara Salutati writes in a Tuscan vernacular familiar from the writings of her admirer Niccolò Machiavelli (1469–1527), while Vittoria Colonna (no. 7) draws heavily on Latinisms to give her verse a classical feel. Corsi and Scarampa, meanwhile, especially in their political verse (nos. 156–57), use a notably vigorous language it is difficult to imagine a female poet using after the advent of Petrarchism, when more squeamish standards of decorum prevailed.

An interesting feature of the early love poetry in this anthology is the prominence of Ovid's *Heroides* as a subtext or source. This is most obvious in Colonna and Salutati, who adopt the Ovidian form of the extended letter-poem directly, with Colonna's capitolo, in particular, closely recalling Ovid's letter from Penelope to Ulysses. Besides these direct imitations, the *Heroides* is also traceable as an influence in two sonnets by Girolama Corsi and Camilla Scarampa, which cast the poet as a deserted woman reproaching a treacherous lover (nos. 2–3). Together with the earlier, thematically analogous, sonnet by Amedea degli Aleardi (no. 1), these poems fascinatingly attest to the formative influence of the *Heroides* on the early tradition of female-authored poetry in Italy. While this influence did not dissipate entirely in the later tradition, it tended, post-1530, to remain the province of socially "irregular" poets such as Gaspara Stampa and Veronica Franco, both of whom authored passionate poems of reproach to absent lovers in the voice of a woman who suspects herself betrayed. Within the more "respectable" and idealizing Petrarchan tradition, while absence from the beloved remains a fundamental motif, the narrative situation portrayed is less commonly that of the woman unhappily enamored of an unfaithful lover than of the pair of eternally faithful lovers—sometimes spouses—separated cruelly by circumstances or death.[47]

The Advent of Petrarchism

Even as the *poesia cortigiana* tradition was at the height of its popular vogue, some poets were beginning to feel the need for a stricter regulation of linguistic norms. *Poesia cortigiana* was characteristically written in an elevated form of the native regional dialect of the poet in question, although generally enriched with Latinisms and with Tuscanisms deriving from the influence of Dante and Petrarch. No universal linguistic standards pertained in the vernacular, as they did in its principal literary competitor, classical Latin. This linguistic diversity was tolerable in a manuscript culture, in which scribes might adapt "foreign" verses to their own linguistic norms, but it posed problems as print began to gain on manuscript as a means of literary circulation, and uniform texts began to be produced for circulation throughout the peninsula. In the face of these pressures, the need for a standard language was increasingly felt in Italy, as it was throughout Europe. Where in centralized nation-states like France or England, the language of the political center gradually imposed itself as dominant, in politically fragmented Italy, such a natural resolution was not likely to be forthcoming, even if some intellectuals argued that the eclectic, "melting-pot" parlance of the papal court might fulfill such a role.

A more realistic solution to this problem began to surface in the first decade of the sixteenth century, when the Venetian poet, intellectual, and courtier Pietro Bembo (1470–1547) began the work on vernacular grammar that would eventually result in his important treatise *Le prose della volgar lingua* (On the Vernacular), first published in 1525. Bembo had worked with the press, editing texts of Dante and Petrarch for the legendary Venetian publisher Aldo Manuzio (1449–1515), and, as a result, he understood the practical problems presented by Italy's lack of a common linguistic standard. As an accomplished humanist, moreover, he was acutely aware of the discrepancy in linguistic regularity between the vernacular and Latin: one accusation snobbish humanists frequently leveled at the "vulgar tongue" was precisely that it lacked grammatical regulation and was merely ruled by the vagaries of usage. To remedy this problem, Bembo proposed a radical solution: that, to ensure a universal standard for the Italian literary vernacular, writers should adhere to the fourteenth-century Tuscan usage of Petrarch and his near-contemporary Giovanni Boccaccio (1313–75). A growing trend within late fifteenth-century Latin humanism, warmly supported by Bembo, advocated the exclusive use as models for imitation of Cicero and Virgil, considered the supreme masters of Latin prose and verse. Bembo took this model, known in Latin as Ciceronianism, and ingeniously adapted it to the vernacular, with Petrarch taking the role of the vernacular Virgil and Boccaccio that of the vernacular Cicero.

Bembo's ideas initially proved controversial because he advocated the use of an anachronistic form of Tuscan in place of contemporary literary idioms that retained some connection with the spoken language. Tuscans, especially, found it offensive to be informed by a Venetian like Bembo that their literary writings should be composed in an antiquated variant of their own modern, spoken idiom, containing words and constructions that sounded odd and ungainly to an educated speaker of the day. Counterintuitive as it may seem, however, Bembo's archaizing solution—which essentially turned literary Italian into a "dead language," like classical Latin—proved eminently functional in practice, as it allowed universal grammatical norms to be established and rules of correct usage to be drawn up. Paradoxically, as well, as the *volgare* moved further from its spoken roots—seemingly an elitist move—literary practice became *more* accessible, rather than less, to a wider ranger of users. Where once the acquisition of a feel for correct literary language required a high level of education and the social opportunity to move in elite circles, the establishment of linguistic and stylistic norms in the 1530s made the attainment of linguistic correctness an accessible aim for any literate person with the leisure to devote to study, especially from the 1540s and 1550s, when aids such as dictionaries, grammars, and rhyme books (*rimari*) became available. The democratizing effects of this linguistic reform were reinforced by the diffusion of print, which made books more available and cheaper, and hence facilitated the spread of literacy. This last development was especially important for women, who were generally educated at home and whose access to literacy was thus crucially dependent on the availability of books within the domestic sphere.[48]

Petrarchism as a Lyric Mode

Petrarchism was the dominant lyric idiom of the sixteenth century and is that of the great majority of the poems in this anthology. The present section is devoted to outlining its key characteristics. As the name suggests, the principal defining feature of Petrarchist lyric was its close fidelity to Petrarch. At the extreme, the Petrarchist poet used no word that had no precedent in Petrarch and drew on Petrarch for her imagery, sentiments, and conceits. This total immersion in a single model attracted much parody at the time, and led to Petrarchism being dismissed by critics during the nineteenth and much of the twentieth century as trite, formulaic, and vacuous, the anti-thesis of the romantic notion of poetry as emotional self-expression.

More recently, critics have begun to look at Petrarchist lyric and at its core poetic practice, imitation, more sympathetically, historicizing them and seeing them on their own terms. The poetry of this era has different ends from modern, postromantic, poetry and inevitably adopts different means. Rather than the kind of idiosyncratic, unique, individual self that romantic lyric posits as its enunciating "I," early modern lyric characteristi-cally fashions a more generic, idealized persona, comparable with the care-fully calibrated social self Castiglione advises the Renaissance courtier and court lady to cultivate in his *Book of the Courtier*. Within this conception of the individual as self-consciously crafted artifact, imitation had a clear con-structive function. Castiglione advises the courtier to frame his social per-sona through the practice of imitation, "stealing" aspects of graceful behav-ior he admires in his peers.[49] Similarly, the Petrarchist poet formed herself as a voice through the appropriation of elements found elsewhere.

The use of imitation as a means of self-fashioning is not the only point of comparison between Petrarchist lyric and the courtly "performance art" Castiglione codified. The stylistic qualities Bembo admired in Petrarch are also quite close to those Castiglione prescribes for the courtier: elegance, grace, moderation (*misura*), and a harmony attained by the balance of oppos-ing qualities. Castiglione advises the young courtier to temper his natural exuberance with gravity and the older courtier to balance his natural grav-ity with occasional lightness.[50] Similarly, Bembo saw the fundamental se-cret of Petrarch's stylistic magic in his blending of the opposing qualities of *gravità* and *piacevolezza* (gravity and charm). Where Dante, in Bembo's view, erred through excessive gravity and a poet like Cino da Pistoia (1270–1336) through excessive sweetness, Petrarch consistently attained a correct and dynamic balance of opposites—the aesthetic equivalent of the Aristote-lian "mean" that Castiglione uses to craft his behavioral ideal.[51] How to at-tain this elusive end in practice was a matter of expert juggling of sound and rhythm, the formal building blocks of poetry. In some of the most interesting passages of the *Prose*, we see Bembo attempting to infer the universal laws of poetic harmony from a meticulous, syllable-by-syllable and phoneme-by-phoneme analysis of Petrarch's verse.[52]

Where the thematics of lyric were concerned, Petrarch once again served as a template, although less completely than in the case of language and style. Petrarch's *Rerum vulgarium fragmenta* (Vernacular Pieces), also known as the "Rime sparse" or "Canzoniere," describes the poet's love for the re-mote and virtuous—and married—Madonna Laura, during the last years of her young life and after her premature death. While the poet's frustrated sexual desire for this unattainable lady is acknowledged early in the work, the emphasis of the poetry is mainly on a more idealized form of love, whereby the poet sees in Laura's beauty and virtue an intimation of the divine beauty and goodness of her Creator and aspires through his love for her, purified of all fleshly yearning, to ascend ultimately to spiritual union with God. This sublimated and spiritualized model of love is often termed "Neoplatonic," in that it has its philosophical roots in the love theory articulated in Plato's *Symposium* and *Phaedrus*. Its presence in lyric poetry is a feature of the medieval Italian lyric tradition that distinguishes it from the prior Provençal tradition of courtly love lyric, which was more sensual in its treatment of love. Petrarch's attitude to the notion of the lady as a "stairway to the Creator" is more skeptical than that of Dante, and his poet figure is portrayed as less successful than Dante's in detaching himself from the thralldom of earthly love.[53] Nonetheless, the *Rerum vulgarium fragmenta* (*RVF*) offered an essentially "honest" model of love, featuring a lover whose erotic aspirations rarely transcend the pleasure of seeing his lady and hearing her voice, and whose descriptions of her physical beauties limit themselves largely to her eyes, lips, hands, and hair.

Petrarch's elegant, chaste, and spiritualized model of love poetry had a strong appeal to Renaissance poets, for reasons that included the social, the intellectual, and the religious. Intellectually, the Neoplatonic model of love had acquired a new interest and resonance since the fifteenth century, when the study of Greek revived in Italy, and the works of Plato and the ancient Neoplatonic philosophers began to be read in the West directly for the first time since classical antiquity. The Florentine philosopher Marsilio Ficino (1433–99) wrote an important commentary on the *Symposium* in the 1480s, and Bembo and Castiglione included elegant vernacular expositions of platonic love theory in their dialogues, *Gli Asolani* (1505) and *The Book of the Courtier*. These vernacular versions heterosexualized the model of Platonic love so that the object of love becomes not a young man or boy, as in the original Platonic model, but a lady, as in the lyric tradition.

One great appeal of Neoplatonic love theory, especially within the princely courts where mixed socializing was common, was that it offered a model for male-female interaction that was both mutually flattering and sexually innocuous. Sublimated love was conceived of as reserved for the noble of heart, while less refined souls were incapable of escaping the gravitational pull of the body. The object of such a love was also noble by definition, as the spiritual dynamic of Neoplatonic love only functioned if the love object was, in her beauty and virtue, an accurate mirror of God. Courtier poets such as Bembo could use this convenient idiom to express their devotion to the ladies of the court, while at the same time advertising their own impeccable manners. One of Bembo's key innovations was to translate an idiom used by Petrarch to describe an exclusive, obsessional love for one woman into something much more flexible and social, functional in both erotic and nonerotic contexts. A sonnet exchange with Veronica Gambara included in this anthology (nos. 132–33) shows him using the language of Neoplatonic love to express an attitude of affection and intellectual respect.

A further appeal of Neoplatonic love theory for intellectuals of Bembo's and Castiglione's generation was that it offered a model of spirituality that evaded institutional contexts. The correct enactment of Neoplatonic love involves a series of meditations on beauty that become progressively more abstracted from the physical love object that originally inspired it. The lover starts by contemplating the beauty of his lady, proceeds to marvel at the beauty of created nature more generally, then proceeds to a contemplation of spiritual beauty, superior to the physical by definition, and ultimately reaches the contemplation of God, beauty's ultimate source. This is a form of religious mysticism, posited on a direct relationship between the lover-worshipper and God, outside any ecclesiastical context. In an age of widespread skepticism about institutional religion, this was a model of spirituality that held indubitable attractions. It is striking how many prominent early-sixteenth-century Petrarchan poets had connections with the Catholic Reform movement, which, like Protestantism, privileged this kind of direct relationship with God. Notable examples are Vittoria Colonna, Veronica Gambara, Benedetto Varchi (1503–65), Lodovico Domenichi (1515–64), Laura Battiferri, and Chiara Matraini.[54]

A defining feature of Italian Petrarchism, deriving from its Platonic philosophical matrix, is its resolutely antimaterialist character, which reflects the Platonic tenet that the material world is merely a shadowy replication of a truer, immaterial world of ideal forms. While the poet dwells on the beloved's physical beauty, that beauty is not valorized in itself but as a signifier of spiritual beauty: hence the importance of the beloved's eyes as a locus of beauty, the eyes being conceived of as the "balcony" of the soul (see esp. no. 5). More generally, Petrarchist verse, following the lesson of Petrarch himself, tends to shrink from the concrete, the corporeal, the temporally located, and the urban, preferring to locate its ideal love stories in a rural, atemporal, mythic-epiphanic space. This is apparent even in a detail such as geographical terminology: although Tullia d'Aragona in one poem identifies herself as being in Rome (no. 10), this kind of geographical precision is unusual. Far more common is the allusive use of river or sea names as geographic markers (Arbia for Siena; Sebeto for Naples; Adria for Venice), giving an ideal, bucolic, Arcadian patina to what was in fact, by contemporary European standards, an intensely urban culture. The world of the court, present

earlier in Boiardo and later in Torquato Tasso (1544–95) as the locus of a
more socialized and competitive erotic practice, is dreamily absent in classic
Petrarchist verse.

This same tendency toward idealism and abstraction is also apparent at
a linguistic level in Petrarchism. In a classic article on Petrarch's own lyric
language, applicable equally to his sixteenth-century imitators, Gianfranco
Contini identifies as the defining characteristics of this language its rarified
character and its extreme linguistic selectivity, which Contini defines as
"monolinguism" (*monolinguismo*).[55] Heir to a richly textured and linguisti-
cally eclectic tradition of medieval vernacular lyric, Petrarch consciously
pared down this legacy, eliminating or severely reducing the presence of all
the "foreign" elements that had colored Dante's startling "plurilinguism" in
the *Divine Comedy*: Latinisms, borrowings from French and Provençal, di-
alect terms not familiar to the majority of Italians, colloquialisms, vulgar-
isms, coinages, terms from technical philosophical discourse. Vulgar
language—in its two senses, of popular or plebeian and of scurrilous—is
especially remote from Petrarch's usage. A feature of his language that ap-
pealed to sixteenth-century court audiences was its extreme and unfailing
politeness: this was gentlemanly—or ladylike—poetry, suited to an age in
which manners were becoming ever more precisely codified. Bembo is ex-
plicit on this point, justifying his preference for Petrarch over Dante, among
other things, on the grounds of Petrarch's avoidance of vulgarity. If this
meant a constraint on the subject matter poetry might deal with, it was a
constraint with which Bembo was happy to live: "it is better to be silent
about those things that cannot be spoken of decently, than to sully one's
writing by speaking of them."[56]

Midcentury Petrarchism: Manuscript and Print

Petrarchism established itself first, in the 1520s and 1530s, as an elite poetic
language, favored especially in courtly settings and circulating through the
preferred aristocratic vehicle of manuscript. Although Bembo himself was
relatively open to the world of print culture, he released his work in print
only after a lengthy manuscript prehistory. Some of his verse had been cir-
culating for almost three decades in 1530, when he first published his col-
lected *Rime*. The two principal female Petrarchists of this period, Veronica
Gambara and Vittoria Colonna, illustrate this preference for manuscript
circulation to a very marked extent. Colonna seems to have orchestrated
the production of gift manuscripts of her poetry, but she refused an offer
from Bembo to see her work through the press.[57] Gambara appears to have
been largely unconcerned about the fate of her verse, neither collecting it
in significant manuscript compilations nor encouraging others to perform

this task for her, with the result that her collected verse was not published until 1759. Similar patterns may be seen in some female poets of later generations, especially those of aristocratic birth. Noblewomen poets such as Colonna's cousin by marriage, Costanza d'Avalos Piccolomini (d. c. 1575), or her fellow Neapolitan aristocrat Dianora Sanseverino (d. 1581) appeared occasionally in anthologies but were otherwise invisible to the world of print.[58]

Despite this continuing aristocratic reticence, however, things were already changing by the 1540s. Publishers, especially in Venice, were increasingly alert to the commercial possibilities of vernacular literature. Production costs, and thus the price of books, were coming down as a result of technological innovation. New audiences for literature were opening up, ready to embrace new species of print product, such as collections of vernacular letters, illustrated emblem books, and, most important for this context, lyric anthologies. The first of a new breed of verse anthologies appeared in Venice in 1545 under the title *Rime diverse di molti eccellentissimi autori* (Diverse Lyrics by Numerous Most Excellent Authors) and collected the work of ninety-one contemporary authors, including three women. The editor, Lodovico Domenichi, and the publisher, Gabriele Giolito (in Venice from 1536; d. 1579) were among the key protagonists of this period of print history, the latter the proprietor of the most innovative press in Venice, the former, one of the most prolific and respected of the new class of writer-editors (*poligrafi*) who had risen up to service the literary needs of the presses.[59] The 1545 anthology established a powerful paradigm and was followed by a sequence of similar volumes spanning a quarter of a century and encompassing nine volumes.[60] Collectively, these brought what had been an elite cultural practice into a broader arena, making Petrarchism's court-connoted idiom available to a less socially exalted audience. The female authors included in the 1545 volume make this point very graphically: alongside the expected courtly figures of Colonna and Gambara, we find there the less expected figure of Francesca Baffo, an obscure figure in the circles of the Venetian *poligrafi*, perhaps a courtesan.[61]

The new, less elite typographical literary culture of the 1540s and 1550s offered an ideal space in which female writers could flourish. Indeed, they could serve almost as figureheads for that culture, their novelty as authorial figures underlining *its* novelty, in much the same way as nonelite male writers like Pietro Aretino (1492–1556), who similarly thrived in these years.[62] Pirated editions of Vittoria Colonna's verse began to appear from 1538 and proved immediately popular with the reading public.[63] Once the appeal of women's writing had been established, we begin to find the first authorially sanctioned verse collections by women beginning to appear, the first two, perhaps not coincidentally, appearing in the year of Colonna's death and the following year (1547–48).[64] The authors of these volumes, Tullia d'Aragona and Laura Terracina, were very far from the print-shy, aristocratic model Colonna embodied: indeed, Terracina, more clearly than any other female writer of the century, may be seen as a virtual creation of the press. She appears to have been "discovered" in her native Naples by a bookseller and talent scout, Marcantonio Passero, who introduced her verse to Lodovico Domenichi. Domenichi then edited a collection of her verse with Giolito, signing the dedicatory letter himself. This collection sold well, and Terracina went on to author five further collections of lyrics, as well as a set of reworkings of passages from Lodovico Ariosto's popular chivalric romance *Orlando furioso* that achieved astonishing success, going through twenty reprintings before 1600.[65] The case of Terracina illustrates very clearly the role publishers played in the 1540s and 1550s in promoting women's writing. It also suggests that this initiative was motivated more by commercial than literary considerations. Far the most prolific and popularly successful female poet of the era, Terracina is also by a long measure the most technically incompetent. She features in this collection with a single poem, from her second volume of *Rime* (no. 162).

A different instance of female poets' interaction with the press is offered by Tullia d'Aragona, who published a collection of verse in 1547 and was the first Italian woman actively to collaborate in the publication of her work. D'Aragona may not be seen as an invention of the press in the same way as Terracina: she was Terracina's senior by around a decade and had a name as a poet long before her work began to circulate in print. Nonetheless, d'Aragona's *Rime* is a quintessentially typographical product, and in formal terms was highly original at the time of its production. Rather than simply collecting d'Aragona's own verse, it reconstructs her poetic correspondences with a series of male admirers and collects poetic tributes to her by others: in total, the collection includes work by nineteen poets in addition to d'Aragona, in what has been aptly described as a "virtual salon."[66] The dialogic character of the text was enhanced by its layout, which placed sonnet exchanges side by side in parallel-text mode rather than grouping reply sonnets at the end of the volume with cross-references to the poems they are replying to, as happens, for example, in Bembo's 1535 *Rime*. This typographical innovation proved highly influential, as did, more generally, the model of the so-called choral anthology, representing a poet not as lyric solipsist but as a social being, graciously interacting with a circle of more or less "trophy" friends.

Despite the evidence of Terracina and d'Aragona, it would be a mistake to portray the Petrarchism of the 1540s and 1550s as entirely print-led. Gaspara

Stampa, one of the most compelling and distinctive female voices of the entire tradition, offers a counterexample. Despite living in Venice, the great publishing center of Italy, and being close to many *poligrafi*, writers, and editors for the presses, Stampa published very little during her short lifetime, circulating her lyrics instead in manuscript and performing them to elite audiences in her career as musical virtuosa.[67] Her verse was published only after her death and had little impact in print, by comparison with Terracina's or d'Aragona's. This may have been partly on account of social factors, such as Stampa's nonnoble birth and her sexually irregular lifestyle, which her verse, unlike d'Aragona's, did little to hide (see no. 22). While these considerations did not work to her detriment in her bohemian Venetian coterie, they may well have affected her reception by a broader print audience: a copy of a 1553 anthology containing verse by her in the Biblioteca Nazionale of Florence has a marginal annotation identifying her bluntly as a "Venetian whore" (*puttana venetiana*).[68]

The richness of the tradition of Italian women's lyric in this period is well illustrated by the anthology published in 1559 in Lucca by Lodovico Domenichi, assembling the work of over fifty "most noble and talented women," including many whose work has not survived elsewhere. More than an evaluative or representative anthology such as we are used to today, Domenichi's volume is better viewed as a kind of *wunderkammer* of female talent, privileging rarities and unpublished work.[69] It is immensely valuable as a snapshot of the extent of poetic activity by Italian women within the still thriving manuscript literary culture of the period, illustrating the social matrix within which female Petrarchism developed. A striking feature of the anthology is the relatively small place love poetry, Petrarchism's original core genre, holds within it. Apart from a lengthy sequence of mainly amorous verse by the Sienese poet Virginia Salvi, religious and occasional verse dominates, with social relations among women, whether of friendship or patronage, given particular salience within the occasional verse. The eighteen selections from Domenichi's anthology in the present volume reflect these thematic orientations. Only three are love lyrics (nos. 11–12, 40), while three are political (nos. 161, 163–64) and five are religious (nos. 82, 84, 87, and 90–91). Of the remaining seven, leaving aside two sonnets of existential lament by Isabella Morra (nos. 195–96), the other five all illustrate aspects of female sociability: two sonnets of friendship, by Olimpia Malipiero and Livia Pii (nos. 176 and 181), one sonnet of homage to a "great lady," by Laodomia Forteguerri (no. 147), and a sonnet exchange between Veronica Gambara and Vittoria Colonna (nos. 134–35), one of several poetic correspondences between women showcased in Domenichi's volume.

Midcentury Petrarchism: The New Gravity

Perhaps as a response to the kind of print-led "Petrarchism by the yard" typified by Laura Terracina, an elitist backlash may be detected within the Italian lyric tradition from around the 1550s. The key figure in this development is the Florentine Giovanni Della Casa (1503–56), often considered the greatest lyricist of the Italian sixteenth century and author of a slim, highly curated verse collection that was published posthumously in 1558. Like Bembo, who recognized him as his heir apparent in his last years, Della Casa was a learned poet, equally at home in Latin and the vernacular, and he drew on classical sources as much as vernacular in crafting his dense, intricate, edgy, syntactically convoluted verse. Della Casa's style had a remarkable aura of novelty for readers used to Bembo's relatively simple and perspicacious idiom, and he rapidly acquired imitators. Around a decade after the publication of Della Casa's *Rime*, we find the young Torquato Tasso (1544–95) noting ironically in a lecture that many poets were currently attempting to emulate his style but succeeding only in mimicking the most obvious of his mannerisms, without penetrating to the secrets of his art.[70]

For Tasso, the most brilliant of his followers, Della Casa's claims to greatness lay as much in the "grandeur" and originality of his subject matter as in his mastery of style. Tasso illustrates the point with a reading of Della Casa's remarkable sonnet "Questa vita mortal" (This Mortal Life): a miraculously compact meditation on time, mortality, and the wonders of the created universe that stands at the antithesis of the kind of decorative but frivolous love lyrics with which contemporary lyric anthologies were filled. The thirst for a weightier model of lyric accorded well with the mood of the post-Tridentine era, as a renewed attraction to the religious sublime made the secular, love-centered literature of the first half of the century seem trivial, as well as profane.

Of the poets in the present anthology, it is Laura Battiferri who most closely approximates to the model of lyric Della Casa pioneered, both in the gravity of her subject matter and in the complexity and denseness of her style. Della Casa's stylistic revolution has been described as a rebalancing of Petrarchism away from the *piacevole* (charming) and toward the *grave* (weighty).[71] Measured against all the components of stylistic gravity recognized by contemporaries (consonant-heavy rhymes; complex, hypotactic sentences; the use of enjambment to break rhythms; a preference for three-rhyme metrical schemes, especially asymmetric ones, in the tercets of sonnets) Battiferri consistently falls on the *grave* side of the equation. Other sixteenth-century female poets tending to the *grave* include Maddalena Campiglia, Livia Spinola, and Maddalena Salvetti, as well as, much earlier,

Vittoria Colonna, who anticipates some tendencies in Della Casa. Poets tending to the *piacevole*, meanwhile, include Gaspara Stampa and Francesca Turina, both colloquial at times in their syntax and showing a strong preference for two-rhyme tercet schemes.[72]

Petrarchism after Trent: The Age of Tasso

With the exception of Tasso himself, unquestionably the finest lyric poet of his day, the Italian lyric tradition after around 1560 has been relatively little studied, except in so far as it appears to offer stylistic anticipations of the seventeenth-century Baroque. Only very recently has any kind of overview of the lyric production of this period become available, and much detailed research remains to be done.[73] This neglect is unfortunate because later sixteenth-century lyric has much to recommend it. While retaining a basic continuity at the level of lexis, late sixteenth-century Petrarchism innovated very significantly thematically and stylistically, to the extent that it should perhaps be viewed as a new lyric tradition, rather than simply a "phase."

Perhaps the most striking innovations of the period were metrical and stylistic. Late-sixteenth-century Italian literature in general is sometimes characterized as "mannerist" or "manneristic," a term transplanted to literature from the history of art, where it signifies a model of art that privileges self-conscious artifice over the imitation of nature. Where lyric poetry is concerned, features that may be perceived as manneristic are insistent wordplay, obtrusive sound patterning or word patterning, unusual or phonetically emphatic rhymes, and arcane metrical schemes. All these things showcase the poet's virtuosity, so that we are conscious of the poem as performance. The effect is quite different from earlier-sixteenth-century verse that aims at a kind of formal transparency and effortlessness, reminiscent of Castiglione's notion of *sprezzatura* (nonchalance), a hiding of art.[74] Taken to extremes, this tendency can result in extraordinary inventions such as the so-called *sonetto continuo*, a sonnet with only two rhyme words, repeated in alternation, sometimes with the rhyme word not used in rhyme in a given line appearing earlier in the line (no. 97). The term *manneristic* also seems well suited to rhetorical devices such as *rapportatio* (see nos. 16, 64, 120, 159, 197, 199), in which sentences or phrases are disassembled and their component grammatical parts lined up in a new order. First popularized by the Venetian poet Domenico Venier (1517–82) in the 1550s, *rapportatio* enjoyed an extraordinary vogue in the later sixteenth century, continuing into the Baroque.[75]

The principal metrical innovation of the later sixteenth century in Italy was the rise of the madrigal form to rival the sonnet as the preferred short lyric meter. This illustrates very well late-sixteenth-century lyric increasing

independence from Petrarch as a model and its restlessness with the con-
straints Petrarchism's strict imitative practice imposed on creativity. The
madrigal is a notably free form of lyric, compared with the sonnet: it may
have any number of lines and be composed of any combination of eleven-
and seven-syllable lines, with any rhyme scheme. It even admits unrhymed
lines, something unthinkable in the sonnet. Characteristic of the later-
sixteenth-century madrigal is extreme brevity and lightness; some poems
encompass a mere seven or eight lines, with seven-syllable lines dominant
over hendecasyllables (see nos. 118 and 120 for examples). Miniature, highly
crafted, jewellike pieces, they thrive on wordplay and "conceits": witty, ar-
cane, or improbable images such the acqueduct of salvation Semidea Poggi
figures in the crucified Christ's side (no. 125) or Isabella Andreini's image of
the lover reduced to dust and trampled under the beloved's feet (no. 68).[76]

The madrigal form was first popularized within the context of love lyric,
and it continued as a primarily erotic form until almost the end of the six-
teenth century. In the mid-1590s, however, the Genoese Benedictine poet
Angelo Grillo (1557–1629), who had perfected his skills in the 1580s as a mad-
rigalist writing love lyric under the pseudonym Livio Celiano, pioneered
the use of the meter in spiritual poetry: an innovation picked up and imi-
tated by Giambattista Marino (1569–1625), generally acknowledged as the
founding father of the Baroque. The combination of light form and weighty
subject matter in Grillo's and Marino's religious lyrics flouted conventional
understandings of decorum yet proved attractive—perhaps partly for this
reason—to the increasingly anticlassical aesthetics of the day. The present
anthology includes religious madrigals by Lucrezia Marinella, Valeria Miani
(d. after 1620), Girolama Castagna, and Semidea Poggi (nos. 118–22 and 125),
all writing after Grillo's and Marino's innovations. Also present is a spiritual
madrigal by Chiara Matraini published in 1590 that intriguingly preempts
Grillo's experiments with the form.

Although the rise of the madrigal was undoubtedly the key metrical de-
velopment of this period, Genoese poet Gabriello Chiabrera (1552–1638) initi-
ated a broader process of metrical experimentation, influenced in part by a
group of French lyricists known as the Pléiade. Chiabrera introduced
new metrical forms into the Italian repertoire, including the *canzonetta* and
scherzo: light, elegant forms with a similar appeal to that of the madrigal,
though longer and hence capable of sustaining a more articulated subject
matter. Chiabrera's chief female imitator was Isabella Andreini, a corre-
spondent of his and far the most metrically adventurous female poet of the
period: her 1601 *Rime* includes poems in nine different metrical forms.[77]
Andreini's Chiabreraesque vein is illustrated here by two scherzi (no. 69–
70), including one, "Deh girate," destined to become one of her most famous

poems. Andreini was also highly regarded as a madrigalist, featuring prominently in the principal seventeenth-century anthologies of the form (see nos. 66–68).

The experimental impulses of the later sixteenth century are apparent even within the traditional Petrarchan meter of the sonnet. Where earlier sixteenth-century Petrarchism, following Petrarch's own lead, had limited itself to a restrained set of metrical schemes, later-sixteenth-century Petrarchism was much freer, and variation in rhyme schemes became a more important and self-conscious element in poets' stylistic self-fashioning. Outstanding in this regard is Maddalena Salvetti, whose 1590 *Rime toscane* deploys sixteen different rhyme schemes in its 104 sonnets, including seven with quatrain schemes that depart from the standard chiastic form, ABBA ABBA. As a comparison, in the 380 sonnets contained in the modern edition of her work (excluding one *sonetto caudato*), Vittoria Colonna employs only nine different schemes in total, and none depart from the standard quatrain form.[78] While Salvetti is unusual in the extent of her metrical inventiveness, she typifies later-sixteenth-century developments more generally. A sample of seventeen occasional sonnets by Maddalena Camiglia from the 1580s and early 1590s show her deploying eight different rhyme schemes, including two with irregular quatrain schemes, while the twenty-eight sonnets of Lucchesia Sbarra's autobiographical sequence deploy seven, again including two with irregular quatrain schemes.[79]

Where thematics are concerned, three main developments may be noted in the later sixteenth century. The first is the rise of religious poetry as an important Petrarchist theme, capable of holding its own quantitatively with the two other great thematic blocks, love poetry and occasional verse. Although spiritual lyrics had begun to figure in Petrarchism from the 1530s, with Vittoria Colonna and Girolamo Malipiero (c. 1480–1547), their popularity vastly increased during the Counter-Reformation, rising to a peak after around 1580. They also acquired a new theoretical legitimacy, especially through the writings of the Venetian poet and preacher Gabriele Fiamma, who argued that the praise of God should be seen as poetry's original vocation, while other themes, such as love and the praise of rulers, were a later, morally suspect deviation. Fiamma advocated an imitative religious poetics on the model of Bembist Petrarchism, but with the psalmist David substituting for Petrarch as the dominant model, at least in theory (in his own poetic practice, Fiamma was sufficiently pragmatic to pay close attention to Petrarch as well).[80]

In his account of the history of poetry, Fiamma gave a prominent place to the Old Testament canticle tradition, which he presents as one of two parallel poetic founding traditions, the other being the mythical Greek tradition of Orpheus, Linus, and Musaeus, the *prisci poetae* (ancient poets) of human-istic lore. Unlike the Greek prisci poetae, the Old Testament tradition in-cludes women, such as Miriam, Deborah, Judith, and the Virgin Mary (as author of the *Magnificat*), giving a powerful biblical sanction to women's presence within the modern tradition of spiritual verse. In evolving this theory, Fiamma was doubtless mindful of the important role women played in the contemporary, Petrarchist religious lyric tradition: he was an admirer of Vittoria Colonna and an acquaintance of Laura Battiferri, whose *Sette salmi* (Seven Penitential Psalms) of 1563 was entirely in consonance with his project (see nos. 93–94 for examples of sonnets taken from this work).[81]

The second important thematic development of the period, less easy to relate to Counter-Reformation cultural tendencies, is the increasing sensu-ality of love lyrics, especially of love lyrics adopting a classicizing pastoral idiom. Already a strong presence since the fourteenth century within the Latin lyric tradition, pastoral vernacular lyrics grew increasingly popular over the course of the sixteenth century, partly due to the new genre of pas-toral drama, which evolved at the court of Ferrara in the mid-1550s.[82] In addition to vernacular versions of classical bucolic forms like the dramatic elegy (practiced, among women writers, by Laura Battiferri and Isabella Andreini), we find increasing numbers of sonnets and madrigals in this pe-riod addressed to love objects whose classicizing names, such as Filli, Clori, Dafne, or Amarinta, evoke the pastoral conventions of idyllic rural life in an ancient, timeless society remote from the pressures of the modern urban or courtly world.[83]

Where these names veil the identity of contemporary women (such as Andreini, who went by the name Filli), love lyrics addressed to them follow the usual, respectable conventions of Petrarchism. Where the addressee is fictional, however—a dreamy imagining of a young, lightly clad, bucolic "nymph," refreshingly free of societal concerns about honor—such pastor-alizing Petrarchist lyrics became the opportunity to explore a more sensual vein from which traditional Petrarchism had forborne. The suitors who voice these lyrics do not limit themselves to admiring their beloved's hair and eyes but also fawn over the beauty of their breasts, and their amorous aspirations are not limited to a word or a smile but extend to kisses or more. An extreme example of the sensual turn in late-sixteenth-century lyric, and a popular choice for musical setting, is Giambattista Guarini's notorious madrigal "Tirsi morir volea" (Tirsi Longed for Death), which portrays a steamy sexual encounter between Tirsi and an unnamed nymph, conclud-ing with their simultaneous "death."

The third important thematic innovation within late-sixteenth-century lyric is the increasing importance of domestic and familial affections as a subject for lyric. Like spiritual verse, this was not entirely new in the late sixteenth century. Precedents existed, especially in a postmortem context: one of Bembo's most famous compositions, for example, was a canzone mourning the death of his brother. The marital love poetry of a poet like Vittoria Colonna, later imitated by other southern poets like Berardino Rota (1508–75) and Bernardo Tasso (1493–1569), may arguably also be placed in this category in that it differs sharply in character from the extramarital "unattainable loves" in which Petrarchism had traditionally specialized. This poetry of domestic affection gained a greater prominence in the post-Tridentine period, plausibly in response to the same kind of moralizing impulses that encouraged the rise of religious poetry in the same period. The thematic range of this lyric vein also widened to embrace themes such as the death of children, a tragically common experience at this time.[84] An example of the richness and diversity of the affective bonds celebrated in lyric poetry in this period may be seen in a volume of verse published in 1600 by two Venetian poets, Orsatto Giustinian (1538–1603) and Celio Magno (1536–1602), the former a contact of Maddalena Campiglia, the latter of Lucrezia Marinella. Besides love poetry addressed to traditional, nebulous beloveds, Giustinian and Magno's *Rime* includes several lyrics by the two poets expressing their passionate friendship with one another; a cycle of fifteen sonnets by Giustinian celebrating his thirty-five-year marriage to Candiana de' Garzoni; a shorter cycle by Giustinian mourning the death of his mother; and canzoni by Magno on the death of his own father and of Giustinian's mother, the latter a victim of the devastating plague that hit Venice in 1575–76.[85]

Female poets engaged with these three thematic novelties to differing extents, as is predictable. Their engagement with religious lyric was enthusiastic, as previously discussed. Far less frequented, as might be expected, was the sensual, pastoralizing vein of poetry explored by poets like Guarini. The only female poet to attempt this fashionable model of poetry was Isabella Andreini, who stood a little outside the "respectable" mainstream of women's poetry by virtue of her professional status as an actress. Andreini handled the delicate problem of decorum by the ingenious expedient of adopting both male and female voices in her love poetry and allocating most of the more sensual of her poems to a male voice. The prefatory sonnet to her 1601 *Rime* (no. 65) breezily outlines this ventriloquizing poetics and presents Andreini's lyric "performances" as an extension of her work on the stage. Although Andreini was unique among female poets of the time in venturing into sensual territory in her lyrics, she was not alone in deploying a male voice in her love poetry. Earlier in the century, we see this distancing device in Laura Terracina and Gaspara Stampa; contemporary with Andreini, in Orsina Cavaletti, Moderata Fonte, and Lucchesia Sbarra (nos. 63–64, 71–72).[86]

More productive, for women, than the shift to the sensual in love poetry, was the tendency for the late-sixteenth-century love lyric to extend its affective range beyond the erotic. The trend toward "domestic Petrarchism" is exemplified by Francesca Turina and Lucchesia Sbarra, both of whom composed verse on the death of their sons (nos. 184–85, 187), and Turina also on the death of her husband (nos. 55–59); and also by Veneranda Bragadin (c. 1566–post 1619), whose *Rime* of 1619 includes verse mourning her mother and husband (no. 186). Turina's verse is especially original, breaking with the thematic boundaries of Petrarchism in ways barely envisaged by the male-authored tradition. It would be difficult to think of anything within the lyric output of this period that resembles the long autobiographical sequence of verse that Turina composed from the 1570s onward, publishing it in 1628, toward the end of her life. The poems tell her story from her infancy and childhood (nos. 202–5), through her marriage (nos. 36–38), and the birth and upbringing of her sons, to her struggles as a widow, and finally to her old age (no. 211). The sequence composes a remarkable poetic autobiography, bending Petrarchist language to a subject matter now entirely remote from conventional Petrarchist thematics. One poem describes her breastfeeding one of her infant sons (no. 180), while others speak of a miscarriage she endured in her husband's absence, her pride in watching her young grandsons compete in a joust, the graying of her hair, the fall of a tooth.[87]

Sui generis as it is, Turina's autobiographical verse is representative of late Petrarchism in one important respect: this may be seen as the period in which the Petrarchist lyric tradition began seriously to engage with the material and social world. As noted earlier, a marked tendency to abstraction characterized the classic Petrarchism of the age of Bembo and Colonna. Although a sonnet of Colonna's speaks of her husband returning from battle and showing her his "beautiful scars," and a poem of Gaspara Stampa's imagines the poet's beloved hunting wild boar and entertaining guests on his country estate, this type of narrative detail was exceptional in the lyric of this period.[88] Later-sixteenth-century Petrarchism, by contrast, began to allow space to the narrative and the particular. An entire subgenre of late-sixteenth-century erotic madrigal, for example, focused on details of the lady's dress and her often whimsical and distinctive adornment: a striking shift from Petrarch, where we encounter only the most generic references to Laura's "gown" or her "veil."

The tendency to the concrete and narrative in later-sixteenth-century Petrarchism is present in a very marked form in Veronica Franco. Although she draws on the Petrarchan tradition in style and lexis, Franco is much closer thematically and in her tone to the Roman elegiac poets in her wry, sensual, narratively embedded treatment of love. In one poem (no. 34) she takes us into the midst of a lovers' quarrel, showing the poet suspended between fury at her treacherous beloved and hopes for a reconciliation, portrayed in explicitly sexual terms unthinkable in any other female writer of the period. Another (no. 35), almost equally transgressive of Petrarchist norms, has the poet reminiscing about a past, now-cooled, infatuation with a young cleric. One scene in this second poem shows the object of her past fascination preaching a sermon, an episode that places him squarely within the social, urban world of Venice and distances him from the nebulous, decontextualized beloveds that had peopled both men's and women's love lyric. Only Gaspara Stampa's offers a convincing precedent with her concretely portrayed Count, although he remains closer to tradition in certain regards, such as his rural setting and his chivalric ethos, reminiscent of the male beloved of Colonna's amorous verse.

Franco has often been portrayed as "anti-Petrarchist," yet she seems less so when contextualized with reference to the Petrarchism of her own, post-1560 era than to a generic, chronologically undifferentiated model. Sixteenth-century Petrarchism, in general, is highly "socialized" by comparison with the fourteenth-century archtype of Petrarch himself, incorporating far higher doses of occasional and political verse and showcasing sonnet exchanges. This tendency was exacerbated in the later sixteenth century, when occasional verse came to occupy an ever greater place within Petrarchist production, and its thematics became ever more ramified and various. A characteristic publication model in the period was the verse collection that brought together poems by various authors on a particular subject, such as a marriage or a death; a battle; the award of a doctorate; or the arrival or departure of a government official. Three poems in this anthology derive from such thematic collections: a Latin poem by Ersilia Spolverini commemorating the departure of a Venetian governor's wife from her home town of Verona (no. 154); a sonnet by Laura Battiferri mourning the death of Eleonora of Toledo (no. 188); and a sonnet by an anonymous "Gentildonna palermitana" commemorating the execution of a noblewoman accused of involvement in a murder (no. 189). Also assimilable to this type of verse, though not taken from a thematic anthology, is a poem by Catella Marchesi mourning the murder of a wife by her husband on suspicion of adultery (no. 191). All illustrate well the tendency to an ever more socially embedded lyric tradition, whose ideal locus of lyric production was no longer the hermetic rural solitude of Petrarch's beloved Vaucluse (which means literally "closed valley") but the intricate, ritualized, social world of the late-Renaissance city or court.

The Advent of the Baroque

In several respects, such as its taste for rhetorical artifice and its emphasis on wit and wordplay, the lyric poetry of the late sixteenth century anticipates the later, seventeenth-century style of verse that is conventionally designated "Baroque." Nonetheless, it still makes good historical sense to locate the stylistic watershed in the early years of the new century, following the publication of Giambattista Marino's seminal 1602 *Rime*. Certainly, it is in the wake of Marino's belated and striking publishing debut that we begin to find a widespread awareness developing of the novelty represented by the "new lyric." In a letter of 1604, Angelo Grillo speaks of Marino having "hit on the taste of these times, as enamored of novelty and caprice in poetry as past ages were of purity and refinement."[89] Less sympathetically, Francesco Visdomini in 1609 complained of "monstrous sonnets" filled with "high-sounding words," "outrageous metaphors" and "senses so obscure that we cannot understand them ourselves."[90]

The new Baroque style was historically destined to prove less amenable to female poets than the Petrarchism that had preceded it. Although some poets, such as Lucrezia Marinella and Lucchesia Sbarra, seized eagerly on the new style, and we can see traces of it also in Semidea Poggi, it would be difficult to speak of a tradition of Baroque lyric by women, as we can so convincingly speak of a tradition of female-authored Petrarchism. One problem may have been that the showy, "rule-breaking" character of Baroque lyric was less compatible with the behavior to which elite women were socialized than the more measured and chaste language of Petrarchism.[91] The same went for the poet's ethos, as evinced by the two traditions' founding fathers: Marino's louche and swashbuckling persona made him less of a feasible role model for female poets than the courtly, sober Bembo, the founder of Petrarchism, a cardinal for the last eight years of his life.

Another feature of the Baroque poetic tradition that contributed to women's marginalization as authors of lyric was the highly sensual character of its love lyric: a trend already apparent in the late sixteenth century, as we have seen, but carried to new heights by Marino. Like Guarini, Marino tends to locate his more explicitly erotic poems in a pastoral dreamscape, where "realist" conventions of honor and sexual morality may be set aside. Although the poetic lady remains a vision of beauty in Marino, that beauty has entirely relinquished the function of moral and spiritual edification that Petrarchism and neoplatonism had attributed to it. Rather than as a sign of her inner, spiritual perfection, the lady's physical beauty is celebrated as an end in itself and as a trigger of sexual desire, sometimes not without a degree of hostility or aggression: gloating warnings of the deterioration age would wreak on the lady's beauty became a recognized subtheme in Italian lyric at this time.

This new and less worshipful configuration of the poetic lady had negative implications for women as poets. Petrarchist lyric had crafted a feminine ideal that combined physical beauty with chastity, intelligence, and moral and spiritual refinement. This allowed a space for the female poet, who could be treated as a "living Laura," a vocal embodiment of the ideal.[92] Baroque lyric was considerably less accommodating to the female voice in this regard. Where Bembo privileged women as interlocutors to the extent of including two poetic exchanges with women among only five in total featured in his 1535 *Rime* (nos. 130–33), Marino's copious output of poetic correspondence, by contrast, includes only one exchange with a woman (ironically, with Margherita Sarrocchi, with whom he later and quite poisonously fell out).

It is barely an exaggeration, then, to state that the tradition of women's lyric in Italy came to an end with the demise of Petrarchism—essentially at the end of the sixteenth century, though with some afterlife in the following few decades. Although women continued to write in the seventeenth century in Italy, it was on a far lesser scale than in the previous century, and, in an increasingly misogynistic age, more of their energies than before were expended on polemic and self-defense.[93] This shift is reflected in this volume, which includes polemical sonnets from this period by Sarra Copio and Veneranda Bragadin (nos. 173–74). While women continued to write and publish after the 1620s, their lyric production dwindled sharply. The only three new female lyric poets to emerge between 1620 and 1680 whose works attained significant circulation were Margherita Costa (d. c. 1657), a Roman singer and courtesan; Isabetta Coreglia (fl. 1628–50), a Lucchese musical virtuosa; and Francesca Farnese (1593–1651), an aristocratic Clarissan nun.[94] None of these three are included in this anthology, partly in order to preserve the coherence of the collection, as principally representative of a single, though long-lived and evolving, tradition. The only poems that have been included that seem datable to beyond the 1620s are a late madrigal by Francesca Turina (no. 211) and a sonnet by Silvestra Collalto (no. 207), included for its interesting intertextual references to Lucchesia Sbarra, and its wry and topical theme of the silencing of the female poet, a theme also found in Coreglia and Costa.[95]

Beyond Tuscan: Latin and Greek Verse

The vast majority of surviving early modern Italian female-authored texts are written in Tuscan, and specifically in the archaic, fourteenth-century model of Tuscan adopted from the 1520s or 1530s as the dominant Italian literary language. Verse in Latin was much rarer, especially after the fifteenth century, when humanistic Latin ceased to be the dominant literary language, and a relatively low percentage of it appears to have survived. Women educated to a standard that allowed them to write poetry in Latin tended on the whole to be of extremely high status, and such women were those least likely to have their verse published. Women such as Camilla Valenti (c. 1523–44) and Renea Pico (d. 1607), respectively niece and great-granddaughter of Veronica Gambara, are documented as having written verse in the vernacular and Latin, while Pico is supposed also to have written in Greek.[96] None of either woman's poetry appears to have survived.

This anthology contains six poems in Latin, one by the fifteenth-century humanist Isotta Nogarola (no. 192), one by the famous singer and erudite Tarquinia Molza (no. 112), one by the far less well-known Ersilia Spolverini (no. 154). The remaining three are by the Florentine nun Lorenza Strozzi (nos. 102–4), author of the most substantial collection of Latin verse surviving by an Italian woman of this period, a volume of hymns published in Florence in 1588. One poem in Greek is also included (no. 170), by the remarkable Olimpia Morata (1526–55), one of the most learned Italian women of the entire period and the most radical religious thinker of the poets in this volume. Morata, tragically, lost most of her writings during the disruptions following the sacking of Schweinfurt, in Germany, where she had moved with her Protestant husband, although several of her poems in Latin and Greek do survive, including a series of psalm adaptations in Greek.[97]

Beyond Tuscan: Dialect Verse

In addition to Tuscan and the classical languages, poetry was also composed in regional dialects in sixteenth-century Italy, including Genoese, Neapolitan, Sicilian, Venetian, and the rural Paduan dialect named *pavan*.[98] Verse composed in these dialects tended to be comic and sometimes vulgar, differentiating itself quite deliberately from the high standards of decorum that were customary in Tuscan "high literature." For this reason, women, bound by stricter behavioral standards than men, tended not to participate in the dialect tradition. Although we find Veronica Franco, in one famous poem not included in the present anthology, offering to "duel" with a poetic enemy in "the vernacular Venetian tongue," no writings by her in any language other than Tuscan survive.[99]

It is fascinating, therefore, to discover that four women of the mainland Veneto published a tiny group of poems in *pavan* in the 1580s: Maddalena Campiglia, Issicratea Monte, Bianca Nievo Angaran (c. 1531–88), and Maria Azzalina.[100] Two of these poems—by Monte (no. 209) and Campiglia (no. 210)—are included here. The female poets who contributed to this tradition did not indulge in vulgarity; nor did they assume a rustic pseudonym, as was usual among male poets. It would not be accurate, however, to say that they wrote entirely as themselves: rather, they adopted the naïve and "unlettered" persona characteristic of verse within the *pavan* tradition, Monte, for example, referring to Petrarch as "pre' Cecco" (Father Frank). The bantering, though respectful, exchanges between female and male *pavan* poets are interesting for the rich sense they give of women's social and cultural life in the cities of the Veneto, far the most flourishing centers for women's literary production in the period after the Council of Trent.[101] They also offer a welcome glimpse of humor, otherwise mainly visible in this anthology in the wry, self-aware love poems of Gaspara Stampa and Veronica Franco, in a zestful sonnet of resistance to love by Camilla Scarampa (no. 167), in Girolama Corsi's sprightly *barzelletta* dramatizing a husband-wife relationship (no. 208), and in the aged and toothless Francesca Turina's wistful madrigal on her nostalgia for solid food (no. 211).

The Afterlife of Early Modern Italian Women's Lyric

The history of the reception of the lyric tradition presented in this volume is by no means a linear one. Sixteenth- and early-seventeenth-century women's lyric enjoyed a first revival in Italy in the final decade of the seventeenth century with the beginning of the classicizing Arcadian movement, which returned the idiom of sixteenth-century Petrarchism to fashion. Between 1692 and 1701, the Naples-based French publisher Antonio Bulifon (1646–c. 1707) republished works by Vittoria Colonna, Veronica Gambara, Isabella Morra, Tullia d'Aragona, Lucrezia Marinella, Laura Battiferri, and Isabella Andreini, as well as reissuing Lodovico Domenichi's anthology of female poetry of 1559.[102] At the same time, contemporary women were once more beginning to contribute to the lyric tradition, as they had not for almost a century. By 1726, the Venetian writer and editor Luisa Bergalli was able proudly to unfurl in her *Componimenti poetici delle più illustri rimatrici d'ogni secolo* (Poetical Compositions by the Most Illustrious Female Poets of All Ages) a tradition of female-authored verse stretching back to the origins of Italian literature and forward to the Arcadian lyric of her own age.

Bergalli's anthology is important as the most complete and comprehensive reconstruction of Italian Renaissance women's lyric prior to the present collection. Unlike most nineteenth- and twentieth-century collections, it does not bisect the sixteenth century following the Council of Trent and ignore subsequent lyric production. Excluding "fakes"—early female poets invented by overenthusiastic male compatriots—Bergalli has verse by 166 poets active between the early fifteenth and the mid-seventeenth century.[103]

Eight of these are fifteenth century; ninety-four were active between 1500 and 1575; and the remaining sixty-four between 1575 and around 1650 (the numbers in the 1500–75 section are boosted by the availability of Lodovico Domenichi's 1559 anthology, all but two of whose fifty-three poets are included in Bergalli's collection).[104]

The prominence accorded to the later period is illustrated still more clearly if we look at the best-represented pre-1650 poets in the collection.

35	Gaspara Stampa
26	Lucia Colao (listed as *incerta*, "unidentified author"), Vittoria Colonna
23	Laura Battiferri
18	Isabella Andreini, Veronica Gambara
15	Maddalena Salvetti
14	Lucrezia Marinella, Lucchesia Sbarra, Olimpia Malipiero, Tullia d'Aragona
13	Laura Terracina
12	Chiara Matraini
10	Veneranda Bragadin

Of these fourteen poets, six wrote exclusively after the closure of the Council of Trent (Colao, Andreini, Salvetti, Marinella, Sbarra, and Bragadin). All are virtually unknown to modern criticism, with the exceptions of Andreini and Marinella, the latter of whom is renowned for her narrative and polemical writings, while her lyric poetry remains virtually unknown. Other poets from the later period well represented in Bergalli are Orsina Cavaletti, with eight poems, and Moderata Fonte and Maddalena Campiglia, with six.

Bergalli is important in the history of the reception of women's lyric not least for her rediscovery of Gaspara Stampa, who had been practically forgotten since 1554, when her verse was first published. Not only did Bergalli give Stampa the preeminent place in her 1726 anthology, but she also reedited Stampa's entire collected verse in 1738.[105] This was a momentous development, as Stampa would from this point take an increasingly dominant place within the canon of Italian women's lyric, rising to challenge more stably canonical figures such as Colonna and Gambara in the nineteenth century, and coming to be regarded by many critics in the twentieth century as the greatest female Italian poet of all time. Another eighteenth-century milestone was Felice Rizzardi's fine 1759 edition of the verse and letters of Veronica Gambara, whose collected work had not been available in print before this time. Both the Stampa and the Gambara edition are illustrations of the immense importance of localism in Italian literary scholarship. Rizzardi's edition was published in Brescia, near Gambara's birthplace of Pralboino, and is dedicated to a member of the Gambara family. Bergalli's edition of Stampa was published in Venice, and was coedited by Antonio Rambaldo da Collalto, a descendant of Collaltino da Collalto, whom Stampa had immortalized (not entirely flatteringly) in her verse.[106]

Another moment when early modern women's lyric resurfaced as a subject of scholarly and critical attention was the late nineteenth century, like the early eighteenth, a time when contemporary women's writing was flourishing. A search on the ICCU online catalog of books in Italian libraries for Vittoria Colonna as author lists twenty-two publications for the nineteenth century: one before 1860, seven in the 1860s and 1870s, and fourteen between 1881 and 1900. Similar results are yielded for the equivalent search for Veronica Gambara and Gaspara Stampa, with, respectively, ten and six publications, sixteen in total, of which three appeared before 1860, four in the 1860s and 1870s, and nine in the last two decades of the century.[107] As in the earlier phase of interest, female scholars were active in work on these authors, with Pia Mestica Chiappetti (1847–82), for example, producing new editions of Gambara and Stampa.[108] Nor was interest in sixteenth-century Italian women's writing in this period limited to Italy: Vittoria Colonna enjoyed something of a vogue in Victorian England, partly on account of her friendship with Michelangelo, and Maud F. Jerrold published a lengthy biography of her—still the best account of her life—in 1906.[109] In Italy, female poets continued to profit from researches motivated by local interests, proceeding with great vigor under the impulse of positivism, a critical tradition that privileged historical contextualization. Important biographical work was carried out in this period, for example, on Maddalena Campiglia, by the Vicenza historian Bernardo Morsolin (1834–99), and Issicratea Monte, by the Paduan classicist Vincenzo de Vit (1810–92).[110]

The late-nineteenth-century studies and editions of early modern female poets often attributed to these women exemplary character and an inspirational role. A very clear example of this attitude is the edition of Colonna, Gambara, and Stampa published in 1882 by the poet Olindo Guerrini (1845–1916). Guerrini's preface ends with a peroration underlining the excellence of the three poets and proposing them as an exemplum of women's potential: "collected here together, they speak to our modern-day women, showing them that what people say about female inferiority is untrue."[111] Similar emphases are found in Enrico Comba's *Donne illustri italiane proposte ad esempio alle giovinette* (Illustrious Italian Women Proposed as Examples to Young Girls), first published in 1872, which includes Colonna, Gambara, Tullia d'Aragona, and Laura Battiferri among its aspirational figures.[112]

Very different in attitude to this bien-pensant late-nineteenth-century feminism is the attitude we find in an early-twentieth-century figure such as Abdelkader Salza, who published three studies between 1913 and 1917 intended to demonstrate that Gaspara Stampa was a courtesan, rather than an impassioned young noblewoman, as most eighteenth- and nineteenth-century readers had thought.[113] Salza may have been inspired by Enrico Celani's edition of Tullia d'Aragona in 1891, a work that helped bring the sixteenth-century figure of the courtesan back into historical and critical attention.[114] As part of his rebranding campaign, Salza published an edition of Stampa's verse in 1913 in a joint volume with that of the known courtesan Veronica Franco.[115] The gesture is particularly striking when we consider that Guerrini's popular 1882 edition had grouped Stampa with Colonna and Gambara partly on social grounds: his volume is entitled *Rime di tre gentildonne del secolo XVI* (Verse by Three Gentlewomen of the Sixteenth Century).

Eccentric in some respects, Salza's prurient research initiative is typical of the period. The early twentieth century in Italy witnessed a misogynistic reaction against late-nineteenth-century feminism that offers a parallel with the similar "misogynistic turn" of the early seventeenth century. As literature and art turned to stridently new aesthetic ideals, most notably with Futurism, female writers were often used to emblematize the "feebleness," "effeminacy," and sentimentality of the older, rejected aesthetic. At the same time, new or revitalized biologically essentialist conceptions of women's writing began to be framed, notably by the revered philosopher and critic Benedetto Croce (1866–1952), one of the great formative figures of twentieth-century literary historiography. Croce's role in the history of the reception of early modern Italian women's writing is a complex one. On the one hand, he did more, arguably, than any twentieth-century critic in researching and promulgating knowledge of women's writing, doing important work in particular on Isabella Morra, Laura Terracina, and Veronica Franco. On the other hand, Croce contributed to the formation of a heavily reductive and stereotypical notion of the character and potential of "feminine literature" (*letteratura femminile*), which he regarded as typically defective in form but redeemed by its emotional immediacy, and as writing that demanded to be read in an autobiographical key as an outpouring of heartfelt emotion.[116] Although he framed this view in regard to the female-authored literary production of his own era, he applied it also to some past Italian figures, notably Gaspara Stampa, whose verse he extolled as a kind of "diary" and a "document of passions truly lived."[117]

In conjunction with the more general, postromantic tendency to dismiss Petrarchism as trite and uninteresting, Croce's prescriptive notion of *letteratura femminile* deeply shaped the twentieth-century reception history of early modern women's verse. Those who fared best tended to be those who could be construed as rebels against Petrarchism, those with colorful biographies, and love poets. Those who fared least well tended to be figures such as Veronica Gambara and Vittoria Colonna, seen as too conformist in their lives to be of compelling biographical interest and too orthodoxly Petrarchist in their verse to be convincingly construed as "other" to their male colleagues. Poets like Laura Battiferri, who barely touched the subject of love, were also ill suited to twentieth-century critical perspectives.[118] Not until late in the century, with the increased influence of sociohistorical approaches to literature, did critical approaches develop that were tooled to the analysis of occasional and encomiastic poetry. A landmark study in this regard, in terms of English-language criticism, was Ann Rosalind Jones's 1990 *The Currency of Eros*, with its reading of Tullia d'Aragona's intensely dialogic *Rime* as an exercise in self-fashioning and social "negotiation."[119] Victoria Kirkham's closely contextualized studies of Battiferri also exemplify this trend.[120]

A further factor that acted to narrow the canon of early modern women's lyric in the twentieth century was Italian criticism's relentless secularism and its near-universal neglect of literary work written after the Council of Trent, especially works religious in their subject matter. This made for an extremely limited vision of women's lyric output, very different from the ecumenical panorama Luisa Bergalli had presented in her *Componimenti* two centuries before. The only phase of women's lyric production that received any critical attention was that of the first half of the sixteenth century, down to around 1560, while knowledge of their later production was so slight that generations of critics repeated Carlo Dionisotti's lapidary 1967 pronouncement that women formed a "group" in Italian literature only in a short period from around 1538 to 1560 as though it were an unassailable fact.[121] Within these chronological limitations, the amount of attention a poet received depended as much on her biographical interest as anything else.

The narrowness of the female lyric "canon" in the twentieth century is well illustrated if we look at the statistics of women's inclusion in the principal anthologies of Renaissance lyric poetry published during this period.[122] Although verse by women tends to be reasonably well represented, the canon of poets represented is distinctly narrow, and weighted very heavily toward the classic period of Petrarchism, with Veronica Franco very often the sole representative of the later sixteenth-century tradition. The canon of female Renaissance poets was more or less stabilized with Luigi Baldacci's 1957 *Lirici del Cinquecento*, important for its enthusiastic rediscovery of Chiara

Matraini. Baldacci's choice of female poets (Stampa, Franco, Matraini, Veronica Gambara, Tullia d'Aragona, Laura Battiferri, Isabella Morra, Vittoria Colonna, Barbara Torelli Strozzi) survives nearly intact into Roberto Gigliucci and Jacqueline Risset's *La lirica rinascimentale*, published in 2000, the only changes being the omission of Barbara Torelli and the substitution of Laura Terracina for Laura Battiferri.[123] Slightly broader, and with some opening toward the later period, is the selection of female poets in Daniele Ponchiroli's 1958 *Lirici del Cinquecento*, which includes the same poets as Baldacci, with the exception of Matraini, augmented by Laura Terracina, Isabella Andreini, and Francesca Turina.[124] The collectively edited *Lirici europei del Cinquecento*, of 2004, contains virtually the same poets as Ponchiroli, only substituting Tarquinia Molza for Francesca Turina.

The handful of all-female anthologies produced in the twentieth century tend to share the same tendencies of the general anthologies. Francesco Flora's 1962 *Gaspara Stampa e altre poetesse del '500*, for example, limits its choices to Stampa, Franco, Colonna, Gambara, Matraini, Morra, d'Aragona, and Barbara Torelli, while Stefano Bianchi's 2003 *Poetesse del Cinquecento* includes the same poets, except omitting Torelli and adding Terracina and Isabella Andreini.[125] The only recent collection to attempt a broader survey is Laura Anna Stortoni's 1997 *Women Poets of the Italian Renaissance*, which includes poems by nineteen women, including some distinctly neglected voices such as Camilla Scarampa, Lucia Bertani (1521–67), and Olimpia Malipiero (after 1523–69). Stortoni's choices include, unusually, three poets active after 1560: Franco, Andreini, and Moderata Fonte (with Fonte represented, however, by extracts from her nonlyric works).[126] To find an anthology with a broader representation of post-1560 voices, it is necessary to turn back to Jolanda de Blasi's 1930 *Antologia delle scrittrici italiane*, which includes fourteen female poets active between the fifteenth and seventeenth centuries, including four from the later period: Orsina Cavaletti, Lucchesia Sbarra, Catella Marchesi, and Veneranda Bragadin.[127]

What changes most in the general lyric anthologies of the twentieth century is not the canon of female poets but the weighting of individual poets within it. Down to around the 1980s, the early twentieth-century preference for Stampa is overwhelming. Stampa is far the dominant poet quantitatively, male or female, in Baldacci's *Lirici*, with eighty-one poems to the fifty-three of her nearest competitor, Michelangelo. Chiara Matraini is present with thirty-nine poems; Colonna and Gambara with, respectively, twelve and six.[128] The historicizing tendencies of later twentieth-century criticism prompted a shift to a more even distribution and one reflecting more accurately the emphases of the period. Gigliucci and Risset's leading female poets are Colonna with fourteen poems, Stampa with twelve, and

Gambara with nine, while Stortoni's are Colonna with sixteen, Stampa with fourteen, and Gambara with nine. In the sixteenth-century volume of their *Antologia della poesia italiana* (1997) for Einaudi, Carlo Ossola and Cesare Segre include Stampa and Matraini with, respectively, three and two poems, in a general survey of secular Petrarchism, and Colonna with nine poems in a separate section on religious poetry. The new attention to spiritual lyrics evinced by Ossola and Segre's anthology has become a marked trend since around the late 1990s: *Lirici europei* also includes a section on religious verse, including Colonna and Laura Battiferri, though the selection from Battiferri is limited to poems appearing in her mainly secular 1560 *Primo libro*.[129]

Beyond anthologies, studies of women's lyric have flourished especially since the 1980s, with critical editions now available of Colonna (1982), Matraini (1989), Gambara (1995), Morra (2000), and Virginia Salvi (Eisenbichler 2012a). Other landmarks are the publication, between 1998 and 2011, of bilingual editions of Franco, Colonna, Battiferri, Matraini, Stampa, Sarra Copio, and Olimpia Morata in the series *The Other Voice in Early Modern Europe*.[130] Especially welcome, among these, are the edition of Battiferri, which illustrates in print for the first time Battiferri's late career, documented by a manuscript in the Biblioteca Casanatense, and the edition of Stampa, the first modern collection to restore the order of poems in the original, 1554 edition of Stampa's *Rime*. The new millennium has also seen the reemergence of the highly original and long neglected voice of Francesca Turina, now available in Italian and, in selection, in English.[131] Much scholarship, however, remains to be done, especially in the period after 1580, where it would be desirable to see editions of Maddalena Salvetti, Lucrezia Marinella, Lorenza Strozzi, Lucchesia Sbarra, and Lucia Colao.

Anthologizing Early Modern Italian Women's Verse

The present volume is the first modern anthology of early modern Italian women's poetry to represent the whole chronological arc of female lyric production, from the fifteenth century to the mid-seventeenth. In this chronological comprehensiveness, it follows the precedent of Luisa Bergalli's 1726 anthology of female-authored poetry, discussed in the previous section. Around 90 of the 211 poems here were composed after 1560. The vast majority of these texts are not available in English, and many are available in Italian only in the early editions in which they were originally published. Many of their authors (Maddalena Salvetti, Lucchesia Sbarra, Veneranda Bragadin, Semidea Poggi, Leonora Bernardi) were practically unknown to the critical tradition before my 2011 book, *The Prodigious Muse*. Others (Moderata Fonte, Lucrezia Marinella, Maddalena Campiglia) have been researched quite intensively in recent years as narrative and dramatic poets, and as polemicists, but their lyric poetry remains almost unknown.

The anthology is organized thematically, rather than by author, as is customary, although the chronological list of authors in appendix A allows readers to use the book as a more conventional, author-based collection if desired. The reasons for my choice of a thematic ordering are partly positive, partly negative. On the positive side, grouping poems on similar themes allows clear illustration of the workings of imitation and the use and adaptation of poetic topoi or commonplaces, both useful things to grasp when trying to understand the poetry of this period. On the negative side, getting away from an ordering by author permits an escape from the biographical approaches that have traditionally dominated the study of women's poetry and have still not entirely dissipated. Poems by women have very consistently tended to be read as transcriptions of their life experience rather than artistic exercises, an approach that can be especially misguided in a poetic culture as relatively stylized and "unconfessional" as this. While there is clearly a place for readings that place a single author's poems in dialogue with one another, this is perhaps best left to other contexts, such as monographic editions. This anthology seeks to reconstruct a lyric *tradition*—or, more precisely, a subtradition within Italian lyric—and an arrangement that encourages dialogic readings seems best fitted to the project in hand.

Besides the core thematic fields of amatory and religious verse, which together occupy around 60 percent of the volume, much space has also been given to verse on other subjects. One section focuses on correspondence verse and sonnet-exchanges, a key thematic subgenre in sixteenth-century verse and one of great importance in establishing women's public profile as writers. Other sections are devoted to political and polemical verse, to encomiastic verse addressed to patrons and dedicatees, to verse addressed to friends and to family members, and to comic and dialect verse. The thematic divisions introduced here are an organizing device intended solely to facilitate negotiation of the volume. They have no pretension to define thematic subgenres that would have been recognizable to readers of the period, who were generally happy with the catch-all category of *rime varie* (various verse) for poems outside the categories of amorous or spiritual, at least down to the Baroque period, when minuter divisions became popular, such as Marino's "amorous, maritime, pastoral, heroic, lugubrious, moral, sacred, and various."[132]

In respect of selection criteria, I have sought in this anthology to balance diversity with coherence. Although I have attempted to provide a broad and eclectic sample of women's verse, I have concentrated largely on the

Petrarchist tradition, far the dominant lyric tradition of Renaissance Italy, and the one that most successfully traversed thematic boundaries. Where amorous and "various" verse are concerned, this does not present problems, since no important alternative traditions exist. In the case of religious verse, however, this collection's Petrarchist bias does imply significant exclusions. Alternative traditions such as the *lauda* and the neo-Latin hymn have only relatively modest representation here (no. 73; nos. 102–4), while traditions such as fifteenth-century convent poetry and psalm translation are excluded altogether.[133] A dedicated anthology of religious poetry by Italian women would ideally be required to represent this diverse body of literature in full.

Where individual poems are concerned, in addition to scholarly considerations of historical representativeness, I have attempted to choose texts that have something to recommend them artistically, whether on grounds of thematic originality, vividness of expression, emotional power, wit, formal sophistication, or rhetorical dexterity. This task was facilitated by the very considerable quantity of Italian female-authored verse surviving from this period, which allowed for an extreme selectivity on my part. To give some measure of this, Lodovico Domenichi's 1559 anthology of verse by Italian women contains 325 poems in total, only 18 of which are included in the selection in this anthology, around 5.5 percent.[134] Similarly, Gaspara Stampa's 1554 *Rime* contains 311 poems, of which 17 appear here; the modern edition of Vittoria Colonna's verse, 390, of which 26 appear here; Francesca Turina's 1628 *Rime*, 328, of which 14 appear here— around 4 to 6 percent in each case.

Although literary quality was an important consideration in my selection, I have interpreted this criterion quite flexibly, admitting poems with formal irregularities or stylistic unevenness where they seem to me to demonstrate compensatory virtues (see, for example, nos. 172, 206). I have also made an effort to remain flexible, and historically sensitive, in my assessment of what constitutes literary merit, remaining alert both to the qualities of spontaneity and emotional truth that modern, postromantic tastes tend to privilege in lyric poetry and to the qualities of formal poise and technical mastery that held such a high place in sixteenth-century evaluations of verse. For example, I have included various examples of "novelty" verse, such as the cento (no. 52), the *trasmutazione* (no. 60), the *sonetto continuo* (nos. 97, 183), and the *contrafactum* (nos. 99–100, 182): species of verse it would be difficult to equate with any modern notion of the expressive vocation of lyric but which embody ideals of "artfulness" and technical virtuosity that the later sixteenth century, in particular, greatly prized.

Despite my commitment to literary quality as a prime selection criterion, I do not wish to present this anthology as anything amounting to a new canon. While I am convinced that each of the poems contained here has a just claim on the reader's interest, I am very far from wishing to suggest that these are the "best" female-authored lyrics of this period in Italy or that poems excluded from this anthology are necessarily inferior to those that have been included. Aside from the intrinsically subjective character of such evaluative judgments—made more difficult in this case since they involve weighing solidly canonical figures against almost entirely unknown ones—a selection made entirely on grounds of literary excellence might risk ending up skewed too far toward established "greats" such as Stampa and Colonna, already available in good modern editions, while excluding lesser known but worthwhile and interesting poets, many of difficult accessibility in Italian and entirely unavailable in English. Without privileging the unpublished or the difficult of access for its own sake, I have given especially sympathetic consideration to works of high quality not available in print or in modern editions. The resulting selection has no pretensions to definitiveness. Rather, I have aimed here to put together a fresh and stimulating collection of lyrics, which gives a true sense of the range and richness of early modern Italian women's verse.

Note on Meter, Rhythm, and Rhyme

Meter

Terms marked with an asterisk are explained in the glossary.

ballata

The ballata was a single- or multi-strophe poem characterized by the presence of a refrain of one or more lines. It was practiced in both secular and religious contexts from the thirteenth century. It offered a degree of freedom in construction, admitting both hendecasyllables (eleven-syllable lines) and *settenari* (seven-syllable lines). After the refrain (*ripresa*), it is made up of strophes composed of two *piedi* with an even number of lines and a *sirma* using the last rhyme of the piedi and ending with the last rhyme of the *ritornello* (see the entry for "canzone" below for the terms *piedi* and *sirma*). At its weightiest, a ballad might have the scheme xyyx (*ripresa*) ab.ab (*piedi*) bccx (*sirma*) + xyyx (*ripresa*). A lighter ballad might be xx ab.ab bx + xx.

barzelletta

The *barzelletta* was a subspecies of the ballata, which emerged in the fourteenth century and reached the peak of its popularity in the fifteenth. It is composed of *ottonari* (eight-syllable lines) and classically comprises a four-line refrain (*ripresa*), rhymed xyyx, followed by a series of eight-line strophes, each subdivided into two *piedi* and a *sirma* (see the entry for "canzone" for these terms), with the last rhyme or two rhymes of the *sirma* reprising the rhymes of the *ripresa*. The most common schemes are xyyx ababbccx or xyyx ababbyyx. The latter is the scheme of the most famous poem in this meter, Lorenzo de' Medici's carnival song "Quant'è bella giovinezza," which emphasizes the refrain by repeating its last two lines in their entirety at the end of each strophe.

canzone

Found from the thirteenth century, the canzone was praised by Dante as the weightiest form of vernacular lyric and the one most suited to grave subject matter. It is fundamental in Petrarch, whose *RVF* includes twenty-nine poems in this form. The canzone is longer than the sonnet, and is composed of a series of strophes of identical metrical form and rhyme scheme, generally followed by a shorter *congedo* (farewell). In Petrarch, the canzone is composed of hendecasyllables (eleven-syllable lines) and *settenari* (seven-syllable lines), though some of his predecessors also used *quinari* (five-syllable lines). The number of lines in a canzone stanza can vary considerably: Petrarch's shortest have seven lines, his longest twenty. The proportion of short lines to long is another important variable: Petrarch's ethereal love canzone "Chiare, fresche e dolci acque," for example, has nine *settenari* to four hendecasyllables in each strophe, while Bembo's weighty elegaic "Alma cortese, che dal mondo errante" has only one *settenario* in its twenty-line strophes.

Canzone strophes conventionally fall into two parts, known as the *fronte* and the *sirma*. Strictly, the *fronte* is only termed a *fronte* if it is metrically indivisible, and *piedi* when it is divisible into two metrically identical segments. Similarly, a *sirma* is known as a *sirma* when indivisible, and as *volte* when it divides into two metrically identical parts. Petrarch's favored scheme, which became far the most common in Petrarchism, is a canzone composed of two *piedi* and a *sirma*. The rhymes of the *sirma* are generally different from those of the *piedi*, with the exception of the first rhyme, which repeats the last rhyme of the *piedi*, a device known as *concatenatio* (lit. "chaining together"). The *sirma* generally concludes with a juxtaposed rhyme (*rima baciata*), though Petrarch does not observe this as an absolute rule. The canzoni included in this anthology (see appendix B for a listing) generally follow the Petrarchan model described here, although in two cases (nos. 87 and 98), the *fronte* is not obviously divisible into *piedi*. Since the *fronte* in both cases is symmetrical, however (AB-BA, ABC-CBA), it is likely that canzoni of this type were still understood as adhering to the *piedi-sirma* model, though with the *piedi* in a relation of specularity rather than replication. (See Beltrami 1991, 261, for commentary on Bembo's "A quai sembianze Amor Madonna agguaglia," whose *piedi* take this chiastic form.)

capitolo

The *capitolo* was a composition of various length, using the meter of terza rima, which Dante evolved for his *Divine Comedy*. This consists of a series of three-line hendecasyllabic stanzas interlinked by the use of chain rhymes carried over from one stanza to the next, on the pattern ABA, BCB, CDC, DED . . . YZY Z. Terza rima was used largely for narrative and for moral or political verse in the thirteenth and fourteenth centuries (a famous example being Petrarch's *Trionfi*), but it became popular in the fifteenth and early sixteenth century as a lyric and elegiac meter and as a vehicle for amorous verse epistles (see nos. 7–8). The rise of Petrarchism in the 1520s and 1530s had the effect of displacing the *capitolo* as an elevated lyric form, since it was not among the forms sanctified by use in the *RVF*, and it was used in the later sixteenth century largely as a vehicle for Horatian satire (a tradition initiated by Ariosto) and comic-burlesque verse, a fifteenth-century tradition brought to new heights by Francesco Berni (1497–1535). The form of the amorous *capitolo* survived, however, in Venice, where we see it used by Gaspara Stampa and, with greater originality, by Veronica Franco (see nos. 34–35).

elegaic distichs

This verse form originated in ancient Greek verse and was subsequently used extensively within both the ancient Roman and the neo-Latin traditions. It consists of alternating hexameter and pentameter lines (for description of these lines, see the section on rhythm in Latin poetry below).

hexameter

Stichic (non-strophic) hexameters constitute the standard meter for epic poetry in Greek and Latin poetry, but they were also used by Theocritus and Virgil for their pastoral eclogues, and by Horace for his verse epistles, and they were deployed by neo-Latin poets for a range of subject matter. (For a structural description of the hexameter, see the section on rhythm in Latin poetry below.)

madrigal

The poetic madrigal of the sixteenth century is a single-strophe composition made up from eleven- and seven-syllable lines in a free distribution, though generally terminating with a rhymed couplet. There is no set rhyme scheme, and the madrigal, unlike most Italian lyric forms current at the time, admits unrhymed lines. In the later sixteenth and earlier seventeenth century, madrigals tended to become shorter and more epigrammatic, and the proportion of seven- to eleven-syllable lines tends to be higher. The term "madrigal" in an earlier context (thirteenth-fourteenth century) refers to a different form, composed of hendecasyllabic *terzine* followed by a couplet, a single line, or a pair of couplets (see Beltrami 1991, 326–28). "Madrigal" in a musical context means something different again: simply a through-composed (as opposed to strophic) secular song, setting a poetic text, which does not have to be a madrigal in metrical terms.

Sapphic verse

Sapphic verse (also known as Sapphics), is a strophic verse form consisting of four-line stanzas, each made up of three hendecasyllables, followed by a shorter, five-syllable line known as an Adonic or adonean line. First used by the ancient Greek poet Sappho, it was later used in Roman verse, most famously by Catullus and Horace, and was not uncommon in the neo-Latin tradition. It is occasionally found in vernacular verse, as, for example, in Gaspara Stampa's "Di chi ti lagni, o mio diletto e fido" (Stampa 2010, 252–54, no. 220).

scherzo

A light, madrigalesque form invented by the late sixteenth-century Genoese poet Gabriello Chiabrera, the *scherzo* (lit. "joke") was most commonly made up of six-line stanzas made up of four and eight-syllable lines, rhymed aaBccB (see no. 69), although Isabella Andreini uses the term more broadly, to encompass also poems in *sesta rima* (see no. 70).

sesta rima

Sesta rima is essentially a lighter version of the popular narrative form of ottava rima, used in the great narrative works of the period, such as Ariosto's *Orlando Furioso* and Tasso's *Gerusalemme liberata*. It consists of six-line stanzas, rhymed ababcc, which may be in hendecasyllables, or in shorter lines such as *settenari* or *ottonari*, of seven and eight syllables respectively. Shakespeare used this form, with iambic pentameters, in his *Venus and Adonis*.

sestina

An eccentric and notoriously difficult form, the sestina was invented by the troubadour Arnaut Daniel and used by Dante and Petrarch, who includes nine poems in this form in his *RVF*, including one double sestina. The single sestina consists of six, six-line stanzas, all hendecasyllables in the Italian form, followed by a *congedo of three lines. There are six rhyme-words, each of which must occur in each stanza according to a set pattern, in which rhymes migrate in from the extremes to the center, starting from the last rhyme of the previous stanza: ABCDEF, FAEBDC, CFDABE, ECBFAD, DEACFB, BDFECA. Petrarch's double sestina (332) repeats this pattern. All six rhyme words occur in the *congedo*, three internally, three in rhyme. In the Italian sestina (as opposed to the Provençal), the order of the rhyme words in the *congedo* is free.

sonetto caudato

A more elaborate version of the *sonetto ritornellato* (q.v.), which developed rather later, in the fourteenth century, the *sonetto caudato* is, literally, a sonnet "with a tail." Following the fourteen hendecasyllabic lines of the conventional sonnet, it continues with a seven-syllable line rhymed with the last line of the sonnet and a rhyming hendecasyllabic couplet (generally dEE, as *sonetti caudati* tend to use the two-rhyme scheme CDC DCD in their sestet). This unit may be followed by any number of additional tercets on the same model, with the short initial line repeating the rhyme of the previous rhyming couplet (dEE eFF fGG, etc.) The form was generally used within the so-called comic-realist tradition of verse rather than the more elevated Petrarchan tradition: a classic (unusually employing the rhyme scheme CDE CDE in its sestet) is Michelangelo's sonnet describing his painting of the Sistine ceiling, "I' ho già fatto un gozzo in questo stento."

sonetto continuo

The *sonetto continuo*, as defined by the fourteenth-century theorist Antonio da Tempo, is one that uses the same two rhymes, A and B, in the quatrains and tercets. Very rare in earlier lyric production, the form enjoyed a brief fashion in the later sixteenth century, when it was used by poets such as Domenico Venier, Gabriele Fiamma, and Torquato Tasso (Zaja 2009, 275 and n. 83), all of whom use not simply the same rhymes, but the same, antithetical rhyme words, *vita* and *morte* ("life" and "death"). An even more virtuosistic variant seemingly invented by the Neapolitan spiritual poet Ferrante Carafa, who includes examples in his *L'Austria* (1573), uses both rhyme words in every line, one in rhyme and one outside it (for an example, see no. 97).

sonetto ritornellato

Related to the *sonetto caudato* (q.v.), this is a sonnet with a hendecasyllabic line added, in rhyme with the last line of the sonnet proper or, alternatively, a sonnet followed by a hendecasyallbic rhymed couplet, unrhymed with the rest of the poem. This sonnet form was mainly practiced in the early stages of the Italian poetic tradition, in the thirteenth century.

sonnet

Dating from the thirteenth century, the sonnet is one of the earliest Italian vernacular verse forms, and far the most common during the period covered here. Unlike the sestina and canzone, it is not an adapted Provençal form but was developed by the first lyric poets to write in an Italian dialect, the Sicilian school: specifically, its invention is often attributed to Giacomo da Lentini (fl. 1233–40). It consists of fourteen hendecasyllable lines, organized into two main segments, the first of eight lines (the octave, subdivided into two quatrains), the second of six (the sestet, subdivided into two tercets). Far the most common rhyme scheme for the octave is ABBA ABBA, although some variants are possible, such as ABAB ABAB, ABAB BABA, and ABAB BAAB. The most common schemes for the sestet are CDE CDE and CDC DCD, with CDE DCE and CDE EDC the most usual Petrarchan variants and CDE CED a somewhat controversial sixteenth-century novelty. Three-rhyme sestet schemes were generally considered more "grave" or "weighty" in the sixteenth century than "sweeter" or more "pleasing" two-rhyme schemes such as CDC DCD (Afribo 2001, 135, also, more generally, Afribo 2001, 132–150, and Afribo 2009, 166–72 for exhaustive discussion of rhyme schemes in sixteenth-century verse). For discussion of female poets' metrical choices in the sonnet, see appendix C.

stanze

The term *stanze* was commonly used in the sixteenth century to refer to a short, variable-length lyric, or lyric-narrative, composition in ottava rima, the meter most commonly used for narrative verse in Italy. An ottava rima stanza is composed of eight hendecasyllabic lines, rhymed ABABABCC. No precedent for the use of the form is found in Petrarch, but the existence of a poem in ottava rima stanzas by Bembo gave it some degree of legitimacy within Petrarchism, and it remained sufficiently popular in the sixteenth century for anthologies devoted specifically to poems in *stanze* to be published. See Calitti 2004 for the history of the form.

Rhythm: Vernacular Verse

Far the most frequent line length in Italian verse of this period is the hendecasyallble, which fulfils the same function in Italian lyric as the iambic pentameter in English. As in English verse, the rhythm of the line is determined by the distribution of accented, or stressed, words. In the Italian hendecasyllable, the most ubiquitous stress falls on the tenth syllable, a stress pattern called *piano* (plain). This was considered the most harmonious rhythm and is easy to attain, since the vast majority of Italian words are proparoxytone (i.e., stressed on the penultimate syllable). *Versi sdruccioli,* rhymes with words stressed on the antepenultimate syllable (*credìbile*, *furono*), were permitted, but frowned on, in Petrarchism, and mainly found in comic and pastoral verse in the sixteenth century. *Versi tronchi*, ending with a word stressed on the final syllable (*verità*, *vedrà*) are, again, admissible, but uncommon.

Aside from the stress on the tenth syllable, the other main stress in the line falls on the fourth syllable or the sixth, producing what are called, respectively *a minore* and *a maiore* lines. An *a minore* line effectively opens with a four-syllable hemistich, stressed on the last syllable or a five-syllable one stressed on the penultimate. Examples are Colonna's no. 41, l. 5: *Giusta cagión / a lamentar m'invoglia*; and Stampa's no. 13, l. 1: *Voi ch'ascoltáte / in queste meste rime* (note that juxtaposed vowels in adjacent words generally elide in Italian verse, a phenomenon called synaloepha, so that the twelve syllables of Stampa's line are eleven, for metrical purposes, with the *e* and *i* of *ascoltate in* eliding). An *a maiore* line, generally regarded as "graver" or weightier, consists of a long hemistich of six or seven syllables, stressed, again, on the last or the penultimate syllable. Examples are Colonna's no. 79, l. 1: *Vorrei che 'l vero sol / cui sempre invoco*; and Livia Spinola's no. 54, l. 1: *Qual vite che dell'orno / è sciolta unquanco*).

Besides these principal stresses, hendecasyllables also generally contain secondary stresses, which can be distributed quite freely. The most common pattern in *a minore* lines is to have a stress on the eighth syllable (4-8-10), though it may also, less usually, fall on the seventh (4-7-10). In the case of evenly stressed lines (4-8-10) it is not uncommon to have further stresses on the sixth and/or the second (4-6-8-10; 2-4-6-8-10), making for a regular, iambic rhythm. *A maiore* lines generally have a stressed syllable before the sixth, most usually the second or third, and may also have a stress on the eighth.

Petrarchan norms dictate for the most part harmonious, subtle, and unemphatic rhythms, but more marked effects could be achieved with irregular stresses. Although stressed syllables in Italian verse are usually preceded and followed by unstressed, it is not impossible to encounter two stressed syllables in succession at the junction of the two hemistichs of a hendecasyllable, in the fourth and fifth syllables or the sixth and seventh (Beltrami 1991, 50). An example is a line like Maddalena Campiglia's no. 105, l. 4, *nel tenace, mondan visco terreno*, where the sixth and seventh syllables, *-dan* and *vis-*, are both stressed. Even more dramatic in its rhythms, and distinctly post-Petrarchan in its self-conscious irregularity, is the first quatrain of Lucrezia Marinella's sonnet "Tremò la terra e 'l mar, pianse l'Inferno" (no. 113), which uses a series of strongly stressed oxytonic verbs (*Tremò, s'aprìo, s'oscurò, mugghiò*) on unexpected syllables to produce an intentionally disharmonious rhythm, mimicking the effects of cosmic disharmony Marinella is describing.

Rhythm: Latin and Greek Verse

Elite verse in the classical languages is quantitative, rather than qualitative, in its meters, in the sense that lines of verse are patterned by syllable length, rather than stress, as in most European vernaculars. The fundamental metrical unit in the classical languages is the foot, of which the most common types are the spondee and the dactyl. The spondee is made up of two long syllables (syllables containing long verbs, whether intrinsically long, or contextually long, because preceding complex consonants). The dactyl is made up of a long syllable followed by two short ones.

Common poetic meters such as the hexameter and pentameter are made up of different patterns of feet. The hexameter has six feet, of which the fifth is almost always a dactyl and the sixth generally a spondee (though its second syllable is termed *anceps*, which means that it may be either short or long). The first four feet may be either spondees or dactyls. The pentameter is bipartite, with a caesura in the middle, and two dactyls followed by a long syllable on either side of it. The dactyls in the first hemistich can be substituted by spondees, but those in the second hemistich must remain dactyls.

Quantitative meter was replaced in most medieval Latin poetry by qualitative meters, based on stress. One of the great humanistic literary "reforms," along with the introduction of classicizing diction and orthography, was a return to the quantitative meter of classical poetry. All the neo-Latin poetry in this anthology is classicizing in its metrical practice. Aside from straight stichic hexameters (no. 154) and elegiac couplets combining hexameters and pentameters (nos. 112 and 192), the other Latin verse form found here is the Sapphic stanza, which combines hendecasyllables (eleven-syllable lines) with a shorter, five-syllable, adonian line (nos. 102–4).

Rhyme

The mastery of rhyme was one of the essential skills of Italian verse and is showcased in the practice of composing replies to sonnets *per le rime* (using the same rhymes as the original). From around the 1560s, a more extreme version of this exercise arose, using the same actual rhyme words (*per le desinenze*, in the terminology of Girolamo Ruscelli).[135] This is part of a more general tendency in the late sixteenth century toward complex and showy rhyme schemes, manifested in its most extreme form in the *sonetto continuo*, which uses the same two rhymes throughout.

Outside this kind of novelty form, rhymes of words with identical sense and orthography (*rime identiche*) were rare, and generally considered an error. A popular form of embellished rhyme was, however, the homonymous rhyme or *rima equivoca*, which has the same orthography, but a different sense (e.g., *sole* in the adjectival sense of "alone," in the feminine plural, and *sole* in the nominative sense of "sun"). Also considered embellishments were composite rhymes (*rime composte*), in which two or more words are involved in a rhyme (*mentr'io/morio*); rich rhymes (*rime ricche*), which share phonemes besides those necessary for the rhyme (*secondo* with *giocondo*). Some rich rhymes are also "derivative rhymes," in which the rhyme words are etymologically related, (*degna/sdegna*), "inclusive rhymes" (*rime inclusive*), where one rhyme word is contained within the other (*face/sface; fere/sfere*); or "grammatical rhymes" (*rime grammatiche*), where the rhymes share the same grammatical form (*cantando/lagrimando*).

Aside from these forms of speciality rhyme, a less precise distinction is worth noting between vocalic and consonantal rhymes. Italian is an easy language to rhyme in, since many words end in widely shared sequences of simple vowels or dipthongs and simple consonants (e.g.,*-are, -ire, -ato, -ito, -ore, -ura, -ano, -ono, -uono, -ieno*). The majority of rhymes in use in Petrarchist lyric take this relatively easy and unobtrusive form (see, for example, nos. 19 and 37 for poems whose whole rhyme scheme is composed of them). This gives special prominence to more difficult, consonant-rich rhymes, which offer fewer options for rhyming. The combination of vocalic and consonant-rich rhymes in the same poem contributed to the intricacy of its soundscape and served to demonstrate the poet's skill, while a concentration of consonantal rhymes was sometimes used to expressive ends (see, for example, nos. 17 and 157). Some theorists distinguished between "ascending" poems, which moved from lighter rhymes in the quatrains to weightier ones in the quatrains, and "descending" poems, which reversed this dynamic. The former were considered more "grave."

Translation, Transcription, and Editing Criteria

The translations in this anthology do not aspire to be texts that can stand independently as artistic creations. My assumption is that many, if not most, readers of this collection will know some Italian, even if not perhaps enough to make sense of a sixteenth-century sonnet, and will wish to read the translations alongside the Italian as an aid to comprehension rather than as self-standing texts. A prose translation or paraphrase remaining reasonably close to the original seems the most practical solution in these circumstances, rather than a translation set out as verse, especially one that attempts to incorporate rhyme, which inevitably results in a looser relationship with the text.

Even though I have privileged utility over art to this extent, I have not taken the route of a pure literal crib, which would make the book virtually unusable to readers with no knowledge of Italian. Rather, I have aimed for the middle ground of a studied prose translation that attempts to capture something of the tone and diction of the original, even while sacrificing its rhythm, and which I hope can be read with pleasure. I have translated essentially into modern English, with a few archaizing lexical choices and a degree of—mitigated—reflection of the often convoluted syntax of the originals. My aim has been to produce translations sufficiently removed from modern English to retain a reminder of the historical "otherness" of the originals, while still being easily comprehensible. In the case of more obscure texts, I have sometimes translated more freely in order to bring out the sense of the poem, for example reordering clauses within sentences or supplying the logical subject for verbs.

The texts in this anthology have been taken from the most reliable early printed sources or manuscripts available. In the case of many of poems reproduced here, all that is available is a single printed text or manuscript, so that editorial problems do not arise. Where this is not the case, I have consulted different versions of the texts and noted any significant variations in the commentary, though without attempting to provide a formal critical edition, which would have gone beyond the scope of this project. Where textual variants among early editions are an issue, I have for the most part preferred to follow whatever seemed to me the best single extant version, so that the text given here corresponds to one concretely available to readers in the sixteenth century. In a few cases, however, where no single version of a text seemed satisfactory, I have amalgamated readings from more than one version. Where I have done this, it is indicated in the commentary.

Attribution is not generally too thorny a problem with the texts reproduced in this anthology. From around the 1540s onward, print publication became increasingly habitual as a mode of circulation of literary texts in Italy, and most of the poems included here were published during their authors' lifetime, quite often with their involvement. A well-documented case is that of Laura Battiferri, who seems to have been very closely involved in the publication of her *Primo libro delle opere toscane* (1560). Gaspara Stampa's *Rime* were published shortly after her death by her sister, and several finished manuscripts exist of Vittoria Colonna's verse that were copied under her supervision. Of course, the fact that a text was printed or copied under a given author's name, close to the time of writing, cannot be taken as an absolute guarantee of authorship: even in Stampa's *Rime*, we find a sonnet attributed in other sources to Francesco Berni (1497–1535) and various poems by Francesco Maria Molza (1489–1544) are found interpolated in early printed editions of Vittoria Colonna.[136] In some cases, such as the many poems in Lodovico Domenichi's 1559 anthology that are not found elsewhere, and whose authors are poorly documented, we are left with no alternative than to rely on the integrity and competence (and perhaps the luck) of a sixteenth-century editor. In a very few cases I have included poems for which the only source I have is a later, eighteenth-century work of erudition (nos. 39 and 207).

Only two poems need special discussion in this context. The first is "Dhe, non esser Iason, s'io son Medea" (no. 1), which is found attributed in manuscripts to two different male authors, Nastagio da Montalcino and Antonio di Ser Guido de' Magnoli, as well as to Amedea degli Aleardi. In this case, I retain the attribution to Aleardi conjecturally, on the grounds that the manuscripts containing the best version of the text attribute it to her and that one of the alternative authors to whom it has been attributed, Magnoli, has been shown to have been a serial plagiarist.[137] It is possible that the sonnet is by a male acquaintance of Aleardi writing in her voice, but, in the absence of any positive evidence to this effect, there seems no particular reason to favor this hypothesis.

The second poem of problematic attribution is "Vinca gli sdegni e l'odio vostro antico" (no. 158), which was traditionally attributed to Veronica Gambara, but was reattributed to Vittoria Colonna by Gambara's, and Colonna's, modern editor, Alan Bullock.[138] Bullock based his reattribution on the fact that the sonnet appears in a sixteenth-century Sienese manuscript with an attribution to Colonna, but he gives no convincing reason why this attribution should be thought more authoritative than that of, say, Lodovico Domenichi, who published the sonnet under Gambara's name in 1545, when both women were still alive. The attribution survived into several later-sixteenth-century anthologies, suggesting that its authorship was not questioned at the time.[139] I have preferred to retain the attribution to Gambara here and have taken the text from early printed editions rather than the Sienese manuscript used by Bullock, which seems corrupt in one line.[140]

Questions of attribution aside, the lyrics of Veronica Gambara and Vittoria Colonna present the most testing editorial problems of any body of verse in this anthology. Both authors' writings circulated widely in manuscript and print during their lifetimes, but neither made any attempt to collect her verse into a single authoritative version. The editorial problems that arise from this situation are especially acute in the case of Gambara's mature verse and of Colonna's amorous lyrics. Although an attempt at a modern critical edition has been made in the case of both poets (Colonna 1982; Gambara 1995, both edited by Alan Bullock), the Colonna edition in particular has struggled to find scholarly acceptance. While Bullock's edition of Colonna's religious verse, based on a collection published in 1546 by Vincenzo Valgrisi, has proved relatively uncontroversial, his edition of Colonna's love lyrics has been justly criticized as being overly reliant on a single manuscript (Florence, Biblioteca Nazionale Centrale II. IX. 30), which Bullock regards as having been compiled under Colonna's supervision. As critics such as Tobia Toscano have noted, there is no firm external evidence for this claim, and the text conveyed in the Florentine manuscript is not self-evidently superior to other competing versions; indeed, in some cases, it is patently corrupt.[141]

In this unsatisfactory situation, until a true critical edition of Colonna's amorous verse is available, any attempt to reproduce segments of this body of work is fraught with difficulty. The versions here are based on a scrutiny of early printed editions down to 1560, along with the Florentine manuscript on which Bullock based his edition, another important manuscript in the Biblioteca Universitaria of Bologna, and a manuscript in the Biblioteca Nazionale in Naples that Toscano has edited (Colonna 1998). Where the differences between the printed and manuscript versions are insignificant, I have preferred to cite printed sources, since they represent the form in which most sixteenth-century readers would have encountered Colonna's verse. Only where the manuscript versions are a significant improvement on the printed editions (nos. 44, 45, and 48) have I used the manuscript sources. With the exception of two poems that were not published until the nineteenth century (nos. 49 and 50) the order of the poems in this anthology reflects that in early printed editions, rather than that in Bullock's edition, although I have cited the numbering of Bullock's edition to facilitate comparison (A1:1, etc.). It should be noted that the selection here incorporates poems from both Bullock's A1 and A2 sequences, the latter of which, labeled *rime amorose disperse*, is made up of poems that do not appear in MS BNCF II. IX. 30. In early printed editions, poems from the A1 and A2 sequences appear side by side, and the evaluative distinction implied by Bullock's division does not pertain.

The texts in this anthology are reproduced in a lightly modernized version, as is customary in Italian editions of early texts. Some recent editors of Italian texts of this period have preferred systematically to preserve archaic linguistic and orthographic features from early editions, but this seemed inappropriate in the case of an anthology drawing texts from a wide range of printed and manuscript sources showing varying editorial criteria and relatively few of which can be reliably thought to transmit the author's original spelling or punctuation.

The editorial changes that have been made are as follows:

- *U* and *v* have been distinguished according to modern usage.
- *H* used for (pseudo-) etymological purposes has been removed.
- *J* in intervocalic or initial position has been altered to *i* (in both Italian and Latin). In final position, it has been rendered by *ii* or *i* as appropriate.
- The Latinate spelling *-ti* followed by a vowel has been changed to *-zi* in vernacular texts (e.g., *otio* → *ozio*; *gratia* → *grazia*).
- The Latinate spelling *ph* has been modernized to *f* in vernacular texts.
- *Et* and the ampersand symbol (&) have been converted to *e/ed* as appropriate (with attention to scansion).
- Word boundaries have in some cases been changed to correspond to modern usage (e.g., *perché, benché, purché* for *per ché, ben ché, pur ché; nei* for *ne i, degli* for *de gli*). *Poiché* for *poi che* has been modernized only where the meaning is "since" in a causal, rather than a temporal, sense.
- Variant spellings of *allor(a), talor(a),* and *ognor(a)* (e.g., *alhora, tal hor, ogn'hora*) have been standardized to follow modern usage.
- Capitalization, punctuation, and accents have been changed to follow modern usage. The accented form has been preferred in the discretionary cases of *sé stesso/a* and *sé medesimo/a*. Pronouns and possessive adjectives referring to God and Christ have not been capitalized, except in instances where it assists comprehension.
- Where the coalescence of adjacent vowels across a word break (synaloepha) has been marked orthographically (e.g. *mi'ardente* in no. 16, l. 4; *dolc'ombra* in no. 33, ll. 14 and 17), the normal word division has generally been restored (*mio ardente; dolce ombra*), except in some less obtrusive instances (e.g., *senz'alma* in no. 55, l. 11).
- The nexus *c'ha* (*che ha*) has been standardized as *ch'ha*; *c'hanno* as *ch'hanno*.

Other archaic features of texts, such as the use of single consonants where modern Italian would use double and vice versa, and uses of the definite article that do not correspond to modern Italian (e.g., *il spirto*) have been retained.

The editorial practice described applies to all poems I have transcribed myself from printed or manuscript sources, with a few exceptions, discussed below. In the relatively few cases where I have taken the text of poems from later editions or from secondary sources, I have obviously had to rely on the transcription practices of the editors of these works, which may differ from my own. Where I have drawn from later sources, this is generally either because the original was unavailable (nos. 39 and 207) or because the work is found in a number of different manuscript sources, and no critical edition has yet been produced (as is the case with Camilla Scarampa's verse).

I have pursued a transcription practice different from my usual one in the case of a few poems of exceptional linguistic interest, whose language differs notably from the relatively "modern" and easily modernized linguistic and orthographic norms of Petrarchism. In these cases, I have provided a more diplomatic transcription, supplying punctuation, accents, diaeresis marks, and, where necessary, especially in the case of manuscript sources, word divisions, but not otherwise altering the language. The poems in question are no. 1 (Amedea degli Aleardi, "Deh, non esser Iason s'io son Medea"), no. 7 (Vittoria Colonna, "Eccelso mio Signor, questa ti scrivo"), no. 8 (Barbara Salutati, "Ardeva il petto mio, ardeva l'alma"), no. 73 (Lucrezia Tornabuoni, "Echo el Re forte"), and the three poems by Girolama Corsi Ramos (nos. 2, 156, 208). A modernized version of no. 7 is available in Colonna 1982 (A2:1), modernized versions of Corsi's poems are available in Rossi 1890, and modernized versions of no. 73 are available in various print sources. The two poems in *pavan* by Issicratea Monte and Maddalena Campiglia (nos. 209–10) have been transcribed without linguistic modification other than that detailed in their respective commentaries.

The editions of reference used in the commentaries on the poems in this volume are as follows: Alighieri 2001; Ariosto 1976; Bembo 1960; Buonarroti 1991; Colonna 1982; Della Casa 2001; de' Medici 1992; Ovid 1984; Petrarca 1996a, 1996b; Sannazaro 1990; Tasso 1980, 1994; Turina 2010. Poems from these sources are identified by poem number (or canto and line number in the case of the narrative works), rather than page number to facilitate searching in other editions, where available. For the *Rime* of Antonio Tebaldeo and Celio Magno, and for Sannazaro's *Rime disperse*, I have used the electronic editions available on the Biblioteca Italiana site, run by Sapienza—Università di Roma (www.bibliotecaitaliana.it/). All quotations from the Bible are from the King James Version.

The date given alongside each poet's name in the anthology is that of the first publication of the material included, in the case of works printed during the author's lifetime or soon after it, and of approximate date of composition, in the case of unpublished works. In some cases, the date of first publication may differ considerably from that of composition, as in the case of Francesca Turina, who is documented as writing from the 1570s, but who did not publish the majority of her verse until 1628.

The convention adopted for writers' surnames in most cases in this volume is that usual in modern Italian, whereby a single, uninflected form of the name is used for both men and women. The archaic usage whereby surnames inflect to the feminine when used of women has been used in some cases where it has become more familiar in modern critical usage than the uninflected form, such as those of Lucrezia Marinella (not Marinelli), Olimpia Morata (not Morato), and Francesca Turina (not Turini or Turrini). In most cases, the natal surnames of poets have been used, following common practice, but occasionally, where authors are better known by their married names, these have been used (Orsina Cavaletti, not Orsina Bertolaio; Virginia Salvi, not Virginia Martini or Virginia Casolani; Ersilia Spolverini, not Ersilia Sebastiani).

Abbreviations

GL	*Gerusalemme liberata* (Tasso 1980)
Inf.	*Inferno* (Alighieri 2001)
Met.	*Metamorphoses* (Ovid 1984)
OF	*Orlando Furioso* (Ariosto 1976)
Par.	*Paradiso* (Alighieri 2001)
Purg.	*Purgatorio* (Alighieri 2001)
RD	Sannazaro, *Rime disperse*
RVF	*Rerum vulgarium fragmenta* (Petrarca 1996a)
TC	*Triumphus cupidinis* (*Triumph of Love*) (Petrarca 1996b)
TF	*Triumphus fame* (*Triumph of Fame*) (Petrarca 1996b)
TP	*Triumphus pudicitiae* (*Triumph of Chastity*) (Petrarca 1996b)
TT	*Triumphus temporis* (*Triumph of Time*) (Petrarca 1996b)

NOTES

[1] Rome, Biblioteca Casanatense, MS 4280 (*Oratione di Curtio Gonzaga in lode della lingua italiana*): "Et se la prisca etade d'una sol Saffo si gloriò tanto, che dovrem far noi . . . delle tante . . . donne nostre passate e . . . presenti, splendore et stupore del nostro secolo[?]" The academy in which Gonzaga delivered his oration was the Accademia delle Notti Vaticane, founded by Cardinal Carlo Borromeo (1538–84). Gonzaga names seventeen modern Italian women writers in his discussion, from the generation of Veronica Gambara (1485–1550) and Vittoria Colonna (c. 1490–1547) onward.

[2] ("tanto tempo per le barbariche ingiurie sepolte"): Terracina 1548, 53r, letter from "Il Caudio" of 23 February 1546.

[3] ("donne in superlativo grado eccellentissime, che con l'opere loro hanno fatto stupir il mondo e mostrato che non meno il sesso femminile che 'l maschile è atto ad apprender qual si voglia più difficile ed oscura disciplina"): Querini 1597, 29. Querini makes reference to the still living Ersilia Spolverini (no. 154), as well as to the now legendary Isotta Nogarola (no. 192).

[4] Domenichi 1559; Della Chiesa 1620. Domenichi's anthology is discussed later in this introduction. For Della Chiesa, see Cox 2011, 23, 221–22.

[5] Erdmann 1999, 206–21.

[6] Erdmann 1999, 199–206, 224–25. These figures do not include reprints.

[7] Cox 2008, xxvi–xxvii, 278 n. 165.

[8] Cox 2008, 235–45.

[9] A single poem is attributed to Tarabotti in a nineteenth-century source (Ray and Westwater 2005, 27 n. 9). A selection of encomiastic and correspondence verse by Sarrocchi is found in Verdile 1989–90. For Torelli, see Torelli forthcoming.

[10] Cox 2008, 119–20.

[11] Cox and Sampson 2004, 31–32, 106.

[12] Cox 2008, 118; Cox 2011, 16–19.

[13] For the seventeenth-century downturn in the fortunes of Italian women's writing, see Cox 2008, 204–8. For Arcadia, see Cox 2008, 229–32, and the bibliography cited in Cox 2008, 374 n. 5.

[14] On women's attainments in the visual arts and music in this period, see Newcomb 1986; Bowers 1986; Riley 1988; Durante and Martellotti 1989a; Garrard 1994; Jacobs 1997; Carter 1999; and Cusick 2009. On actresses, see Nicholson 1999; Andrews 2000; and Henke 2002, 85–105.

[15] See Andreini 1601, 150; Bà 2009, 128–31 (for Turina); *Rime* 1587, 212–13 (for Cavaletti); and Fonte 1997, 153–54. Cavaletti also wrote a poem to Peverara's colleague in the Ferrarese *concerto delle donne*, Livia d'Arco (*Rime* 1587, 212).

[16] For discussion of Bronzini, see Jordan 1990, 266–69; Cusick 2005; Harness 2006, 43, 137–40; Cox 2008, 190–91; Cusick 2009, esp. xx, 194–95, 340 n. 10; and Ross 2009, 107–9.

[17] For overviews of the political history of the period, see Hay and Law 1989, 149–281; and Hanlon 2000, 33–75.

[18] On relations between the Ottoman Empire and Christian Europe in this period, see Goffman 2002.

[19] For a contextualized study of Sienese women's political verse, see Eisenbichler 2012b.

[20] Good summaries of critical trends in this area may be found in Ditchfield 2004 and Laven 2006. For overviews of the Catholic religious history of this period, see Bireley 1999; Mullett 1999; and Hanlon 2000, 104–35.

[21] A study of Colonna's religious poetry within the context of Catholic Reform thought is Brundin 2008. See also D'Elia 2006.

[22] On Colonna's post-Tridentine fortunes, see Cox 2011, 56–57.

[23] For an overview of female-authored religious lyric in this period, see Cox 2011, 55–76.

[24] For fuller discussion of the material in this paragraph, see Cox 2011, 19–32.

[25] For Mary's status in Catholicism in this period, see Haskins 2008; also Warner 1976 and Pelikan 1996. For fuller discussions of Mary within female-authored Italian lyric, see Russell 2000; Brundin 2001; and Cox 2011, 65–69.

[26] On Mary Magdalene, see Haskins 1993. For a fuller discussion of her place in Counter-Reformation Italian women's lyric, see Cox 2011, 72–76.

[27] Mary Magdalene is also referenced in nos. 87 and 127.

[28] Fonte 1997, 89–91.

[29] Overviews of early modern women's place in the family and their economic position may be found in Wiesner 2008, 55–100, 101–37.

[30] For an overview of early modern thinking on women, see Wiesner 2008, 17–49. For more detail on the Aristotelian tradition, see Maclean 1980 and Allen 2002, 65–179.

[31] For studies of various aspects of Italian sixteenth-century convent culture, see Monson 1995; Weaver 2002; Lowe 2003; Nelson 2008; Pomata and Zarri 2009; and Weaver 2009.

[32] The five are Laura Beatrice Cappello, Girolama Castellani, Semidea Poggi, Lorenza Strozzi, and Battista Vernazza. For discussion of nuns' participation in Italian literary culture, see Cox 2008, 16–17, and Cox 2011, 7–11.

[33] See Cox 2008, 17–34, and Cox 2009a.

[34] See Notes on Authors.

[35] Groto 2007, 298–99, 337, 362.

[36] On the status of Venetian *cittadini*, see Grubb 2000.

[37] On Terracina's social position, see Cox 2008, 85, 295 n. 8.

[38] Detailed studies of the lifestyle of Venetian courtesans may be found in Santore 1988 and Fortini Brown 2004, 159–87.

[39] Bandello 1992–96, 194 (3.42).

[40] This is not a reflection of the occasionally salacious character of Franco's verse (see no. 34); a collection of encomiastic verse she edited in 1575 and her sober and often moralizing 1580 *Lettere* were also printed without details of the publisher's name.

[41] For bibliography on actresses, see n. 14 above.

[42] The suggestion was first made, with rather obsessive insistence, by Abdelkader Salza in two articles of 1913. The episode is discussed later in this introduction. See also Tylus 2010, 4–5.

[43] I have adopted the spelling "Sarra" suggested by Don Harrán, in his *recent* edition of Copio's writing, on the basis of the usage found in contemporary documents. Earlier criticism uses the spelling "Sara."

[44] Outstanding Italian Jewish cultural figures in this period include the dramatist Leone de' Sommi (c. 1525–90), the composer Salamone Rossi (c. 1570–1630), and the writer and religious polemicist Leone Modena (1571–1648), the last a mentor of Copio's.

[45] See Harrán 2009, 5–6.

[46] Cox 2008, 49–50.

[47] For absence as a theme, see especially no. 32, also nos. 4, 6–8, 10–11, 28–29, and 38. For death, see nos. 40–59.

[48] See Cox 2008, 57–58, 82–83, for further discussion of the material in this paragraph.

[49] Castiglione 2002, 31–32 (1.26).

[50] Castiglione 2002, 78–79 (2.15–16).

[51] On the correct balance of the *grave* and *piacevole* in poetry, see Bembo 1960, 146 (2.9). On the centrality of the Aristotelian mean in Castiglione's aesthetic theory, see Woodhouse 1978, esp. 4, 72–73, 78, 100, 102, 119–20, 154.

[52] See, for example, Bembo 1960, 139–40, 142–43, 166–67 (2.6, 2.8, 2.17) on the opening lines of Petrarch's first sonnet.

[53] The phrase "stairway to the Creator" (*scala al fattor*) is found in Petrarca 1996, 1366 (canzone 360, l. 139).

[54] On the relationship between the Petrarchan poetic tradition and the Italian Reform movement, see Brundin 2008.

[55] Contini 1970. Although Contini's analysis has been justly criticized as over-schematic (see Afribo 2009, 9, 35–37), it is still helpful in broad terms in characterizing Petrarchist language.

[56] Bembo 1960, 138 (2.5) ("da tacere è quel tanto, che sporre non si può acconciamente, più tosto che, sponendolo, macchiarne l'altra scrittura"). Bembo illustrates the point with a violent image from the *Inferno* comparing sinners tearing at their scab-encrusted flesh to fishmongers descaling a large-scaled fish.

[57] Richardson 2009, 17.

[58] See Cox 2008, 85–88, 103.

[59] On Giolito, see, most exhaustively, Coppens and Nuovo 2005. On Domenichi, see Piscini 1991. The 1545 anthology is available in a modern edition: Tomasi and Zaja 2001.

[60] On the series of lyric anthologies that followed the 1545 *Rime*, see Clubb and Clubb 1991; Robin 2007, 205–42; and the online database ALI RASTA (http://rasta.unipv.it/).

[61] For Baffo, see Cox 2008, 297–98 n. 27. On the democratizing effects of the lyric anthologies, see Robin 2007, 56–57.

[62] This point was first made in an important essay by Carlo Dionisotti, first published in 1967: see Dionisotti 1999, 237–46.

[63] For a list of early printed editions of Colonna's verse, to 1560, see Colonna 1982, 258–68.

[64] The two volumes are Tullia d'Aragona's *Rime della Signora Tullia d'Aragona e di diversi a lei* (1547) and Laura Terracina's *Rime* (1548). Both works are presented as having been published against the author's will (see Cox 2008, 81), but this seems a transparent modesty screen.

[65] Cox 2008, 237. On Terracina's relationship with Domenichi, see Robin 2007, 60–61. Domenichi was also instrumental in launching the print career of Chiara Matraini: see Cox 2008, 296 n. 15.

[66] Kirkham 1996, 353.

[67] On Stampa's "poetry for performance," see Smarr 1991.

[68] See Tylus 2010, 4 n. 9, for comment.

[69] The collecting metaphor is drawn from Shemek 2005. On Domenichi's anthology, see Cox 2008, 105–6 and the bibliography cited in Cox 2008, 307 n. 118; see also Eschrich 2009, who emphasizes particularly the element of female sociability in the volume.

[70] Tasso 1875. See also the online edition on the Biblioteca Italiana site (www.bibliotecaitaliana.it/). For discussion of Della Casa's influence on contemporary and subsequent poets, see Afribo 2009, 209–35.

[71] Afribo 2001. For Laura Battiferri's connections with Della Casa's poetic "school," see Afribo 2009, 217 and 224.

[72] See Appendix C.

[73] The overview is Bruscagli 2007.

[74] Veronica Gambara's verse offers a particularly good example of this "nonchalant" style: see, for example, nos. 40, 134, and 193.

[75] On *rapportatio* in the verse of the Baroque poet, Giovanni Battista Marino, see Besomi 1969, 213–27.

[76] In a brief theoretical discussion of the madrigal in Moderata Fonte's dialogue *The Worth of Women*, Fonte has her poet-speaker Corinna describe the form as having "one might almost say, more conceits than they have words" (Fonte 1997, 223).

[77] Cox 2011, 55 and 297 n. 24.

⁷⁸ My analysis is based on Colonna 1982. It omits "Vinca gli sdegni e l'odio vostro antico" for reasons explained later in this introduction, and also three sonnets so irregular in their rhyme schemes that their texts may be assumed to be corrupt (A2:7; S1:55; S2:18).

⁷⁹ Aside from the poems contained in this anthology, other sonnets taken into account in this analysis are those in Campiglia 1585; Zarrabini 1586; Rossi, 1587; Calderari 1588; and Ducchi 1607 (first published in 1587). For further discussion of meter in the sonnet, see Appendix C.

⁸⁰ For discussion of Fiamma's theory, see Cox 2011, 32–34.

⁸¹ On Fiamma's admiration for Colonna and acquaintance with Battiferri, see Cox 2011, 34, 36. Battiferri's "Sette salmi" is available in a modern edition: Battiferri 2005.

⁸² For overviews of the role of pastoral in Italian sixteenth-century culture, see Sampson 2006 and Gerbino 2009.

⁸³ For discussion of women's participation in the tradition of pastoral eclogue, see Cox 2011, 115–18.

⁸⁴ Cox 2011, 78–79.

⁸⁵ Giustinian and Magno 1600. Giustinian's marital love poetry is available in a modern edition: Giustinian 2001.

⁸⁶ For Terracina and Stampa, see Terracina 1548, 33r–46v, and Stampa 2010, 252–54 (no. 220).

⁸⁷ A bilingual edition is available: Turina 2009.

⁸⁸ Colonna 1982, 33 (A1:61) and no. 24 of this anthology.

⁸⁹ Durante and Martellotti 1989b, 211: "Il Marino, in somma, a mio parere, ha colpito nel gusto di questi tempi; amatori altrettanto della novità, et del capriccio delle poesie, quanto peraventura i passati della candidezza, et della coltura."

⁹⁰ Massini 1609, †3v–†4r ("sonettoni . . . a guisa di Pitonesse . . . parole sonanti . . . translazioni smoderate . . . sensi così oscuri, che noi stessi non gl'intendiamo"). For comment, see Volpi 2005, 39.

⁹¹ Cox 2008, 208–9.

⁹² Cox 2005.

⁹³ Cox 2008, 210–12; Cox 2011, 218–19, 236–49.

⁹⁴ For discussions of Costa and Coreglia, see Cox 2008, 209–10, 213–16. For samples of Costa's verse, see Costa-Zalessow 1982, 146–52, and Morandini 2001, 114–24. For samples of Farnese's, see Morandini 2001, 127–31.

⁹⁵ Cox 2008, 225, 227.

⁹⁶ Cox 2011, 265.

⁹⁷ Morata's works are available in a bilingual modern edition: Morata 2003. Selections of Latin verse by Angela and Isotta Nogarola, Morata, and Strozzi may be found in Brown et al. 2002. Marian Latin verse by Strozzi, Molza, and the Bolognese nun Febronia Pannolini (fl. 1601) is found in Piastra 2002, while Anselmi et al. 2004, 329–31, has examples of verse by Molza in Latin and Greek. For discussion of the tradition of Latin poetry by women, see Stevenson 2005.

⁹⁸ These languages are grouped here as "dialects" for convenience, although the distinction between languages and dialects is notoriously imprecise. Venetian, in particular, as the language of an independent state, used in official contexts, stretches the usual definition of a dialect.

⁹⁹ ("la lingua volgar venezïana"): Franco 1999, 166.

¹⁰⁰ Milani 1983.

[101] Cox 2008, 144–46.

[102] On Bulifon's activity, see Cox 2008, 230.

[103] On some of the "fakes" in Bergalli's collection, see Cox 2008, 181, 270 n. 96, 350 n. 67. These include most of her pre-fifteenth-century poets. For critical discussion of her anthology, see Chemello 2000 and Curran 2005.

[104] The exceptions are the anonymous "P.S.M." and Maria da San Gallo (based on the list of poets in Domenichi in Shemek 2005, 252–53).

[105] Stampa 1738. For discussion of the edition, from differing perspectives, see Curran 2005, 266–67, and Jones 2005, 299–300.

[106] Venetian patriotism is also a consideration in Bergalli's choices for her 1726 anthology: seven of her top fourteen pre-1650 poets were Venetian or from the Veneto (Stampa, Colao, Andreini, Marinella, Sbarra, Malipiero, Bragadin).

[107] ICCU catalog, www.iccu.sbn.it/, accessed September 30, 2012. Duplicate titles have been omitted.

[108] Stampa 1877; Gambara 1879.

[109] On Colonna's Victorian reception, see Ostermark-Johansen 1999.

[110] Morsolin 1883; De Vit 1883.

[111] Guerrini 1882, 10: "Unite qui insieme, [queste tre autrici] parlano alle nostre donne ammonendole che non è vero quello che si dice della inferiorità femminile." Guerrini's edition was republished in 1930.

[112] See Kirkham 2005, 184–85 and 194–95 n. 19.

[113] For discussion and references, see Tylus 2010, 4.

[114] D'Aragona 1891. For discussion, see Jones 2005, 291–95.

[115] Franco and Stampa 1913. For discussion of the edition, which notoriously reordered the two poets' verse to construct an "edifying" biography, culminating in religious repentance, see Jones 2005, 295–99.

[116] For summaries of Croce's views on women's writing, see Quondam 1974, 173–74; Re 2000, 190–91; and Zancan 2012, 117–18.

[117] ("documento di passioni realmente vissute"): *Pagine sparse: Serie prima*, first published 1887, cited in Zancan 2012, 118. Salza's 1913 edition of Stampa and Franco was published in a series, Scrittori d'Italia, that had been founded by Croce, and his critical approach is heavily indebted to Croce.

[118] On Battiferri's distinctly meager twentieth-century fortunes, see Kirkham 2005, 186.

[119] Jones 1990, 103–17.

[120] See especially Kirkham 1996 and Battiferri 2006.

[121] For discussion, see Cox 2008, xx–xxi, 131–37, and Cox 2011.

[122] For a more detailed treatment of the reception of sixteenth-century Italian women poets, contextualized with regard to the reception of Petrarchism generally, see Quondam 1974, esp. 133–53.

[123] Baldacci 1975; Gigliucci 2000.

[124] I consulted the revised edition by Guido Davico Bonino, of 1968. Another anthology of the late 1950s, Giacinto Spagnoletti's *Il petrarchismo* (1959), has poems by Colonna, Stampa, Matraini, Morra, and Franco.

[125] Barbara Torelli (c. 1475–post 1533) was long accredited with the authorship of a single, striking, sonnet mourning the death by murder of her poet husband, Ercole Strozzi. It was convincingly shown by Angelo Monteverdi in the late 1950s and 1960s to have been a forgery by the editor of the volume in which it first appears (Baruffaldi 1713).

[126] Other anthologies of writings by Italian women covering the period after 1560 include Costa-Zalessow 1982, Arslan et al. 1991, and Morandini 2001; none, however, are limited to lyric.

[127] De Blasi's other writers are Colonna, Gambara, Scarampa, d'Aragona, Matraini, Morra, Stampa, Malipiero, Virginia Salvi, and Aurelia Petrucci. For an analysis of the collection, see Insana 2005.

[128] Ponchiroli, less extreme in his choices, includes eighteen poems by Stampa, and, respectively, ten and eight by Colonna and Gambara. Spagnoletti's *Il petrarchismo* has twelve poems by Stampa and six by Matraini to only two by Colonna, while Gambara does not appear.

[129] On the new critical interest in religious literature among Italian critics in recent years, see Cox 2011, xv, and the bibliography cited in 288 n. 175, 289 n. 191 and 193, 290–91 n. 208–9.

[130] Franco 1999; Morata 2003; Colonna 2005; Battiferri 2006; Matraini 2007; Copio 2009; Stampa 2010. Two other editions nearing completion at the time of writing, of Veronica Gambara, by Molly Martin and Paola Ugolini, and of Tullia d'Aragona, by Julia Hairston. The series was started by the University of Chicago Press and is now published by the Centre for Reformation and Renaissance Studies, Toronto.

[131] See Turina 2005, 2009, 2010.

[132] See the complete title of Marino 1602.

[133] For examples, with English translation, of psalm translations, see Morata 2003 (Greek) and Battiferri 2006 (vernacular). Battiferri's psalm translations have been published in full in Italian: Battiferri 2005. For fifteenth-century convent poetry, see the references in Cox 2008, 269–70 n. 92–95.

[134] I thank Anna Wainwright for this calculation.

[135] See Ruscelli 1559, clviii, for the rules governing this kind of risposta, which Ruscelli identifies as an invention of "the moderns."

[136] Forni 2008, 292; Bullock 1977.

[137] The case against Aleardi's authorship is made in Sabbadini 1911. See Grayson 1971, 40–41 n. 9–11, for discussion of the issue, and 32–35 of the same essay on Magnoli's plagiaristic tendencies.

[138] See Bullock 1971 and Bullock 1973, esp. 128–31. Bullock prints the poem as Colonna's in Colonna 1982 as E29 (p. 217).

[139] By contrast, Gambara's ottava rima poem "Quando miro la terra ornata e bella" was published multiple times in the sixteenth century under Colonna's name but was then authoritatively reattributed to Gambara by Girolamo Ruscelli in an anthology of 1553. Ruscelli cited evidence that Colonna had denied her authorship of the poem, and Gambara claimed it: see Bullock 1973, 116–17 and n. 6.

[140] Colonna 1982, 217 has "bagna il Mar Indo valle o colle aprico," in place of "bagna il mar, cinge valle e colle aprico" in the early printed editions. Bullock's version translates "wherever the Indian Sea bathes a valley or sunny hill."

[141] For a critique of Bullock's edition and its premises, see Toscano 2000, 25–84.

Amorous Verse

In vita

Amedea degli Aleardi (c. 1405)

I

Deh, non esser Iason, s'io son Medea;
duro Theseo, io son la tua Hadriana,
e ben ché non sia Tysbe a la fontana,
Dido serò per lo crudele Enea.   4
Vieni a veder s'io son quel ch'io solea,
ch'el c'è il bianco color ma non la grana.
Deh, lassa un poco 'sta tua voglia strana,
se non morte per passer si accogliea.   8
Pensa le amare lacrime di amore
le quai bagnando il mio palido volto
ti furon già sì dolce di sapore.   11
Cara speranza, Amor, chi mi t'ha tolto?
Se non vieni a por fine al mio dolore
io haggio al bianco collo il lazo avolto   14
per por con una morte fine a mille,
né non mi mancharà l'ardir di Phille.

Ah, do not be Jason, though I be Medea. Heartless Theseus, I am your
Ariadne; and, even if I am not Thisbe at the fountain, I shall be Dido to
your cruel Aeneas. Come and see for yourself whether I am as I used
to be. The white color remains to me, but not the crimson. Ah, for one
moment, abandon this strange desire of yours, lest I die of sorrow.
Think of the bitter tears of love that were once so sweet to your taste
when they used to bathe my pale face. Dear hope, my love, who has
taken you from me? If you do not come to put an end to my suffering,
I have the noose already round my white neck to put an end to a thousand
deaths with a single one; nor will I lack the boldness of Phyllis.

Sonetto ritornellato ABBA ABBA CDC DCD EE. Modena Biblioteca Estense, MS α.
N.7.28 (with *Dhe* in ll. 1 and 7 corrected to *Deh*). This sonnet is one of the earliest Italian
poems with a fairly strong claim to female authorship. It is attributed to Amedea degli
Aleardi in two manuscripts, in Udine and Modena. The one used here gives the poet's
name as Medea and identifies the addressee as a Count Malaspina of Verona. The poet
compares herself to five famous women of classical mythology, three abandoned by
their lovers (Medea, Ariadne, and Dido) and two who kill themselves in the belief that
their lovers are dead or unfaithful (Thisbe and Phyllis). The poem's principal subtext,
alluded to in l. 16, is Phyllis's epistle to her lover Demophon in Ovid's *Heroides*, pur-
ported to be written on the day of her death. Stark and simple for the most part in its
language, Aleardi's sonnet is not without stylistic ornamentation: note the word-play
of *Iason* / *io son* in l. 1 and *amare/amore* in l. 9. The meaning of l. 8 is obscure.

Girolama Corsi (1490s)

2 ⌒

Io me ne vo, non già del tutto esciolta,
ch'Amor mi tiene ancor sotto suo impero,
ma tu che sei per altra fato altero
ancor dirai:—Oimè, chi mi t'a tolta?—   4
Perché ogniuna non n'ha la fede acolta
in sé, né l'amor suo iusto né entero.
Mai oro né argento el mio pensiero
volse contra di te pur una volta.   8
Io piango nel partir; tu, poi partita.
Io me ne vo, contento el tuo desio,
fuor de la patria tua come sbandita.   11
Or vivi lieto, restati cum Dio,
ché se dipoi mil'anni havesti vita
convien che ti ricordi el servir mio.   14

Away I go, not yet quite free, for Love still holds me in his thrall; but
you who disdain me now for another, will live to say "Alas, who took
her from me?" Not every woman harbors faith in her heart; not every
woman is whole and true in her love. Never did gold or silver turn my
thoughts against you a single time. I lament in leaving; you will weep
when I am gone. Away I go, just as you desire, going hence from your
homeland like an exile. Now fare you well and God be with you—for
you will not forget my devotion, even if you live a thousand years.

Sonnet ABBA ABBA CDC DCD. Venice, Biblioteca Marciana, MS IX, 270 [6367], 8v.
Corsi's sonnet, recorded in a manuscript compiled by the diarist Marin Sanudo
(1466–1536), has the heading "To her Venetian lover" ("Ad amicum venetum"). An-
other poem is addressed to the same figure and refers to the same unhappy love
triangle. Both this poem and Corsi's other "Ad amicum venetum" sonnet, which
speaks more explicitly of the sexual nature of the liaison, have the air of poems
originating in an actual love affair, probably not originally intended for circulation.
A likely source here is Ovid's letter from Oenone to Paris (*Heroides* 5), a line of
which (143) is echoed in ll. 7–8. As in Ovid, in protesting the nonmercenary charac-
ter of her love, the speaker may be tacitly accusing the "other woman." The single
consonants in *fato* (3) and *acolta* (5) probably reflect the scribe's Venetian linguistic
background.

Camilla Scarampa (1490s)

3

Chiaro conosco vostra fiera voglia,
per ch'ella si dimostra a più d'un segno,
et ben ch'assai mi offenda il vostro sdegno
in me cresce l'amor quanto la doglia.   4
Mancherà il spirto e questa afflitta spoglia
pria che la fé che già vi diedi in pegno;
né tanto puotrà forza né ingegno
che quel pensier d'amarvi mi si toglia.   8
Né pur altra da vui mercede attendo
di un tristo, lungo, e doloroso pianto:
questo il premio sarà de' duri affanni.   11
Ma voi n'acquisterete un cotal vanto
che ciascun puotrà dir, se ben comprendo,
—costui fu nido d'amorosi inganni!—   14

I plainly perceive your cruel intent, which betrays itself by more than
one sign, yet, though your scorn greatly wounds me, my love grows in
me along with my pain. My spirit will perish, and these wearied bones,
before the faith dies that I pledged to you, nor will any force or cunning
be sufficient to remove me from my resolve to love you. Nor do I expect
any return at your hands other than miserable, long, painful weeping.
Such will be the reward for my suffering. But you will acquire such
fame from this that all will be able to say, if I have understood rightly,
"This man was a nest of amorous deceits!"

Sonnet ABBA ABBA CDE DCE. Leone 1962, 299. Non-Petrarchan usages here in-
clude *puotrà* for *potrà* and the definite article *il*, rather than *lo*, before *spirto* (*vui* for
voi at l. 9, a survival from early Sicilian lyric, is used by Petrarch, for example, in
sonnet 134). The sonnet is especially interesting for its thematic anticipation of
Gaspara Stampa's poems of amorous recrimination (esp. no. 20). Scarampa's self-
representation as devoted, *Heroides*-like abandoned lover is unusual within her
small corpus of surviving poems, several of which instead represent her as deter-
minedly set against love (see nos. 166–67). Striking here are the beginning of the
sonnet, with its dramatic portrayal of the suspicious poet piecing together clues of
her lover's betrayal, and the end, with its sharp shift in tone, from lament to accusa-
tion. Line 1 is particularly intricate in its soundscape, with its interlinked patterns of
*consonance and *assonance, the twinned consonant clusters—*osco/ostra* continu-
ing into the *dimostra* of l. 3.

Veronica Gambara (c. 1500–18)

4

Quando sarà ch'io mora
Amor, se 'n questa cruda dipartita
non può tanto dolor finir mia vita?
Qualor avien ch'io pensi
quel che dir me volea l'ultimo sguardo   5
e 'l partir lento e tardo,
con quei sospir sì accensi,
come pon star in me l'anima e i sensi?
S'allor ch'io gli odii dire
quell'ultime parole in tanto ardore   10
non mi s'aperse il core,
e non potei morire,
quando potrò mai più di vita uscire?
Io n'uscirò, ch'a tant'aspro martire
non potrò già durar, vedermi priva   15
e sì lungi da lui, e che sia viva!

When shall I die, then, Love, if in this cruel parting, so great a pain
cannot end my life? When I think of what that last look meant, and that
slow, tardy leaving, and those burning sighs, how can my soul and my
senses remain in me? If, when I heard him speak those last words with
such ardor, my heart did not open, and I could not die, when shall I ever
be able to depart from life? Yet depart from it I shall, for I cannot last in
such cruel torment, seeing myself bereft and so far from him—and yet
still in life!

Madrigal aBBcDdcCeFfeEEGG. Gambara 1995, 59. This poem, unpublished in her
lifetime, has been conjecturally identified by Gambara's modern editor as one of
her earliest surviving works. The theme of a parting between lovers was popular in
fifteenth-century *poesia cortigiana*, although in male-authored lyric, it is usually the
poet who leaves, rather than the beloved. Gambara uses the irregular rhythms and
short lines of the madrigal effectively here to evoke the poet's emotional agitation.
The structure of the poem is *chiastic, with two shorter, three-line segments at the
beginning and end (1–3, 14–16) focused on the poet's anguish and two longer, five-
line segments in the middle (4–8, 9–13) incorporating fragments of embedded narra-
tion. This pattern is underlined by the similar rhyme scheme of the opening and
closing segments (aBB EGG), and their closure on the words *vita* and *viva*. Note the
anagrammatic pun of *mora/amor* in ll. 1–2.

5

Occhi lucenti e belli:
come esser può ch'in un medesmo instante
nascan da voi sì nove forme e tante?
Lieti, mesti, superbi, umili, alteri
vi mostrate in un punto, onde di speme   5
e di timor m'empiete,
e tanti effetti dolci, acerbi, e feri
nel cor arso per voi vengono insieme
ad ogn'or che volete.
Or poiché voi mia vita e morte sete,   10
occhi felici, occhi beati e cari
siate sempre sereni, allegri, e chiari.

Shining, lovely eyes: how can it be that in one same instant you give
rise to so many new, wondrous forms? Gay, sad, proud, humble,
haughty you show yourselves in one instant, filling me with hope and
with fear. These effects, sweet, bitter, cruel, you cause all at once in my
burned heart whenever you wish. Now, since you are death and life to
me, happy eyes, dear, blessed eyes, pray ever be serene, blithe, and
bright.

Madrigal aBBCDeCDeEFF. Ruscelli 1553a, 5 (*fieri* in l. 7 amended to *feri* on the basis
of Gambara 1995). This is one of Gambara's most famous madrigals, frequently set
to music, most famously by Luca Marenzio (1553–99). It shows her in her lightest,
most mellifluous mode. Description of the physical beauties of the beloved, central
to male-authored Petrarchist verse, posed problems of decorum for female poets.
Gambara finds an elegant solution here, as elsewhere, concentrating solely on the
eyes, in Neoplatonic theory the noblest element in physical beauty, the "windows of
the soul." *Nove*, in l. 3, essentially means "new" but can also have connotations of
"remarkable" or "miraculous"; hence the translation "new, wondrous forms."

6

Ombroso colle, amene e verdi piante,
liete piagge, profonde e grate valli,
correnti, freschi e lucidi cristalli,
conforto spesso a le mie pene tante;   4
segrete selve reverende e sante,
folti boschetti e solitari calli,
süavi fiori persi, bianchi, e gialli
oppressi da celesti e sacre piante;   8
a voi, piangendo, già miei duri stenti
narrai più volte, or a voi tutti insieme
voglio parte scoprir de' miei contenti: 11
dopo lunghe fatiche e doglie estreme
vidi del mio bel Sole i raggi ardenti
quando di veder lor manco ebbi speme.   14

Shady hill, green and lovely trees, blessed slopes, deep and pleasant
valleys, fresh, flowing, bright crystal waters—you who have so often
been of comfort in my great miseries; secret, holy, venerable forests,
dense thickets and solitary paths, sweet flowers, darkest carmine,
white, and yellow, trodden by heavenly and sacred feet. Often to you,
weeping, I told my hard sufferings; now to all of you together I wish to
confide a part of my joy. After long travails and desperate anguish, just
when I least hoped to, I saw the burning rays of my beautiful sun.

Sonnet ABBA ABBA CDC DCD. Gambara 1890, 29. This sonnet describing the poet's
joyful reunion with her beloved is often assumed to date from the time of Gamba-
ra's marriage. The poem demonstrates Gambara's characteristic use of idyllic natu-
ral description (cf. no. 193). It is used here to particular effect, in a long decorative
invocation, moving from the externalized landscape of the first quatrain to the more
subjectivized, "secret," "solitary" scenes of the second and setting off the relatively
spare language of the final tercet. The *topos of calling on a landscape to witness
the poet's emotion is frequent in Petrarchism: see Petrarch's canzone 126 and Ia-
copo Sannazaro's sonnets 46 and 88, the first perhaps the source for Gambara's
"folti boschetti" (6), the second for the rhyme words *valli/cristalli/gialli/calli*, and
the *fiori persi . . . e gialli* of l. 7. Note the *rima equivoca on "piante," in the sense of
trees/soles in ll. 1 and 8.

Vittoria Colonna (1512)

7

Eccelso mio Signor, questa ti scrivo
per te narrar tra quante dubie voglie,
tra quanti aspri martir dogliosa io vivo.   3
Non sperava da te tormento e doglie,
ché se 'l favor del Ciel t'era propicio
perdute non sarian l'opime spoglie.   6
Non credeva un Marchese et un Fabrizio,
l'un sposo e l'altro padre, al mio dolore
fussi sì crudo e dispietato inicio.   9
Del padre la pietà, di te l'amore,
come doi angui rabidi affamati
rodendo stavan sempre nel mio core.   12
Credeva più benigni haver i fati,
ché tanti sacrificij e voti tanti
il rettor de l'Inferno harrian placati.   15
Non era tempio alcun che de' miei pianti
non fusse madefatto, né figura
che non avesse di miei voti alquanti.   18
Io credo lor dispiacque tanta cura,
tanto mio lacrimar, cotanti voti,
ché spiace a Dio l'amor fuor di misura.   21
Benché li fatti tuoi a 'l ciel sian noti,
e quei del padre mio volan tant'alto
che mai di fama e gloria seran voti,   24
ma hor in questo periglioso assalto,
in questa pugna horrenda e dispietata
che m'ha fatto la mente, il cor di smalto   27
la vostra gran virtù s'è dimostrata
d'un Hettor, d'un Achille; ma che fia
questo per me, dolente, abandonata?   30
Sempre dubiosa fu la mente mia;
chi me videva mesta iudicava
che me offendessi absentia o gelosia,   33
ma io, misera me! sempre pensava
l'ardito tuo valor, l'animo audace,
con che s'accorda mal fortuna prava.   36
Altri chiedevan guerra; io sempre pace,
dicendo: —assai mi fia s'el mio Marchese
meco quïeto nel suo stato giace—.   39

Non nuoce a voi seguir le dubie imprese,
m'a noi, dogliose, afflitte, ch'espettando
semo da dubio e da timore offese.   42
Voi, spinti dal furor, non ripensando
ad altro ch'ad honor, contr'il periglio
soleti con gran furia andar gridando.   45
Noi timide nel cor, meste nel ciglio
semo per voi; e la sorella il frate,
la sposa il sposo, vol la madre il figlio;   48
ma io, misera! cerco e 'l sposo e patre
e frate e figlio; sono in questo loco
sposa, figlia, sorella e vecchia matre.   51
Son figlia per natura, e poi per gioco
di legge natural sposa; sorella
e madre son per amoroso foco.   54
Mai venia peligrin da cui novella
non cercassi saper, cosa per cosa,
per far la mente mia gioiosa e bella,   57
quando, ad un punto, il scoglio dove posa
il corpo mio, che già lo spirto è teco,
vidi coprir di nebbia tenebrosa,   60
e l'aria tutta mi pareva un speco
di caligine nera; il mal bubone
cantò in quel giorno tenebroso e cieco.   63
Il lago a cui Typheo le membra oppone
boglieva tutto, o spaventevol mostro!
il dì de Pasca, la gentil stagione.   66
Era coi venti Eulo al lito nostro,
piangeano le syrene e li delphini,
li pesci ancor; il mar pareva inchiostro;   69
piangean intorno a quel li dei marini,
sentend'ad Ischia dir:—Hoggi, Vittoria,
sei stata di disgracia a li confini,   72
bench'in salute et in eterna gloria
sia converso il dolor; ch'el padre e sposo
salvi son, benché presi con memoria—.   75
Alhor con volto mesto e tenebroso,
piangendo, a la magnanima Costanza
narrai l'augurio mesto e spaventoso.   78
Ella me cohortò, com'è sua usanza,
dicendo:—No 'l pensar, ch'un caso strano

sarebbe, sendo vinta tal possanza—.   81
—Non può da li sinistri esser lontano—,
diss'io,—un ch'è animoso a li gran fatti,
non temendo menar l'ardita mano.   84
Chi d'ambiduo costor trascorre gli atti
vedrà tanto d'ardir pronto e veloce;
non han con la Fortuna tregua o patti—.   87
Et ecco il nuncio rio con mesta voce
fandoci chiaro tutto il mal successo,
ché la memoria il petto ognhor mi coce.   90
Se Vittoria volevi io t'era a presso,
ma tu, lasciando me, lassasti lei,
e cerca ognun seguir chi fuge adesso.   93
Nocque a Pompeo, come saper tu dei,
lasciar Cornelia, et a Catone ancora
nocque lassando Marsia in pianti rei.   96
Seguir se deve il sposo dentro e fora,
e s'egli pate affanno, ella patisca,
e lieto lieta, e se vi more mora;   99
a quel che arrisca l'un l'altro s'arrisca;
equali in vita, equali siano in morte,
e ciò che avien a lui a lei sortisca.   102
Felice Mitridate e sua consorte,
che faceste equalmente di fortuna
i fausti giorni e le disgratie torte!   105
Tu vivi lieto, e non hai doglia alcuna,
ché, pensando di fama il novo acquisto,
non curi farme del tuo amor digiuna;   108
ma io con volto disdegnoso e tristo,
servo il tuo letto abandonato e solo,
tenendo con la speme il dolor misto,   111
e col vostro gioir tempr'il mio duolo.

[1–3] My august lord, I write this to tell you among how many doubts and fears I am miserably living, among how many harsh scourges. [4–6] I was not expecting such torment and pain from you; for if the heavens had been favorable, the rich spoils would not have been lost. [7–9] I could not believe that a Marquis and a Fabrizio, the one my husband, the other my father, could have been the cruel and pitiless origin of my woes. [10–12] My devotion to my father, my passion for you were like two rabid famished serpents constantly gnawing at my heart.

[13–15] I thought the fates would look more benignly on me, that all my sacrifices and vows would have placated the lord of hell! [16–18] There was no temple that was not soaked in my tears, no image that had not had some of my vows. [19–21] Perhaps they were displeased by so much anxious care, so many tears, so many vows; for love without measure is displeasing to God. [22–24] Although your deeds are already known even to the heavens, while those of my father already fly so high that they will never be devoid of fame and glory, [25–27] still, in this perilous assault, this fierce and horrendous battle that has turned my mind and heart to stone, [28–30] you showed yourself to have the greatness of a Hector, an Achilles. But what do I care for that, grieving and abandoned as I am! [31–33] My mind was always filled with foreboding, so that those who saw me so sad thought I was suffering from your absence or from jealousy. [34–36] But, alas! I was constantly thinking of your bold valor, your audacious spirit, which ill accords with malevolent fortune. [37–39] Others preached war, but I was for peace, saying to myself: "It will be quite enough if my Marquis can remain safely here with me." [40–42] You men are not harmed by attempting your bold enterprises, but what of us women, suffering, afflicted, torn apart by fear and doubt as we wait for you? [43–45] You, fueled by fury, thinking of nothing but honor, delight to race furiously into the face of danger, [46–48] while we wait, fearful at heart, sad-eyed on your account; the sister longs for her brother, the bride her husband, the mother her son. [49–51] But I, alas! long for husband and father, brother and son; I feel myself at the same time bride, daughter, sister, and aged mother. [52–54] I am daughter by nature, bride by the play of natural law; sister and mother by my amorous fire. [55–57] Never did a pilgrim come to these shores from whom I did not eagerly seek news and ask for every detail, hoping that it would bring relief and joy to my mind. [58–60] But then this rock on which my body abides (for my spirit is with you) I saw suddenly covered with a thick black mist; [61–63] and the air all around seemed to me a cave; the sea, black vapor; a night owl sang on that blind and mournful day. [64–66] The lake where Typhon once lurked began to boil— horrible portent!—on Easter day in the soft season of spring. [67–69] Aeolus was there at our shores with his winds; the sirens and dolphins were weeping, and the fishes too; the sea looked like ink. [70–72] All around the sea gods were weeping, hearing Ischia itself saying: "Today, Vittoria, you have been at the brink of disaster; [73–75] but know that your sorrow will be changed to hope and eternal glory, for your father and husband are both safe, though fatefully captured." [76–78] Then

with a sad and shadowed face, weeping, I told the great-souled Costanza
this sad and fearful portent. [79–81] She exhorted me as is her wont,
saying: "Do not believe it; for it would be strange if such great prowess
were defeated." [82–84] "But a man cannot be far from mishap," I
replied, "when he is so dauntless in the face of danger, not fearing to
advance his bold hand. [85–87] Look at the deeds of both; they are both
men of such daring, swift to risk themselves; neither offers truces or
pacts to Fortune." [88–90] And now there arrived the cruel messenger
to recount the whole calamity to us in somber tones. Even the mere
memory of it burns me through! [91–93] If you wanted Victory [*Vittoria*],
I could have been at your side; but you, in leaving me, also left her, and
now all seek to follow her as she flees. [94–96] It harmed Pompey, as you
must know, to leave his wife Cornelia; and Cato too regretted leaving
his wife Marcia weeping. [97–99] A wife should follow her husband
at home and abroad; if he suffers hardship, let her suffer too; if he is
fortunate, let her share in his happiness; if he dies, let her die alongside
him. [100–102] What one spouse risks, the other should risk; they are
equal in life; let them be equal in death; what he undergoes, let her too
undergo. [103–5] O happy Mithridates and his wife, who equally shared
in all Fortune brought, both the days of victory and the distress that
followed! [106–8] But you are blithe and have no care; thinking only of
how to increase your fame; you do not care that you are leaving me
hungering for your love. [109–11] But I remain, miserable and angry,
waiting in your lonely abandoned bed, mingling my sorrow with some
faint hope; [112] only the thought of your happiness softens my grief.

Capitolo. Luna 1536, Gg1r–Gg2r (ampersands expanded to *et* in ll. 7 and 73; *quel* at l. 23
amended to *quei*; *mar* to *mal* at l. 62; *facesti* in l. 105 to *faceste*, on the basis of Colonna
1982; ll. 61–62 seem corrupt in the original). This is one of only a handful of surviv-
ing poems by Colonna dating to the years of her marriage, and it attests to her early
formation within the *poesia cortigiana* tradition, in which the *capitolo* was a much-
favored form. The poem refers to the capture and imprisonment of Colonna's
father and husband, both military leaders of great renown, after the horrendous
Battle of Ravenna in 1512, and its composition can presumably be dated to that year.
As a verse epistle addressed by an "abandoned woman" to the man she loves, it con-
sciously imitates Ovid's *Heroides*, especially Ovid's letter from Penelope to Ulysses.
In fact, Colonna's *capitolo* can be located within a microgenre of late-fifteenth- and
early-sixteenth-century *heroides* written in the voices of contemporary women (Cox
2008, 49–50). Colonna's is the only one actually written by a woman.

One great interest of the poem lies in Colonna's deft self-mythologizing. Aside
from the use of Ovid as a model, which already allies the poet ideally with the hero-
ines of classical mythology, she compares herself explicitly toward the end with

three famous classical women, Cornelia, wife of Pompey; Marcia, wife of Cato; and Hypiscratea, wife of Mithridates VI of Pontus (ruled c. 120–63 BC), famed for having followed her husband into battle cross-dressed as a serving man. Together with the earlier comparisons of the poet's father and husband to the Homeric heroes Hector and Achilles (29) and the classical allusions contained in the description of the island of Ischia, near Naples, where Colonna lived with her aunt by marriage, Costanza d'Avalos (the "great-souled Costanza" of l. 77, not to be confused with the younger Costanza d'Avalos, the author of no. 89), these references serve to cast the events and protagonists of the poem in a glamorizing neoclassical light.

The poem divides broadly into three segments, with a discursive opening and ending broken by the long narrative episode of ll. 55–90, recounting in darkly portentous tones the arrival of the ill news at Ischia. (Typhon, at l. 64, is a mythological monster purportedly buried under Ischia; Aeolus, at l. 67, the mythological ruler of the winds). A shift of tone can be noted between the opening and the end. Where the initial discursive passage, taking its cue from the *Heroides*, portrays men and women contrastively, men as creatures of war, women of peace (43–47), the end passage proposes a more "heroic" and equal relationship between the sexes (97–102), embodied in that between Mithridates and Hypsicratea.

Colonna's language in this poem is notably Latinate, as is her orthography: note, for example, *lacrimar* in l. 20; and *frate/patre/matre* in rhyme at ll. 46–52. *Opime spoglie*, in l. 6, translates the Latin *spolia opima*, a technical term meaning the arms, dress, and effects of an enemy commander slain in battle and taken as a trophy. *Madefatto*, in l. 17, is a coinage based on the Latin *madefactus* (soaked); *bubone* in l. 62 a Latinism meaning "owl" (*bubo* in Latin); *cohortò* in l. 80, a coinage based on the Latin verb *cohortor* (to exhort or give courage to). The striking passage at ll. 52–54 echoes a passage in Petrarch's *TC* (2:55–56) describing the Carthaginian Massinissa's devotion to the Roman general Scipio ("Padre m'era in onore, in amor figlio / fratel ne gli anni": He was my father in honor, in love my son, / my brother in years). For a detailed reading of this poem, see Vecce 1993. On Ovid's *Heroides* as an inspiration for sixteenth-century female poets, see Phillippy 1992.

Barbara Salutati (?1520s)

8

Ardeva il petto mio, ardeva l'alma,
ardeva tutta in un süave focho
che m'adornava d'amorosa palma.   3
Benediceva sempre il tempo e 'loco
quando ne prese e ne congiunse amore
a' dolci fatti, all'amoroso gioco.   6
Poscia che per così alto valore
che in petto viril si chiude et serra
era infiammata d'amoroso ardore,   9
beata sola i' mi chiamavo in terra,
ancor che posta intra timore e speme
vivessi sempre in amorosa guerra.   12
Un raro frutto di sì nobil seme
coglieva, dove si potea vedere
cortesia e valore uniti insieme.   15
Per me volgean tutte l'amiche isphere,
ver me gli amici lumi erono intenti
per duplicar l'amoroso piacere.   18
Suoi razzi il sol mostrava più lucenti,
vedesi il ciel da ogni parte bello,
tutti i nimici lumi erono spenti.   21
La terra anchor si pareggiava a quello:
ogni bene, ogni gratia e virtute era
raccolta drento al mio povero ostello.   24
Per me ridea lieta primavera;
gli amorosi animai si veden fora
e nascondesi ogni inimica fera.   27
Aveno in cima le verde erbe i fiori,
et lieti intorno a quella si vedea
gire scherzando i pargholetti amori.   30
Mentre così felice io mi vivea
Fortuna, ch'el mio male e brama e vuole,
ver me si volse impetüosa e rea.   33
In uno instante si coperse il sole
per folta e grossa nebbia e l'aer puro
si turbò tutto assai più che non suole.   36
Il Ciel si fece tenebroso e scuro
e le nemiche stele apparson tutte
presaghe sol del mio danno futuro.   39

L'erbette ch'eron pria verde e asciutte
divener seche e molli, e sopra a quelle
apparvon spine ischolorite e brutte.   42
Le fere ch'amor fea leggiadre e belle
si dispartirno e dipoi venno fora
quelle ch'a Dio e al ciel forno rebelle.   45
I parvoletti amor fuggirsi ancora
tutti sdegnosi e per più lieta via
volaro al Ciel tutto turbato allora.   48
Maraviglia non è che questo sia,
poscia che gli ha cercati altri paesi
l'unicha vita della vita mia.   51
Io benedico tutti i passi spesi
per honorarti, e benedico sempre
l'hora che ti conobbi, i giorni e mesi.   54
Non mai perciò sarà ch'io non mi stempre
pel desiderio dell'esserti appresso
e che l'immagin tua non contempre.   57
I pensier miei tutti in non cale ho messo,
e sol bramosa e lachrimosa attendo
la ritornata nel tempo premesso,   60
et quel trapasso e numerando spendo
i giorni e mesi e col sol par ch'io sdegni
il qual non va com'io vorrei correndo.   63
E se non fussi li amorosi pegni
che mi donasti, certo in uno exemplo
darei di me giù ne' tartarei regni;   66
ma parte l'uno e hor l'altro contemplo
la rimembranza per sì grati doni
è al tutto cagion che non mi stemplo.   69
Alhor chiam'io felice dove poni
l'onorate tua piante, e dove arriva
delle tuo voglie gli amorosi suoni,   72
et me poi che d'udirgli ne son priva
chiamo infelice, ma sol la speranza
del tuo tosto ritorno mi tien viva.   75
Questo fa ch'io non mora, perché sanza
la tuo presenza non saprei che farmi
per far minor la voglia, che mancanza!   78
Or se tu brami com'io credo darmi
in questa absentia tua qualche conforto

voglia spesso scrivendo vicitarmi,   81
accioché il parlar tuo cognoscha schorto,
imagini la voce e quella mano
ch'era già di mie affanni fine e porto.   84
Cognoscerò anchor che non invano
io tanto t'amo, perciò prego voglia
l'alterato mio petto render sano.   87
Di nuovo prego ch'a questa mia voglia
tu sia cortese e tal mi doni aita
che si mitighi in parte la mia doglia,   90
E come già fu certa la partita
sia il tuo ritorno e più là non soggiorni
se brami o speri ritrovarmi in vita   93
et far beati i miei futuri giorni.

[1–3] My heart was burning; my soul was burning; I was burning all through in a gentle fire, which adorned me with an amorous palm. [4–6] I blessed the time and the place when Love captured us and brought us together to such sweet doings, to the amorous game, [7–9] since it was for such high valor, enclosed within such a manly breast, that I was inflamed with amorous ardor. [10–12] I alone of all women called myself blessed on earth, even though, suspended between fear and hope, I lived consumed by amorous strife. [13–15] A rare fruit of such noble seed I gathered, uniting courtesy and valor. [16–18] The heavens turned benignly in their spheres for me, and every friendly star was bent on multiplying my amorous delight. [19–21] The sun showed its rays more brightly; the sky was clear and lovely in every part; all evil stars were extinguished. [22–24] The earth, too, equaled the heavens in its beauty; all goods, all graces and virtues were enclosed within my poor dwelling. [25–27] For me spring laughed gaily; the amorous animals could be seen at play, while all cruel beasts were far from sight; [28–30] the green grass was scattered with flowers and gaily all around little *amoretti* could be seen frolicking. [31–33] While I was living so happily, Fortune, who seeks and wishes my harm, turned against me, impetuous and cruel. [34–36] In an instant, the sun vanished in thick and dense fog and the pure air was all disturbed, beyond the usual course of nature. [37–39] The sky filled with dark shadows, and the evil stars all appeared, presaging only my future harm. [40–42] The grass that first was green and dry became dead and dank and within it grew ugly and discolored thorns; [43–45] the beasts Love had made so sprightly and beautiful all disappeared, and those other beasts, hateful

to God and the heavens, came out in their place. [46–48] The little
amoretti also flew away through the darkened sky, filled with anger and
seeking a happier place. [49–51] Let it not be wondered that all this
should have happened, since you who are the only life of my life left to
seek other lands. [52–54] I bless every step I have ever taken to honor
you, and I shall always bless the hour when I first met you and the days
and months. [55–57] Even so, I cannot cease to pine away from the
desire to be close to you, and always I see your image before my eyes.
[58–60] All other concerns are now as nothing to me; all I can do is wait
in tears and hope for your return at the time fixed. [61–63] I pass my
time counting the days and months and find myself furious with the
sun when it does not rush forward in its course as swiftly as I would
wish. [64–66] If it were not for the amorous pledges you left to me,
certainly I would plunge down to the Tartarean realms, making an
example of my love. [67–69] Now I gaze at one of them, now the other;
my gratitude for these lovely gifts is the only reason why I do not
entirely fall apart. [70–72] Then I call happy every spot where you place
your honored feet and every place where the loving sounds of your
wishes reach, [73–75] but I, who am too far to hear them, I call unhappy;
only the hope of your swift return keeps me alive. [76–78] This alone
keeps me from dying because, without you, I do not know what I could
do to lessen my desire. How great my loss! [79–81] Now, if you wish—as
I believe—to give me some relief in your absence, I pray you often to
visit me with your writings, [82–84] so that I may once again hear your
speech and imagine the voice and hand that were once the happy end
and port of all my sufferings. [85–87] Then, too, I shall know that it is
not in vain that I so love you; so I beg of you, give health to my troubled
breast. [88–90] I pray once more that you will courteously grant this
wish and give me such help as can mitigate my suffering in part,
[91–93] and, just as your parting was certain, so may your return be. Do
not linger there any longer if you hope or desire to find me still alive
[94] and to make blessed all my future days.

Capitolo. Florence, Biblioteca Laurenziana, MS Antinori 161, 109r–111v. This *capitolo*
is attributed in the manuscript to "la Barbara" and is grouped with another short
poem attributed to the same poet, a love poem to her by Niccolò Machiavelli, and a
poem by Machiavelli written in her voice. Given Machiavelli's well-attested associa-
tion with the musical virtuosa and possible courtesan Barbara Salutati, an attribution
to her seems credible. This makes the poem a rare early surviving example of the
poetic activity of a nonaristocratic woman, complementing the remarkable series of
letters by the Florence-based courtesan Camilla Pisana of around 1515–17 (Fedi 1996).

Linguistically, this text is quite distinctive. Salutati's language shows notable morphological differences from the Petrarchan model of Tuscan codified by Pietro Bembo (see introduction) and is much closer to the modern Florentine idiom familiar from Machiavelli's writings (note especially "erono" as the imperfect third-person plural, the alternation between *il* and *el* for the masculine definite article, and the fluctuating treatment of agreement in possessives [*tua piante, tuo voglie* in ll. 71–72]). Another feature of Salutati's language that differentiates it from Bembo's model is the use of Latinate spellings (*exemplo, lacrimosa*). Resistance to Bembo's linguistic model endured in Tuscany longer than elsewhere in Italy, down to the 1540s, so this linguistic characterization does not help date the work.

As a *capitolo* written to an absent lover, recounting the poet's distress, Salutati's poem recalls Vittoria Colonna's (no. 7) metrically and thematically, though it is less sophisticated and agile in its style and less assertive in its authorial persona. Fundamentally, the model is that of Ovid's *Heroides*, much imitated in the vernacular at this time. Salutati's poem is far less of a conventional *heroid* than Colonna's, delaying its direct address to the lover until l. 53. The first half of the poem, following its dramatic in medias res opening, recounts the poet's happiness in love, and the turn to unhappiness occasioned by the absence of her lover in an extended exercise in *pathetic fallacy: her happiness is figured in terms of a smiling spring landscape, her unhappiness as a sinister blighted one. The second half of the poem shows the poet pleading the case for her lover's return. Lines 79–84, requesting letters from him during his absence, have a self-referential aspect, emphasizing as they do the power of a letter to convey the absent correspondent's voice, as does this poem. *Amorosi pegni* at l. 64, may be a reference to the couple's children, as "pledges" was often used metaphorically in this sense, following the Latin *pignora* (see notes to no. 192). Lines 52–54 echo the opening of Petrarch's sonnet 61, already imitated in ll. 4–5. The *lieta primavera* of l. 25 may echo of a line in Angelo Poliziano's *Stanze per la giostra* (1478), 1:72, l. 6, from an episode that may have influenced the opening amorous landscape of Salutati's *capitolo* more generally.

Tullia d'Aragona (1547)

9

Qual vaga Filomela che fuggita
è da l'odiata gabbia e in superba
vista sen' va tra gli arboscelli e l'erba,
tornata in libertate e in lieta vita;   4
er'io dagli amorosi lacci uscita,
schernendo ogni martìre e pena acerba
de l'incredibil duol ch'in sé riserba
qual ha per troppo amar l'alma smarrita.   8
Ben avev'io ritolte (ahi stella fera!)
dal tempio di Ciprigna le mie spoglie,
e di lor pregio me n'andava altera;   11
quand'a me Amor:—le tue ritrose voglie
muterò—disse; e femmi prigioniera
di tua virtù per rinovar mie doglie.   14

Like a lovely nightingale who has flown from the hated cage and escapes, a glorious vision, to the bushes and fields, returning to her happy life in liberty—just so was I having escaped from the bonds of love, scorning the torment and bitter pain that is reserved for those who have lost their souls through excessive love. I had withdrawn my spoils from the temple of Venus (alas, cruel star!), and was flaunting them proudly, when Love spoke, saying "I will change your rebellious desires," and, in order to renew my suffering, he made me a prisoner of your valor.

Sonnet ABBA ABBA CDC DCD. D'Aragona 1547, 10r. Like another of d'Aragona's sonnets ("Amore un tempo in così lento foco"), this poem describes the poet's recovery from one love and relapse into another. This departs from the Petrarchan model of the obsessive lifetime love and anticipates the same theme in Gaspara Stampa (nos. 25–26). The reference in l. 10 may be to a text by the Greek sophist Philostratus that describes nymphs offering up beauty aids such as mirrors to Venus to ensure them success in love (Ciprigna is a name for Venus, referring to her Cypriot origins). A famous version of the Philostratus scene, by Titian, hung in the ducal palace in Ferrara, and the image may derive from d'Aragona's visits to that city in the 1530s. The image of the poet as nightingale probably alludes to d'Aragona's fame as singer. "Cruel star" (9) refers to the belief that the stars governed men's fates. For a reading of the poem, see Jones 1990, 115–17.

IO

Se forse per pietà del mio languire
al suon del tristo pianto in questo loco
ten' vieni a me, che tutta fiamma e foco
ardomi e struggo colma di disire,   4
vago augellino, e meco il mio martìre
ch'in pena volge ogni passato gioco,
piangi cantando in suon dolente e roco,
veggendomi del duol quasi perire;   8
pregoti per l'ardor che sì m'addoglia,
ne voli in quella amena e cruda valle
ov'è chi sol può darmi e morte e vita,   11
e cantando gli di' che cangi voglia,
volgendo a Roma 'l viso e a lei le spalle,
se vuol l'alma trovar col corpo unita.   14

If, by chance, out of pity for my suffering, hearing the sound of my sad plaints, you have come to me, charming little bird, as I burn, all fire and flame, and melt, burdened with desire; if you are weeping alongside me as you sing in a hoarse, sorrowing tone, lamenting my torment, which turns all past joys to sorrow, and watching me almost perish with grief—if this is true, then I beg you, in the name of the burning love that so grieves me, to fly to that lovely and cruel valley where that man is who alone can give me life or death. Tell him, singing, to change his plans, turning his face to Rome and his back to that place, if he wishes to find me with my soul and body still conjoined.

Sonnet ABBA ABBA CDE CDE. d'Aragona 1547, 11r (*angellino* in l. 5 corrected to *augellino*). Although d'Aragona's love poems are hard to date, this is probably datable to the 1520–30s, since the poet locates herself in Rome. The *topos of an address to a "little bird" (*augelletto, augellino*) is common in Petrarchist poetry: see Petrarch's sonnet 353 for the model, and Francesca Turina (no. 37) for another example. Lines 3–4, with their dramatic *enjambment and their imagery of fire, flame, and melting, offer an unusually emphatic and explicit description of physical passion for a female poet of the era, underlined by the rhythmically anomalous strong stress at the beginning of l. 4, which creates a dramatic effect. The poem is constructed as a single, long, syntactically complex sentence beginning with two "if" clauses addressed to the little bird, whose identity is revealed only at l. 5.

Virginia Salvi (1553–59)

II

Mentre le vaghe ed onorate sponde
de la Tressa pass'io, l'alta sembianza
del mio bel Sol, ch'ogni altro bello avanza
miro entro quelle chiare e felici onde.   4
Ivi mi fermo, e 'l chiamo; ei non risponde,
ché git'è a ravvivar l'altrui speranza
per più mia doglia e per antica usanza
de l'ozio, che lo chiama e lo confonde.   8
Tal ch'io mesta men'vo, dove già fui
seco mirando i bei ridenti fiori,
e dico:—Qui posossi, e qui sorrise;   11
qui la man gli baciai; qui pur m'ancise,
ché mi disse: "Felici i nostri amori
saranno"—. Or vivo, e pur son senza lui.   14

While I wander along the lovely, honored banks of the Tressa, I gaze in those bright and happy waters at the glorious semblance of my beautiful Sun, the fairest of all men. I stop and call to him, but he does not reply, for he has departed to revive another's hopes, to make my misery complete, lured away by his old habit of restlessness, which calls and confounds him. So I now walk in sadness where once I strolled alongside him, gazing on the fair laughing flowers. I tell myself: "Here he stopped, and here he smiled. Here I kissed his hand, and here he slew me, saying, 'Our love will be a happy one.'" Now I live, yet without him.

Sonnet ABBA ABBA CDE EDC. Domenichi 1559, 175. Virginia Salvi was active as a poet from at least 1540, and verse of hers first appeared in print in 1544. Her love lyrics may have been part of a narrative sequence, as they include both *in vita* and *in morte* poems. The present sonnet is interesting for its narrative concreteness and for the hint in ll. 7–8 at a certain waywardness in the beloved (the term I have translated "restlessness" literally means "leisure" or "idleness"). Also interesting are the opening lines, which have the poet see a reflection of her beloved as she gazes into the waters of the Tressa (a river running near Siena). Although this may simply reflect the Petrarchan *topos of the beloved's image imprinting itself on the landscape (see, for example, *RVF* 129), it also recalls the myth of Narcissus, who fell in love with his own reflection: an evocative allusion, given that the Neoplatonic lover was said to fuse spiritually with the object of his love. In that case, the poet would embody both Narcissus and Echo: we see her at ll. 13–14 echoing her lover's words.

12

Se quel ch'amo di voi non è mortale
convien ch'eterno sia quest'amor mio,
e s'infinito è in me l'alto desio,
fassi a la sua cagion in tutto eguale.   4
E se tant'è, scacciate il vano e frale
timor che fa lo stato nostro rio;
e vivete secur, ch'io non desio,
né prezzo altra d'Amor fiamma né strale.   8
Tutti i nodi in me sciolse allor ch'avvinse
il vostro laccio intorno all'alma mia,
e spense ogni altro ardor quand'ei l'accese.   11
Ragione il laccio ordì; Tempo lo strinse;
per elezïon fui vostra, e non desia
il cor piu glorïose o belle imprese.   14

If what I love in you is not mortal, then my love cannot be other than
eternal; and, if my noble desire for you is infinite, it is so out of likeness
to its cause. If this is the case, then banish the vain, weak fear that is
poisoning our happy state. Live secure, for I do not desire or prize
any other flame or arrow of love. Love untied all knots in me in the
moment when he clasped your leash around my soul and quenched all
other ardors when he lit it with his fire. Reason secured the leash; Time
pulled it tight. I was yours by election, and my heart desires no finer or
more glorious feat.

Sonnet ABBA ABBA CDE CDE. Domenichi 1559, 182. Several of Salvi's love poems
address the theme of jealousy, relatively rare in women's poetry of this era. Here
the poet seeks to dissuade her lover of his fear that she will abandon him for an-
other man. The sonnet overturns contemporary stereotypes of feminine fickleness
and sensuality, arguing that the poet's love is rooted in rational choice and that its
Neoplatonic, spiritual character guarantees its permanence. It is the male lover
who is associated with the traditionally feminine traits of "frailty" and fear (5–6).
The logical, quasi-syllogistic tone of the first quatrain, and the crisp syntax of the
tercets enhance the impression of rational control. Salvi's tercets closely echo Vit-
toria Colonna's A1:7, which expresses the same adamant devotion in an *in morte*
context, while the description of love for a noble soul as a glorious feat (l. 14) recalls
the heroic treatment of love we find in Gaspara Stampa.

Gaspara Stampa (1554)
13

Voi ch'ascoltate in queste meste rime,
in questi mesti, in questi oscuri accenti
il suon degli amorosi miei lamenti
e de le pene mie tra l'altre prime,　　4
ove fia chi valor apprezzi e stime,
gloria, non che perdon, de' miei lamenti
spero trovar fra le ben nate genti,
poiché la lor cagione è sì sublime.　　8
E spero ancor che debba dir qualcuna
—Felicissima lei, da che sostenne
per sì chiara cagion danno sì chiaro!　　11
Deh, perché tant'amor, tanta fortuna
per sì nobil signor a me non venne,
ch'anch'io n'andrei con tanta donna a paro?　　14

All you who listen in these sad rhymes, these sad and dismal utterances,
to the sound of my amorous laments and my sufferings, exceeding
those of all others—wherever a soul may be found who prizes and
esteems valor, I hope among gentlefolk to find glory, not merely
pardon, for my laments, since their cause is so sublime. And I hope
one day some woman will say: "O most happy she, who suffered such
famous pain for a cause so famous! Alas! Why was I not fated to
experience such good fortune and endure such great love for so noble
a lord, that I might be the equal of so great a lady!"

Sonnet ABBA ABBA CDE CDE. Stampa 1554, 1. The quatrains of Stampa's proemial
sonnet reprise the first sonnet of Petrarch's *RVF*, while the sestet structurally echoes
that of Bembo's sonnet 141, a tribute to Giovanni della Casa. Through this ambi-
tious imitative strategy, Stampa associates herself with the three most distin-
guished male lyricists of the distant and immediate past and the present day. The
main stylistic characteristics of Stampa's verse are on display: her relatively simple,
colloquial syntax (note the *anacoluthon in the quatrains); her rhythmic, almost
sing-song, sound patterning, especially noticeable in ll. 1–2; and her insistent use of
rhetorical figures of *parallelism and repetition like the *chiasmus of l. 11. The iden-
tical rhyme *lamenti* in ll. 3 and 6 would have been considered a technical error (*la-
menti* in l. 6 is corrected to *tormenti* in Stampa 1738). *Altre* (others) in l. 4 is feminine:
perhaps with a view to Ovid's *Heroides*, the poet announces her superiority in suf-
fering to all women who have loved.

14

Chi vuol conoscer, donne, il mio signore,
miri un signor di vago e dolce aspetto,
giovane d'anni e vecchio d'intelletto,
imagin de la gloria e del valore: 4
di pelo biondo e di vivo colore,
di persona alta e spazioso petto,
e finalmente in ogni opra perfetto,
fuor ch'un poco (oimè lassa!) empio in amore.   8
E chi vuol poi conoscer me, rimiri
una donna in effetti ed in sembiante
imagin de la morte e de' martiri,   11
un albergo di fé salda e costante,
una che, perché pianga, arda e sospiri,
non fa pietoso il suo crudele amante.   14

Ladies, if you wish to know my lord, look on a lord of comely and
gentle aspect, young in age and old in wisdom, the image of glory and
valor: blond of hair and bright of visage, tall in his person and broad of
chest, and finally perfect in all his deeds, except that he is a little—alas,
poor me!—villainous in love. And whoever should wish to know me, let
her look once more, and she will see a woman in truth and appearance
the image of death and torment, a haven of firm and constant faith: one
who, however she weeps, burns, and sighs, cannot wring pity from her
cruel lover.

Sonnet ABBA ABBA CDC DCD. Stampa 1554, 4. Detailed physical description of the
beloved's beauty, though a theme of enormous centrality in the male-authored love
lyrics of the period, barely features in the female-authored tradition. Stampa's de-
scription of the handsome, blond Collalto is practically unique. The address to an
audience of "ladies" is characteristic of Stampa, who frequently constructs her love
as a spectacle. This may reflect performance dynamics, in that Stampa appears to
have sung or declaimed her verse, as well as circulating it in writing (Smarr 1991). If
this sonnet was performed, it is not difficult to imagine that the unexpected twist of
l. 8, with the accusation of erotic iniquity smuggled in at the end of an otherwise
exemplary portrait, would have been especially effective. The *Chi vuol* incipit de-
rives from Petrarch's sonnet 248.

15

Se così come sono abietta e vile
donna posso portar sì alto foco,
perché non debbo aver almeno un poco
di ritraggerlo al mondo e vena e stile?   4
S'Amor con novo, insolito focile,
ov'io non potea gir, m'alzò a tal loco,
perché non può non con usato gioco
far la pena e la penna in me simìle?   8
E, se non può per forza di natura,
puollo almen per miracolo, che spesso
vince, trapassa e rompe ogni misura.   11
Come ciò sia non posso dir espresso;
io provo ben che per mia gran ventura
mi sento il cor di novo stile impresso.   14

If, although I am an abject and base woman, I can sustain such a noble
fire, why should I not have at least a little vein and style to portray it to
the world? If Love with his new, unwonted firesteel exalted me to a
place I could not reach alone, why can he not, with an unaccustomed
trick, make my pain and pen alike? And if he cannot do this by natural
means, he might at least by a miracle, for often he vanquishes and
breaks and defies all limits. How this may have come about I cannot
explain, yet I feel that, by my great good fortune, my heart has been
imprinted with a new style.

Sonnet ABBA ABBA CDC DCD. Stampa 1554, 5. Although the motif of love for an
exalted object as ennobling for the poet was an established *topos in love lyric since
the pre-Petrarchan era, it takes on a particular significance in Stampa, a commoner
in love with a nobleman and a merchant's daughter appropriating a model of poetry
long associated with the aristocracy and the courts. Here, the poet calls on Love to
give her the eloquence to transcend her "base" state and express her noble suffer-
ings in a fittingly noble style. By the final tercet, the miracle she is calling for ap-
pears to have been achieved, and she feels herself newly inspired. The association
made in the sonnet between the poet's love suffering and her poetry, underscored
by l. 8's pun on *pena* and *penna*, encourages us to draw an analogy between the re-
markable and unique quality of both. The metaphor of Love as a *focile* (firesteel)—
used in a tinderbox to strike sparks—derives from Petrarch's sonnet 185.

16

Altri mai foco, stral, prigione o nodo
sì vivo e acuto e sì aspra e sì stretto
non arse, impiagò, tenne e strinse il petto,
quanto 'l mio ardente, acuto, acerba e sodo.   4
Né qual io moro e nasco e peno e godo,
mor'altra e nasce e pena ed ha diletto,
per fermo e vario e bello e crudo aspetto,
che 'n voci e 'n carte spesso accuso e lodo.   8
Né fûro ad altrui mai le gioie care,
quanto è a me quando mi doglio e sfaccio,
mirando a le mie luci or fosche or chiare.   11
Mi dorrà sol se mi trarrà d'impaccio,
fin che potrò e viver ed amare,
lo stral e 'l foco e la prigione e 'l laccio.   14

Never did fire, arrow, prison, or knot, so fierce and sharp, so harsh and tight, ever burn, wound, restrain, or bind any breast, in such an ardent, sharp, cruel, unyielding manner. Nor has any other woman been born and died and suffered and relished as I am born and die and suffer and delight in that stable and mutable and lovely and cruel aspect, which in voice and on paper I oftentimes praise and accuse. Nor did ever lover so prize his joy as I prize my suffering, as I melt gazing on his eyes, now dark, now bright. I will only complain if, while I still live and can love, I am rescued from the arrow and the fire and the prison and the leash.

Sonnet ABBA ABBA CDC DCD. Stampa 1554, 14. The opening and closing lines of this virtuosistic sonnet employ the fashionable device of *rapportatio*, of which the Venetian poet Domenico Venier had recently offered a striking example with his sonnet "Non punse, arse, o legò stral, fiamma, o laccio" (Never did an arrow, flame, or leash so pierce, burn, or tie). In the rest of the poem, Stampa uses similar correlative constructions to underline the unique and miraculous nature of the poet's love, varying the poem's soundscape notably, especially in the quatrains, from the dense, consonant-rich, *s*-dominated ll. 2–3, to the more open and varied sounds of ll. 4–8, with rhythmic *polysyndeton. The unusual mixture of denunciation and praise in Stampa's love poetry is pointed up in ll. 7–8 and justified by the baffling and contradictory character of its object. "In voice and on paper," in l. 8, refers to Stampa's practice of performing her love poetry, as well as circulating it in a written form.

17

Dura è la stella mia, maggior durezza
è quella del mio Conte: egli mi fugge,
i' seguo lui; altri per me si strugge,
i' non posso mirar altra bellezza.   4
Odio chi m'ama ed amo chi mi sprezza;
verso chi m'è umìle il mio cor rugge,
i' son umìl con chi mia speme adugge;
a così stranio cibo ho l'alma avezza.   8
Egli ognor dà cagione a novo sdegno,
essi mi cercan dar conforto e pace:
i' lasso questi ed a quell'un m'attegno.   11
Così ne la tua scola, Amor, si face
sempre il contrario di quel ch'egli è degno:
l'umìl si sprezza e l'empio si compiace.   14

Harsh is my star; still greater harshness is that of my Count. He flees me, and I follow him; another melts for me, but I can admire no other beauty. I hate those who love me and love him who despises me; my heart roars against my humble suitors, while I humble myself toward him who cruelly chokes my dreams. To such a strange diet is my soul accustomed. He gives me cause for ever new anger, while they try to offer me comfort and peace, yet I leave them behind and cleave only to him. Thus in your school, Love, do we always do the contrary of what is deserved: the humble is scorned, while the cruel wins the day.

Sonnet ABBA ABBA CDC DCD. Stampa 1554, 22. This sonnet frustratedly analyzes the irrationality of love, which leads lovers to desire unattainable objects while scorning those who love them. The theme has a strong literary tradition, especially in Ariosto, the second canto of whose *Orlando furioso* (1532) opens with a lament against the injustice of love. The sonnet has a strategic importance in Stampa's collection, as it underlines the poet figure's attractiveness, which might otherwise be undermined by her invidious position as spurned lover to the heartless Count. The quatrains of the sonnet, with their jagged double-consonant rhymes, deploy a phonetically "hard" poetry to explore the hardness of the beloved, in a manner pioneered by Dante in his "stony rhymes" (*rime petrose*). *Adugge/fugge/strugge* is found in rhyme in Petrarch's canzone 264, and *adugge/rugge* in his sonnet 56. *Stranio cibo*, in l. 8, derives from Petrarch's canzone 207.

18

Piangete, donne, e poiché la mia morte
non move il Signor mio crudo e lontano,
voi che sète di cor dolce ed umano,
aprite di pietade almen le porte.   4
Piangete meco la mia acerba sorte,
chiamando Amor, il ciel empio, inumano,
e lei, che mi ferì, spietata mano,
che mi vegga morir e lo comporte.   8
E, poi ch'io sarò cenere e favilla,
dica alcuna di voi mesta e pietosa,
sentita del mio foco una scintilla: 11
—Sotto quest'aspra pietra giace ascosa
l'infelice e fidissima Anassilla,
raro essempio di fede alta amorosa—.   14

Weep, ladies, and since my death does not move my cruel and distant lord, you, at least, who are sweet and kindly of heart, open the doors to pity. Weep with me my bitter fate, calling Love and the heavens iniquitous and unkind, and that unpitying hand that wounded me and now watches me dying and looks on. And once I am nought but ashes and sparks, let one of you say in sorrowful, pitying tones, "Beneath this cruel stone lies hidden the unhappy and most faithful Anassilla, a rare paragon of noble amorous faith."

Sonnet ABBA ABBA CDC DCD. Stampa 1554, 46. A lengthy sequence in Stampa's *Rime* recounts the poet's misery during an extended absence of Collalto in France in 1549, when he fought alongside French troops in an attack on English-held Boulogne. The micro-sequence from which this sonnet comes portrays the poet as brought close to death by Collalto's neglect. Here she imagines herself, dramatically, incinerated by love, reduced to "ashes and sparks." The address to an audience of ladies is fairly frequent in Stampa's verse (cf. no. 14), as is the motif of the poet as amorous *exemplum (cf. no. 13). Anassilla is Stampa's *senhal in the *Rime*, deriving from the Latin name for the river Piave, which flowed through Collalto's estates near Treviso. The epitaph of the final tercet is written in a notably grave style, with its three double *s*'s, its Latinism *fidissimo* and its two examples of *concorso di vocali (*fidissima Anassilla; alta amorosa*). Note also the inclusive rhymes *umano/inumano* and *porte/comporte*.

19

Novo e raro miracol di Natura,
ma non novo né raro a quel Signore
che 'l mondo tutto va chiamando Amore,
che 'l tutto adopra fuor d'ogni misura: 4
il valor che degli altri il pregio fura,
del mio Signor, che vince ogni valore,
è vinto, lassa, sol dal mio dolore,
dolor, a petto a cui null'altro dura.   8
Quant'ei tutt'altri cavalieri eccede
in esser bello, nobile ed ardito,
tanto è vinto da me, da la mia fede.   11
Miracol fuor d'Amor mai non udito;
dolor, che chi nol prova non lo crede:
lassa, ch'io sola vinco l'infinito!   14

What a strange and rare marvel of Nature! (Though not so strange or
rare to that lord the world likes to call Love, whose every act is without
measure.) The valor of my lord, which steals the prize from all others
and vanquishes all valor, is vanquished—alas!—only by my suffering, a
suffering beside which no comparison can stand. Just as he exceeds all
other knights in being fair, noble, and bold, so he is defeated by me and
my faithfulness. A marvel that would be unthinkable outside the realm
of love, a suffering unimaginable to anyone who has not felt it: alas,
I alone vanquish the infinite!

Sonnet ABBA ABBA CDC DCD. Stampa 1554, 48. This is one of the most famous of
Stampa's sonnets, not least for its remarkable last line, in which Stampa's heroic
construction of her poetic persona reaches an extreme. It illustrates well Stampa's
characteristic use of repetition to articulate her verse ("novo . . . raro" in ll. 1–2;
"che 'l tutto" in 3–4; *valor/valore* in 5–6; *dolore/dolor* in 7–8, a case of *anadiplosis;
vincere and its derivatives in 6, 7, 11, and 14). The light irony of the description of
Love in ll. 2–3 (echoing Petrarch's *TC* 1.76) is also characteristic of Stampa, whose
tragic-romantic self-dramatization is offset by an element of playful wit that distin-
guishes her from her Petrarchist peers. The representation of the female lover's de-
votion and faith as representing a heroism alternative to and comparable to the
male beloved's martial prowess is reminiscent of Ovid's *Heroides*, a powerful influ-
ence on Stampa's love poetry (see Phillippy 1992).

20

A che, Conte, assalir chi non repugna?
A che gittar per terra chi si rende?
A che contender con chi non contende?
Con chi avete mai sempre fra l'ugna?   4
Sapete che co' morti non si pugna;
ché lo splendor d'un cavalier offende,
e 'l vostro più, che l'ali oggimai stende
dove non so s'altrui chiarezza aggiugna.   8
Guardate che la fama de le tante
vostre vittorie poi non renda oscura,
Signor, quest'una sola, e non ammante.   11
Io per me stimerei mia gran ventura
l'esser veduta al vostro carro innante;
ma voi del vostro onor abiate cura.   14

Count, what is the use of attacking someone who offers no defense?
Of throwing to the ground someone who has already surrendered?
Fighting one who does not fight in return? Why must you always have
me in your claws? Be informed that it is not proper to fight with the
dead, for this can sully a knight's splendor—all the more so one like
you, whose glory outshines that of all others in our day. My lord, you
must ensure that the fame of all your great victories is not dimmed and
shrouded by this last one. For my part, I would esteem it a great fortune
to be seen before your chariot—but you should have some care for your
honor.

Sonnet ABBA ABBA CDC DCD. Stampa 1554, 50. A striking feature of Stampa's love
lyrics is that they not only praise the beloved but also frequently accuse him of
neglect and infidelity. A precedent existed in male Petrarchists' complaints of their
ladies' cruelty, but this was a disguised compliment since this harshness was seen to
stem from their rigorous chastity. A sonnet by Camilla Scarampa (no. 3) offers a more
apposite point of comparison. Stampa's insistence on the damage Collalto's treat-
ment of her may do to his reputation underlines the power of her verse to shape
perceptions of him, offsetting her frequent self-presentation as abject victim. The
language of this sonnet is unusually vigorous and aggressive, though softened at
points by flattery (7–8) and wit. The dominance of consonant-heavy rhymes and the
sequence of *end-stopped lines in the first quatrain offer a marked difference from
Stampa's generally mellifluous style. Lines 12–13 allude to Roman generals' custom
of displaying their captives as trophies during their triumphs.

21

Con quai degne accoglienze o quai parole
raccorrò io il mio gradito amante,
che torna a me con tante glorie e tante,
quante in un sol non vide forse il sole?   4
Qual color or di rose, or di vïole
fia 'l mio? Qual cor or saldo, ed or tremante,
condotta innanzi a quel divin sembiante,
ch'ardir e téma insieme dar mi suole?   8
Osarò io con queste fide braccia
cingerli il caro collo ed accostare
la mia tremante a la sua viva faccia?   11
Lassa, che, pur a tanto ben pensare,
temo che 'l cor di gioia non si sfaccia:
chi l'ha provato se lo può pensare.   14

What welcome shall I give my adored lover? With what words shall
I greet him, when he returns to me laden with greater glories than
the sun has ever seen in one man? What color shall I turn, now that
of roses, now of lilies? How shall my heart feel—now steady, now
trembling—in the presence of that divine visage, which inspires in me
both boldness and fear? Shall I dare to clasp his dear neck with these
faithful arms of mine and bring my trembling face close to his bright
one? Alas, I fear that, even thinking of such pleasure, my heart will
break with joy. Whoever has known this can imagine how I feel.

Sonnet ABBA ABBA CDC DCD. Stampa 1554, 54 (*penare* in l. 12 corrected to *pensare*).
In its representation of a reciprocated physical love, this sonnet is remote from
Petrarchist norms and closer to the *poesia cortigiana* tradition. The quatrains of the
poem are insistently patterned through devices of repetition: the *anaphora of
"Quai . . . qual . . . qual" in ll. 1, 5, and 6; the *polysyndeton of "or . . . or," in 5 and 6;
the wordplay on "sol . . . sole" in 4, and the typically Petrarchan antithetical couplet
of "ardir e téma" in 8. The vivid first tercet, with its two strong *enjambments, gains
its effectiveness partly by contrast with the highly patterned quatrains. The final
tercet's rhymes present a problem: *pensare* seems required for the sense in l. 12, yet
the text has *penare* (to suffer). This may be an editorial correction of what was origi-
nally an identical rhyme (see also no. 13). *Viole* (lilies), in l. 5, literally means "[white]
violets," with possible allusion to Petrarch's 224, l. 8.

22

O notte, a me più chiara e più beata
che i più beati giorni ed i più chiari,
notte degna da' primi e da' più rari
ingegni esser, non pur da me, lodata;   4
tu de le gioie mie sola sei stata
fida ministra; tu tutti gli amari
de la mia vita hai fatto dolci e cari,
resomi in braccio lui che m'ha legata.   8
Sol mi mancò che non divenni allora
la fortunata Alcmena, a cui ste' tanto
più de l'usato a ritornar l'aurora.   11
Pur così bene io non potrò mai tanto
dir di te, notte candida, ch'ancora
da la materia non sia vinto il canto.   14

O night, brighter to me and more blessed than the most bright and blessed days: night worthy of being praised by the rarest and finest intellects, not merely by me. You alone have been the faithful minister of my bliss, you have rendered all the bitterness of my life dear and sweet to me, by bringing to my arms the man who has bound me. All that was missing from me then was that I did not become that happy Alcmena, for whom dawn so delayed her usual coming. Shining night, I can never praise you so highly that my song will not be outstripped by its subject.

Sonnet ABBA ABBA CDC DCD. Stampa 1554, 56. In its subject matter, a rapturous reminiscence of a night of love, this sonnet is extremely unusual within Petrarchist lyric. It is closer to the more sensual traditions of classical elegy and *poesia cortigiana* than to the sublimated erotic tradition of orthodox Petrarchism. Thematic parallels are offered by Propertius's elegy 2.15, with its opening paradox of the "bright night" (*nox candida*), echoed by Stampa in l. 13, or by Lorenzo de' Medici's sonnet 107 ("O veramente felice e beata / notte"), with which it shares its first rhyme word. The mythological reference in ll. 9–11 is to Jove's adulterous night of love with Alcmena, when he artificially extended the hours of darkness to protract his pleasure. The sonnet rests for its effect partly on the poet's public celebration of what she might be expected to keep silent about, for reasons of decorum. This lends a hint of irony to her remark in ll. 3–4 that her night with her lover deserves to be hymned by the greatest and rarest intellects.

23

Signor, io so che 'n me non son più viva,
e veggo omai ch'ancor in voi son morta,
e l'alma ch'io vi diedi non sopporta
che stia più meco vostra voglia schiva.   4
E questo pianto che da me deriva,
non so chi 'l mova per l'usata porta,
né chi mova la mano e le sia scorta,
quando avien che di voi tal volta scriva.   8
Strano e fiero miracol veramente,
che altri sia viva e non sia viva e pèra,
e senta tutto e non senta niente;   11
sì che può dirsi la mia forma vera,
da chi ben mira a sì vario accidente,
un'imagine d'Eco e di Chimera.   14

My lord, I know I no longer live in me, and I see now that in you, too,
I am dead. The soul I gave you can no longer bear to see itself shunned
by your desire. So these tears that still flow from me, I know not who
moves them through their accustomed gates; nor who moves my
hand and acts as its guide when it sometimes comes to write of you. A
strange and cruel miracle indeed, to be alive and not alive, and to
perish, to feel everything and nothing. He who studies these so diverse
effects will recognize my true form as an image of Echo and Chimera.

Sonnet ABBA ABBA CDC DCD. Stampa 1554, 67. The notion of love as a "living
death" was a Petrarchist commonplace (see nos. 29, 68), but Stampa gives the *to-
pos remarkable vitality in this sonnet. Especially striking is the evocation of mental
self-alienation in ll. 5–8, reminiscent of the speech of the mad Orlando in *OF* 23.106–
8. The mythological references in l. 14 are to Echo, the nymph who loved Narcissus
and pined away after his death, leaving only her disembodied voice, and to the
Chimera, a female monster combining elements of a lioness, snake, and goat. The
term also metaphorically meant a fantastic and impossible imagining, so the defini-
tion of the poet's "true form" as that of a chimera is ironic and *oxymoronic. Stylistic
features to note in the poem are the *polysyndeton of ll. 10–11; the inclusive rhyme of
porta/sopporta (3, 6), and the juxtaposition of *viva* and *morta* in rhyme position (1–2).

24

—Or sopra il forte e veloce destriero—,
io dico meco—segue lepre o cerva
il mio bel Sole, or rapida caterva
d'uccelli con falconi o con sparviero.   4
Or assal con lo spiedo il cignal fiero,
quando animoso il suo venir osserva;
or a l'opre di Marte, or di Minerva
rivolge l'alto e saggio suo pensiero.   8
Or mangia, or dorme, or leva ed or ragiona,
or vagheggia il suo colle, or con l'umana
sua maniera trattiene ogni persona—.   11
Così, Signor, bench'io vi sia lontana,
sì fattamente Amor mi punge e sprona,
ch'ogni vostr'opra m'è presente e piana.   14

"Now on his strong, fast steed," I tell myself, "my fair Sun is coursing after hares or deer; now he is hunting a swift flock of birds with his falcons or hawk. Now with his spear he is assailing the fierce boar, boldly facing it as it rushes toward him. Now he is turning his lofty, sage thoughts to the pursuits of Mars or Minerva; now he is eating, now sleeping, now waking, now speaking. Now he gazes fondly on his hill, now converses charmingly with all around." Thus, my lord, although I am far from you, Love goads and spurs me in such a way that your every action is present and plain to me.

Sonnet ABBA ABBA CDC DCD. Stampa 1554, 78. A unusual thematic feature of Stampa's love lyrics is the degree of agency and individuality they give to the figure of the beloved, who is usually little more than an abstracted ideal of beauty in Petrarchist lyric. This imagined representation of Collalto engaged in the sporting and intellectual pursuits of the ideal Renaissance gentleman underlines his aristocratic ethos, while the almost narcissistic self-sufficiency she portrays in him—the "hill" (*colle*) he gazes on fondly in l. 10, is a *senhal Stampa uses for Collalto himself in some poems—contrasts sharply with the poet's obsessive love. This sonnet represents an extreme case of Stampa's characteristic syntactic simplicity: the entire visionary segment of the quatrains and first tercet is constructed purely of simple declarative sentences starting *anaphorically with *or* (now). Minerva and Mars (7) were the Roman gods, respectively, of wisdom and war or, in the favored Renaissance formula, letters and arms.

25

Amor m'ha fatto tal ch'io vivo in foco,
qual nova salamandra al mondo, e quale
l'altro di lei non men stranio animale,
che vive e spira nel medesmo loco.   4
Le mie delizie son tutte e 'l mio gioco
viver ardendo e non sentire il male,
e non curar ch'ei che m'induce a tale
abbia di me pietà molto né poco.   8
A pena era anche estinto il primo ardore,
che accese l'altro Amore, a quel ch'io sento
fin qui per prova, più vivo e maggiore.   11
E io d'arder amando non mi pento,
purché chi m'ha di novo tolto il core
resti de l'arder mio pago e contento.   14

Love has made me such that I live in the fire, like a miraculous
salamander, or like that other animal, no less strange than she, who
lives and breathes in the same place. All my pleasure, all I delight in, is
to live burning and not feel the pain and not to care whether he who
leads me to this torment feels for me little or much. Hardly had my first
flames been extinguished, when another love flared, still more power-
ful and keen, to judge from what I have felt to date. And I do not regret
this burning in love, just so long as he who has newly taken my heart is
satisfied and content that I burn.

Sonnet ABBA ABBA CDC DCD. Stampa 1554, 108. This sonnet is from a short
sequence in Stampa's *Rime* describing the end of one love and the beginning of an-
other. Critics have sometimes held these to refer to the end of Stampa's affair with
Collalto and the beginning of a new one with a lover, sometimes identified as Bar-
tolomeo Zen. It should be remembered, however, that there is no external evidence
for these events in Stampa's life and that the theme of a return to love after a brief
escape has precedents in Tullia d'Aragona (no. 9). The sonnet constructs the poet
heroically as fated to love, in a manner that transcends the rather contingent figure
of the beloved: a significant departure from Petrarchism, although Stampa borrows
the image of the salamander, reputedly capable of living in flames, from Petrarch's
canzone 207. The other fire-living animal of ll. 3–4 may be the phoenix (see no. 48).
A paraphrase of l. 6 of this poem, one of Stampa's most striking lines, was used as a
motto by the late-romantic poet Gabriele d'Annunzio (1863–1938).

26

A mezo il mare ch'io varcai tre anni
fra dubbi venti, ed era quasi in porto,
m'ha ricondotta Amor, che a sì gran torto
è ne' travagli miei pronto e ne' danni;   4
e per doppiare a' miei disiri i vanni
un sì chiaro oriente agli occhi ha pòrto,
che, rimirando lui, prendo conforto,
e par che manco il travagliar m'affanni.   8
Un foco eguale al primo foco io sento,
e, se in sì poco spazio questo è tale,
che de l'altro non sia maggior, pavento.   11
Ma che poss'io, se m'è l'arder fatale,
se volontariamente andar consento
d'un foco in altro e d'un in altro male?   14

Into the midst of that sea I was three years in the crossing, beset by treacherous winds, Love has driven me back when I was almost at harbor, swift as he always is to work to my travail and harm. And to quicken the wings of my desire, he has placed such a clear dawn before my eyes that the sight of it comforts me and all my troubles seem to afflict me less. I feel a fire equal to the first fire and, if it has grown such in so short a space of time, I fear it may be greater than the last. But what can I do, if to burn is my fate, and if, of my own will, I consent to go from one fire to another and from one evil to the next?

Sonnet ABBA ABBA CDC DCD. Stampa 1554, 114. This poem is on the same theme as no. 25 but combines the imagery of love as fire with another popular Petrarchan metaphor, of the life of the lover as a dangerous sea voyage, beset with the winds of passion (see for example Petrarch's sonnet 189). The final tercet offers a powerful statement of the poet's enslavement to love, presented in a logic-defying manner as both predestined and voluntary. An effective formal feature is the contrast between the stately, almost cumbersome penultimate line, with its paired consonants (-*nt*, -*nt*, -*nd*, -*ns*, -*nt*), and the much swifter and phonetically lighter final line, which echoes l. 9 in its neatly parallel structures. Note the *rima equivoca* at ll. 2 and 6 (the second *porto* is a poetic variant for the usual past particle *portato*).

27

—Dimmi per la tua face,
Amor, e per gli strali,
per questi, che mi dan colpi mortali,
e quella, che mi sface,
onde avien che non osi   5
ferir il mio signore,
altero de' tuoi strazi e del mio core,
in sembianti pietosi?—
—Ove anniderò poi—
mi risponde ei—s'io perdo gli occhi suoi?—   10

"Tell me, Love, by your brand and your arrows—the arrows that rain mortal blows on me, the brand that undoes me—why it is that you do not wound my lord, who proudly flaunts your torments and my heart, and soften him to pity?" "And where shall I make my nest," he rejoins, "if I lose his eyes?"

Madrigal abBacdDceE. Stampa 1554, 168. The long sonnet sequence in Stampa's *Rime* is followed by a short sequence of madrigals, which show her at her most witty and playful. Here the poet urges Love to work his magic on the impervious beloved, and Love refuses, on the ground that the beloved's eyes are his favored launching-pad for attacks. Love is portrayed as armed not only with arrows but also with his less common attribute of a burning brand or torch. The poise and wit of this madrigal, as well as its shortness and metrical lightness (*settenari* dominate over hendecasyllables) are reminiscent of later-sixteenth-century fashions. The witty inclusive rhyme *face/sface*, describing the cause and effect of the poet's emotional meltdown, underline the *chiastic structure of the first metrical segment (abBa), repeated in the second (cdDc) before the concluding couplet.

28

Il cor verrebbe teco
nel tuo partir, Signore,
s'egli fosse più meco,
poi che con gli occhi tuoi mi prese Amore.
Dunque verranno teco i sospir miei,   5
che sol mi son restati
fidi compagni e grati,
e le voci e gli omei;
e se vedi mancarti la lor scorta,
pensa ch'io sarò morta.   10

My heart would come with you on your departure, my lord, if I still had it with me after Love took me prisoner through your eyes. What will come with are you my sighs, which are all that remain to me, my trusted and dear companions—those, and my cries and complaints. If you see you are lacking their escort, then know I am dead.

Madrigal abaBCddcEe. Stampa 1554, 170. Unusually, Stampa addresses the beloved here using the familiar *tu* form rather than the more honorific *voi*, making it dubious whether this madrigal was part of the sequence for Collalto. The poem starts with the familiar *topos of the poet's heart having departed her body to be with her lover but continues more originally with the image of her sighs and laments—presumably as embodied in her verse—accompanying him on his travels. The image recalls the mythological figure of Echo, Narcissus's lover, existing only as a disembodied voice (cf. no. 23, where Stampa explicitly recalls this figure).

Chiara Matraini (1555 and 1597; see Notes on Authors)
29

Smarrissi il cor, ghiacciossi il sangue quando,
dipinto di pietà, l'almo mio Sole
udii con dolci ed umili parole
dirmi, e con un sospiro:—O mio sostegno,
mesto men vo, ma 'l cor ti lascio in pegno—.   5
In questo, l'aspro suo dolore accolto
sfogò per gli occhi, e 'mpalidì il bel volto.
Quel ch'io divenni allor, sasselo Amore,
e sallo bene ogni invescato core,
ché quasi morta, in voce rotta e frale,   10
a gran pena formai:—Signor mio, vale—
e più non potei dire
ché mi sentì morire.

My heart failed and my blood froze when I heard my fair Sun, his face
infused with pity, saying with a sigh, in sweet, simple words, "My
staunch one, I am sad to leave you, but my heart remains with you as a
pledge." As he spoke, the sorrow he had been holding back was released
through his eyes, and his lovely face grew pale. What I felt at that
moment only Love can know, and those whose hearts are in thrall to
love. Close to death, I could barely utter these words, in a broken and
frail voice: "My lord, farewell." More I could not say, for I felt myself die.

Madrigal ABBCCDDEEFFgg. Matraini 1597, 44v (*e 'mpalidì* in l. 7 corrected from
o'npalidì; *in pegno* corrected from *impegno* in l. 5). This dramatic madrigal, recalling
a parting from the beloved, is thematically reminiscent of Veronica Gambara's
madrigal "Quando sarà ch'io mora" (no. 4), which similarly represents the love
described as reciprocal and gives the beloved an unwonted degree of agency and
affect. Especially effective here is the use of two shorter, seven-syllable lines—the
only ones in the poem—in the two closing lines, evoking the poet's voicelessness.
The madrigal was set to music by three composers: Bonardo Francesco Perissone
(1565), Francesco Portinaro (1568), and Francesco Vecoli (1575).

30

Fera son io di quest'ombroso loco,
che vo con la saetta in mezzo al core,
fuggendo (lassa) il fin del mio dolore,
e cerco chi mi strugge a poco a poco.   4
E com'augel che fra le penne il foco
si sente acceso, onde volando fuore
dal dolce nido suo, mentre l'ardore
fugge, con l'ale più raccende il foco,   8
tal'io fra queste frondi a l'aura estiva,
con l'ali del desio volando in alto,
cerco il foco fuggir che meco porto.   11
Ma quanto vado più di riva in riva,
per fuggire 'l mio mal, con fiero assalto
lunga morte procaccio al viver corto.   14

I am a wild creature of this shadowy place, who seeks pitifully to flee
the end of her pain, with an arrow through her heart, and searches out
the enemy who is destroying her little by little. I am like a bird who
feels her feathers take fire and seeks to fly her sweet nest, but, as she
attempts to flee the burning, fans the fire higher with her wings. Just so,
among these leaves in the summer air, as I soar on the wings of desire,
I attempt to flee the fire I carry with me. But however I try to flee my
cruel fate, flitting across the river banks, all I do, with a fierce assault,
is to secure a long death for my short life.

Sonnet ABBA ABBA CDE CDE. Matraini 1597, 46r. Matraini draws on two images
here to express the torment of love, that of a fleeing wounded deer, used by Virgil of
Dido in the fourth book of the *Aeneid* (68–73; cf. Petrarch no. 209, 9–11), and that of
a bird set alight by a forest fire, whose attempt to escape in flight succeeds only in
fanning its flames. The poem's success depends in part on its changing rhythms,
the *end-stopped lines of the first quatrain and tercet contrasting with the more
broken rhythms of the second. Not always the most technically correct of poets,
Matraini here anomalously rhymes *foco* with itself, in ll. 5 and 8. Line 9 reworks ele-
ments from the incipit of Petrarch's sonnet 279, including *l'aura estiva* in rhyme.

31

Alti son questi monti ed alti sono
li miei pensier, di cui l'alma s'ingombra:
questi, sol piante sterili gli adombra,
le mie speranze senza frutto sono.   4
Scendon fonti da lor con alto suono,
contrari venti alle lor cime ed ombra
di nubi stanno, e 'l duol da me disgombra
pianto e sospir, di cui sempre ragiono.   8
Nemiche fere in essi, empie e rapaci, .
s'annidan solo, e nel mio petto alberga
fiera doglia, che 'l cor m'ange e divora;   11
godon pur questi le superne faci
qualor vil nebbia almo seren disperga,
ma non vedo mai 'l Sol che l'alma adora.   14

Lofty are these mountains and lofty are the cares with which my soul
is burdened. Only leafless trees shadow their slopes, and my hopes are
without fruit. Water gushes down from their springs with a thundrous
sound, and warring winds and shadowy clouds linger at their peaks;
tears and sighs flow from me, prompted by pain, of which I ever speak.
Only cruel, voracious beasts lurk in these parts; my breast harbors fierce
pain, which devours my heart. Yet these mounts still enjoy the great
blaze of the heavens whenever a lovely calm dispels their base mists,
while I never see the Sun my soul adores.

Sonnet ABBA ABBA CDE CDE. Matraini 1597, 46r–v. This sonnet hyperbolically
compares the poet's sufferings during her beloved's absence to a mountainous land-
scape, perhaps that of the Garfagnana north of Matraini's native Lucca. As in no. 30,
Matraini includes an identical rhyme in this sonnet (*sono* in ll. 1 and 4), although,
given the insistency of her repetition of sounds in the poem (the two *alti son[o]* of
l. 1 are echoed closely, for example, by the *alto suono* in rhyme in l. 5), this apparent
error may be intentional. A notable feature of the poem is the frequent and marked
*enjambment, used to particular effect in ll. 1–2, 7–8, and 10–11. In conjunction with
the consonant-rich rhymes, -*ombra* and -*erga*, and the *concorso di vocali* of the last
two lines (*nebbia almo*; *alma adora*), this would have helped define the poem stylisti-
cally as *grave*. For the enriched rhyme sequence *ingombra/adombra/disgombra/ombra*,
see Petrarch's sonnets 38 and 327.

32

Viva mia bella e dolce calamita,
che, partendo, con sì mirabil modo
stringeste l'alma in quel tenace nodo
ch'a voi sol la terrà più sempre unita;   4
non è la mente mia da voi smarrita,
se ben, lontana da voi, di voi non godo
l'amata vista; anzi via più sempre odo
da voi chiamarmi, ove il desio m'invita.   8
Per voi sì ricco laccio Amor m'avinse
di salda e pura fede al collo intorno,
ch'ogn'altra umil catena sdegna il core.   11
Sciolse ogni nodo quando questo strinse,
e ruppe l'arco con vittoria il giorno,
ch'in me fe' eterno l'ultimo suo ardore.   14

Sweet, beautiful, living magnet, who, in your leaving, so marvelously bound my soul in that tenacious knot which will ever bind it to you, my mind has not wandered from you, even though, far from you, I cannot enjoy your beloved sight; rather, I hear myself ever more called by you where desire invites. Through you, Love bound such a rich leash round my neck, made of solid, pure faith, that my heart scorns to wear any lesser chain. All other knots loosed when this one was tightened, and the bow was victoriously broken that day when Love made eternal in me his utmost fire.

Sonnet ABBA ABBA CDE CDE. Matraini 1555, 44 (*a* in l. 6 amended to *da*). A test of love's purity, in Neoplatonic theory, was its ability to survive distance. A love that transcended the body should be capable of enduring in the beloved's physical absence, as here. The unusual image of the beloved as magnet derives from Petrarch's canzone 135 (30), which also supplies the adjectives *viva* and *dolce*. Matraini combines this with the common metaphor of love as a knot (*nodo*) and the common, but reworked, image of love as a *laccio* (here a "leash," rather than, more conventionally, a "noose" or "trap"). This same sense of *laccio* is found in Vittoria Colonna's A1:7 ("Di cosò nobil fiamma Amor mi cinse"), which Matraini echoes in her tercets, as does Virginia Salvi in no. 12.

33

Freschi, ombrosi, fioriti e verdi colli
dov'or si siede dolcemente a l'ombra
quello ch'ovunque va riporta il giorno,
e movendo i be' pie' fra la fresca erba,
fa dove tocca il terren lieto e verde,
deh fossi'io pianta in voi di lauro o mirto.   6

Io mi torrei di star dentro ad un mirto,
o 'n verde lauro in cima agli alti colli,
sol per vederlo quando entro il bel verde
sen viene a diportar soletto a l'ombra,
ov'alcun fior non è sì bello in erba,
che non s'inchini a lui la notte e 'l giorno.   12

Lassa, quanto sperar debb'io quel giorno,
ch'a la dolce ombra d'un bel verde mirto,
cogliendo seco fiori, or frondi, or erba,
mi senta dir da lui fra lieti colli
in un bel prato assisa alla dolce ombra:
—Meco sempre starai, fin ch'io sia verde—.   18

Non sentii fiamma ne l'età più verde
e lieta andava più di giorno in giorno
fuggendo Amor per l'alte selve a l'ombra,
cercando intorno a' fonti edera e mirto,
quando voce udii dir dagli alti colli:
—Ferma i be' passi qui tra' fiori e l'erba—.   24

Qual si fe' Glauco nel gustar de l'erba,
sentii mutarmi allor tra l'erba verde
e trarmi da un desio, che per i colli
mi fe' seguire il mio bel Sol quel giorno,
che m'arde or sì, che non di lauro o mirto
potrà giovarmi, o de la notte l'ombra.   30

Nulla mi pò da lui far scudo od ombra
né per forza d'incanto, o virtù d'erba
sannolo i campi, i poggi, ogn'antro e mirto,
ma una speranza sol mi mantien verde
dicendo:—Tosto ancor vedrai quel giorno,
che tornerà il tuo Sol da' lieti colli—.   36

Deh qual giorno sarà, ch'a la dolce ombra
de' colli, seco qui fra la fresca erba
corona tesserò di lauro o mirto?

Fresh, shady, flowery, green hills, where that man now sits sweetly
in the shade who, wherever he goes, brings the day with him and, as
he moves his fair feet amid the fresh grasses, makes the earth spring
happy and green. Oh, if I could be a tree among you of laurel or
myrtle!

I would choose to be encased within a myrtle, or in a green laurel
atop the high hills, solely to see him, when within the lovely green,
he comes to disport himself all alone in the shade, where there is no
flower so lovely amid the grass that does not bow to him by night
and by day.

Alas, how long must I await that day, when, in the sweet shade of a fair
green myrtle, as I gather flowers with him and leaves and grass, I hear
him say to me amid the smiling hills, as I sit in a lovely meadow
beneath the shade: "You will be with me always, as long as I live [lit.
remain green]."

I felt no flames when my years were green; my happiness grew from
day to day, as I fled from Love through the trees in the shade, and
sought ivy and myrtle among the springs. Then I heard a voice from
the high hills, saying, "Halt your fair footsteps there amid the flowers
and the grass."

As Glaucus became when he tasted of the herb, I felt myself change
then amid the green grass, and I was drawn by a desire that made me
follow my beautiful Sun across the hills that day: that Sun which burns
me now so the shadow of laurel or myrtle cannot help me, nor that of
the night.

Nothing can serve me as shield or shade against him, neither by force
of magic or the virtue of herbs. The fields know it, and the hills, and
each cave and myrtle. But one sole hope keeps me green, saying,
"Soon you will see the day when your Sun will return from those
blithe hills."

Oh when will that day come when, in the sweet shade of the hills,
sitting with him among the fresh grass I shall weave a crown of laurel
or myrtle?

Sestina. Matraini 1555, 46–48 (*senti* in l. 26 corrected to *sentii*). Relatively few female poets in this period attempted the sestina, one of the most difficult of poetic forms. In addition to Matraini, who included two in her *Rime* of 1555, neither of which survives in the later, revised version, we have sestinas by Tullia d'Aragona, Gaspara Stampa, Laura Battiferri, and Isabella Andreini.

The hermetic, incantatory character typical of the sestina form is enhanced in this poem by patterns of secondary repetition within the stanzas. *Verde* occurs in the second stanza in l. 2 out of rhyme, as well as in rhyme in l. 3; *ombra* in l. 2 of the third stanza as well as in rhyme in l. 5; *erba* in l. 2 of the fifth stanza, as well as in l. 1 in rhyme (the translation renders the word in its two different senses, "herb" and "grass"). The phrase "lauro o mirto" (laurel or myrtle) is repeated in stanzas 1 and 5 and the *congedo*, and the two trees—symbolic, respectively, of poetic glory and of love—are found juxtaposed in stanza 2.

A distinctive characteristic of Matraini's poetry is her occasional borrowing of entire lines from other authors, mainly Dante, Petrarch, Bembo, and Colonna (see Matraini 2007, 217–37). Here, at l. 25, she quotes a line from Dante's *Paradiso* 1.68, referring to the myth of Glaucus, the fisherman who discovered a mysterious herb that made him immortal, an appropriate image here for the effects of Neoplatonic love. The opening line of the sestina is also a near-quotation of the opening line of Petrarch's sonnet 243 ("Fresco, ombroso, fiorito, e verde colle"), while the opening stanzas more generally recall Petrarch's dreamlike visions of Laura, goddesslike, in an idyllic landscape (see, for example, canzone 126), as well as Dante's description of Matelda in the earthly paradise in canto 28 of *Purgatorio*, where she wanders *soletta*, gathering flowers, just as the beloved here disports himself *soletto* (10).

In speaking of the poet's desire to be encased in a tree (7–8), Matraini may be thinking of the classical notion of a dryad or tree-nymph, or of the mythological Daphne, transformed into a laurel tree to escape the lust of Apollo. Ariosto, in the *Orlando Furioso*, portrays the hapless Astolfo encased in a myrtle tree through a spell placed on him by the enchantress Alcina, but the context of the passage is too comic and irreverent to imagine Matraini wishing to evoke it here.

An irregularity of this sestina is that it omits one of the rhyme words, *verde*, from the *congedo*, where it should technically occur with all the others. This is probably intentional. Since green symbolizes hope, its omission lends an ominous tone to the *congedo*: will the blissful reunion the poet is dreaming of ever occur?

Veronica Franco (1575)

34

Non più parole: ai fatti, in campo, a l'armi,
ch'io voglio, risoluta di morire,
da sì grave molestia liberarmi.   3
Non so se 'l mio "cartel" si debba dire,
in quanto do risposta provocata:
ma perché in rissa de' nomi venire?   6
Se vuoi, da te mi chiamo disfidata;
e, se non, ti disfido; o in ogni via
la prendo, e ogni occasïon m'è grata.   9
Il campo o l'armi elegger a te stia,
ch'io prenderò quel che tu lascerai;
anzi pur ambo nel tuo arbitrio sia.   12
Tosto son certa che t'accorgerai
quanto ingrato e di fede mancatore
fosti e quanto tradito a torto m'hai.   15
E se non cede l'ira al troppo amore,
con queste proprie mani, arditamente,
ti trarrò fuor del petto il vivo core.   18
La falsa lingua, ch'in mio danno mente,
sterperò da radice, pria ben morsa
dentro 'l palato dal suo proprio dente;   21
e, se mia vita in ciò non fia soccorsa,
pur disperata prenderò in diletto
d'esser al sangue in vendetta ricorsa;   24
poi col coltel medesmo il proprio petto,
de la tua occision sazia e contenta,
forse aprirò, pentita de l'effetto.   27
Or, mentre sono al vendicarmi intenta,
entra in steccato, amante empio e rubello,
e qualunque armi vuoi tosto appresenta.   30
Vuoi per campo il segreto albergo, quello
che de l'amare mie dolcezze tante
mi fu ministro insidïoso e fello?   33
Or mi si para il mio letto davante,
ov'in grembo t'accolsi, e ch'ancor l'orme
serba dei corpi in sen l'un l'altro stante.   36
Per me in lui non si gode e non si dorme,
ma 'l lagrimar de la notte e del giorno
vien che in fiume di pianto mi trasforme.   39

Ma pur questo medesimo soggiorno,
che fu de le mie gioie amato nido,
dov'or sola in tormento e 'n duol soggiorno,   42
per campo eleggi, accioch'altrove il grido
non giunga, ma qui teco resti spento,
del tuo inganno ver'me, crudel infido: 45
qui vieni, e pien di pessimo talento
accomodato al tristo officio porta
ferro acuto e da man ch'abbia ardimento.   48
Quell'arma, che da te mi sarà pòrta,
prenderò volentier, ma più, se molto
tagli, e da offender sia ben salda e corta.   51
Dal petto ignudo ogni arnese sia tolto,
al fin ch'ei, disarmato a le ferite,
possa 'l valor mostrar dentro a sé accolto.   54
Altri non s'impedisca in questa lite,
ma da noi soli due, ad uscio chiuso,
rimosso ogni padrin, sia diffinita.   57
Quest'è d'arditi cavalier buon uso,
ch'attendon senza strepito a purgarsi,
se si senton l'onor di macchie infuso: 60
così o vengon soli ad accordarsi,
o, se strada non trovano di pace,
pòn del sangue a vicenda saziarsi.   63
Di tal modo combatter a me piace,
e d'acerba vendetta al desir mio
questa maniera serve e sodisface.   66
Benché far del tuo sangue un largo rio
spero senz'alcun dubbio, anzi son certa,
senza una stilla spargerne sol io;   69
ma, se da te mi sia la pace offerta?
se la via prendi, l'armi poste in terra,
a le risse d'amor del letto aperta?   72
Debbo continuar teco anco in guerra,
poiché, chi non perdona altrui richiesto,
con nota di viltà trascorre ed erra?   75
Quando tu meco pur venissi a questo,
per aventura io non mi partirei
da quel ch'è convenevole e onesto.   78
Forse nel letto ancor ti seguirei,
e quivi, teco guerreggiando stesa,

in alcun modo non ti cederei: 81
per soverchiar la tua sì indegna offesa
ti verrei sopra, e nel contrasto ardita,
scaldandoti ancor tu ne la difesa,   84
teco morrei d'egual colpo ferita.
O mie vane speranze, onde la sorte
crudel a pianger più sempre m'invita.   87
Ma pur sostienti, cor sicuro e forte,
e con l'ultimo strazio di quell'empio
vendica mille tue con la sua morte;   90
poi, con quel ferro ancor tronca il tuo scempio.

[1–3] No more words: to deeds, to the field, to arms! For I have resolved, prepared for death, to free myself of this great vexation. [4–6] I do not know whether this should properly be called a challenge, because I am responding to a provocation—but why fight about terms? [7–9] If you like, I will call myself challenged; if not, then I challenge you. Either way, I am happy, and seize the opportunity with pleasure. [10–12] You may have the choice of place or weapon, just as you prefer. I'll take whichever you leave—or why don't you choose both? [13–15] Soon I am sure you will recognize how untrustworthy and faithless you were and how you have wronged and betrayed me. [16–18] And if my wrath does not cede to my all too great love, with these very hands, I will boldly tear your living heart from your breast. [19–21] That false tongue of yours, which lies, to my harm, I will rip out from the root, though you will first bite it through with your own teeth. [22–24] Even if I do not escape with my own life intact, I will still delight, in my desperation, to have had recourse to a vendetta in blood; [25–27] indeed, sated and content after your death, I may perhaps use the same knife to open my own breast, repenting of what I have done. [28–30] So while I meditate my revenge, get into the jousting ground, vile, lawless lover, and present your weapon now, whichever you have chosen. [31–33] Do you wish for our battlefield that secret chamber which was the treacherous, cruel minister to me of so many bitter sweetnesses? [34–36] I see my bed before me, where I welcomed you in my lap, and which still retains the impress of our two bodies, locked together. [37–39] Now I do not take my pleasure there, nor can I sleep: my weeping, day and night, transforms me into a river of tears. [40–42] Yes, why don't you choose this as our battlefield, this once beloved nest of my joys, where now I dwell in sorrow and in torment? [43–45] That way, news of your betrayal of me, vile traitor, will not reach outside these walls but will die within them, along with you. [46–48] Come here, and filled with wicked desire as is fitting for your grim purpose, bring a sharp blade and a bold hand. [49–51] I will happily seize the weapon you bring, especially if it is one that pierces, a sturdy dagger for the attack. [52–54] Let all armor be removed from our naked breasts so that, disarmed against attack, they may show forth the valor they harbor within. [55–57] Let no one else intervene in this battle; we alone shall engage, behind closed doors, without seconds. [58–60] This is the proper practice of bold knights, who fight to purge their honor in this discreet fashion, if they feel it has been stained; [61–63] either they try quietly to reach some accommodation, or, if there can be no peace accord, they mutually agree to sate themselves with blood. [64–66] This is the mode of combat that I like; this manner of cruel vendetta is just what my desire demands. [67–69] Although I am quite certain I will make a great river of your blood without spilling a drop of my own; [70–72] what if you were to offer me the option of peace? If you were to choose the path of a skirmish of love on the bed, laying our weapons aside? [73–75] Should I then continue at war with you, given that the man who does not offer pardon when it is asked errs against chivalry? [76–78] If you were to offer me this, perhaps I would not depart from what is fitting and honest. [79–81] Perhaps I would follow you into the bed, and fighting alongside you, I would not yield in any fashion; [82–84] to subjugate you in your shameful offense against me, I would wrestle you beneath me, and, battling boldly away, while you too became heated in your defense, [85–87] I would die alongside you, both wounded by the same blow. O vain hopes, whither my cruel fate leads me, to cause me to weep all the more! [88–90] But endure, strong and steadfast heart, and with the last destruction of this evil man, avenge a thousand of your own deaths with one of his; [91] then with that same blade put an end to your torment.

Capitolo. Franco 1575, 25r–26v (*arme* at l. 49 corrected to *arma*; *servo* in l. 66 to *serve*). This *capitolo* comes from the first, dialogic, section of Veronica Franco's *Terze rime*, in which poems by her are paired with others by, or purportedly by, men, some rejected admirers and others actual or prospective lovers. This poem is followed by a conciliatory response from the lover accused here of treachery and faithlessness: he defends himself against these accusations and professes devotion, having clearly decided to take the peace option offered at ll. 70–72.

Franco uses the meandering rhythms of the *capitolo* form to portray drifts of thought and desire, as the poet's initial fury against her errant lover gradually mutates into a sexual fantasy about their reconciliation, simmering already from ll. 31–33 and coming to a head in ll. 79–85, before being recognized as a "vain hope" at l. 86. At the same time, considered in its epistolary function, as a poem addressed to the lover, this seemingly artless self-revelation is clearly a calculated sexual lure, intended to bring about precisely the capitulation we see in the lover's response.

The sexual explicitness of Franco's verse differentiates her from other female poets of the period, even those who make reference to a physically consummated relationship (see no. 22). While Franco's status as a courtesan is sometimes adduced as the reason for this, a contrast with Tullia d'Aragona's polite, Neoplatonic love poetry shows that the equation cannot be made automatically. More relevant is, perhaps, that Franco was writing at a time when Counter-Reformation moral rigorism had made the participation of courtesans in literary culture less acceptable. Without an incentive to present herself as "honest" and publicly acceptable, like d'Aragona, Franco may have felt a more provocative persona would serve her better. Furthermore, there was considerable interest in Venice at this time in the Roman, sensual tradition of love elegy, as practiced by poets such as Ovid and Propertius (Franco imitates a poem from Ovid's *Amores* directly in her *capitolo* 20).

The use of dueling imagery was something of a trademark of Franco's; she used it also in nonerotic contexts, such as her *capitolo* 16, where it serves as a metaphor for verbal combat in a response to a satirical poet who had attacked her. While implicitly masculinizes her poetic persona—critics have noted an analogy with the widespread practice of transvestitism among Venetian courtesans—a literary precedent for the fighting woman existed in the figure of the female knights of romance, who were portrayed fighting in armor and frequently being mistaken for men.

A poem that depends crucially at moments on sexual double entendre presents particular problems of translation. A case in point is the lingering description at ll. 50–51 of the assailant's sturdy assault weapon. *Corta* (lit. "short") here seems best understood as defining a particular kind of close-combat weapon (as in the phrase *essere ai ferri corti*: "to be at daggers drawn"); hence my translation of it in a nominative form as "dagger."

35

Quel che ascoso nel cor tenni gran tempo
con doglia tal, ch'a la lingua contese
narrar le mie ragioni a miglior tempo;   3
quelle dolci d'amor amare offese,
che di scovrirle tanto altri val meno,
quanto ha più di far ciò le voglie accese;   6
or che la piaga s'è saldata al seno
col rivoltar degli anni, onde le cose
mutan di qua giù stato e vengon meno,   9
vengo a narrar, poiché, se ben noiose
a sentir fûro, ne la rimembranza
or mi si volgon liete e dilettose.   12
Così spesso di far altri ha in usanza
dopo 'l corso periglio, e maggiormente
se d'uscirne fu scarsa la speranza.   15
Or sicura ho 'l pericolo a la mente,
quando da' be' vostri occhi e dal bel volto
contra me spinse Amor la face ardente: 18
ed a piagarmi in mille guise volto,
dal fiume ancor de la vostra eloquenza
il foco del mio incendio avea raccolto.   21
L'abito vago e la gentil presenza,
la grazia e le maniere al mondo sole,
e de le virtù chiare l'eccellenza,   24
fur ne la vista mia lucido sole,
che m'abbagliar e m'arser di lontano,
sì ch'a tal segno andar Febo non suole.   27
Ben mi fec'io solecchio de la mano,
ma contra sì possente e fermo oggetto
ogni riparo mio fu frale e vano;   30
pur rimasi ferita in mezzo 'l petto,
sì che, perduto poscia ogni altro schermo,
arder del vostro amor fu 'l cor costretto: 33
e con l'animo in ciò costante e fermo
vi seguitai; ma mover non potea
il piede stretto d'assai nodi e infermo.   36
Tanta a me intorno guardia si facea,
che da assai men dal cielo a Danae Giove
in pioggia d'oro in grembo non cadea.   39

Ma l'ali che 'l pensier dispiega e move,
chi troncar mi potèo, se mi fu chiuso
al mio arbitrio l'andar co' piedi altrove?   42
Pronto lo spirto a voi venìa per uso,
né tardava il suo volo, per trovarsi
del grave pianto mio bagnato e infuso.   45
E bench'al mio bisogno aiuti scarsi
fosser questi, vivendo mi mantenni,
come in necessità spesso suol farsi;   48
e così sobria in mia fame divenni,
ch'assai men che d'odor nel mio digiuno
sol di memoria il cor pascer convenni.   51
Così, senza trovar conforto alcuno,
la soverchia d'amor pena soffersi,
in stato miserabile importuno: 54
nel qual ciò che i tormenti miei diversi
far non poter, col tempo i miei pensieri
vari da quel ch'esser solean poi fersi.   57
Voi ve n'andaste a popoli stranieri
ed io rimasi in preda di quel foco,
che senza voi miei dì fea tristi e neri;   60
ma procedendo l'ore, a poco a poco
del bisogno convenni far virtute,
e dar ad altre cure entro a me loco.   63
Questa fu del mio mal vera salute:
così divenne alfin la mente sana
da le profonde mie gravi ferute: 66
il vostro andar in regïon lontana
saldò 'l colpo, benché la cicatrice
render non si potesse in tutto vana.   69
Forse stata sarei lieta e felice
nel potervi goder a mio talento,
e forse in ciò sarei stata infelice.   72
La gran sovrabondanza del contento
potrìa la somma gioia aver cangiato
in noioso e gravissimo tormento;   75
e se da me 'n disparte foste andato,
in tempo di mio tanto e di tal bene,
infinito il mio duol sarebbe stato.   78
Così non volse 'l ciel liete e serene
far l'ore mie, per non ridurmi tosto

in prova di più acerbe e dure pene.   81
Ond'io di quanto fu da lui disposto
restar debbo contenta; e pur non posso
non desiar ch'avenisse l'opposto.   84
Da quel che sia 'l mio desiderio mosso
in questo stato, non so farne stima,
ché s'è da me quel primo amor rimosso.   87
Quanto cangiato in voi da quel di prima
veggo 'l bel volto! Oh in quanto breve corso
tutto rode qua giuso il tempo e lima!   90
Di molta gente nel comun concorso
quante volte vi vidi e v'ascoltai,
e dal bel vostro sguardo ebbi soccorso.   93
E, se ben il mio amor non vi mostrai,
o che 'l faceste a caso, o per qual sia
altra cagion, benigno vi trovai;   96
perch'ora in una ed ora in altra via
di devoto parlar, con atto umano,
volgeste a me la fronte umile e pia;   99
e, nel contar il ben del ciel sovrano,
v'affisaste a guardarmi e mi stendeste,
or larghe or giunte, l'una e l'altra mano: 102
ed altre cose simili faceste,
ond'io tolsi a sperar che del mio amore
cautamente pietoso v'accorgeste.   105
Quinci s'accrebbe forte il mio dolore
di non poter al gusto d'ambo noi
goder la vita in gioia ed in dolzore.   108
Mesi ed anni trascorsero da poi,
ond'a me variar convenne stile,
com'ancor forse far convenne a voi.   111
Or vi miro non poco dissimìle
da quel che solevate esser davante,
de l'età vostra in sul fiorito aprile.   114
Oh che divino angelico sembiante,
quel vostro, atto a scaldar ogni cor era
d'agghiacciato e durissimo diamante.   117
Or, dopo così lieta primavera,
forma d'autunno, assai più che d'estate,
varia vestite assai da la primiera.   120
E, se ben in viril robusta etate,

l'oro de la lanugine in argento
rivolto, quasi vecchio vi mostrate;   123
benché punto nel viso non s'è spento
quel lume di beltà chiara e serena,
ch'abbaglia chi mirarvi ardisce intento.   126
Questa con la memoria mi rimena
del vostro aspetto a la prima figura,
ond'ebbi già per voi sì crudel pena;   129
e, mentre 'l pensier mio stima e misura,
e pareggia l'effige di quegli anni
con questa de l'età d'or più matura,   132
di fuor sento scaldarmi il petto e i panni,
senza che però 'l cor dentro si mova,
per la memoria de' passati affanni.   135
In questo l'alma un certo affetto prova,
ch'io non so qual ei sia; se non che vosco
l'esser e 'l ragionar mi piace e giova;   138
e, se 'l giudicio non ho sordo e losco,
quest'è de l'amicizia la presenza,
ch'al volto ed a la voce io la conosco . . .   141

[1–3] That which for a long time I kept hidden in my heart, with such pain that it prevented my tongue from pleading my cause at the time I should have—[4–6] those sweet and bitter wounds of love which we are worse at revealing when we most burn to do so—[7–9] now that the wound has healed within my breast with the turning of the years, whereby all mortal things change their state and die, [10–12] I now come to recount. If these things were painful to live through, they now, in my memory, have become happy and pleasing. [13–15] We often like to look back thus after running some danger, especially if we had little hope of escape. [16–18] Now, from a position of safety, I look back on that dangerous time when Love thrust his burning brand at me from your lovely eyes and handsome face [19–21] and, determined to wound me in a thousand ways, stoked the flames of my fire also through the river of your eloquence. [22–24] Your fine dress, your noble presence, your peerless grace and virtues, your splendid talents [25–27] were a bright sun in my eyes that dazzled and burned me from afar, outdoing Phoebus himself. [28–30] Try as I might to shield myself with my hand, against such a powerful, unmoving object, every remedy I tried was frail and in vain. [31–33] I was pierced straight through my breast, and, deprived of any other protection, my heart was constrained to burn

with love for you; [34–36] and with my soul, firm and constant, I
followed you, though I could not move my feet, weak as they were and
shackled by many knots. [37–39] So strict a surveillance did I suffer then
that Danaë was far less well guarded when Jove rained into her lap in a
shower of gold. [40–42] But the wings that thought unfurls and moves—
who could curb them, even though I was prevented from going with
my feet where I willed? [43–45] My spirit used to fly to you always, nor
did the fact that it was bathed and drenched in my tears hamper its
flight. [46–48] And although these visits were scarce help to me in my
great need, I managed to survive on them, as people do in times of
famine. [49–51] So sparing did I become in my hunger that I learned to
feed my fasting heart simply on memory, far less of a nutriment even
than smell. [52–54] Thus, bereft of all consolation, I suffered the ex-
treme pain of love in a wretched, importunate state, [55–57] but what all
my torments did not achieve, time eventually did: my thoughts began
to become different from what they had been. [58–60] You went off to
foreign parts, and I remained in prey to that fire which, without your
presence, made my days sad and black; [61–63] but, as the hours proceeded,
little by little, I made a virtue of necessity and started to allow other
thoughts and cares into my mind. [64–66] This was the healing of my
malady; thus eventually my mind recovered from its deep and cruel
injuries. [67–69] Your going off to a distant place was what closed the
wound, though it could not entirely remove the scar. [70–72] Maybe I
would have been blithe and happy if I could have enjoyed you as I
wished, and maybe I would have been unhappy. [73–75] The sheer
superabundance of my pleasure might have turned my great joy into
the cruelest of torments, [76–78] for if you had left while I was enjoying
such delight, then my pain would truly have been infinite. [79–81]
Heaven did not wish to make my hours happy and serene only to thrust
me then into a crueler and graver torment. [82–84] So I resolved to be
content with what the fates had determined, yet still I cannot help
wishing the contrary had happened. [85–87] I cannot guess how my
desire has moved me to feel this, nor can I decide what to make of it, for
that first love I felt for you has all gone. [88–90] How changed in you
since that first day do I see your lovely face! Ah, in what a brief course
Time gnaws at all things here below and rasps them away with his file!
[91–93] How many times I saw you and listened to you among the flocks
of people and drew comfort from your lovely gaze! [94–96] And if I
never showed you my love, whether you did this by chance or for some
other reason, I found you benign. [97–99] At one moment or another in
your devout speaking, with a kindly air, you would turn your humble

and pious brow in my direction, [100–102] and, as you spoke of the good of heaven on high, you would fix me with your gaze and extend your hands to me, now spread wide, now clasped— [103–5] and other, similar things, so that I began to hope you were aware of my love and cautiously returned it. [106–8] This greatly increased my pain, that we could not enjoy life in pleasure and sweetness, as was the desire of both. [109–11] Months and years then passed, and I had to change my style, as you did perhaps also. [112–14] Now I see you no little different from how you used to be in the blooming April of your years. [115–17] Oh what a divine angelic semblance was yours, fit to warm even a heart of frozen hardest diamond! [118–20] Now, after such a happy spring, you have taken on the guise of autumn, more than summer, very far from your earlier self. [121–23] And, though you are still in the age of robust manhood, the gold of your beard turned to silver, you seem almost old, [124–26] although that glimmer of bright serene beauty has not been extinguished in your face that can still blind those who dare to look at you closely. [127–29] This remaining beauty draws me back in my memory to that earlier aspect of yours that made me suffer so cruelly, [130–32] and, as my thought judges and measures and compares the image of your youth with this new one of your maturer years, [133–35] I feel my breast and my garments beginning to warm, though without my heart moving within at the memory of my past sufferings [136–38]. Meanwhile, my soul feels a certain emotion, I know not what—only that I like to be with you and to speak to you, [139–41] and, if my judgment is not deaf and blunt, I think I am in the presence of friendship. I recognize its face and its voice . . .

Capitolo (extract). Franco 1575, 40v–43r. The *capitolo* from which this extract is drawn (no. 19), is one of Franco's most original compositions and is generally considered her masterpiece in Italian-language criticism. It is addressed to a man who was once the object of a powerful attraction on the part of the poet and who has returned to the city after a long absence, at a time when her love for him has long since cooled. The poem narrates the history of the poet's infatuation and records with forensic precision her emotions on renewing acquaintance with the object of this attraction, now much aged. It continues after this extract with an offer of friendship and an expression of hope that the relationship may be continued through correspondence when the poem's addressee once again departs from Venice.

One of the great thematic novelties of this poem is its realist, quasi-novelistic account of the decline of love over time. This was entirely contrary to the Petrarchan and Neoplatonic tradition, in which a spiritualized love is shown to be capable of transcending physical distance and even death. While poets such as

Tullia d'Aragona and Gaspara Stampa had defied this tradition by speaking in their verse of a new love following the demise of the old (nos. 9 and 25–26), Franco breaks new ground with this nuanced description of the effects of time on emotion, which adeptly exploits the leisurely, meandering rhythms of the *capitolo* form. Her most likely source, echoed in the opening lines, comes from outside the lyric tradition entirely: Boccaccio's description in the proem to the *Decameron* of a past love-affair, which, though it caused him intense suffering at the time of the experience, remains to him now as a pleasing memory. Lines 13–15 of Franco's *capitolo* may also recall Dante's *Inf.* 1.22–24.

A further thematic novelty of the poem (88–90, 112–23) is its reflection on the dimming effects of time on male beauty. Although the ephemerality of beauty was a frequent theme of both love lyric and moralistic literature, it was for the most part exclusively applied to women. Most female-authored writing tended, for reasons of decorum, to privilege spiritual beauty over physical in describing the love object, and Franco's "frankness" in portraying a love with its roots in the physical is unusual. In some respects, nothing could be further from Petrarch, yet an important subtext of the poem, contradicted, but also echoed, is Petrarch's famous sonnet 90, which recalls Laura's youthful beauty and acknowledges its diminution over time, while vowing that this does not diminish his love.

In ll. 97–102, the poet recalls her past pleasure in watching her beloved preaching. Only at this point in the poem is the man revealed as a priest, by conventional moral standards hardly an appropriate object of desire. Franco is at her most mischievous in this account of an enamored young girl ignoring the content of a priest's sermon to concentrate on his looks and reading a message of personal seduction into his emotive and gestural preaching style. Particularly subtle is her description of the preacher's face as *pia* (99), playing on the double meaning of the adjective. Although in its primary sense (pious or merciful), the word is clearly wholly appropriate in describing a cleric, *pio* had acquired a secondary meaning within love lyric, meaning, effectively, "receptive to [the poet's] love" (see, e.g., no. 25, l. 8; no. 27, l. 8; no. 69, ll. 3 and 39).

Phoebus, in l. 27, is Apollo, in his guise as sun god; here, the word is used metonymically to mean the sun. Danaë (38), in Greek mythology, was a princess of Argos imprisoned in a tower by her father after a prophecy warned that he would be killed by her son. Jove penetrated her seclusion, entering the tower in the guise of a shower of gold, and impregnated her. The allusion is particularly charged given Franco's courtesan status, as the myth of Danaë was sometimes seen as an allegory of prostitution. Franco's reference to the Danaë-like state of confinement in which she was kept at the time of her infatuation suggests she may be speaking of the time of her short-lived marriage to a physician during her teens. At ll. 49–51, Franco's description of herself as living on memory, not simply on smell, is a reminiscence of the tercets of Petrarch's sonnet 191 (which probably also supplied the word *dolzore* in l. 108; see below). The reference is to Pliny the Elder's account of an Indian tribe, the Astomi, who lacked mouths and nourished themselves purely on odors (*Natural History* 7.25).

Rather oddly, Franco's first rhyme in this *capitolo*, *tempo/tempo*, looks to be an identical one, of a kind generally considered illegitimate. *Tempo* is used, however, first in an uncountable, then in a countable sense, so Franco may have considered it two different words. More classic equivocal rhymes are *volto/volto* at ll. 17 and 19, and *sole/sole/suole* at 23, 25, and 27, while other noteworthy rhymes include the inclusive *felice/infelice* (70–72); the punning *dolore/dolzore* (106, 108), and the recherché *vosco/losco* at (137–39). *Dolzore* is a rare Provençalism used only once by Petrarch in the *RVF* (no. 191), as is also *rimembranza*, at l. 11 (no. 67). The phrase "il petto e i panni" (133) echoes Petrarch's *TC* 1:57.

Francesca Turina (1628)

36

Se penato hai fuor del paterno tetto,
misera vita mia, fin da la cuna,
gioisci, che propizia or tua fortuna
si volge e arreca in sen pace e diletto.   4
Sposo d'alto valor, d'alto intelletto
t'appresta; spoglia ormai la veste bruna,
spiega le ricche gioie ad una ad una,
e lieta te ne adorna 'l crine e 'l petto.   8
Mira come è pomposo a te venuto,
che vuol col sacro anel sua sposa farti;
odi il cortese suo dolce saluto.   11
T'allegra, ch'hai ragion di rallegrarti,
ché se fra i monti hai pene sostenuto,
goderai lieta in più felici parti.   14

My wretched life, if you have suffered in exile from your paternal roof
since the cradle, now rejoice, for your fortune has turned auspicious
and harbors peace and pleasure for you in her breast. She has readied for
you a bridegroom of high worth and intellect. Cast off your dark dress,
unfurl your rich jewels, one by one, and happily adorn your locks and
your breast. See in how fine a guise he has come to you, wishing with
his sacred ring to make you his bride. Hear his greeting, courteous
and sweet. Be happy, as you have reason to be happy, for if among the
mountains you have suffered grief, you will live now blithely in happier
parts.

Sonnet ABBA ABBA CDC DCD. Turina 1628, 130. The only substantial surviving
body of first-person love poetry by an Italian woman after 1575 is that of Francesca
Turina to her husband, Giulio Bufalini (1504–83). Twenty-three *in morte* poems were
published in Turina 1595; four *in vita* poems in Guaccimani 1623, and a longer
sequence of *in vita* and *in morte* poems in Turina 1628. The dates of composition are
hard to ascertain. The originality of Turina's love poetry lies in its combination of
conventional, Petrarchan, lyric-introspective elements with a more concrete, quasi-
novelistic narrative of events. Here, the poet describes the moment of her betrothal
in the present tense, in simple, almost naïve language, evoking her girlish pleasure
at the prospect of marriage. It would be difficult to guess from the poem that Bu-
falini was his bride's senior by half a century at the time they were wed (c. 1573). For
the past tribulations referred to in ll. 1–2 and 13, see no. 202.

37

Vago augellin, che per quei rami ombrosi
dolce cantavi a minüir mie pene,
di sentirti al mio cor gran desir viene
per fare in tutto i giorni miei giocosi.　　4
Deh vieni, e teco mena i più famosi
cantor che quella selva in sen ritiene,
ché goderete in queste rive amene,
ed a l'estivo dì starete ascosi.　　8
Il boschetto vi attende, e 'l bel giardino
là dove in fra le fronde e l'onda e l'ora
gareggian mormorando a me vicino.　　11
A cantar sorgeremo in sul mattino:
io con le Muse invocarò l'aurora,
e voi col vostro gorgheggiar divino.　　14

Lovely little bird, who, among those shady branches, used to sing so
sweetly to mitigate my sorrows, a great desire comes to my heart to
hear you again, to make my days complete in their joy. Come, and bring
with you the most famous singers that forest nurtures in its breast, for
you will have the pleasure of these fair waters and be hidden from the
heat of the summer day. The little wood awaits you, and the lovely
garden where, among the leaves, the ripples and the breeze compete in
their murmuring beside me. We will rise together before sunrise: I will
herald the dawn with the Muses, and you with your warbling divine.

Sonnet ABBA ABBA CDC CDC. Turina 1628, 135. At her best, Turina is a supremely
musical poet, as this sonnet well attests. The poet calls on the birds that consoled
her during her melancholy girlhood to come to the garden of her marital home to
share her joy. Although the sonnet is not explicitly a love poem, its position in the
narrative sequence of the *Rime* encourages us to read it as such, and it locates itself
within the tradition of love poems addressed to "little birds," called on to sympa-
thize with the lover's plight (see no. 10). Lines 12–13 recall l. 9 of Petrarch's sonnet
219, as well as l. 3 of a spiritual sonnet by Celio Magno (no. 129), also addressed to a
"vago augelletto." Turina's sonnet brilliantly exploits the implicit comparison between
the poetic voice and birdsong, achieving particular onomatopoeic effects in lines 10–
11 and 14. Bembo's sonnet 4 addresses a bird as "singer" (*cantor*), but Turina's pairing
of the term with *famosi* (5–6) wittily transfers to the woodlands the cult of celebrity
singers so alive in her day.

38

Mentre del Tebro i liquefatti argenti
corron sonanti, e per gli obliqui calli
guizzano i pesci un contro l'altro ardenti,
ché guida Amor ne l'acque anco i suoi balli, 4
su le rive di fior vermigli e gialli
sparse e d'erbette e degli umor sorgenti,
m'assido, e al suon dei limpidi cristalli
accordo i lagrimosi miei lamenti. 8
Tanti pesci non ha questo e quel gorgo,
né tante frondi e fior le sponde amene,
quante lagrime allor dagli occhi sgorgo. 11
Tante 'l lido non ha minute arene,
né mover tante foglie al vento scorgo,
che non sian più le mie gravose pene. 14

While the melted silvers of the Tiber run murmuringly past and fish dart ardently along their oblique paths (for Love leads his dances in the waters as well), I sit on the riverbank, strewn with vermilion and yellow flowers and new grass and rising sap and, to the sound of the bright crystals, accord my tearful laments. So many fish do not dwell in this or that rapid, nor do the lovely banks have so many flowers and fronds, as I pour out tears from my eyes. So many minute grains of sand the seashore does not have, nor do I see so many leaves moving in the wind that my heavy sorrows are not more.

Sonnet ABAB BABA CDC DCD. Turina 1628, 143. This sonnet forms part of a sequence describing the poet's misery during a long absence of her husband's early in their marriage. These poems may have been composed at the time, as a 1575 letter from Turina's husband, sent from Rome, mentions her sending him love poetry (Torrioli 1940, 19). A version of this sonnet with a variant last line was published in Guaccimani 1623, 48. Like no. 37, this sonnet implicitly assimilates the poet's voice to a natural sound, this time that of flowing water, and it is keenly attentive to sound effects, drawing extensively on the liquid *l*. The B rhyme was probably suggested by Petrarch's sonnet 219, which coincides on two rhyme words, although Turina gives a distinctive rhythm to her quatrains by using alternating rhymes instead of the usual *chiastic form. The hyperbolic comparisons in the tercets are a poetic commonplace, though a likely source is the opening of Petrarch's sestina 237. A striking feature of the tercets is the flamboyant rhyme sequence *gorgo/sgorgo/scorgo*.

Lucrezia della Valle (pre-1622)
39

Non con la fiamma dell'impura face,
non con lo stral che le vil'alme fere,
il cor mi punse e accrescemi il pensiere
l'altero Dio, ch'ogni durezza sface,   4
ma con quel foco suo dolce e vivace,
che tolse in pria dalle celesti sfere,
e con quella saetta, il cui potere
anche ai spirti gentil diletta e piace.   8
Quindi egli avvien che dall'acceso petto
escan le voci mie legate in rima
per far palese la sua gioia altrui.   11
Santo Amor, deh, non far ch'ove diletto
ebbi nel farmi a te ligia da prima,
dica in fin, lassa me, qual son, qual fui?   14

Not with the flame from the tainted brand, not with the arrow that wounds base souls, did that proud God who melts all hardness pierce my heart and burden me with anxious care; rather, he wounded me with that sweet living fire he first took from the celestial spheres and with that dart that pleases and delights even the noblest souls. This is the reason why from my burning breast there issue words bound in rhyme, to reveal its joy to others. Sacred Love, do not permit that, having delighted in first entering your service, I should say at the end, alas, wretched me, what am I? what have I been?

Sonnet ABBA ABBA CDE CDE. Spiriti 1750, 103 n. 1. The impression given by the printed record that first-person love poetry by women practically disappeared after the 1560s may be misleading. This accomplished proemial sonnet is all that remains of a substantial love *canzoniere* by the late-sixteenth-century Calabrian poet Lucrezia della Valle, which survived in manuscript at least until the eighteenth century. The quatrains of the sonnet make the classic Neoplatonic distinction between a "vulgar" love, centered on the body, and the higher love that has its source in divine beauty (6), of which only the spiritually noble are capable. The passage is intricately constructed: note especially the two inclusive rhymes *face/sface* (1 and 4) and *fere/sfere* (2 and 6). The purity of the love recounted should serve as guarantor of its "joy" (11), but the final tercet introduces the possibility of more traditional petrarchan love anguish. The concluding phrase echoes l. 30 of Petrarch's canzone 23 ("lasso, che son, che fui!").

In morte

Veronica Gambara (c. 1518)

40

Quel nodo in cui la mia beata sorte
per ordine del ciel legommi e strinse,
con grave mio dolor sciolse e discinse
quella crudel che 'l mondo chiama morte;   4
e fu l'affanno sì gravoso e forte
che tutti i miei piaceri a un tratto estinse,
e, se non che ragione al fin pur vinse,
fatto avrei mie giornate e brevi e corte.   8
Ma téma sol di non andar in parte
troppo lontana a quella ove 'l bel viso
risplende sopra ogni lucente stella   11
mitigato ha 'l dolor, ché 'ngegno o arte
far nol potea, sperando in Paradiso
l'alma veder oltre le belle bella.   14

That knot in which my happy fate, by order of heaven, bound and tied me, to my great sorrow was loosened and untied by that cruel creature the world calls death. This grief was so harsh and oppressive that all my pleasures were extinguished in one moment, and, if reason had not at last triumphed, I would have made my days brief and short. Fear that I might go to a place remote from where that fair face shines above every gleaming star was the sole thing that mitigated my pain, for intellect and art could not reach it—fear and the hope to see in Paradise the soul that is the fairest of the fair.

Sonnet ABBA ABBA CDE CDE. Ruscelli 1553a, 16. Since Gambara's husband died in 1518, this sonnet probably dates from before Vittoria Colonna's more famous poetry of widowhood. It is a good example of the lucid, even-toned, melodious style that characterizes Gambara's mature verse. Thematically interesting is the very explicit allusion to suicide as a potential response to the grief of bereavement in ll. 7–8 and the religiously based explanation in the tercets for the poet's rejection of this choice. Gambara may here be attempting to evolve a specifically Christian ideal of marital devotion to counterpose to classical exempla of wives who manifested their love of their husbands in suicide following their death (see similarly no. 48). A noteworthy formal feature of the poem is its pervasive *enjambment, apparent especially in the tercets, whose fluidity contrasts with the more stately rhythms of the quatrains, with their *synonymous doublets (2, 3, 5, 8). The last words of the poem echo the end of the first line of Petrarch's sonnet 289.

Vittoria Colonna (1525–38)

41

Scrivo sol per sfogar l'interna doglia
ch'al cor mandar le luci al mondo sole,
e non per giunger lume al mio bel Sole
al chiaro spirto, a l'onorata spoglia.　　4
Giusta cagion a lamentar m'invoglia;
ch'io scemi la sua gloria assai mi dole;
per altra voce e più sagge parole
convien ch'a Morte il gran nome si toglia.　　8
La pura fe', l'ardor, l'intensa pena
mi scusi appo ciascun, ché 'l grave pianto
è tal che tempo né ragion l'affrena.　　11
Amaro lagrimar, non dolce canto,
foschi sospiri e non voce serena,
di stil no, ma di duol mi danno il vanto.　　14

I write solely to salve the suffering that those bright eyes, peerless in this world, caused my heart, and not to add luster to my lovely Sun, to his radiant spirit and honored remains. A just cause leads me to lament, and it sorely pains me that I may detract from his glory; his great name deserves to be rescued from death by a loftier voice and wiser words. May my pure faith, my ardor, my intense grief excuse me, for my mourning is such that neither reason nor time can restrain it. Bitter weeping, not sweet song; dark sighs, not a serene voice: my verse boasts not of style but of woe.

Sonnet ABBA ABBA CDC DCD. Colonna 1560, 5 [A1:1] (with *il* inserted before *vanto* on the basis of Colonna 1558, 1). Colonna's mourning poetry for her husband, Ferrante d'Avalos, brought her to national fame in Italy in the 1530s. The image of this golden soldier-poet couple embodied the Renaissance ideal of excellence in arms and letters, while Colonna's devotion to the task of memorializing her dead husband helped domesticate the still exotic figure of the erudite woman. In her opening sonnet, Colonna proclaims a poetics of pure emotion, with no pretension to literary refinement, but this is belied by the poem's mastery of rhetorical ornament: note the *alliteration in the first line, the emphatic *antithesis of the final tercet, and the juxtaposed *rima equivoca* in ll. 2–3. Line 5 quotes almost verbatim the equivalent line of one of Petrarch's mourning sonnets for Laura, 276, while the "foschi sospir" of l. 13 recall the "rime . . . fosche" of another, 293, which also supplies the notion of writing solely to "relieve the sorrowing heart."

42

A le vittorie tue, mio lume eterno,
non diede il tempo o la stagion favore;
la spada, la virtù, l'invitto core
fûr li ministri tuoi l'estate e 'l verno.   4
Prudente antiveder, divin governo
vinser le forze averse in sì brevi ore
che 'l modo a l'alte imprese accrebbe onore
non men che l'opre al grande animo interno.   8
Viva gente, reali animi alteri,
larghi fiumi, erti monti, alme cittadi
da l'ardir tuo fûr debellate e vinte.   11
Salisti al mondo i più pregiati gradi;
or godi in Ciel d'altri trïonfi veri,
d'altre frondi le tempie ornate e cinte.   14

The time and the season, my eternal light, gave no advantage to your victories; your sword, your courage, your dauntless heart were your instruments, in summer and winter alike. Prudent foresight, divine leadership, vanquished the enemy forces in such a brief hour that the manner of your victory added luster to your lofty endeavors, just as your deeds added luster to your fine inner spirit. Keen foes, proud royal spirits, wide rivers, steep mountains, fair cities were conquered and vanquished by your daring. You ascended in this world to the highest honors; now in heaven you enjoy different, true triumphs, your temples adorned and crowned by different wreaths.

Sonnet ABBA ABBA CDE DCE. Colonna 1558, 52 [A1:6]. While the persona of the Petrarchan lover-poet proved relatively easily appropriable by female poets, the construction of the male love object proved more of a problem. Colonna finds a solution by substituting the virile attributes of courage and daring for the beauty and chastity that had traditionally adorned the female love object. Here she devotes ll. 1–11 to her husband's military prowess, changing the focus to his heavenly triumph only in the final tercet, which counterposes the laurel wreaths awarded to successful Roman generals with the Christian crown of the palm, symbol of spiritual salvation. The repetition of *altri/altre* in ll. 13–14 may allude to the *congedo* of Petrarch's conversional sestina 142.

43

Quand'io dal caro scoglio miro intorno
la terra e 'l ciel ne la vermiglia aurora,
quante nebbie nel cor son nate allora
scaccia la vaga vista e 'l chiaro giorno.   4
S'erge il pensier col sole, ond'io ritorno
al mio, che 'l ciel di maggior luce onora;
e da quest'alto par che ad or ad ora
richiami l'alma al suo dolce soggiorno.   8
Per l'essempio d'Elia non con l'ardente
celeste carro ma col proprio aurato
venir se 'l finge l'amorosa mente   11
a cangiarne l'umil doglioso stato
con l'alto eterno; e in quel momento sente
lo spirto un raggio de l'ardor beato.   14

As I gaze from this dear rock at the land and sea in the crimson dawn,
all the mists that have arisen in my heart are dispelled by the lovely
vista and the clear day. My thoughts rise with the sun, leading me back
to my own Sun, who honors heaven with a greater light and who
seems to be calling my soul back from this high cliff to its sweet natural
abode. On the model of Elijah, not in a burning, heavenly chariot but
in his own golden one, my amorous mind imagines him coming, to
change my base, dolorous condition with that high, eternal state, and
in that moment, my spirit feels a ray of the ardor of the blessed.

Sonnet ABBA ABBA CDC DCD. Colonna 1558, 268 [A2:13] (*alto* in l. 7 corrected from
altro). Although the theme of the poet's mystic communion with her husband's soul
in heaven is frequent in Colonna, this sonnet is unusual for the precision with
which it locates her moment of epiphany. She is portrayed at dawn in Ischia ("this
dear rock") watching the sun dispelling the early morning mist from the sky, in
anticipation of the manner in which contemplation of her own "Sun" will allow her
to glimpse the beatitude of heaven through the veil of the flesh. The reference to
Elijah in ll. 9–10 may have been inspired by Bembo's speech on Neoplatonic love in
Castiglione's *Courtier* 4.69, where Elijah's ascent to heaven in a fiery chariot (2 Kings
2:11) symbolizes the spiritual ecstasy that is the ultimate end of human love in its
purest form. Colonna juxtaposes this image with the more secular and erotic one of
the golden chariot of the classical sun god Apollo, which the poet imagines descend-
ing to carry her off.

44

Questo sol ch'oggi agli occhi nostri splende,
di grave ingiuria carco e d'alto scorno
io vidi un tempo; or di sé il mondo adorno,
fertil la terra e 'l ciel lucido rende,   4
perché con l'altro mio più non contende,
ch'or lampeggiando nel divin soggiorno
d'uno ardor santo e d'un perpetuo giorno
dinanzi al vero Sol s'alluma e accende.   8
Quei raggi, quel calor, quell'alma luce
m'infiamman sì che questa or sento e scorgo
discolorata, mesta, afflitta e nera.   11
Caduchi effetti il vostro alfin produce;
fa 'l mio beata l'alma, onde m'accorgo
di spregiar l'uno e gir dell'altro altera.   14

This sun that is shining before your eyes today, I once saw much injured and despised. Now, it is decking the world in beauty, awakening the earth to fertility, and lighting up the skies, for it no longer has to compete with mine, which now gleams above, in its celestial home, burning with a holy ardor in perpetual daylight, flaming and glowing before the true Sun. Those rays, that warmth, that lofty light so inflame me that this other light now seems to me discolored, sad, afflicted, and dark. Your sun can produce only mortal effects, while mine renders the soul blessed, so that I am resolved to despise the one, and glory in the other.

Sonnet ABBA ABBA CDE CDE. Bologna, Biblioteca Universitaria, MS 828 (1250), 24v [A1:21]. The conceit of the rivalry between "two suns," the physical sun and the beloved, is found in Petrarch's no. 219 and in Bembo's no. 86. Colonna develops it with panache in this sonnet, complicating it religiously with the introduction of a third, "true" sun, God (8), of whose spiritual light the light of the second sun, the soul of her dead husband, is a reflection. The sound-patterning in this highly rhetorical sonnet is exceptionally dense and intricate, with the consonant-rich rhymes of the quatrains reinforced by the inclusive rhyme *soggiorno/giorno*, and the phonetically paired duplets *alluma/accende* and *sento/scorgo* at the ends of ll. 8 and 10. Line 1 is also very calculated, with sound pairings in *questo/nostri*, *sol/splende*, and *oggi/occhi*.

45

Nodriva il cor d'una speranza viva,
fondata e colta in sì nobil terreno
che 'l frutto promettea giocondo e ameno;
morte la svelse allor che la fioriva.   4
Gionser insieme i bei pensieri a riva,
mutosse in notte oscura il dì sereno,
e 'l nettar dolce in aspero veleno;
sol la memoria nel dolor s'avviva.   8
Ond'io d'interno ardor sovente avvampo;
parmi udir l'alto suon delle parole
gionger concento all'armonia celeste,   11
e veggio il folgorar del chiaro lampo
che dentro il mio pensiero avanza il sole.
Che fia vederlo fuor d'umana veste?   14

I once nourished my heart with a living hope, planted and tended in
so noble a terrain that it promised to bring forth fair and pleasant fruit;
death uprooted it while it was still in flower. My happy thoughts then
all at once ran to ground; balmy day turned to dark night, and sweet
nectar into bitter poison. Memory alone stirs fresh life within my
sorrow. And so I often blaze with hidden ardor; I seem to hear the lofty
sound of his words blending with the harmony of heaven, and I see the
lightning-flash of that bright flame that, within my thoughts, outshines
the sun. What will it be to see him beyond human guise?

Sonnet ABBA ABBA CDE CDE. Bologna, Biblioteca Universitaria, MS 828 (1250), 12r
[A1:3] (*avvanza* corrected to *avanza* in l. 13). One of the finest of Colonna's poems of
widowhood, this sonnet looks forward to the mystical vein within her later reli-
gious verse. The opening phrase, *Nodriva il cor*, quotes the second line of the pro-
emial sonnet of Petrarch's *Canzoniere*, while the last line echoes the closing line of
the last of his *Trionfi* (the *Triumph of Eternity*)—a bold gesture on Colonna's part, as
it invites us to read this sonnet as encapsulating the moral-erotic trajectory of those
two works. Colonna's rhyming here is particularly dense, with inclusive rhymes at
ll. 1 and 8 and at 4 and 5. That between *viva* and *avviva* is especially effective, mark-
ing the resurrection in memory and spirit of the beloved whose physical death has
been described in ll. 4–7. "Interno ardor" in the striking l. 9 is a characteristic phrase
for Colonna, who uses *ardere* and its derivatives insistently in both her erotic and
religious verse.

46

Qual tigre dietro a chi le invola e toglie
il caro pegno (o mia dogliosa sorte!)
cors'io, seguendo l'empia e cruda Morte
ricca allor de l'amate e care spoglie.   4
Ma, per colmarmi il cor d'interne doglie,
sdegnosa a l'entrar mio chiuse le porte,
ché con far nostre vite manche e corte
non empia le bramose ingorde voglie.   8
Vuol troncar l'ali ai bei nostri desiri
quando han preso spedito e largo volo
per gir del cader loro alta e superba.   11
Uopo non l'è ch'a numer grande aspiri,
certa d'averne tutti; elegge solo
l'ore più dolci per parer più acerba.   14

Like a tigress after the hunter who has stolen and snatched away her
dear offspring—alas, my wretched fate!—so I ran, following cruel,
heinous Death, who was laden with that beloved, dear prey. But, to fill
my heart with inner grief, she disdainfully slammed the door, blocking
my path, for cutting our lives short is not enough to satisfy her voracious
greed: instead, she wants to break the wings of our finest desires so she
can preen herself in triumph as she watches us fall. She has no need to
aspire to numbers, certain one day to have us all; she concentrates
merely on picking the sweetest moment, so that she may seem the
more bitter.

Sonnet ABBA ABBA CDE CDE. Colonna 1558, 138 [A2:8]. A frequent theme of Colonna's widowhood verse is her longing for death. Here, the theme is handled with unusual vigor, with the poet cheated of her desire to die alongside her husband by a malevolent personified Death. The striking initial image of the tigress chasing the hunter who has stolen her young derives ultimately from the bestiary tradition, mediated through the opening lines of Bembo's sonnet 67. Line 6 echoes ll. 20–21 of a canzone by the fourteenth-century Pisan poet Fazio degli Uberti (Sonetti 1527, 103v, "Lasso, che quando immaginando vegno"). The sprightly, combative tone of this poem contrasts with Colonna's usual gravity, and, together with stylistic features such as the frequent *synonymous doublets and the casual syntax (ché as conjunction at l. 7) may indicate that this was a relatively early composition. The use of maternal love as an analogy for marital love recalls Colonna's no. 7 (54).

47 ⟶

Tralucer dentro al mortal vel cosparte,
quasi lampe cui serra un chiaro vetro,
mille luci vid'io, ma non mi spetro
dal mondo sì ch'io le depinga in carte.   4
Amor ne l'alma accesa a parte a parte
vere l'impresse già molti anni a dietro,
onde ei spinge il desir ed io m'arretro
da l'opra ch'ogni ardir da sé disparte.   8
E s'avien pur ch'i'ombreggi un picciol raggio
del mio gran Sol, da lagrime e sospiri
quasi da pioggia o nebbia par velato.   11
S'in amarlo fu audace, in tacer saggio
sia almeno il cor, ch'omai sdegna il beato
spirto che mortal lingua a tanto aspiri.   14

Gleaming scattered within their mortal veil, like lamps behind clear glass, a thousand lights I saw; yet I cannot disburden myself of the world so I may paint them on the page. Love little by little impressed them deep on my burning soul many years ago, and now he spurs my desire while I hold back from this task that daunts the highest daring. And if it yet happens that I shadow forth some slight ray of my great Sun, it appears veiled by tears and sighs, as if by rain or mist. If it was bold in loving him, let my heart now at least be wise in keeping silent, for now his blessed spirit disdains that a mortal tongue should aspire so high.

Sonnet ABBA ABBA CDE CED. Colonna 1558, 19–20 [A2:28]. This sonnet explores the theme, already present in no. 41, of the poet's inability to express the glories of her beloved. It is notable for the shimmering mystical language of the opening lines, reminiscent of Colonna's later visionary spiritual lyrics. The "lights" the poet saw gleaming in her living husband are the spiritual beauties that showed forth through the "clear glass" of his physical being (*chiaro*, in l. 2, has the sense of "bright" or "famous," as well as "clear"). In Neoplatonic erotic theory, it is these gleams of the spirit that are the true source of love. Stylistically, the poem is notable for its pairing of two very similar consonant-heavy rhymes in the quatrains (*-arte, -etro*), with an inclusive rhyme at ll. 5 and 8, and also for the *assonance and *concorso di vocali of l. 5. This stylistic boldness underlines the "daring" of the poet's erotic and poetic enterprise (8), which amounts to an attempt to grasp the divine through mortal means.

48

Mentre la nave mia, longe dal porto,
priva del suo nochier che vive in cielo,
fugge l'onde turbate in questo scoglio,
per dar al lungo mal breve conforto,
vorrei narrar con puro acceso zelo   5
parte della cagion ond'io mi doglio,
e di quelle il martir che da l'orgoglio
di nimica fortuna e d'Amor empio
ebber più chiaro nome e maggior danno
col mio più grave affanno   10
paragonar, acciò che 'l duro scempio
conosca il mondo non aver esempio.

Laodamia e Penelope un casto ardente
pensier mi rapresenta, e veggio l'una
aspettar molto in dolorose tempre,   15
e l'altra aver, con le speranze spente,
il desir vivo, e d'ogni ben digiuna
convenirli di mal notrirsi sempre;
ma par la speme a quella il duol contempre,
quest'il fin lieto fa beata, ond'io   20
non veggio il danno lor mostrarsi eterno,
e 'l mio tormento interno
sperar non fa minor, né toglie oblio,
ma col tempo il duol cresce, arde il desio.

Arianna e Medea, dogliose, erranti,   25
odo di molto ardir, di poca fede
dolersi, in van biasmando il proprio errore;
ma se d'un tal servir da tali amanti
fu il guiderdone d'aspra e ria mercede
disdegno e crudeltà tolse il dolore;   30
e 'l mio bel Sol ognor pena ed ardore
manda dal Ciel coi rai nel miser petto,
di fiamma oggi e di fede albergo vero;
né sdegno unqua il pensero,
né speranza o timor, pena o diletto   35
volse dal primo suo divino obietto.

Porzia sovra d'ogn'altra me rivolse
tant'al suo danno che sovente insieme
piansi l'acerbo martir nostro equale;
ma parmi il tempo che costei si dolse   40
quasi un breve sospir; con poca speme
d'altra vita miglior le diede altr'ale;
e nel mio cor dolor vivo e mortale
siede mai sempre, e de l'alma serena
vita immortal questa speranza toglie   45
forza a l'ardite voglie;
né pur sol il timor d'eterna pena,
ma 'l gir longi al mio Sol la man raffrena.

Esempi poi di veri e falsi amori
ir ne veggio mill'altri in varia schiera,   50
ch'al miglior tempo lor fuggì la spene;
ma basti vincer quest'altri e maggiori
ché pareggiar a quei mia fiamma altera
forsi sdegna quel Sol che la sostiene,
ché quante io leggo indegne o giuste pene,   55
da mobil fede o impetüosa morte
tutte spente le scorgo in tempo breve;
animo fiero o leve
aperse al sdegno o al furor le porte,
e fe' le vite a lor dogliose e corte.   60

Onde a che volger più l'antiche carte
de' mali altrui, né far de l'infelice
schiera moderna paragon ancora,
se 'nferior ne l'altre chiare parte,
e 'n questa del dolor quasi fenice   65
mi veggio rinovar nel foco ognora?
Perché 'l mio vivo Sol dentro innamora
l'anima accesa e la copre e rinforza
d'un schermo tal che minor luce sdegna,
e su dal Ciel l'insegna   70
d'amar e sofferir, ond'ella a forza
in sì gran mal sostien quest'umil scorza.

Canzon, tra' vivi qui fuor di speranza
va' sola, e di' ch'avanza
mia pena ogn'altra, e la cagion può tanto   75
che m'è nettar il foco, ambrosia il pianto.

While my ship, far from port and deprived of her helmsman, who is now in heaven, flees from the tumultuous waves and takes harbor on this rock, to give some brief respite to my long suffering, I shall recount with a pure inflamed passion part of that cause for which I grieve. And I shall measure myself against those ladies whose contest with hostile Fortune and cruel Love has earned them the brightest fame and the greatest harm, comparing their torments with my graver affliction so the world will know my harsh suffering knows no match.

A chaste ardent thought first conjures to me Laodamia and Penelope. I see one waiting long in her misery, while the other saw her hopes spent while her desire was still alive, and lived on, starved of all good and feeding only on pain. But the anguish of the one was tempered by hope, and the other was blessed by a happy outcome, so the harm they suffered was not eternal. But my inner torment is not mitigated by hope or canceled by oblivion: time passes, and my pain grows, my desire burns.

I hear of Ariadne and Medea, wandering in their pain, complaining of their lovers' great boldness and little faith, and lamenting in vain their own errors; but if their amorous service to such lovers brought them only a bitter and harsh recompense, cruelty and contempt soon arose in them to replace love. But my fair Sun still beams rays of ardor and pain from the heavens into my languishing breast, still today the true abode of flames and of faith; nor did anger ever turn my thoughts—nor hope or fear, pain or delight—from the first divine object of my love.

Porcia above all others drew me so to her pain that I often wept together with her over our same cruel torment. But the time she suffered seems to me merely that of a brief sigh; with little hope of another, better life, she fled from this. But, in my heart, living mortal pain presides always, and my rash promptings are held back by the hope of immortal life. Nor does only the prospect of eternal punishment restrain my hand but the thought of being far from my Sun.

I see a thousand more examples of true and false love troop pass in a diverse horde, all of whom saw their hopes dashed in the midst of their joy. But let it be enough for me to have conquered these few towering examples, for to compare my lofty flame to others is perhaps something the Sun who sustains it would scorn. For however many torments I read about, worthy and unworthy, all soon find their end, whether through change of heart or impetuous death. A fierce soul or a changeable one opens the door to anger or madness, making their lives painful but brief.

So why continue to turn the ancient pages that tell of others' ills, or to look for peers in the unhappy ranks of modern lovers? I may be less than these heroines in their other fine qualities, but in my pain I am like the phoenix, eternally renewing myself in the fire. My living Sun fills my burning soul with love from within, covering it and stoking it so that it disdains all lesser lights, and from heaven he teaches me to love and to suffer, sustaining the humble shell of my body in this great pain by which it is racked.

Song, among the living here, bereft of all hope, go wandering alone, and tell that my pain advances all others and that its cause is such that the fire is nectar to me and my weeping ambrosia to my lips.

Canzone ABCABCCDEeDD + EeDD. Florence BNCF MS II. IX. 30, 51v–54r, with various amendations (see below) [A1:89]. In her mature verse, Colonna writes almost exclusively in sonnets, but this rare canzone is one of the finest of her widowhood poems, reminiscent of no. 7 for its use of classical heroines in the poet's self-fashioning. The classical figures mentioned are, in order, Penelope, the famously faithful wife of Odysseus, who waited, fending off her suitors for twenty years until her husband's return to Ithaca; Laodamia, wife of Protesilaus, a Greek warrior killed by the Trojans, who committed suicide to join him in Hades; Ariadne, who was abandoned by Theseus, whom she had saved from the Minotaur, but later rescued by and married to Dionysius; Medea, who was abandoned by Jason for Glauce and who later avenged herself by killing Glauce (and, in some versions, her children with Jason); and, finally—the only example from history, rather than myth—Porcia, wife and confidante of Caesar's assassin Brutus, who killed herself after hearing a false rumor of his death. Colonna portrays Porcia as an exemplum especially dear to her, in a manner that was probably intended to call attention to the parallels between her and this Roman heroine, as both the daughter and wife of famous men. Contemporary readers would probably have been aware of the speech attributed to Porcia in Plutarch's *Life of Brutus* in which Porcia argues that her status as the daughter of Cato and the wife of Brutus lifts her above the normal limitations of womankind (Cox 2009, 69–70). The same argument is implicit in Colonna's heroic self-portrayal as daughter and wife in no. 7.

In the successive stanzas of the poem, Colonna weighs the suffering of these classical heroines against her own and finds theirs wanting. Unlike Penelope, her grief has no hope of a happy ending; unlike Arianna or Medea, who loved unworthy objects, she cannot find relief through anger and emotional self-distancing; unlike Laodomia and Porcia, she cannot escape her grief through suicide without risking eternal damnation (compare Gambara's no. 40, the close of whose l. 8 is perhaps echoed in Colonna's l. 60). These distinctions differentiate the restrained, passive, Christian mode of love martyrdom Colonna is describing here from the more dramatic, pagan, model, typically ending in violence or suicide. The inadmissibility of external outlets for the sufferings of love means that they must be suffered as a purely internal torment (22), lived in a spirit of submission to God's will. Colonna's reflection on these themes is conducted in implicit dialogue with Ovid's *Heroides*, her inspiration in no. 7, which includes Penelope, Laodamia, Aridane, and Medea among its "heroines." Another subtext is Dante's portrayal of the circle of lust in Hell, echoed in stanza 5's vision of a "horde" (*schiera*) of amorous exempla (cf. *Inf.* 5.41, 5.85). Through this intertextual dialogue, Colonna underlines the literary novelty represented by her Christian-Stoic model of morally controlled amorous grieving and implicitly differentiates herself from the great classical model for the female love poet represented by Sappho, whom Ovid presents in the *Heroides* as precisely the kind of "excessive," suicidal love heroine that Colonna disavows here.

Among the stylistic features of the poem may be noted the rich rhyme *tempre/contempre* (15, 19); the *chiasmus of l. 24; the use in rhyme position of the semantically related *erranti/errore* (25, 27), which marks off the morally errant Ariadne and Medea from the other heroines; and the *oxymoron *vivo e mortale* (43), at first sight simply reiterating the conventional Petrarchan "love as living death" motif, but also readable in context as a more complex allusion to the poem's Christian-Neoplatonic erotics, in which a mortal love acts as a conduit to the immortal. The phrase "volger l'antiche carte" (61) echoes Petrarch's canzone 28, l. 77, and Sannazaro's canzone 69, l. 19. The phoenix, proposed in the penultimate stanza as an emblem for the poet's love, was a mythical Arabian bird, the sole in its species, said to regenerate itself by burning. It signifies both uniqueness and immortality, especially immortality attained through love, and was hence a frequent symbol for the Christian soul.

"Mentre la nave mia" presents significant editorial problems, in that two distinct versions exist, probably representing two distinct authorial redactions. That found in MS Florence BNCF II. IX. 30 is generally superior to that found in early printed editions, and it may represent a later redaction of the poem. There are points, however, where the manuscript version's deviation from the texts in the printed editions may reflect scribal errors or omissions rather than authorial intent, and I have amended the version here accordingly, using the edition in Colonna 1558 (374–87) as a control. The substantive amendments are as follows: "casto" has been inserted in l. 13; "fu beato" in l. 20 has been amended to "fa beata"; "l'acerbo piansi martir" at l. 39 has been amended to "piansi l'acerbo martir"; "impetuoso Marte" at l. 56 has been amended to "impetuosa morte." Of the other variants found in early printed editions, such as Colonna 1558, 374–87, the version of ll. 28–29 is worth recording, as in some ways superior to the manuscript version given here: (378) "ma se il volubil ciel, gl'infidi amanti / diero a tanto servir'aspra mercede" (but if the fickle heavens and their faithless lovers rewarded their great devotion so harshly).

49

Sogno felice e man santa che sciolse
il cor da vari nodi e antichi danni,
e da dubbie speranze e chiari inganni
a la strada del ver dritta il rivolse.　　4
Quante in un'ora dalla mente tolse
imagin false impresse per molt'anni,
e l'alma de' suoi dolci acerbi affanni
pentimento e dolor per frutto colse.　　8
Non squarciò nube mai con tal furore
impetüoso fulgor come 'l velo
che 'l voler chiuse, la ragion aperse.　　11
Me riformò la man che formò il Cielo,
e sì pietoso al mio priego s'offerse
ch'ancor lieto ne trema ardendo il core.　　14

Happy dream and sacred hand that freed my heart from various knots and ancient scars and returned it from its dubious hopes and clear errors back on to the straight path of right. How many false images, imprinted for many years, in one sole hour it swept from my mind, while my soul gathered from its sweet, bitter torments the fruit of repentance and sorrow. Never did an irresistible lightning bolt tear through a cloud with such fury as that veil that closed my desire and opened my reason. The hand that heaven formed re-formed me and so pityingly offered itself to my prayer that my heart still blithely trembles, burning, in its wake.

Sonnet ABBA ABBA CDE DEC. Colonna 1840, 387 [A1:84]. This mysterious sonnet, unpublished until the nineteenth century, seems to recount a dream in which the soul of the poet's husband, visiting from heaven, releases her from the residual bonds of sensual love and redirects her to the Dantean *diritta via* (*Inf.* 1.3). We are perhaps supposed to imagine a dream on the lines of Petrarch's edifying vision of Laura in heaven in sonnet 302, which coincides with this poem in two rhyme words in the tercets (*velo/Cielo*), and in its emphasis on the dead beloved's hand (ll. 5 and 12 in Petrarch; 1 and 12 here). The moralizing discourse of the quatrains, speaking of a clear-cut elimination of desire (8), is complicated, however, by the description of the poet's past love sufferings as "sweet" as well as bitter (7) and by the sensuality of the imagery of the tercets (the searing lightning-bolt of ll. 9–10, the trembling heart of l. 14).

50

Occhi, piangeno tanto
che voi perdiate il lume ed io il timore
di non veder più mai luce minore;
ché se bastò mio ardir, vostro vigore,
a penetrar il cielo,   5
sdegnar debbiamo ogni altra vista in terra,
e con l'imagin bella sculta al cuore,
scarca d'ogni altro zelo,
contempliamo il valor ch'ivi si serra,
e arem per breve guerra   10
eterna pace. A lei debito onore
darem, fugendo d'Atteon l'errore.

Eyes, let us weep so much that you lose your sight and I the fear of
never again seeing a lesser light, for if my boldness and your vigor were
such as to let us penetrate heaven, we should disdain all other, earthly
sights. With the lovely image sculpted on our heart, untouched by any
other desire, let us contemplate the good it locks within; then we will
have eternal peace in exchange for brief war. We will give it its rightful
honor, avoiding Actaeon's error.

Madrigal aBBBcDBcDdBB. Bologna, Biblioteca Universitaria, MS 828 (1250), 35v
[A2:52] (*perdiati* in l. 2 corrected to *perdiate*; *penestrar* in l. 5 corrected to *penetrar*).
One of very few surviving madrigals by Colonna, this poem is preserved in a single
manuscript. It is conceptually highly compressed, in a manner that prefigures the
later sixteenth-century madrigal tradition. The poet aspires to weep so much that
she becomes blind and can concentrate without distraction on her inner vision of
her beloved in heaven, which will eventually lead her to salvation (10–11). Divine
vision is here posited in an edifying and platonizing vein as transcendence of the
shadowy world of the senses. Cutting against this, however, is the troubling and
sacrilegious model of divine vision evoked in l. 12: the huntsman Actaeon, who, in
Greek mythology, was turned into a stag and devoured by his own hounds when he
stumbled upon the goddess Artemis naked. Together with ll. 4–5, where the poet
and her eyes are said to have boldly "penetrated" heaven, the Actaeon reference of
the last line introduces a transgressive, Promethean element into the poem, recall-
ing the closing lines of no. 47, where she reproaches herself for her audacity in aspir-
ing to encompass the divine with mortal words. The first person plural ending
"-eno" in "piangeno" (l. 1) is not uncommon in early-sixteenth-century texts.

Chiara Matraini (1555 and 1597; see Notes on Authors)

51

Vivo mio foco, ond'io solea aver vita,
qual arbor verde o fior da sua radice,
dolce de' miei pensier ora beatrice,
chi mi darà fra tanta doglia aita?   4
Lassa, da me s'è l'anima partita,
né morir posso, né di viver lice,
e grido e piango:—Ahi misera infelice,
la tua gioia amorosa ove n'è gita?   8
Ove son le speranze indi raccolte?—.
Son, ohimè, morte, e null'altro che pianto
mi veggio a fronte e quel ch'io men vorrei.   11
Le dolci rime in lagrime son volte,
che verso sopra il negro e tristo manto;
o congiurati incontra, uomini e dei!   14

Living fire, from whom I drew life, like a green tree or flower from its
roots, sweet breeze who used to bless my thoughts, who will now give
me help in this great misery? Wretched me, my soul has departed, yet
I cannot die; nor may I live, so that I cry out, weeping, "Alas, poor
unhappy creature, whither has your amorous joy vanished? Where are
the hopes that you harvested from it?" They are dead, alas, and before
me I see nothing but weeping and what I least wish for. My sweet
rhymes have turned to tears that flow over my black, dismal mantle.
O men and gods, conspired to my ill!

Sonnet ABBA ABBA CDE CDE. Matraini 1555, 94. Like some of Matraini's other *in
morte* poems, this sonnet shows the poet despairing over her beloved's death with-
out any suggestion of Christian consolation. There are precedents for this dark vein
in Petrarch, though he also provides a model for the more consolatory tradition
that speaks of the beloved in heaven. Striking especially here is the last line, which
portrays the poet in neopagan language as object of the enmity of men and the
gods. The reference may be to the violent circumstances of her beloved's death (see
Notes on Authors). Line 3 is quoted almost verbatim from Petrarch's sonnet 191. As
in Petrarch, the word *ora*, a variant of *aura*, here signifies "breeze," completing a
dense sequence of metaphors in the first quatrain that sees the beloved transmute
from life-giving fire to life-giving root to consolatory breeze. Line 12 combines
echoes of Dante's canzone incipit "Le dolci rime d'amor ch'io solia" with the last
line of Petrarch's sonnet 292.

52

Occhi miei, oscurato è il vostro Sole
così l'alta mia luce è a me sparita
e, per quel che ne speri, è al Ciel salita,
ma miracol non è: da tal si vuole.   4
Passò com'una stella che in Ciel vole
nell'età sua più bella e più fiorita.
Ahi dispietata Morte, ahi crudel vita,
via men d'ogni sventura altra mi duole.   8
Rimasta senza 'l lume ch'amai tanto,
vomene in guisa d'orbo, senza luce,
che non sa dove vada, e pur si parte;   11
Così è il mio cantar converso in pianto.
O mia forte ventura, a che m'adduce
veder l'alte speranze a terra sparte!   14

Alas, my eyes, your Sun has been obscured; the light that came from on high has vanished from my sight, and, I hope, has ascended to heaven, through no miracle but His will. He passed like a shooting star in the flower of his youth. Alas, pitiless death! Cruel life! No other misfortune can match this. Alone, without that light that I so loved, I grope around like a blind man who sets off into the darkness not knowing where he is going. Thus my song is turned to weeping. Harsh fate, to what has it brought me to see my high hopes scattered on the ground!

Sonnet ABBA ABBA CDE CDE. Matraini 1597, 51v. This is an example of a cento, a poem made up entirely of lines taken from another poet and restitched to make a new work. Though also practiced by male poets, the form was especially associated with female, as its most famous practitioner was Faltonia Proba (4thC C.E.), who wrote a Christianized cento based on Virgil. The main female writers of centos in the period covered by this book are Laura Terracina and Isabella Andreini. Matraini drew her component lines from Petrarch, as did most Renaissance writers of centos (from, in order, poems 275, 1; 327, l. 6; 91, l. 3; 207, l. 42; 233, l. 13; 278, l. 1; 324, l. 4; 267, l. 11; 292, l. 10; 18, ll. 7–8; 332, l. 34; 207, l. 73). Line 14 is the only line not taken from Petrarch, although l. 46 of Petrarch's 331 reads "or mie speranze sparte." The first four lines of Matraini's sonnet quote a Petrarchan cento by Vittoria Colonna (A1:15), complicating the poetic genealogy implied here. See also no. 53 for an explicit tribute to Colonna by Matraini.

53

Quanto l'alta Colonna il suo gran Sole
avanzò in Ciel mentre che i santi carmi
cantava in terra, e ne' più saldi marmi
l'opre di lui intagliava eterne e sole,   4
tanto l'alto suo stile avanzar suole
mio ingegno, onde non posso a tanto alzarmi.
Però conviensi e la vettoria e l'arme
rendere a lei, che 'l mondo onora e cole.   8
Ella qui morta e in Ciel bella e viva
merita sol la glorïosa palma
e corona di lauro, edera, oliva;   11
ma voi di ricca e prezïosa salma
meritate, e di fiamma ardente e viva
ornata aver di me sempre mai l'alma.   14

Just as the lofty Colonna advanced her great Sun in heaven as she sang
her holy songs here on earth and sculpted his eternal, peerless deeds in
the most lasting marble, so too does her lofty style advance my intellect:
I cannot rise so high, and must give the victory and surrender my
weapons to her whom the world honors and worships. She alone, dead
on earth and beautiful and living in heaven, merits the glorious palm
and the laurel, ivy, and olive wreath, but you deserve me to adorn your
soul with a rich and precious body, and with live and ardent fire.

Sonnet ABBA ABBA CDC DCD. Rabitti 1985, 241. This fascinating tribute sonnet to
Vittoria Colonna, unpublished in Matraini's lifetime, is found in a manuscript in
the Vatican. The first quatrain praises Colonna for her memorialization of her hus-
band's feats and perhaps also for advancing his passage through Purgatory with her
prayers (although Matraini flatteringly places him already in heaven, following the
logic of his epithet of the "Sun": *cielo* means both "heaven" and "sky"). The second
quatrain puns on another meaning of the verb *avanzare* (to outstrip or outdo). In ll.
10–11, the palm is symbolic of victory and salvation; the laurel, of poetic or military
glory; the ivy, of immortality and fidelity; and the olive, of wisdom (as sacred to
Athena). The striking imagery in ll. 12–14 posits *in morte* verse as a kind of necro-
mancy, reclothing the beloved's soul in a new, immortal poetic "body." Lines 3–4
draw instead on a more conventional sculptural analogy.

Livia Spinola (1591)

54

Qual vite che dell'orno è sciolta unquanco
cui s'avviticchia a terra, incolta langue,
e calcata or dal gregge ed or dall'angue
d'empio veleno aspersa, alfin vien manco;   4
tal io giacea dal duolo oppressa, e bianco
avea il volto e quasi il corpo esangue,
ch'era agghiacciato tra le vene il sangue,
né trar potea più molto il debil fianco,   8
quando tu, del mio fin pietoso, desti,
Castel, soccorso al viver frale e in carte
formasti vivo il mio consorte amato.   11
E tanto il valor tuo nell'opra ergesti
che, col pennel ch'Amor sostenne in parte,
in dar la vita a un uom, tre vite hai dato.   14

Just as a vine, when it has come loose from the ash tree that anchors it to earth, languishes unnourished and finally withers, trodden by the herd and spread with evil poison by snakes, so too I was lying stricken with grief, my face white and my body almost bloodless, for the blood had frozen in my veins, and I could barely drag along my weakened limbs. Then you, pitying my plight, Castello, gave succor to my frail life and formed my beloved consort alive upon the page. So high did your genius rise in this work that, with the brush Love held for you in part, in giving life to one man, you gave three lives.

Sonnet ABBA ABBA CDE CDE. *Scelta* 1591 *(prima parte)*, 35. Descriptions of the beloved's portrait were an established Petrarchist subgenre (Bolzoni 2008, 2010), but this kind of *ekphrastic verse gained new popularity in the Baroque. Among the initiators of the trend was Livia Spinola's cousin by marriage, Angelo Grillo, who wrote extensively in praise of Bernardo Castello (1557–1629), the same artist referred to here. Spinola's opening image of the widow as a climbing vine torn loose from her support tree relies on the *topos of the "marriage" of elm tree and vine (Demetz 1958). Torquato Tasso, a friend of Grillo's, is Spinola's likely source for the tragic version of this topos (*GL* 20, 99), as also for the juxtaposed rhyme *esangue/sangue* (*GL* 8, 61, and various lyrics). The "three lives" of the closing *conceit are those of the painted figure, true enough to seem alive; the poet's husband, resuscitated in the portrait; and the poet herself, saved from death by grief. The phrase "in carte formasti" (10–11) echoes Petrarch's sonnet 77, l. 7.

Francesca Turina (1595 and 1628)

55

Morte, se ben fatto hai l'ultima possa
d'incenerir quella terrena scorza,
non fia però, che per tuo inganno o forza,
la mia candida fé sia spenta o scossa.   4
Quel ardor marital ch'andò per l'ossa
nel core, ond'arsi, il suo vigor rinforza,
né tempo il tempra, o di questi occhi ammorza
onda di pianto nubilosa e grossa.   8
Ahi, se goder non l'ho potuto in vita,
se concesso mi fu per breve spazio,
se, rimasa senz'alma e senza vita,   11
s'è 'l cor del mondo fastidito e sazio,
se cheggio a Morte incontro morte aita,
Morte, pon' fine a così lungo strazio.   14

Death, though you have exerted your utmost power in reducing those
earthly remains to ash, it shall never be that, through your deceptions
or violence, my stainless faith is extinguished or shaken. That marital
love that seared through my bones to my heart, so I burned, only
reinforces its vigor, nor does time temper it, or lessen in my eyes this
wave of cloudy, thick tears. Alas, if I could not enjoy him in life, if he
was conceded to me only for a brief moment, if, as I linger here without
my soul and life, my heart has become weary and sick of the world, if
I plead against Death only the succor of death—then Death, put an
end to this long torment.

Sonnet ABBA ABBA CDC DCD. Turina 1595, 150. Turina's first secular published
verse was a sequence of poems mourning her husband's death. Although Vittoria
Colonna's *in morte* verse served as a model (see no. 58), Turina's style is very differ-
ent from Colonna's, less *grave* and more simple and direct. Especially distinctive
here is the physicality of the language, with the image of love searing through the
bones to the heart and the adjective *grosso* (found nowhere in Petrarch's *RVF*) ap-
plied to her tears. The use of two phonetically similar consonant-rich rhymes in the
quatrains (*-ossa* and *-orza*) gives this portion of the sonnet a distinctive, dense, harsh
soundscape, reinforced by the pairing of *spenta* and *scossa* (4), and *tempo* and *tempra*
(7). The colloquial tercets abandon the *enjambment of the second quatrain for a
series of *end-stopped lines punctuated by *anaphora and repetitive rhymes, includ-
ing an identical rhyme on *vita*. Line 13 echoes Petrarch's 327, l. 7.

56

Ne l'atro abito mio si rappresenta
la mestizia che albergo entro nel core,
che, vie più dentro che non mostra fuore,
lassa, m'ancide insidïosa e lenta;   4
né scema il grave duol che mi tormenta
per volger d'anni, anzi si fa maggiore,
ond'amo sol quel funeral colore,
ch'il mio vedovo stato mi rammenta.   8
O dura impresa, o dolorosa insegna
de l'empia Morte, e sol de la mia vita,
e del grado presagio afflitto e mesto.   11
Ahi, chi mi fa d'ogni letizia indegna,
ne l'età mia più verde e più fiorita?
Come il ben tardi viene e fugge presto!   14

My black garb pictures the sadness I harbor in my heart, which is killing me, alas! insidiously and slowly, far more than my outward guise shows. Nor does the grave sorrow that torments me wane with the years; rather it grows, so that I love alone that funerary color, which reminds me of my widowed state. Oh harsh device and dolorous ensign of cruel Death, sole presage of my life and my miserable, afflicted state. Alas, who is it that makes me unworthy of all happiness, in the greenest and most flowering age of my life? How good comes to us late, and flees soon!

Sonnet ABBA ABBA CDE CDE. Turina 1595, 152. Athough a sonnet of Vittoria Colonna's (A1:27) alludes to the dark clothes of her widowhood, and Chiara Matraini refers in another to her "black, dismal mantle" (no. 51), this sonnet of Turina's is unusual in thematizing her mourning dress as symbol of her grief. Especially striking, after the slow, reflective rhythms of the quatrains, is the outburst of the first tercet, underlined by the alliterative *isocolon of l. 9 and the dramatic *antithesis of *Morte* and *vita* in l. 10. An *impresa* (9) was a visual emblem or "device," expressive of a given individual's identity or values. Mourning dress is both Death's device and his ensign or military flag. The last line of the poem, which takes the form of a *sententia* (maxim), recalls similar closes in Petrarch, such as those to sonnets 1 and 311.

57

Spinta talor d'ardente alto desio,
con gli occhi al cielo e 'l cor tutto rivolto,
vonne ove giace il mio signor sepolto
tra l'ombre del silenzio e de l'oblio;   4
quivi, resi gli onori debiti a Dio,
mi stringo e struggo e di nove onde il volto
spargo e sospiro: ahi, pensier vano e stolto,
se quel vuo' che non puote esser più mio!   8
Con la voce del cor prego e richiamo,
e dico lui:—Deh, sarà mai quel giorno
ch'io ponga fine al duolo ed a la vita?   11
Sarà ch'io torni a quel che cotanto amo,
sciolta dal corpo, ove han pace e soggiorno
quei che son scritti al libro della vita?—   14

Prompted by an ardent high desire, with my eyes and whole heart turned to heaven, I sometimes go where my lord lies buried amid the shadows of silence and oblivion. There, having given due honor to God, I shrink and melt and sigh and flood my face anew with tears. Alas, vain foolish thought, to want what can no longer be mine! With the voice of my heart, I pray and call to him, saying: "Ah, when will that day come when I shall find an end to my sorrow and my life? Will it ever be that I return to him I so love, free of this body, in the peaceful abode of those who are written within the book of life?"

Sonnet ABBA ABBA CDE CDE. Turina 1595, 155 (*ghiace* in l. 3 corrected to *giace*). Like no. 56, this sonnet demonstrates Turina's attention to the concrete and narrative in her widowhood verse. The poet is also seen visiting her husband's tomb in several poems in Turina 1628, including two in which she sees his coffin opened, presumably for reburial (nos. 180–81). This focus on her husband's mortal remains, rather than his immortal soul, could be seen as morally suspect; hence the emphasis in ll. 2 and 5 of this sonnet on the religious sentiments accompanying the visit. The opening lines of the poem are mainly *end-stopped, lending drama to the concentrated description of the poet's ouburst of grief in ll. 6–7, marked by a strong *enjambment and emphatic *alliteration. The reference in l. 14 to those "written in the book of life" presumably means simply "the blessed," without reference to the Calvinist doctrine of predestination. The phrase occurs frequently in the Book of Revelation, most notably at 20:12–15.

58

Porti, Vittoria, il vanto
di stil, non di dolore,
ché de la vena onde si strugge il core
l'arte ho minor, ma non minore il pianto.
Tu chiamasti Parnaso; ei ti rispose,   5
al suon di dotte, angeliche parole,
con rime alte e famose,
adornandone il ciel del tuo bel Sole.
Misera, io piango, e male
Pindo ascolta il mio dire semplice e frale;   10
ch'io crederei, s'eguale
fosse 'l mio stile a la pietade e al zelo,
ornar anch'io d'un novo Sole il cielo.

Vittoria, you carry the palm of style, not of sorrow, for in the vein that
melts the heart, my art may be lesser, but my affliction is not less. You
called Parnassus, and Parnassus responded, to the sound of learned,
angelic words, with sublime, famous verses, adorning heaven with your
fair Sun. Poor wretch that I am, I weep, and Pindus barely listens to my
simple, frail voice. But, if my style were equal to my devotion and
passion, I too would think to adorn the heavens with a new sun.

Madrigal abBACDcDeEeFF. Turina 1595, 172. Turina's 1595 sequence concludes with
a tribute to Vittoria Colonna as poet of widowhood, reminiscent of Chiara Matraini's
sonnet on the same theme (no. 53). A factor in Turina's homage may have been her
relationship with the Colonna family, with whom she lived later in her life (see
Notes on Authors). Turina here modestly contrasts her "simple and frail" style with
Colonna's "learned" one, though professing herself Colonna's equal in marital devo-
tion. The distinction accurately captures the difference between Colonna's dense,
sometimes challenging style and Turina's more limpid one. The choice of the mad-
rigal form for this tribute, rather than Colonna's signature form, the sonnet, under-
lines this difference. The first lines of the madrigal quote and elegantly contradict
the closing line of the opening sonnet of Colonna's love sequence (no. 41), while ll. 8
and 13 echo a line from Ariosto's tribute to Colonna in OF (37.17, l. 8). Parnassus (5)
and Pindus (10) were mountains in Greece with associations with Apollo and the
Muses; they are paired in Virgil's tenth eclogue, l. 11.

59

Sopra il ritratto del Sig. suo consorte

Diletto mio, che 'l sol mi rassomigli
e quanto bello sei, tanto fedele,
ché non rispondi e stai così crudele,
e qual solevi già non mi consigli?   4
Non vedi tu con quai feroci artigli
squarcia Fortuna del desio le vele?
Forse tu desto al suon di mie querele
a soccorrer venisti i miei perigli?   8
Ben riconosco le sembianze e gli occhi
del mio signore e la bell'aria umana:
e l'ardente desio fa che ti tocchi.   11
Lassa! Ma pasco il sen d'un'ombra vana,
e dico fra pensier' torbidi e sciocchi:—
misera, di dolor vôi farti insana?—   14

On Her Husband's Portrait

My darling one, you who to my eyes resemble the sun, as faithful as
you are lovely, why do you not respond? Why are you so cruel, not
counseling me as was once your wont? Can you not see with what fierce
claws Fortune is tearing at the veils of my desire? Perhaps you have
come to help me in my peril, awakened by the sound of my laments? I
recognize very well the features and eyes of my lord and his kindly air,
and my ardent desire makes me touch you. Alas! I am feeding my breast
with a vain shadow and tell myself amid my troubled, foolish thoughts,
"Poor wretch, will you let grief drive you mad?"

Sonnet ABBA ABBA CDC DCD. Turina 1628, 172. Poems on or addressing portraits
of the beloved were a recognized subgenre of Petrarchism (see nos. 54, 152). This son-
net of Turina's is distinctive within the genre, for the dynamism and ambiguity of its
treatment of the theme. While the capacity of portraits to evoke presence and their
disconcerting unresponsiveness were established *topoi, Turina vivifies them by hav-
ing her poet "madly" address the portrait directly, as though it were her living hus-
band or his ghost. The use of a title indicating the poem's theme (a device that became
common from the later sixteenth century) frees Turina to dramatize the poet's delu-
sion directly within the poem, without the need for narrative contextualization. The
motif of touch as breaking the illusion in the final tercet recalls Dante's portrayal of
his protagonist's attempt to embrace the shade of his friend Casella in *Purg.* 2.79–81, an
allusion reinforced by the term *ombra* (shade or shadow) in the next line.

Ventriloquized Love Poetry

Dianora Sanseverino (pre-1545)
60

[1] La bella Bradamante che sé stessa
non tanto amava, quanto il suo Ruggiero,
veggendol sì dubbioso in la promessa
che l'era per lei fatta d'amor vero,
una lettra gli scrisse, acciò per essa   5
riconoscesse falso il suo pensiero,
ed eron tai parole in quel bel foglio:—
Ruggier, qual sempre fui tal'esser voglio.

[2] Se sempre ritrovasti in me l'amore,
in me la fede immobile e sincera,   10
non pensare ritrovarla unqua minore
o vadi autunno, o passi primavera.
Sol vo' che riguardiamo al nostro onore
ché, machiati ambi due d'altra maniera,
giamai di pianto asciugarei le gote   15
fin'alla morte, o più, se più si pote.

[3] Non miro, o mio Ruggier, la tua possanza
fra gl'altri cavalier, né 'l tuo gran merto,
né di Merlino l'alta rimembranza
che 'l futuro mio ben mi fece certo;   20
non miro tua beltà ch'ogni altra avanza,
ma sol per osservar ciò ch'io t'ho offerto
io t'amo sempre e sempre amar ti voglio
o siam'Amor benigno, o m'usi orgoglio.

[4] Non so per qual cagione a dubitare   25
ti sei mosso Ruggier de la fe' mia,
se già perch'io son donna a te non pare,
che mobile per comun difetto sia.
Ma mancar potrà prima l'acqua al mare
che mai promessa a te mancata fia,   30
e le speranze sien d'effetto vote,
o me Fortun'in alto, o in basso ruote.

[5] Deh, guarda, o mio Ruggier, che sei fregiato
di tant'alti trofei, fra tante schiere:
non ti mostrar verso chi t'ama ingrato,   35
né cangiar mai per tempo le bandiere.
Ed io ch'oro disprezzo, regno e stato,

senza favor d'altrui vo' sostenere
ch'essendo quella stessa ch'esser soglio
immobil son di vera fede scoglio.   40

[6] Già non mi spiace ancor che del tuo petto
tali sospizïon venghino e tante,
poi ch'il vero amator sempr'è in sospetto,
come lo provo in me, sospetta amante,
ché pensand'altro amor v'abbi interdetto,   45
qual foglia secca in arbore tremante
resto, e qual nave in mar che gir non puote,
ché d'ogni intorno il vento e il mar percuote.

[7] Ma che penso, ove sono, a che parl'io,
lasciando trasportarmi a tant'errore?   50
Chi sarà mai che turbi il piacer mio?
Chi scioglie 'l mio col tuo legato cuore?
Misera me, non lo consente Dio
ch'altro de l'amor mio sia possessore,
perché non dee mutarsi in sempiterno   55
né già mai per bonaccia, né per verno.

[8] All'ultimo per farne paragone,
e qual pronta a mostrar mia spada e lancia,
dico che Ruggier voglio, e non Leone,
se ben Carlo volesse e tutta Francia.   60
Non potran far Beatrice e 'l padre Amone
ch'altri che il mio Ruggier ponghi in bilancia,
ché non da poi ch'el cor diedi in governo
luogo mutai, né mutarò in eterno—.

[1] The lovely Bradamante, who loved her Ruggiero more even than herself, seeing him so doubting of the pledge she had made him of her true love, wrote him a letter to apprise him of his error, and these were her words, set out on a fair page: *"Ruggiero, as I ever was, so shall I be.*

[2] "If you always found love in me and an unchanging, sincere loyalty, do not think to find it ever less, with the coming of autumn or the passing of spring. I only wish us to think of our honor, for, if we were to stain it, never would my cheeks be dry of tears, *until death or beyond it, if that may be.*

[3] "Ruggiero, in loving you, I am not swayed by your knightly prowess, nor your great merit. My noble memory of Merlin, and the future good

he predicted, do not sway me, nor your beauty, which advances all others. I love you, and will love you always, solely in faith to the promise I gave you, *whether love treats me kindly or uses me ill.*

[4] "I do not know, Ruggiero, what reason has led you to doubt of my faith, unless you think that because I am a woman, I must be fickle, through a common fault. But the waters will desert the sea before I will fail in my promise and dash your hopes, *whether Fortune bears me on high or casts me low.*

[5] "Ah, Ruggiero, you who are adorned with so many noble trophies, won on so many fields, do not show yourself ungrateful to her who loves you. Do not change your colors. I despise gold, power, and high estate and wish to prove, alone and without support from others, that, being the woman I have ever been, *I am an umoving rock of true loyalty.*

[6] "It does not displease me that such suspicions arise in your breast, for the true lover is always racked by suspicion. I feel this in myself, suspicious lover that I am. When I think that another love may have intervened with you, I remain like a dry leaf trembling on the bough, or a ship mired in the sea, *battered on all sides by the wind and the waves.*

[7] "But what am I thinking? Where am I? What am I saying, allowing myself to rave in this manner? Who can disturb my happiness? Who free my heart from yours, to which it is bound? Alas, God will not permit, nor that anyone else should ever possess my love; for my heart must never change, *in fair weather or winter's chill.*

[8] "Finally, to come to the test, as I am keen to show off the skills of my sword and lance, I say I want Ruggiero, and not Leone, even if Charlemagne wills it and the whole of France. Beatrice and my father Amone cannot force me to weigh another man against my Ruggiero; for ever since I gave my heart to him, *I have not shifted an inch and shall not for ever more."*

Stanze (with the last lines of each stanza successive lines from Ariosto, *Orlando furioso*, 44, 61). Bologna, Biblioteca Universitaria, MS 828 (1250), 213r–14v (*die'* at l. 55 amended to *dee*; *parrangon* at l. 57 amended to *paragon*).

One sign of the extraordinary popular success of Ariosto's great chivalric romance, *Orlando furioso* (1532) is the existence of so many derivative works, ranging from full-scale narrative continuations to musical settings of individual stanzas. Among these meta-Ariostan works, a particularly interesting segment is represented by *trasmutazioni*, poetic reworkings of sections of the *Furioso* incorporating lines from the source text at regular intervals, in a structured manner. Petrarch's verse attracted the same treatment. A novelty within the Ariostan tradition of *trasmutazioni* was that some poems in this genre do not simply appropriate lines for insertion into an independent, first-person lyric but import the narrative context of the passage chosen for transmutation and voice the sentiments of the relevant fictional character. Other examples of this are found in Laura Terracina's 1548 *Rime*, which has a series of *lamenti* attributed to characters in the *Furioso* and incorporating Ariostan lines.

The present poem, one of very few compositions by Dianora Sanseverino to survive, seems to have attained quite a degree of notice when it first began to circulate. It was published in Venice in 1545 by Leonardo Furlan in a collection of *trasmutazioni* by various authors (Agnelli and Ravegnani 1933, 2:200–202). Furlan was a street performer as well as a publisher, and it is likely that the work featured in his performance repertoire (on the literary dimension of such performances, see Salzberg 2010). The circulation of Sanseverino's poem is further attested by the existence of a musical version of the first stanza by the Sicilian composer Giandomenico Martoretta, published in 1548 (see Balsano 1988, xvii). It also seems to have inspired a Spanish *trasmutazione* of the same Ariostan passage by the poet and romance-writer Alonso Nuñez de Reinoso (Ravasini 2003).

The text given here derives from a manuscript in Bologna that attributes it to "the Princess of Bisignano" (Sanseverino's father was the prince of Bisignano, in Calabria). It is considerably more correct than that of the 1545 printed edition, which is reproduced in Fatini 1910, 97–98, although I have used Fatini's edition to supply a few words that are unreadable in the Bologna manuscript as a result of physical damage (in ll. 45, 48, 60, and 64).

The source text of Sanseverino's poem is a stanza of the *Furioso* that was particularly favored for declamation and musical setting, deriving from the episode near the end of the poem in which the warrior heroine Bradamante finds herself under threat of being compelled to marry the Byzantine prince Leone rather than her beloved Ruggiero. Hearing reports that Ruggiero fears the temptation of this royal match may be testing her loyalty, she sends a message to him confirming her undying love, consisting of six stanzas, of which the one reworked by Sanseverino is the first. Merlin, in stanza 3, is the long-dead but still-prophesizing Arthurian wizard, who in canto 3 of the poem reveals to Bradamante that she and Ruggiero will found the dynasty of the Este, Ariosto's patrons. Beatrice and Amone, in the final stanza, are Bradamante's parents, who are in favor of the match with Leone. This stanza sets out Bradamante's escape plan: she will ask the Emperor Charlemagne to grant that she be allowed to marry only a man who can defeat her in single combat, confident that only Ruggiero will be capable of such a feat. Her parents foil the plan by locking her away on their country estate.

Sanseverino expands on the Ariostan stanza mainly by embroidering Bradamante's adamantine fidelity, which, as stanza 4 underlines, contradicts the misogynistic orthodoxy that saw women as more fickle than men because they were supposedly less rational and more swayed by their senses. Stanza 3 reinforces this by portraying Bradamante's love as a rational, contractual commitment, rather than a superficial attraction that might waver with time. The listing of Ruggiero's merits in this stanza, especially his outstanding strength and beauty, echoes his own assessment of his attractions in *OF* 44, 49. In her representation of a heroically rendered feminine ideal of fidelity, Sanseverino recalls the Ovidian *Heroides* tradition, an association she reinforces by representing Bradamante's speech explicitly as the text of a letter, where in Ariosto is it a message sent via a lady-in-waiting, which may be conceived of as either written or oral.

Where form is concerned, the chief skill of the *trasmutazione* lay in the naturalness with which it succeeded in incorporating its borrowed lines. Sanseverino succeeds better in this than Terracina, whose meshing together of source text and original material is often strikingly inept. The most elegantly managed transition is probably that in stanza 6, in which Sanseverino appropriates Ariosto's line describing the rock of the previous line battered by the waves and winds and uses it to describe the storm-tossed ship she introduces as a simile for Bradamante's suspicion-ravaged state. The description in this stanza of Bradamante's jealousy draws on Ariosto's depiction of her earlier in the poem, where she is driven almost to distraction by the suspicion that Marfisa—in fact Ruggiero's sister—is his new love.

Vincenza Armani (pre-1569)
61

[1] Notte felice e lieta,
prescritta al piacer mio,
onde l'alma s'acqueta
del suo dolce desio,
notte in c'ho ferma spene   5
por fine alle mie pene.

[2] Pur fugge or mentre io canto
il tempo e già s'appressa
l'ora bramata tanto,
ch'oggi è a mercé promessa   10
della mia lunga noia,
principio alla mia gioia.

[3] Placido amico sonno,
deh vieni, occupa i sensi
di quei che sturbar puonno   15
i miei piaceri immensi,
tal ch'io senza suspetto
goda il mio ben perfetto.

[4] Ecco pur giunta è l'ora
prefissa a piacer tanto   20
ond'io senza dimora
prendo il notturno manto
ed al luogo m'invio
dove alberga il cuor mio.

[5] L'uscio ch'io tocco appena   25
mi sento aprir pian piano
poi cheta indi mi mena
una invisibil mano.
Io con tremante passo
lieto guidar mi lasso.   30

[6] Giunto al felice loco,
ch'è al mio piacer parato
dove risplende il foco
ripiglio alquanto il fiato,
e poi, la lingua sciolta,   35
io parlo ed ella ascolta.

[7] —Dunque è, ben mio, pur vero
ch'io sia da voi degnato,
qui, dove esser già spero,
felice, anzi beato?   40
Son desto, oppor sogn'io?
Troppo contento è il mio.

[8] Non merta la mia pena,
sofferta, e 'l mio tormento,
una de mille appena   45
gioie che per voi sento,
e mercé vostra ottengo
quel di ch'io sono indegno —.

[9] Ella:—Per la tua fede
e per tuo merto—dice—   50
d'amor ti si concede
quel che ad altri non lice,
e cogliere è a te dato
quel che è a ciascun vietato.

[10] Dolce io l'ammiro e insieme   55
con lei ringrazio Amore,
che in gioie alme e supreme
bear voglia il mio core;
poi nel piacer perduto
la miro e resto muto.   60

[11] Dolce ella sorridendo
mentre mi legge in viso
l'alto desio che ardendo
tien me da me diviso
rende all'alma il vigore   65
che per dolcezza more.

[12] E con le belle braccia
mi cinge il collo e tace,
e 'l cor con l'alma allaccia
che di desio si sface,   70
ond'io di piacer pieno
le bacio il petto e 'l seno.

[13] E da sua bocca bella
poi colgo il cibo grato;

io muto e tacita ella,   75
lieta ella ed io beato,
partiam l'alte faville
coi baci a mille a mille.

[14] Quel che succede poi
Amor solo il può dire,   80
perché ebri ambidue noi
nel colmo del gioire,
perdiam ne i gaudi immensi
l'alma, gli spirti e i sensi.

[1] Happy and joyful night, ordained for my pleasure, when the soul
will slake its sweet desire—night I firmly hope will put an end to my
sufferings.

[2] Time flies as I sing, and already the hour approaches that I have been
longing for. I have been promised my reward tonight, an end to my
misery and the beginning of my joy.

[3] Peaceful friendly sleep, come, invade the senses of all those who can
disturb my immense pleasure, so I may enjoy perfect happiness without
fear.

[4] Now the hour has come that is destined to such great pleasure, so I seize
my night cloak and make my way to that place where my heart resides.

[5] I lightly knock at the door and hear it softly open; then an invisible
hand draws me in. With trembling steps, I happily let myself be
guided.

[6] Reaching that blissful place where my pleasure awaits, I recover
myself a little before the gleam of the fire. Then, my tongue loosed,
I speak and she listens.

[7] "Can it really be true, my love, that you have deigned to receive me
here, where I hope to be made happy, indeed blessed? Is it true or am
I dreaming? Too great is my contentment.

[8] "The suffering and torment I have undergone do not merit me a
single one of those joys you have given me. Through your kindness,
I am granted a gift far beyond my desert."

[9] She replies: "Your fidelity and worth have earned you what Love
concedes to no other; you will be allowed to take what to all others is
forbidden."

[10] I gaze at her softly and give thanks both to her and to Love, who has granted that my heart be blessed in the supreme and highest joy. Then, lost in pleasure, I gaze on her and fall mute.

[11] She smiles sweetly, reading in my visage the ardent desire that divides me from myself, and restores my vigor, which had been drowning in sweetness.

[12] And with her lovely arms she clasps my neck and is silent, binding my heart and soul to her, as they melt with desire. Filled with pleasure, I shower her breast with kisses.

[13] Then I sup greedily on the nectar of her lovely mouth. I am silent and she does not speak; she is in bliss and I in ecstasy, and we share the sparks of our love in a thousand kisses.

[14] What happened next Love alone can tell, for we two were drunk with pleasure at the height of our mutual joy; in our immense bliss, we lost our souls, our spirit, and our senses.

Sesta rima (settenari). Valerini 1570, 39r–40r. This *sesta rima* narrative in the voice of a male lover, describing an assignation with his beloved, is among a handful of poems attributed to Armani by her lover and fellow actor, Adriano Valerini, who published them after her death. Although the sexual character of the love described is unusual within female-authored verse in this period, there are sufficient continuities with the work of Gaspara Stampa (no. 22), Veronica Franco, and Isabella Andreini for the attribution to be credible. The poem was probably intended for performance, perhaps by Armani herself: in a published oration praising Armani written after her death, Valerini speaks of her playing both male and female parts. The combination of love narrative and dialogue (in stanzas 7–9) recalls traditions of popular song, but apart from a few anomalous forms (*sturbar puonno*), the poem's language is elevated, incorporating Petrarchan images such as the lover "divided from himself" (64; cf. Petrarch's sonnet 292, l. 3).

Fiammetta Soderini (1571)

62

[1] Febo nell'ocean tuffato avendo
il biondo crine e' bei raggi lucenti,
mesta sen giva, lacrimando e ardendo,
Filli lungi 'l chiaro Arno in foschi accenti;
e gl'umidi occhi al vago ciel volgendo: 5
—Or che taccion—dicea—tutti i viventi,
dal basso cerchio tuo, Cinzia serena,
degnati d'ascoltar l'alta mia pena.

[2] Mentre ch'intorno le più ardenti stelle
t'inchinan reverenti e fan corona,   10
e che per te quest'onde chiare e belle
splendon più che pe 'l Sol fra l'alba e nona,
se per Endimïon vive fiammelle
t'arsero il cor, sì come si ragiona,
pietosa ferma il luminoso viso   15
fin che in te gl'occhi lamentando affiso.

[3] Or che in te queste luci oscure e meste
volgo, o del ciel maggior lampa notturna,
e ch'io più spargo lagrime per queste
rive, che d'Arno onde non versa l'urna,   20
deh, fa' che 'l mio lamento impresso reste
nella tua fronte lucida ed eburna;
sì che la donna onor del Mar Tirreno
scorga lontan da lei qual foco ho in seno.

[4] Mostra nel volto tuo, candida Luna,   25
al mio bel Sol, che, poiché il suo splendore
a quest'occhi contese empia fortuna,
altro non scorser mai ch'ombra ed orrore,
e che, da che 'l dì nasce a ch'ei s'imbruna
sempre ov'ella il piè volga i' volgo il core: 30
il cor che, sol con lei da lei disgiunto,
non fu per altro cor trafitto e punto [. . .]

[8] Non possa tanta terra, e tanto cielo,
che s'interpon fra noi, Virginia bella,
spegner quel che mostrasti ardente zelo,
mentre teco mi strinse amica stella.   60
Io pria che te non ami, esser di gelo

vedrassi il foco e Amor senza quadrella,
l'edra dritta e spedita e torto il pino,
e caso uman frenar voler divino.

[9] Crederò io, che 'l suon delle querele   65
meste, ch'io spargo quì fra morta e viva,
aggiunga al seno illustre e alla fedele
orecchia tua, che già grata mi udiva?
Deh, sì, ch'esser non puo desir crudele
dove somma virtù nasce e deriva;   70
renditi dunque tanto spazio mia,
quanto il ciel fa che da te lungi io stia.

[10] Ché come a tua beltà farmi vicina
mi si concede e dir mio duol profondo,
se di rigido cerro in piaggia alpina,   75
o d'elce nata in cupo ombroso fondo
fusti, o di scoglio in seno a la marina,
d'impetrar non tem'io viver giocondo
da te; ché gli angosciosi miei tormenti
tigri pietosi far ponno e serpenti.   80

[11] Sovvengati del dì che le ostinate
mie luci non sapean da te partire;
delle mie guance pallide e bagnate,
di me che volli e non potei morire:
di quelle brevi parolette grate   85
che pur scemano alquanto il mio martire:
—Va, Filli, che restando io vengo teco—.
O dì ch'io sempre alla memoria arreco!

[12] Ma, deh, perche sì tosto i bianchi rai
dopo l'alpestre Golfolina ascondi,   90
o sorella del Sol, mentre i miei guai
narrando all'ombra vo di queste frondi?
Ciò forse avvien per la pietade ch'hai,
che un petto sol tanto martir circondi;
o pur da' lunghi miei lamenti offesa   95
sei più veloce oltre a quei monti scesa?

[13] Vattene ornata d'argentato arnese
più queta parte e più lieta illustrando;
e il tuo drappel d'eterne fiamme accese

teco sen venga e me quì lasci in bando.   100
Quest'alma lasci, oimè, lassa, che scese
qui sol per gir miseramente amando:
ché chi vive, com'io, senza il suo bene
mal fa, se un sol momento è senza pene—.

[1] Phoebus having plunged his blond locks and lovely gleaming rays
into the ocean, Filli was wandering wretchedly, weeping and burning,
along the bright Arno, lamenting in dark tones. Turning her damp eyes
to the beautiful heavens, "Now that all living things are silent," she said,
"serene Cynthia, from your low circle, deign to hear my noble suffering.

[2] "While the most ardent stars of the sky gather round you in reverence,
crowning you, and you are making these bright and lovely waves shine
more than the sun between dawn and nones, if for Endymion bright
flames burned your heart, as men say, piteously linger here for as long
as I fix my eyes, lamenting, on your luminous face.

[3] "While I am turning these dismal, sad eyes on you, O greatest night
lamp of the heavens; while I am weeping more tears on these banks
than Arno pours waves from its urn, pray, let my lament leave its
impression on your shining, ivory brow, so that the lady who is the
honor of the Tyrrhenian Sea may descry at a distance the great fire
I nurture in my breast.

[4] "Bright moon, show my lovely Sun in your expression that, since
cruel Fortune denied her splendor to my eyes, they have seen nothing
but shadow and darkness, and that, from the dawning of the day to its
darkening, my heart follows her, wherever her foot moves: that heart
which, always with her though separated from her, has never been
pierced or wounded by any other heart [. . .]

[8] "All the land and all the sea that lies between us, lovely Virginia,
cannot extinguish that ardent affection you showed when a friendly star
bound us together. Before I cease to love you, fire will be seen to freeze
and Love to roam without his quiver; ivy will be straight and true and
pines twisted, and human vagaries halt divine will.

[9] "Can I believe that the sound of the sad laments that issue here from
me, as I languish between life and death, will ever arrive at your
illustrious breast and your faithful ear, which used to listen to me so
kindly? Surely yes, for a cruel desire cannot coexist with the highest
virtue. Be mine, then, for whatever length of time the heavens destine
you to be absent from me.

[10] "For as soon as I am able to approach your beauty more nearly and speak of my profound suffering, if you were not born of a rigid fir tree on some alpine slope, or some holm oak in a deep shady hollow, or a rock in the bosom of the shore, I shall not fear to beg you for my happiness, since my anguished torments could make tigers merciful and serpents.

[11] "Remember that day when my obstinate eyes could not bring themselves to leave you; remember my pale, tear-stained cheeks and how I wanted to die, yet could not; remember those few welcome little words with which still in some measure assuage my suffering: 'Go, Filli, for, though I stay I come with you.' Oh day I shall always carry in my memory!

[12] "But, alas, why so soon are you hiding your white rays behind the steep Golfolina, sister of the Sun, while I am recounting my woes to you in the shadow of these trees? Perhaps it is because of the pity you feel that a sole breast can harbor so much suffering, or perhaps it is through weariness of my long laments that you have descended beyond those mountains more swiftly?

[13] "Go, then, adorned with your silvery apparel, to illumine more peaceful and happier parts; let your band of eternal flaming fires go with you and leave me here in exile. Leave this soul behind, alas—this soul which descended here on earth only to wander wretchedly loving: for he who, like me, is living without his love, does wrong to be a moment without woe."

Stanze. Ferentilli 1571, 309–12 (*splendan* in l. 12 corrected to *splendon; fuste* in l. 77 corrected to *fusti; tuo* in l. 104 corrected to *suo*). This composition, published in an anthology of ottava rima lyrics, is one of very few poems by Soderini to survive. The poem is headed "For the Most Illustrious Lady of Piombino" ("Per l'Illustrissima Signora di Piombino"), allowing us to identify the recipient as the Genoese Virginia Fieschi (1530–97), wife of Jacopo VI d'Appiano, lord of Piombino, on the Tyrrhenian coast in southern Tuscany. The speaker, Filli, is most likely intended to represent Soderini herself, although it is possible that she represents a third person known to both. In its use of erotic language to express the poet's relationship to a high-status lady, it has analogies with the tradition represented by nos. 142, 147, and 150–52. Here, however, the status disjunction between speaker and addressee is less marked, and the relationship portrayed is more intimate: Filli addresses Virginia using the familiar *tu* form and reports fond words from her beloved in stanza 11. Without external evidence, it is difficult to say more about the nature of the relationship evoked in the poem. While it might be tempting to see it as an early expression of same-sex love between women, it needs to be remembered that erotic discourses were deployed in this period to express various types of relationship, including some we would not regard today as erotic or romantic, in a manner encouraged by Neoplatonic erotic theory, which constructed love as a "union of souls."

The poem consists principally of a long reported lament addressed by Filli to the moon goddess Cynthia or Diana, sister of the sun god Apollo (the Phoebus of l. 1), pleading with her to convey her love laments to her distant beloved. The name Filli is suggestive of pastoral literature, but Virginia Fieschi is addressed under her own name (58) and the references to the Arno River and Golfolina anchor the poem to a precise geographic setting, on the river, south of Florence. Soderini handles the *topos of the address to the moon decoratively, and even perhaps with a touch of humor in stanza 12, when Filli recognizes that the moon has not heeded her plea to it to linger. The omitted stanzas (5–7) contain further reflections on the paradoxical state of the lover, existing and speaking in the absence of her heart and soul, which are figured as having remained with the beloved. The "low circle" of the moon in l. 7 refers to the notion that the planets circled round the earth in a series of ascending orbits. The moon's was the lowest. Nones, in l. 12, was around three o'clock in the afternoon, the fifth of the canonical hours into which the day was divided. Endymion, in l. 13, was a handsome shepherd beloved by Diana, the only known love of the goddess of chastity.

Orsina Cavaletti (1587)

63

Sdegno la fiamma estinse,
e rintuzzò lo strale e sciolse il nodo
che m'arse, che mi punse, e che m'avinse;
né di legame il core
paventa, né di piaga né d'ardore;   5
né cura se baleni,
perfida, o s'hai quegli occhi tuoi sereni;
ché lieto fuor de l'amoroso impaccio
sprezza l'incendio e le quadrella e 'l laccio.

Wrath extinguished the flame and blunted the arrow and loosed the
knot that burned, pierced, and bound me. My heart does not fear
binding nor wounding nor burning, nor does it care whether you flash
lightning, perfidious woman, or whether calm reigns in those eyes of
yours, for happy beyond the encumbrance of eros, it scorns the fire, the
arrows, and the noose.

Madrigal aBAcCdDEE. *Rime* 1587, 211. This madrigal is found in the first printed
verse anthology to privilege the madrigal form, reflecting a powerful new trend in
Italian verse (see pp. 18–19). The speaker's gender is not revealed explicitly, but *per-
fida* in l. 7 defines the love object as female, so, if we assume the heterosexual para-
digm usual in the love poetry of the period, this poem reads as male-voiced. Poems
in the voice of a disdainful lover who has escaped the bounds of love were a popular
subgenre of love lyric in Ferrara in this period, reflecting a more general shift away
from an idealizing Petrarchan to an edgier, more "realist" representation of love.
Striking stylistically here is Cavaletti's use of the favored mannerist device of *rap-
portatio* in ll. 1–3, 5, and 9. The beginning and end of the madrigal are united pho-
netically by the preponderance of consonant-heavy words, in and out of rhyme.
Cavaletti's madrigal was set to music by five composers, including Monteverdi,
between 1586 and 1619.

Moderata Fonte (pre-1592)

64

Deh, come cieco io sono
della mente, foss'io degli occhi ancora,
per non veder, oimè, quel che m'accora;
o pur, sì come io veggio
pur troppo, oimè, con gli occhi della fronte,   5
le luci avess'io ancor de l'alma pronte;
che così amore o sdegno
di me compita avrebbe intera palma,
sendo Argo o talpa tutta e d'occhi e d'alma.

Oh, if only I could be blind in my eyes, as I am in my mind, so I could
not see, alas! that which tears at my heart—or, since I see all too much
with my eyes, would that the eyes of my mind were equally sharp. For
then love or anger would have complete and perfect victory over me,
and I would be Argos, or entirely a mole, blind both in eyes and in soul.

Madrigal aBBcDDeFF. Fonte 1600, 135. This artful madrigal, with its three unrhymed
settenari alternating with rhymed hendecasyllables, is thematically and stylistically
close to no. 63: the implied narrative context is the unidealizing one of a lover in
prey to an unsuitable love object and hoping to escape. Cavaletti and her school are
probably a direct influence, as Fonte seems to have been in touch with Ferrarese
literary circles (Cox 2011, 307 n. 160). The poem is found in Fonte's dialogue *The
Worth of Women*, where it is cited as an example of the conceptually hypercom-
pressed character of the madrigal form (see introduction, n. 76). While not formally
employing *rapportatio, like no. 63, Fonte's madrigal operates in a similar manner,
requiring the reader to correlate the two conceits of ll. 1–3 (the blind lover, unaware
of his lady's betrayal) and ll. 4–6 (the disillusioned lover who has recovered the "clear
sight" of reason) with the corresponding elements in ll. 7–9 (love and the mole for
the blind lover; anger and Argos, a many-eyed monster in Greek mythology, for the
disillusioned lover). Fonte's speaker Leonora in *The Worth of Women* refers to such
patterns as *regressi* or *corrispondenzie* (Fonte 1997, 223). The sound patterning of the
poem is intricate: of the rhymes, *ancora/accora* are nearly identical phonetically,
pronte/fronte rich, and *palma/alma* inclusive, while the repetitions *veggio/veder* (3–4
and *per/pur/pur* (3–5) help bind together the two semantically disjunctive tercets
with which the poem begins.

Isabella Andreini (1601)
65

S'alcun fia mai che i versi miei negletti
legga, non creda a questi finti ardori:
ché ne le scene imaginati amori
usa a trattar con non leali affetti,　　4
con bugiardi non men con finti detti
de le Muse spiegai gli alti furori,
talor piangendo i falsi miei dolori,
talor cantando i falsi miei diletti.　　8
E come ne' teatri or donne ed ora
uom fei rappresentando in vario stile
quanto volle insegnar natura ed arte,　　11
così la stella mia seguendo ancora,
di fuggitiva età nel verde aprile,
vergai con vario stil ben mille carte.　　14

Should anyone ever come to read these careless verses, let him not believe in these feigned ardors: for on the stage, accustomed to acting imagined loves with insincere affects and feigned, lying words, I have often expressed the poetic furor of the Muses, sometimes weeping my false sorrows, sometimes singing my false delights. And just as in the theater, acting now women, now men, I showed in varied style all that nature and art can teach, so, following my star, in the green April of my fleeting time, I penned in varied style many a thousand leaves.

Sonnet ABBA ABBA CDE CDE. Andreini 1601, 1. The opening sonnet of Andreini's *Rime* wittily undermines the central fiction of most love lyric, that it conveys the author's own experience. Targeted especially is the proemial sonnet of Tasso's *Rime*, which opens, "True were these joys and ardors" (*Vere fur queste gioie e questi ardori*). Although the histrionic model of love lyric Andreini proposes as an alternative was probably suggested by her experience as an actress, she may also have been influenced by the Aristotelian poetic theory of Pomponio Torelli (1539–1608), which regards lyric as a form of quasi-dramatic mimesis. Despite her allusion to her verse as "careless" (1), Andreini uses her proemial sonnet, like Gaspara Stampa (no. 13), to locate herself within the most prestigious tradition of male-authored lyric. The pairing of *piangere* and *cantare* (7–8) derives from Bembo's opening sonnet; *con vario stile* (10, 14) from Petrarch's. Both phrases are already echoed in Tasso's proemial sonnet (l. 2).

66

Sdegno, campione audace,
incontra a te arma di ghiaccio il core
perch'io non tema più fiamma d'amore;
ma non sì tosto poi
m'appar degli occhi tuoi l'ardente face,   5
che 'l suo gielo si sface.
Folle guerrier, indarno vittoria attende
chi con arme di giel col sol contende.

Anger, my bold champion, arms my heart against you with ice, so I need no longer fear the flames of love, but no sooner does the burning brand of your eyes appear before me than his ice melts. Foolish warrior! He who contends against the sun with weapons of ice awaits victory in vain.

Madrigal aBBcAaDD. Andreini 1601, 9. Like nos. 63–64, this madrigal addresses the fashionable theme of *amoroso sdegno* (amorous anger). The poem has no grammatical markers indicative of the sex of the speaker, though the traditional gendering of *sdegno* poems was male-voiced. Andreini combines dueling metaphors here with traditional Petrarchan fire-and-ice imagery, mingling the two to surreal effect in the last line. A burning brand was among the attributes of Cupid, god of love; hence l. 5 perhaps implicitly references the poetic *topos of Love taking up residence in the beloved's eyes (cf. no. 27). A formal feature to note is the juxtaposed inclusive rhyme *face/sface* in ll. 5–6, whose echo effect is reinforced by the internal rhyme *poi/tuoi* in ll. 4–5, and the phonetically similar *che 'l* and *giel* in l. 7. The climatic last line is set off by the slow line before it, with its many consonant clusters and *concorso di vocali.*

67

Qualor, candida e vaga,
sovra quel che la cinge, oscuro manto,
quella man che sì dolce il cor m'impiaga
scopre Madonna, io del mio duol mi vanto,
e dico:—Ah, non risplende   5
sì chiara mai nel suo notturno velo
stella d'amor nel Cielo—.
Insidïoso intanto
tra le vedove bende
contra me novi lacci Amor pur tende.   10

Whenever my lady reveals that hand which so sweetly wounds my heart, pure white and lovely on the dark mantle that frames it, I glory in my sufferings and say, "Ah, no star of love shines so brightly on heaven's nocturnal veil." Insidiously, meanwhile, within a widow's weeds, Love is preparing new traps for me.

Madrigal aBABcDdbcC. Andreini 1601, 88. Poems praising the beauty of the lady's hand were an established subgenre of Petrarchism, to the extent that a *canzoniere* by the fifteenth-century poet Giusto de' Conti, is entitled *La bella mano* (The Beautiful Hand). The unveiling of the hand, by taking off a glove, was seen as highly erotic, as a synecdochic suggestion of further disrobing. This slight, graceful madrigal is characteristically post-Petrarchist in that it does not assume a single love but a succession of loves (10). Widows as love objects are not uncommon in Baroque love poetry, not least because of the potential they offer for chromatic contrasts, such as that described here, between the black of their garments and the lady's white skin.

68 ⟶

Tu m'uccidesti e già son fatta polve
(o miracol possente!),
polve che spira e d'amor fiamma sente
e là dove si volge il tuo sembiante,
per mio maggior tormento,   5
ivi mi porta il vento,
perch'io sostenga, disprezzata amante,
l'ingiuria ancor de le tue crude piante.

You killed me and I am now dust (o potent miracle!)—dust that breathes
and feels love's flame. Wherever your semblance goes, the wind carries
me, to keep me in torment, so that I may suffer, despised lover that I
am, the injury too of your cruel soles.

Madrigal AbBCddCC. Andreini 1601, 100–101. This female-voiced madrigal gives a
witty twist to the *topos of the lover driven to his death through the pain of un-
requited love. Here, reduced to dust, she is wafted by the wind to be trampled be-
neath her callously indifferent beloved's feet. The *conceit is developed relatively
simply, with the only touches of rhetorical ornamentation provided by the juxta-
posed inclusive rhyme *possente/sente* (2–3), the alliteration of *possente/polve* (2–3), and
the *concorso di vocali* of *disprezzata amante* and *ingiuria ancor* (7–8).

69

Deh girate,
luci amate,
pietosetto quel bel guardo
che mi fugge,
che mi strugge,   5
onde 'n un m'agghiaccio ed ardo.

O pupille,
che tranquille
serenate l'aria intorno:
sarà mai   10
che i be' rai,
faccian lieto un mio sol giorno?

Dolce scocchi
da quegli occhi
più del Sol vaghi ed ardenti   15
pio splendore,
che ristore,
care luci, i miei tormenti.

Deh fiammeggi,
deh lampeggi,   20
in quel labro un dolce riso,
in quel labro
di cinabro,
che m'hà 'l cor dal sen diviso.

Amorosa,   25
grazïosa,
di rubini colorita,
tocca il vento
d'un accento,
bocca ond'esca la mia vita.   30

Se v'aprite,
se scoprite,
belle rose amate e care,
vostre perle,
a vederle   35
riderà la terra e 'l mare.

Non si nieghi
a' miei preghi
per pietà giusta mercede.
(ahi) languire,   40
(ahi) perire
deve amando tanta fede?

No, ch'io scerno
al governo
di quei chiari onesti lumi   45
amor vero,
per cui spero
pria gioir, ch' i' mi consumi.

No, che dice
la beatrice   50
bocca, ov'or le grazie stanno:—
Avrai, taci,
mille baci,
degno premio a tanto affanno—.

Come, beloved eyes, turn on me with a little pity that lovely gaze that
flees me, that melts me, so I freeze and burn at the same moment.

O pupils that, so tranquil, make all around serene. Will it ever be that
those lovely rays make happy one sole day of mine?

Sweet, you shoot from those eyes, lovelier than the sun and more
ardent, a merciful beam that heals, dear shining eyes, my torments.

Look! There flames, there flashes, a sweet smile on those lips: on those
vermilion lips that have stolen my heart from my breast.

Loving, gracious, the colour of rubies, you touch the breeze with a
voice, mouth from which my life issues.

If you open, lovely roses, dear and beloved, if you reveal your pearls, the
earth and sky will laugh to see them.

Do not deny to my prayers their deserved response in your kindness.
Must such loving faith, alas! languish and perish?

No, for I can see, at the helm of those clear honest eyes, true love, so
that I hope to be happy before I consume myself with desire.

No, for that blessing mouth, the home of the graces, says, "Be silent, and
you will have a thousand kisses, a worthy reward for your suffering."

Scherzo. Andreini 1601, 115–17. Andreini's *Rime* of 1601 is notable for its metrical virtuosity, using eleven verse forms in total, including blank-verse poems, sestinas, *capitoli*, and centos, as well as the fashionable *scherzo* and *canzonetta*. Andreini exploits the lightness and compression of the *scherzo* admirably well in "Deh girate" achieving almost haiku-like effects. The gender of the speaker is not identifiable. The first three strophes address the lover's eyes (compare Veronica Gambara's no. 5), but, in the next three, the poem becomes more sensual as the focus shifts to the mouth, culminating in a promise of secret kisses. "Deh girate" reflects a general shift in late-sixteenth-century verse toward less sublimated representations of love. The simplicity of Andreini's language and the frequent, quasi-naïve repetitions, are typical of the contemporary madrigal tradition, as is the decorative diminutive *pietosetto* (3). The stylistic ideal resembles the *mignardise* of the French Pléiade, which influenced Italian poetry largely through the mediation of Gabriello Chiabrera, a poetic correspondent of Andreini's and initiator of the *scherzo* form. "Deh girate" was one of Andreini's most famous poems: it was set to music several times and even inspired a parody (Andreini 2005, 15–16). The metaphor of Love as helmsman of the lover's ship, in the penultimate stanza, derives from Petrarch's sonnet 189.

70

Movea dolce un zefiretto
i suoi tepidi sospiri,
e, lasciando l'aureo letto,
fiammeggiò per gli alti giri
l'alba e 'l mondo colorìo,   5
mentre rose e gigli aprìo,

quando ninfa Amor m'offerse,
ch'adornò d'altra alba i campi.
Forse Pari in Ida scerse
così chiari ardenti lampi?   10
No, che Venere si crede
finta allor che costei vede.

Ella ornava gli ornamenti
col sembiante pellegrino,
e gioivan gli elementi   15
vagheggiando il bel divino,
e su l'oro dei capelli,
ridean lieti i fior novelli.

Febo uscì de l'onde fuore,
ma poich'egli in terra scorse   20
d'alti raggi altro splendore,
saggio indietro il camin torse,
ché se fosse in ciel comparso
fora stato e vinto ed arso.

Le fresche aure matutine   25
s'infiammaro al dolce foco
de le labbra porporine;
de le labbra ov'oggi han loco
di rubin vive facelle,
ch'ardon l'alme, ardon le stelle.   30

Il bel petto ove biancheggia
di sue nevi il giglio pieno
con mille occhi il ciel vaghegghia,
né so ancor se 'n quel bel seno
scendon guardi o scendon baci,   35
del mio ben ladri rapaci.

Pure nevi, che accendete
le faville ond'io tutt'ardo,
morte voi, voi tomba sete
del famelico mio sguardo: 40
del mio sguardo che, fenice,
nel morir divien felice.

Dolci pomi ed acerbetti
pur quel candido sentiero
veggio in voi ch'almi diletti   45
mi promette; per voi spero
che, tra neve e neve ardendo,
vada l'alma al ciel salendo.

Ma perch'altri ov'io non poggi,
a me solo Amor gentile   50
scopri i duo nevosi poggi
che fiorir fan vago aprile;
che lampeggian fiamme d'oro;
a te gloria, a me tesoro.

O se tanto mi concedi   55
Amor, vedi nel mio canto
dirà Clio tuo nobil vanto.

A sweet little zephyr was breathing its warm sighs, and Dawn, leaving her golden couch, flamed through the upper spheres, and colored the world, opening roses and lilies,

when Love offered up to me a nymph who adorned the fields with another dawn. Perhaps Paris on Ida saw such bright ardent beams? No, for Venus would seem feigned if he saw this one.

She was adorning her ornaments with her peerless looks, and the elements rejoiced around her, gazing raptly on her divine beauty. On the gold of her hair, bright spring flowers laughed.

Phoebus rose from the waves, but on seeing a different splendor with glorious rays, he wisely turned his steps homeward. Had he appeared in the sky, he would have been vanquished and burned.

The fresh morning breezes were catching fire on the sweet flame of her crimson lips, those lips where there linger live sparks of ruby that burn men's souls, burn the heavens themselves.

The heavens gaze with a thousand eyes on her lovely breast, on which there gleamed the full lily of her snows; nor can I tell whether they shower down on it only looks or also kisses, rapacious thieves of what I desire.

Pure snows, that set alight the sparks that have me aflame: you are the death, the tomb you are of my famished gaze, that gaze which, like the phoenix, finds happiness in death.

Sweet unripe apples, I see between you that white path that promises to lead me to delight; I hope through you, as I burn between snow and snow, my soul will ascend to heaven.

But so that others cannot climb where I do not, gentle Love, reveal those snowy hills to me alone, which bring lovely April into bloom, which flash flames of gold—your glory, my treasure.

Concede this to me, Love, and you will see in my song Clio telling your noble tales.

Sesta rima (ottonari). Andreini 1601, 178–80. Andreini terms this a *scherzo*, though it is in a different, less ethereal, meter than no. 69. The poem is written in a sensual, classicizing vein popular with male poets at this time. Although the gender of the speaker is not explicit, the poem would probably have been read as male-voiced. The first stanza of the poem, describing dawn "rising from her golden couch," alludes to the classical personification of dawn in the figure of the goddess Aurora. The second stanza alludes to the Greek hero Paris's judgment of the relative beauty of three naked goddesses Juno, Venus, and Minerva, on Mount Ida (Paris chose Venus, as is implicit here). Comparison of the beauties of the beloved to that of the three goddesses, or Venus specifically, was a *topos in Petrarchist lyric, used especially famously in two sonnets by Pietro Bembo and Giovanni della Casa (see no. 151 below). Similarly, in the fourth stanza, the competition between the actual sun (Phoebus, or Apollo, was the sun god) and the metaphorical sun represented by the beloved was an established poetic *topos, popularized especially by Vittoria Colonna (see nos. 44 and 147), but it is here given a characteristically light and witty turn.

   This playful reworking of Petrarchist commonplaces reaches a climax in the eighth stanza, where the fire-and-ice imagery traditionally used in Petrarchist lyric to express the tortured emotions of the lover is redeployed in a sensual image of the burning lover tracing his imaginary way between the nymph's snowy breasts (46–48). Similarly, the traditionally spiritual Neoplatonic language of love as a means to ascend to heaven is used in the final line of the stanza in a distinctly unspiritual sense. The image of love resulting in a "happy death," in the previous stanza, demands to be read in a similar, sensual key, typical of the era (see introduction, p. 31).

The poem concludes (56–57) with the poet promising Love that he or she will return the god's favors by singing his praises with Clio, muse of history. This may be a hint from Andreini that she herself was contemplating a "history" of Love's deeds, perhaps along the lines of Ercole Udine's well-received miniature epic on the Cupid and Psyche theme (*La Psiche*, 1598), which was dedicated to one of Andreini's principal patrons, Leonora Medici Gonzaga, duchess of Mantua. For evidence that Andreini was writing an epic at the time of her death, see Belloni 1893, 286 n. 4.

A discussion of a musical setting of this poem is found in MacNeil 2005, 135–40.

Lucchesia Sbarra (1610)

71

Fattosi in Tiro toro il gran tonante,
pria su l'arena e poi ne la sals'onda
trasse l'onor de la Sidonia sponda,
né sdegna ella montar ferino amante.   4
Varca Teti Anfitrite e spinge inante
un Triton, che la regge e la seconda,
e spira ovunque va luce gioconda,
qualora è il mar più torbido e sonante.   8
Ed a voi, cruda, par che vi dispiaccia,
ch'io porti in su la penna il vostro volto,
che pace mi promette, indi la nega.   11
Ahi, quanto è ver che Amor torto mi faccia
mentre vuol ch'abbia in voi tutto il cor volto,
et Iole mi lusinga e non mi piega.   14

Having made himself a bull in Tyre, the great Thunderer carried the
honor of the Sidonian shore first onto the sand, then onto the salt
waves, nor did she disdain to mount this feral lover. Thetis embarks on
Amphitrite, spurring forward a Triton who supports and transports her,
and, wherever she goes a joyous light breathes, even when the sea is at
its most turbulent and loud. Yet you, cruel one, seem to be displeased
that I carry on the point of my pen that face of yours that promises me
peace, then denies it. Alas, how true it is that Love does me wrong
when he rules that I should have my heart wholly fixed on you, while
Iole courts me and I do not bend.

Sonnet ABBA ABBA CDE CDE. Sbarra 1610, E3v. With Lucrezia Marinella, Sbarra
was the female poet of her generation who embraced the novelties of the Baroque
most enthusiastically. This aspect of her verse is well exemplified in her male-voiced
love sonnets, with their extravagant conceits and exuberant wordplay. The first
quatrain refers to the myth of Jove's abduction of Europa, disguised as a bull, while
the second shows the sea nymph Thetis, mother of Achilles, drawn across the sea
by a Triton or merman. (Amphitrite, though the name of a sea goddess, is here in-
tended simply as an epithet for the sea.) Although Iole (14) is a figure in Greek my-
thology, the name is probably here chosen simply to evoke a pastoral context of
love rivalries between shepherds and nymphs as found in contemporary pastoral
drama. Stylistically, the most striking thing in the sonnet is the wordplay in the
tongue-twisting first line, though note also the *alliteration across the transition of
ll. 3–4 and in ll. 10–11, and the *rima equivoca* on *volto* in ll. 10 and 13.

72

A che, bella e crudel, tender le reti
ed ingorda ingannar pennuti augelli,
e piegar con le man verdi arbuscelli,
e col piede salir faggi e abeti?   4
Ormai desio sì folle in te s'acqueti,
e se pur preda vuoi, gli occhi e i capelli
scuopri, e sian l'esca questi e rete quelli
per far i tuoi prigion contenti e lieti.   8
In così ricca rete, a così dolce
d'ambrosia esca soave, in sì tersi ori,
ch'Amor di propria man porge e dispiega,   11
volano a gara insieme anime e cuori;
ch'ogni restio pensiero inebria e molce,
e vago l'uom d'esservi preso prega.   14

Lovely cruel lady, why spread your nets and greedily ensnare the feathered birds? Why bend the green bushes with your hands and scale beeches and firs with your feet? Let this mad desire be quieted in you, and if you still long for prey, reveal your eyes and hair: one will be the bait, one the net that will keep your prisoners happy and gay. Souls and hearts vie together to rush into such a rich net, to such a sweet and lovely ambrosial bait, into such bright threads of gold that Love with his own hands proffers and disposes. All resisting thoughts are inebriated and softened, and men plead to be prisoners made.

Sonnet ABBA ABBA CDE DCE. Sbarra 1610, E5v. The representation of the lady hunting in this sonnet exemplifies the trend in Baroque love lyric toward a more active and kinetic love object and literalizes the Petrarchan metaphors of love as snare and of the lady's golden hair as a net. It is paired in Sbarra's *Rime* with a sonnet describing the lady fishing, a *topos found in the lyrics of Giambattista Marino, a poet Sbarra much admired. The first quatrain of the sonnet, with its *end-stopped lines and emphatic *polysyndeton, contrasts with the syntactic and rhythmic fluidity of what follows: note especially ll. 9–12, where the sense flows across the tercet break, and the decorative, consonant-rich soundscape and broken rhythms of ll. 9–10 give way to the breezy *assonance of l. 12. The rhymes *augelli*/*arboscelli* and *molce*/*dolce* probably both derive from Tasso (see *GL* 7.5, 12.84, 14.61, 15.65).

Religious
Verse

Lucrezia Tornabuoni (before 1482)

73

Echo el Re forte,
echo el Re forte:
aprite quelle porte!

[1] O principe infernale,
non fate resistenza:
egli è il re celestiale,
che vien con gran potenza.
Fategli riverenza   5
levate via le porte. *Echo el Re forte . . .*

[2] Chi è questo potente,
che vien con tal victoria?
Egli è 'l signor possente,
egli è 'l signor di gloria.   10
Aúto ha la victoria,
egli ha vinto la morte. *Echo el Re forte . . .*

[3] Egli ha vinto la guerra,
durata già molt'anni
e fe' tremar la terra   15
per cavarci d'affanni.
Riempier vuol gli scanni
per ristorar suo corte. *Echo el Re forte . . .*

[4] E' vuole el padre antico
e la sua compagnia.   20
Abel, vero suo amicho,
Noè, si metta in via,
Moisè, qui non stia:
venite alla gran chorte. *Echo el Re forte . . .*

[5] O Abraam patriarcha,   25
seghuite il gran signore;
la promessa non varcha;
venuto è il redemptore;
venghane il gran cantore
a far degna la corte. *Echo el Re forte . . .*   30

[6] O Giovanni Baptista,
or su, sanza dimoro,
non perdere di vista

su nell'eterno coro;
e Symïon con loro   35
drieto a sé fa la scorte. *Echo el Re forte . . .*

[7] O parvoli innocenti,
innanzi a tutti gite,
or siate voi contenti
delle aúte ferite;   40
o gemme, o margarite,
adorate la corte. *Echo el Re forte . . .*

[8] Venuti siete al regno
tanto desiderato,
poi che nel santo legno   45
i' fu' morto e straziato
e ho ricomperato
tutta l'humana sorte. *Echo el Re forte . . .*

Here is the strong king. Here is the strong king. Open those gates!

[1] O Prince of Hell, do not resist: he is the heavenly king, coming in great power. Do him reverence; throw open the gates. *Here is the strong king . . .*

[2] Who is this mighty one who comes in such triumph? He is the powerful lord; he is the lord of glory. He has triumphed; he has defeated death. *Here is the strong king . . .*

[3] He has won the war that lasted long years and made the earth tremble, to save us from our woes. He seeks to replenish heaven's ranks, to restore his court. *Here is the strong king . . .*

[4] He wants the ancient father and his companions. Abel, his true friend, and Noah, get on your way; Moses, do not wait: come to the great court. *Here is the strong king . . .*

[5] O patriarch Abraham follow the great lord. He does not fail in his promise: the Redeemer has come. Let the great singer come to adorn his court. *Here is the strong king . . .*

[6] O John the Baptist, now come quickly, don't lose sight of the heavenly choir; and Simeon with them follows on behind. *Here is the strong king . . .*

[7] O little Innocents, leading on ahead, now be happy in your wounds; you little jewels, you pearls, worship his court. *Here is the strong king . . .*

[8] You have come to the kingdom you so longed for, now that on the holy rood I have died and been martyred, redeeming the human race. *Here is the strong king . . .*

Ballata xx ababbx xx, with the first line of the refrain repeated. *Laude* 1485, 68v–69v (*effe* in l. 15 amended to *e fe'*; *anthico* in l. 19 amended to *antico*; *chaute* in l. 40 to *aúte*). Six *laude* (praise songs) by Lucrezia Tornabuoni de' Medici, first published in a Florentine anthology of *laude* that came out in 1486 (or 1485 using the Florentine dating system of the time), may well be the earliest poems by a secular woman to appear in print. Four of the six poems, including this one, have the same metrical form and are accompanied by the annotation, "It is sung like (*cantasi come*) 'Ben venga maggio.'" The reference is to a famous secular *ballata* celebrating the coming of spring by the greatest Tuscan poet of the age, Angelo Poliziano (1454–94), a friend of Tornabuoni's and a client of her husband's family, the Medici. Such religious *contrafacta* of secular songs were a frequent phenomenon of the time. The *ritornello* ("Echo el Re forte, echo el Re forte / aprite quelle porte") was repeated at the end of each strophe.

"Echo el re forte" takes as its subject Christ's "harrowing of Hell," his supposed descent into the underworld between his death and resurrection to release the souls of the righteous who had died and been condemned to Hell before his death on the cross had redeemed mankind. This episode is not found in the gospels but is attested by the later Apostles' Creed and formed part of Christian dogma from the thirteenth century. Tornabuoni's account of the harrowing draws both on Psalm 24:7–8 ("Lift up your heads, O ye gates, and be ye lift up, o everlasting doors, and the King of glory shall come in / . . . the Lord strong and mighty"; compare stanzas 1–2 of Tornabuoni's poem), and on Virgil's eyewitness account of the episode in Canto 4 of Dante's *Inferno*, where he describes Christ as a "powerful man, crowned with a sign of victory" ("un possente / con segno di vittoria coronato" [53–54]; compare stanza 2 of Tornabuoni's poem).

The specific figures whom Tornabuoni describes as being rescued from hell are the first man, Adam ("the ancient father" of l. 19), responsible for the Fall; his son Abel; Noah, the sole survivor, with his family, of the great flood described in Genesis 6–8; Moses, the prophet and lawgiver whose deeds are described in the Book of Exodus; the patriarch Abraham, whose life is recounted in Genesis 11–25; David ("the great singer"), supposed author of the Psalms; John the Baptist, who prophesized Christ's coming; Simeon (Luke 2:25–35), who recognized the infant Christ as the Messiah; and the Innocents, the infant boys massacred by Herod shortly after Christ's birth (Matthew 2:16–18). The first six of these figures derive from the account in Dante (*Inf.* 4.55–58), who lists them in the same order. John the Baptist's presence may be dictated in part by his status as patron saint of Florence, although he was also said in apocryphal texts to have prophesized Christ's coming in Hell, as he had on earth. It is possible that the word translated "companions" here (*compagnia*) refers instead to Adam's orginal companion, Eve.

The language of Tornabuoni's *lauda* is clear, robust, and popular, as was customary within this tradition. Its syntax is simple and its grammar occasionally loose (see esp. ll. 35–36). Devices of repetition are frequent, like the *anaphora of ll. 9–13, the *polyptoton of 11–12 and 28–29, and the *isocolon of ll. 9–10 and 41. Together with the closely placed rhymes, these help give a rhythmic feel to the whole, presumably enhanced by the musical setting.

A curious feature of Tornabuoni's poem is the shift of speaker in the final stanza, where we hear Christ, who had earlier been referred to in the third person, speaking directly to the rescued souls, now in Heaven. In a monophonic performance, it would be possible to underline this change by having a new singer for the last stanza, although polyphonic settings of *laude* were more common in fifteenth-century Florence.

Vittoria Colonna (pre-1546)

74

Poi che 'l mio casto amor gran tempo tenne
l'alma di fama accesa, ed ella un angue
in sen nudrìò, per cui dolente or langue,
volta al Signor, onde il rimedio venne,　　4
i santi chiodi omai sieno mie penne,
e puro inchiostro il prezïoso sangue,
vergata carta il sacro corpo exangue,
sì ch'io scriva per me quel ch'ei sostenne.　　8
Chiamar qui non convien Parnaso o Delo,
ch'ad altra acqua s'aspira, ad altro monte
si poggia, u' piede uman per sé non sale.　　11
Quel Sol, che alluma gli elementi e 'l cielo,
prego ch'aprendo il suo lucido fonte
mi porga umor a la gran sete eguale.　　14

After my chaste love had long kept my soul burning for fame,
nurturing a serpent in its breast, so that it now lies ailing, turning now
to the Lord, from whom the remedy came, let my pens now be his holy
nails and my pure ink his precious blood; let my scriven paper be his
bloodless sacred body, so that I may write for myself what he endured.
I shall not call here on Parnassus or Delos: it is to a different water that
I aspire, and a different mountain that I climb, where no human foot
can ascend by itself. I pray the Sun who lights the elements and the
heavens that, opening his bright fount, he proffer me fluid equal to my
great thirst.

Sonnet ABBA ABBA CDE CDE. *Souce*: Colonna 1546, 4r. The proemial sonnet of Colonna's *Rime spirituali* dramatically announces her poetic "conversion." After identifying the poet's former, secular verse as a sinful distraction (the serpent metaphor of l. 2 recalling Genesis), it launches into a striking description of her new religious poetics, rooted in Christ's passion, in the vigorous, *end-stopped ll. 5–7. Colonna's imagery here seems inspired by 2 Corinthians 3:3, perhaps mediated through medieval religious texts. Line 7's paper-skin equation had special force in a culture that habitually used parchment; note also that *vergata* means both "lined" (of paper) and "beaten." The tercets speak of the poet's rejection of secular poetry, symbolized by Parnasuss (see no. 58) and Delos (a shrine sacred to Apollo, god of poetry), although the myth of the poetic springs on Mount Helicon may have informed the imagery of l. 13. Line 10, with its rich *assonance and *concorso di vocali, echoes the *congedo of Petrarch's conversional sestina 142.

75

Spiego ver voi, Signor, indarno l'ale
prima che 'l vostro caldo interno vento
m'apra l'aria d'intorno qualor sento
vincer da novo ardir l'antico male.   4
Che giunga a l'infinito opra mortale
vostro dono è, però che in un momento
la può far degna; ch'io da me pavento
di cader col pensier quand'ei più sale.   8
Bramo quel raggio di che 'l ciel s'alluma,
che scaccia dense nebbie, e quella accesa
secreta fiamma ch'ogni gel consuma,   11
perché poi lieve al caldo ed a la bruma,
tutta al divino onor l'anima intesa
si mova al volo altero in altra piuma.   14

Lord, I try in vain to open my wings toward you until your burning
inner wind clears the air around me, so that I feel the old evil conquered
by a new daring. That a mortal being can attain the infinite is your
gift, for you can make us worthy of it in an instant; by myself, I fear to
plummet when my thought aspires too high. I yearn for that ray that
illumines heaven and clears the densest mist, and for that burning
secret flame that consumes all ice, so my soul, careless of heat and cold
and fixed wholly on divine honor, may soar up lightly on its noble flight
on new wings.

Sonnet ABBA ABBA CDC CDC. Colonna 1546, 6r. One great theme of Colonna's
religious verse is the poet's aspiration to ascend spiritually to the contemplation of
God. Here, she speaks in theological terms of how such mystical experiences are
possible: they rely on divine grace, which alone can conquer the stain of original sin
(the *antico male* of l. 4) and empower a mortal being to ascend to the divine. Colon-
na's emphasis on grace over effort or desert reflects her closeness to reformist cir-
cles. Grace is figured metaphorically in terms of light and "inner flame" (9–11) and
as a logic-defying "hot wind" (2) that is both internal to the soul and capable of
clearing the air around it. Its power to release the soul from the burden of sin is
evoked in the sound patterning of the tercets, which move from the consonant-rich
texture of the first tercet (note especially the opening of l. 10) to the much lighter
vocalic soundscape of the second. Structurally, the poem is characterized by fre-
quent *enjambment, used to particular effect between ll. 10–11.

76

Se 'l breve suon che sol quest'aer frale
circonda e move, e l'aura che raccoglie
lo spirto dentro e poi l'apre e discioglie
soavemente in voce egra e mortale,   4
con tal dolcezza il cor sovente assale
che d'ogni cura vil s'erge e ritoglie,
sprona, accende 'l pensier, drizza le voglie
per gir volando al ciel con leggiere ale,   8
che fia quand'udirà con vivo zelo
la celeste armonia l'anima pura
sol con l'orecchia interna intenta al vero   11
dinanzi al suo fattor nel sommo Cielo,
u' non si perde mai tuono o misura,
né si discorda il bel concento altero?   14

If the brief sound that this frail air alone surrounds and moves, and the breath that our spirit gathers within us to open and unfold so sweetly in a weak mortal voice, can so often assail our heart with such sweetness that it lifts our spirits and divides us from all our cares, spurs us and fires our thoughts, and drives our desires heavenward flying on light wings—what, then, will it be when our pure soul will listen with bright zeal to the harmonies of the heavens, hearing with our inner ear alone, keenly tuned to the true, before our maker in Paradise, where tone and rhythm never fail, nor does the lovely high harmony ever discord?

Sonnet ABBA ABBA CDE CDE. Colonna 1546, 10v. This sonnet, composed of a single, complex sentence, flowing freely across the line breaks, offers a good illustration of Colonna's technical mastery of the form. It recalls the poetic ideal Colonna adumbrates in a letter to Bembo of 1530 in which she compliments her correspondent on writing a sonnet that sounds like "well-ordered prose," its rhymes sufficiently self-effacing for their harmony to be heard "in the soul before they are in the ear" (Dionisotti 2002, 122). The tercets of the poem refer to the notion that the spheres of the planets as they circle the earth emit a celestial harmony, expressive of the divinely created beauty of the universe. The sonnet's comparison of this heavenly music with the pale shadow of it constituted by human vocal music may reflect Boethius's distinction in *De musica* between *musica humana*, the natural harmony of the human body and soul, and *musica universalis*, the higher harmony of the spheres.

77

Vorrei l'orecchia aver qui chiusa e sorda
per udir coi pensier più fermi e intenti
l'alte angeliche voci e i dolci accenti
che vera pace in vero amor concorda.   4
Spira un aer vital tra corda e corda,
divino e puro in quei vivi instrumenti,
e sì move ad un fine i lor concenti
che l'eterna armonia mai non discorda.   8
Amor alza le voci, amor le abbassa,
ordina e batte equal l'ampia misura
che non mai fuor del segno invan percote;   11
sempre è più dolce il suon, se ben ei passa
per le mutanze in più diverse note,
ché chi compone il canto ivi n'ha cura.   14

I wish I could have my earthly ear sealed and deaf so I could listen more
keenly and sharply in my mind to the voices of the angels on high and
the sweet sounds that come from true concord united with true love.
A vital air breathes between string and string, divine and pure, in those
living instruments, and their melodies are so pitched that they never
discord with the eternal harmonies. Love lifts their voices, Love lowers
them, Love orders and beats their stately rhythm, always equal, with no
beat falling vainly out of time. The sound is ever sweeter as the harmo-
nies change, for he who directs the song has it in his care.

Sonnet ABBA ABBA CDE CED. Colonna 1546, 10v. This sonnet is thematically simi-
lar to no. 76, but, rather than aspiring to hear the "music of the spheres" after death,
the poet describes a mystical, earthly anticipation of this experience, the auditory
equivalent of the vision of paradise she describes in no. 80. Especially effective are
ll. 5–6, with their bold and beautiful metaphor of the angels as "living instruments."
The chiastic rhythmic organization of these two lines, with the even, regular rhythms
of the second half of l. 5 and the first of l. 6 flanked by more irregular rhythms at the
beginning of l. 5 and the end of l. 6, contributes to the effect. The rhythmic quality of
the sonnet, appropriate to its theme, is enhanced by the phonetically emphatic
character of its A and B rhymes; by the repetition of *corda* in the rhymes of ll. 4, 5,
and 8; by the *isocolon of l. 9, and the repetition of *vera* in l. 4. Note also the allit-
eration of l. 14.

78

Qual digiuno augellin, che vede e ode
batter l'ali a la madre intorno quando
li reca il nudrimento, ond'egli amando
il cibo e quella si rallegra e gode,   4
e dentro al nido suo si strugge e rode
per desio di seguirla anch'ei volando,
e la ringrazia, in tal modo cantando
che par ch'oltra il poter la lingua snode: 8
tal io, qualor il caldo raggio e vivo
del divin Sole onde nudrisco il core
più de l'usato lucido lampeggia,   11
movo la penna, mossa da l'amore
interno, e, senza ch'io stessa m'aveggia
di quel ch'io dico, le Sue lodi scrivo.   14

Like a hungry baby bird who sees and hears his mother beating her wings around him when she brings him sustenance, so he rejoices and exults, loving her and the food she brings, and sits yearning and pining in his nest with the desire to follow her in flight, and thanks her, singing, in such a way that he seems to unknot his tongue far beyond its power; so too I, when the warm, vivid ray of the divine Sun that nurtures my heart shines more dazzlingly than usual, move my pen, moved by the love inside me, and, without being aware of what I am saying, write in his praise.

Sonnet ABBA ABBA CDE DEC. Colonna 1546, 15r. This remarkable sonnet is more Dantean in character than Petrarchan, even though local Petrarchan elements are apparent in *nudrisco il core* (10; cf. Petrarch's no. 1, l. 2), and *snodare*, used of the tongue (8; cf. Petrarch, canzone 125, l. 41). The opening simile, comparing the poet to a baby bird being fed by its mother, is developed with an **enargeia* characteristic of Dante and recalls the image in *Paradiso* 23.1–12 of Beatrice as a mother bird awaiting the dawn so she can feed her young. Also Dantean is the notion of the poet's pen as moving to the dictation of Love (12–13; cf. *Purg.* 24.52–54). Colonna's emphasis on the spontaneous, quasi-instinctual nature of her spiritual lyrics anticipates the notion, fundamental to Counter-Reformation religious poetics, that praise of God was poetry's natural vocation. The poem's frequent **enjambment contributes to this air of spontaneity, while the use of present participles in rhyme (3, 6, and 7) contributes to its dynamism.

79

Vorrei che 'l vero Sol, cui sempre invoco,
mandasse un lampo eterno entro la mente,
e non sì breve raggio che sovente
le va girando intorno a poco a poco,   4
ma riscaldasse il cor col santo foco
che serba dentro in sé viva ed ardente
fiamma, e queste faville tarde e lente
m'ardesser molto in ogni tempo e loco.   8
Lo spirto è ben dal caldo ardor compunto,
e sereno dal bel lume il desio,
ma non ho da me forza a l'alta impresa.   11
Deh! Fa', Signor, con un miracol, ch'io
mi veggia intorno lucida in un punto,
e tutta dentro in ogni parte accesa.   14

I would that the true Sun, on whom I always call, would send a flash
of eternal lightning into my mind and not this slight ray that often
circles feebly around it. I would that he would heat my heart with his
sacred fire, which nurtures within it a live, ardent flame, so these slow
and lame sparks would burn me greatly in every place and time. My
spirit has been pricked by the burning heat and my desire made serene
by his beautiful light, but I have no strength in myself for this great
enterprise. Lord! Make it by a miracle that I see myself in an instant
brilliant with light all around and, within, all aflame in every part.

Sonnet ABBA ABBA CDE DCE. Colonna 1546, 17r. This sonnet expresses a frequent
theme in Colonna, the poet's inability to ascend to the more powerful level of faith
she senses lies just beyond her reach. This effectively takes the place of the peniten-
tial verse practiced by poets like Petrarch who represent themselves as sinners
awaiting conversion. The sonnet plays with the twin metaphors of light and heat,
expressive of spiritual illumination and desire for the divine. The sharp stylistic
shift from the calm, even rhythms and rational, almost prosaic, diction of the first
tercet, to the dramatic visionary language of the second dramatizes precisely the
spiritual leap the poet is calling for here. Also striking is the contrast between the
long, wistful, subjective sentence in the quatrains, expressing the poet's wish for a
spiritual breakthrough, and the urgent imperative of l. 12, reminiscent of the incipit
of Michelangelo's sonnet 274.

80

In forma di musaico un alto muro
d'animate scintille alate e preste,
con catene d'amor sì ben conteste
che l'una porge a l'altra il lume puro,   4
senza ombra che vi formi il chiaro e scuro
ma pur vivo splendor del Sol celeste
che le adorna, incolora, ordina e veste,
d'intorno a Dio col mio pensier figuro;   8
e quella, poi, che in velo uman per gloria
seconda onora il ciel, più presso al vero
lume del figlio ed a la luce prima,   11
la cui beltà non mai vivo pensero
ombrar poteo, non che ritrar memoria
in carte, e men lodarla ingegno in rima.   14

In the form of a mosaic, a high wall of winged swift live sparks of fire, bound together so well with chains of love that each offers its pure light to the others, without any shadow that gives shape through chiaroscuro but only the bright splendor of the heavenly Sun, which adorns, colors, and orders them and clothes them in light—this I figure in my thought, arrayed around God. Then, closest to the true luster of her Son and to the first Light, I see Her whom the heavens honor in human guise as their second glory. No mortal thought can adumbrate her beauty, nor can memory portray it on paper, still less human intellect praise it in verse.

Sonnet ABBA ABBA CDE DCE. Colonna 1546, 19v. Colonna is in Dantean territory again here with this stunning vision of paradise as a living mosaic of blessed souls glittering in the light of God. The imagery presumably reflects her acquaintance with the Paleochristian mosaics of Rome. The surreal quality of the imagery (e.g., "winged sparks") is intended to convey the transcendental character of the reality described. The main verb, *figuro*, is delayed until the end of the octave, allowing the celestial vision to be presented unmediated. The tercets of the poem foreground the figure of the Virgin, presented in a kind of trinity in ll. 9–11 with the Father and Son. In l. 11, a precise theological distinction is encapsulated in the terms *lume* for Christ and *luce* for God: *lux*, in scholastic theology, was properly reserved for the originatory divine source of light, while *lumen* was this light as it was transmitted to the world. In the *ineffability topos of the final tercet, *ritrar*, translated as "portray," also has the sense of "bring back."

81

Se per serbar la notte il vivo ardore
dei carboni da noi la sera accensi
nel legno incenerito arso conviensi
coprirli, sì che non si mostrin fore,   4
quanto più si conviene a tutte l'ore
chiuder in modo d'ogn'intorno i sensi,
che sian ministri a serbar vivi e intensi
i bei spirti divini entro nel core?   8
Se s'apre in questa fredda notte oscura
per noi la porta a l'inimico vento
le scintille del cor dureran poco;   11
ordinar ne convien con sottil cura
il senso, onde non sia de l'alma spento,
per le insidie di fuor, l'interno foco.   14

If to keep the coals we set aflame in the evening alive and smoldering overnight, we must cover them within the burnt and cindered log so they are quite hidden, how much more should we at all hours shelter our senses so they can minister to the fine divine spirits we harbor in our heart, keeping them vivid and alive? If we open the door to the enemy wind in this cold dark night, the sparks of our heart will last little. We must order our senses with the subtlest of care so the wiles of the world do not stifle our soul's inner fire.

Sonnet. ABBA ABBA CDE CDE. Colonna 1546, 23r (*de* in l. 13 amended from *da*). Thematically, this poem is central to Colonna's *rime spirituali*, in that it makes the basis of the poet's mysticism explicit. The bodily senses, seen in many ascetic practices of Christianity in purely negative terms as conduits of sin, are not presented here as something to be repressed. They must rather be preserved from contamination by the outer, mortal world so they can play their true role within the inner realm of the spirit. The results of this spiritual discipline may be seen in mystical sonnets (e.g., nos. 77 and 80) that redeploy the senses of vision and hearing to spiritual ends. The positioning of *vivo ardore* and *interno foco* at the end of the first and last lines of the poem give special emphasis to Colonna's core image of the "inner fire," counterposed here to the phonetically leaden, consonant-heavy *fredda notte oscura* of the mortal world in l. 9.

82

Eterna luna, alor che fra 'l Sol vero
e gli occhi nostri il tuo mortal ponesti,
lui non macchiasti, e specchio a noi porgesti
da mirar fiso nel suo lume altero;   4
non l'adombrasti, ma quel denso e nero
velo del primo error coi santi onesti
tuoi prieghi e i vivi suoi raggi rendesti
d'ombroso e grave, candido e leggiero.   8
Col chiaro che da lui prendi, l'oscuro
de le notti ne togli, e la serena
tua luce il calor suo tempra sovente;   11
ché sopra il mondo errante il latte puro
che qui il nudrì, quasi rugiada, affrena
de la giusta ira sua l'effetto ardente.   14

Eternal moon, when you placed your mortal self between the true Sun and our eyes, you make no blemish on his light but offered us a mirror so we could look straight into his high brightness; you did not dim his light, but with your holy pure prayers and his bright rays, you made limpid and light that dense black veil of man's first error where it had once been heavy and dim. With the brightness you draw from him you remove the darkness from our nights and temper his heat with your serene light, for the pure milk with which you nourished him, falling like dew over the errant world, cools the burning heat of his just wrath.

Sonnet ABBA ABBA CDE CDE. Colonna 1546, 31v. This is the most theologically dense of the sonnets Colonna dedicated to the Virgin. The quatrains describe Mary's role in the Incarnation in a manner that strongly emphasizes her agency: she is the subject of all five verbs, all in the phonetically assertive second person of the past definitive tense (*-asti, -esti*), three of which are in rhyme. In ll. 6–7, her prayers are given equal weighting with God's grace in effecting humanity's redemption from sin. The light imagery of the quatrains in general, and especially the phrase "Lui non macchiasti" (3) are suggestive of the doctrine of Mary's innate freedom from original sin (the Immaculate Conception), which, though not dogma, was widely believed in this period and contributed to her effective deification within Catholic culture. The image of Mary as moon, reflecting God's light, was traditional, as is the less common association of Mary with dew in the final tercet.

83

Vergine pura, che dai raggi ardenti
del vero Sol ti godi eterno giorno,
il cui bel lume in questo vil soggiorno
tenne i begli occhi tuoi paghi e contenti,   4
uomo il vedesti e Dio quando i lucenti
suoi spirti fer l'albergo umile adorno
di chiari lumi e timidi d'intorno
i tuoi ministri al grand'ufficio intenti.   8
Immortal Dio nascosto in mortal velo
l'adorasti Signor, figlio il nudristi,
l'amasti sposo, e l'onorasti padre;   11
prega Lui dunque che i miei giorni tristi
ritorni in lieti, e tu, donna del cielo,
vogli in questo desio mostrarti madre.   14

Pure Virgin, you who enjoy eternal day from the burning rays of the
true Sun, whose beautiful light kept your eyes happy and content in the
base sojourn of this earthly life: you saw him man and God when his
shining spirits adorned the humble stable with bright beams while,
timidly all around, your attendants went about their great task. Immortal
God hidden in a mortal veil: you adored him as your Lord, nurtured
him as your son, loved him as your spouse, honored him as your father.
Entreat of him, then, that my sad days be turned to happy, and, Lady of
Heaven, in this desire pray show yourself a mother.

Sonnet ABBA ABBA CDE DCE. Colonna 1546, 29r. The most anthologized of Colon-
na's Marian sonnets, "Vergine pura" was also set to music by Philippe de Monte and
Pietro Vinci. The poem's *incipit invites comparison with the opening of the last
canto of Dante's Paradiso and the final poem of Petrarch's RVF. The quatrains juxta-
pose the Virgin's heavenly contemplation of God with her maternal enjoyment of
Christ through a calibration of light effects, from the brilliant day of ll. 1–2 to the
mysterious light-in-darkness of 5–7. Lines 9–11 describe Mary's relationship with her
son-father-spouse in a manner reminiscent both of Colonna's models (Par. 33.1; RVF
366, ll. 28, 47) and also of her own no. 7 (49–51). Stylistic features to note include the
juxtaposed inclusive rhyme of ll. 2–3 and the *zeugma of 5–8. The "shining spirits"
of l. 6 are the angels present at Christ's birth, the mysterious "attendants" of l. 8
perhaps the shepherds (Toscano 2000, 76).

84

Donna accesa animosa, e da l'errante
vulgo lontana, in soletario albergo
parmi lieta veder, lasciando a tergo
quanto non piace al vero eterno amante,   4
e, fermato il desio, fermar le piante
sovra un gran monte; ond'io mi specchio e tergo
nel bello exempio, e l'alma drizzo ed ergo
dietro l'orme beate e l'opre sante.   8
L'alta spelonca sua questo alto scoglio
mi rassembra, e 'l gran sol il suo gran foco
ch'ogni animo gentil anco riscalda.   11
In tal pensier da vil nodo mi scioglio,
pregando lei con voce ardita e balda
m'impetri dal Signor appo sé loco.   14

Dauntless ardent lady, remote from the errant masses, I see you happily going to your solitary abode, leaving far behind you all that does not please your true eternal Lover, until, on a great mountain, where your desire at last fixes, there you fix your feet. I mirror myself and polish myself in your lovely example, turning my soul after your blessed footsteps and lifting it to your holy deeds. Her lofty cave I compare to this high rock, and this great sun to that great fire of hers that still warms every noble soul. In such thoughts, I escape the base knots that entangle me, and I pray to her with a bold, fearless voice that she seek me a place beside her at the side of the Lord.

Sonnet ABBA ABBA CDE CED. Colonna 1546, 34r. In a letter to Costanza d'Avalos, published in 1545, Colonna speaks of Mary Magdalene and Catherine of Alexandria as the great religious role models for women, besides the Virgin (Brundin 2001, 79–80). Here, the poet speaks of Magdalene as her "mirror," and the similarity between them is underlined by references to their energy and boldness (*animosa*, l. 1; *voce ardita e balda*, l. 13). The phrase "mi specchio e tergo" derives from Petrarch's sonnet 146, where it similarly falls in the sixth line. Colonna gives the phrase salience through an equivocal rhyme with *tergo* in the sense of "back" (3). The references to the poet's physical context in the first tercet ("high rock," "great sun") locate the composition in Ischia (cf. no. 43). The "great mountain" of l. 6 is Saint-Baume, in Provence, where medieval legend told that Mary Magdalene spent her last years as a cave-dwelling hermit. For a discussion of the sonnet in conjunction with Titian's *Pitti Magdalene*, painted for Colonna, see Debby 2003.

Veronica Gambara (c. 1538–40)

85

O gran misterio e sol per fede inteso!
Fatto è 'l bel corpo tuo tempio di Dio,
Vergine santa, e 'n quello, umile e pio,
è per propria virtù dal ciel disceso.   4
Fu de l'umiltà tua sì forte acceso
e tanto di salvarne ebbe desio,
ch'in te si chiuse, e di te fuor uscìo
non tocco il virginal chiostro od offeso.   8
Creossi in te, come nel bianco vello
la celeste rugiada, arida essendo
la terra, ed egli sol d'acqua ripieno.   11
Questo l'effetto fu, fu il segno quello,
però teco cantiamo oggi dicendo:
—Gloria al Signor non mai lodato appieno—.   14

Oh great mystery, only to be understood through faith! Holy Virgin,
your lovely body has become God's temple, and He has descended into
it, humble and pious, through his own power. He was so fired with love
for your humility, so desirous of saving us, that he sealed himself within
you and then ushered forth, without touching or harming your virginal
cloister. There grew in you, as on the white fleece, the heavenly dew,
while the land was arid and he alone filled with water. This was the
effect; that, the sign; hence we sing today along with you, saying "Glory
to the Lord, exceeding all praise!"

Sonnet ABBA ABBA CDE CDE. Atanagi 1565, 195r. This is one of two sonnets medi-
tating on the Incarnation that Gambara sent to Pietro Bembo in 1538–40 (Gambara
1995, 155); the second follows (no. 86). In this sonnet, Gambara focuses on the Vir-
gin, emphasizing the humility and faith that led her to be chosen as an instrument
of salvation. Lines 7–8 stress not only her miraculous virginity but also her exemp-
tion from the pains of childbirth, which were inflicted on Eve (Genesis 3:16) as a
punishment for her sin: an oblique reference to the doctrine of the Immaculate
Conception, which held that Mary, alone of all humanity, was without the stain of
original sin. The beautiful imagery of the first tercet derives from Judges 6:36–37,
where Gideon lays a fleece on the ground and it is covered with dew, while the rest
of the land remains bare. The reading of the bedewed fleece as a *type for Mary was
traditional. The final tercet, speaking of the faithful singing "with" Mary, may be
an allusion to Mary's canticle, the *Magnificat* (Luke 1:46–55).

86

Oggi per mezzo tuo, Vergine pura,
si mostra in terra sì mirabil cosa
che piena di stupor resta pensosa,
mirando l'opra, e cede la Natura.   4
Fatto uomo è Dio e, sotto umana cura,
vestito di mortal carne noiosa,
restò qual era, e la divina ascosa
sua essenza tenne in pueril figura.   8
Misto non fu, né fu diviso mai,
ma sempre Dio e sempre uomo verace,
quanto possente in ciel tanto nel mondo.   11
Volgi dunque ver me, Vergine, i rai
de la tua grazia, e 'l senso mio capace
fa' di questo misterio alto e profondo.   14

Today, by means of you, pure Virgin, such a miraculous thing is seen here on earth that Nature is left pensive, marveling at this work, and gives herself up for defeated. God is made human, and under human care, clothed in our wearisome mortal dress, he remained what he was, retaining his divine hidden essence in the guise of a child. Not mixed was he ever, nor divided, but always God and a true man, as powerful in heaven as on earth. Turn, then, Virgin, the rays of your grace on me, and make my mortal mind apt to grasp this mystery, so high and profound.

Sonnet ABBA ABBA CDE CDE. Atanagi 1565, 195r (*e* in l. 5 amended to *è* on the basis of Gambara 1995). Gambara's second sonnet on the Incarnation seems to have been written for a particular feast, to judge from the opening: perhaps the Annunciation (25 April), or Christmas, given the reference to Christ as a child in l. 8. The poem is impressive for the lucidity with which it condenses the theological mystery of Christ's dual nature, divine and human, established at the Council of Nicaea (325 CE). Especially striking is the *enjambment at ll. 7–8, which dramatizes the "hiddenness" of God's essence by delaying the noun. The appearances of the Virgin at the opening and close of the sonnet pair her role as physical conduit of the incarnation with a parallel role of intellectual and spiritual mediation between God and humanity. The initial address to Mary as *Vergine pura* may be an echo of Colonna's sonnet (no. 83), with which this poem has thematic analogies.

Isabella Morra (pre-1546)
87

[1] Signor, che insino a qui (tua gran mercede),
con questa vista mia caduca e frale
spregiar m'hai fatto ogni beltà mortale,
fammi di tanto ben per grazia erede
che sempre ami te sol con pura fede   5
e spregie per innanzi ogni altro oggetto,
con sì verace affetto,
ch'ogniun m'additi per tua fida amante
in questo mondo errante,
ch'altro non è senza il tuo amor celeste   10
ch'un procelloso mar pien di tempeste.

[2] Signor, che di tua man fattura sei,
ov'ogni ingegno s'affatica in vano:
ritrarre in versi il tuo bel volto umano
or sol per disfogare i desir miei,   15
ad altri no, ma a me sola vorrei;
ed iscolpirmi il tuo celeste velo,
qual fu quando dal Cielo
scendesti ad abitar la bassa terra
ed a tor l'uom di guerra.   20
Questa grazia, Signor, mi sia concessa
ch'io mostri co 'l mio stil te a me stessa.

[3] Signor, nel piano spazio di tua fronte
la bellezza del Ciel tutta scolpita
si scorge, e con giustizia insieme unita   25
de l'alta tua pietade il vivo fonte,
e le pie voglie a perdonarci pronte.
Ombre de i lumi venerandi e sacri,
di Dio bei simulacra;
ciglia, del cor fenestre, onde si mostra   30
l'alma salute nostra;
occhi che date al sol la vera luce,
che per voi soli a noi chiara riluce.

[4] Signor, co' gli occhi tuoi pien di salute
consoli i buoni ed ammonisci i rei   35
a darsi in colpa di lor falli rei;
in lor s'impara che cosa è virtute.

O mia e tutte l'altre lingue mute,
perché non dite ancor de' suoi capelli,
tanto del sol più belli   40
quanto è più bello e chiaro egli del sole?
O chiome uniche e sole,
che, vibrando dal capo insino al collo,
di nuova luce se ne adorna Apollo.

[5] Signor, da questa tua divina bocca   45
di perle e di rubini, escon di fore
dolci parole, ch'ogni afflitto core
sgombran di duolo e sol piacer vi fiocca
e di letizia eterna ogniun trabocca.
Guancie di fior celesti adorne e piane   50
a le speranze umane;
corpo in cui si rinchiuse il Cielo e Dio,
a te consacro il mio:
la mente mia qual fu la tua statura
con gli occhi interni già scorge e misura.   55

[6] Signor, le mani tue non dirò belle
per non scemar co 'l nome lor beltade,
mani, che molto innanzi ad ogni etade
ci fabricar la luna, il sol, le stelle:
se queste chiare son, quai saran elle?   60
Felice terra, in cui le sacre piante
stampar tante orme sante.
A la vaghezza del tuo bianco piede
il Ciel s'inchina e cede.
Felice lei, che con l'aurate chiome   65
le cinse e si scarcò de l'aspre some.

[7] Canzon, quanto sei folle,
poiché nel mar de la beltà di Dio
con sì caldo desio
credesti entrare. Or ch'hai 'l camin smarrito,   70
restati fuor, ché non ne vedi il lito.

[1] Lord, who, until now, through your great mercy, have made me
despise all human beauty with this frail, mortal sight of mine, make
me through your grace heir to such bounty that I may always love you
with pure faith and despise henceforth all other objects, with such true
passion that all will point to me as your true lover in this errant world,

which is nothing more without your heavenly love than a stormy, wind-tossed sea.

[2] Lord, you who are the creation of your own hands, solely as an outlet for my desires, and for myself only, not for others, I would portray in verse your lovely human face, a task that defies any mortal mind. I would sculpt your heavenly veil as it was when from heaven you descended to live on this base earth, to rescue man from war. Lord, concede me this grace, that I may show you to myself with my pen.

[3] Lord, on the plain of your brow, all the beauty of heaven may be seen sculpted, united with justice and the living fountain of your mercy and your merciful wishes quick to pardon us. Lashes, shadowing those venerable, sacred lights, beautiful images of God, windows of the heart, where our happy salvation shows itself: eyes that endow the sun with its true light, so that only through you does it shine for us so brightly.

[4] Lord, with your eyes full of salvation, you console the good and admonish the wicked to repent of their wicked errors; from your eyes we learn what virtue is. O my tongue, mute like all others before this sight, why do you not also speak of his hair, as much more beautiful than the sun as He is himself lovelier and brighter than the sun? O matchless, peerless locks, which, tumbling from head to neck adorn Apollo himself with new light.

[5] Lord, from this divine mouth of yours, of rubies and pearls, sweet words issue that ease the pain of every afflicted heart so that pleasure alone rains into us and we overflow with eternal joy. Cheeks adorned with celestial flowers, smooth to human hopes, body in which God and heaven enclosed themselves, I consecrate mine to you, while with the inner eyes of my mind I intuit and measure how tall you stood.

[6] Lord, your hands I shall not call beautiful, as the term cannot do justice to their beauty, hands that long before any age built for us the moon, the sun, the stars. If *they* are bright, then what must be those be? Happy ground on which your sacred footsteps marked so many holy prints. Before the loveliness of your white foot heaven itself bows and yields. Happy that woman who with her golden locks embraced those feet and threw off her heavy burden.

[7] Song, you are quite mad to think you could embark with such warm desire on the great sea of God's beauty. Now you have lost your way, remain on the high sea, for the shore is no longer in sight.

Canzone ABBAACcDdEE—cDdEE. Dolce 1556, 235–38. This canzone of Morra's reg-
enders and converts to a religious use the *topos of the *blazon*: a segmentalized de-
scription of the beauties of a woman, usually, as here, descending from the head to
the feet. The model of beauty used here for the poet's imagining of Christ is that of
the Petrarchan lady, with her golden hair and "rubies and pearls" mouth. The philo-
sophical premise of the poem is the Neoplatonic one that the beauty of a human
body is an irradiation of the immaterial, divine beauty of the soul that informs it
and, hence, of that soul's creator, God. Logically, then, Christ, as the creator him-
self, embodied, must represent the epitome of human physical beauty. Morra com-
bines physical description with evocations of God's power and goodness to attempt
to master the incarnational paradox of a figure who is together God and man
(cf. no. 86).

Apollo, in stanza 4, was the Roman sun god and here signifies the physical sun,
as opposed to the spiritual sun of Christ. Christ was frequently associated with
Apollo in Neoplatonically inflected Christian texts, and Apollo's conventional por-
trayal as a handsome, golden-haired youth influenced some Renaissance artistic
representations of Christ (notably Michelangelo's in the Sistine Chapel *Last Judg-
ment*). Morra's allusion here may have been intended to help the reader envisage her
distinctly Apollonian Christ. The "woman" of stanza 6 is Mary Magdalene, identi-
fied in later Christian culture with the unnamed female sinner in the gospel of
Luke 7:37–50, who washes Christ's feet and dries them with her hair (cf. nos. 106,
120). Her "heavy burden" is that of her sins, which Christ announces are forgiven to
her "because she loved much."

The rhyme scheme of this canzone, shared with another canzone by Morra, is
unusual for the number of juxtaposed rhymes it uses (all lines except the first are
rhymed with the following or previous line). Proximity of rhyme words was seen
as a feature of a "charming" (*piacevole*) style rather than a "weighty" (*grave*) one.
The prominence of rhyme in the canzone is enhanced by the quite frequent use of
equivocal rhymes (*rei/rei* in ll. 35–36; *sole/sole* in 41–42) and inclusive rhymes (*luce/
riluce* in ll. 32–33; *bocca/trabocca* in 45–49). The use of the same word, *Signor*, at the
beginning of each stanza, recalls Petrarch's canzone 366, which uses *Vergine* in the
same manner. The effect, in both cases, is to give the canzone a prayerlike rhythm.

A substantially different, shorter, five-stanza version of this canzone was pub-
lished in 1552. Variants include "la tua *sola* amante" ("your only lover," in place of
"your faithful lover") in l. 8 and "*scendendo* dal capo insino al collo" (falling from head
to neck) in l. 32 (43 in the 1556 edition). The version in the 1556 edition substitutes the
more vivid *vibrando* (literally "wielding," as of a weapon), used by Petrarch in son-
net 198, where the breeze is said to "wield" Laura's hair. Morra, anomalously, uses
the verb intransitively. Line 51 of the 1552 version directly quotes a line from Pe-
trarch's visionary description of Laura's beauty in canzone 126, (l. 10, "aer sacro
sereno"), reinforcing the association of Laura with Christ.

Gaspara Stampa (1554)
88

Mesta e pentita de' miei gravi errori
e del mio vaneggiar tanto e sì lieve,
e d'aver speso questo tempo breve
de la vita fugace in vani amori,   4
a te, Signor, ch'intenerisci i cori,
e rendi calda la gelata neve,
e fai soave ogn'aspro peso e greve
a chiunque accendi di tuoi santi ardori,   8
ricorro, e prego che mi porghi mano
a trarmi fuor del pelago, onde uscire,
s'io tentassi da me, sarebbe vano.   11
Tu volesti per noi, Signor, morire,
tu ricomprasti tutto il seme umano;
dolce Signor, non mi lasciar perire!   14

Sorrowing and repentant for my grave errors, and my long, foolish raving, and for spending this brief time of our fleeting life in vain loves, to you, Lord, you who soften hearts and warm cold snow and make the heaviest burden easy to whomever you set aflame with your holy ardors—to you I turn and pray you to reach out your hand and draw me from this cruel sea, for if I were to try through my own efforts, it would be in vain. Lord, you chose to die for us; you redeemed the whole human race. Dear Lord, do not let me perish!

Sonnet ABBA ABBA CDC DCD. Stampa 1554, 148. Stampa's *Rime* includes a short sequence of religious sonnets, all penitential in theme. In this fine example, the term *vaneggiar* (2) recalls Petrarch's first sonnet, whose penitential character Stampa had ignored in her direct imitation (no. 13), while the image of God lightening the burden of his followers (7) recalls Matthew 11:30 ("my burden is light"). Stampa makes effective use here of devices of repetition, especially *anaphora and *polysyndeton, using the anaphora of ll. 12–13 to set off by contrast the dramatic and moving last line. An unusual feature of the sonnet is its breach of the division between octave and sestet with the long delayed main verb *rincorro*. Lines 1–11 are composed of a single sentence, highly structured in the quatrains and more fluid in the first tercet, giving climactic emphasis to the *end-stopped lines of the final tercet, where the metaphorical language of ll. 6–10 (snow, burden, fire, sea) gives way to a starker and simpler style.

Costanza d'Avalos (before 1558)
89 ⟶

Se 'l vero Sol coverto d'uman velo
volse patir tormenti e crudel morte
sol per aprir le già serrate porte
che vietavano a noi l'entrare al cielo,   4
perché son'io con vivo e mortal zelo
sì pronta a desïar per vie distorte
di prolungar la vita in duol sì forte,
che, se di fuor appar, più dentro il celo?   8
Ora che 'l divin foco accende il core,
intepedisca e mora ogni altra voglia,
e la sua fiamma purghi il vano errore,   11
e mi dimostri che con pianto e doglia
si corre al ciel, s'acquista il vivo Amore,
vinto il mondo, il nimico, e la sua spoglia.   14

If the true Sun, clothed in human veil, was willing to suffer torture and cruel death in order to open the closed doors that once barred us from heaven, then why am I, with such a lively and deathly urge, so eager to seek to prolong my days by twisted paths when I suffer misery so acute that, even if it appears without, I hide far more within? Now the divine fire has set my heart alight, may all other desires grow tepid and die, and its flame purge my vain error and show me that through tears and pain we race to heaven and win the life-giving Love, conquering the world and the enemy and his spoil.

Sonnet ABBA ABBA CDC DCD. Colonna 1558, n.p. (appended). Costanza d'Avalos was Vittoria Colonna's cousin by marriage and shared her reformist religious sympathies. In this sonnet, one of very few that survive by her, the poet, in a state of misery perhaps following a bereavement (7–8), reproaches herself for her stubborn attachment to life, which she contrasts with Christ's willingness to embrace death (1–4). The survival urge (lit. "zeal") of l. 5 is "lively" in the sense of "keen," and "deathly" in the sense that it leads to spiritual ruin: a piece of *oxymoronic wordplay that, along with the quasi-homonymous rhyme *cielo/celo*, lends an air of quiet artifice to the quatrains. The tercets are strong, with the dramatic *enjambment of ll. 12–13, which juxtaposes earthly misery and spiritual escape, contrasting with the *end-stopped ll. 9–11. The "enemy" of l. 14 is the devil; his "spoil," probably the mortal body, left behind in the race to heaven (*spoglia* can also mean "husk" or "remains").

Girolama Castellani (1559)

90

Pargolette, beate, alme innocenti,
che fuor del nostro tenebroso orrore
or vi godete il sempiterno onore
quasi stelle nel ciel chiare e lucenti,   4
per quei, ch'oggi di morte aspri tormenti
sentiste, quando al crudo empio signore
col sangue l'ira acquetaste, e il furore,
uccise in braccio a le madri dolenti,   8
di me, che vie più fero ed orgoglioso
tiranno opprime, e con più lunga guerra
afflige ognor, vi stringa il cor pietade,   11
pregando l'infinita alta bontade
ch'anch'io lasci il mio fral sciolta da terra
e venga a goder vosco il mio riposo.   14

Blessed little innocent souls, who, far from this shadowy darkness, now rejoice in eternal honor like bright shining stars in heaven, for the sake of that bitter death torment you underwent today, when the cruel, evil lord slaked his fury and ire with your blood as you were slain in the arms of your grieving mothers, let your hearts be moved with pity for me, oppressed as I am by a far more savage and proud tyrant who assaults me with a longer war. Pray for me to the infinite high goodness that I too may leave behind my husk and, freed from earth, come and enjoy my repose with you.

Sonnet ABBA ABBA CDE EDC. Domenichi 1559, 61. The Bolognese Dominican Girolama Castellani was the first Italian nun to see her verse published under her name in her lifetime and the first nun who is documented using a modern, Petrarchist style. Here, she commemorates the infants massacred by Herod in Bethlehem shortly after Christ's birth (Matthew 2:13–23) on their feast day (December 28), concluding with a prayer to their souls to intercede for her with God in her struggle against the devil, the "tyrant" of ll. 9–10. The subjective, penitential aspect of the sonnet distinguishes it from Vittoria Colonna's poem on these same infant martyrs (S1:25), though Castellani's incipit may echo the *pargoletti amori* ("little cherubs") of Colonna's l. 13. Castellani's sonnet is constructed of a single sentence, flowing across the octave-sestet break, which nevertheless marks a thematic transition. In its fluidity, it offers a good example of Colonna's ideal of the "prosaic" sonnet (see commentary to no. 76).

Olimpia Malipiero (1559)
91

Oggi 'l celeste pelicano il petto
sacro s'aperse, e diè co 'l sangue vita
a' figli, e oggi la bontà infinita
ci diè 'l gran saggio del suo amor perfetto;   4
oggi nuova fenice arse d'affetto
amoroso nel legno; oggi sbandita
fu morte, ed oggi la grazia smarrita
trovò mercede nel divin cospetto.   8
Vero oggi cigno si mostrò col canto
dolce ed estremo, ch'a pietà commosse
il ciel, la terra, gli elementi, e 'l mondo;   11
oggi è quel serpe celebrato tanto,
ch'in lui mirando del nemico scosse
fûr l'empie forze, ed ei tratto al profondo.   14

Today the heavenly pelican opened his sacred breast, nurturing his offspring with his blood. Today the infinite goodness gave us the great evidence of his perfect love. Today the great phoenix burned with amorous passion on his tree; today death was banished, and grace, long lost to us, found favor in the sight of the divine. Today he showed himself a true swan, with his sweet, final song, which moved to pity the heavens, the earth, the elements and the world. Today did that holy serpent triumph, for, when the Enemy gazed on him, his forces were smashed and he was drawn to the depths.

Sonnet ABBA ABBA CDE CDE. Domenichi 1559, 141. Meditations on Good Friday, the day of Christ's death, were an established subgenre of religious lyric (see also no. 105). While many such poems focused on Christ's suffering, Malipiero's sees the Passion through the lens of the Resurrection, celebrating it as the moment of humanity's redemption. The sonnet's most notable feature is its animal imagery, mainly traditional, but made striking by juxtaposition. The pelican, in medieval bestiaries, was said to revive its dead chicks with its blood, making it an apt symbol for Christ, while swans, generally mute, were said to sing sweetly just before they died. The serpent symbolized Christ through association with an Old Testament *type, Moses's bronze serpent in Numbers 21:9. For the phoenix, see no. 48. The poem is unified by the insistent repetition of *oggi*, varied from its usual initial position in l. 9, where it follows *vero*, with *concorso di vocali*. The "Enemy" of l. 13 is Satan, defeated in his plan to destroy mankind.

Laura Battiferri (1560–89)

92

Servo fedel, che in alta croce affisso
oggi simìle al tuo signor per morte
salisti al ciel, fra le bell'alme accorte,
in Dio con dolci e maggior chiodi fisso;   4
a te del cielo, a me di questo abisso
furo aperte in tal giorno ambe le porte;
tu lassù vivi, io quaggiù in doppia morte
un'anno men del sesto lustro ho visso,   8
né so ancor s'io son giunta al mezzo, o s'io
son presso al fin di mia giornata, ed anco,
che più mi duol, s'entrarò in porto mai.   11
Almo Andrea, priega umil dunque oggi Dio,
che 'n tal tempesta, e 'n sì continui guai,
sia l'alma pronta, quanto il corpo è stanco.   14

Faithful servant, who, on this day, affixed to a high cross like your Lord,
rose to heaven through death to live among those lovely, wise souls,
fixed in God with sweet and greater nails; to you the gates of heaven, to
me those of this abyss were opened on this same day. You live on high
while I, below, in double death, have lived one year less than my third
decade. I cannot know whether I have yet reached the middle of my
day or whether I am close to its end; nor yet, which grieves me more,
whether I shall ever enter in port. Bountiful Andrew, humbly pray God
for me today that in this tempest and these endless travails, my soul be
as ready as my body is weary.

Sonnet ABBA ABBA CDE CED. Battiferri 1560, 44 (*apperte* in l. 6 corrected to *aperte*).
One of several poems by Battiferri presented as written on her birthday, November
30 (cf. no. 198), this sonnet addresses Christ's disciple, St. Andrew, whose feast falls
on that day. Battiferri takes the date as marking the day of Andrew's martyrdom by
crucifixion. The sonnet plays on the Christian paradox that true life lies in Heaven,
while life on earth is a form of death (indeed, a "double death" [7], in that the body
is subject to mortality and the soul to the spiritual death of sin). A secondary mean-
ing of *giornata* (day; l. 10) is "a day of battle" or, by extension "a battle," and Battiferri
may have intended this as a metaphor for life, along with the tempestuous sea voy-
age implied by *porto* (11) and *tempesta* (13) (the "port" signifies salvation). The inclu-
sive rhyme *affisso/fisso* underlines the bold *conceit of Andrew's "sweet nailing" to
God in Heaven. The last line echoes that of Petrarch's sonnet 208.

93

Verace Apollo, a cui ben vero amore
impiagò 'l fianco di pietoso strale;
ed a prender fra noi forma mortale
già ti constrinse non mortale ardore: 4
ecco colei, lo cui gelato core
de l'onesto arder tuo non calse, o cale,
l'errante Dafne, ch'ognor fugge, quale
notturno augello, il tuo divin splendore. 8
Eccol'al fine in duro tronco volta
e tu pur l'ami e segui e cerchi ornare
tuo santo crin di sua negletta fronde. 11
O grand'amore, o pietà rara e molta,
chi si fugge seguir, chi t'odia amare:
amar chi tante frodi in sé nasconde. 14

True Apollo, you whose flank was pierced by the merciful arrow of truest love and who were constrained by an ardor more than mortal to take on mortal form here on earth: here is she whose icy heart was not touched by your honest burning, and remains untouched by it—that errant Daphne, who still flees your divine splendor like some bird of the night. Here she is now, at last transformed into an unfeeling trunk, and yet you still love her and pursue her and seek to adorn your sacred locks with her heedless leaves. O greatest of loves! O rare and vast mercy, to seek her who flees you, to love her who hates you, to love a creature who harbors such deceptions within.

Sonnet ABBA ABBA CDE CDE. Battiferri 1564, f3v. This tour de force penitential sonnet transforms for religious ends the core myth of Petrarch's love lyrics, that of the love of Apollo, god of poetry, for the nymph Daphne ("laurel" in Greek). In the myth, Daphne flees Apollo and is transformed into a laurel tree to preserve her virginity. The evergreen laurel hence becomes sacred to the god and symbolizes poetic immortality. Here the poet, herself named Laura like Petrarch's beloved, becomes Daphne, while Apollo is Christ, a frequent identification (see notes on no. 87). The myth thus comes to express Christ's love for the sinful human soul, with Daphne's arborification symbolizing the sinner's spiritual "hardening." Besides Petrarch, there is an echo of Colonna in the *Ecco colei . . .* construction (5–6; cf. S1:8, ll. 13–14), while the repetition of *calse/cale* (6) echoes Bembo's canzone 142, l. 181. Note also the further repetitions and wordplay in l. 1 (*verace/vero*); ll. 3–4 (*mortale/mortale*); and ll. 13–14 (*amare/amar*).

94

Come padre pietoso, che l'amato
figlio vagando or d'uno in altro errore
gir vede pur del cammin dritto fuore
ch'ei lungo tempo già gl'abbia segnato,   4
ch'or con volto benigno, or con turbato,
or lo minaccia, or prega a tutte l'ore,
per ritornarlo al più vero e migliore
sentier nel primo suo felice stato,   8
così tu vero, e piu d'ogn'altro pio
supremo Padre, me tua figlia errante,
ch'a tua viva sembianza in ciel creasti,   11
perché quest'alma torni ond'ella uscìo,
con dolci e amarissimi contrasti
tenti ridurla a le tue leggi sante.   14

Like a kind father who sees his beloved son straying from one sin to
another, far from the path of righteousness he has long taught him and
who, with a face now loving, now wrathful, threatens and pleads with
him, trying to return him to the truer and better path and restore him
to his happier state—in just the same manner, true and more than any
other merciful supreme Father, seeing your daughter, created in heaven
in your living image, so errant, in order that this soul may return
whence it came, with sweet and most bitter scolding, you seek to lead
me back to your holy laws.

Sonnet ABBA ABBA CDE CED. Battiferri 1564, f4r. Battiferri's technical mastery of
the sonnet form is well displayed in this supremely controlled sonnet, consisting
of a sole sentence developing an extended analogy in the style of an *epic simile
(cf. no. 78). Variety is attained through modulations of pace and sound, with the
fluid, *enjambment-rich first quatrain followed by the choppier, patterned ll. 5–6,
whose *anaphoric repetition of or is underlined by the repetition of the same sound
in ore, while the tercets build phonetically to a climax of "gravity" in the striking l.
13 before falling off gently at the end. One effective device lost in the translation is
the highly compressed *chiastic juxtaposition of supreme Father and errant daugh-
ter in l. 10 (the first person pronoun has been transferred in translation to l. 14,
where the original has "soul" as the object). Cammin dritto at l. 3 recalls the diritta
via of the opening of Dante's Inferno (Inf. 1.3).

95

Questo foco sì ardente e questa fiamma
ch'esce del petto tuo, dolce Signore,
avvampa così il mio d'acceso ardore
ch'ognor via più m'infoca e più m'infiamma;   4
e questo ferro, che la destra mamma
tua aperse tutta ed indi passò al core,
trapassa tanto il mio dentro e di fuore
che per dolcezza manco a dramma a dramma;   8
m'impiagan tutta queste piaghe sante,
questa corona mi trafigge e punge,
e teco ogn'or m'inchiodan questi chiodi.   11
Possente Amor, ch'al sempiterno Amante
l'anime lega con sì stretti nodi,
e mai per tempo alcun non le disgiunge!   14

This burning fire and this flame that issues from your breast, dear Lord,
sets mine alight with such blazing ardor that it ignites and inflames me
ever more fiercely, and this spear, which tore open your right breast
and went through to your heart, pierces mine through and through,
making me swoon, dram by dram, by its sweetness. Your holy wounds
wound me wholly; this crown pierces and stabs me; these nails nail me
as they do you. Such potent love, that can bind the soul to the eternal
Lover with such tight bonds and never for the whole of time release it!

Sonnet ABBA ABBA CDE CED. Rome, Biblioteca Casanatense MS 3229, 48v. Intense imaginative reliving of Christ's passion was a fundamental spiritual practice in this period, formalized in such works as Ignatius Loyola's *Spiritual Exercises*. This sonnet expresses the ideal of identification with Christ's suffering so absolute as to enable the worshipper physically to share quasi-stigmatically in his agony. The erotic and masochistic character of Battiferri's language is striking here, with the image of the poet pierced and swooning with sweetness at ll. 7–8 recalling Bernini's *St. Theresa in Ecstasy* (although the gendering of the poem's erotics is complicated by the fact that the poet's "perforability" is modelled on Christ's). Notable stylistically is Battiferri's insistent use of devices of repetition, such as the inclusive rhyme *fiamma/infiamma* (1, 4) and the *polyptota of *impiagan/piaghe* (9); *inchiodan/chiodi* (11); *Amor/Amante* (12). For the *dramma/fiamma/infiamma* rhyme, see the commentary to Colonna's no. 160.

96

—Nella mia amata e tanto eletta
vigna, ch'io già piantai con tanto amore,
e poi co'l sangue mio, co 'l mio sudore
rigai, ingrassai, rendei sì pura e netta,   4
ite, o cari operai, ch'a voi s'aspetta
farla ampia sì che dove nasce e more
il sol, spanda i suoi rami e 'l frutto e 'l fiore,
e torni al secol rio l'età perfetta.   8
Né temete per le fatiche e stenti,
né tormento, né morte aspra e acerba,
della mia Compagnia guerrieri invitti: 11
tant'alto è 'l premio alfin che vi si serba,
qui dove sete eternamente ascritti,
ché sol render vi può paghi e contenti—.   14

"Into my beloved and ardently chosen vineyard, which I once planted with such burning love and then watered, nurtured, and rendered so clean and so pure with my own sweat and blood, go, my dear workers, for the task lies before you to extend it so wide that it spreads its branches and fruits and flowers even unto where the sun rises and where it goes to rest, so the perfect age may return to these depraved times. Fearless warriors of my Company, do not fear on account of the pains and labors that await you, nor the torments, nor the risk of a harsh, early death: so high is the prize that awaits you here above, where your names are eternally written. This alone can makes you happy and content."

Sonnet ABBA ABBA CDE DEC. Rome, Biblioteca Casanatense MS 3229, 52v. The Jesuits were one of the most representative clerical orders of Counter-Reformation Europe, active in education and evangelism. Battiferri was close to the order, leaving the Jesuits a legacy in her will. Here, in a sustained exercise in *prosopopoeia, Battiferri has Christ speak to his "dear workers," urging them to continue their missionary work in the face of danger and suffering (martyrdom, alluded to in l. 10, was a very literal threat). Syntactically fluid and marked by *enjambment, especially in the quatrains (1–2, 5–7), the poem draws on the biblical image of the Lord's vineyard in Isaiah 5 and John 15:1–9, perhaps echoing Colonna's S1:12. The "perfect age" of l. 8 refers to the classical Arcadian myth of a primeval "golden age" of innocence. Citing this myth through Christ's mouth, Battiferri elegantly harmonizes the humanistic and Christian influences in her verse. The last words of the poem, *paghi e contenti*, echo Colonna's no. 83, l. 4.

97

Quel che la terra feo di nulla e 'l cielo,
e poi dal ciel per noi discese in terra,
la bassa terra unendo all'alto cielo,
con gran stupor del cielo e della terra;   4
per portar questa terra insino al cielo
e gl'onori del ciel dare alla terra,
morto e sepolto in terra, al fine in cielo
salendo aperse il cielo a questa terra.   8
Gl'indegni della terra e più del cielo,
Tu, gran Signor del cielo e della terra,
tolti da terra avar riporti in cielo.   11
Stupisci meco, ciel; stupisci, terra,
poiché vedi la terra ir sopra 'l cielo,
e per me, terra, il ciel porto sotterra.   14

He who made earth and heaven from nothing and then descended from
heaven to earth for us, uniting the lowly earth to the high heaven, to
the wonderment of both heaven and earth, to carry this earth up to
heaven and give heaven's honors to earth, having died and been buried
on earth, he rose to heaven and opened up heaven to this earth. Great
Lord of heaven and earth, you take us poor sinners, unworthy of earth
and still less of heaven, and raising us from the miserly earth, carry us
back to heaven. Marvel, heaven, alongside me; and you, earth, marvel
also; for you see earth ascending above heaven, while, I, vile earth, drag
heaven down beneath the earth.

Sonetto continuo ABAB ABAB ABA BAB. Rome, Biblioteca Casanatense MS 3229,
59v–60r. Battiferri's late spiritual verse includes two examples of the unusual form
of sonnet known as a *sonetto continuo*. This one is particularly virtuosistic, as the
two repeated rhyme words, *cielo* and *terra*, occur twice in each line, one in rhyme,
the other internally. This was a variant introduced by the Neapolitan poet Ferrante
Carafa (1509–87), in two sonnets using *Cristo* and *Maria* as its rhymes (Carafa 1573,
116v, 119r). Battiferri uses this hypermannerist form here with expressive intent,
to meditate on the central mystery of the Christian faith, the Incarnation, which
"made heaven earth," through God's assumption of mortal flesh, and "made earth
heaven," by redeeming mankind from original sin, and enabling salvation. The last
line, which encases *ciel* between two occurrences of *terra*, gives a penitential inflec-
tion to the poem, reminding us that the sinner each day "buries Christ" through
her sins.

Moderata Fonte (1581)
98

[1] S'angelico pensier, puro intelletto,
de' secreti del ciel misteri immensi
appena ombrar potria l'almo disegno;
come indegna aspirar poss'io a quel segno,
che trapassa e confonde i nostri sensi,   5
col fallace mio stil d'errori obietto?
Signor, tu che a spiegar l'alto concetto,
che né scoprir né imaginar si puote,
mi sproni, infiammi, e scorgi;
tanta virtù mi porgi,   10
ch'almen fra' tuoi s'intendan le mie note.
Piovan le grazie tue nel duro seno,
arido e vil terreno,
e fioriscan le glorie al mondo ignote.
Ma pria mi squarcia il velo,   15
ch'adombra a l'alma il bel sentier del cielo.

[2] Mentre per obedir l'almo e supremo
voler del sommo padre il sacro verbo
veggio abbassar per noi, levar dal centro,
e ch'io risguardo poi me stessa dentro   20
tanti error vani, onde 'l nimico acerbo
s'arma per trarmi seco al fondo estremo,
di vergogna e paura avampo e tremo;
né 'l cor pensar, né può la lingua esporre
quel ch'altri non comprende,   25
e sol sé stesso intende.
Onde la mente a sua pietà ricorre,
e 'l giogo altier d'una tremenda croce,
ch'altrui dà spirto e voce
fia 'l mio Parnaso, ove altra fonte scorre   30
da le sacrate vene.
e fian gli angeli pii le mie Camene.

[3] Era fra 'l cielo e noi tal lite accesa,
che né d'angel valea, né d'uom virtute
per ricomporci in amicizia e in pace,   35
quando al verbo divin, che in fronte giace
del paterno splendor, darci salute
piacque, e 'n nostro favor tolse l'impresa.

Egli ch'acquetar sol l'aspra contesa
poteo, lasciò le parti alme e divine,   40
e portò insieme unita
la morte con la vita,
l'ombra col sole, e col principio il fine.
Egli pagò per noi quanto dobbiamo
dal dì che nacque Adamo,   45
prima cagion di tante empie ruine;
e poich'altro non valse,
col suo morir nostra ragion prevalse.

[4] Ahi, che fra 'l suo gran Padre, e l'uman seme
si pone amico, e si fa scudo e muro: 50
ma fero premio, o mediator, riporti,
poich'al ciel noi mandando ingiurie e torti,
e 'l ciel a noi più d'un castigo duro,
la colpa e l'ira in te ridonda insieme.
Tu prendi umana spoglia e ci dai speme   55
di vestirci di gloria; e tu consenti,
carco de' nostri errori,
versar pianto e sudori.
Tu fai stupir fin le tartaree genti,
mentre, per noi saziar d'ambrosia e manna,   60
tua bontà ti condanna
a patir fame, onde t'assalti e tenti
il Re del pianto eterno,
per insegnarci a superar l'Inferno.

[5] E se discorro col pensier più avante,   65
io ti veggio, Signor, mandar ne l'orto
notturni preghi al Ciel, donde sei sceso,
ed in pregando esser tradito e preso,
per dar a noi nel nostro orar conforto,
sforzato no, ma in tuo voler costante,   70
e benché tu ti veggia offerto a tante
pene ed obbrobrii, o Dio, sì non ti cale
del proprio strazio, quanto
perché d'un dolor tanto
non scorgi il frutto a l'alto merto eguale.   75
Ingrata stirpe! Or non fûr mai gli Ebrei
nel tuo mortal sì rei,
come ne l'alma noi, ch'assai più vale,

col perverso volere,
che di continuo ti percote e fere.   80

[6] Ahi, che per islegar l'aspra catena
de l'alme a' danni propri intente e pronte,
indegno laccio il sacro collo annoda.
Ahi, che per far che l'uom riposi e goda,
veggio sudar quella benigna fronte,   85
che 'l Paradiso agli angeli asserena.
Quella testa, che 'l ciel, l'acqua, e l'arena
formò ad un cenno, or va di spine avinta
sotto 'l divin diadema,
di che l'Inferno trema,   90
per far la mia d'eterna gloria cinta.
Al fin la dura trave ascende invitto,
sanguinoso e trafitto,
onde la morte in sé medesma è vinta,
e, perché 'l morto viva,   95
more il principio onde la vita è viva.

[7] Ma benché al fin sì rara morte impetre
stupende essequie, onde pietà ed orrore
conturba il cielo, e 'l sol si rende oscuro,
e gli angeli ammirati al caso duro   100
piangono, e 'l mondo trema, e di dolore
spezzansi i monti e l'insensate pietre;
benché lascin le tombe oscure e tetre
gl'inceneriti corpi, e 'l vel diviso
resti del sacro tempio,   105
non però il mio cor empio
può da qualche pietà restar conquiso.
Ahi, se giace il gran Dio de la natura
in poca sepoltura,
ch'ha 'l mondo in pugno e calca il paradiso,   110
fia questo cor men lasso
d'angel, ciel, terra, sol, polve, ombra e sasso?

[8] Signor, che mentre in ciel col Padre regni,
giaci col corpo spento
in novo monumento,   115
e vai con l'alma ai più profondi regni,
deh, poni teco ogni mio error sotterra;

indi quest'alma afferra,
e trai del limbo de' pensieri indegni,
acciò dal velo umano   120
sciolta al fin voli al suo Fattor in mano.

[1] If angelic thought, pure intellect, could barely adumbrate the lovely design of the secrets of heaven and their immense mysteries, how can I, in my unworthiness, aspire to that unfathomable, thought-transcending aim with my fallacious, error-bound pen? Lord, you who spur, inflame, and guide me to speak of that exalted concept that can be neither discovered nor imagined, give me such power that my notes may at least be heard among those who are yours. Pray, rain down your graces into my obdurate breast, an arid and base terrain, so that glories unknown to the world may flourish there. But first rend that veil that hides from the soul the lovely path to heaven.

[2] As I watch the sacred Word, obeying the supreme will of the great Father, abase himself for us and move from the center, and as I then, looking into myself, see so many vain errors, the weapons of our cruel enemy as he seeks to drag me to the depths, I burn and tremble with shame and fear. The heart cannot conceive, nor the tongue express him who cannot be understood by others, but only by himself. So my mind takes shelter in his compassion; and the proud yoke of a fearsome Cross, which gives us spirit and voice, will be my Parnassus, where a different fount flows from those sacred veins; and the pitying angels will be my Muses.

[3] Such a quarrel had broken out between us and heaven that neither the power of angels nor men could serve to reconcile us in friendship and peace, when it pleased the divine Word, who resides on the brow of his Father's splendor, to give us salvation, and he took on this enterprise as our champion. He, who alone could settle this cruel contest, left the lovely divine realm and brought with him death melded with life, the shadow with the sun, and the beginning with the end. He paid for us what we owed from the day of the birth of Adam, the first cause of this dreadful ruination. And since nought else would suffice, he won our cause for us through his death.

[4] Ah, between his great Father and the human race he places himself, a friend to us, and makes himself our shield and wall. But you will have a cruel reward for this, O Mediator, for, as we inflict on heaven endless injuries and wrongs and heaven showers on us more than one harsh punishment, the guilt and wrath redound both together on you. You

take on human form and give us the hope that we may garb ourselves in glory, and you consent, laden with our errors, to pour out sweat and tears. You stun the hordes of Hell, and, so we may feed on ambrosia and manna, your goodness condemns you to hunger, while the King of eternal weeping assaults you and tempts you, so we can learn to overcome Hell.

[5] And if I look forward in my thought, I see you, Lord, in the garden, offering up nocturnal prayers to heaven, from which you descended, and, as you pray, you are betrayed and captured, to give us comfort in our own prayers. You do not go forced, but of your own constant will, and although you see yourself subjected to so many sufferings and insults, this pains you less, O Lord, than that you see the fruit of it not worthy of your great sacrifice. Ungrateful race! The Jews were never so cruel to your body as we are to your soul, a far graver crime, as our perverse will strikes and wounds you without cease.

[6] Alas, to break the harsh chains of our souls, so intent on their own harm, he suffers a vile noose to surround his sacred neck. Alas, so that man may find repose and joy, I see drenched in sweat that mild brow that makes Paradise serene for the angels. That head, which with one nod formed the heavens, the waters, and the earth, is now crowned with thorns beneath that divine diadem at which Hell trembles, so that mine may be crowned with eternal glory. And at last, he ascends that hard beam, unvanquished, bloody, and pierced, so that death is defeated in death, and so that the dead may live, the source dies whereby life itself lives.

[7] Such a rare death demands stupendous exequies, so the heavens are disturbed by pity and horror, and the Sun turns dark, and the angels, marveling at this cruel event, weep, and the earth trembles, and the mountains and insensate stones break with grief, while the dead, dissolved to ash, leave their dark and obscure tombs, and the veil of the temple is rent. Yet even so, my wicked heart continues to resist all compassion. Alas, if the great God of nature, who holds the world in his grasp and treads on heaven with his feet, is lying in a poor tomb, will this heart be less pitying than angel, heaven, earth, dust, shadow, and stone?

[8] Lord, you who, while you rule in heaven with your Father, lie in your wasted body in a new monument, and descend in spirit into the depths, I beg you, take all my errors below the ground with you, and there seize this soul and rescue it from the limbo of unworthy thoughts, so that, at last, released from its mortal veil, it can fly into the hand of its Maker.

Canzone ABCCBAADeeDFfDgG + *congedo* DeeDFfDgG. Fonte 1582, 50–54 (*Fia* in l. III corrected from *Fra*). Although Fonte's biographer, Giovanni Niccolò Doglioni, speaks of her having written much lyric verse, most of this is lost, apart from a few occasional lyrics in collectively authored volumes and a few poems inserted in her dialogue *The Worth of Women*. This powerful canzone, published at the end of her 1582 narrative work *The Passion of Christ*, is her only surviving religious lyric. In its original published context, it works as complementary to Fonte's narrative of the Passion, illustrating the manner in which that narration can be incorporated the reader's own penitential meditations.

The first two stanzas of the poem constitute a long, metapoetic *captatio benevolentiae*, reflecting on the poet's inadequacy to the task of confronting the great theological mystery of the Incarnation, intrinsically beyond the compass of human understanding. These stanze make no reference to the poet's intellectual weakness, or the "imbecillity" of her sex, as was common in such passages in female-authored works in this period. The grounds for her doubts of her abilities are, rather, moral-theological (as a mortal and a sinner, she is unworthy to approach this sacred theme), and her conventional modesty is offset by her statement in the first stanza that God himself is inspiring her to write. The notion in the closing lines of the second stanza that Mount Calvary will henceforth be the poet's Parnassus and Christ's blood her Pierian or Castalian spring echoes the closing lines of Vittoria Colonna's no. 74, though a punning reference to her pseudonym, Fonte (fountain) may be intended in the *altra fonte* of l. 30. The relatively rare term *Camene* (Latin: *Camenae*) for the Muses probably derives from Ariosto's *OF* 46.17. Fonte may have chosen it here over the more usual *Muse* because of the original association of the Camenae with water: they were archaic nymph goddesses of springs.

The next five stanzas narrate and meditate on the story of the Incarnation and Passion, starting from the theological premise (stanza 3): humankind has fallen out of God's grace following Adam and Eve's sin and is condemned to spiritual death until it is redeemed by Christ's voluntary expiatory sacrifice. Stanza 4, mainly devoted to rehearsing the theological implications of the Incarnation, ends with a reference (62–64) to the devil's unsuccessful attempt to tempt Christ following his fast of forty days in the desert, as recounted in the gospels of Matthew, Mark, and Luke. Stanza 5 alludes to the episodes of the Agony in the Garden and Christ's arrest and the various punishments and humiliations inflicted on him before the crucifixion, while stanza 6 describes the crucifixion and stanza 7 the miraculous cosmic events following Christ's death. The *congedo* takes the narration to the moment of the harrowing of Hell, prior to the Resurrection, when Christ descended into Limbo to rescue the souls of the righteous (see no. 73). Narration is, in each case, accompanied by meditation. While stanzas 3, 4, and 6 emphasize the profundity of humankind's debt of gratitude to God, stanzas 5 and 7 stress the inadequacy of its meeting of that debt, with stanza 5 noting humankind's continuing "crucifixion" of Christ through its addiction to sin, and stanza 7 lamenting the poet's own inability to feel the pity and horror of Christ's passion as powerfully as she ought. This more personal focus of the end of stanza 7 continues into the *congedo*, where the poet calls on Christ to bury her errors with Him in His tomb and to rescue her soul from the Limbo of sin.

In linking meditation on Christ's passion with personal, penitential meditation, Fonte's canzone represents a tradition of verse of great popularity in Counter-Reformation Italy (see no. 113 for another example). This model of verse may be seen as a literary reflection of contemporary meditative practices, as formalized in works such as Ignatius Loyola's *Spiritual Exercises* and Luis de Granada's *Book of Prayer and Meditation*. Meditation on the five "sorrowful mysteries," from the Agony in the Garden to the Crucifixion, was also part of the ritual stipulated within the devotion of the Rosary. Within the general spectrum of Passion-related literature, Fonte's canzone is noteworthy for the relative austerity of its treatment of Christ's physical sufferings and the exclusivity of its focus on their theological significance. From a theological perspective, one significant detail is her imputation of the sin of the Fall entirely to Adam, without mention of Eve (stanza 3). This may be in part due to the exclusively Christocentric character of the poem—the canzone also omits mention of the Virgin—but it may also reflect Fonte's pro-feminist sympathies. Her later dialogue, *The Worth of Women*, contains an account of the Fall that tends largely to exculpate Eve (Fonte 1997, 93–94).

Although the canzone is essentially Petrarchan in its language and style, Fonte shows a taste for paradoxical wordplay at the end of the fifth stanza (94–96) that brings her close to the proto-Baroque trends of her day. The passage brings to a head the series of antitheses developed in the previous stanze, contrasting Christ's sufferings with the spiritual boons the Incarnation brought to humanity. Other rhetorical ornaments include the mild *rapportatio* of l. 23; the juxtaposed inclusive rhyme at ll. 47–48, and the noun pile-up of 112, recalling Petrarch's famous "fior, frondi, erbe, ombre, antri, onde, aure soavi" (sonnet 303, l. 5).

Lucia Colao (1570s–80s)

99

Io amo sì di quel lume l'assalto,
ove il mio ben e la mia vita alberga,
che non come fanciul timido a verga,
ma corro ardita a lui, qual Curzio al salto.   4
Né fia già mai che faticoso e alto
loco mi stanchi, e il mio voler non s'erga,
acciò che grazia tal non si disperga,
ond'io rimanga poi qual freddo smalto.   8
Già capir non potei, né creder volsi,
or m'avveggio, che quanto il cor si strugge
a questo foco è più beato e degno.   11
Se per altezza alcun timido fugge
da tanta impresa, io per me non mi sciolsi
dal mondo, ma per fede io n'ho tal pegno.   14

I so love the assault of that light in which my good and life reside that I run to it, not like a timid child, urged on by the rod, but boldly, like Curtius to his leap. May no high and weary path ever tire me and my desire cease to drive me onward, so that this grace does not disperse, leaving me like cold brittle enamel. I could never understand or bring myself to believe what I now see: that the more the heart melts in this fire, the more blessed it is and the finer. Some timid souls may fly from such a daunting and high task, but I did not free myself from the world through my own merit; it is through faith that I have this great pledge.

Sonnet ABBA ABBA CDE DCE, with the rhyme words of Petrarch's sonnet 39 (substituting *degno* for *indegno* in l. 11). Bergalli 1726, 2:5. A familiar sixteenth-century subgenre of spiritual verse was that of religious *contrafacta: religious "remakings" of secular poems using the same rhymes or rhyme words as the originals. The practice was popularized by the Venetian Franciscan Girolamo Malipiero in the 1530s and gained currency in the late Cinquecento, with the growing taste for overt virtuosity in poetry (see introduction). Colao, a specialist in contrafacta, here succeeds against the odds in crafting a plausible poem, despite the constraints of the form, converting Petrarch's description of his timorousness before the "assault" of his earthly love into an account of the fearlessness inspired by her love for the divine. The reference to Curtius's leap in l. 4 is to the legend told in Livy of the hero Marcus Curtius, who leapt into a mysterious abyss that had opened in Rome, sacrificing himself to placate the gods.

100

Solo sperando, i suoi fecondi campi
solca l'agricoltore a passi lenti,
e gli occhi fermi tien mirando intenti
come l'aratro suo la terra stampi: 4
così del mio bel Sole i chiari lampi
miro, bench'io mi trovi tra le genti;
e tanto sono i miei sensi contenti,
che il cor d'un dolce foco par che avvampi.   8
Onde per tal diletto e monti e piaggie
e fiumi e selve e le più chiare tempre
seguir mi piace, e quanto sprezza altrui,   11
e quelle vie stimate aspre e selvaggie,
soavi e piane mi si mostran sempre,
che il mio Lume stia meco ed io con Lui.   14

Possessed by hope, the slow-paced farmer plows his fertile fields, his
eyes fixed intently before him, gazing at his harrow as it scores through
the earth. Just so do I gaze on the bright light of my lovely Sun, even
when I find myself lost among the crowds, and my senses are so slaked
by this vision that my heart seems to blaze with a sweet fire. This
delight makes me search out mountains and plains and rivers and
woods, and the clearest objects and what others despise, and those
roads considered most hard and wild seem easy and smooth, just as
long as my Light is with me and I with Him.

Sonnet ABBA ABBA CDE CDE (using the rhyme words of Petrarch's sonnet 35, ex-
cept for those in ll. 5 and 7). Bergalli 1726, 2:4. Like no. 99, this sonnet rewrites in a
spiritual key a love lyric by Petrarch, this time one of his most famous. Colao's bold-
est innovation is the *epic simile of the first quatrain, describing a farmer ploughing
his field, intently watching the bare earth where one day crops will spring. The
image conveys the fixity with which the poet attends to God, ignoring worldly dis-
tractions and concentrating on the future "fruits" of her faith. Also effective in this
regard is the foregrounding of *solo sperando* (lit. "only hoping") in the first line. Some
elements in the poem recall the earlier, less accomplished spiritual reworking of the
sonnet by Girolamo Malipiero, notably the image in l. 14 of the poet as eternally
accompanied by Christ (replacing Eros in Petrarch), although Colao softens Mal-
piero's *Iesù* to the lyrical epithet *il mio Lume*. The sense of the borrowed rhyme
word, *tempre*, in l. 10 is not entirely clear.

Battista Vernazza (pre-1587)

101

È questo il dì cui nel bell'orto nacque
mistica Rosa e si mostrò foriera
di pace etterna, onde fiaccò l'altera
testa il gran Verme e sotto ai piè le giacque.   4
L'aure più pure e le più limpide acque
le stanno intorno insin dall'alba a sera,
e de' mistici fior tutta la schiera
sa che in lei tanto il suo Fattor si piacque.   8
Nel suo bel seno immacolato e pio
ubbidiente, e in estasi d'amore,
il Verbo esinanito all'uom s'unìo.   11
Su, dunque, canti, suoni, e inni d'onore,
ché nasce madre, figlia e sposa a Dio
e, se tanto dir lece, ognun l'adore.   14

This is the day, when in the lovely orchard a mystical Rose was born and showed herself a herald of eternal peace, for she crushed the proud head of the great Worm, and he lay under her feet. The purest airs and the clearest waters surround her from dawn to evening, and all the throng of mystic flowers know that her Maker so greatly delighted in himself in her. In her lovely breast, immaculate and pious, obediently and in an ecstasy of love, the Word, self-abased, united itself with man. Come, then, songs, music, and hymns of honor, for the mother, daughter, and bride of God is born. If it is licit to speak so, let all adore her.

Sonnet ABBA ABBA CDC DCD. Vernazza 1819, 3. This sonnet, written for the feast of Mary's birth (September 8), locates that event in heaven, reflecting the notion that the Virgin was conceived in God's mind ab aeterno. Lines 3–4 celebrate Mary's "defeat of the devil" through her role in the Incarnation. The description of the devil as a serpent or "worm" recalls his role in the Fall, and perhaps echoes Dante's *Inf.* 34, 108, where Lucifer is described as an "evil worm." *Esinanire*, in l. 11, translates the Latin *exinanio*, used in Paul's letter to the Philippians 2:7, in a similar context. The conditional clause in l. 14 ("if it is licit") reflects an awareness that worship should be reserved for God. Petrarch uses a similar phrase in his canzone 366, l. 99, to excuse his addressing Mary as goddess (*dea*), a turn of phrase echoed in another sonnet by Vernazza that addresses Mary as "Most powerful Goddess" (Vernazza 1819, 1). Line 8, with its allusion to God "delighting in himself" in Mary refers to the notion that man is made in God's image.

Lorenza Strozzi (1588)

102

prima currentis celebratur anni
nunc dies sacro puero dicata,
Patre divorum genito, pudica et
matre Maria.   4

legis antiquae monumenta servans,
sanguinem fudit tener innocensque;
factus in terris homo, Patris iram
abstulit inde.   8

nam parens primus scoelus omne traxit,
foemina pomum sibi dante mortis:
ianuas coeli subitoque clausit,
summa potestas.   12

natus e coelu peregrinus orbi
crimen antiqui patris omne soluit
lucidas coeli reserando portas,
sanguine puro.   16

nomen inducunt soboli parentes
dulce, praeclarum, iugiter vocandum.
nomen aeternum, super omne nomen
nomen Iesu.   20

o puer nostri decus orbis, atque
gloria et splendor, tribuas precamur
perfrui nobis sine fine pace
mortis in hora. Amen.   24

Now we celebrate the first day of the year, dedicated to the holy Child, born to the Father of the gods and to the chaste mother Mary.

Obeying the dictates of the old law, he sheds his blood, though tender and innocent. Made a man on the earth, he draws away from it the Father's wrath.

For the first father brought with him all sin, a woman giving him the apple of death; the supreme power at once closed the gates of heaven.

Born of heaven, a pilgrim in the world, he wipes clean the sin of the ancient father, opening the shining portals of heaven with his pure blood.

The parents name their offspring, calling him at once by the sweet and most excellent eternal name, name above all names, Jesus.

O child, honor of our world and glory and splendor, we pray you concede us peace without end in the hour of our death. Amen.

Sapphics. Strozzi 1588, 1–2. Far the most substantial body of Latin verse by an early modern Italian woman is a collection of hymns by the Florentine Dominican Lorenza Strozzi, published at the end of her long life in 1588. The collection comprises 104 hymns, themed to Christian feasts throughout the year and presumably intended for performance during divine office at Strozzi's convent, San Niccolò, in Prato. Although Strozzi uses six different meters in the collection, the dominant meter is the Sapphic stanza, whose invention by Sappho, a "most learned woman" (*doctissima foemina*), Strozzi recalls in her dedicatory letter. Strozzi uses this especially for her lighter, narrative-dominated hymns, such as those for saints' feast days and feasts celebrating events told in the gospels, reserving heavier meters for more theologically dense topics (see Stevenson 2002, 118–19, for an example). The heading before this first hymn, for the Feast of the Circumcision (January 1), notes that it may be sung to the tune of "Ut queant laxis," a famous eighth-century hymn. For each meter subsequently introduced in the collection, another familiar hymn tune is similarly adduced.

The Feast of the Circumcision commemorated both the circumcision of Christ and his naming, recounted with great brevity in Luke 2:21. The theological importance of the circumcision lay in the fact that it was the occasion when Christ's blood was first shed; hence, it could be seen as prefiguring his redemption of humanity from sin through the Crucifixion, as here in stanzas 2–4. Implicit in Strozzi's treatment is the notion of Christ as a "new Adam," reversing the Fall, articulated in Romans 5:18–19.

An intriguing feature of Strozzi's hymn is its intertextual relationship with Horace's ode 1.2 ("Iam satis terris"), which Strozzi cites in the heading to the poem as a classical precedent for the metrical form she is adopting. Horace's violence-haunted poem speaks of a collective, ancestral sin that is yet to be expiated and augurs the arrival of a savior, figured in the heaven-sent Mercury, incarnated in Augustus. The thematic consonance between Horace's ode and Strozzi's Christian hymn is sufficiently close to invite comparison between them, and implicitly to confer on "Iam satis terris" something of the same air of miraculously anticipating Christianity as had traditionally been accorded to Virgil's fourth eclogue, with its annunciation of a messianic birth. This has strategic importance in legitimizing Strozzi's use of Horace as a model and, more generally, the classicizing decorum of her language in the collection, which is exemplified here most strikingly in her allusion to the Christian God as "father of the gods" (3). Although neo-Latin humanistic hymnody was an established tradition (see Moss 1986 and, for examples, Piastra 2002, 240–51, 260–64, 270–73, 290–96), the use of classicizing language in Christian contexts was still a distinctive and far from automatic choice, especially for a woman and a nun.

The second edition of Strozzi's hymns (Strozzi 1601, 2) has a variant version of ll. 17–18: "nomen imponunt soboli parentes / iugiter cunctis simul invocandum" (the parents name their offspring, calling [his name] out at once to all present). The edition was prepared by Strozzi's nephew, and it is not clear whether the variants introduced there derive from an alternative text of Strozzi's hymns in his possession or whether they are editorial interpolations.

103

nunc Dei dicam ac hominis parentem,
atque Regina venerabor orbis
et decus mundi, superoque regni
voce sonora.   4

quam Dei summi paranymphus alto
missus e coelo radians salutat:
ex ea narrans fore nasciturum
numen Olympi.   8

tunc silet Virgo, pavefacta luce.
Gabriel secretum aperitque, dicens:
"alma nunc gaude sociata Patri
Omnipotenti,   12

qui simul coelum regit, atque terram,
quem tremunt omnes, Erebo manentes;
te sibi in matrem legit, atque sponsam
lege marita."   16

"quomodo," quaerit, "copula mariti
dum caret voto, generatur infans?"
nuncius partum referat futurum
mira loquendo.   20

annuit dictis penitus Maria:
et sacrum flamen penetravit alvum,
nesciam culpae, intemerata linquens
membra puellae.   24

gaudio in terris homines fruuntur,
angeli et laudes modulando cantant:
Inferus plangit cuneus dolore
atque pavescit.   28

Alme qui coelum bonitate summa
aspicis, semper genus atque nostrum,
Matris immensae precibus rogamus
visere coelos.   32

Now I shall tell of the mother of God and man and venerate the queen
of this world, the glory of earth and heaven, with a resounding voice.

A shining bridesman, sent down by God from highest heaven, greets her, telling her there will be born from her an Olympian god.

The Virgin is silent, fearing the light. Gabriel reveals his secret unto her, saying, "Now rejoice, blessed one, conjoined to the Father Omnipotent.

"who reigns over both heaven and earth; whom all fear, condemned to Erebus; he chooses you for his mother and his lawful wife."

"How," she asks, "Will I bear a child, while I am not yet joined to a husband?" The messenger tells her of the future birth, saying things of wonder.

Mary assented within to what he said, and a breath penetrated her sacred womb, untouched by sin, leaving inviolate the girl's body.

Men on earth rejoice, and angels sing sweet praises. The infernal squadron laments, stricken, and quakes.

O bountiful one who gazes on heaven, in your supreme goodness, and watches over the human race, we ask that, by the prayers of the great Mother, we may behold heaven. Amen.

Sapphics. Strozzi 1588, 24–25 (*hunc* corrected to *nunc* in l. 1; *superique* to *superoque* in l. 3; *paranimphus* to *paranymphus* in l. 5; *omne* to *omnes* in l. 14; *viscere* to *visere* in last line). Strozzi's hymn for the Annunciation gives a highly succinct version of the narrative recounted in Luke 1:26–38, which tells of the angel Gabriel announcing Christ's forthcoming birth to the Virgin Mary, her confusion and apprehension, his explanation, and her assent. It follows a common pattern of Strozzi's sapphic hymns, consisting of an exordial stanza announcing the subject, a narrative, and a concluding invocation beseeching protection from the holy figure to whom the hymn is addressed. The brevity of the stanza form encourages concision, and Strozzi's narrative proceeds essentially by snapshots, except in stanzas 3–4, where the announcing angel's speech crosses the stanza boundary. Strozzi's language is notably classicizing throughout, reaching for periphrases such as *numen Olympi* for Christ at l. 8, *Erebus* and *Inferus* (the classical Underworld) for Hell at ll. 14 and 27, and *sacrum flamen* for Holy Ghost at l. 22 (where the usual Church Latin would be *Spiritus Sanctus*). Even the one apparent exception proves the rule: the postclassical, late-Latin *paranymphus* (5), meaning "best man" or "bridesman," is found in a classically trained patristic writer like Augustine and presumably qualifies on that score.

As in no. 102, Strozzi draws on Horace as a model, especially his "Carmen saeculare," a hymn to Apollo and Diana, and his ode 1:12 ("Quem virum aut heroa lyri vel acri"), which begins with a sequence of praise of the gods. One of the adonic lines here (*lege marita*; l. 16) is identical to an adonic line in the "Carmen saeculare," while *dicam* (I shall tell of) in the opening stanza recalls Horace's similar use of the same verb form in the opening lines of the fourth and seventh stanzas of ode 1:12. The epithet *almus*, applied to God in l. 29, may also derive from the "Carmen saeculare," l. 9, where it is applied, again in the vocative, to Apollo. Elsewhere, in her hymn on the birth of the Virgin, Strozzi quotes an entire line verbatim from ode 1:12 (Stevenson 2002, 122, l. 29; cf. "Carmina," 1:12, l. 49).

Strozzi 1601, 28, corrects some of the typographic errors of the 1588 edition and has a variant version of ll. 17–18: "Quomodo . . . face nuptiali / dum caret virgo" (How, when a young girl is unmarried [lit. "lacks the nuptial torch"]).

104

lumen e coelo rutilans sereno
ambitum mundi penetrando lustrat
et super cunctos residet fideles
orbe repleto.   4

iam dies clarus decimus refulget,
qua Dei natus superos revisit,
dona promittens sacra Patre ab alto
flaminis illis.   8

turba quae Christo famulando corde,
arce tunc montis Syon alma stabat,
munus espectans iubaris superni
tertia in hora.   12

ecce promissum repetente coetu
adfuit numen, fragor atque magnus
intonans alto, Deus ipse coelo
terruit orbem.   16

terruit gentes sonus aethre factus;
ignis at magnus residens quievit
divi ubi existunt, Domini fideles
lumine magno.   20

in modum linguae, super omne pectus
tunc iacet numen, radiis corruscans,
fortia ad poenas faciendo corda
discipulorum.   24

omnium linguis resonare verba
audiunt hostes, pavidique fiunt
et mero dicunt famulos Iesu
esse repletos.   28

Petrus at verbis nimiisque signis
falsa mentiri, monuit rebelles,
praedicat cunctis populis et urbis
dona Tonantis.   32

protinus fortes timidum pavorem
mentibus facti iugiter repellunt

et pati mortem cupiunt cruentum
nomine Christi.   36

sit tibi semper, Deus alme noster,
gloria et splendor, decus et potestas
qui tuis donas sine fine lumen
pneumatos almi. Amen.   40

A rosy light gleams down from the serene heavens, penetrating the earth's orbit, and settles over all the faithful, filling the world.

Now the tenth day is shining forth since the man born of God returned to heaven, promising holy gifts from his high Father to his priests.

The happy throng that served Christ in its heart was waiting on the fruitful summit of Mount Zion, waiting for the gift of the heavenly light at the third hour.

Then, see, the promised divine presence was there, striking the group, and, thundering on high with a mighty clamor, God himself struck fear on the earth.

This sound in the ether made the people fearful, and a great fire hung in the air, consoling all the faithful of the Lord God with its great light.

In the form of a tongue, the godhead is now lying on each man's breast, gleaming with bright rays, making the disciples' hearts strong against pain.

The enemies hear words sounding in the languages of all men and are filled with fear, and they say the servants of Jesus have drunk of unmixed wine.

But Peter warns the faithless that they are speaking falsely with many words and signs, and he preaches the gifts of the Thunderer to every people and city.

Made strong, they constantly banish timid fear from their minds and crave to suffer cruel death in the name of Christ.

Bountiful God, let Thine be ever glory and splendor, honor and power, Thou who givest to Thy followers the eternal light of the life-giving Spirit.

Sapphics. Strozzi 1588, 40–41. The feast of Pentecost, celebrated ten days after Ascension Day, commemorates the episode recounted in Acts of the Apostles, when, in accordance with the promise of the risen Christ (Acts 1:8), the "gift of tongues" descended on the apostles, enabling them to preach the Christian gospel in every language on earth (Acts 2:1–6). The feast had special significance for Strozzi's order, the Dominicans, as the "order of preachers," and the earliest general chapters of the order were held over Pentecost in 1220–21. Strozzi narrates the event dramatically, beginning in medias res with a dawn scene before recalling Christ's promise to the disciples in stanza 2, and giving great emphasis in stanzas 4 and 5 to the cosmic sound effects accompanying the miracle (in the Acts described as a "mighty rushing wind"). The transition between the stanzas, *terruit orbem / terruit gentes,* echoes almost verbatim the transition between the first and second stanzas of Horace's ode "Iam satis terris" (see no. 102).

As elsewhere, Strozzi employs classical terms in preference to more familiar Christian ones, describing God at l. 32 as *Tonans* ("the Thunderer," an eptithet of Jove) and apostles at l. 8 as *flamines,* a Roman term for priests involved in the worship of the official public cults of the city (each assigned to a single god; hence the appropriateness in this case). *Superos,* in l. 6, translated "heaven," is also a classical term (lit. "those on high"). As in no. 103, the usual term for the Holy Spirit, Spiritus Sanctus, is avoided in favor of classical *periphrasis, numen* (divinity) at ll. 14 and 22, and *pneuma* in the final line. The use of the Greek word *pneuma* is especially interesting since *agia pneuma* is the New Testament term that the Latin Vulgate translates as *spiritus sanctus* (for example in Acts 2:4). This usage opens the possibility that Strozzi was familiar with the Greek New Testament. Her brother, Ciriaco Strozzi (1504–65), was a distinguished scholar of Greek.

Strozzi 1601, 47–48, has a variant version, differing most significantly at ll. 7–8, which read "pollicens illis veneranda sancti / munera spiritus" (promising them sacred gifts of the holy spirit).

Maddalena Campiglia (1586–88)

105 ⌐⌐

Signor, se per amor, per pianger molto,
e aver non sol d'odori un vaso pieno,
ma il cor di doglia, il cor che visse involto
nel tenace, mondan visco terreno,   4
fûr rimesse a colei le colpe apieno,
che con l'umor che le piovea dal volto
lavò i tuoi piedi e se gli strinse al seno,
poi gli asciugò co 'l crin sparso e disciolto,   8
oggi che fosti al duro legno affisso,
per dar con la tua morte eterna vita
a ogn'alma che in te sol si fida e crede,   11
d'un'altra Maddalena, ch'or si chiede
perdon, assorba iniquità infinita
de l'alta tua bontà l'immenso abisso.   14

Lord, if by love, by much weeping, by having not only a vase filled
with unguents but a heart filled with sorrow (that same heart that had
formerly lived mired in the viscous birdlime of the world), the woman
who bathed your feet with the tears raining from her eyes then clasped
them to her breast and dried them with her loosened hair received full
absolution for her sins, then today, when you were nailed to that hard
wood to give eternal life through your death to all souls who believe
and trust in you alone, absorb the infinite iniquity of another Magdalene,
who now asks your pardon, in the immense abyss of your great
goodness.

Sonnet ABAB BABA CDE EDC. Zarrabini 1586, i2v–3r. The most interesting of
Maddalena Campiglia's surviving religious sonnets are those on her name saint,
Mary Magdalene (see also no. 106). The present one recounts the story of Magda-
lene's supposed washing and anointing of Christ's feet and his absolution of her sins
(found in Luke 7:36–48, where it is attributed to an anonymous sinful woman). The
poet, meditating on Christ's death and redemption of mankind on Good Friday (the
"today" of l. 9), asks him to forgive her sins, as "another Magdalene." The *per amor*
of l. 1 may allude to Luke 7:47: "her sins, which are many, are forgiven her, because
she loved much." Notable stylistic features of the sonnet are its syntactic control (it
is composed of a single sentence), its unusual rhyme scheme, and its inclusive and
near-equivocal rhymes (*pieno/apieno*; *volto/involto*; note also the juxtaposed *chiede/
crede*). The rhyme *affisso/abisso* is found in Petrarch's sonnet 145.

106

Ecco la Maddalena ai piedi santi
del Salvator venir: non avrà core
chi non compate a questa vista e fuore
di duol non mostra segno ai duri pianti.   4
Entra dogliosa, passa, e umile inanti
al suo Signor s'inchina, e del suo errore
chiede perdon pentita, e in caldo umore
tutta par che si sfaccia, e con tremanti   8
gesti lava felice quelle piante.
Dolce le bascia indi, le asciuga poi
coll'aureo crin disannellato e incolto;   11
poi söave le stringe, ed ei rivolto
la rimira benigno, assolve, e i suoi
peccati cangia in caste voglie e sante.   14

Watch Magdalene come to the holy feet of her Savior. No one with a
heart could watch such a sight without pity or fail to express sorrow at
her bitter laments. She enters, sorrowing, comes forward, and humbly
kneels before her Lord, penitently asking forgiveness for her sin; then
in hot tears she seems utterly to melt, and with trembling movements
she happily washes those feet. She kisses them and dries them with her
golden hair, uncurled and unkempt; then she holds them to her softly.
He, turning to her, looks at her kindly, absolves her and changes her
sins into chaste and holy desires.

Sonnet ABBA ABBA CDE EDC. Morsolin 1882, 63. Unpublished in her lifetime, this
sonnet is found in a 1588 letter Campiglia sent to a literary acquaintance, Francesco
Melchiori. It narrates the apocryphal story of Magdalene's washing of Christ's feet,
also alluded to in no. 105. Campiglia treats it here in a dramatic, present-tense narra-
tive mode, given fluency by insistent *enjambment. Particularly dramatic are ll. 8–9,
where Magdalene's melting into tears of repentence is accompanied by a "melting"
of the usual syntactic break between octave and sestet. Campiglia was sufficiently
concerned about this to consult with Melchiori whether it was an "acceptable
error" (error comportabile). She also consults him on the legitimacy of using the near-
identical rhymes -anti and -ante. An alternative ending supplied in the letter corrects
both these "flaws" and also introduces the adjectives "immaculate" and "pure" to
qualify "feet" in l. 9, mitigating what Campiglia may have felt to be the excessive
sensuality of the earlier version.

Chiara Matraini (1590–1597)

107 ⌒

Poi che l'antico Prometeo formata
ebbe di terra qui l'umana gente,
ascese al Cielo e una favilla ardente
tolse dall'alta sua rota infocata;   4
e con sì degna preda alma e pregiata,
(ritornato dal Cielo immantenente),
die' vita a quella e spirito lucente,
del cui splendor sarà sempre illustrata.   8
Tal io, volendo dar spirito e vita
de' miei concetti alle figliuole morte,
convien che al Sol del gran Mobile ascenda,   11
e della gloria sua, larga, infinita,
una scintilla del suo lume apporte
in esse, ond'io con lor chiara risplenda.   14

When the ancient Prometheus had formed the human race with clay, he ascended to heaven and took a spark from its high fiery wheel; and with this great prey, so lovely and prized, having returned immediately from heaven, he gave life to his creation and a bright spirit with whose splendor it will always shine. In just the same way, when I wish to give spirit and life to the dead daughters of my thoughts, it behoves me to ascend to the Sun of the great sphere and from his vast, infinite glory to transfer a scintilla of his light into them so that I and they will shine bright.

Sonnet ABBA ABBA CDE CDE. Matraini 1597, 62v (*Mobile* corrected from *Nobile* in l. 11). Matraini's revised 1597 *Rime* contains several new religious poems whose date of original composition is difficult to ascertain. This sonnet may be read as a state-ment of Matraini's religious poetics: poetry crafted by human means is dead clay until animated by the spark of divine inspiration. Prometheus, in Greek myth, was a Titan said to have crafted humankind and to have stolen fire from heaven as a gift for it. Already in ancient sources, this fire was seen as a metaphor for human wis-dom, while in Christian readings it often came to signify the immortal soul. *Chiara*, in l. 14, a characteristic play on the poet's name, is translated as "bright," but also carried the metaphorical sense of "famous." Matraini's gendering of her poems as female (10) may just reflect the gender of the Italian word *rime*, though there are other instances of female poets describing their works metaphorically as their daughters (e.g., Campiglia 2004, 48–49).

108

Speme del sommo ben, che 'l dolce e chiaro
fonte del mio gioir cresci ed inondi,
l'erbe m'infiori e gli arboscei m'infrondi
e purghi ogni mio dolce almo d'amaro,   4
sali innanzi al gran Sol, mai non avaro
de' suoi raggi beati al cor profondi
ed ergi ivi il pensier, che non affondi
il nettar dolce, prezïoso, e caro.   8
Ivi canta 'l bel foco, ove 'l mio ghiaccio
fia trasformato, entro nell'alma assiso,
e lieta ogn'ombra ne discaccia e 'l gelo,   11
tanto ch'io possa alla sua grazia in braccio,
altera stella, sovr'alzarmi al Cielo
a quasi angel volar nel Paradiso.   14

Hope of the supreme good, which swells and floods the sweet and clear
fountain of my joy, springing flowers on my shoots and green leaves
on my saplings and purging all that is bitter from my sweetness, fly up
before the great Sun, who never fails to pour down his blessed rays
deep into our hearts; raise my thoughts to that place, so His sweet,
precious, beloved nectar be not vainly spilled. There sing of the lovely
fire in which the ice frozen in my soul will be transfigured, and drive
all shadows and cold away in your happiness so that I can rise into the
arms of His grace, a proud star, and fly like an angel to Paradise.

Sonnet ABBA ABBA CDE CED. Matraini 1597, 64v–65r. This sonnet offers a fascinat-
ing case of a religious *contrafactum of what had been a secular love sonnet, "Viva
speme d'Amor, che 'l dolce e chiaro" (Rabitti 1985, 247–48). The revisions are mini-
mal, the most significant being the beginning of l. 5, which earlier read "Sali in alto
al mio Sol" ("Ascend to my Sun," with the Sun serving as a metaphor for the be-
loved, in this case his soul in heaven). The poem's most notable feature is its tum-
bling superabundance of metaphors, from the flowing waters, springing leaves,
pouring rays and flooding nectar of the quatrains to the ice-melting fire, shadow-
dispelling light, and angelic flight of the tercets. The sound-patterning is especially
intense in the quatrains, with the *consonance of *speme/sommo* (1), the *assonance
and consonance of *almo/amaro* (4), the echoing verb sequence *inondi/infiori/infrondi*
in ll. 2–3, and the very close rhymes *chiaro/caro* (1, 8) and *amaro/avaro* (4, 5).

109

Prego allo Spirito Santo

Spirto ch'ovunque vuoi sempremai spiri,
deh, spira un dolce fuoco
nel vivo nido della mia fenice;
tal ch'ogni suo mortale a poco a poco
ardendo mora, e di sua morte elice   5
nov'augel, che volando al cielo aspiri.
Ecco ch'aprendo l'ale
cerca nel fin di sé farsi immortale.

Prayer to the Holy Spirit

Spirit who always wafts where'er you wish, pray breathe a sweet fire
into the live nest of my phoenix so what is mortal in it may little by
little die burning, and may in its death give rise to a new bird that
aspires to the sky, taking wing. See—opening its wings, it strives in its
end to find eternal life.

Madrigal AbCBCAdD. Matraini 1590, 71 (*Nov'augel* corrected from *Non'augel*). While,
in her *Rime*, Matraini remains metrically within Petrarchan norms, her *Brief Dis-
course on the Life and Virtues of the Most Blessed Virgin* of 1590 participates in the late-
sixteenth-century vogue for madrigals, containing (excluding paratexts) thirteen
madrigals to only six sonnets. This example is also close to late-sixteenth-century
modes in its taste for wordplay, which here serves to articulate the sense of the
poem. The first six lines divide into a "breath" sequence in ll. 1–2 and 6 and a "death"
sequence in ll. 4–5, marked, respectively, by the *polyptota *Spirto/spiri/spira/aspiri*
and *mortale/mora/morte*, the latter picked up again, and semantically negated, in the
final line's *immortale*. Another preciosity is added by the incidence of two inclusive
rhymes (*spiri/aspiri* and *ale/immortale*) among only four rhymes in total. A third
rhyme (*fenice/elice*) probably derives from Petrarch's sonnet 321. For the metaphor
of the phoenix, see no. 48.

Livia Spinola (1591)

IIO

Sopra l'effigie della Vergine che tiene in grembo il figliuol morto
Chi del barbaro fin l'acerba sorte
unqua non vide, e la gran spoglia ancisa,
se in costei sola il guardo intento affisa
vedrà l'altrui nella sua propria morte;   4
perché, mentre con luci afflitte e smorte
ella sostiene il figlio in terra assisa,
sì l'offre il duolo altrui da sé divisa
che le piaghe onde ei muore in lei son scorte.   8
Tela felice in cui vivace appare
questa gran meraviglia, ond'altri ammira
la man che 'n Cristo uccise anco Maria,   11
Ma più felice il zelo ond'ella spira
questo sacrato senso in note chiare:
la pietà d'un pittor fe' l'opra pia.   14

On an Image of the Virgin Holding Her Dead Son in Her Lap

Even one who had never seen that cruelly fated brutal end and His great mortal remains, merely by fixing his gaze on her could see the other's death in her own, for while with afflicted and deadened eyes she holds her son, seated on the ground, she is so lost to herself in the other's pain that his death wounds may be seen also in her. Happy canvas on which this great miracle appears with such vividness that we marvel at the hand that, with Christ, killed also Mary. Yet happier still the zeal with which it breathes this sacred sense in clear notes: a painter's pity gave piety to his work.

Sonnet ABBA ABBA CDE DCE. *Scelta* 1591 (*prima parte*), 34 (title taken from the volume index). Like her other poem in this volume (no. 54), this sonnet of Spinola's alludes to an artwork, this time a painting of the type known as a pietà, representing the Virgin holding the dead Christ. The poem's central *conceit is that the Virgin in the image may be seen as an image herself, so vividly does her grief represent Christ's suffering. The last line contains an untranslatable pun, as *pietà* in Italian means both "compassion" and "piety." The poem reflects the Counter-Reformation ideal of a religious art capable of stirring powerful emotions (*affetti*) mimetically in its viewers, in a manner, the poem suggests, only possible if the painter or poet is imbued with religious zeal. Spinola's sonnet is typical of the age in its formal artifice: note especially the *zeugma of l. 4, and the phonetically close quatrain rhyme sequences (*sorte/morte/smorte/scorte*; *ancisa/affisa/assisa*). The sense of l. 7 is unclear.

Leonora Bernardi (1591)

III

[1] Se pur fin su negli stellanti chiostri
talor penetrar osa
presontüosa ancor lingua mortale,
anch'io vorrei, ma con lodati inchiostri
mio core aprirti, o santa e glorïosa   5
Vergine, e gran desio m'impenna l'ale;
ma a dir le maraviglie altere e sole
di te, mio vivo Sole,
gran spavento ritragge il cor mentr'io
di lui penso che 'n Po cadde e morio.   10

[2] Musa, tu dunque a cui d'eterni allori
nel più vero Elicona
degna corona il crin adorna e cinge;
tu le tenebre mie co' tuoi splendori
rischiara, e 'l canto avviva, e tu perdona,   15
Vergin, se penna umil tue lodi pinge;
tu sostenta lo stil, tu porgi aita,
alla virtù smarrita;
mostra il sentier, che senza te non scerno,
battuta nave in mar senza governo.   20

[3] Già tra le meraviglie al mondo rade
scampò vergine pia
da fama ria, portando acqua col cribro,
gentil fidanza in tenebrosa etade;
e tu l'infamia d'Eva, onde peria   25
il mondo, purghi, e già non corri al Tibro
ma nel tuo seno, a Dio gradito tempio,
Vergine senz'essempio,
di grazie accogli il fiume, e da quell'acque
vita ebbe vita e morte estinta giacque.   30

[4] Ecco vedova ebrea che 'n treccia, e 'n gonna,
con famosa pietate,
tra schiere armate si fidò soletta,
poi riede vincitrice, altiera donna;
e tu, Vergine ebrea, tanto più grate   35
spoglie riporti, quanto più perfetta
sei tu d'ogn'altra; ecco l'empio Oloferne

già ne le parti inferne
per te legato, ecco inaudita e nova
pace a' mortali, e 'n Ciel letizia a prova.   40

[5] Veggio di regia stirpe e d'alto core
sposa che 'n bel sembiante
al Rege avante supplice s'inchina
e 'l popol trae di grave rischio fuore.
Tu dell'eccelso e sempiterno amante,   45
sposa, figliuola, e madre, e 'n ciel regina,
tutte le grazie impetri, e peccatrice
turba rendi felice.
Tu ci liberi ognor da orribil morte,
o noi beati, o nostra altera sorte!   50

[6] Or tu che da' celesti e santi giri,
Vergine eletta e pura
in valle oscura e 'n grave aspro periglio,
mi vedi omai di sì lunghi martiri,
di questa vita tenebrosa e dura,   55
deh, ti mova pietà; prega il tuo figlio
che si degni col suo beato lume,
com'è pur suo costume,
risguardar quest'afflitta anima stanca
d'ogn'altro aiuto omai povera e manca.   60

[7] Già sai, Vergine pia, che poco è lunge
il quartodecimo anno
che 'n grave affanno io son misera involta,
e 'l core or trema or doglia afflige e punge.
Deh, volgi a me dal tuo beato scanno   65
le sante luci, e 'l umil prego ascolta
di quest'indegna tua devota ancella.
Sgombra, benigna stella,
sgombra tante procelle, e rasserena
la vita d'atro orror, di morte piena.   70

[8] E se tal grazia, tua mercede, impetro,
spero più che mai lieta
con fronte queta, il volgo e suoi pensieri
avere a scherno; allor saran di vetro
suoi vani sforzi, se divino aqueta   75
favor le rie tempeste, e i turbi fieri.

O mia celeste Dea, ecco l'umìle,
se ben con roco stile,
fida serva a' tuoi piè. La mia salute,
opra sia di tua man, di tua virtute.   80

[9] Va', poverella mia, non ti smarrire.
Se ben al gran desire
non hai manto conforme, un puro zelo
fu con pietà sempre raccolto in cielo.

[1] If even on high, within the starry cloisters, sometimes a mortal tongue dares presumptuously to venture, I too would open my heart to you with a worthy pen, holy and glorious Virgin, and a great desire feathers my wings. But from telling your rare and lofty virtues, my living Sun, a great fear impedes my heart, as I think of him who fell into the Po and died.

[2] Muse, you whose locks are adorned and circled by a noble crown of eternal laurels in the true Helicon, dispel my shadows with your splendor and give life to my song. And you, Virgin, forgiving that a humble pen paints your praises, sustain my pen and lend support to my scattered powers. Show me the way, for I cannot discern it without you, a battered ship on the ocean with no one at the helm.

[3] Once among the rare miracles of the world, a holy virgin escaped from ill fame, carrying water in a sieve, a noble sign of faith in an age of shadows; and you purge the world of the infamy of Eve, from which it was perishing. You do not run to the Tiber, but in the beloved temple to God in your breast, matchless Virgin, you gather up the river of grace and from those waters life has life, and death lies slain.

[4] Here is the Hebrew widow who, in skirts and braids, with famous piety entrusted herself all alone amid the armed throng, from which she returned in triumph, a great lady; and you, Hebrew Virgin, bring back finer spoils, as one more perfect than any other woman. Here is the wicked Holofernes bound by you in the regions of hell; here is a new and unwonted peace sent to mortals, and joy in heaven to vie with it.

[5] I see a bride of regal blood and high heart, who, in lovely guise, bows a supplicant before the king and draws her people safely from mortal risk. You, bride, daughter, and mother of the supreme and eternal lover, queen of heaven, ask all graces for us, rendering happy your errant horde. You free us at every hour from fearful death. How blessed we are, how lofty our fate!

[6] Now, Virgin choice and pure, you who from the celestial and holy spheres see me in a dark valley and in grave cruel danger, suffering such long torments in this hard life of shadows, let pity move you, pray your son that he deign with his sacred light, as he is wont, to shield this weary and afflicted soul, lacking and bereft of all succour.

[7] Merciful Virgin, you know it is almost the fourteenth year I have been, alas, enveloped in grave suffering. Now my heart trembles, now it is afflicted and pierced by pain. Turn your holy eyes on me from your blessed dwelling and listen to the humble prayer of your unworthy devoted handmaiden. Banish, kind star—banish these storm clouds and bring peace to my life, full of black horror and death.

[8] And if I should attain such a grace through your mercy, I hope that, happy as never before, I shall defy the vulgar throng and its thoughts with a quiet brow, for then all its vain efforts will be as glass, and if divine favor calms the cruel storms and fierce blasts, my heavenly goddess, here is your humble faithful servant at your feet, though her style be hoarse. Let my salvation be the work of your power and your hand.

[9] Go, poor little creature, do not lose your way. Even if you do not have the garb my great desire wished for you, pure-hearted zeal was always welcome in heaven.

Canzone AbCABCDdEE+DdEE, without *concatenatio* and with internal rhyme in l. 3. Scelta 1591 (*prima parte*), 50–53 (*ali* in l. 6 amended to *ale*; *dhe* in l. 65 amended to *deh*). Very little lyric verse by Leonora Bernardi survives, but this fine Marian canzone, praised in a sonnet by Angelo Grillo (no. 140), shows her to have been a highly accomplished poet. The eight-stanza poem falls into three parts. In the first (stanzas 1–2), the *captatio benevolentiae, the poet speaks of her inadequacy to the task she has set herself here, of praising the Virgin. In the second part (stanzas 3–5), she embarks on her task of praise, comparing the Virgin to three famous female classical and Old Testament figures: Tuccia, the Vestal Virgin accused of unchastity who miraculously proved her innocence by carrying water in a sieve (stanza 3); Judith, the widow of Betulia who, in the apocryphal Book of Judith rescued her people by killing the enemy general Holofernes; and Esther, who, in the Book of Esther, intervened with her husband, the Persian king Ahasuerus, to save the Jewish people of his kingdom from destruction. The third part of the canzone, before the *congedo*, shows the poet asking the Virgin to intercede for her and rescue her from current, unspecified, woes, which she describes in stanza 7 as having lasted over the past fourteen years. We do not know enough of Bernardi's life to conjecture what these sufferings were.

The three stanze praising the Virgin by reference to famous women invite comparison with Vittoria Colonna's no. 48, which makes similar use of exempla of famous women, although Colonna's are all classical. Judith and Esther were frequently cited in the religious literature of the period as *types of the Virgin. The Virgin, like Judith, rescued her people from destruction (in this case, spiritual) through her role in the Incarnation, defeating the Devil in the process, as Judith had defeated Holofernes. She also resembles Esther in respect of her mediatory interventions with God on behalf of humankind. All three of these women acted as agents of divine providence, but the presence of the secular example, Tuccia, invites a reading of these three stanze as celebratory of women's virtues, rather than purely of the greatness of God.

An interesting feature of the poem is its very dense intertextual relationship with the poetry of Petrarch and Tasso. Where Tasso is concerned, this is especially apparent in the second stanza, which very closely tracks the second stanza of Tasso's *GL* in its invocation of the heavenly Muse. The term *stellanti chiostri*, in l. 1, is also frequent enough in Tasso's religious lyrics to be understood as a deliberate echo here (see Piatti 2007, 67). Bernardi's allusion to the Tuccia story in the third stanza closely imitates a passage in Petrarch's *TP*, 148–51. The phrase *gentil fidanza* also derives from Petrarch's *Trionfi* (*TF* 2:67). Another echo of Petrarch is found in the last line of the first stanza, the second half of which precisely echoes l. 20 of Petrarch's canzone 105: the reference is to to the myth of Phaeton, who borrowed the chariot of the sun from Apollo and was struck down by Jove with a thunderbolt. The last line of the second stanza (20) also contains a Petrarchan allusion (*RVF* 132, l. 11: "mi trovo in alto mar senza governo"), while the description of Judith in stanza 4 echoes both *TC* 3:55 and *RVF* 121, l. 4. The phrase *beato scanno* in l. 65 is a rare quotation from Dante (*Inf.* 2.112), while the address to the canzone in the *congedo* as *poverella mia* returns to Petrarch (canzone 125).

Aside from this ornament through allusion, Bernardi's canzone shows a high degree of rhetorical ornamentation, which belies her description of her "humble pen" in the first stanza and her "crude style" in stanza 8. Especially notable for its rhetorical embellishment is stanza 1, whose rhymes include the inclusive, consonant-rich *chiostri/inchiostri*, the composite *mentr'io/morìo*, and the equivocal *sole/Sole*.

Tarquinia Molza (1601)

112

Felsina clara virum ingeniis, et clarior almae
   quod frueris vera Virginis effigie
quae sic ad vivum Lucae est expressa per artem
   ipsa sibi ut similes vix queat esse magis.
sed tamen inde tibi surgit quoque gloria maior,   5
   quod datur haec ipsa Matre iubente Dea.
ergo illi referas tanto pro munere grates
   et certam dubiis hinc pete rebus opem.
namque sui quae μνημόσυνον tibi dulce reliquit,
   credibile est votis velle favere tuis.   10

Felsina, you are famous for your men's intellects, yet more famous still because you can boast the true image of the bountiful Virgin, captured by Luke's art so true to life that she could hardly be more similar to herself. The fame you derive from this image is the greater because it is given to you by the divine Mother herself. Give thanks to her, then, for such a great gift, and call on her certain help in uncertain times. For she who left you such a sweet memento of herself will surely listen kindly to your prayers.

Elegaic distichs. Segni 1601, 61. This poem comes from a large anthology of verse in the vernacular, Latin, and Greek, put together in 1601 to celebrate a famous sacred icon of the Virgin held in the sanctuary of the Monte della Guardia in Bologna, an image claimed to have been painted by the evangelist Luke. The custodianship of this revered cult object became a political issue in the later sixteenth century as the ecclesiastical authorities attempted to reallocate it away from the Dominican nuns of the convent of San Mattia, who had traditionally had charge of the sanctuary. The 1601 volume was one of a number of literary initiatives intended to support the case for the nuns (Callegari and McHugh 2011, 35–36). Another female-authored Latin poem from the collection, by the Bolognese Dominican Febronia Pannolini, is reprinted with an Italian translation in Piastra 2002, 280.

    Molza's epigram opens with an allusion to Bologna's ancient fame as a university city (Felsina is a classical name for Bologna, deriving from the Etruscan), before going on to note the greater fame deriving to the city from the possession of the icon. The third distich alludes to the legend of the icon's arrival in Bologna, carried from Byzantium by a pilgrim directed to bring it to Bologna by the Virgin herself. Molza inserts the Greek word μνημόσυνον (*mnemosynon*), a reminder or memorial, in the penultimate line, perhaps mindful of the use of the term in the Greek New Testament, especially in Matthew 26:13 and Mark 14:9.

Lucrezia Marinella (1603)

113

Tremò la terra e 'l mar, pianse lo 'nferno;
s'aprìr le tombe e del gran Tempio il velo;
s'oscurò il sol, si mostrò irato il cielo;
mugghiò il mar, mugghiò l'aria e 'l Lago Averno,   4
mentre fra chiodi, spine e lancie, e scherno
e felle, e di timore il crudo gelo,
e d'amor fiamma, e d'empia morte il telo
languivi, o del gran Padre figlio eterno,   8
ed io non piango? Ed io pur spesso i marmi
vidi l'acque stillar, far fonti e fiumi.
Nuda son di pietà, d'impietà imago;   11
ma s'io ti miro, uscir di veder parmi
pianto e sangue dal corpo e da' bei lumi
come del mio rigor fatto presago.   14

The earth trembled, and the sea and Hell wept; the tombs opened, and
the veil of the Great Temple was rent; the Sun darkened; the heavens
lowered; the sea roared; the air roared, and the Avernian Lake, while
amid nails, thorns, and lances and contempt and hyssop and the cruel
ice of fear and the flames of love and the spear of black death you
languished, O eternal son of the great Father—and still I do not weep?
Yet I have often seen waters drip from the very stones, springs and
rivers flow from them. I am naked of pity, an image of cruelty: but if
I gaze on you, I seem to see tears and blood coming from your body
and your beautiful eyes, as if you could foresee my hardness.

Sonnet ABBA ABBA CDE CDE. Marinella 1603, 4r (*s'aprìr* in l. 3 substituted for *s'aprìo*).
Published only a year after the appearance of Giambattista Marino's seminal *Rime*,
Marinella's *Rime sacre* is the first verse collection by an Italian woman to embrace the
stylistic novelties of the Baroque. Her extravagant style is well exemplified in this
sonnet, which shares the subject of stanza 7 of Moderata Fonte's no. 98: the poet's
inability to feel to the full the pathos of Christ's passion, as reflected in the cosmic
chaos following his death. The treatment of this chaos in the quatrains is dramatic,
using broken and irregular rhythms to particular effect. Insistent repetition (for
example, of the past historic verbs in ll. 2–3) and *polysyndeton (6–7) lend this pas-
sage an oratorical feel. The final tercet, where the language simplifies, evokes con-
templation of a visual depiction of the crucifixion as the poem's narrative context.
Lake Avernus, near Naples (4), was thought in classical times to be the entrance to
Hades.

114

Di glorie oggi, di gemme e di splendori
coronata e vestita, al ciel ascende
la Vergine santa, e più fiammeggia e splende
che 'l puro sol dopo i primieri albori.   4
Scende nembo di rai, nembo di fiori,
che da le intatte nevi il candor prende,
sovra lei; già per lei dal ciel discende
schiera lucente di celesti amori.   8
Tuona e rimbomba, in un ride e sfavilla
l'aria d'intorno, e sbalza l'acque al cielo
per gioia il mar, di fiori il pian si veste.   11
Cristo con voce e fronte alma e tranquilla
dolce l'accoglie, e di stellato velo
la cinge, e 'l crin d'alta beltà celeste.   14

In glories today, in gems and splendors crowned and garbed, the holy
Virgin ascends to heaven, flaming and gleaming more than the pure
sun as it rises at dawn. A shower of rays descends on her, a shower of
petals that take their whiteness from her untouched snows, and a
shining throng of celestial amoretti pours down from heaven around
her. The air all around thunders and resounds, laughs and sparkles, the
sea throws up its waters to the heavens in its joy, and the plains adorn
themselves with flowers. Christ with a tranquil and benign brow and
voice sweetly welcomes her and garbs her in a veil of stars, crowning
her locks with high celestial beauty.

Sonnet ABBA ABBA CDE CDE. Marinella 1603, 7v (*suora* in l. 7 corrected to *sovra*).
This exuberant sonnet on the Virgin's Assumption was Marinella's most antholo-
gized and reprinted poem. The subject had special connotations in Venice, as the
never-conquered republic identified itself with the Virgin, an association Marinella
underlines in her patriotic epic *Enrico*. The quatrains are highly structured, with
the ascending movement of the Virgin-rising sun of the first quatrain balanced by
the descending movement of the second, a point underlined by the parallel close of
ll. 2 and 7. While the falling clouds of rays and amoretti reflect the visual tradition
(see, for example, Titian's *Assumption* in the Frari and Veronese's in the Accademia),
the image of falling petals may owe something to Petrarch's canzone 126, stanza 4.
The "untouched snows" of l. 6 refer to the whiteness of Mary's skin as well as to her
virginity. The final tercet recalls representations of the Coronation of the Virgin.
Stellato velo (13) may derive from Tasso (*GL* 6.103).

115

Ardi in giel d'onestade, ardi d'amore
e ardendo nuovo incendio a l'alma appresti,
e mentre nuove fiamme al petto desti
ed ardi sol di lui che t'arde il core,   4
guati il Ciel, batti il petto, e sciogli fuore
da' begli occhi divini i pianti onesti;
Dio, che ti mira, porge a' sensi mesti
liete dolcezze di celeste ardore.   8
Con le tue fiamme sante il Cielo accendi,
che t'accende e t'infiamma, e ardi; egli arde,
tu de' folgori suoi, ei del tuo foco,   11
ed abbrusciando qual fenice prendi
divine forme; e 'l Ciel par che ti guarde,
prendendo del tuo ardor letizia e gioco.   14

You burn in the ice of chastity, you burn with love, and, as you burn,
you stoke a new fire in your soul, and while new flames arise in your
breast and you burn for him alone who burns your heart, you gaze at
the sky, beating your breast and honest tears flow from your lovely
divine eyes. God, as he looks on you, soothes your weary senses with
happy balms of heavenly ardor, and with your holy flames you set
heaven alight as it fires you and inflames you; you burn; it burns—you,
from its lightning shafts; it, from your fire—and in flames like the
phoenix you take on divine forms, and it seems as though heaven is
gazing on you and taking joy and delight in your burning.

Sonnet ABBA ABBA CDE CDE. Marinella 1603, 15r. A distinctive feature of Mari-
nella's *Rime sacre* is the attention it gives to female saints, especially martyrs: of fif-
teen saints featured, nine are female, and six of these martyrs. This sonnet de-
scribes the martyrdom of St. Agnes, who was beheaded after an attempt to burn
her at the stake failed. The sonnet describes the saint burning in spiritual ardor at
the moment of her death. *Polyptoton is the sonnet's governing device. *Ardere* and
its derivatives occur nine times in it, *accendere* twice, and *fiamma/infiammare* three
times. The fire-ice *oxymoron of the first line is adapted from Petrarchan erotic
verse, and martyrdom is conceived of in notably erotic terms throughout, espe-
cially in the climactic line of the octave, showing "sweetnesses" (translated "balms")
pouring from heaven as consolation to the senses. For the image of the phoenix, see
no. 48.

116

Fra 'l candor di ligustri ardente rosa
che de l'eterno Sole a i chiari lampi
cresci, t'orni, t'abbelli, ardi e avvampi
d'amor vero al suo ardor dolce e pietosa.   4
Tu con faccia dimessa e vergognosa
apri il seno al suo lume, e i lieti ed ampi
vezzosi orti del cielo, e gli alti campi
orni fresca e vermiglia e rugiadosa.   8
Lucida perla, i vivi tuoi candori,
cinta d'eterne gemme al tu'oriente
discopri, e di beltà pure fiammelle: 11
candido giglio infra ridenti fiori;
maraviglioso sol chiaro e lucente
d'undici mila cinto elette stelle.   14

Amid the candor of lilies an ardent rose, you grow, blossom, bloom,
and burn in the brilliant rays of the eternal sun, flaming with true love
at His sweet and merciful ardor; with meek and shamefast visage you
open your breast to His light and adorn the broad happy laughing
orchards and the vast fields of heaven, fresh and vermilion and dewy.
A gleaming pearl, girded with eternal gems and pure flames of beauty,
you uncover your living whiteness to your Orient: a candid lily among
bright flowers, a wondrous sun, clear and shining, with eleven thousand
precious stars arrayed around you.

Sonnet ABBA ABBA CDE CDE. Marinella 1603, 16r. Like the previous selection, this
sonnet celebrates a virgin martyr, St. Ursula, whose legend speaks of her being
martyred by the Huns in Cologne along with her 11,000 virgin companions. Ursula
is portrayed here not at the moment of death, like Agnes in the previous sonnet, but
rather enjoying the reward for her sufferings in heaven. Divine ecstasy is evoked
here in self-consciously gorgeous and highly visual language, especially in the ter-
cets, where the images of Ursula as pearl, lily, and sun follow in rapid succession,
taking over from the extended rose metaphor of the quatrains. By l. 13, the saint has
usurped the sun metaphor more conventionally accorded to God in l. 2. While the
presence of Ursula's 11,000 virgins is most explicit in l. 14, they may be glimpsed
earlier in the lilies of l. 1 and the gems and flames of 10–11. "Orient" as a metaphor
for God or Paradise is probably an echo of Petrarch's canzone 28, l. 15.

117

Ad una sua donna chiamata Margherita, la qual pose l'imagine di San
Francesco nella cassa di uno specchio

Tu che 'n vil specchio già di vetro privo,
lume di cinque lumi adorno metti,
di Cristo essempio, un di que' saggi eletti,
ch'abbracciar povertà non ebbe a schivo,   4
scopri come lo spirto invitto e divo
fra sassi e fiere odiando alteri tetti,
palme, illustri vittorie, onor perfetti
celesti accolse in Dio felice e vivo.   8
—Ora in tal specchio, o giovanetti amanti,
imparate polir, far tersa e bella
l'anima, ch'è rugosa, egra e smarrita.   11
Pria convienla lavar con larghi pianti,
farla al ben di qua giù cieca e rubella—
così grida invitando Margherita.   14

To a Servant of Hers, Margherita, Who Placed an Image of St. Francis in the Frame of a Mirror

You who, in a base mirror, bereft of glass, place a living model of Christ,
a light adorned with five lights, one of those elect sages who did not
disdain to embrace poverty—you show us how his dauntless, divine
spirit, living among rocks and wild beasts and despising rich dwellings,
won palms of victory, famous triumphs, and perfect celestial honors,
happy and thriving in God. "In this mirror, young lovers, learn to refine
and groom your soul to beauty, now wrinkled, haggard, and ailing.
First you must bathe it in copious tears, and make it blind and immune
to the goods of this world"—this invitation Margherita cries out.

Sonnet ABBA ABBA CDE CDE. Marinella 1603, 18v (*bella e tersa* in l. 10 corrected to
tersa e bella). An important novelty of late Petrarchist lyric was the increasing use of
titles to explain poems' narrative context. This allowed for obliquity and allusive-
ness in the poems themselves, as here: without the mention of St. Francis in the ti-
tle, it would be impossible to identify the "model of Christ" of l. 3 or the "five lights"
(Francis's stigmata: see nos. 118–19) of l. 2. The poem displays the *arguzia* (wit) that
was prized in baroque lyric, literalizing the metaphor of saints as "mirrors" for
Christian virtue and paradoxically juxtaposing the implied physical beauty of the
worldly young lovers of ll. 9–11 with their ugliness of soul. The use of direct speech
from a source whose identity is revealed only late in a poem was a convention (see
no. 154). The unexpected appearance of a servant as protagonist here may reflect
the Franciscan theme of the spiritual superiority of poverty to riches.

118

Glorïoso Francesco,
ardi fra fredde nevi
ai dì più freddi e brevi
qual nel foco di Dio, spirto beato.
Per te non gela il ghiaccio o morde il fiato   5
di Borea, ma sì in Dio
appaghi il tuo desio;
e godi e speri e spiri
ne l'eterna sembianza e 'l vero ammiri.

119

O serafico eroe,
ardi fra fredde nevi, ardi d'amore;
giaci stanco e ferito;
languendo miri il Feritor gradito,
e, di vil'antro in tenebroso orrore,   5
vivi lieto e beato,
riverito dal mondo e da Dio amato.

Glorious Francis, on the coldest and shortest days of the year, you burn amid cold snows as if in the fire of God, blessed spirit. The ice does not freeze you, nor Boreas's breath bite; rather, you sate your desire in God and relish and hope and breathe in the eternal vision, gazing and wondering at the true.

Seraphic hero, you burn in cold snows, burn with love; you lie weary and wounded, languidly gazing on Him who has inflicted your welcome wounds, and within the dread darkness of a vile cave, you live happy and blessed, revered by the world and beloved by God.

Madrigals abbCCddeE and aBcCDeE. Marinella 1603, 24r. Marinella's *Rime sacre* concludes with a series of short religious madrigals in the style of Angelo Grillo, already imitated by Marino. The two given here are addressed to St Francis, a saint for whom Marinella had particular devotion (Cox 2011, 144). They describe Francis's receipt of the stigmata in the winter snow of Mt. Verna, drawing on the fire-ice *oxymoron familiar from Petrarchan love poetry. The implicit eroticism of the treatment is more explicit in no. 119. No. 118 is especially reminiscent of Grillo in its preference for short lines (six out of nine) and juxtaposed rhymes, as well as its simple and sometimes quasi-naïve language (note in ll. 2–3 the repetition of *freddi/fredde* and the near-repetition of *Ardi / ai di*) and its liking for wordplay (the *speri e spiri* of l. 8). Boreas in l. 6, was a classical wind god, bringer of the north wind. The implicit metaphor of Francis's stigmatization as a duel in "Serafico eroe" was common in Baroque poetry on the theme: see Maggi 2008, which includes discussion of Marinella's Franciscan verse.

120

Converte la Maddalena

Del suo Signor le piante
la pentita unge e d'aspro pianto asperge;
con le rose e con l'oro
de la bocca e del crin le bacia e terge,
ond'egli in dolce suono   5
disse, aprendo di grazie ampio tesoro,
—Va', che n'hai già perdono—.
Ed ella in santo zelo
arse, surse, partì, diè lodi al Cielo.

He Converts Mary Magdalene

The penitent oils the feet of her Lord and waters them with bitter tears;
with the roses and gold of her mouth and hair, she kisses and dries
them. At last he spoke sweetly, opening a rich treasury of grace, "Go,
for your sins are forgiven." And she, in holy zeal, burned, rose, left, gave
thanks to Heaven.

Madrigal aBcBdCdeE. Bozi 1614, 26r (*con* in l. 3 amended from *co* in both cases). This
madrigal appeared in a curious anthology of religious lyrics published in 1614 but
probably compiled around at least a decade earlier, consisting of a complete account
of the life, passion, and resurrection of Christ, narrated in 250 madrigals, each by a
different author. The poems were commissioned by the Venetian patrician Leon-
ardo Sanudo (1544–1607), who had a penchant for such themed compilations: he is
best known for *The Triumph of Dori* (1598), a collection of twenty-nine musical mad-
rigals commissioned from different composers in honor of his bride. Sanudo's reli-
gious collection includes poems by twelve women, ranging from luminaries like
Marinella to figures not attested elsewhere (see no. 121). Marinella narrates Mary
Magdalene's conversion and her washing of Christ's feet, a popular subject for reli-
gious verse (see no. 106) in a fashionably short and metrically light madrigal of nine
lines, with five *settenari* to four hendecaysllables. The poem shows the same taste
for wordplay and rhetorical elaboration within an appearance of simplicity as nos.
118–19. Note especially the play on *piante/pianto* and *aspro/asperge* in ll. 1–2, the *rap-
portatio of 3–4, and the *asyndeton of 9.

Girolama Castagna (pre-1607)

121

È predicata da Anna profetessa per Messia

S'avea per cella un cielo
fatt'entro al sacro Tempio
Anna pudica a l'Ebraismo essempio;
e in vedovile velo
già per sedici lustri   5
del pargoletto nato
predicea in avvenire i fatti illustri;
e tu stuolo ostinato
non vedi in tanto lume
il tuo umanato nume?   10
Sol casta tortorella
lo mira e ammira e Redentor l'appella.

The Prophetess Anna Hails Him as Messiah

She had made herself a celestial cell within the holy Temple, chaste
Anna, a lesson to the Hebrew faith, and in her widow's veil for more
than eighty long years, she had prophesized the bright deeds of the
Child that would be born. And you, stubborn throng, in all this light,
you cannot see our Deity made man? A sole, chaste turtle dove, she
gazes and marvels and calls him Redeemer.

Madrigal abBacdCdeefF. Bozi 1614, 10v. An interesting feature of the biblical verse
collection in which this poem is found (see no. 120) is that the female poets were
given gender-appropriate subjects, focused on female protagonists. Here, Girolama
Castagna recounts an episode in Luke 2:22–38 in which the infant Christ is taken to
the Temple by his parents and encounters two early witnesses to his status as Mes-
siah, Simeon and Anna. Anna is described in the gospel as a prophetess and long-
time widow, who lives within the Temple (Luke gives the length of Anna's widow-
hood as eighty-four years; Castagna as sixteen lustrums, a Roman measure of a
five-year period). Castagna uses Anna as an exemplum of faith, and an implicit re-
proach to those incapable of embracing God's truth even in the "light" of the Chris-
tian era (9–10). The brevity of the lines (nine *settenari* to only three hendecasylla-
bles), and the frequent wordplay and sound-patterning (*cella/cielo* in l. 1; *lustri/
illustri* in 5 and 7; *umanato nume* in 10; *mira e ammira* in 12) give this madrigal a mod-
ish, Baroque feel; it is close stylistically to Lucrezia Marinella's madrigal style
(nos. 118–20).

Valeria Miani (pre-1607)

122

Appare a Maddalena

Carca di quel languir di cui maggiore
non può far il dolore
stava la sconsolata peccatrice;
quando ecco d'improviso chi le dice:
—Maria?—e qui conobbe e le fu nota   5
la voce della santa effigie ignota.
Diss'ella allor—Maestro?—E pur volea
più dir, ma non potea.
O donna aventurata
da Dio cotanto amata;   10
poiché te sola elesse messaggiera
de la Resurrezion sua santa e vera.

He Appears to Magdalene

Laden with as great a languor as ever sorrow could provoke was the
inconsolable sinful woman, when suddenly someone spoke, "Mary?"
And she knew and recognized the voice of the unrecognized holy
figure. "Master?" she said then, and she wished to speak more but could
not. O happiest of women, so beloved of God that he chose you alone as
the messenger of his holy and true Resurrection.

Madrigal AaBBCCDdeeFF. Bozi 1614, 60v. This madrigal, from the same collection
as nos. 120–21, is one of a handful of surviving lyrics by the Paduan Valeria Miani,
better known as a playwright. Recounting the episode of Christ's appearance to
Mary Magdalene after his resurrection, Miani focuses on the most dramatic mo-
ment of dialogue between the two in her gospel source (5–7; John 20:16). It may not
be too fanciful to see the influence of her background in drama here. The madrigal,
of twelve lines with hendecasyllables dominant, is rhymed in couplets throughout.
Miani's style is less self-consciously "artful" than Marinella's or Castagna's, though
note the dramatically effective rich rhyme *nota/ignota* at ll. 5–6 and the grammati-
cal rhyme *volea/potea* at 7–8. The transition to a *settenario* at l. 8, and the line's
simplicity of language, recall the close of Matraini's no. 29. The last two lines of
Miani's poem have a concentration of sibilant consonants, giving emphasis to the
semantically key *messaggiera*, perhaps intended here to recall Magdalene's epithet
apostola apostolorum (apostle to the apostles; the meaning of the Greek *apostolos* is
"messenger").

Maddalena Salvetti (1611)

123

Alto Signor, ch'al popol tuo piovesti,
in ermo clima, già dolci rugiade,
quel popol tuo a cui sicure strade
nel procelloso mar pria gli facesti,
quello per cui sorgesti   5
d'un vivo sasso duro
un fonte chiaro e puro,
deh, rinovella omai gran Padre, in questi
miei giorni afflitti e stanchi,
l'istessi essempi, pria che 'l crin s'imbianchi.   10
Piovi pietose stille
a me della tua grazia a mille a mille,
tal che questo mio core,
più duro, oimè, ch'un duro sasso assai,
stilli per gli occhi un chiaro fonte omai,   15
onde in quest'aspro mar d'orrido gelo
s'apra una strada di salire al cielo.

Lord on High, who once rained down on your people sweet dews in a
harsh climate and drove sure paths for them through the turbulent sea
and raised for them from a living hard stone a pure and clear fountain—
Lord, in these weary and afflicted days of mine, before my hair whitens,
renew these same miracles in me. Rain down on me merciful drops of
your grace, thousands upon thousands, so this heart of mine, harder,
alas! by far than a stone, distills through my eyes a clear fountain, and
in this cruel sea of fearsome ice, a path opens to lead me to heaven.

Madrigal ABBAaccAdDeEfGGHH. Salvetti 1611, 62v (misnumbered 58v). Salvetti's
small collection of religious lyrics is distinctive within female-authored *rime spiri-*
tuali for its theological and moral emphases. This madrigal draws on imagery from
Exodus 14–17, recounting Moses's leading of the Isaraelites out their captivity in
Egypt. The references are to the raining of manna in a "dew" from heaven in the
desert, the miraculous parting of the Red Sea, and Moses's striking of a fountain
from a rock in the desert. The poet calls on God to repeat these miracles for her,
raining down grace, which will wring tears from her stony, impenitent soul and
open a path to heaven. The heading of the poem refers to the Old Testament images
as "figures," alluding to the theory, dating back to Paul and the Church Fathers,
whereby the Old Testament was seen as a prefiguration of the truths of the New.
This mode of reading is implicit in Salvetti's use of the Exodus material here as a
figure, or *type, for Christian salvation. The length of this madrigal (seventeen lines)
and its relative weightiness (twelve hendecasyllables to six *settenari*) distinguish it
from the fashionable lighter model used by Lucrezia Marinella (nos. 118–20).

Semidea Poggi (1623)

124

—Qual sole, o pellegrin, da l'orïente
vedesti uscir con più dorati raggi?
Qual più mirasti mai ne' tuoi viaggi
Espero a sera scintillar lucente?   4
Dillo, se il cielo a' tuoi desii clemente
ti dia guide e nocchier esperti e saggi,
e non soffra giamai, che fieri oltraggi
d'iniquo predator turbin la mente—.   8
—Dirol: Non fiammeggiò luce più bella
per seren quando aggiorna e quando imbruna
tra quelle mar che fanno il mondo adorno   11
di Maria, ch'è del mar fidata stella,
di Maria, ch'è la notte unica luna
di Maria, ch'è l'aurora al far del giorno—.   14

"What Sun, O pilgrim, did you see rising from the East with the most
golden rays? What in all your journeying was the Hesperus you saw
most brightly gleaming? Tell me, and may the heavens, merciful to
your desire, give you always the wisest and most practiced guides and
helmsmen and grant that your peace is not disturbed by a cruel preda-
tor's fierce attacks." "I shall tell you: no light shone so lovely in a clear
sky at dawn or dusk above those seas that adorn the world as does Mary,
who is the trusted star of the sea; as does Mary, who is the sole moon of
the night; as does Mary, who is dawn at the breaking of the day."

Sonnet ABBA ABBA CDE CDE. Poggi 1623, 58. This sonnet, cast entirely in dia-
logue, draws on traditional images of life as a pilgrimage and the Virgin as guiding
light. Its novelty lies in its long development of the literal sense of these metaphors
and its withholding of their referent until the final tercet. This unveiling corre-
sponds with a stylistic shift, from the syntactically sinuous and lexically elevated ll.
1–11 to the three *end-stopped lines (12–14), with their strong *anaphora and simple,
almost popular language. Mary's name is capitalized in the original in these lines.
The optative subjunctive construction of ll. 4–8, auguring the pilgrim a safe jour-
ney, is frequent in Dante's *Divine Comedy*, in addresses to the souls encountered.
Hesperus, in l. 4, is the evening, or morning, star, Venus, while "del mar . . . stella"
(12) translates the Latin *stella maris*, one of Mary's traditional appellations. For the
assocation of Mary with the moon, see no. 82.

125

Da le vene del Cielo,
mio Salvator, mio Dio,
per l'acquedotto del costato pio,
scatorì nel mirare,
misto d'acqua e di sangue   5
sacro e salubre fonte,
ch'ha virtù di sanar chi giace e langue:
probatica de l'alme, in ch'io m'affondi,
e n'escano i miei sensi integri e mondi.

From the veins of heaven, my Savior, my God, through the aqueduct
of his blessed side, there sprang as I watched a holy and health-giving
fountain of blood mixed with water, with the power to heal those who
lie ailing: a Probatic Pool for souls, in which I immerse myself, and
from which my senses emerge whole and pure.

Madrigal abBcdeDFF. Poggi 1623, 59, headed "Al Santissimo costato di Nostro
Signore" (To the Holy Side [lit. Ribcage] of Our Lord). This madrigal, like those of
Lucrezia Marinella (nos. 118–20), falls within the tradition of religious madrigal
initiated by Angelo Grillo. Poggi is closer than Marinella to Grillo and Marino in
the boldness of her *conceits: Christ's side wound as aqueduct ferrying blood from
the "veins" of heaven into a curative "Probatic Pool" for souls on earth (the refer-
ence is to the Pool of Bethseda, mentioned in John 5:2–4: in the Vulgate version, a
miraculous curative pool outside Jerusalem where the sick gathered, hoping for a
cure). Three lines in this poem (1, 4, 6) have no rhyme, lending more emphasis to
the two couplets, especially the hendecasyllabic l. 7–8, which introduce the figure
of the poet and round off the *conceit. Line 4 speaks of the fountain of Christ's
blood springing forth as the poet watches, evoking legends of miraculous cruci-
fixes that bleed or shed tears.

Francesca Turina (1628)

126

O querce antiche, o duri cerri, o faggi,
alteri pini e verdeggianti abeti,
ove a menar i dì tranquilli e lieti
son giunta in questi lochi ermi e selvaggi,   4
qui faranno i pensier dritti vïaggi
al ciel, e in Dio staran fissi e quïeti;
qui svelar suol gli arcani più secreti
il divin lume con gl'immensi raggi.   8
Chi non vorria fuggir l'aspre procelle
di questo Egeo di vita e 'n voi far stanza
per gustar di là sù cose sì belle?   11
Qui dolce sopra ogni mortal usanza
cantan gli augelli in queste parti e in quelle,
onde ebra l'alma nell'orar s'avanza.   14

Ancient oaks, sturdy holms, beeches, lofty pines, green-growing firs, I
have come to spend my happy, peaceful days in these bleak wild places.
Here my thoughts will travel directly to heaven, and in God they will
be fixed and quieted; here, the divine light with His immense rays
reveals his most hidden secrets. Who would not wish to flee the cruel
tempests of this Aegean of life, to come to dwell here and taste such
lovely things from on high? Here on all sides the birds sing sweet more
sweetly than any mortal usage, so the soul rushes onward intoxicated
with prayer.

Sonnet ABBA ABBA CDC DCD. Turina 1628, 223. This fine sonnet, headed "Rivolgi-
mento a Dio" (Turning to God), opens a sequence of religious verse in Turina's
collected *Rime*. The context is the poet's return to her childhood home of Carpegna,
on the northern border of Tuscany, near St. Francis's heremitic retreat at La Verna.
The poem celebrates the aptness of the wild landscape of the area for visionary
mediation in Turina's characteristically limpid, musical language. The description
of God in l. 8 revealing his secrets "with immense rays" may reflect the traditional
iconography of Francis's receipt of the stigmata. "Aegean" in l. 10, used by antono-
masia to mean "an ocean," was a common metaphor in sixteenth-century verse, but
Turina may have been thinking of a phrase in Giovanni della Casa's sonnet 62: "'n
questo Egeo che vita ha nome" (in this Aegean we call life). *Quercie* and *cerri* (1) pres-
ent translation problems, as both are types of oak (the *cerro*, which I have translated
"holm," is more precisely a Turkey oak or *quercus cerris*).

127

O se, mentre dal volgo m'allontano
fra l'erbe e i fior per vie remote e torte,
avessi d'incontrar cotanta sorte
il mio Giesù sotto sembiante umano   4
(quel ch'altrui quasi peregrin mondano
mostrossi allor che ritornò da morte),
quanto il pensar di lui gioia m'apporte
gli scoprirei con parlar dolce e piano,   8
e d'amor lagrimando a lui davante
prostrata umilmente, gli vorrei
mille volte baciar l'amate piante.   11
O come e quante volte io gli direi
—Abbi pietà di me, cortese amante
ch'in te solo riposto ho i pensier miei—.   14

And if, while I was wandering far from the crowds among the flowers and grass along secret winding ways, I should have such fortune as to meet with my Jesus in human form, as he showed himself in the guise of a wordly pilgrim that time when he returned from death, with words sweet and low, I would confide in him how great a joy I have thinking of him, and weeping with love, I would long to prostrate myself humbly before him and kiss his beloved feet a thousand times. O how I would repeat to him, and how often, "Have pity on me, courteous lover, for in you alone have I placed all my care."

Sonnet ABBA ABBA CDC DCD. Turina 1628, 232. Some of the most intriguing of Turina's religious sonnets recount visions or fantasies occurring during the rural meditations she speaks of in no. 126. In one sonnet, she speaks of seeing the penitent Magdalene in a cave; in another, the Virgin, Magdalene, and John lamenting over the dead Christ (Turina 1628, 224, 234). The present sonnet imagines a meeting with the risen Christ, who is figured initially as a pilgrim, as in the account of his meeting with the disciples on the road to Emmaus (Luke 24, 13–16); the tercets, however, figure the encounter in a manner recalling his appearance to Magdalene in the noli me tangere scene familiar from pictorial tradition (Cox 2011, 75). The faintly illicit, erotic character of the religious fantasy recounted here may determine the adjectivization applied to the *vie* of l. 2: *torto* means literally "winding" but also has the metaphorical meaning of "morally dubious." *Diaeresis must be assumed in *vorrei* and *miei* (10, 14).

128

Cristo al pozzo

Chi non saria, Gesù, preso e conquiso
veder la faccia tua così vermiglia,
mista col bel candore a meraviglia,
umidi i bei crin d'oro intorno al viso?   4
Stanco, anelante, sopra il pozzo assiso,
con fisse luci e con penose ciglia,
a l'aura estiva refrigerio piglia
il monarca immortal del Paradiso,   8
le labra asciutte e la serena fronte
chino riposi su la bianca mano,
spirando tutto amor, tutto bellezza.   11
Deh, corri, anima ingrata, al vivo fonte
ch'estinguer puote ogni desire insano,
e resta ebra d'amore e di dolcezza.   14

Christ at the Well

Who would not be captured and conquered, Jesus, seeing the crimson
of your cheeks so wondrously mingled with their lovely pallor and your
beautiful golden locks damp around your face? Weary, panting, seated
on the well, with fixed eyes and aching brows, the immortal Monarch
of Paradise takes refreshment from the summer breeze; you lean your
dry lips and your serene brow on your white hand, breathing love and
beauty from every pore. Run, ungrateful soul, to the bright fountain
that can extinguish every unhealthy desire, there to become drunk on
love and sweetness.

Sonnet ABBA ABBA CDE CDE. Turina 1628, 247. Like no. 127, this sonnet projects
the poet imaginatively into the role of a New Testament female protagonist, this
time the Samaritan woman of John 4:1–42 who encountered Christ at the well where
he was resting, and offered him water. Like the noli me tangere episode, which in-
spired no. 127, Christ's encounter with the Samaritan woman was quite frequently
depicted in art, and Turina may have been inspired by visual prototypes in her
imagining of the episode. The eroticized description of Christ's beauty recalls that
in Isabella Morra's no. 87, though Turina's description is more vivid and dynamic.
The last tercet, figuring divine love and grace through the metaphor of an inebriat-
ing fountain, recalls Christ's words to the Samaritan woman (John 4:10) that he can
offer her "living water" that will eternally quench her thirst.

129

Il sesso femminile narra le sue prerogative e possanza

Io non già da vil fango ebbi i natali
ma quando l'uomo assomigliossi a Dio
trassi dal gran conforto il viver mio
e spirai dal perfetto aure vitali.   4
Morte già m'appressò l'arco e gli strali
quando uccidere il mondo ebbi in desio,
e s'al uom chiusi il ciel, anco poss'io
spalancarli lassù gl'archi fatali.   8
Dal Olimpo stellato all'ime arene
piombando a volo in questa terrea mole
angiol sublime ad annunciar lo viene.   11
Chi crea l'impone e chi redime il vuole;
chi procede il consente, e quindi avviene
che dal mar di Maria sorge il mio sole.   14

The Female Sex Narrates its Prerogatives and Power

I did not have my origins in base mud, but when man took on God's
form, I drew my life from this great consolation and breathed vital airs
from this perfection. Death proffered me his bow and arrows when I
wished to slay the world, but, if I closed heaven to man, I can also open
the fatal arches on high. From the starry Olympus to the base sands, a
sublime angel came to announce it, plummeting down on his wings to
this terrestrial mass. He who creates imposes it; he who redeems wishes
it; he who acts concedes it—and thus it is that from the ocean of Mary
there rises my sun.

Sonnet ABBA ABBA CDC DCD. San Giustino, Archivio Bufalini, Inventario Azzi
MS 185, sez. IV, c. 293 (*all'ime* corrected from *al ime*). This remarkable unpublished
sonnet traces the theological status of women from Creation to Incarnation. The
first quatrain draws on an interpretation of Genesis developed in the 1520s by Hen-
ricus Cornelius Agrippa and subsequently much disseminated in texts praising
women, whereby women's intrinsic superiority to men was proved, among other
things, by the fact that they were created from nobler matter (Adam's rib, rather
than clay). Lines 5–6 recount Eve's part in the Fall, while the remainder of the poem
narrates how the slur placed on womankind by Eve was removed by the Virgin's
role in the redemption of humanity through her bearing of Christ. The elegant
*conceit of the last line is underlined by the *alliteration and *assonance of *mar/
Maria*, *sorge/sole*, and the pun on Mary's name.

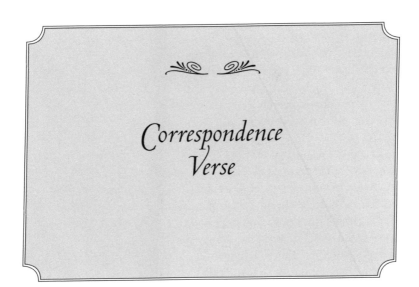

*Correspondence
Verse*

Vittoria Colonna–Pietro Bembo

130

Ahi quanto fu al mio Sol contrario il fato,
che con l'alta virtù dei raggi suoi
pria non v'accese, che mill'anni e poi
voi sareste più chiaro, ei più lodato.   4
Il nome suo col vostro stile ornato,
che dà scorno agli antichi, invidia a noi,
a mal grado del tempo avreste voi
dal secondo morir sempre guardato.   8
Potess'io almeno mandar nel vostro petto
l'ardor ch'io sento, o voi nel mio l'ingegno
per far la rima a quel gran merto eguale,   11
ché così temo il ciel ne prenda a sdegno:
voi, perch'avete preso altro suggetto,
me, che ardisco parlar d'un lume tale.   14

131

Cingi le costei tempie de l'amato
da te già in volto umano arboscel, poi
ch'ella sorvola i più leggiadri tuoi
poeti col suo verso alto e purgato;   4
e se 'n donna valor, bel petto armato
d'onestà, real sangue onorar vuoi,
onora lei, cui par, Febo, non puoi
veder qua giù, tanto dal ciel l'è dato.   8
Felice lui ch'è sol conforme obietto
a l'ampio stile, e dal beato regno
vede amor santo quanto pote e vale;   11
e lei ben nata, che sì chiaro segno
stampa del marital suo casto affetto,
e con gran passi a vera gloria sale.   14

Alas, how cruel fate was to my Sun, that with the great power of his rays he did not strike you earlier so that in a thousand years and more you would be more famous, he more praised. Adorned with your style, which leaves the ancients in its wake and fills us with envy, his name would have been preserved by you from the second death, in defiance of time. If only I could at least send into your breast the ardor I feel, or you into mine the genius that would let me make verse equal to his great merit! As it is, I fear heaven will be angered with us—with you because you have chosen another subject, with me because I dare to speak of so great a light.

Crown her temples with that beloved plant you once loved in human form since she soars above your most elegant poets with her lofty, refined verse. If you wish to honor in a woman true worth, a fair breast armed with chastity, the highest birth, then honor her, Phoebus, whose peer you cannot see on earth, so great are heaven's gifts to her. Happy that man who is the sole deserving object of her noble style and who sees from the realm of the blessed the power and worth of holy Love; and well born she, who is stamping such a brilliant mark of her chaste marital affection and ascending to true glory with great strides.

Sonnets ABBA ABBA CDE DCE, using same rhymes. Bembo 1535, 42v, appendix (*merto* in l. 11 of no. 130 corrected from *merito* on the basis of Colonna 1560; *voi/poi* in ll. 7–8 of no. 131 corrected to *vuoi/puoi*). The habit of exchanging sonnets with other poets, familiar from the thirteenth century onward, enjoyed an immense vogue in the sixteenth century, when such correspondence verse came to occupy an ever-increasing space in published verse collections. The initiating poem in such exchanges was called the *proposta*, the reply poem the *risposta*. *Risposte* often, though not always, used the same rhymes, or even the same rhyme words, as the original, making them a considerable test of poetic skill.

Although not the first surviving sonnet exchange between a female and a male poet, this exchange between Colonna and Bembo is of exceptional historical importance. Colonna sent her sonnet to Bembo in 1530 through intermediaries, and he was evidently much struck by its quality. In one letter, he describes it as "grave, noble, ingenious, and altogether excellent in its invention, order, and style" (the three key components of eloquence in classical rhetorical theory); in another, he talks of the poem having exceeded his expectations of women's literary capacities by far. The exchange was published in 1535, in the second edition of Bembo's *Rime*, with a small selection of sonnet exchanges, including one with Veronica Gambara (nos. 132–33). This may be seen as marking female poets' moment of cultural "arrival," given Bembo's enormous prestige.

As usual in sonnet exchanges, it is the junior poet who writes the *proposta*, and Colonna positions herself in her sonnet deferentially with respect to Bembo. The premise of the poem is that Colonna's husband, Ferrante d'Avalos, referred to in the first line by her customary metaphor of the Sun, deserved a greater poet than her to immortalize him. As in no. 41, Colonna modestly presents herself as a weak poet distinguished only by the strength of her love, although her claim is, as there, belied by the sophistication of her poetry and the elevation of her style. The quatrains develop a parallel between Bembo's excellence as poet and d'Avalos's excellence as poetic subject while the tercets complicate this binary relation by introducing a third, antithetical figure, the poet herself, inferior to both men in genius but distinguished

by her uxorial "ardor." Much of the poem's success rests on the limpidity and sup-
pleness with which Colonna handles these geometries, counterposing *voi/ei* and
suo/vostro in a parallel and a *chiastic structure in the pivotal ll. 4–5 of the quatrains
and similarly contrasting *io/voi* and *me/voi* in the *chiastic l. 10 and the parallel
clauses of ll. 13–14. "Second death" (8) means the death of a person's name through
historical oblivion.

Bembo replies in a sonnet whose quatrains are addressed to Apollo, god of
poetry (the Phoebus of l. 7), demanding that he crown Colonna as a laureate (the
"plant" of ll. 1–2 is the laurel, sacred to Apollo and symbolic of poetic glory). Bembo
crafts Colonna here as a new female ideal, combining traditional feminine attri-
butes such as chastity and marital devotion with the more "virile" quality of poetic
eloquence. Adding to this virilization are the metaphor of chastity as "armor" (5) and
the use of *valore* in the same line, a word that has connotations of "valor" or "prow-
ess" in military contexts, as well as moral worth. Notable also are the emphasis in
the tercets on the grandeur of Colonna's style (*ampio* in l. 10, translated as "noble,"
means literally "ample") and the dynamism and energy conferred by the verb
stampa, prominently placed at the beginning of l. 13, and by the striking closing im-
age of Colonna "striding" toward fame.

Veronica Gambara–Pietro Bembo (c. 1530)

132

A l'ardente desio ch'ognior m'accende
di seguir nel camin ch'al ciel conduce
sol voi mancava, o mia serena luce,
per discacciar la nebbia che m'offende.   4
Or poiché 'l vostro raggio in me risplende,
per quella strada ch'a ben far ne induce,
vengo dietro di voi, fidato duce,
che 'l mio voler più oltra non si stende.   8
Bassi pensieri in me non han più loco;
ogni vil voglia è spenta, e sol d'onore
e di rara virtù l'alma si pasce,   11
dolce mio caro ed onorato foco
poscia che dal gentil vostro calore
eterna fama e vera gloria nasce.   14

133

Quel dolce suon, per cui chiaro s'intende
quanto raggio del ciel in voi riluce,
nel laccio, in ch'io già fui, mi riconduce
dopo tant'anni, e preso a voi mi rende.   4
Sento la bella man che 'l nodo prende,
e strigne sì che 'l fin de la mia luce
mi s'avicina, e chi di fuor traluce
né rifugge da lei, né si difende: 8
ch'ogni pena per voi gli sembra gioco,
e 'l morir vita; ond'io ringrazio Amore,
che m'ebbe poco men sin da le fasce,   11
e 'l vostro ingegno, a cui lodar son roco,
e l'antico desio, che nel mio core,
qual fior di primavera, apre e rinasce.   14

In the ardent desire that has always fired me to follow the path that
leads to heaven, you alone were lacking, my dear serene light, to dispel
the obscuring mists; but now that your ray is shining in me, trusted
leader, I can follow you along the way of righteousness, for this is now
entirely my end. Base thoughts I have banished; every low desire is
spent, and my soul now feeds solely on honor and rare virtue, O my
dear, sweet, and honored fire, since from your gentle warmth eternal
fame and true glory are born.

That sweet sound, which clearly shows how bright a heavenly ray shines within you, now leads me back, after so many years, into the noose in which I was once caught and renders me to you as a captive. I feel your lovely hand taking the knot and so tightening it that my death seems nigh, but my soul neither flees from you nor offers any defense, for every pain it suffers for you seems rather a joy, and death becomes life. And so I thank Love, who has been my lord since my earliest days, and your fine mind, which I praise without cease, and that former desire that unfurls within my heart and is reborn like a flower in spring.

Sonnets ABBA ABBA CDE CDE, using same rhymes. Bembo 1535, 42r and appendix. Like the previous one (nos. 130 and 131), this sonnet exchange dates to around 1530 and was published in Bembo's *Rime* of 1535. Its tone is much warmer, however: while Colonna and Bembo were not personally acquainted, Gambara and Bembo had family connections and had known one another for several decades by this time (their first sonnet exchange dates to 1504, when Gambara was nineteen). Gambara positions herself in her sonnet in a position of discipleship to Bembo, spiritual, moral, and, implicitly, poetic: his teaching will both show her the way to heaven and to righteousness (2, 6) and lead her fame and glory (14). Appropriately, her sonnet shows a precise observance of the linguistic and stylistic norms of Petrarchism as Bembo had taught them and employs a dense web of Petrarchan allusion in making its argument: ll. 2 and 6 closely echo ll. 3 and 7 of Petrarch's canzone 72, where Laura is given the same guiding role that Gambara attributes to Bembo here. The term *fidato duce* (7) similarly derives from Petrarch's description of Laura as his "fida e cara" duce in sonnet 357, l. 2, while the image of Bembo's ray shining through the poet's mind in l. 5 echoes Petrarch's sonnet 95, l. 9, where Laura, again, has the role given to Bembo.

   Bembo replies to this barrage of Petrarchan quotation with a counter-barrage of his own, drawn in some cases from Gambara's own sources. The rhyme *luce/traluce* (part of a linked inclusive sequence, *luce/traluce/riluce*, which echoes Gambara's *duce/conduce/induce*) derives from sonnet 357, while *traluce* also occurs in rhyme in the first stanza of canzone 72 and out of rhyme in sonnet 95. A new Petrarchan source is sonnet 199, whose opening, "O bella man, che mi destringi 'l core," is echoed in ll. 5–6. Bembo's language is more overtly erotic than Gambara's and constructs their relationship quite explicitly as a Neoplatonic love affair. Together, however, the two poems constitute a textbook exercise in how Petrarch's erotic language might be adapted to describe a nonerotic relationship of mutual esteem and regard between a male and female poet. Unlike the conventional poetic lady, who conquers through her beauty, Bembo represents Gambara's seductive power as deriving from her poetry (the "sweet sound" of l. 1) and from her intellect (12); even the "beautiful hand" (5) has become the writing hand of the female poet—and, metonymically, her poetry itself—rather than the passive object of aesthetic appreciation it is in Petrarch.

Veronica Gambara–Vittoria Colonna (c. 1532)

134

O de la nostra etade unica gloria,
donna saggia, leggiadra, anzi divina,
a la qual reverente oggi s'inchina
chiunque è degno di famosa istoria,   4
ben fia eterna di voi qua giù memoria,
né potrà il tempo con la sua ruina
far del bel nome vostro empia rapina,
ma di lui porterete alma vittoria.   8
Il sesso nostro un sacro e nobil tempio
dovria, come già a Palla e a Febo, farvi
di ricchi marmi e di finissim'oro.   11
E poiché di virtù siete l'essempio,
vorrei, donna, poter tanto lodarvi,
quanto vi reverisco, amo e adoro.   14

135

Di novo il cielo de l'antica gloria
orna la nostra etade, e sua ruina
prescrive, poscia che tra noi destina
spirto ch'ha di beltà doppia vittoria.   4
Di voi, ben degno d'immortal istoria,
bella donna, ragiono, a cui s'inchina
chi più di bello ottiene, e la divina
interna parte vince ogni memoria.   8
Faranvi i chiari spirti eterno tempio,
la carta il marmo fia, l'inchiostro l'oro,
che 'l ver constringe lor sempre a lodarvi.   11
Morte col primo o col secondo ed empio
morso il tempo non ponno omai levarvi
d'immortal fama il bel ricco tesoro.   14

Oh unique glory of our age! Wise and graceful lady—nay, divine—
before whom all those living who are worthy of fame's annals bow in
reverence, your immortality on earth is now quite assured. Time with
his all his ruination will not now be able to snatch away your lovely
name; instead, you will carry off a fine victory [*vittoria*] over him. Our
sex should erect a sacred and noble temple to you, as once they were
raised to Pallas and Phoebus, adorned with rich marbles and the most
refined gold. And since you are the epitome of virtue, I would wish,

lady, to be so capable of speaking your praise as I am of revering, loving, and worshiping you.

Once more, heaven adorns our age with ancient glory and proscribes its ruin, since it destines to us a spirit who has a double victory of beauty. Of you, worthy of immortal history, I am speaking, beautiful lady, to whom those who boast the greatest beauty bow, while your divine internal part is unmatched. The brightest spirits will shape for you an eternal temple, with paper as its marble and ink as its gold, for the truth constrains them always to praise you. Death with the first bite, nor Time with the cruel second can now steal from you the fine rich treasure of immortal fame.

Sonnets (no. 134) ABBA ABBA CDE CDE; (no. 135) ABBA ABBA CDE CED, using the same rhyme words in different order (*per le confuse*). Colonna 1558, 389–90, 330. Gambara and Colonna engaged in two sonnet exchanges in around 1532, with Gambara providing the *proposta* in each case. The two exchanges gained an iconic status among female poets, with Gambara's sonnet in particular, the more successful of the two, being much imitated (see nos. 153, 163). The opening line of Gambara's sonnet echoes Ovid's *Letters from Pontus* 2.8, l. 25 ("saecli decus indelebile nostri": undying glory of our age), while the B rhymes of the quatrains echo Petrarch's sonnet 167, which portrays the singing Laura as a "sweet siren of heaven," an appropriate reminiscence in a poem to Colonna. Phoebus and Pallas (10) are Apollo and Minerva, gods, respectively, of poetry and wisdom, while *virtù*, of which Colonna is said to be the epitome in l. 12, means "moral virtue" but also "talent," especially creative or intellectual. *Vittoria* (8) puns on Colonna's "lovely name," alluded to in the previous line.

Bembo commented in a letter of 1532 of one exchange he had seen between Colonna and Gambara that, while he liked both poems, Colonna's reply was "more labored" (*di più fatica*) since it was an answer *per le rime*. That is certainly the case here, where the *risposta* is distinctly inferior as a poem to the *proposta*. Colonna makes things especially difficult for herself by using the same actual rhyme words, not just the same rhymes, as Gambara in her *proposta*: an unusual choice in the 1530s, although it became fashionable later in the century (see no. 141). Thematically, Colonna picks up Gambara's concern with immortalization and the role of poetry in constructing fame, while the tercets develop Gambara's image of the temple, which here becomes explicitly a poetic monument, created in paper and ink. Both poems are highly self-referential in regard to their own participation in the process of mutual poetic immortalization: the subtext of their temple imagery may be Horace's description of his poetry as a "monument more lasting than bronze" (ode 3.30).

Tullia d'Aragona–Girolamo Muzio (1547)

136

Fiamma gentil che da gl'interni lumi
con dolce folgorar in me discendi,
mio intenso affetto lietamente prendi,
com'è usanza a tuoi santi costumi;   4
poiché con l'alta tua luce m'allumi
e sì soavemente il cor m'accendi
ch'ardendo lieto vive e lo difendi
che forza di vil foco nol consumi.   8
E con la lingua fai che 'l rozo ingegno,
caldo dal caldo tuo, cerchi inalzarsi
per cantar tue virtuti in mille parti;   11
io spero ancor a l'età tarda farsi
noto che fosti tal, che stil più degno
uopo era, e che mi fu gloria l'amarti.   14

137

Quai d'eloquenza fien sì chiari fiumi,
luce che d'alto ardor mio core incendi,
ch'aguagli tua virtù? Se là 've splendi
a superno desio l'anime impiumi?   4
Come dinanzi a Borea nebbie e fumi,
così di là, dove tu i raggi stendi,
fugge ogni vil pensier, sì ch'a noi rendi
la vita in terra dei celesti numi.   8
E poich'a me non son tuoi lumi scarsi
di quel splendor che, da l'eterno regno
in te disceso, tu fra noi comparti;   11
di quel c'ho dentro e fuor non può mostrarsi,
faranno al mondo manifesto segno
l'amarti, il celebrarti e l'onorarti.   14

Gentle flame that through my inner eyes descends within me like sweet lightning, graciously accept my intense affection, as you are so kindly wont, for your noble light illumines me and sets my heart aflame so softly that it lives happily burning, defended from being consumed by any baser fire. And with your tongue, you urge my unfinished mind, heated by your heat, to raise itself up in order to sing your praises in a thousand parts. I hope to convey to the centuries to come that you were such a man as to require a finer style to praise you, and that it was my glory to have loved you.

What bright rivers of eloquence could do justice to your virtue, O light that fires my heart with noble ardor, if, wherever it gleams, you feather the wings of men's souls to aspire to the highest desire? Just as all mists and vapors are dispersed by the north wind, so all base thoughts take flight wherever your rays extend, making the life of your followers here on earth that of the celestial gods. And since your fair beams do not deny me that splendor that descended into you from the eternal realm and that you share among us, let what I have within and cannot express manifest itself to the world through my loving you, praising you, and honoring you.

Sonnets ABBA ABBA CDE DCE. d'Aragona 1547, 14r. Although Gambara, Colonna, and Bembo pioneered the female-male sonnet exchange, it was popularized by d'Aragona and Laura Terracina, whose verse collections of the late 1540s contain such a high quotient of correspondence verse that they have been termed "choral anthologies" (see introduction). Girolamo Muzio (1496–1576) was, together with Benedetto Varchi, one of d'Aragona's principal poetic admirers, featuring in the *Rime* with thirty sonnets and an eclogue. D'Aragona's sonnet echoes the imagery of Gambara's no. 132, representing Muzio's spiritual and poetic guidance in terms of illumination and heat transfer, although the language is more sensual, particularly in ll. 1–2 and 10. The rhyming in the quatrains is intricate, with the rich rhymes *lumi/allumi* and *discendi/accendi* further enhanced by the juxtaposition of the grammatically and phonetically parallel *m'allumi/m'accendi*. More generally, the poem is rich in sound patterning: note the *consonance of l. 5, the *alliteration of l. 10, and the pairings of *accendi/ardendo* and *farsi/fosti* across the transitions between ll. 6–7 and 12–13.

Muzio's reply converts the Neoplatonic motif of the lady as conduit to the divine from the "private" model found, for example, in Bembo's sonnet to Gambara (no. 133), in which the lady serves as individual muse and guide to the poet, into a more public model, where she serves not only the poet but an entire community, the *noi* (7,11), in the same way. Although this generalization of the lady's role has precedents in Dante's Christlike Beatrice, it may also be seen in context as an idealization of the social and cultural role of a courtesan like d'Aragona, who was an object of adulation to multiple admirers. Muzio's insistence on d'Aragona's salvific influence on her followers is pointed, given the moralizing commonplace that saw courtesans as a corrupting presence in society. This is particularly the case in the context of the publication of the *Rime* (the composition of the sonnet may date to around a decade earlier): shortly before the collection appeared, d'Aragona had famously fought to defend herself against a law introduced in Florence, where she was living, which constrained any woman defined as a prostitute to wear a distinguishing yellow veil (Basile 2001).

Agnolo Bronzino–Laura Battiferri (1560)

138

Io giuro a voi per quella viva fronde
di cui voi fuste al sacro fonte pianta,
e per quella di lui cortese e santa
fiamma, che regge il ciel, la terra e l'onde,   4
ch'alla sua felice ombra in sì gioconde
note ho veduto tal ch'onesta canta
ch'io tengo a vile omai qual più si vanta
e dolcezza maggior non viemmi altronde;   8
ché se le fortunate Oretta e Bice
onora il mondo, all'altrui senno ed opra
sì dee non men ch'ai lor merti dar vanto.   11
Voi per proprio valor Laura e Beatrice
vincete, e sète ai lor pregi di sopra,
e forse ai loro amanti in stile e canto.   14

139

Sì come al fonte ebb'io larghe e seconde
le stelle a impormi il nome, avess'io tanta
grazia da lor pur'anco avuta quanta
a voi novello Apelle Apollo infonde,   4
ch'oggi le vostre altere rime, donde
verace amor di falso velo ammanta
il vero, a me con gran ragion cotanta
lode darian, ch'a lor sol corrisponde,   8
e forse delle due non men felice
sarei, che stanno a tutte l'altre sopra
co' lor casti amator per sempre a canto.   11
Ma poiché 'n questa etate a voi sol lice
dar doppia vita altrui, perché non s'opra
per voi ch'io con voi viva altrettanto?   14

I swear to you by that bright frond of which you became a plant at the sacred fount, and by the gentle holy flame of him who rules the sky, the earth, and the waves, that, in its happy shade, I have heard a lady sing in such fair and honest notes that I now hold vile all that which is most prized and know no higher sweetness. For if the world honors those lucky two, Oretta and Bice, they have others' wit and labor to thank for it no less than their own merits. You defeat Laura and Beatrice through your worth and outdo their proudest boasts, just as perhaps you outdo their lovers in pen and song.

If only, just as the stars smiled kindly on me at the fount when they gave me my name, they had lavished on me that grace that is infused in you, new Apelles, by Apollo. For then your fine verses, in which true love conceals the truth with a false veil, would rightly give that praise to me that is only owing to them. Then perhaps I would indeed be happier than the two who are famed beyond all other ladies, with their chaste lovers forever at their side. But since in our own age, you alone have the gift of giving a double life to others, why do you not strive that I, with you, should live on in such a way?

Sonnets ABBA ABBA CDE CDE, using same rhymes. Battiferri 1560, 82. Battiferri was married to the sculptor Bartolomeo Ammannati, and the sonnet exchanges in her first verse collection included correspondences with the artists Agnolo Bronzino (1503–72) and Benvenuto Cellini (1500–71), who followed Michelangelo in practicing poetry as well as the plastic arts. This exchange with Bronzino explores the theme of the lady as both the object of poetry and as poet herself, a theme also foregrounded in Bronzino's famous portrait of Battiferri, now in Palazzo Vecchio (Kirkham 1998; Plazzotta 1998). The "bright frond" of the opening of Bronzino's sonnet is the laurel, symbolic of poetic inspiration. Battiferri "became a laurel at the sacred fount" in the sense that she was christened Laura. "He who rules the skies, the earth, and the waves" is probably Love, rather than God. Bronzino's mention of Battiferri's *onestà* (6) may reflect residual qualms over the moral propriety of poetry as a practice for women. In the tercets, Bronzino speaks of the new Laura's superiority to Petrarch's Laura and Dante's Beatrice (Oretta and Bice are diminutives, used here to comic effect), in that she is capable of attaining fame through her own efforts and not simply by acting as muse to others. The sonnet ends audaciously by comparing Battiferri as poet to Dante and Petrarch themselves.

Battiferri, in her reply, turns the compliment, praising Bronzino for his double gift of poetry and painting (the *Apelle-Apollo* quip of l. 4 was a habitual compliment for artist-poets: Apelles was one of the most famous painters of antiquity, Apollo the god of poetry), and ending by inviting him to immortalize her through this double gift in the same way that Dante and Petrarch did Beatrice and Laura. In ll. 6–7, the poet modestly suggest that Bronzino's lavish praise for her verse is undeserved, but this modesty is belied by the technical sophistication she displays in the sonnet. Syntactically complex and *enjambment-rich, the poem is also notable for its wordplay and elaborate sound-patterning. *Assonance and *consonance are pervasive, especially in ll. 4 and 14, and across the line transition between 1 and 2, while ll. 6–7 combines phonetic couplings such as *amor/ammanta* and *velo/vero* with *polyptota such as *verace/vero*.

Angelo Grillo–Leonora Bernardi (1589)

140

E sì chiare, e sì belle, e sì devote
voci, e pregar sì pio, sì caldo zelo
al ciel non tornerà? Se vien dal cielo,
e 'l detta il ciel, celesti son le note?   4
Leonora su sovra l'eccelse rote,
qua giù lasciando il suo corporeo velo,
non l'udì con la mente? Apollo in Delo
l'insegnò? Tanto sa? Cotanto puote?   8
L'udì, l'apprese, e parve dir Maria:
—Figlia, ch'offristi a me lo spirto e 'l core,
vie più d'ogni altra affettuosa e pura: 11
divo spirto, alta tromba e santo ardore
eccoti in vece. Ah, da mie lodi impura
lingua fia lunge, e tu mia Musa sia—.   14

141

Se le mie preci ed umili e devote,
piene, quanto poss'io, d'acceso zelo
celeste messaggier portando al cielo,
le spiegherà con vive ardenti note,   4
forse salir sovra l'eccelse rote
potrò, sgravata del terrestre velo,
sprezzando il lusinghiero Apollo e Delo,
che 'n ciel solo ogni ben trovar si puote.   8
Tu in terra, Angel divin, caro a Maria,
a cui sacrasti già devoto il core,
prega per me, che puoi, con mente pura: 11
ch'accesa l'alma, e nel suo santo ardore
purgata e monda d'ogni macchia impura,
sua serva, e non del tutto indegna, io sia.   14

And will such clear, fine, devout words, such pious prayer, such warm zeal not reach Heaven? If it comes from Heaven, if Heaven dictates it, if heavenly are its notes? Did Leonora not hear it in her mind on high, above the sublime spheres, leaving her corporeal veil far beneath her? Did Apollo teach it to her in Delos? Can she know so much? Do so much? Mary heard it, welcomed it, and seemed to say: "Daughter, you who have offered me your spirit and heart, more impassioned and pure than any other woman, a divine spirit, lofty trumpet, and holy ardor

shall be yours in exchange. Let impure tongues refrain from my praises:
you shall be my Muse."

If my humble and devout prayers, full as I can make them of burning
zeal, are carried to heaven by a celestial messenger and voiced with
vivid ardent notes, then perhaps I shall be able to soar above the
sublime spheres, freed of my terrestrial veil, despising the flatteries of
Apollo and Delos, for only in heaven may all good be found. You on
earth, divine Angel, dear to Mary, to whom you long ago devoutly
pledged your heart, pray for me, for you can, with a pure mind, that
with my soul on fire and purged in her holy flame and freed from every
stain of impurity, I may be her not wholly unworthy handmaid.

Sonnets ABBA ABBA CDE DEC, with same rhyme words in same order (*eccotti* at
l. 13 of no. 140 corrrected to *eccoti*). Grillo 1589, 26r, 113v. Grillo's **proposta* here, un-
usually, is an appreciation of a particular poem rather than a generic tribute. As
Giulio Guastavini's notes to the volume indicate (Grillo 1589, e3v), the sonnet refers
to Bernardi's Marian canzone (no. 111), to whose aspiration to be heard in heaven,
expressed in the first stanza and the congedo, it alludes in its opening lines. The
quatrains of Grillo's sonnet develop the conceit that Bernardi's canzone must have
been inspired by heaven itself, given its literary excellence and piety. The tercets, in
an exercise in **prosopopoeia*, have the Virgin elect Benardi as her chosen poet on the
grounds of her devotion (11), giving her in return the eloquence necessary to praise
her in a fitting manner. The underlying conceit is that of Mary as celestial Muse,
developed by Bernardi in the second stanza of her canzone. The description of Ber-
nardi as *affettuosa* (11) is significant, since *affetti* (affects, emotions) were conceived of
as central within Counter-Reformation religious poetics.

   Bernardi's reply succeeds astonishingly well within the difficult constraints of a
reply using the same rhyme words, showing very little of the strain apparent in a
poem like Vittoria Colonna's no. 135. Where Grillo's sonnet had allocated part of her
poetic success to divine inspiration and part to natural talent and skill, symbolized
by the classical god of poetry, Apollo (7–8), Bernardi modestly disavows this, re-
nouncing Apollo (7) and presenting her verses merely as "humble, devout prayers"
(1). Bernardi's skill, is, however, much on display here. The sound patterning of her
sonnet is quite intricate, with **alliteration* and **assonance* used throughout, par-
ticularly in the tercets, for harmony and variety, and some quite showy effects, such
as the *celeste/cielo* **polyptoton* (3), echoing Grillo's play on the same words in l. 4 of
his sonnet, and the **chiastic* balancing of sounds in l. 13 (*purgata/monda/macchia/
impura*), the *monda/macchia* pairing again echoing a similar device in Grillo's son-
net, *lingua/lunge* (14). The pun on Grillo's Christian name, *Angelo* (9), translates into
a religious context the **senhal* device of secular Petrarchism and clarifies the refer-
ence to the "celestial messenger" (3) who will amplify her humble prayers with his
own "vivid, ardent notes."

Maddalena Campiglia–Curzio Gonzaga (1591)

142

Curzio, impiumando al mio pensier sovente
l'ali, pur poggio al mio desir conteso;
quindi appagando quella brama ardente
che m'ave il cor di strania piaga offeso,   4
o me felice se restasser spente
le mie forze vitali, allor che reso,
mercè d'Amor, l'idolo mio lucente
mi vien, l'alma sgombrando il mortal peso.   8
Puro spirto l'ambrosia andrei libando
da l'avorio e da l'ostro, qual da fiore
suol in vago giardin ape ingegnosa,   11
e paga di celeste almo licore,
l'avida mia fame lunga amorosa,
sarei beata a pieno in lei mirando.   14

143

Qualor movo il pensier, alzo la mente,
a contemplar d'amor lo spirto acceso
di voi, Campiglia illustre, immantenente
son da infinita meraviglia preso.   4
Ma qual altro più degno, o più eccellente
è in terra obietto, o in maggior stima asceso
di quel, che singolar da l'altra gente
vi face, co 'l suo bel dal ciel disceso?   8
Beata lei, che può bearvi quando
in dir sue lodi con perpetuo onore
v'alzate ove uman stil giunger non osa,   11
rendendo lei col vostro alto valore
sopra ogn'altra felice e glorïosa,
ond'io lieto vi inchino ambi ammirando.   14

Curzio, often, feathering the wings of my thought, I fly up toward my contested desire, to appease that ardent yearning that has violated my heart with such a strange wound. By Love's mercy, my shining idol is then restored to me, and releases my soul from all mortal weight: how happy should I be then if all my vital forces were spent! A pure spirit, the ambrosia I would go sucking from her ivory and crimson, just as the ingenious bee does from a flower in a lovely garden, and having sated my avid long amorous hunger with this heavenly sweet liquor, I would be fully blessed, gazing on her.

Whenever I move my thought and lift my mind to contemplate your spirit, inflamed with love, illustrious Campiglia, I am at once seized by infinite wonderment. But what other more worthy or excellent object is there on earth, or more revered, than the one who makes you singular among all others, with her heaven-descended beauty? Blessed she, who can bless you when in speaking her praise with perpetual honor you raise yourself where a human pen dares not go, rendering her with your great talent happy and glorious above all other women so that I joyfully bow before you, admiring you both.

Sonnets ABAB ABAB CDE DEC. Gonzaga 1591, Lv3, 165. Maddalena Campiglia had a close literary relationship with the aristocratic Mantuan poet Curzio Gonzaga (1536–99) and played a role in the publication of several of his works in the 1590s. This intriguing exchange between the two celebrates Campiglia's love for Isabella Pallavicino Lupi, Marchioness of Soragna (c. 1545–1623), who was co-dedicatee, with Gonzaga, of Campiglia's pastoral *Flori* (1588). Campiglia's sonnet presents this love in the highest Neoplatonic terms as rapt spiritual contemplation of beauty. The first quatrain describes the poet's soul winging itself to contemplate the beauties of her distant beloved, while the second quatrain and the tercets evoke a further level of ecstatic contemplation, evocative of the Christian soul's vision of God. The idolatrous elements in the poem are noteworthy for a work written at the height of the Counter-Reformation: not only is the beloved referred to explicitly as an "idol" (7), but the disembodied character of the erotic ecstasy (5–6) and its provision to the beholder of absolute beatitude (*beata a pieno*, l. 14) intentionally conflate the experiences of erotic rapture and divine vision. Although an element of idolatry is intrinsic to the Petrarchan tradition (Durling 1971), this may be read in context partly as a compliment to Isabella Pallavicino's "divine" status as a ruler: Campiglia's pastoral eclogue *Calisa* (1589) figures her as a woodland goddess.

An especially striking feature of the sonnet is the sensuality of the first tercet's image of the lovestruck poet as a bee sucking ambrosia from her beloved's rapturously contemplated physical beauty. "Ivory and crimson" was a conventional metaphorical description for the lady's pink and white complexion, similar to the English "milk and roses" (*ostro*, from the Latin *ostrum*, originally signified a purple dye). Although a tradition existed of quasi-erotic verse addressed by female poets to their patrons (see nos. 147 and 150–51), the use of this device has a special charge in Campiglia, who consistently thematizes female-female desire in her works (Cox 2011, 104, 116–17). Campiglia's reference to her love as a "strange wound" (*strania piaga*) at l. 4 may allude to the perceived exoticism of the love described, though it also echoes Petrarch's description of feeding on the "strange food" (*stranio cibo*) of his love in *canzone* 207, l. 41. The same canzone (in l. 26) supplies the phrase *fame amorosa* in the tercets.

Gonzaga replies to this unconventional sonnet in more conventional terms, celebrating Campiglia and Isabella Pallavicino as an exceptional conjunction of poet and muse. The construction of the sonnet gives equal weight to both women and emphasizes the reciprocal character of their relationship, especially in the tercets, elegantly brought to a close on the phonetically assertive phrase *ambi ammirando*. Gonzaga follows Campiglia in her arcane, non-Petrarchan rhyme scheme and adds further preciosity with the rich rhyme sequence *acceso/asceso/disceso*, and the *polyptoton of *beata/bearvi* (9). The phrase *fatto singolar da l'altra gente* (7) echoes l. 4 of Petrarch's sonnet 292, but it may also allude to Campiglia's cultivated aura of "singularity" and exceptionalism (Cox 2011, 117).

Angelo Ingegneri–Isabella Andreini (1605)

144

In ischietto vestir vera bellezza
meglio riluce, e in verde prato erboso
talor vie più che in bel giardino ombroso
di Natura il valor s'ama e s'apprezza,   4
così, bench'abbia il favellar vaghezza
quand'egli è di color ricco e pomposo,
più chiaro splende un'artificio ascoso
se pura il copre e semplice dolcezza.   8
Donna, ch'or tutta bella, or tutta ornata,
or l'uno e l'altro, i più contrari affetti
con istupor altrui sempre imitate,   11
di par ne gite ognor chiara e lodata:
più forte allor che i bei soavi detti
con minor arte, o men palese, usate.   14

145

Un bel sembiante in abito negletto
sua grazia perde; ai risguardanti è grato
vie più colto giardin che verde prato:
l'aborre sol chi sprezza almo diletto.   4
Così piu degno è pellegrin concetto,
quand'altri di bei detti il rende ornato.
Ciò non tocca al mio dir, cui fu negato
quel che in te sol risplende, Angel perfetto.   8
Arte non ho per ricoprir con l'arte
mio stil, che, in tutto di dolcezza privo,
loda non merta di celeste canto.   11
Deh, saggio tu (se di lodarmi a schivo
non hai), del vero dir pria dammi parte,
e confuso non sia co 'l biasimo il vanto.   14

In a simple dress, true beauty shines forth more brightly, and we often cherish and prize the wonders of Nature more in a green grassy meadow than in a fine shady garden. Just so, although richly colored and ornamented speech may be lovely, a hidden artifice shines more brilliantly when veiled in pure and simple sweetness. Lady, sometimes wholly beautiful, sometimes wholly adorned, sometimes a mixture of both, you imitate the most diverse affects to the amazement of all. You are famed and lauded in both guises, but more so when you use your lovely sweet words with a lesser art, or a less obvious one.

A lovely semblance carelessly dressed loses its grace, and onlookers far prefer a cultivated garden to a green meadow; none despise it except those who disdain sweet delight. In the same manner, a choice thought has more merit in our eyes when it is adorned by fine words. I do not speak of my own verse, for I was denied the talent that shines only in you, perfect Angel. I do not have the art to conceal art in my style, which, deprived of all sweetness, does not merit the praise of heavenly song. Come, be wise: if you do not disdain to laud me, share your true words with me in advance, so that your praise is not mingled with blame.

Sonnets (no. 144) ABBA ABBA CDE CDE; (no. 145) ABBA ABBA CDE DCE. Andreini 1605, 74–75. Andreini's two verse collections (1601, 1605), include significant quantities of correspondence verse, with Andreini generally supplying the *risposta*. Her practice is either to reply with no observation of rhymes, as here, or to reply using the same rhyme words. This exchange with the dramatist Angelo Ingegneri, from the 1605 collection, is a rare example of an exchange between poets containing something other than pure compliment. Ingegneri's *proposta* is rather one of aesthetic advice. He expresses a strong preference for simplicity over artifice in Andreini's verse, probably distinguishing between the "artless" style of her madrigals and *scherzi* and the more rhetorically elaborate style she sometimes used in "graver" forms such as the sonnet and the moral canzonetta. Ingegneri's recommendation of "pure, sweet simplicity" as the manner most suited to Andreini may seem at first sight patronizing, particularly in the light of nineteenth- and twentieth-century critical ideologies that identified spontaneity and artlessness as the most laudable qualities of women's writing. However, the mention of "hidden artifice" (7) and "unobvious art" (14) make it clear that Ingegneri is speaking of an assumed "artful artlessness," reminiscent of Castiglione's notion of *sprezzatura*, rather than the natural expression of a supposed "simple soul."

Andreini's reply, though polite and complimentary, has a touch of frostiness about it, particularly in the final tercet, which suggests that she disapproves of Ingegneri's innovation of introducing a critical element into a genre of verse that was conventionally purely encomiastic in character. Where the substantive argument is concerned, Andreini offers in the quatrains a trenchant defense of artifice as superior to natural beauty: a position of considerable topicality at the time of publication with the assertion of the Baroque.

Encomia of
Rulers & Patrons

Tullia d'Aragona to Cosimo de' Medici (1547)

146

Se gli antichi pastor di rose e fiori
sparsero i tempii e vaporar gli altari
d'incenso a Pan, sol perché dolci e cari
avea fatto a le ninfe i loro amori: 4
quai fior degg'io, Signor, quai deggio odori
sparger al nome vostro, che sian pari
ai merti vostri, e tante e così rari
ch'ognor spargete in me grazie e favori?   8
Nessun per certo tempio, altare o dono
trovar si può di così gran valore
ch'a vostra alta bontà sia pregio eguale.   11
Sia dunque il petto vostro, u' tutte sono
le virtù, tempio; altare, il saggio core;
vittima l'alma mia, se tanto vale.   14

If the shepherds of old strewed their temples with roses and flowers and burned incense to Pan on their altars merely because he had made their love sweet and welcome to their nymphs, what flowers should I, my Lord, and what odors offer up to your name that might correspond to your merits and to the many and rare graces and favors you have showered on me? Certainly, no temple, altar, or offering may be found of such great value that it may equal your great goodness. Let, then, your breast, which harbors all virtues, be my temple, your wise heart my altar, and let the sacrificial victim be my soul, if it merits such an end.

Sonnet ABBA ABBA CDE CDE. d'Aragona 1547, 3r. The opening sonnet of Tullia d'Aragona's *Rime* offers her verse to the dedicatee, Cosimo I de' Medici, duke of Florence, who had recently granted her immunity from sumptuary laws applying on prostitutes on the grounds of her status as poet (Basile 2001). Her gift of verse is figured in the guise of a sacrifice to a god, drawing on the classical myth of Arcadia, a utopian primitive pastoral society that worshipped the rustic satyr god Pan. An earlier version of d'Aragona's sonnet has Venus as the deity of l. 3 (see d'Aragona 1891, 6). Stylistically, d'Aragona's sonnet is characterized by insistent *enjambment and *parallelism. The quatrains are dominated by binary structures (note the *isocolon of l. 2 and the mild *rapportatio of 7–8), with ternary patterning taking over in the tercets. The beginning of l. 14 echoes l. 5 of Colonna's sonnet A1:55, which may have inspired the poem's sacrificial imagery more generally.

Laodomia Forteguerri to Margaret of Austria (1559)
147

A che il tuo Febo col mio Sol contende,
superbo ciel, se il primo onor gli ha tolto?
Torna fra selve o stia nel mar sepolto
mentre con più bei raggi il mio risplende.　　4
Picciola nube tua gran luce offende
e poca nebbia oscura il suo bel volto;
il mio tra nubi (ahi lassa!) e nebbie avvolto,
più gran chiarezza e maggior lume rende.　　8
Quando il tuo porta fuor de l'onde il giorno,
se non squarciasse il vel che l'aria adombra,
non faria di sua vista il mondo adorno;　　11
il mio non toglie il vel né l'aria sgombra,
ma somigliando a sé ciò ch'ha d'intorno,
fiammeggiar fa le nubi e splender l'ombra.　　14

Proud sky, why does your Phoebus contend with my sun, when mine
has taken from it the first honors? Go back to the woods or stay buried
in the sea, while mine shines with far lovelier rays. A small cloud can
obscure your lovely face, while mine, though wrapped—alas!—in
clouds and in mists, yet gives off greater brilliance and more light.
When your sun carries the day out of the waves, if it did not rend
asunder the veil shadowing the air, it would not adorn the world with
its fair sight. Mine does not remove its veil nor unburden the air, but,
pervading all that lies around it, it makes the clouds flame and the
shadows shine.

Sonnet ABBA ABBA CDC DCD. *Rime* 1559, 102. A remarkable sequence of sonnets by
Forteguerri addressed to Margaret of Austria (1522–86), daughter of the Emperor
Charles V, initiated an intriguing tradition of female-authored poems to female
patrons drawing on erotic language (see nos. 142 and 150–52). This sonnet, probably
written in the late 1530s, models itself closely on Vittoria Colonna's no. 44, borrow-
ing several rhyme words from it (*contende/rende/[ri]splende*; *adorno/giorno*) along
with its central conceit of the "competing suns." Forteguerri's first line also echoes
l. 4 of Lorenzo de' Medici's no. 87, the proemial sonnet of his *Comento*. The allusion
has special meaning, in that Margaret was the widow of Lorenzo's great-grandson,
Alessandro de' Medici, duke of Florence. Phoebus (1), is Apollo, the sun god, here
used simply to designate the sun. The clouds, mists, and shadows of ll. 8 and 14
probably refer to the dress and affect of widowhood. For discussion of Forteguerri's
poetry for Margaret, see Eisenbichler 2012b, 114–36.

Laura Battiferri to Eleonora of Toledo (1560)

148

Felicissima donna, a cui s'inchina
l'Arno superbo e la bell'Arbia ancora,
poscia ch'ad ambo ordine e legge ognora
date, sola di lor degna reina;   4
una, cui suo volere e 'l ciel destina
voi che cotanto sovra ogn'altra onora
riverir e cantar, bench'uopo fôra
a dire a pien di voi lingua divina,   8
queste, del picciol suo sterile ingegno
povero dono, incolte rime nuove
sacra oggi e porge al vostro alto valore.   11
Non le sdegnate, prego, che 'l gran Giove,
che fece e muove il sol, non prende a sdegno
l'umili offerte d'un divoto core.   14

Most happy lady, to whom the proud Arno and the lovely Arbia make
their reverences, now that you give order and law to both, sole worthy
queen of these cities, one destined by her will and the heavens to revere
and to sing of you, honoring you above all other ladies, consecrates
to you today these artless new verses, a poor gift of her feeble, sterile
intellect, offering them up to your great valor, although fully to speak
of you would require the tongue of a god. Do not disdain them, pray,
for the great Jove, who made the sun and moves it, does not scorn the
humble offerings of a devout heart.

Sonnet ABBA ABBA CDE DCE. Battiferri 1560, 122. This sonnet, the closing poem of
Battiferri's *First Book of Tuscan Poems*, is addressed to her dedicatee, Eleonora of To-
ledo (1522–62), duchess of Florence. The volume was published not long after Flor-
ence's acquisition of Siena, and Eleonora is portrayed in the first quatrain receiving
tribute from the two cities, designated through conventional *periphrasis by their
respective rivers, the Arno and the Arbia. The harmony of the image disguises a far
messier reality (for which see the notes to no. 164). Battiferri complements her
queenly vision of Eleonora with a self-deprecating portrayal of herself as poet, in-
troduced by the modest and anonymous *una* of the beginning of the second qua-
train, sharply contrasted with *Felicissima donna*, in parallel position in the first. De-
spite this modesty, Battiferri portrays her poet as destined by heaven to celebrate
Eleonora (5–7), and the sonnet is an ambitious one, employing complex *hypotactic
syntax, extensive *enjambment, and *concorso di vocali (2–3).

Moderata Fonte to Francesco de' Medici (1581)

149

Folta, frondosa e verdeggiante selva
di sacri onor, non di cipressi o palme,
produce il suol de le tue belle ed alme
virtù, là 've ogni stil vago s'inselva.   4
In lei non s'ode aspra feroce belva
fremir, ma dolce suon di ben nate alme,
che porta (o gran Signor) tuoi pregi e palme
di cittade in città, di selva in selva.   8
Io, che d'entrar fra li sentier diversi
e fra l'immense vie bramo ed ardisco,
per quale or deggio incaminar miei versi?   11
Scopriran li tuoi merti? O 'l valor prisco
degli avi illustri? O pur n'andran dispersi?
Ma gloria è porsi ad onorato risco.   14

A dense, leafy, verdant forest, made up of sacred honors, not cypresses
or palms, springs from the soil of your fine, noble virtues, in which
every polished pen seeks shelter. No cry of cruel, ferocious beast
trembles through this forest, but the sweet sound of well-born souls
carrying the fame, O great Lord, of your trophies and triumphs from
city to city, forest to forest. I, who yearn and dare to venture through
the many paths and great avenues of these woods—along which shall
I direct my verses? Will my words reveal your merits? Or the ancient
valor of your illustrious forebears? Or will they be scattered to the
wind? But an honorable risk is a glory in itself.

Sonnet ABBA ABBA CDC DCD. Fonte 1581, n.p. The first securely attributed work
of secular fiction published by an Italian woman, Fonte's chivalric romance, *Il Flori-
doro*, was dedicated to Francesco de' Medici, grand duke of Tuscany (1541–87), and
his Venetian consort, Bianca Cappello. *Il Floridoro* is a dynastic epic in the tradition
of Virgil and Ariosto, incorporating praise of the Medici and representing their fic-
tional heroic ancestors. Fonte's dedicatory sonnet has a virtuosistic character, with
its proto-Baroque *conceit figuring Francesco's virtues as a fertile terrain growing a
"forest" of praise and its playful, punning use of equivocal and identical rhymes in
ll. 1, 4, and 8. *S'inselva* in l. 4 (literally "to enforest oneself"), is found in rhyme with
selva/belva in Angelo Poliziano's fifteenth-century Medicean epic, *Stanze per la gios-
tra* (1.32). Poliziano may also have inspired Fonte's unusual, classicizing use of *tu*
rather than *voi* to address the patron, although this is also found in Tasso's *GL*.

Maddalena Salvetti to Christine of Lorraine (1590)

150

Quand'io veggio nel ciel sorger l'aurora,
coronata di gigli e di vïole,
Amor m'assale e la fronte scolora
membrando lei che scolorir ne suole;   4
e quando veggio il bel nascente sole,
cinto del lume suo, che 'l mondo onora,
poggiar l'erto cammin, divengo allora
neve, pensando a le bellezze sole.   8
Quando poi notte il bel carro stellato
gira per l'ampio e spazïoso albergo,
non mi concede Amor più lieto stato,   11
ch'a quel gli occhi in un tempo e la mente ergo
al viso suo di più bei lumi ornato,
onde lungi da lei sol pianto aspergo.   14

When I see dawn rise in the sky, crowned with lilies and violets, Love assails me and my brow grows pale, thinking of her who always makes me pale; and when I see the beautiful rising Sun on its steep path, girded by her light, to which the world pays homage, then I become snow as I think of her matchless beauties. Then, when night drives her fair starry chariot through the ample reaches of the sky, Love concedes me no happier state, for I raise my eyes to the heavens and my mind to her face, adorned with lovelier stars still, so that, far from her, I can do nothing but weep.

Sonnet ABAB BAAB CDC DCD. Salvetti 1590, 69–70. Shortly after the arrival in Florence as grand duchess of the French princess Christine of Lorraine in 1589, Maddalena Salvetti published a remarkable *canzoniere* of poems addressed to her, mingling the erotic language we find in verse addressed to patrons by poets like Laodomia Forteguerri and Maddalena Campiglia (nos. 142, 147) with the straight encomiastic discourse of a poet like Laura Battiferri (no. 148). Salvetti's lyrics are notable for their rich intertexuality. Here she draws on the thirteenth-century poet Guido Guinizelli for the *amor m'assale* of l. 3 (Contini 1960, 2:468); on Bembo's canzone 162, l. 58 for the closing *pianto aspergo*, in rhyme with *albergo*; and perhaps on Tasso's sonnet 509 ("O d'eroi figlia illustre, o d'eroi sposa") for the very unusual rhyme scheme (although Petrarch's sonnet 210 also has this scheme). More generally, the "night" section in the first tercet echoes Petrarch's sonnet 164, whose l. 3 is close to Salvetti's ll. 9–10.

151

Se nel bel colle Ideo vostra bellezza
fusse stata presente al gran pastore
per cui de l'Asia il trïonfante onore
girò Fortuna all'ultima bassezza,   4
Venere non avria tanta alterezza,
de l'aureo pomo, e per l'ondoso umore
la bella greca il suo lascivo amore
non avria avuto di seguir vaghezza.   8
E se quel gran pittor vista l'avesse,
quando a ritrarne una beltà perfetta,
di tante belle il più bel fior s'elesse,   11
stupido al bel che 'l ciel formò sì raro,
voi sola per sua Idea s'avrebbe eletta
e fatto il nome suo sonar più chiaro.   14

If on the lovely Idean Mount your beauty had been present to that great shepherd on whose account the triumphal honors of Asia were plunged to the lowest depths by Fortune, Venus would not have enjoyed such pride in the golden apple and the beautiful Grecian would not have desired to follow her lascivious love across the wave-tossed deep. And if that painter had seen you, who to paint a perfect beauty chose the finest flowers of so many belles, stupefied by the rare loveliness formed by heaven, he would have chosen you alone as his Idea and, in doing so, would have made his name resound with more fame.

Sonnet ABBA ABBA CDC EDE. Salvetti 1590, 17–18. In the quatrains of this erudite sonnet, Salvetti alludes to the Judgment of Paris, where the Greek hero Paris judged between the beauty of the three goddesses Venus, Minerva, and Juno, and to the tragic aftermath of this story, Paris's abduction of Helen, which led to the Trojan War (3–4). The tercets refer to a story told of the Greek painter Zeuxis, who strove to evoke Helen's insuperable beauty by fusing the most beautiful features of several models. Salvetti's principal source in combining these mythological references is Ariosto (*OF* 11.70–71), who uses similar elements to compliment the beauty of a "new Helen," Olimpia, but Salvetti's quatrains also echo famous works by Bembo (sonnet 133) and Della Casa (sonnet 36) that draw on the Judgment of Paris myth. In this densely intertextual context, the Zeuxis allusion becomes wittily (and audaciously) self-referential: we see Salvetti here, like Zeuxis, drawing on various beautiful models to create a more beautiful whole.

152

Son questi que' crin d'oro al mondo soli
ch'empion di luce la terrena mole?
Son questi quei begli occhi, anzi quei soli
che di lor fanno invidïoso il sole?   4
È questa quella bocca onde uscir suole,
Amor, il suono, onde mill'alme involi?
È questo il petto, onde sovente voli
scherzando fra i ligustri e le viole?   8
È questa quella bella e bianca mano,
non di donna mortal, ma di divina,
ch'a quanto cinge il mar devria por freno?   11
O quanto è quel pensier fallace e vano,
celeste dea, che tua beltà destina
con natural color ritrarre a pieno!   14

Are these those golden locks, without peer in this world, that flood the whole globe with light? Are these those beautiful eyes, or rather those suns that make the sun seethe with envy? Is this that mouth from which there issue, Love, those sounds through which you steal so many souls? Is this that breast, where you so often flit blithely among the lilies and violets? Is this that lovely, white hand, not that of a mortal lady but a divine one—the hand that deserves to hold the reins of all that is encircled by the sea? Ah, how fallacious and vain, celestial Goddess, is the thought of capturing your beauty with the colors that Nature provides!

Sonnet ABAB BAAB CDE CDE. Salvetti 1590, 19. Like no. 151, this sonnet reworks a famous poem by Bembo (sonnet 20), already emulatively reworked by Della Casa (in his sonnet 34). Like Bembo's and Della Casa's poems, Salvetti's sonnet implicitly locates the poet before a portrait of the beloved (a narrative context made explicit at the beginning of the sonnet that follows, which refers to a "skilled painter . . . chosen for this great task"). As in many Renaissance sonnets on portraits (Bolzoni 2008; 2010), an implicit context is the *paragone* or contest between painting and poetry, both tested to the extreme by the task of capturing the beloved's unearthly beauty. Line 14's judgment that "natural colors" cannot suffice for the task has a self-referential quality, as it calls our attention to Salvetti's sonnet's extreme formal artificiality, apparent in its arcane rhyme scheme and the equivocal and rich rhymes of the quatrains (*soli/soli/sole/suole*; *involi/voli/viole*).

153

Alma felice e glorïosa donna,
luce di questa notte ombrosa e nera
che da la più lucente ed alta spera
scendeste dentro a la terrena gonna,   4
o de la bella Esperia alta colonna
cui tempo non potrà, che 'l mondo impera,
sveller, né pur crollar Fortuna fera,
tal è l'alto valor che in voi s'indonna,   8
se me, che in grembo de la bella Flora
nacqui e nudrita fui data dal cielo
a schivar de le donne i vili uffici,   11
sotto l'ombra real del vostro velo
accogliete benigna, i cieli amici
forse avrò sì che vivrò eterna ancora.   14

Happy soul and glorious lady, light of this dark and gloomy night, you
who from the highest and most brilliant sphere descended to clothe
yourself in worldly flesh; O lofty column, the mainstay of our lovely
Italy, who cannot be uprooted by Time, ruler of this world, nor shaken
by the evils of Fortune, so great is the valor you embody, if you should
benignly welcome beneath the royal shadow of your veil me, a woman
born in the city of lovely Flora, and whom heaven has graced to escape
the base occupations of women, then perhaps the heavens will so smile
on me that I too shall live eternally.

Sonnet ABBA ABBA CDE DEC. Salvetti 1590, 28–29. Couched in straight encomi-
astic language without erotic overtones, this sonnet reworks the tradition of female
poets' verse in praise of other women as knowingly as nos. 151–52 rework Bembo
and Della Casa. Salvetti's closest model is Laura Battiferri's no. 148, which similarly
pairs the patron, described in the octave, with the poet, in the sestet. Also echoed
are Battiferri's no. 188 (compare its l. 9 with l. 11 here) and Veronica Gambara's no.
134 (compare ll. 6–7 in both poems). The image of Christine as heaven-sent (3–4)
derives from Neoplatonic traditions of representing the lady as an angelic figure,
but it takes on new significance applied to a ruler, as an allusion to monarchs' quasi-
divine status. The rhyme *donna/s'indonna* (1, 8), deriving from Dante (*Par 7*, 11–13), is
used here in a gender-conscious manner (*s'indonna* means literally "enwoman").

Ersilia Spolverini to Chiara Dolfin (1596)

154

Athesis

"Naïadum vos pulchra manus, vos humida aquarum
numina, quae vestris nostros augetis honores,
has dum perpetuis cumulatis fontibus undas,
prompta quidem semper mandata capescere nostra,
et parere mihi, iubeam quaecunque, parata;   5
praecipites alio undarum convertite gressus,
vel primos celeri ad fontes revocate recursu,
et nostros prisco latices educite ab alveo.
Illa illa Adriacae gentis generosa propago
dotibus ingenii, morum probitate, lepore,   10
forma, opibus, fama, factisque ornata suorum,
gnatorum sobole insignis, tantique mariti
laudibus illustris, Cornelia nomine Clara
(proh dolor!) ad patrias nunc regressura penates
discessum accelerat gaudens, ubi praemia gestis   15
digna suis referat, multoque ornetur honore;
et mea foelicem ut subito vehat unda carinam
mandat, et ut duro mihi pondere terga premantur.
ergone consuetos effundet vena liquores,
tantorumque erit ipsa modo mihi causa malorum?   20
ergo ministerio tam tristi inserviet unda,
perpetuae ut surgant averso sole tenebrae
et nigra obducant nostras velamina ripas?
haud equidem, sed quisque suos contendat ad ortus,
seque cavernosis terrae penetralibus abdat: 25
turgidus aut largos fluvius tam crescat ob imbres,
et circum resonent ingenti murmure fluctus,
ut metuat dubio corpus committere dorso
Clara suum nostro, et tardet pavefacta recessum.
quid loquor infelix? pectus quae vana volutat?   30
quod cupit, id se posse putat. num semita forsan
tutior in terris deerit, quae subtrahat illam
undarum imperio, tempestatumque furori?
quid faciam infelix, iuxta si exardeat ira
servitio fraudata meo? Si taedet amicam   35
decessuram adeo, quid si hinc inimica recedat?
defendet valida obsequium quae causa negatum,
si Pater Adriacus nostris succenseat ausis?

mens ubi consistit tantis agitata procellis?
Eia age, vincat amor, nec amatae desit amicum   40
servitium Dominae concedat nostra voluntas;
egregiae fidei serventis noscat amoris
signa mei, gravibus dum pareo iussibus istis.
temperet ergo suos insanos unda furores,
et lignum suavis pulsum demulceat aura   45
mollia ne tristes turbent praecordia curae,
nec gelidum admittat facies formosa timorem,
sed reditu aspiciat foelici laeta parentem
tellurem. Interea mihi sit medicina doloris,
quod tam pulchro humeros ornarit pondere nostros,   50
Et sit lympharum semper vis tanta mearum
ut valeant pelagi fluctus superare tumentes
visurae Dominam, et Venetum penetrare recessus."
Altisonis Athesim fundentem talia dictis
audiit in ripis pascens armenta Lycoris.   55

The Adige

[1–5] "Oh lovely band of Naiads, damp goddesses of the waters, you who augment our honors with your own, just as you augment these waves with your perpetually renewing springs, always ready to follow our commands, and primed to obey me, whatever I command: [6–10] turn the headlong course of your waves elsewhere, or call them back to their original fount in a swift retreat, and lead our waters back to their ancient womb. For she, she, that noble scion of the Adriatic race, endowed with keenness of mind, probity of manners, charm, [11–15] beauty, wealth, and reputation; adorned by the deeds of her ancestors, proud in the fresh shoots of her offspring, glorying in the splendors of her great husband, Cornelia of famous name, is now (alas!) preparing to return to the hearth of her homeland and eagerly hastes her parting, where her deeds [16–20] will be rewarded by worthy praise and she will be adorned with great honor; she orders that a happy keel at once launch on the waves and weigh my back with its cruel burden. Shall it really be the case that, in pouring forth my usual waters, I shall be the cause of so many ills? [21–25] Shall my waves serve such a miserable office, as perpetual shadows rise above a fleeing sun and black veils envelop our banks? No, indeed: instead, let each of you hurry back to her source and haste into the cavernous depths of the earth, [26–30] and let my river swell from heavy rainfall and the waves resound with a crashing roar so that Clara fears to entrust herself to our precarious, fluctuating surface and timidly delays her leaving. But what am I saying, poor wretch? What vain thoughts is my heart turning over? [31–35] It believes that what it wishes, it may have. Is a safer land route lacking to preserve her from the empire of the waves and the fury of the storms? And what shall I do, poor wretch, if she is filled with wrath at being cheated of my service? If I offend her now, as a friend, [36–40] when she is about to depart, what if she leaves an enemy? Will I have any sound argument to defend my refusal to carry her if Father Adriatic is enraged by my impudence? Where is my mind wandering, tossed by so many storms? Come now, let Love triumph; [41–45] let us not permit our beloved Lady to be without our friendly service; may she recognize in me the signs of a noble servant's faithful love as I prepare to obey her painful commands. May my waters temper their mad fury, and may a soft breeze gently speed her vessel, [46–50] so that no bitter cares disturb her tender heart. Let frigid fear not trouble her fair aspect, but let her happily anticipate her joyful return to her homeland. Meanwhile, let it be medicine to my sorrow to think that such a lovely burden was carried on our shoulders, [51–55] which will ever hence give such power to my waters that they will conquer the swelling waves of the ocean and penetrate the sea-blue depths, knowing they are to see our Lady." These lofty words Lycoris heard Athesis pouring forth as she pastured her flocks on his banks.

Stichic hexameters. Palermo 1596, 191–93 (*meorum* in l. 50 amended to *mearum*). A popular subgenre of occasional poetry within the cities of Venice's mainland empire in the late sixteenth century was verse celebrating the arrival or departure of the Venetian officials sent as governors or magistrates. When these officials brought their wives with them, the poetic tribute volumes marking their departure sometimes incorporated a section of poems in praise of the wife as well as the husband. It is here that female poets most frequently made an appearance (Cox 2011, 310 n. 201), although the gender division was not absolute.

The poem given here, by Ersilia Spolverini, commemorates the departure from Verona of Chiara Dolfin, wife of Giovanni Cornaro (1551–1629), a future doge. A study of its context (Smith 2009) observes that Cornaro and Dolfin seem quite freely to have flouted the strict regulations the Venetian government had put in place to limit social interaction between the governor and the subject populace, impressing the Veronese elite with the elegance of their lifestyle and the lavishness of their entertaining. The same study notes that Dolfin gave birth to one of the couple's twelve children, a son, Luigi, during her stay in Verona: again, an experience that must have increased her closeness to the elite women of the city, given the intense female sociability that surrounded the experience of childbirth at this time.

Spolverini's literary celebration of Chiara Dolfin constitutes one of the most sustained bodies of encomiastic work written by a woman in praise of a female

patron at this time, along with Maddalena Campiglia's praises of Isabella Pallavi-
cino Lupi (no. 142), and Maddalena Salvetti's in praise of Christine of Lorraine (nos.
150–53). In addition to this Latin poem, Spolvernini honored Dolfin and her family
in a twenty-four-page vernacular oration and four vernacular poems (two sonnets
and a canzone, along with a madrigal celebrating Luigi Cornaro's birth). A dialect
poem by the Veronese poet Giovanni Fratta included in the anthology from which
the text of this poem is taken seems to indicate that the oration was commissioned
from Spolverini by the ladies of Verona and delivered by her at a parting ceremony
for Chiara Dolfin (Cox 2011, 358 n. 20).

In an extended exercise in *prosopopoeia, Spolverini's poem is written in the
voice of the river god of the Adige, which flows through Verona, traumatized at the
thought of being forced to conduct Chiara Dolfin back to her home city, leaving
Verona bereaved. That Dolfin left for Venice by boat is confirmed by the poem by
Fratta just cited, which comically portrays the farewell ceremonies interrupted at
one point by a boatman reminding her it is time to depart. In Spolverini's poem, the
Adige's speech is handled with a certain wit, with the swift-flowing river heroically
resolving to prevent Chiara's leaving through a violent swelling of his waters before
tamely realizing that it would not be difficult for her to foil his plans by simply tak-
ing an alternative land route. The emphasis on submission and devoted servitude at
ll. 39–42 is clearly ideological, in a poem voiced by an embodiment of one of Ven-
ice's subject cities and addressed to a representative of the Venetian ruling class.

Less complex and erudite than Nogarola's no. 192, Spolverini's poem refers to
classical mythology mainly for the generic notions of river gods and Naiads, or wa-
ter nymphs. There is also relatively little by way of classical allusion, though phrase
mollia praecordia (45) occurs in a famous passage of Ovid's describing the metamor-
phosis of Daphne (*Met.* 1:549). There is some punning, in keeping with the light tone
of the poem. "Cornelia nomine Clara" (13) means both "Cornara, Chiara by name"
and "Cornara, famous for her name" (the Cornaro family claimed descent from the
ancient Roman *gens Cornelia*; hence *Cornelia* for Cornara, the feminine form of Chi-
ara Dolfin's married name). *Venetum* (52) means both "sea-blue" and "Venetian" (the
mouth of the Adige lies south of Venice, below Chioggia, so we have to imagine its
waters fighting their way through the Adriatic to make their way to Venice and
Chiara).

The poet herself makes a modest appearance at the end of the poem in the pas-
toral guise of the shepherdess Lycoris, said to have heard the laments of the Adige
as she pastured her flocks on its banks. The name Lycoris may be intended to recall
the classical figure of that name, mentioned, for example, in Virgil's tenth eclogue.
Spolverini may also, however, have been influenced by contemporary pastoral
drama, and perhaps specifically by Maddalena Campiglia's drama *Flori*, published
in nearby Vicenza in 1588, in which Licori is the name of the heroine's closest friend.

Isabella Cervoni to Maria de' Medici (1600)

155

[1] Donna real, che, dentro a nobil velo
quanto covrisse mai bellissima alma
puro spirto divino accolto avete,
ed infiammate di perpetuo zelo,
vie più de l'altre glorïosa ed alma,   5
a riverirvi chi di gloria ha sete;
mentr'a gara venire a voi vedete
le provincie a scovrir quant'oggi al mondo
questa degna di voi grandezza piaccia,
udire i vostri onor non vi dispiaccia   10
con volto e cor giocondo
da verginella a voi serva e divota.
Vicina, né remota
parte sarà de l'universo, dove
non s'oda il suon de' vostri almi splendori;   15
e con diverse e nuove
fogge allettare ad adorarvi i cori [. . .]

[4] De la beltà, che Dio larga possiede,
sì vivo raggio in voi, Donna, risplende,
e tale indi esce lume agli occhi nostri
che chi di rimirarvi è degno, vede   55
il vero fonte donde a noi discende
l'eterna luce de' celesti chiostri.
Con fida scorta de' begli occhi vostri
la mente nostra per sicura via
a la prima bellezza si conduce.   60
Ivi contempla la divina luce,
ivi sé stessa oblia,
ivi conosce 'l bello, il buono, e 'l vero,
ivi l'esempio intero
vede de l'alma vostra a pien perfetta,   65
e d'amore infiammata alto e divino,
tanto in Dio si diletta,
che ripigliare a noi non sa il camino [. . .]

[8] Grave consiglio ne le donne antiche,   120
qual gemma in or, refulse; e spesso tolse
altri da sdegno, incendio, e da rapina.
D'Ataulfo le voglie empie, nimiche

Placidia mitigò sì, che rivolse
l'odio in amor, né Roma andò in ruina.   125
Tal consiglio a Traian diede Plotina,
che de la propria laude il fe' bramoso,
e al ben de le provincie assai più desto.
Risvegliò Teodosio Eudossa, e presto
lo rese più zeloso   130
del divin culto e vita più serena.
Quella ancor dea terrena
Clotilde, tanto saggia e tanto pia,
induce il primo Clodoveo, che tolta
da' suoi l'idolatria,   135
corre al battesmo ed il Vangelo ascolta.

[9] Livia in Augusto il naturale instinto
de la severità cangiò in clemenza;
ond'è il suo nome ancor tanto lodato.
Teodelinda il suo Agilulfo avvinto   140
ne' lacci d'eresia con gran prudenza
sciolse, e lo rese a Pietro e a Dio sì grato.
Costume appresso i greci ancor fu usato
di voler nel governo e ne' perigli
de le donne il parer, che sempre piacque.   145
Né a' Galli usare de le lor donne spiacque
i saggi e pii consigli,
se trattar si dovea di guerra o pace.
O giudizio fallace
de l'uom, che de la donna il grave ingegno   150
pospone al suo; né vede che sovente
la donna arriva al segno
ov'ella al par di lui resta eccellente [. . .]

[*congedo*] Canzon, la dea terrena a cui t'invio
sparge sì largo di virtute il rio;
in tanta altezza è posta,
tanto avanza in bellezza il bello umano,   225
ch'alto ingegno e sovrano
né con lo stil, né col pensier v'arriva;
ond'a far le sue lodi alme, immortali,
uopo è, che donna e diva
n'accolga a l'ombra de le sue grand'ali.   230

[1] Royal lady, you who harbor a pure divine spirit within a veil as noble as ever covered a most beautiful soul; you who, far more glorious and lovely than any other woman, inflame all who yearn for glory to reverence you with perpetual zeal, while you watch the provinces flock toward you to reveal how greatly your deserved elevation pleases the world, do not disdain to listen with a joyous face and heart to a young virgin, your servant and worshipper, as she tells your honors. There will be no part of the universe, near or far, where the echo of your fine splendors is not heard and hearts are not lured to adore you in new, diverse, remarkable ways.

[4] So bright a ray shines in you, Lady, of the vast beauty of God, and such a light issues forth from it to our eyes that he who is privileged to gaze on you sees the true fountain from which there descends to us the eternal light of the heavenly cloisters. With the trusty guide of your lovely eyes, our minds are led on a safe path to the primal beauty. There it contemplates the divine light; there it forgets itself; there it learns the beautiful, the good, and the true; there it sees the true pattern of your soul in its full perfection; and inflamed with high, divine love, it so delights in God, that it knows not how to find the way of return.

[8] Grave counsel shone in the ladies of old like a gem set in gold and often saved those around them from wrath, fire, and pillage. Placidia so mitigated the evil, fierce desires of Ataulf that she muted his hatred into love, and Rome did not perish. Plotina counseled Trajan in such a way that she made him desirous of his own honor and alive to the good of his lands. Eudocia roused Theodosius from his slumber and soon made him more zealous of divine worship and a more serene life. So too that earthly goddess Clothilde, so wise and pious, induced the first Clovis, who, lured away from his idolatry, hastened to be baptized and to listen to the gospels.

[9] Livia changed Augustus's natural instinct of severity into clemency, wherefore his name is still so lauded. Theodelinda, with her great prudence, rescued her Agilulf, who had been enmeshed in the bonds of heresy, and made him beloved of Peter and God. It was the custom of the Greeks, too, in rule and in danger to seek the opinion of their women, which was always pleasing to them; nor did the Gauls disdain to make use of the wise and pious counsels of their women when it came to treat of war or of peace. O false judgment of men, who think women's weighty intellect inferior to theirs, failing to see that women often rise to a point where they match men in excellence.

[*congedo*] Song, from the earthly goddess to whom I send you there flows such a wide river of virtue, and so highly is she placed and so greatly does she outshine human beauty in her loveliness, that even the most lofty and sovereign intellect cannot reach her with pen or with thought. To frame her lovely and immortal praises, it is needful that a lady and goddess should shelter me under the shade of her great wings.

Canzone ABCABCCDEEdFfGHgH + EEdFfGHgH. Cervoni 1600, C3v–D3v. Following the lead of her father, Giovanni Cervoni, Isabella Cervoni specialized in encomiastic compositions, mainly addressed to members of the Medici family and commemorating specific events. Her favored metrical form was the canzone, and her productions were characteristically weighty: the canzone excerpted here has thirteen stanzas of seventeen principally hendecasyllabic lines, with a *congedo*. The canzone is one of three published together in 1600 in a volume by Cervoni celebrating the marriage of Maria de' Medici, niece of the grand duke of Tuscany, to King Henri IV of France. The first of the three canzoni is devoted to the couple, the second to Henri, and the third to Maria.

The extracts given are the first stanza, in which Cervoni, presenting herself in her characteristic guise as a *verginella*, promises Maria a tribute of praise that will be heard throughout the universe and trumpets the novelty of her verse (I have translated *nuove* in l. 16 in its two senses of "new" and "remarkable"; cf. no. 5). In the fourth stanza, the third of four devoted to Maria's physical and spiritual beauty, Cervoni praises her in Neoplatonic terms as a reflection of divine beauty who leads onlookers to contemplate the beauty and good of heaven. Interesting here is the way in which the Neoplatonic notion of the lady's salvific function with regard to her lover is generalized to an entire community, in keeping with the political context. The four stanzas devoted to Maria's virtues (6–9) draw on classical exempla of famous women as points of comparison. The two stanzas given here (8–9) pointedly focus on the function of the queen consort in government. Cervoni uses the historical erudition she also amply displays in her 1598 *Oration to Pope Clement VIII* (see no. 165) to propose examples of consorts who positively influenced their husbands in government, privileging especially those who tempered their husbands' severity or effected their religious conversion. Her examples are, in order, Aelia Galla Placidia (c. 390–450 CE), daughter of the Roman emperor Theodosius I and married to the Visigoth king Ataulf; Pompeia Plotina (d. c. 121 CE), wife of the Emperor Trajan; Aelia Eudocia (c. 401–60 CE), wife of the Eastern Roman Emperor, Theodosius II; Clothilde (?475–545 CE), wife of the Frankish king Clovis I; Livia (58 BCE–29 CE), wife of the Emperor Augustus; and Theodelinda (d. 627 CE), wife of the Lombard king Agilulf. The moral, that women equal men in intelligence and judgment, is spelled out at the end of stanza 9.

Clothilde and Theodelinda both were noted for having converted their husbands to Catholicism from the competing creed of Arianism. Henri IV had been a Huguenot before converting to Catholicism in 1593, shortly before becoming king of France (an occasion Cervoni marked with a canzone), and Maria is clearly implicitly posited here as a valuable agent in consolidating the king's faith. The *congedo* of the canzone ends, typically for Cervoni, with a request for patronage (229–30): less secure than a noblewoman like Maddalena Salvetti, she clearly hoped to make a living, as well as a name, through her pen. The phrase "donna e diva" (229) is found in rhyme in Petrarch's sonnet 107 (6), but more relevant to Cervoni, given the Medicean context, may be the opening line of Tullia d'Aragona's sonnet to Eleonora of Toledo, "O qual vi debb'io dire, o donna o diva" (d'Aragona 1547, 5r).

Stylistically, Cervoni's canzone has a somewhat workaday quality, although certain refinements may be noted, such as the paired rich rhymes *piaccia/dispiaccia* and *piacque/spiacque* in stanzas 1 and 9. As her *Orazione* attests, Cervoni had an interest in rhetoric, and her verse sometimes takes on an oratorical tone, as in ll. 61–65, with their insistent *anaphora.

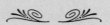

Political Verse

Girolama Corsi (1494)

156

Nel bel paese mio toscho gentile
vassene il gallo, ognhor bechando el grano,
e le galine che li viene a mano
tutte l'alletta e chiama a suo chovile.   4
Oymè, marzocho, come fosti vile
a darli il passo e tuo governo in mano!
Tempo non ci verà molto lontano
che habito mutarai, 'dioma e stile.   8
Ma se 'l leone, el cui potere è tanto,
metter volesse fuor per te l'artiglio,
vedresti al gallo spenachiato el manto   11
ché sol col mover d'un rubesto ciglio
fa tremar l'universo tutto quanto;
pensa de' gali s'el faria scompiglio!   14
Sì che prendi consiglio;
richore a lui del tuo commesso fallo,
vedi che in la tua paglia chova el gallo,   17
perhò cercha cazarlo
prima che el basilischo esca de l'uovo
che nascer diè quest'anno a tempo nuovo.   20

Into my fine, noble land of Tuscany goes the Gaulish rooster, pecking at his grain, and all the hens that come his way he lures and calls to his lair. Alas, Marzocco, how cowardly and base to give him free passage and deliver yourself into his hand! The time will not be long in coming when you change your clothes, language, and customs. But if the lion, whose power is so great, were to put out his claw for you, then you would see the rooster's coat plucked. One flicker of his mighty brows can make the whole universe shudder: think of what it could do to a few roosters! Take counsel; turn to the lion and confess your fault; think that the rooster is brooding in your straw. Chase him out before the basilisk hatches from its egg, as it must this coming year.

Sonetto caudato ABBA ABBA CDC DCD + dEE eFF. Venice, Biblioteca Marciana, MS IX, 270 [6367], 12v–13r. This sonnet responds to the French invasion of Italy in 1494, which marked the start of the long and devastating series of campaigns known as the Italian Wars. As the French king Charles VIII descended through France with his army, Piero de' Medici, effectively head of Florence, was sent out to treat with him and offered humiliating terms of capitulation. The Florentines expelled the Medici and reestablished a republic, but the new government offered no resistance to Charles, inviting him into the city in what was widely read as an admission of defeat. In 1495, after the French had conquered Naples, a league was formed among the Pope (Alexander VI), Spain, Milan, the Empire, and Venice to expel the French. This poem was presumably written prior to the formation of the league, as Corsi calls on her home town, Florence, to seek military assistance from her adoptive town, Venice, against the French. *Gallo* (2) is a pun, meaning both "rooster" and "Gaul" or "Gaulish." The *Marzocco* was the Florentine lion emblem, while the lion of l. 9 is the lion of St Mark, emblem of Venice. The basilisk of the last lines was a mythical venomous snake, said to be hatched by a rooster from the egg of a serpent or toad: here it stands for the disastrous results of the French invasion generally, waiting to be "hatched." In its aggressive, scornful tone, especially apparent in the exclamation of ll. 5–6, the poem recalls the Dantean tradition of political polemic (for a famous example, see *Purg.* 6.76–151). It is difficult to think of any equivalent to this scathing, robust language in the later, more polite, tradition of female-authored Petrarchist verse.

Camilla Scarampa (?1498)

157

Misera Italia, il ciel pur te minaccia:
una voce me intona nell'orecchia,
ché se non svegli tua virtute vecchia,
convien ch'ogni tua pompa si disfaccia.   4
Sciolta non sei ancor dell'un de' braccia
de' barbari, che l'altro s'apparecchia.
Chi vuol veder miseria in te si specchia,
poi, lagrimando, per pietà s'agghiaccia;   8
ché per le nostre tante adverse voglie,
de 'sti rabiosi can sei fatta preda,
che van stracciando le tue belle spoglie.   11
Or tal lo proverà, che par nol creda:
saran commune tante amare doglie.
Chiudemi gli occhi, Dio, che ciò non veda.   14

Wretched Italy, heaven still threatens you. A voice thunders in my ear
that if you do not revive your ancient prowess, all your splendors will
be undone. You have barely escaped from one of the arms of the
barbarians when the next awaits you. Whoever wants to see
wretchedness should mirror himself in you then, weeping, freeze in
pity, for in punishment for our perverse desires, you have been made
prey by these dogs who are now tearing away at your fair remains.
Those will soon feel the truth of this who seem now not to believe it: all
these bitter woes will be common to all. Close my eyes, God, that I
shall not see that day.

Sonnet ABBA ABBA CDC DCD. Leone 1962, 298. This sonnet, with its powerful last
line, was probably composed at the time of the second French invasion of Italy, in
1499, when Milan, where Scarampa had lived for most of the 1490s at the court of
Lodovico Sforza, fell into French hands. Scarampa predicts a more general misery
for her country if it does not recover the military might that distinguished it in
Roman times (the "ancient prowess" of l. 3: *virtute*, sometimes meaning "virtue," is
used here in the Latin sense of "manliness," "fortitude," or "power"). The sonnet
consciously recalls Petrarch's great political canzone 128 in its counterposition of
civilized Roman Italy, with the "barbarity" of the northern European nations. Scar-
ampa uses discordant consonantal rhymes in the quatrains (-*accia*/*ecchia*) to lend a
phonetic harshness to the poem reflective of the harsh realities it describes, while
l. 10 is characterized by what Giuseppe Leone in 1962 (298) called an "unfeminine
vigor" of tone ("non femminile vigore dell'accento").

Veronica Gambara (c. 1537–49)
158

Vinca gli sdegni e l'odio vostro antico,
Carlo e Francesco, il nome sacro e santo
di Cristo, e di Sua fe' vi caglia tanto
quanto a voi più d'ogn'altro è stato amico.   4
L'arme vostre a domar l'empio nimico
di lui sian pronte, e non tenete in pianto
non pur l'Italia, ma l'Europa, e quanto
bagna il mar, cinge valle o colle aprico.   8
Il gran Pastor, a cui le chiavi date
furon del cielo, a voi si volge e prega
che de le greggie sue pietà vi prenda.   11
Possa più in voi che 'l sdegno la pietate,
coppia real; un sol desio vi accenda:
di vendicar chi Gesù sprezza o nega.   14

Charles and Francis, let your anger and ancient hatred be defeated by
the sacred, holy name of Christ. His faith should move you all the more,
as he has been kinder to you than to all other men. Let your weapons
be readied to subdue his wicked enemy; cease to keep in woe not
merely Italy but the whole of Europe, wherever is bathed by the sea or
clasped by a valley or sun-drenched hill. The great Shepherd, to whom
the keys were given by heaven, is turning to you and praying you to
take pity on his flocks. Royal pair, may mercy prove stronger in you
than anger, and let one sole desire enflame you, to avenge yourselves
against those who despise or deny Christ.

Sonnet ABBA ABBA CDE CED. Ruscelli 1553a, 2. This sonnet was probably written
around 1537, when the "great shepherd" (9), Pope Paul III, was urging peace talks to
end the endemic conflict between the Emperor Charles V and Francis I of France.
The poem is traditionally attributed to Gambara; a suggested reattribution to Col-
onna (Bullock 1971) rests on thin ground. Although the sonnet is ostensibly even-
handed, its call for both rulers to devote themselves to a crusade against the Turks—a
priority for Charles—reflects Gambara's imperial sympathies. In keeping with its
portentous subject matter, the poem adopts a sober, majestic, oratorical style, rich
in *enjambment. Structurally crucial is the parallel between ll. 1–2 and 12–13, both
opening with a jussive subjunctive (*Vinca/possa*), followed by a vocative, the first bi-
nary ("Carlo e Francesco"), the second unitary ("coppia real"), reflecting the poem's
call for the two rulers' wills to unite. Also effective is the postponement of the sub-
ject of the initial verb *vinca* until ll. 2–3.

159

Mira, Signor, la stanca navicella
di Pietro che nel mar da fieri venti
spinta va errando e par che si lamenti
di questa fluttüosa e ria procella.   4
Mira che sola in questa parte e in quella
smarrita corre e con dogliosi accenti
ti dimanda soccorso, e tu consenti
che finor possa in lei nemica stella?   8
Nave senza nocchier, senza pastore
non può star gregge, che da l'onde l'una,
l'altro è da' lupi travagliata e morto;   11
Signor, dunque, provedi, e il tuo favore
spira a chi sappia in la maggior fortuna
questa barca condur felice in porto.   14

Lord, look down upon the weary little boat of Peter, which wanders, driven by cruel winds, and seems to complain of this fierce turbulent storm. Look at it how all strays alone and lost and in pitiful tones begs you for help. Can you consent that a malign star should have such power over its fate? A ship cannot endure without a helmsman, without a shepherd a flock; one is ravaged by the waves, the other killed by wolves. Lord, therefore, provide, and breathe your grace into whoever can, at the height of this storm, guide your boat happily into harbor.

Sonnet ABBA ABBA CDE CDE. Gambara 1995, 167 (with changes to punctuation and *travagliato* in l. 11 amended to *travagliata*). Written before a papal conclave, probably that following Paul III's death in 1549, this sonnet expresses the poet's anxiety at the state of the Church and augurs a successful outcome to the election. The image of the Church as ship was traditional, figuring, for example, in Dante's *Purg.* 32.129. *Fortuna* (13) has the metaphorical meaning of "storm" but also evokes the classical notion of Fortune as a capricious goddess ruling worldly affairs. The phrase *stanca navicella* occurs in l. 39 of Petrarch's canzone 206, in rhyme with *quella/stella/procella*, while l. 2's *fieri venti* in rhyme is found in Petrarch's sonnet 235 (9). The sonnet's most striking stylistic device is the extended *rapportatio of ll. 9–11, combined with *zeugma. The metaphors of the unhelmed ship and unshepherded flock are pursued in parallel throughout; hence my emendation of l. 11 (*travagliata* applies to the feminine *nave*).

Vittoria Colonna (1541)
160

Prego il Padre divin che tanta fiamma
mandi del foco suo nel vostro core,
Padre nostro terren, che de l'ardore
de l'ira umana in voi non resti dramma.   4
Non mai da fier leone inerme damma
fuggì come da voi l'indegno amore
fuggirà del mortal caduco onore,
se di quel di là su l'alma s'infiamma.   8
Vedransi allor venir gli armenti lieti
al santo grembo, caldo de la face
che 'l gran lume del ciel gli accese in terra.   11
Così le sacre glorïose reti
saran già colme; e con la verga in pace
si rese il mondo e non con l'armi in guerra.   14

I pray the divine Father to fill your heart with such a great flame of his
fire, earthly Father, that no dram can remain in you of burning human
anger. Never did a harmless hind flee a cruel lion as the unworthy love
of mortal, fleeting honor will flee from you once your soul is aflame
with heavenly love. Then shall we see the happy herds flocking to your
holy lap, warmed by the brand the great light of Heaven lit for it on
earth. Thus will the sacred glorious nets be filled; for the world yielded
to the rod of peace, not to the weapons of war.

Sonnet ABBA ABBA CDE CDE. Colonna 1548, 107. Colonna addressed this powerful
sonnet to Pope Paul III (Alessandro Farnese) in 1541, while in retreat in a convent
in Orvieto. Paul was at the time at war with Colonna's brother, Ascanio, whom he
would eventually expel from the family's strongholds in the papal states. Vittoria
Colonna played an important diplomatic role in the conflict, and this sonnet is in-
teresting not least as a masterly work of propaganda, masking trenchant denuncia-
tion beneath its polite tones. Paul is reproached for his unchristian aggression (3–4)
and for his attachment to worldly honor (6–7), while the Petrine and apostolic imag-
ery of the tercets (John 21.17: "feed my sheep"; Matthew 4.19: "I will make you fishers
of men") obliquely underlines his dereliction of his nurturing role as vicar of Christ,
the "light" of l. 11. The *fiamma/infiamma* rhyme derives from Petrarch's canzone 270,
ll. 17–18; the *dramma/fiamma* rhyme from *Purg.* 30.47–49. On the poem's context, see
Robin 2007, 79–101.

Aurelia Petrucci (pre-1542)

161

Dove sta il tuo valor, patria mia cara,
poiché il giogo servile, misera, scordi,
e solo nutri in te pensieri discordi,
prodiga del tuo mal, del bene avara?   4
A l'altrui spese, poco accorta, impara
che fa la civil gara e in te rimordi
gli animi falsi e rei, fatti concordi
a tuo sol danno, a servitute amara.   8
Fa' de le membra sparse un corpo solo,
ed un giusto voler sia legge a tutti,
ch'allor io ti dirò di valor degna.   11
Così tem'io, anzi vegg'io, ch'in duolo
verrai, misera, ognor piena di lutti;
ché così avvien dove discordia regna.   14

Where is your valor, my dear homeland? You wretchedly ignore your yoke of servitude and nurture in yourself only warring thoughts, prodigal with your own ill, avaricious of good. Reckless one, learn at others' expense the cost of civil strife, and curb those false, dangerous spirits, united only in conspiring to your harm and bitter servitude. Gather your scattered limbs into one sole body and let one just will be law to all: then only I will call you worthy of the name of valor. As it is, I fear—nay, I already see—that you will come to grief, poor wretch, ever filled with sorrow, for such is the consequence where discord reigns.

Sonnet ABBA ABBA CDE CDE. Domenichi 1559, 9. This sonnet, warning against the effects of political factionalism in republican Siena, was composed by a member of the dynasty that had ruled the city as lords in the early decades of the sixteenth century. While the "single body and will" Petrucci calls for (9–10) may refer simply to civic unity, she may also be advocating one-man rule as a solution: tellingly, Lodovico Domenichi chose the sonnet to head his 1559 anthology of verse by Italian women, published shortly after Siena's annexation by the Medici duchy of Tuscany. A possible subtext of this poem is Ambrogio Lorenzetti's fresco cycle of *Good and Bad Government* in Siena's main council chamber, contrasting a city at peace with one shattered by discord. Where in Lorenzetti a personified Concordia is seen uniting Siena's citizenry, here, with bitter irony, the Sienese are *concordi* (7) only in working for the city's harm. The inclusive rhyme with *discordi* (3) underlines the point. For a reading of the sonnet, see Eisenbichler 2012b, 73–76.

Laura Terracina (1549)
162

Valoroso Signor, nella cui mente
ogni saggio pensier nasce e alberga,
onde convien che di virtude ardente
a Dio sovente l'intelletto s'erga,
poiché il monarca sacro d'occidente   5
t'ha di noi posto in man la degna verga,
non ti sdegnar, s'una tua vile ancella
a te volge la semplice favella.

A te si volge, non già per lodarte,
ché non trova parole al pregio uguali;   10
né mai potrà forza d'ingegno o d'arte
agguagliar mai tuoi meriti immortali,
e 'l ciel non può più glorïoso farte,
né prestar al tuo corso più grand'ali:
ma prega sol ch'ascolti il prego umile,   15
ch'ella ti porge in questo basso stile.

Vergine vaga assai leggiadra e bella,
Signor, la penna mia sforza e l'inchiostro;
e quanto io scrivo in carte, al cor detta ella,
solo impetrar sperando il favor vostro.   20
Me dunque udendo ascoltarete quella,
ch'il desio d'ambidue qui vi dimostro:
e s'elle pronte sono a darvi il core,
siate voi pronto a farli ancor favore.

Quella Ninfa gentil che da l'estremo   25
occidente, signor, t'ebbe in soccorso;
ond'or difesa l'hai da Polifemo,
or da l'Arpie, dal lupo, ed or da l'orso,
mentre lieta gioiva nel supremo
de l'allegrezze in un bel prato, morso   30
gli ha dato un velenoso e perfido angue;
tal che presso al morir giacendo langue.

O velenosa e mortal peste ria,
odio civil, che non guasti e consumi!
Che meraviglia se la ninfa mia,   35
Partenope leggiadra, arder presumi,
se per te la superba monarchia

cadde di Roma con suoi tanti numi?
Or questa è, signor mio, che meco chiede
a te favore e ti offre amore e fede.   40

A te certo offre amore, che non ha dove
di te lagnarsi e si lamenta a torto,
e l'odio e l'ira son rivolti altrove,
ché l'un vorrebbe l'altro amico morto,
e per ciò su l'aurate treccie piove   45
gran fiamma il ciel da l'occidente a l'orto,
ché gli abitanti d'una istessa terra
da lor sciaccian la pace e braman guerra.

Chi pensò mai che ne l'eccelse e forti
mura ch'ergere al ciel facesti voi,   50
tante e sì fiere immagini di morti
sì tosto si chiudessero fra noi?
Ben puoi, Napoli mia, ciechi e mal accorti
sempre chiamare i cittadini tuoi,
ché fuor d'ogni saper, d'ogni consiglio   55
han la fama e l'onor posto in periglio.

E se non era la discreta aita
del gran Toledo tuo che ben s'accorse,
Napoli in sul fiorir eri fornita.
Egli al dritto camin tuoi passi torse;   60
egli da morte ritornotti in vita.
Omai che pensi? A che ti veggo in forse?
Corri a chi te forte ama col tuo regno,
e che di ciò mostrato ha più d'un segno.

Ecco ch'ella ne vien pensosa in vista   65
e chiede mercé, grida soccorso omai.
Se onor e fama per ben far s'acquista,
tranne, Signor, che puoi, da tanti lai.
Noi saremo lieti allor che l'alma vista
ne mostrerai con più lucenti rai.   70
Quella può contentar nostri desiri,
purch'una volta sol lieto ci miri.

Né convien, Signor mio, volger la mente
e la memoria ai già passati danni.
Sommergi in Lete il giusto sdegno ardente,   75

e con lui tutti gli altri orditi inganni:
ch'il Monarca celeste immantinente
trae ciascun peccator d'eterni affanni
che pentito da lui cerca mercede,
e lo fa d'immortal tesoro erede.   80

Valorous lord, in whose mind every sage thought is born and dwells so that your intellect, burning with virtue, often soars to God, since the sacred monarch of the west has placed the noble baton of our governance in your hand, let it not arouse your scorn if a vile handmaiden addresses her simple words to you.

She turns to you not to praise you, for she can find no words equal to your worth; nor, indeed, can the power of intellect and art ever match your immortal merits, while heaven itself is not sufficient to add to your glory or lend swifter wings to your flight. All that she asks is that you listen to the humble prayer that she offers up to you in this lowly style.

A Virgin of great beauty and loveliness, lord, compels my pen and ink, and whatever I write on these pages, she dictates in my heart, only wishing to beg for your favor. Thus in listening to me, you will hear the words of her, for I am laying out here the desire of both our hearts, and if we two are ready to give you our hearts, pray be equally ready to give us your favor.

That noble nymph, to whose aid you came, lord, from the far west, and whom you have defended now from Polyphemus, and now from the Harpies, the wolf and the bear, while she was happily lying in the fullness of bliss in a lovely meadow, was stung by a venomous and perfidious serpent, so that now she languishes close to death.

O venomous and mortal evil plague, civil strife, what do you not ruin and consume! What wonder if you dare burn my nymph, lovely Parthenope, when through you the splendid monarchy of Rome fell, with its many gods. Parthenope it is, my lord, who together with me begs your favor and pledges you her love and faith.

She pledges her love to you, for sure, for she has no reason to complain of you, and she laments in vain. Hatred and wrath are directed elsewhere, for one friend wishes to see the other dead. For this reason on her golden locks a great flame rains down from heaven, from where the sun sets to where it rises, for the inhabitants of one same city banish peace from themselves and yearn only for war.

Who would have thought that the lofty, strong walls that you raised
to the heavens would soon embrace so many and such cruel images of
death? My Naples, well may you call your citizens blind and foolish,
since they have imperiled their fame and honor outside the bounds of
all reason and good counsel.

And if it were not for the wise aid of your great Toledo, who saw
what was needed, Naples, you would have run your life's course while
in the fullness of your flourishing. He turned your steps back to the right
path; he restored you from death to life. Now, what are you thinking?
Why do I see you hesitate? Run with your whole realm to him who loves
you greatly and has given you many signs of this love.

See how Parthenope comes, pensive of visage, asking for mercy, nay,
crying now for help. If honor and fame may be acquired through good
deeds, lord, rescue us from so much suffering, for you can. Then we
will rejoice, when you show your noble visage to us with brighter eyes.
Look kindly on us but once, and it will be enough to content our
desires.

Nor, my lord, should you turn your mind and memory back to past ills.
Submerge in Lethe your righteous burning wrath, and with it all the
deceptions and plots, for the celestial Monarch immediately rescues any
sinner who begs mercy from him from eternal suffering and makes him
instead heir to immortal treasures.

Stanze. Terracina 1549, 8–11 (*lul* corrected to *lui* in penultimate line). Although she
also wrote sonnets, Terracina was happier within the less demanding metrical form
of ottava rima. Of around fifty poems in her 1548 *Rime* with named addressees, for
example, only seven are sonnets, the remainder *stanze* and *strambotti* (single-octave
poems). The long stanza composition that opens her *Seconde rime* of 1549, addressed
to the Spanish Viceroy of Naples, Don Pedro Alvarez de Toledo (1484–1553), offers a
characteristic example of Terracina's use of this form.

Although formally unrefined to the point of ineptitude, the poem is of notable
historical interest, written as it was in the wake of the rebellion in Naples that broke
out in May 1547 following Toledo's ultimately failed attempt to introduce the Span-
ish Inquisition in the city. The 1547 rebellion was led by powerful elements within
the Neapolitan aristocracy and may be seen as an episode in the protracted power
struggle between this formerly dominant elite and the new Spanish government.
The Terracina family, of the minor Neapolitan nobility, were Spanish loyalists, and
Laura Terracina's uncle, Domenico Terracina, aroused hatred for his support for
the viceroy both in 1547 and at earlier moments of social tension in the 1530s (Maroi
1913, 30–31, 45–46). Laura Terracina writes from a clear position of loyalism here,

condemning the 1547 rebellion as the result of "blindness and folly" (53) and representing Toledo as the wise father of his city and sole bulwark between it and the horrors of civil war. She concludes the poem, however, with a plea for clemency and forgiveness, perhaps reflecting her connections of clientelage with many of the aristocratic families associated with the rebellion (Terracina's *Seconde rime* and *Quarte rime* contain sonnets to Isabella Villamarina, princess of Salerno, wife of the leader of the uprising, Ferrante Sanseverino).

The volume of verse in which this poem appears was published in Florence, home to Don Pedro of Toledo's daughter, Eleonora, the wife of the city's ruler, Cosimo I de' Medici (see nos. 148, 188). It seems almost certain that this was more than a coincidence, especially when we consider that it was published by the ducal printer Lorenzo Torrentino and that this was the only work Terracina published in Florence. It may be that Eleonora herself, or Cosimo, facilitated the publication through an intermediary such as Lodovico Domenichi or Benedetto Varchi. The Florentine context helps account for the prominence given to the poem to Don Pedro within the collection, where it appears as the first text.

In this politically high-profile poem, Terracina makes an effort to elevate what she accurately terms her "lowly style" (16), gesturing toward the rhetorical device of *prosopopoeia in her invocation of the personified city of Naples and including a prominent citation of the incipit of Petrarch's political sonnet 136 at ll. 45–46. This allusion to Petrarch's famous diatribe against the corruption of the papal court has political resonance, since relations between Charles V, Toledo's superior, and Pope Paul III were notoriously strained at the time. Parthenope (36) was a mythological siren enamored of Odysseus, said to have been buried in Naples and hence an icon of the city. Terracina's self-association with Parthenope, here as paired virgin supplicants, has an obvious patriotic dimension but also serves as oblique self-compliment, since Parthenope, as siren, was a singer of miraculous power. The other mythological references in the poem, in ll. 27–28, are to Polyphemus, the one-eyed cannibalistic Cyclops tricked by Odysseus in Homer, and the Harpies, the female bird-monsters who plague Aeneas in Virgil. They probably stand generically for irrational foes and serve implicitly to underline Toledo's status as epic hero. Lethe (75) was the river of forgetfulness, one of the five rivers of the Greek underworld.

A point of ideological interest in the poem is the use of *monarca* in the first and last stanzas (5, 77) to designate, respectively, the Emperor and God. More baffling is the reference to civil strife bringing about the fall of the Roman "monarchy" (37), where a reference to the republic might be expected. The reference to "lofty, strong walls" (49–50) refers to the ambitious new fortification system constructed in Naples in Toledo's vice-regency, tax appropriations for which had caused the first rebellion against his rule. The image of these walls filling with "cruel images of death" is poetically the strongest moment of the poem.

Claudia della Rovere (1550s)
163

Qui dove noi viviam franchi e securi,
mercé del valor vostro alto e sovrano,
timidi già per lo nimico ispano
siam stati in giorni tenebrosi e oscuri;   4
ond'acciò che per sempre eterna duri
la chiara fama de l'invitta mano
vostra, Signor, convien, che tutto 'l piano
e 'l monte fregi darvi ognor procuri.   8
Pochi i metalli son, men sono i marmi
atti a capir vostre vittorie tante,
ché si convien'a voi piu lunga istoria.   11
Uopo saria di quel che cantò l'armi
del figliulo d'Anchise a far memoria
degna di voi, cui non va alcuno innante.   14

Here where we now live free and happy, thanks to your lofty and
sovereign valor, timidly we once cowered from the Spanish foe in dark
and benighted days; so, now, in order that the bright fame of your
dauntless hand may ever flourish, it is fitting that the whole of the plain
and the mount should ever strive to deck you with praise. Few are the
metals, fewer the marbles that are fit to encompass your countless
victories, for a longer history is owing to you. To make a fitting memorial
for you, we would need him who sang the arms of the son of Anchises,
for you are peerless in this world.

Sonnet ABBA ABBA CDE CED. Domenichi 1559, 32 (with *pochi* in l. 4 amended from
poco). This sonnet documents the final phase in the grueling sequence of wars on
Italian territory that began with the French invasions of the 1490s (nos. 156–57). It is
addressed to Charles de Cossé, Comte de Brissac (1506–63), leader of the French
army sent to combat the entrenched Spanish-Imperial forces in della Rovere's
native Piedmont in 1551–59. *Franchi* (1) is a pun, meaning both "free" and "French,"
while the injunction in ll. 7–8 to the "plain" and the "mount" to praise Brissac may
be a punning reference to the literal meaning of Piedmont (foot of the mount). Line
13 alludes to Virgil, whose *Aeneid* celebrates the Trojan hero Aeneas, son of Anchises
("sings the arms of" echoes the "arma . . . cano" of Virgil's first line). For the implicit
parallel between verse memorials and statuary in the first tercet, see Gambara's no.
134, which may be echoed here in the *memoria/istoria* rhyme.

Virginia Salvi (post 1555)
164

Afflitti e mesti intorno a l'alte sponde
del Tebro altiero i cari figli vanno
de la mia patria, e 'l grave acerbo affanno
ciascun nel petto suo dolente asconde.   4
Miran lungi il bel colle ove s'infonde
ira, sdegno, furor, rapina e danno
dal famelico augello, in cui si stanno
ingorde voglie a null'altre seconde.   8
Spargon per l'aria alti sospiri ardenti;
versan dagli occhi largo pianto ognora:
muovon i sassi i lor giusti lamenti.   11
Piange, Reina mia, la vosta Flora,
più di tutt'altre mesta, e son possenti
i vostri rai far che di duol non mora.   14

Sad and afflicted, along the great banks of the ancient Tiber go the
dear children of my homeland, hiding the burden of keen pain in their
suffering breasts. From far off, they gaze on that lovely hill, now filled
with wrath, scorn, fury, pillage, and ruin by that ravening bird, whose
greed is second to none. They breathe great burning sighs into the air,
their eyes pour an unceasing flow of tears, the stones themselves are
moved by their just laments. My Queen, your Flora weeps, more
wretched than any other; only the power of your distant rays keep her
from dying of sorrow.

Sonnet ABBA ABBA CDC DCD. Domenichi 1559, 197 (*del* in l. 7 amended to *dal*). Siena
in the 1530s–50s produced a remarkable cluster of female poets, several of whom
wrote on their city's turbulent political history (see also no. 161). Virginia Salvi came
from a leading family within the city's pro-French, anti-Imperial faction and went
into exile in Rome after the imperial conquest of 1555, after which Siena passed under
the rule of Cosimo de' Medici, duke of Florence. This sonnet, addressed to the
Italian-born French queen Caterina de' Medici (1519–89), laments Siena's rule by op-
pressors emblematized by the eagle of the Empire (the "ravening bird" of l. 7). The
final tercet, with its reference to Florence's oppression under Cosimo, is especially
charged, given that Catherine had a strong dynastic claim to Florence herself.
Other poems by Salvi are more explicit in calling on France to invade Florence
(Eisenbichler 2003, 89–92). The "rays" of l. 14 are Catherine's eyes.

Isabella Cervoni (1598)
165

[1] Divino Atlante, a cui commesso ha 'l pondo,
sovra le spalle il Re de l'universo
e posto in man del cielo ambe le chiavi;
invitti eroi, ch'avete oggi del mondo
la miglior parte e la più bella, e perso   5
quasi quel ch'acquistar già gli antichi avi:
io, che cantar solea dolci e soavi
versi, e già scrissi il pentimento vero
del re de' Franchi, e 'l prego e il perdono;
io che, con grave suono,   10
di Cesare cantai l'eccelso impero,
per inasprirlo contra 'l fero Trace;
io, che la mano audace
d'altri biasmai a quel sacro Collegio
che pur parte vede ora   15
di quel predissi allora,
quasi Cassandra non avuto in pregio:
a voi parlo; a voi dir m'accingo cose
che nel petto tener non posso ascose.

[2] Spiegato avea di già l'aquila altera   20
l'ali, e poggiando ad or ad or più ardita
contr'oriente ad oscurar la luna,
con gli artigli e col rostro avea la fera
nostra nimica in più parti ferita:
e de le tane tolte già più d'una,   25
quando, non so se fato o pur Fortuna,
(caso da me più giorni anteveduto)
nel più bel volo tarpa a lei le penne.
Oh cielo, e quando avvenne
ne' tempi andati quel ch'or s'è veduto   30
con poco onor nel popolo di Cristo?
È questo il grande acquisto
che'l Transilvano e Cesare speraro
contra l'Asia feroce,
per innalzar la croce   35
là dove a Costantin regnar fu caro?
Ma forse a ragion cade esto flagello
per pena a chi s'è fatto a Dio rubello.

[3] Io dico e dissi e dirò fin ch'io viva
che chi si trova in duro laccio preso,   40
cui l'avarizia o la superbia annodi,
non giunge mai co' suoi pensieri a riva
nel largo mare ov'ognun resta offeso
da le tempeste sue, da le sue frodi.
Quasi vipere son, ch'in mille modi   45
mordon quei che più ponno; anzi tiranni,
ch'a la ragion comandano ed al senso.
Quindi nasce un'immenso
desio, che fa che l'uom s'infiammi a' danni
d'altri, e protervo le crud'armi adopre.   50
Quindi tosto si scopre
fra' più potenti la discordia pazza,
che quanto più ne arreca
travagli e più n'accieca,
più del nostro fallir ride e gavazza.   55
Questa co 'l seme suo n'ha sempre il frutto
prodotto acerbo al cristianesmo tutto.

[4] Quel pensier generoso e pio, quel senno,
che suol ne' sommi re svegliare sdegni
contra chi mai la santa chiesa offenda,   60
vostri, ch'al ben commun convenir denno,
animi alteri a racquistare i regni
persi di Cristo, e non rancore, incenda.
L'onor vostr'è che l'un l'altro difenda,
e contra 'l popol timido ed imbelle   65
volgiate l'armi, e non contra voi stessi.
Duo gran re d'odio impressi
dunque hanno i cori e d'empie voglie e felle
in sanguinosa e sempiterna guerra?
Dunque inondar la terra   70
del cristian sangue vi diletta e giova?
L'armi e gli scettri in mano
vi pose il Re sovrano,
non per usargli un contra l'altro a prova;
ma contro 'l Turco abbassando la lancia,   75
per ornar di trionfi e Spagna e Francia.

[5] Tu che 'l nome "cattolico" ritieni,
e che comandi a novo mondo, or'hai

volto lo stocco contra il re de' Franchi?
Sei tanto involto ne' pensier terreni,   80
che non t'accorgi omai che te ne vai
al fin degli anni che già sono stanchi?
Quando per te quella corona manchi,
e 'l desiderio tuo saziato resti,
che onor, che lode, e che mercede sia?   85
Dirà la gente pia.
di te:—senza pietà real fu questi,
di quel bramoso che dispiace al Cielo—.
Ahi, re pien di buon zelo,
quanto meglio saria voltar l'insegne   90
e spronar le tue voglie
là dove a ricche spoglie
Giesù ti chiama contra genti indegne?
Oprar non deve un re cristian (né erro)
contr'altro re cristiano il foco e 'l ferro.   95

[6] Il giusto Dio quand'i peccati nostri
han di remissïon passato 'l segno;
ed a sua maiestà pur troppo lesa.
giust'è che la giustizia sua dimostri;
e col coltel de la vendetta degno   100
ne dia gastigo e vendichi l'offesa.
Te vede accinto a non lodata impresa:
te, che pur devi la religione
difender, suo campione e figlio amato,
ed ella in dubbio stato   105
posta, di te si lagna e con ragione,
il cui ferro il suo popol fere e ancide.
Non senti come stride
e chiede aita la Garonna e 'l Reno
contra la fera spada,   110
che per ogni contrada,
macchia del sangue suo tutto 'l terreno?
Pur di bei detti nostra legge è piena:
premio al ben fare, al mal'oprar la pena [. . .]

[congedo] Canzon, se tra i furor, gli sdegni e l'armi,   305
che mantengono ancora in piè la lite,
non è chi al grande e bel desir risponda,
va pur lieta e gioconda

di qua da l'Alpi; ivi saranno udite
le tue ragioni e forse poste in opra.   310
Non parlo io, ma di sopra
vien chi detta la voce a l'intelletto
di verginella pura,
la qual resta sicura,
che, se fia 'l nodo de la Lega stretto,   315
vedremo ove splend'or la luna indegna,
drizzar di Cristo la reale insegna.

[1] Divine Atlas, on whose shoulders the King of the Universe has placed the world's weight, and into whose hands he has given the keys of heaven; dauntless Heroes, who rule the best and finest part of the world (and who have lost almost all your ancient ancestors gained), I, who was used to sing sweet and soft verses; I who wrote of the true penitence of the French king and his prayer and his pardon; I who, in grave tones, sang of Caesar's sublime empire, to stir him to battle against the fierce Thracian; I who complained of another's bold hand to that sacred College, which now sees to be true what I then predicted in part, like a despised Cassandra—to you I speak. I shall speak to you of things I cannot keep concealed in my breast.

[2] The proud eagle had spread its wings and, soaring ever more boldly against the east to obscure the moon, had wounded our savage enemy in many places with its claws and beak and rooted our foes out of their dens, when, either because fate willed it or through chance Fortune (as I had already foreseen), in its finest flight, its wings were cut back. Oh heavens! When did we ever see Christ's folk suffer so greatly in past times, with so little honor? Was this the great conquest the Transylvanian and Caesar hoped for against fierce Asia, to raise the cross where Constantine so fondly ruled? But perhaps this scourge falls fairly on those whose have betrayed our faith.

[3] I say, and always said, and shall say until I die that whoever finds himself caught in the harsh noose knotted by avarice or pride will never reach safe harbor in the vast sea whose storms and deceptions assail us. These vices are like vipers, which bite the most powerful in a thousand ways; nay, tyrants who command their reason and senses both. Thence is born a vast desire that inflames men to harm others and arrogantly to wield their cruel weapons. Thence mad Discord is often revealed among our rulers—she who, the more she wearies us with travails and blinds us, the more she mocks and relishes our downfall. She it is who, with her seed, has always produced bitter fruits for all of Christendom.

[4] May that noble and pious ideal, that concern which so often awakes wrath in the highest monarchs against any who offend against the most holy church—may that ideal, and not rancor, inflame your proud spirits, framed for the common good, to reacquire the lost kingdoms of Christ. Your honor resides in defending one another and in turning your weapons against that timid and defenseless people, not against each other. Shall it be that two great kings have their hearts so stamped with hatred and with evil, fell desires, in a bloody and eternal war? Does it so please you to drown the earth in Christian blood? The Supreme Lord placed your weapons and scepters in your hands not to test them against one another, but to train your lance against the Turk and hence to adorn Spain and France with triumphs.

[5] You who retain the name of "Catholic" and who command the new world, do you turn your sword against the king of France? Are you so wrapped in worldly thoughts that it does not occur to you that you are coming to the end of your long, wearied years? If that crown were to fall, if your desire were to be sated, what honor, what praise, what reward would you reap? The faithful will say of you, "That man was without the piety fitting a king: he hungered for that on which Heaven frowns." Alas, zealous king, how much better would you do to turn your banners and spur your will there where Jesus calls you against a base foe and rich spoils await? Unless I err, a Christian king should not use flame and iron against another Christian king.

[6] It is just that God, in his justice, stand in judgment when our sins have passed the point of remission, and injured his majesty too greatly, and that he punish us with his worthy avenging blade to redress the offense he has received. He sees you girded for a battle undeserving of praise—you, who should defend religion, his champion and beloved son. Our faith, which you have endangered, complains of you, and rightly, when your weapon strikes and slays her own people. Do you not hear how Garonne and Rhine wail and cry for help against the fierce sword that stains the earth with blood on all sides? And yet our faith is full of fine sayings: rewards for well-doing, punishment for ill.

[congedo] Canzone, if, amid the furor, amid the wrath and the clash of arms that keep this quarrel alive, you find no one who corresponds to your lofty, fine desires, go, nonetheless, happy and blithe, beyond the Alps; there your arguments will be heard and perhaps will see fruit. I do not speak myself: the voice comes from on high that dictates to this

pure little virgin. I rest assured that, if the knot of the League is pulled tight, we will see, where there now blazes the unworthy moon, Christ's regal banner lofted on high.

Canzone ABCABCCDEeDFfGhhGII + CDEeDFfGhhGII. Cervoni 1598, n.p. [extract]. A political crisis was occasioned in 1598 when the last Este ruler of Ferrara, Alfonso II, died. Although a member of a minor branch of the family claimed the duchy, Pope Clement VIII (Ippolito Aldobrandini) took advantage of the dynastic impasse to recoup the city for direct papal rule. Shortly after the resolution of this crisis, Isabella Cervoni published a substantial prose essay, cast in the form of a deliberative oration addressed to the Pope, disputing the issue of whether military force was justified in such circumstances. She accompanied the oration with a lengthy canzone urging the rulers of Europe to unite in a crusade and with a sonnet addressed to Clement, reiterating the theme of the canzone. Collectively, these three works make up a strikingly assertive whole, staging Cervoni as advisor to spiritual and temporal princes. She underlines the boldness of this self-positioning at the beginning of the oration, calling attention to her apparent lack of authority for such a task. "What will the world say when it hears my words on such high matters, so remote from the nature and quality of a simple young virgin?"

Cervoni's canzone "Ai prencipi cristiani" (To the Christian Rulers), as it is described on the title page of the volume, is massive even by her normal standards, containing sixteen stanzas of nineteen lines each and a thirteen-line *congedo*—317 lines in total, by comparison with the 230 of her canzone for 1600 Maria de' Medici (no. 155). The sheer size of the poem is part of its message, underlining the weight of its theme. It was probably composed some time prior to the oration on the Ferrara crisis with which it was published. The second stanza's reference to a sudden, devastating setback in a war against the Ottomans that appeared previously to have been going well (20–28), is probably to the Battle of Keresztes in October 1596, when Hapsburg-Transylvanian forces were defeated by an Ottoman army under Mehmet III. A date of 1596–97 would also square well with the references to Franco-Spanish conflict in stanzas 5–6. Henri IV of France and Philip II of Spain were at war for most of the 1590s, but a resolution was reached at the Peace of Vervins in May 1598.

As an unsolicited political address to the rulers of Europe, Cervoni's canzone places itself within the tradition of Petrarch's great political canzone "Italia mia," (128) of whose l. 56 there may be an echo in l. 5. Cervoni's prime intertext is, however, canto 17 of Ariosto's *Orlando furioso*, two passages of which she echoes closely: the proem (stanzas 1–5), in which the poet speaks of tyrannical rulers as a punishment from heaven, and the "digression" at stanzas 73–79, in which he upbraids the rulers of Europe for devoting themselves to aggressions against one another instead of uniting against their common enemy, the Turk. The first of these passages is quoted directly in ll. 96–97 (cf. *OF* 17.1, ll. 1–2). The second is echoed most directly in l. 75 (cf. *OF* 17.74, l. 1), in 77 (cf. *.OF* 17.75, ll. 1–2), and in the juxtaposed *Cristo/ acquisto* rhyme of 31–32 (cf. *OF* 17.74, ll. 7–8). Further echoes of Ariosto are found in l. 39, a direct quotation of *OF* 16.2, l. 1; in the personified description of Discord in ll. 52–55 (cf. *OF* 27.100, ll. 1 and 5); in the phrase *timido ed imbelle*, used (incongruously) to describe the Ottomans at l. 65 (cf. *OF* 39.20, l. 8); and in the coupling of *Garonna* and *Reno* in l. 109 (cf. *OF* 27.101, l. 7).

Among female-authored political texts, an important thematic precedent for Cervoni's canzone is offered by Veronica Gambara's much-published no. 158, which similarly calls on the rulers of Europe to forget their differences and unite against the Turk. A more distant model may be St. Catherine of Siena's letters to Popes Gregory XI and Urban VI, which offer a precedent for a lowly *verginella* presuming to advise a pope. Catherine is particularly likely to have been influential because she was a local, Tuscan saint, born not far from Cervoni's birthplace, Colle di Val d'Elsa. A further female authorizing figure, whom Cervoni cites at l. 17, is Cassandra, the daughter of King Priam of Troy, granted the power of prophecy by Apollo but doomed never to have her prophecies believed.

Despite her bold self-presentation as speaker of unwelcome truths, Cervoni is careful not to offend potential patrons in her canzone. Her chief opprobrium is reserved for Philip II of Spain, at a safe distance and opposed by the Tuscan grand duke Ferdinando I de' Medici, who sided with Henri IV in the Spanish-French conflict. Clement VIII's policy also tended toward an attempt to free the papacy from its traditional dependency on Spain. Later in the canzone, Cervoni is careful to shower with praise Gianfrancesco Aldobrandini (1545–1601), the husband of a niece of the pope, who was entrusted on several occasions with the command of the pope's armies. The rulers of Parma, Urbino, and Mantua also come in for praise, as do the republic of Venice and, naturally, the "demigod" Ferdinando de' Medici himself.

Stylistically, Cervoni exerts herself here to maintain a "weighty" style appropriate to her momentous subject matter: the "grave suono" (10) she opposes to her former "dolci e soavi versi" (7–8). She succeeds well in the opening stanzas, given here, which are certainly the strongest in the poem, along with the *congedo*, though her inspiration slackens elsewhere. Especially notable is her use of alliteration, consonance, and assonance to lend emphasis and phonetic cohesion: see, for example, *l'aquila altera / l'ali* in ll. 20–21 (also featuring *concorso di vocali*); *nostra nimica* and *tane tolte* (24–25); *danni/d'altri* (49–50); and *commun convenir, animi alteri*, and *racquistar i regni* (61–62). Also noteworthy is Cervoni's use of *hypotaxis, particularly obvious in the first stanza, which is composed of a single long sentence, articulated through *anaphora (*io che* in ll. 7, 11, and 13; *a voi . . . a voi* in 18), and featuring a bold *zeugma in ll. 4–5 (*perso* depends grammatically on the *avete* of l. 4: "have lost").

Atlas (1) was a mythological giant who bore the heavens on his shoulders. The "two keys" of the pope (3) are his powers of "binding and loosing" (Matthew 16.19), encompassing actions such as the remission of sins and excommunication. Caesar (11) was used as a generic name for emperors, presumably used here of the Holy Roman emperor Rudolf II (1552–1612). Cervoni speaks of having urged him to fight against the Turks in a canzone that does not appear to have survived (the classicizing term "Thracians" for Turks was common in this period). The canzoni on Henri IV's conversion to Catholicism and on Clement VIII's benediction of him alluded to in ll. 8–9, were published in 1597 by Giorgio Marescotti, while the canzone addressed to the College of Cardinals (13–14) appears to be lost. The eagle and the moon, in the allegorical passage at ll. 20–28, were the emblems, respectively, of the Hapsburg emperors and the Ottomans. "The Transylvanian" (33) was Sigismund Báthory (1572–1613), ruler of Transylvania, at this time an independent principality. Constantine (36) was the first Roman emperor to convert to Christianity. His seat was Constantinople or Byzantium (modern-day Istanbul), occupied by the Turks after 1453.

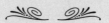

Polemical &
Manifesto Verse

Camilla Scarampa (1490s)
166 ⟶

Biasimi pur chi vuol la mia durezza,
ché seguir voglio il casto mio pensero,
il qual mi scorge per il buon sentero,
che fa gli spirti miei vaghi d'altezza.   4
Fugga pur gioventù, venga vecchiezza,
ché sol nella virtù mi fido e spero,
e per lei il mio cor sdegnoso e altero
disprezza quanto il cieco vulgo apprezza.   8
Né d'altro che di questa più mi cale,
ed ho di lei sì la mia mente accesa
che ogn'altra mi par opra vana e frale.   11
E però vo' seguir l'alta mia impresa,
poiché beltà senza virtù non vale;
non sia chi faccia al mio voler contesa.   14

Let him who wishes blame my hardness: I am resolved to follow my
chaste intent, which guides me along the righteous path, filling my
spirits with a yearning for greatness. Flee, youth; come, age: I put my
faith only in virtue, and my disdainful, proud soul despises what the
blind hordes prize. So aflame is my mind with the desire for virtue that
all other labors seem to me vain and feeble. So let me follow my lofty
ambition, for beauty without virtue is worthless. Let no man contest
my will.

Sonnet ABBA ABBA CDC DCD. Leone 1962, 298 (*pensiero* and *sentiero* in ll. 2–3
amended to *pensero* and *sentero* on the basis of Florence, BNCF MS Palatino 221, 22r).
An early biography of Scarampa speaks of her resisting marriage to pursue her
studies (Cox 2008, 46–47), and this sonnet appears to be a manifesto of this intent.
As such, it offers interesting parallels with Moderata Fonte's no. 171. In constructing
her combative poetic persona, Scarampa wittily plays off the characteristics of
hardness and haughtiness male poets frequently attribute to their obdurately chaste
ladies. A likely source for the poem is Petrarch's sonnet 263, which celebrates Lau-
ra's commitment to chastity in similarly heroizing terms, while his sonnet 229 may
have supplied the hard rhyme *-ezza* of the quatrains, duplicated in the pairing of
disprezza/apprezza (8). Another phonetically assertive line is 5, with its two hemis-
tichs bound, respectively, by *consonance and *alliteration. *Virtù* (6, 13), translated
as "virtue," can also signify intellectual or creative talent.

167

Amor, tu vien ver me sì pien d'orgoglio
volando con inganni hor basso hor alto,
credendo forse darmi un grave assalto;
non ti convien, ch'io son qual esser soglio.   4
Com'al turbato mar un saldo scoglio
sarà contra di te mio cor di smalto
et di ciò lieta me ne glorio e exalto
et però teco contrastar io voglio.   8
Sì ch'a tua posta le tue ale spiega,
vien pur come tu vuoi armato in campo,
ché tua forza a la mia convien che piega.   11
De la vittoria già tutta m'avampo
et se l'advien ch'io pur ti prenda et lega,
non sperar da mie man trovar più scampo.   14

Love, you come at me so full of pride, flying with feints, now low, now high, thinking perhaps to inflict a grave assault on me. It will not avail, for I am as I am wont, a resisting rock in a stormy ocean. My heart will be stone against you. I glory and exalt, delighting in this thought, and am happy to meet you in battle. So spread your wings at your leisure and come to the field armed as you wish, for your strength must perforce bend to mine. Already, I am all afire at my victory, and if it chances that I capture and bind you, do not think to find mercy at my hands.

Sonnet ABBA ABBA CDC DCD. Rozzo 1982, 430. Similar in theme to no. 166, this sonnet illustrates the "expressive vigor" Ugo Rozzo atttibutes to Scarampa. The image of Love as a winged assailant reflects traditional figurations of the god Cupid, while the reference to the poet capturing him (13) may be to Petrarch's *Triumph of Chastity*, where Laura is seen taking Cupid prisoner and beating him, as revenge for the "thousands of women" who have suffered at his hands (*TP* 118–26). The A rhymes of the poem derive from a sonnet by Scarampa's contemporary Antonio Tebaldeo (no. 28), echoed very explicitly in the closing phrase of l. 4. *Smalto* (6), translated "stone" means, literally, "enamel."

Tullia d'Aragona (1547)
168

Bernardo, ben potea bastarvi averne
co 'l dolce dir, ch'a voi natura infonde,
qui dove 'l re de' fiumi ha più chiare onde,
acceso i cuori a le sante opre eterne: 4
che se pur sono in voi pure l'interne
voglie e la vita al vestir corrisponde,
non uom di frale carne e d'ossa immonde,
ma sete un voi de le schiere superne.   8
Or le finte apparenze e 'l ballo, e 'l suono
chiesti dal tempo e da l'antica usanza,
a che così da voi vietati sono?   11
Non fôra santità, fôra arroganza
torre il libero arbitrio, il maggior dono
che Dio ne die' ne la primiera stanza.   14

Bernardo, it should have been quite enough for you, with that sweet eloquence that nature infused in you, to have fired hearts with enthusiasm for holy eternal works, here where the king of rivers has its clearest waves; for if your inward desires are pure, and your life truly corresponds to your habit, you are truly not a man of frail flesh and foul bones but one of the angelic hosts. But the masks and dancing and music demanded by the season and by ancient custom—why would you prohibit them in this way? It is not saintliness but arrogance to take from us the gift of free will, the greatest gift God gave us within our first dwelling on earth.

Sonnet ABBA ABBA CDC DCD. d'Aragona 1547, 9r. D'Aragona was in Ferrara during a 1537 visit by the charismatic Sienese preacher Bernardo Ochino (1487–1564), who later scandalized the Catholic Church with his departure for protestant Geneva in 1542. Ochino appears from this sonnet to have preached against the observation of carnival, traditionally a time of often riotous partying before Lent. D'Aragona defends carnival festivities in the first tercet on grounds of custom and in the second, more audaciously, on theological grounds: man must have the opportunity to sin, or the cardinal doctrine of free will, as practiced by Adam and Eve in the Garden of Eden (l. 14's "first dwelling"), is undermined. The quatrains of the poem, though highly complimentary toward Ochino, nonetheless manage to insinuate the possibility of hypocrisy on his part in ll. 5–6 (a tacit accusation that presumably gained a new resonance for Catholic readers after his "defection"). The "king of rivers" (3) is the Po (cf. Petrarch's sonnet 180, l. 9).

169

Poiché mi die' natura a voi simìle
forma e materia, o fosse il gran Fattore,
non pensate ch'ancor disio d'onore
mi desse e bei pensier, Manel gentile?   4
Dunque credete me cotanto vile
ch'io non osi mostrar, cantando, fore,
quel che dentro n'ancide altero ardore,
se bene a voi non ho pari lo stile?   8
Non lo crediate, no, Piero, ch'anch'io
fatico ognor per appressarmi al cielo
e lasciar del mio nome in terra fama.   11
Non contenda rea sorte il bel disio,
ché, pria che l'alma dal corporeo velo
si scioglia, sazierò forse mia brama.   14

Since Nature, or our great Maker, gave me matter and form similar to
yours, noble Manelli, do you think they did not also give me a desire for
honor, and fine thoughts? Do you truly believe me so base that I should
not venture to tell in my song of the lofty love that is slaying me from
within? Do not think so, no, Piero, for I too labor at all hours to bring
myself nearer the heavens and to leave fame on earth for my name. May
cruel fate not contest my fine desire, for before my soul dissolves from
its mortal veil, perhaps I shall satisfy my craving.

Sonnet ABBA ABBA CDE CDE. d'Aragona 1547, 9v. This sonnet, addressed to a Flo-
rentine banker, Piero Manelli, defends the legitimacy of d'Aragona's literary ambi-
tions and, by extension, those of women in general. D'Aragona replies with extreme
urbanity to what may well have been a less polite attack on Manelli's part, even
courteously deferring to him as the superior poet (8). The first quatrain, with its
reference to the Aristotelian notions of form and matter, alludes to current debates
over whether women were intrinsically inferior to men, as Aristotle argued, or
whether they shared men's native capacities but were held back by social factors.
The tercets speak feelingly of the poet's urge to fame: note the emphatically placed
brama (14), signifying a craving or strong desire. The sonnet's language is relatively
plain, reflecting its argumentational character, though note the marked *alliter-
ation in l. 14 and the *assonance in l. 7. *Ancide* (7) is a poetic synonym for *uccide*, used
most famously in Petrarch's sonnet 134, l. 7.

Olimpia Morata (pre-1555)
170

οὔποτε μὲν ξυμπᾶσιν ἐνὶ φρεσὶν ἥνδανε ταὐτὸ
  κοὔποτε πᾶσιν ἴσον Ζεὺς παρέδωκε νόον.
ἱππόδαμος Κάστωρ, πὺξ δ᾽ ἦν ἀγαθὸς Πολυδεύκης,
  ἔκγονος ἐξ ταὐτῆς ὄρνιθος ἀμφότερος.
κἀγὼ μὲν θῆλυς γεγαυῖα τὰ θηλυκὰ λεῖπον   5
  νήματα, κερκίδιον, στήμονα, καὶ καλάθους.
Μουσάων δ᾽ ἄγαμαι λειμῶνα τὸν ἀνθεμόεντα
  Παρνάσσου θ᾽ ἱλαροὺς τοῦ διλόφοιο χορούς.
ἄλλαι τέρπονται μὲν ἴσως ἄλλοισι γυναῖκες.
  ταῦτα δέ μοι κῦδος, ταῦτα δὲ χαρμοσύνη.   10

oupote men xumpâsin eni phresin hêndane tauto
  koupote pâsin ison Zeus paredôke noon.
hippodamos Kastôr, pux d'ên agathos Polydeukês,
  ekgonos ex tautês ornithos amphoteros.
kagô men thêlus gegauia ta thêluka leipon   5
  nêmata, kerkidion, stêmona, kai kalathous.
Mousaôn d' agamai leimôna ton anthemoenta
  Parnassou th'hilarous tou dilophoio khorous.
allai terpontai men isôs alloisi gunaikes.
  tauta de moi kudos, tauta de kharmosunê.   10

Never did the same thing please the hearts of all, and never did Zeus grant the same mind to all. Castor is a horse tamer, but Polydeuces is good with his fist, both the offspring of the same bird. And I, though born female, have left feminine things, yarn, shuttle, loom threads, and work baskets. I admire the flowery meadow of the Muses and the pleasant choruses of twin-peaked Parnassus. Other women perhaps delight in other things. These are my glory, these my delight.

Elegaic distichs. Morata 2003, 179 (text slight amended); translation by Holt Parker. Morata was one of few Renaissance women to have written in Greek as well as Latin. This epigram, probably written during her youth at the court of Ferrara, is addressed to an unidentified humanist, Eutychus Pontanus Gallus. Like Tullia d'Aragona's no. 169, it may well have been a response to a provocation, questioning the propriety of Morata's devotion to literary studies. Her poem deliberately ignores the ideological issue, instead airily presenting the choice between literary erudition and weaving as pursuits for women merely as a question of individual taste and inclination. The notion of women abandoning domestic pursuits for poetry was a *topos by the time Morata was writing, a classic statement being Ariosto's *OF* 37.14, ll. 4–6 (see also nos. 153 and 188). Morata focuses specifically on weaving, perhaps mindful of its frequent use as a metaphor for poetic composition. The epigram divides into five semantically self-contained distichs, the first two and last two constructed around binary *parallelisms. Only the middle distich, listing the implements of weaving, breaks this pattern with a quadripartite list (6). Castor and Polydeuces (or Pollux) were the twin sons of Leda, raped by Zeus in the form of a swan (hence his description as a bird). Their counterposed description here echoes that in Horace's ode 1.12, ll. 25–27.

Moderata Fonte (pre-1592)

171

Libero cor nel mio petto soggiorna:
non servo alcun, né d'altri son che mia;
pascomi di modestia e cortesia,
virtù m'essalta e castità m'adorna.   4
Quest'alma a Dio sol cede e a lui ritorna,
benché nel velo uman s'avolga e stia,
e sprezza il mondo e sua perfidia ria
che le semplici menti inganna e scorna.   8
Bellezza, gioventù, piaceri e pompe
nulla stimo, se non ch'a i pensier puri
son trofeo, per mia voglia, e non per sorte.   11
Così negli anni verdi e nei maturi,
poiché fallacia d'uom non m'interrompe,
fama e gloria n'attendo in vita e in morte.   14

A free heart dwells within my breast; I serve no one and am no one's
but my own. Modesty and courtesy are my lifeblood; virtue exalts me
and chastity adorns me. This soul yields only to God, and turns to him
even while it is wrapped in a mortal veil, despising the world and its vile
perfidy, which deceives and undoes simple minds. For beauty, youth,
pleasure, and pomp I care nothing, other than as sacrifices to my pure
intention, embraced through my choice, not through chance. Thus in
my green years and my mature ones, as long as men's deceptions do not
foil me, I expect fame and glory in life and in death.

Sonnet ABBA ABBA CDE DCE. Fonte 1600, 14. This sonnet appears in Fonte's dia-
logue *The Worth of Women*, where it is attributed to a speaker who has resolved to
remain single to pursue her literary career. It is possible that Fonte composed it in
her youth in her own voice, as she married exceptionally late for the period, at
twenty-eight. The second half of l. 2 quotes from a speech from the female knight
Marfisa in Ariosto's *OF* 26.79, l. 7: an apposite allusion, as Marfisa is similarly intent
on glory and impervious to love. Close in theme to Camilla Scarampa's no. 166,
Fonte's sonnet differs in its introduction of a religious inflection in ll. 5–6 and in its
characteristic allusion to men's perfidy in l. 13. Stylistically, the sonnet's conserva-
tism supports the thesis of an early composition date. Formally, it is highly con-
trolled and "correct," rich in balanced binary structures such as the *isocolon of l. 4,
and closer to the style of Bembo and Gambara than the distinctly "late-Petrarchist"
nos. 64, 98, and 149.

Chiara Matraini (1597)

172

Quel sì dolce di gloria ardente sprone,
ch'in le parti del cor profonde impresso
m'avete, oltra di quel ch'ha il desir messo,
quant'al mio andar più duro il fren s'oppone,   4
maledir mi fa i ceppi e la prigione
e gli altrui ingiusti torti e 'l nostro sesso
e 'l giogo e le catene ch'hanno oppresso
il poter de l'ingegno e la ragione,   8
che non mi lascian gire ov'io farei
forse anco il nome mio chiaro, immortale,
e voi n'andreste più superbo e altero.   11
Deh, pur com'esser può che i pensier miei,
qual Dedalo, non trovino ancor l'ale
da fuggir questo laberinto fero?   14

That spur to glory, so sweet and fierce, that you have impressed deep in
my heart, along with the promptings my own desire has placed there,
whenever harsh constraints most cruelly curb my progress, makes me
curse the irons and the prison and the injustices of others and our sex
and the yoke and chains that have oppressed the power of our mind and
reason. These hold me back from going where I would perhaps make
my own name famous and immortal and lift your name proudly to the
skies. Ah, how can it be that my thoughts, like Daedalus, cannot yet
find the wings to flee from this cruel labyrinth?

Sonnet ABBA ABBA CDE CDE. Matraini 1597, 47r–v. Though stylistically not one of
her best, this sonnet of Matraini's is interesting for the trenchancy of its polemic
against the "chains" that held women back from achieving their intellectual poten-
tial. The same theme is found in some of Matraini's prose writings (Cox 2008, 119–
20). A likely time of composition is the 1560s, when Matraini conducted an intense
correspondence with the jurist and poet Cesare Coccapani, the probable addressee
of the sonnet. There are echoes in ll. 1–3 of Gambara's no. 132 (the male poetic men-
tor as inspirational force), but these are tempered by the reference to the poet's own
innate "desire" as a further propulsive force. *Chiaro*, in l. 10 (bright or famous), is a
pun on Matraini's name, again suggesting that she is innately destined to fame. The
last tercet conflates two myths about the ancient Greek inventor, Daedalus: his de-
sign of the deadly labyrinth that enclosed the Minotaur and his invention of wings
to escape from a prison tower.

Veneranda Bragadin (1613)

173

Se i bassi merti tuoi forse ti fero
meritamente a qualche dama odioso,
il cui pudico cor tentar fosti oso,
ma ti scacciò con dir aspro e severo;   4
o se le furie ultrici il latte diero
al tuo mortale, onde sì furioso
le donne offendi, dal cui sen pietoso,
già non uscisti, ma da scoglio fiero,   8
a che co 'l rostro tuo, manca cornice,
laceri tutte? S'è che più d'un cigno
con stil canoro insino al ciel l'estolle?   11
Te stesso offendi, forsennato e folle;
te macchia quel tuo dir aspro e ferigno:
a chi non può lodar, biasmar non lice.   14

Did your low worth perhaps make you deservedly hateful to some lady
whose chaste heart you ventured to assail and were repelled with harsh
and severe words? Were you suckled by the vengeful Furies, so that you
so furiously insult women, from whose kind womb you certainly never
emerged, but from some cruel rock? Why, sinister crow, do you feel
the need to lacerate us all with your beak, when more than one swan
with his sweet style has extolled us to the heavens? You insult yourself,
madman. It is you who are stained by your cruel, feral language. He
who cannot praise has no right to blame.

Sonnet ABBA ABBA CDE EDC. Bragadin 1619, 68. Bragadin's sonnet, written c. 1613,
is a response to a misogynistic work by a Paduan medic and writer, Giovanni Bat-
tista Barbo. It triggered a reply from Barbo in the form of an offensive *capitolo*, to
which Bragadin responded with a virulent prose invective (Cox 2012). *Manca cornice*
(9), translated "sinister crow," is found in Petrarch's sonnet 210. Here it probably
also alludes to Boccaccio's misogynist diatribe, *Il Corbaccio* (The Evil Crow), and
perhaps to a famous scene in Canto 35 of Ariosto's *OF* in which poets of genius are
figured as rare swans, standing out among swarming crows and vultures. Braga-
din's point that true "swans" have consistently extolled women is found in Lucrezia
Marinella's *On the Nobility and Excellence of Women* (1600), her probable inspiration in
her invective against Barbo, as is the accusation in the first quatrain that misogy-
nists' animus against women frequently derives from their own disappointments
in love.

Sarra Copio (1621)

174

Con la tua scorta, ecco, Signor, m'accingo
a la difesa, ove m'oltraggia e sgrida
guerrier che ardisce querelar d'infida
l'alma che, tua mercé, di fede i'cingo.   4
Entro senz'armi in non usato aringo,
né guerra io prendo contra chi mi sfida,
ma, poiché tua pietà, mio Dio, m'affida,
col petto ignudo i colpi suoi respingo;   8
ché se di polve già l'armi formasti
al grand'Abram contra i nemici regi
sì ch'ei di lor fe' memorando scempio,   11
rinova in me, bench'inegual, l'esempio,
e l'inchiostro ch'io spargo fa' ch'or basti
a dimostrar di tua possanza i pregi.   14

See me here, with your aid, Lord, girding myself to face a warrior
who insults and berates me, daring to accuse of faithlessness that soul
which, by your grace, is girt with faith. I am going weaponless into an
unwonted tourney; nor do I offer battle to my challenger, but, trusting,
God, in your mercy, I withstand his blows with an unarmed breast. For
if you once raised arms for the great Abraham from dust when he faced
the enemy kings, so he then destroyed them in a memorable rout,
renew this miracle in me, unworthy though I am, and let the ink I that
spill suffice to demonstrate the virtues of your might.

Sonnet ABBA ABBA CDE ECD. Copio 1621. This sonnet is one of two prefacing a
polemical tract by the Venetian Jewish poet Sarra Copio, written in response to a
letter by a priest, Baldassare Bonifaccio (1585–1659), who had accused her of denying
that the soul was immortal. The use of martial imagery in the quatrains as a meta-
phor for textual "combat" recalls Veronica Franco's *capitolo* 16, although Copio
presents herself in a less belligerent manner, as an unwilling combatant. *Querelare*
(3) has judicial implications, underlining the public quality of Bonifaccio's accusa-
tion, and hence the necessity of response. While Abraham's defeat of the "enemy
kings" (10) is recounted in Genesis 14:13–15, the detail of the miraculous transforma-
tion of dust into weapons is apocryphal (Ginzberg 2003, 1:195). Stylistically, note the
phonetically emphatic, consonant-rich opening, the inclusive rhyme *accingo/cingo*,
the sound pairing *col pe / colpi* (8), and the *alliteration of the last phrase, giving a
resonant close.

Verse of
Friendship & Family Love

In vita

Vittoria Colonna (c. 1540)

175

Figlio e signor, se la tua prima e vera
madre vive prigion, non l'è già tolto
l'anima saggia o 'l chiaro spirto sciolto,
né di tante virtù l'invitta schiera.   4
A me, che sembro andar scarca e leggiera,
e 'n poca terra ho il cor chiuso e sepolto,
convien ch'abbi talor l'occhio rivolto
che la novella tua madre non pera.   8
Tu per gli aperti spacïosi campi
del ciel camini, e non più nebbia o pietra
ritarda o ingombra il tuo spedito corso.   11
Io, grave d'anni, aghiaccio. Or tu, ch'avampi
d'alta fiamma celeste, umil m'impetra
dal commun Padre eterno omai soccorso.   14

Son and lord, if your first and true mother is living a prisoner, that has
not taken her wise soul from her or deprived her of her bright spirit or
her great, undaunted company of virtues. You should sometimes turn
your thought to me, who seem to walk so free and untrammeled, yet
whose heart is closed and buried in a small space of earth, to make sure
that your new mother does not perish. You walk through the spacious
open field of heaven, and no mist or rock can slow or impede your rapid
march. I, heavy with years, freeze; may you, who burn with a high
heavenly flame, humbly pray our common Father for my eternal succor.

Sonnet ABBA ABBA CDE CDE. Colonna 1546, 39r. The addressee of this sonnet,
Cardinal Reginald Pole (1500–58), was a close friend and spiritual counselor of Col-
onna's. The sonnet seems to have been written between 1538, when Pole's mother,
Margaret, was imprisoned for political reasons by Henry VIII, and 1541, when she
was executed. Colonna constructs Margaret Pole as an exemplar of true, steadfast
virtue, in contrast with the poet's own wavering spiritual state. The reference to
the poet's heart being buried *in poca terra*, an echo of Petrarch's canzoni 331 (47) and
366 (121), refers to her grief for her dead husband, felt here as a spiritual weakness.
The sonnet is artfully constructed, with the *enjambments at ll. 9–10 and 12–13 un-
derscored by *alliteration and *assonance, and the "common Father" of l. 14 balanc-
ing the doubled mothers of the quatrains. Further ornament is provided in the ter-
cets by the inclusive rhyme *corso/soccorso* and the quasi-inclusive *pietra/impetra*.

Olimpia Malipiero (1559)
176

Privo di stelle 'l cielo e del mar l'onde
cangiar vedransi tutti in pietra dura,
e al dolce tempo l'aura fresca e pura,
foco e fiamma spirar d'ambe le sponde;   4
ed alla terra i fior, l'erbe e le fronde
mancare, il dì mutarsi in notte oscura,
e gli elementi varïar natura,
e qui nove produr piaghe profonde;   8
gl'augei, le fiere, gl'uomini e gli dei,
ciechi di mente e co' desiri ingordi
l'un l'altro roder senza restar mai,   11
e 'l mondo tutto in sempiterni guai
vedrasi, e giunto 'l fin de' giorni miei
pria che, Minia gentil, di voi mi scordi.   14

First we will see the sky empty of stars and the waves of the sea turning to hard rock, and in the springtime the sweet and fresh breeze breathing fire and flame from shore to shore; the flowers, the grass and leaves will abandon the land and the day transform into deepest night; the elements will change their nature and carve deep gashes once again in the earth. We will see birds, beasts, men, and gods, blinded in reason, ravenous in appetite, gnawing at each other without respite, and the world plunged in eternal tumult; we will see the end of my days on earth before, dear Minia, I will ever forget you.

Sonnet ABBA ABBA CDE ECD. Domenichi 1559, 138 (*cieci* in l. 10 corrected to *ciechi*). Male friendship, considered the highest form of human bond, was a common theme in classical and humanistic literature. Friendship between women was less culturally salient, but we begin to see it emerging as a theme in Italian women's writing from the 1550s (Cox 2008, 115). Here, Olimpia Malipiero writes from Florence to a friend in her native Venice, assuring her of her continuing affection. Minia (14) is the feminine form of the Venetian patrician surname Minio. The poem's simple message, "I will never forget you as long as I live" (13–14), is amplified in ll. 1–12 through a listing of dystopian *adynata. The effect is to ground the women's friendship in the broader, cosmic principle of *amicitia* underpinning the order of the universe, a linkage familiar from Cicero's *On Friendship*. The use of adynata in a friendship context may have been suggested by the opening of Ovid's *Tristia* 1.8, where the exiled poet reproaches a faithless friend.

Laura Beatrice Cappello (1595)

177

Questo ramo d'alloro
le tempie mi cinse,
mentre vago desir il cor mi strinse
di discender al sacro e vivo fonte,
e di poggiar per erto calle al monte   5
ove soggiace de le Muse il coro.
Ma, lassa, or ben m'aveggio
che più tener no 'l deggio,
perch'ei sol nacque a coronar il crine
vostro gentil, che face invidia a l'oro,   10
Angela mia, del ciel ricco tesoro.

178

Questo crin, ch'io disposi
quel dì ch'io mi disposi
lieta al mondo morir, viver a Dio,
fu serbato da me sol con desio,
che le due parti estreme   5
de la vostra ghirlanda hor leghi insieme,
e 'nsieme il laccio mostri
che lega e in un ristringe ambi i cor nostri.

This branch of laurel crowned my temples while a fine desire seized my heart to descend to the sacred living fountain and to climb the steep path to the mountain where the chorus of the Muses has its home. But, alas, now I see I should have it no more, for it was born only to crown your noble head, which gold itself envies, my Angela, rich treasure of heaven.

These locks, which I laid aside on the day when I resolved happily to die to the world and live for God, I saved for one reason, so they could now bind together the ends of your garland and serve at the same time as the tie that binds and laces our hearts together in one.

Madrigals abBCCAddEFF, aaBBcCdD. Guazzo 1595, 13, 534–35. These are the opening and closing poems of the first meter-specific collection of madrigals to be published, a "garland" of poems by various authors in praise of Countess Angela Bianca Beccaria of Pavia, presented in the context of a dialogue and each themed to a particular plant or flower. The choice of poems by Laura Beatrice Cappello, an Augustinian nun, as "alpha and omega" of the collection (Guazzo 1595, 535) evidently reflected the two women's particular intimacy: an anonymous madrigal in the collection *O voi coppia felice* (O Happy Pair) (Guazzo 1595, 538) celebrates their mutual love. The first madrigal here is themed "Laurel" (*Lauro*), the second "Hair" (*Capelli*, with a pun on Cappello's surname). The first madrigal speaks of Cappello's relinquishment of the laurel, understood as the symbol of poetic endeavor, to Beccaria (Beccaria seems from several poems in the *Ghirlanda* to have practiced poetry herself, though no works of hers survive). The second poem, in a proto-Baroque *conceit, describes the poet's hair—cut off, as was customary, when she entered the convent—now being resurrected poetically to bind together Guazzo's "garland," as well as the hearts of the two friends. Highly polished and distinctly modish in their use of the madrigal form, these poems offer fascinating documentation of the extent of some nuns' continuing contacts with secular poetic culture well into the age of the Counter-Reformation. The second poem is especially accomplished, with its intriguing *conceit, abbreviated length, juxtaposed rhymes, and artful *rima equivoca* on *disposi*. Note also the *chiasmus in l. 3.

Lucchesia Sbarra (1611)

179

In molte cose il ciel mi fu cortese,
e sempre il dissi e son per dirlo ancora,
ma più nella stagion che, ornata Flora,
a inghirlandar di novo il Tauro prese;   4
ché gli uomini e gli dei stupidi rese
il parto mio che diedi in luce allora;
per cui d'Adon, la dea che Cipro onora
lasciò la traccia, e al mio bel Sole attese.   8
Non d'Aci Galatea più si ricorda,
ma allo splendor d'un crespo e biondo crine
spera lieta asciugar la chioma e 'l ciglio.   11
Febo il duol di Giacinto omai si scorda,
e bellezze più rare e pellegrine
mira; di Giove sol temo l'artiglio.   14

In many things heaven was kind to me, as I always said and always
shall, but especially in the season when, having adorned Flora, it
garlanded Taurus anew. Men and gods were amazed at the infant I
gave into the light at that time. The goddess whom Cyprus honors left
Adonis to attend to my beautiful Sun; nor did Galatea any longer
remember Acis, but rather, in the shining rays from a curly blond head
did she happily wish to dry her hair and brow. Phoebus forgets now the
pain of Hyacinth and gazes on beauties more rare and choice. I fear
only the claw of Jove.

Sonnet ABBA ABBA CDE CDE. Sbarra 1610, A4r (*Ati* at l. 9 corrected to *Aci*). This
sonnet is found in a sequence in Sbarra's *Rime* describing the birth, short life, and
death of the poet's son Giovanni Battista. Here, she rapturously describes the child's
beauty at his birth in the spring (3–4) using a series of comparisons with male Greek
mythological figures famous for their looks: Adonis, beloved of Venus (the "goddess
Cyprus honors"; l. 7); Acis, beloved of the sea-nymph Galatea; and Hyacinth, be-
loved of Apollo. All died young, a fact that gives the poem an ominous undertone
reinforced by the allusion to Ganymede (14), abducted by Jove in the form of an eagle.
The use of the metaphor of the Sun for the child (8) and the reference to his blond
locks (10) assimilate him to the traditional objects of love poetry, with "crespo . . .
crin" recalling l. 1 of Bembo's sonnet 5, while the mythological references curiously
echo stanza 5 of Celio Magno's homoerotic poem 351 ("Già fu che, stolto, io non
credea possente"), unpublished at the time.

Francesca Turina (1628)
180

Viscere del mio sen, cara pupilla
degli occhi miei, vezzoso pargoletto,
quanto di gioia il cor arde e sfavilla
qualor ti bacio e mi ti stringo al petto.   4
O con che dolce e che materno affetto,
non madre pur, ma ti son fatta ancilla:
or ti vezzeggio, or'a dormir ti alletto,
cantando, e meno in ciò vita tranquilla.   8
Fra l'animate rose la mammella
talor ti porgo e il latte in un col core
ti dono, e 'l prendi tu con gran diletto.   11
Mi ridi e miri e par che in tua favella
dica:—Madre, gradisco un tanto amore,
ma in vece del parlar, prendi l'affetto—.   14

Lifeblood of my womb, apple of my eye, dearest little creature, how
my heart burns and sparks with joy whenever I kiss you and clasp you
to my breast. Oh, with what sweet, maternal feeling I have become
not your mother only but your handmaid. Now I play with you, now I
soothe you to sleep singing, and lead a tranquil life doing these things.
At times I offer my breast to the living rosebuds of your lips, giving you
my heart together with my milk, and you take it with great delight. You
laugh at me and look at me, and it seems as though you are saying in
your own language: "Mother, your great love for me makes me happy.
Take my feelings in place of words."

Sonnet ABAB BABA CDB CDB. Turina 1628, 166. This highly original sonnet cele-
brates the birth of Turina's first son in 1576. Other poems speak of her love for her
second son and her grandsons, though her daughter does not feature in her verse.
The description of the poet's delight in breast-feeding her baby represents a star-
tling thematic novelty within the lyric tradition; it is also historically interesting at
a time when wet nurses were commonly used in families of Turina's social rank.
The poem is almost as anomalous formally as thematically: while Petrarch's sonnet
260 offers some precedent for the unusual rhyme scheme, Turina departs from this
model, and from the lyric tradition generally, by repeating the B rhyme, *-etto*, and
one rhyme word, *affetto*, in the tercets. The A, B, and C rhymes are all, moreover,
phonetically close, in a manner that gives salience to the sole exception, the seman-
tically poignant *core*/*amore* (heart/love).

In morte

Livia Pii (1559)
181

Alma beata, che già al mondo involta
nel tuo bel ma mortal corporeo velo
mi fosti un tempo, or mi sei guida al cielo,
dal terren nodo innanzi tempo sciolta;   4
mentre che al sommo Sol tutta sei volta,
piena di ardente e di verace zelo,
odi i sospir ch'io spargo e il duol ch'io celo
rimira in Lui che il tutto e vede e ascolta.   8
Deh! il mio gran male ora il tuo ben non sceme,
ma ti muova a pietà, che sol me sdegna
Morte, per non por fine alla mia guerra.   11
E s'ancor m'ami in ciel, come già in terra,
impetra dal Signor (bench'io sia indegna)
ch'io goda l'uno e l'altro volto insieme.   14

Blessed soul, you who once were my guide in the world, wrapped in your lovely, but mortal, corporeal veil and who now guide me from heaven, having been released early from your terrestrial bonds, while you gaze on the highest Sun full of ardent, true zeal, hear the sighs that I issue and see the pain that I hide, reflected in Him who hears and sees all. Ah! Do not ignore my suffering in your happiness, but take pity on me, whom alone Death disdains, refusing to put an end to my struggles. And, if you love me in heaven as you once did on earth, beseech of the Lord, despite my unworthiness, that I may gaze one day on the one and the other face.

Sonnet ABBA ABBA CDE EDC. Domenichi 1559, 110. One of the most accomplished of the otherwise unknown poets included in Lodovico Domenichi's 1559 anthology of female poets, Livia Pii features there as the author of four sonnets and the addressee of another. Not enough is known of Pii's life for the identity of the "blessed soul" of this poem to be clear, but we may assume it is a friend or relative, since Pii's husband outlived her. It may well be a woman, as then the grammatically feminine endings of the quatrains (agreeing with *alma*, "soul") would coincide with the gender of the addressee. The sonnet is elegantly constructed and syntactically very fluent, using *enjambment to particular effect in ll. 7–8, and deploying a series of parallel and contrastive binary constructions at ll. 3, 7–10, and 12 to prepare for the striking last line. The "one and other face" (14) are the faces of the "blessed soul" and of God. Beatitude was commonly conceived as consisting in the contemplation of God; hence to look on God's face was synonymous with salvation.

Lucia Colao (1570s–80s)

182

Quanto più desïose l'ali spando
verso di voi, o diletta e fida amica;
tanto piu l'importuno arcier m'intrica
con sue lusinghe e gir mi face errando;   4
pur, il cor di voi vago ora vi mando,
ché viver brama in quella stanza aprica,
là dove ogni celeste odor s'implica,
poiché qua giù visse sempre lagrimando.   8
Ma chi lo guida a voi nel camin dritto,
se non voi stessa, che finora scorto
l'avete, come il popul da l'Egitto?   11
Allor serà sicuro il mio conforto,
che sciolta fia dal termine prescritto
e non sia il veder voi più raro e corto.   14

The more desirously I spread my wings toward you, sweet and trusted friend, the more the importunate archer entangles me with his lures and condemns me to errant wandering; yet now I send my desiring heart to you, for it longs to live in that sunlight space surrounded by celestial odors, having lived here below in a constant state of tears. But who will guide it to you on the path of righteousness, if not you, who have led it on its way so far, like the people out of Egypt? Only then will my comfort be sure, when I will be freed from my prescribed term and my glimpses of you will no longer be rare and brief.

Sonnet ABBA ABBA CDC DCD, with rhyme words from Petrarch's sonnet 139. Treviso, Biblioteca Comunale, MS 3215, appendix 11r. Colao's religious reworkings of Petrarch (see nos. 99–100) include occasional references to a female friend who takes a role as spiritual mentor to the poet in her struggles against love. Here, the friend is in heaven, guiding the poet from above as Moses guided his people out of Egypt (10–11; cf. Exodus 12–13). Colao makes good use of her borrowed rhyme word *Egitto* in an image that implicitly figures sin as a form of enslavement. *Implica* (7), a hapax in *RVF*, meaning "to entangle" or "impede," causes her more problems; I have translated it "surround." The "rare and brief" sightings of the poet's friend (14) are presumably the imaginative visitations of her in heaven described in the quatrains, while the "prescribed term" (13) is the poet's destined term of life. The relationship between this poem and its source text is especially close in the first quatrain: Colao follows Petrarch verbatim until *voi* in l. 2 and co-opts the phrase "gir mi face errando" in l. 4.

Agnese Piccolomini (1596)
183

Già non si deve a te doglia né pianto,
anima bella, ma sol gioia e riso,
lieta vivendo in gioia eterna e riso,
ove arrivar non puote o doglia o pianto.   4
Io (tua mercé) sol vivo in doglia e 'n pianto,
poi che partì da me la gioia e 'l riso,
mentre salisti ov'è sol gioia e riso,
e lasciasti quaggiù sol doglia e pianto.   8
Dunque, spirto felice, ora che 'n cielo
non più mortal com'eri avanti in terra,
godi la vista del gran Re del cielo,   11
pregal per me, ch'ancor vo' errando in terra,
che teco al fin mi riunisca in cielo
sciolta da' duri lacci de la terra.   14

Lovely soul, we do not owe you sorrow or tears but only joy and laughter, since you now live in eternal joy and laughter, where sorrow and tears cannot reach. On account of you, I live only in sorrow and tears, since joy and laughter departed from me when you ascended to the realm of joy and laughter, leaving behind only sorrow and tears. Happy spirit, now that in heaven, no longer mortal, as you were on earth, you delight in the vision of the great king of heaven, pray to him for me, still wandering errant on earth, that I may at last reunite with you in heaven, freed from the cruel bounds of earth.

Sonnet ABBA ABBA CDC DCD. Marchetti 1596, aa4r. Like no. 97, this is an example of the trend in late sixteenth-century poetry toward difficult and artificial rhyme schemes. Though not strictly a *sonetto continuo*, as the rhymes change between quatrains and tercets, it is comparable in terms of its hammering *epistrophe, enhanced in the quatrains by the use of a repeated doublet, not simply a word, at the end of the lines. The sonnet, from a collection in memory of a Sienese gentlewoman, Isabella Marescotti, rehearses the familiar Christian mourning paradox that it is the dead person who is happy and the living who is sad. The poet, identified only by her initials, as "A.P.," and said to have been distinguished in life by an extremely close friendship ("una strettissima amicizia") with Marescotti, is almost certainly the Agnese Piccolomini who figures elsewhere in the collection along with Marescotti's husband Orazio Ballati as chief mourner: several male poets, for example, write mourning verses to Marescotti in Agnese's voice.

Lucchesia Sbarra (1610)

184

Prestami i draghi, o Dea, prestami i pini,
tu che provasti la medesma rabbia,
ond'io non cerchi sol la ferma sabbia,
ma del ciel e del mar tutti i confini.   4
Ma non so che il destin di lui destini;
temo che quel cinghial ferito l'abbia;
conoscoli il mio sangue in su le labbia
e par che 'l mesto cor se lo indovini.   8
Ahi, che 'l mio bello Adon disteso langue,
e Morte ha gli occhi suoi di morte asperso,
e già in bianche viole il viso involve,   11
e queste amare lagrime che io verso
oprato han sì ch'io più non veggo il sangue,
ma sembra agli occhi miei sol poca polve.   14

Lend me your dragons, Goddess, lend me your pines—you who felt the
same fury that drives me to search not only the hard sands but all the
confines of the sky and sea. I do not know what destiny is destined for
him. I fear that the boar has wounded him; I recognize my blood on
its lips and it seems my sad heart divines the truth. Alas, my beautiful
Adonis is lying there languid. Death has strewn death on his eyes and
his face is already fading into pale anemones. These bitter tears I have
shed have blinded me to his blood, which seems to me only dry dust.

Sonnet ABBA ABBA CDE DCE. Sbarra 1610, A6r (misnumbered as A4r; *cingiale* in
l. 6 corrected to *cinghiale*). Sbarra's extravagant Baroque style attains almost surreal
effects here in a poem on the death of her son Giovanni Battista, whose birth we
saw celebrated in an earlier poem (no. 179). The poem refers to two myths: that of
Ceres, the goddess of l. 1, who searched for her daughter Proserpina after her abduc-
tion by Pluto and partly reclaimed her from the underworld, and the more defini-
tively tragic myth of Venus, whose beloved, Adonis, was gored to death by a boar.
The introduction of the boar in l. 6 is the first allusion we have to the Venus-Adonis
myth, confirmed by the naming of Adonis in l. 9. The tercets refer to Adonis's meta-
morphosis, which, in the myth, is into blood-red anemones, reflecting his death
from violence. In Sbarra, these become pale, reflecting what was presumably a
death from illness. The *poca polve* of the last line echoes Petrarch's *TT*, 120, also the
poca polvere of *RVF* 292, l. 8.

185

Anch'io, folle, pensai di secco salce
brandir ferma la lancia in Elicona,
ma poi la vidi al parangon mal buona,
ché a pena mi rimase intiero il calce.   4
Morte meglio di me seppe la falce
oprar, che fere e vince e non ragiona,
e in un tempo la speme e la corona
mi tolse, ond'io sospiro e nulla valce;   8
e mi duol che fortuna oggi interrompa
che quella chioma inannellata e bionda
dove Morte ha girato il ferro adunco   11
or non faccia al mio crin funebre pompa;
ed io qui senza frutto e senza fronda
resti fra ricche piante inutil trunco.   14

I too once, madly, thought to brandish my lance of dry flint in Helicon,
but then I saw it not up to the contest, so that even the hilt barely
remained whole. Death knew better than I how to use the scythe:
Death who wounds and wins and says not a word. He took from me
together my hope and my crown, so I sigh and am good for nothing.
It sorrows me that Fortune today prevents those curling blond locks in
which Death turned his iron hook from being a funereal trophy for my
head; so here I stand without fruit or frond, a useless trunk amid rich
trees.

Sonnet ABBA ABBA CDE CDE. Sbarra 1610, A1or (unnumbered). This sonnet juxta-
poses the poet's sense of artistic failure with her despair at the death of her son; she
concludes by wishing herself dead. The bleakness of the subject matter contrasts
rather oddly with the poem's stylistic verve and bold imagery, which belie the
poet's self-description as failed literary "jouster" (3–4). The unusual rhymes *salce/
calce/falce* derive from Ariosto's *OF* 19.94, from a passage describing a duel in which
the female knight Marfisa fights successfully against male opponents. The use of
valce (= *ci val[e]*) for the fourth rhyme may have been suggested by Della Casa's son-
net 56, which rhymes *felce* and *selce* with *dielce* (= *ce lo diè* [i.e. *diede*]). The poem ends
resonantly, as well as poignantly, with the *isocolon *senza frutto* / *senza fronda* and
the rich sound patterning of the last line (the *fronda* is the laurel to which the poet
once aspired). Line 10 echoes l. 26 of Celio Magno's poem 351, a source also for no. 179.

Veneranda Bragadin (1619)
186

So ch'in ciel vivi, o mia diletta e cara,
so che ti specchi ne l'eterno Bene,
so che sei sciolta da' tormenti e pene
ch'ognor pativi in questa vita amara.   4
So ch'a la mensa prezïosa e rara
del tuo Sposo ti pasci e che in amene
campagne di bei gigli e rose piene
ti diporti là su, lucida e chiara,   8
e i suoni e i canti di angelici cori
senti mai sempre e sei felice a pieno,
onde sentir dovrei gioia e contento;   11
ma poi ch'io viddi il tuo bel lume spento,
sembra un'inferno il mio affannato seno,
ché il senso qua giù regge i nostri cori.   14

I know you live in heaven, beloved and dear one; I know you mirror
yourself in the eternal Good; I know you are free from those torments
and sorrows that you suffered at all times in this bitter life. I know that
you eat at the rare and precious table of your Bridegroom and disport
yourself, shining and bright, in lovely fields filled with beauteous lilies
and roses, hearing the music and song of the angelic choirs, and
experiencing happiness in full. I should feel joy and contentment,
knowing this; yet ever since I saw your lovely light extinguished, my
troubled breast has seemed an inferno, for sense here on earth rules our
hearts.

Sonnet ABBA ABBA CDE EDC. Bragadin 1619, 51. Bragadin's last volume of *Rime*
contains poems mourning the deaths of her husband and her mother, both seem-
ingly recent. This sonnet, for her mother, departs from the literary convention that
represents the poet as consoled by imagining the deceased happy in heaven. Braga-
din rehearses this convention in the quatrains and first tercet, in a carefully man-
aged litany of beatitude, following the *anaphora, *end-stopped lines and simple de-
clarative language of the first quatrain with the more fluid rhythms and decorative,
metaphorical language of the second. The bleak final tercet returns to an unadorned
idiom to contrast the hell of the poet's unredeemed, "sensual" grief with the heav-
enly spiritual consolation she should be feeling. The sestet is bounded by the equiv-
ocal rhyme *cori/cori*, while the octave is similarly framed by the near-identical *cara/
chiara*. Note also the chiming, though nonrhymed, sequences *amaro/amene* (4–6)
and *pene/piene/pieno* (3, 7, 10).

Francesca Turina (c. 1623)

187

Viscere del mio sen, figlio diletto,
figlio di duol, tu notte e dì mi stai
fisso nel cor, anzi tu l'hai dal petto
rapito e teco 'l porti ovunque vai;   4
né spero, ahi lassa, rïaverti mai,
né più conforto o refrigerio aspetto,
e freddo e muto e con trafitti rai
parmi vederti entro il funereo letto.   8
Or sembri dirmi:—Madre pia, ti lasso;
come in vita mi amasti, or dopo morte
di me ti caglia e ne l'estremo passo—.   11
E pur non è che 'l viver mio si scorte:
di ferro è questo sen fatto e di sasso,
ché resta intègro a un duol sì grave e forte.   14

Lifeblood of my womb, beloved son, son of sorrow, night and day you are fixed in my heart; no, you have torn it from my breast and carry it with you now wherever you go. Nor, alas, can I ever hope to have you again; nor do I ever expect relief or comfort. Cold and mute, with rigid eyes, I seem to see you lying on your funerary bed. Now you seem to say to me, "Kind mother, I leave you. As you loved me in life, care for me after my death and at the final passage." And yet my life is not cut short. This breast is made of iron and of stone if it can remain whole before a pain so keen and strong.

Sonnet ABBA BABA CDC DCD. Turina 1628, 206. This sonnet, remarkable for the period in its emotional rawness, relates the author's grief following the death of her younger son Ottavio, who was murdered in 1623 intervening to stop a brawl at a local feast. His elder brother Giulio may have been involved in his death (Torrioli 1940, 27). The sonnet is poignantly in dialogue with Turina's sonnet on Giulio's birth (no. 180), with which it shares an opening phrase, a rhyme (-*etto*), and a passage of recorded speech attributed to the son. Ottavio's imagined plea to his mother to care for him after his death gains purchase from the doctrine of purgatory, whereby the families and friends of the dead could speed their passage to heaven by prayer. *Estremo passo* (11) seems to refer to the divine judgment following death, which established the soul's place in hell, purgatory, or heaven. Those who died violently were especially vulnerable in this judgment since they had not always had time to repent of their sins and receive extreme unction.

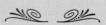

Other
in morte *Verse*

Laura Battiferri on Eleonora of Toledo (1563)
188

Lassa, nel tuo partire, ahi lassa, in quante
lacrime io viva, in quante pene il core,
fatta albergo immortal d'alto dolore:
ben lo veggion dal Ciel tue luci sante.   4
Indi d'amaro umor marmo stillante
il mio Fidia vedrai, ch'eterno onore
non chiede o spera, poi ch'el tuo splendore
sparìo, ch'illustri fea l'opre sue tante;   8
ed io, che già lasciai l'ago e la gonna
per talor gir lungesso Anfriso ed Ea,
di te cantando anchor ch'in basse rime,   11
che sperar deggio più se musa e donna
più non mi sei? Se tu qual pria non stime
quest'umil serva tua, celeste Dea?   14

Alas, since you departed, alas, in what tears I live, in what anguish my
heart, now the immortal abode of high sorrow: your holy eyes can see
this from on high. From there, you will see my Phidias, like a stone
seeping bitter tears, no longer wishing or hoping for eternal honor,
since the splendor vanished that illuminated his many works. And I,
who abandoned the needle and skirt to wander beside Amphrysis and
Aeas, singing of you, though in humble rhymes—what may I now hope
for if you, my muse and lady, are no longer here for me? If you, celestial
Goddess, no longer esteem your humble servant as you did?

Sonnet ABBA ABBA CDE CED. *Poesie* 1563, 67. Eleonora of Toledo, duchess of Flor-
ence, died of malaria at the age of forty in 1562, along with two of her sons. Laura
Battiferri's mourning sonnet for her, though not one of her most polished, is nota-
bly personal and heartfelt. The poet's emphasis falls upon herself and her sculptor
husband Bartolomeo Ammannati (the Phidias of l. 6), their art meaningless after El-
eonora's death. Amphrysis (10) was a river in Thessaly associated with Apollo; Aeas,
a river in Epyrus. Ovid speaks of the gods of both rivers joining Daphne's father in
mourning after his daughter is transfigured into a laurel tree (*Met.* 1.580). The allu-
sion is a rich one, since Daphne is both Battiferri's own *senhal* (nos. 93, 138–39) and a
symbol of poetry's capacity for immortalization. For the *topos of the female poet
"abandoning the needle" to pursue her art (9), see no. 170. Stylistically noteworthy
is the sound sequence *amaro umor marmo* in l. 5.

"Gentildonna palermitana" on Laura Frías (1572)
189

Scemo di Laura il capo, al empio caso
Oreto accolse l'onde e si coperse
di cipressi la terra e 'l ciel s'aperse
e Pandora lasciò più colmo il vaso.   4
Videsi il giorno senza sol rimaso,
e nel pianto e nel duol le fere immerse
s'udì d'intorno. Il ciel come sofferse
che, nato appena, il dì fosse al occaso?   8
Vidersi mirti, olivi, edere e lauri,
cui tempo ingordo mai fronde non toglie,
del vago verde lor nudi e spogliati,   11
e tra muggiti fieri e aspri ululati
l'aria mesta sonò con queste spoglie.
Perso ogg'ha 'l mondo i suoi maggior tesauri.   14

When Laura's head was cut off, the Oreto drew back its waters in horror, cypresses covered the earth, Heaven opened, Pandora let her vase overflow. The day remained sunless, and the beasts of the earth could be heard immersed in pain and weeping. How did Heaven permit that this day, newly born, should already have come to its end? Myrtles, olives, ivy, laurels, a sole leaf of which ravening Time never strips, were now seen naked and despoiled of their lovely green, and amid fierce wails and bitter howling, the mourning air resounded with these spoils. Today, the world has lost its finest treasures.

Sonnet ABBA ABBA CDE EDC. *Rime* 1572, C3r. One of the most thematically fascinating poetic anthologies of this period is a collection of verse published in 1572 in Palermo to mourn the execution of Laura Frías, a noblewoman accused of conspiring with her cousin and lover Alonso Frías to murder her husband Lodovico Serra. The collection was edited by the poet Argisto Giuffredi (d. 1593) and is notably sympathetic to Laura (intriguingly, in a later treatise, Giuffredi spoke against the use of the death penalty, an extremely rare position for the time). The only female poet in the collection, present with two poems, is an unidentified "Palermitan gentlewoman," perhaps Elisabetta Aiutamicristo (d. 1580) or one of the Bonanno sisters (Cox 2011, 10). Oreto (2) is a river near Palermo; the cypress (3) a tree symbolic of mourning; Pandora (4), in Greek mythology, the first woman, famous for having released the ills of the world from a jar. The myrtle (9) was Venus's tree, symbolic of love. For the meanings of the other plants, see no. 53.

Orsina Cavaletti on Maddalena Calepio (1587)

190

Hai pur disciolto, o dispietata Morte,
non solo il nodo che di sua man strinse
Amor, quando la nobil coppia avinse
ne l'asprissime sue dolci ritorte,   4
ma con la curva falce ancora il forte
legame hai tronco onde Imeneo la cinse,
ché le vermiglie rose onde si pinse
il volto, hai rese impallidite e smorte.   8
Pur s'a l'antico padre hai la diletta
figliuola ancisa, e la consorte amata
al giovin sposo e già canuto amante,   11
e la figlia e la sposa nel sembiante
mirano de la bella pargoletta,
in guisa di fenice rinnovata.   14

Cruel Death, not only have you untied the knot that Love himself tied when he bound this noble couple in his most harsh and pleasant fetters; you have also slashed with your curved scythe the powerful bonds with which Hymen tied them, making the crimson roses of her face pallid and drained. Yet if you have killed the dear daughter of an aged father and the beloved wife of a young husband, grown old as a lover, they can still gaze on their daughter and wife, reborn like a phoenix, in the semblance of their lovely little girl.

Sonnet ABBA ABBA CDE ECD. *Rime* 1587, 206. Among the endless examples of occasional verse mourning deaths in this period, this sonnet stands out for the tenderness of its treatment of family affection. The subject, Maddalena Calepio, was the daughter of a Bergamasque aristocrat, Giovanni Paolo Calepio. Several sonnets on her death survive, including one by Tasso. Cavaletti represents Calepio as mourned by her father and husband, who are said to find consolation in her surviving infant daughter, suggesting that Maddalena may have died in childbirth. The marriage is portrayed as a love match: l. 11 has her husband young as a spouse but old (lit. "white-haired") as a lover. Noteworthy formal features of the sonnet include its extensive use of *enjambment, its use of the inclusive rhyme *morte*/*smorte* to frame the octave, and its elegant *oxymoronic description of Love's "asprissime . . . dolci ritorte" in l. 4. *Ritorte* is a non-Petrarchan word probably deriving from Tasso's GL 2.26, where it is used, as here, with *aspre* and in rhyme.

Catella Marchesi on Margherita Martinengo (1597)

191

—S'io 'l feci mai, ch'io venga in odio al cielo,
sì che mi sien contrari uomini e dei;
s'io 'l feci, le mie luci i raggi bei
unqua non veggian del signor di Delo;   4
s'io 'l feci, di Vulcan l'orribil telo
l'estremo fine apporti ai giorni miei;
s'io 'l feci, tra gl'inferni spirti rei
con l'alma scenda il mio corporeo velo;.   8
ma s'io no 'l feci, il re dell'universo
tosto m'accolga nel suo santo albergo,
e a te perdoni il fallo empio e perverso—.   11
Così al consorte Margarita disse,
quand'egli, ogni pietà lasciando a tergo,
il bel petto pudico a lei trafisse.   14

"If I ever did such a thing, may I be hated by heaven, and an enemy to both men and gods. If I ever did such a thing, may my eyes never see the lovely rays of the lord of Delos. If I ever did such a thing, may Vulcan's awful spear bring about the end of my days. If I ever did such a thing, among the black souls of Hell may I descend in my corporeal veil. But if I did not do it, may the King of the Universe soon welcome me into his holy abode, and forgive you this hideous crime." So Margherita said to her spouse, as, leaving all pity behind, he pierced through her fair and chaste breast.

Sonnet ABBA ABBA CDC EDE. Bratteolo 1597, 115r. Margherita Martinengo, daughter of a prominent literary and musical patron, Marcantonio Martinengo (c. 1545–before 1607), was murdered by her husband on suspicion of adultery in March 1595. Her supposed lover strongly denied the accusation and their innocence was widely believed. Numerous poems in the collection of verse put together by Catella Marchesi's tutor Giacomo Bratteolo in 1597 mourn Margherita's undeserved death. Only fourteen at the time of publication, Catella imitates Petrarch's famous canzone 206, similarly structured *anaphorically around the repeated phrase "S'io dissi mai" (If I ever said it), followed by "Ma s'io no 'l dissi." The device had been used in sonnets by several female poets, including Gaspara Stampa and Tullia d'Aragona, the latter of whom adapts the *dissi* (said) to *feci* (did), as Marchesi does here. The "lord of Delos" is the sun god Apollo (here, the sun); "Vulcan's spear" probably the thunderbolt with which Vulcan is customarily depicted.

Verse of
Place & Selfhood

Isotta Nogarola (pre-1466)
192

salvete, o Cyani fontes dulcesque recessus
  in medioque alnis consita silva lacu,
Aonidum salvete choris loca grata sororum
  et quae cum Bromio Phoebus adire solet.
docta mihi quoties quaerenti carmina Musas   5
  profuit in vestro comperiisse sinu.
posthabito quoties Parnasi vertice Apollo
  Libethrique undis haec nemora alta colit.
haec quoque, dum sordent Nysae iuga celsa, feroces
  Liber agens tigres saepe vireta petit.   10
[. . .]
deliciae, o Cyanum, et Nogarolae gentis ocelle,
  Alcinoi atque hortis gratior Hesperidum,
non mirum si iam deserta sede Pelori
  Nympha suburbano constitit hoc Cyane.   40
dux Erebi Aetneis quondam ferus abstulit oris
  Persephonem Cereris pignora cara deae.
Trinacris ingemuit raptam miserata; tulisset
  Persephonae, ah miserae, si potuisset, opem.
flumina creverunt lacrimis fontesque lacusque;   45
  flammarum evomuit latius Aetna globos.
quis credat? tunc Scylla etiam, tunc Scylla doloris
  latratu horrifico maxima signa dedit.
te quoque non solitas memorant fudisse querelas
  miscentem lacrimis saeva Charybdis aquas.   50
ipsae etiam nymphae confectae corda dolore
  errabant scissis lata per arva comis
ac veluti Euantes implebant questibus auras,
  tundentes palmis pectora et ungue genas.
quas inter forma egregia castoque pudore   55
  praeclari Cyane nominis emicuit.
fida una ante alias Cyane comes atque ministra
  haerebat lateri sedula Persephones.
Alma Ceres, dum maternas inviseret arces:
  "Natae," ait, "o Cyane, sit tibi cura meae.   60
hanc tibi commissam, Cyane, fidissima serves,
  nusquam absit, iussis pareat illa tuis."
utraque paruerat, cura utebatur eadem,
  utraque sed Stygiis est superata dolis.

quid faceret? Quo se raperet perterrita custos?   65
   non erat et formae vis metuenda suae?
ipsa amens animi atque ingenti caeca dolore
   torpuit et nuda frigida sedit humo.
tum patriam fugere atque invisa excedere terra
   et petere Ausoniae littora certa fuit.   70
nulla mora. undisonum Siculas quod dividit oras
   finibus Hesperiae traiicit illa fretum.
post varios casus, post multa pericla quievit
   sedibus his longae fessa labore viae.
rus proprio "Cyanum" dixit de nomine, fontes   75
   admirata tuis hic, Arethusa, pares.
ex illo Cyanum prisci didicere parentes,
   sera hoc gaudebit nomine posteritas.
Nympha decus Siculi quondam formosa Pachyni,
   nunc Cyani et nostrae gloria magna domus,   80
floreat o utinam per saecula longa superstes,
   credita tutelae gens Nogarola tuae.
aemula sit vitae Nogarolo a sanguine creta
   atque pudicitiae foemina quaeque tuae.
hanc oro tutare domum natosque nepotesque;   85
   incolume hoc serves, candida nympha, genus.
sic varios nunquam flores mala frigora laedant,
   neve tuos nimius torreat aestus agros.
sic tibi sint liquidi fontes, vernantia circum
   prata nec anguinea sordeat unda lue.   90
quin ea, quot rutilas Pactolus fundit arenas
   vincat, quotque Tagi iactat Iberus opes.

[1–5] Hail, springs of Cyanum and sweet secluded spots, and alder grove planted in the midst of the lake. Hail, places dear to the choruses of the Aonian sisters, where Phoebus and Bromius often linger. How often, casting around for learned verses, [6–10] have I happily discovered the Muses in your bosom! How often has Apollo neglected the Parnassan peak and the waters of Libethra to visit these high glades! Liber, too, scorning the lofty peaks of Nysa, often seeks out this verdure, spurring on his fierce tigers.

[. . .]

[37–40] O Cyanum, delight of the Nogarola, and apple of their eye, lovelier than the gardens of Alcinous or the Hesperides. No wonder if,

departing her haunts on Pelorus, the nymph Cyane takes up her abode
in this rural spot. [41–45] The cruel lord of Erebus once carried off from
Aetna's shores Persephone, beloved daughter of the goddess Ceres.
Trinacris groaned pityingly over her abduction: alas, wretched
Persephone, she would have aided her if she could. The rivers and
springs and lakes swelled with tears, [46–50] and Aetna spewed out her
fireballs far and wide. Who would believe it? Then Scylla, Scylla herself,
gave off the most powerful evidence of her grief in a terrifying howling,
and you, too, fierce Charybdis, so they tell, poured out unwonted
lamentations, mingling tears with your waters. [51–55] The nymphs
themselves, stricken to the heart by grief, wandered in the spacious
fields, tearing at their hair, filling the air with laments like Maenads,
beating their breasts with their palms and scoring their cheeks with
their nails.

Among these nymphs, one shone forth for her noble beauty and
chaste modesty: [56–60] the famous Cyane, Faithful above all others,
Persephone's companion and handmaiden, she clung solicitously ever at
her side. Bountiful Ceres would say, when she visited her maternal
stronghold, "Cyane, please take care of my daughter. [61–65] Keep this
treasure entrusted to you most safely. Let her never leave your sight; let
her always obey your commands." Both obeyed, both were equally
careful, yet the deceptions of Styx vanquished them both. What could
Cyane do? Whither could the terrified guardian take herself? [66–70]
Was not the power of her own beauty a thing to be feared? Frantic in
mind and blinded with her great misery, she grew weary, and sat down,
numb with cold, on the bare earth. Then she resolved to flee her
birthplace and leave the hated land and seek out the Ausonian shores.
[71–75] No lingering: she crossed the strait, loud with waves, that
divides the Sicilian shores from the borders of Hesperia; then, after
many adventures and dangers, she came to rest in these parts, ex-
hausted from her long journey. She called this rural place "Cyanum,"
from her own name, [76–80] marveling at these springs, the equal,
Arethusa, of yours. From that time, the ancient forefathers learned of
Cyanum, and posterity will long delight in this name. Lovely Nymph,
once the honor of Sicilian Pachynum, now the great glory of Cyanum
and our house, [81–85] long may that house flourish, surviving through
the ages, the Nogarolan race entrusted to your care! May every woman
born of the Nogarolan line emulate you in her life and her chastity! I
pray you, guard this house, its children and their children. [86–90] Keep
this race unharmed, O gleaming Nymph, so may harsh frosts never
injure your many diverse flowers or the fierce heat of summer parch

your fields. May your spring be limpid and your meadows verdant; may your water remain free from the blight of serpents. [91–92] Rather, may it outshine the golden sand that streams from the Pactolus, and the treasures of which Iberian Tagus boasts.

Elegaic distichs. Nogarola 1888, 2: 261–64 (*Phebus* changed to *Phoebus* in l. 4; *Libetrique* to *Libethrique* in l. 8; *Nisae* to *Nysae* in l. 9; *chara* to *cara* in l. 42; *lacrymis* to *lachrimis* in ll. 45 and 50). This elegy, celebrating the beauties of the Nogarola family's country estate in Castel d'Azzano, and particularly the now vanished Lake Vacaldo, is Isotta Nogarola's only surviving poem. It was published in 1563 by a descendant, Francesco Nogarola, along with Isotta's dialogue *On Whether Adam or Eve Was the Greater Sinner.* No independent manuscript copies survive. In the sixteenth-century edition, the poem contains a lengthy interpolation by Francesco Nogarola (19–36), recounting a visit to the estate by Giovanni Navagero, an ancestor of his dedicatee, Cardinal Bernardo Navagero. The version given here omits both this and also ll. 11–17, recounting visits by an unnamed member of the Gonzaga family, related to the Nogarola by "love and lineage," and by the distinguished neo-Latin poet Giovanni Pontano (1426–1503). These lines may also be an interpolation. The complete text is available in a modern edition, with a verse translation, in Parker 2002.

The poem is written in elegiac distichs, made up of alternating hexameter and pentameter lines. It is notably polished and classicizing in its lexis and style. Nogarola mythologizes the lake-feeding spring on her family's estate first by portraying it as a haunt of Apollo and the Muses; then by constructing an onomastic myth for it, drawing on the myth of Persephone's abduction by Hades, lord of the Underworld. In Nogarola's version, Persephone's most faithful handmaid, the nymph Cyane, whose name means "spring" or "fountain" in Greek, flees to Italy after the abduction and adopts the lake and spring of Vacaldo as her final resting place. Cyanum, as Nogarola names the spring, hence gains associations both with poetic creativity and with chastity (since Cyane flees to save her endangered virginity), associations that Nogarola underline quite explicitly at ll. 5–6 and 83–84. In this way, the poem constitutes a kind of mythical-topographical portrait of the author, famed for her unusual choice of an unmarried secular life.

The inspiration for Nogarola's Cyane myth is probably Ovid's version of the Persephone story in the *Metamorphoses* (told using the Roman names: Proserpina for Persephone; Dis for Hades; Ceres for Persephone's mother, the earth goddess Demeter). In Ovid's narrative, Cyane, the tutelary nymph or naiad of a Sicilian spring, is seen first attempting to reason with Dis to prevent Proserpina's abduction and then, having failed, dissolving into and fusing with her own spring in her grief (*Met.* 5:409–37). The special role as *custos* (guardian) attributed by Cyane by Ceres is new in Nogarola, and may have been inspired by the third book of Claudian's *The Rape of Proserpina,* where a similar role of *comes* and *custos* is attributed to the nymph Electra (3.170–76), an older, quasi-maternal figure, rather than a contemporary, like Cyane. Also new in Nogarola with respect to Ovid is Cyane's implicit status as a virginal nymph, like Persephone: in Ovid, she has a partner, the river god, Anapis (*Met.* 5.417–18).

Nogarola's poem is replete with allusions to classical mythology. In the opening passage, the Aonian sisters (3) are the nine Muses; Phoebus and Bromius (4) alternate names for, respectively, Apollo, god of poetry and music, and Bacchus, god of wine. These two gods recur at ll. 7–10, Bacchus this time under the epithet of Liber and mounted on a tiger to recall his conquest of India. The presence of Bacchus, as well as Apollo, as tutelary deities of the place, may imply that the Nogarola cultivated vines on their estate. Libethra, in this same passage, was a city near Olympus associated with the Muses and with the ancient poet sage Orpheus, who was buried there, while Mount Nysa, variously located in Africa, India, and Arabia, was the birthplace of Bacchus. Alcinous (38) was a mythical Greek king, father of Nausicaa, whose beautiful garden, featuring two springs, is described in Book 7 of Homer's *Odyssey*. The Hesperides were the nymph custodians of a beautiful garden sacred to Juno, whose golden apples Hercules was ordered to steal as one of his twelve labors.

In the Persephone-Cyane passage (41), the "lord of Erebus" is Hades, lord of the Underworld; Trinacris (43), a name for the "triangular" island of Sicily; Scylla and Charybdis (47–50), two legendary Sicilian perils, respectively a monstrous dog and a whirlpool. Euantes (53), or, more familiarly, Maenads, were followers of Bacchus, named for their howling cries; Styx (64), a river in the Underworld, or, by extension, the Underworld itself; Ausonia and Hesperia (70 and 72) names for the Italian peninsula; Pachynus (79), like Pelorus (39), a classical place name in Sicily. Arethusa (76) was a Sicilian nymph, like Cyane, transformed into a spring on the island of Ortygia in Syracuse to escape the pursuit of the river god Alpheus. The Pactolus (in Turkey) and the Tagus, mentioned in the last lines, were both rivers associated with gold: the Pactolus was where King Midas washed off his golden touch, while Pliny speaks of the Tagus in his *Natural History* as having gold in its bed.

Besides the general Ovidian inspiration, more local classical allusions may be noted. Virgil describes Etna as issuing *globos flammarum* (46) in a dramatic descriptive passage of the *Aeneid* (3.574). *Haerebat lateri* (58) may also be a Virgilian echo, of the *haeret lateri* of *Aeneid* 4.73, where Dido is compared to a deer with an arrow clinging to her side. *Ocellus* (lit. "little eye," a term of endearment) at l. 37, was a word associated with Catullus, born in Verona and hence a compatriot of Nogarola's (see esp. l. 2 of his poem 31 for a contextually similar occurrence). Line 38 may be an allusion to l. 2 of Martial's epigram 4.64, where Julius Martialis's idyllic gardens in Rome are said to be "hortis Hesperidum beatiora."

A few translations here require some comment. A *pignus* (lit. "pledge" or "promise"), used here in the plural of Persephone (42), was a metaphorical term often used for children, on the logic that they were "pledges of love" between spouses; I simply translate "daughter." A *suburbanus* (40), which I translate "rural spot," was used in ancient Rome for a villa or estate in the vicinity of Rome. Here, it is vicinity to Verona that is referenced.

Veronica Gambara (1532)

193

Con quel caldo desio che nascer suole
in petto di chi torna, amando assente,
gli occhi vaghi a vedere e le parole
dolci a scoltar del suo bel foco ardente;
con quel proprio voi, piaggie al mondo sole,   5
fresch'acque, ombrosi colli, e te, possente
più d'altre che 'l sol miri andando intorno,
bella e lieta cittade, a veder torno.

Salve, mia bella patria, e tu, felice
tant'amato dal ciel ricco paese,   10
che 'n guisa di leggiadra alma fenice,
mostri l'alto valor chiaro e palese.
Natura, a te sol madre e pia nudrice,
ha fatto agli altri mille gravi offese,
spogliandoli di quanto avean di buono   15
per farne a te cortese e largo dono.

Non tigri, non leoni e non serpenti
nascono in te, nemici a l'uman seme,
non erbe venenose, a dar possenti
l'acerba morte, allor che men si teme;   20
ma mansüete fiere e lieti armenti
scherzar si veggon per li campi insieme,
pieni d'erbe gentili e vaghi fiori,
spargendo grazïosi e cari odori.

Ma perché a dir di voi, lochi beati,   25
ogn'alto stil saria roco e basso,
il carco d'onorarvi a' più pregiati
sublimi ingegni e glorïosi lasso.
Da me sarete col pensier lodati
e con l'anima sempre, e, ad ogni passo,   30
con la memoria vostra in mezzo il cuore,
quanto fia il mio poter, farovvi onore.

With the warm desire that rises in the breast of those who love in absence, when they return to see the fine eyes and hear the sweet words of their lovely ardent fire—with just that desire, gentle slopes peerless in the world, fresh waters, pleasant hills, and you, mighty above all others the sun gazes on in its travels, beautiful and happy city, I return to see you once more.

Greetings, my lovely homeland, and you happy, blessed land, so beloved by heaven, showing your worth so bright and clear, in the guise of a lovely phoenix. Nature, to you alone a kind mother and nurse, has done grave injury to many other lands, despoiling them of all their goods to make gracious and ample gifts to you.

Not tigers, not lions, not serpents are born in you, enemies to the human race; not venomous plants, capable of dealing bitter death when it is least feared. Gentle beasts and joyous herds gambol together through your fields, filled with gentle plants and fair flowers, spreading their sweet charming odors in the air.

But because to speak of you, blessed lands, any style, however lofty, would be hoarse and crude, I leave the task of honoring you to more distinguished, sublime, and glorious minds. You will always be praised by me in my thoughts and my soul, and, at every step, with your memory lodged deep in my heart, I shall honor you as highly as I can.

Stanze. Ruscelli 1553b, 85v–86r (*disio* in l. 1 amended to *desio*; *matre* in l. 13 amended to *madre*; *tigre* to *tigri* in l. 17; *mezo* to *mezzo* in l. 31). This poem, one of Gambara's most famous, probably dates from 1532 when she visited her family's estates near Brescia for the first time since the family had been exiled from them in 1512 following their support of an anti-Venetian revolt. This circumstance gives a particular emotional charge to the account of the poet's return, and to the phoenix image of stanza 2, which, although applied to the city, which had been sacked by the French in 1512, applies equally to the family's fortunes, restored by the able diplomacy of Veronica and her brothers.

In its evocation of a beautiful landscape, imbued with emotion through the poet's emotional projection, these stanze are reminiscent of Gambara's sonnet *Ombroso colle* (no. 6), with which the first stanza also shares its technique of deferral: the referent of *te* in l. 6 is only revealed in l. 8, as is the main verb of the sentence (*torno*). Gambara praises Brescia and its hinterland in terms that deliberately recall the Arcadia of classical pastoral poetry, with its peaceful, idyllic landscape. More specifically, in the third stanza, she echoes two famous descriptions of the Golden Age in Roman poetry: the *anaphoric repetition of *non* in ll. 17–19 recalls Ovid's *Met.* 1.97–99, while the content of ll. 17–21 (lions, herds, snakes, venomous herbs) echoes ll. 22–25 of Virgil's fourth eclogue. Another classical allusion is found at the beginning of the second stanza, whose "Salve, mia bella patria" suggests l. 12 of Catullus's poem 31 ("Salve, o venusta Sirmio"), and perhaps also, given the emphasis on the richness of the terrain, Virgil's address to Italy in the second of his *Georgics* (173–74): "Salve, magna parens frugum, Saturnia tellus, magna virum" (Hail, Saturnian land, great parent of crops and of men). Catullus's poem 31 may well be a subtext more generally, since, like this poem it describes a return to a beloved place after absence. Given the Veronese connections of her family (her grandmother was

Ginevra Nogarola, sister of Isotta), Gambara may, like Nogarola herself (see no. 192), have felt a particular, local, attachment to his verse.

Early printed versions of this poem differ in their phrasing at a number of points, notably l. 6 (where *ameni* is sometimes found in place of *ombrosi*), and l. 21 (where *fiere mansuete* or *mansuete greggie* are sometimes found in place of *mansuete fiere*; see also Gambara 1995, 104, for a variant version of this line deriving from a manuscript, "ma fiere isnelle e ben pasciuti armenti"). A definitive version would be difficult to establish: Gambara was notably unconcerned about the fate of her poems and made little attempt to assemble an authorized version, despite promptings from friends. Where l. 21 is concerned, a subtext may be l. 40 of Petrarch's great canzone 128, "Italia mia," where a warn-torn Italy is said to harbor together "fiere selvagge et mansuete gregge" (fierce beasts and gentle flocks).

194

Tu che mostrasti al rozzo mondo prima
mutar le dure ghiande in belle spiche,
e festi sì con l'utili fatiche
che dea ti chiama ogni abitato clima;   4
e tu, del cui valor canta ogni rima,
primo a insegnare a quelle genti antiche
piantar le viti ne le piaggie apriche
per trarne poi liquor di tanta stima: 8
se con occhi pietosi e mente umìle
guardarete ambiduo quel che finora,
vostra dolce mercé, dato n'avete,   11
di sangue e latte al più fiorito aprile,
con vino e farro i vostri altari ognora
da me onorar con puro cor vedrete.   14

You who first taught the unschooled world to exchange hard acorns for fair grain, and who did so much through your valuable labors that the whole inhabited globe calls you goddess; and you whose worth is sung in every rhyme, the first to teach those ancient folk to plant their vines on sun-drenched hills and draw forth the liquor we now so prize: if, with pitying eyes and gentle spirit, you watch over the bounty your sweet kindness has given us, then with the freshest blood and milk of spring, with wine and with corn, you will see me honor your altars day and night, pure of heart.

Sonnet ABBA ABBA CDE CDE. Gambara 1995, 100. Closer than most vernacular female poets to the classicizing world of neo-Latin poetry, Gambara here calls on the ancient gods of agriculture and viniculture, Ceres and Bacchus, to supply a good harvest. In return, she offers the kind of sacrifice, of spring lambs, milk, wine, and corn (lit. "spelt") that we see Arcadian shepherds offering up to the gods in classical pastoral verse. Although the poem might seem purely a humanistic exercise, the success of the harvest must have been a living concern each year for Gambara, as ruler of Correggio. The sonnet exemplifies Gambara's mellifluous style, its rhythms enhanced in the quatrains by frequent phonetic pairings (*mostrasti/mondo*; *festi/fatiche*; *chiama/clima*; *rima/primo*; *piantar/piaggie*). The opening address to Ceres and Bacchus recalls lines 7–9 of Virgil's first *Georgic*. Lines 3–4 reflect the theory known as euhumerism, which interprets the classical gods as outstanding historical individuals, later deified by their compatriots.

Isabella Morra

195

Torbido Siri, del mio mal superbo,
or ch'io sento da presso il fin amaro,
fa' tu noto il mio duolo al padre caro,
se mai qui 'l torna il suo destino acerbo.　　4
Dilli come, morendo, disacerbo
l'aspra Fortuna e lo mio fato avaro
e, con esempio miserando e raro,
nome infelice a le tue onde serbo.　　8
Tosto ch'ei giunga a la sassosa riva
(a che pensar m'adduci, o fiera stella?
Come d'ogni mio ben son cassa e priva!)　　11
inqueta l'onde con crudel procella
e di':—Me accrebber sì, mentre fu viva,
non gli occhi, no, ma i fiumi d'Isabella.　　14

Turbid Siri, proud of my ills, now that I feel my bitter death near, make my suffering known to my dear father, if his cruel destiny should ever lead him back to this place. Tell him how, dying, I appease the harshness of Fortune and my miserable fate, and, with my rare and pitiful tale, I bequeath an unhappy name to your waves. When he arrives at this stony bank (alas, cruel star, what are you leading me to think of? How bereft and deprived I am of all hope!) stir up your waters with a cruel storm and tell him: "I was swollen in this same way, while she lived, by the eyes—nay, the rivers—of Isabella."

Sonnet ABBA ABBA CDC DCD. Dolce 1555, 313 (*accreber* in l. 13 corrected to *accrebber*). Although the cruelty of the poet's fate is a frequent Petrarchist theme, it has special force in Morra's verse given her circumstances: during her father's absence as a political exile in France, she lived an isolated life with her brothers, by whom she was eventually murdered (tragically, with the probable connivance of her father, so warmly invoked here). In this sonnet, Morra addresses the river Siri (now Sinni), near her home in Valsinni, in Basilicata, constructing the river as a living monument to her sufferings. Her consciously exemplary self-fashioning anticipates Gaspara Stampa (see especially no. 18): *esempio* (7), has the force of the Latin *exemplum. The positioning of *Torbido Siri* and *Isabella* as the opening and closing words of the poem reinforces the implicit parallel between the turbulent river and the metaphorically turbid emotions of the poet. A striking formal feature of the poem is the inclusive rhyme *acerbo/disacerbo* (4–5).

196

Ecco ch'un'altra volta, o valle inferna,
o fiume alpestre, o ruinati sassi
o ignudi spirti di virtute e cassi,
udrete il pianto e la mia doglia eterna.   4
Ogni monte udirammi, ogni caverna,
ovunqu'io arresti, ovunqu'io mova i passi;
ché Fortuna, che mai salda non stassi,
cresce ognor il mio mal, ognor l'eterna.   8
Deh, mentre ch'io mi lagno e giorno e notte,
o fere, o sassi, o orride ruine,
o selve incolte, o solitarie grotte,   11
ulule, e voi del mal nostro indovine,
piangete meco a voci alte interrotte
il mio più d'altro miserando fine.   14

Once again, o hellish valley, o wild river, o ruined rocks, o spirits bereft
and deprived of all virtue, you will hear my plaint, and my eternal
sorrow. Every mountain will hear me, every cavern, everywhere I
pause, everywhere I pass; for Fortune, who never rests, increases my ills
at every moment, making them eternal. Ah, while I lament both day
and night, o beasts, o rocks, o dread ruins, o pathless woods, o solitary
caves, o night birds, and you who augur our evil—bewail with me in
high, unceasing voices my incomparably pitiful end.

Sonnet ABBA ABBA CDC DCD. *Dolce* 1555, 312 (*una altra* corrected to *un'altra* in l. 1).
Morra's description here of a hellish, dark nature is the antithesis of the pastoralism
of a poem like Gambara's no. 193. Although there is an element of realism here, in
that Morra is describing the wild mountain landscape near her home at Valsinni,
there is clearly also a degree of *pathetic fallacy at work here. The unusual word
ulule (12) probably derives from the Neapolitan poet Jacopo Sannazaro's pastoral
novel *Arcadia* (books 6 and 12, poems), which may also have supplied the phrase
ruinati sassi in l. 2 (book 10, prose). *Solitarie grotte* (12) may derive from Sannazaro's
RD 7* ("Sonanti liti e voi, rigidi scoglie"), thematically close to this poem in its
portrayal of the poet in a bleak landscape attuned to his mood. The last line, present-
ing the poet as an insuperable *exemplum* of suffering, recalls ll. 7–8 of no. 195. Note
the equivocal rhyme, *eterna/eterna*, at ll. 4 and 8.

Laura Battiferri (1560)

197

Non cria, Cecero mio, pietre né fronde
sì dure e tante il tuo canuto seno,
quante 'l mio verde, ancor di calda pieno
speme, alte e salde voglie entro n'asconde;   4
né tante piaghe sì larghe e profonde
ha 'l fianco tuo che mai non verrà meno
quante al mio sento; e non ne vorrei meno
pur una, tanto son dolci e gioconde.   8
Se poggia in alto la tua antica fronte
al ciel sormonta il mio nuovo desire;
se tu stai fermo, io sempre immobile sono;   11
se del fiero Aquilon sprezzi l'ardire,
io quel del volgo audace: oh sia chi conte
quel che teco e fra me taccio e ragiono!   14

My Ceceri, your snowy breast does not nurture stones or leaves as hard or many as my green one, still filled with warm hope, harbors within it lofty and puissant desires. Your flank, which will stand always, does not have so many wide, deep gashes as I feel in my own; yet I would not be without a single one of these wounds, so sweet and pleasurable are they. If your ancient brow soars on high, my unwonted yearning aspires to the heavens; if you stand firm, I am unmovable; if you scorn the insolence of cruel Aquilo, I scorn that of the vulgar throng. Oh, who could tell what I speak of and conceal with you and to myself!

Sonnet ABBA ABBA CDE DCE. Battiferri 1560, 35. Although Battiferri's poetic mentor Benedetto Varchi addresses a sonnet to Mount Ceceri, near Fiesole (Varchi 1555, 18), Battiferri's main source for this sonnet appears to be Chiara Matraini's thematically analogous no. 31. Battiferri follows Matraini in rhyming a word with itself, the *meno* of ll. 6–7: a repetition underscored through the parallelism of the preceding *non verrà / non ne vorrei*. While Matraini's poet suffers the stereotypical pains of love, the nature of Battiferri's poet's emotions is more mysterious, though her anticipation of hostility from the "vulgar throng" might point to her literary ambitions. The sonnet shows the influence of Della Casa in its extensive use of *enjambment, and it makes artful use of devices of parallelism such as *rapportatio* ("pietre . . . fronde / dure . . . tante"). The concluding phrase is intriguing, juxtaposing inward and outward dialogues, revelation and concealment. Aquilo (12) was the Roman god of the north wind.

198

Quando nell'ocean l'altera fronte
inchina il sole, e 'l nostro mondo imbruna,
e dal più basso ciel la fredda luna
sormonta e fa d'argento ogn'alto monte,   4
partesi il buon pastor dal chiaro fonte,
e la sua greggie alla sua mandra aduna
e 'l stanco pellegrin raccoglie in una
le forze stanche al suo voler mal pronte;   8
ed io che veggio avvicinar la notte,
e volar l'ore e i giorni, gli anni e i lustri,
e già dal quinto indietro mi rivolgo,   11
il passo affretto, e prima che s'annotte,
lo stuol de' pensier miei sparsi raccolgo
per fargli in cielo eternamente illustri.   14

When the sun lowers his proud brow into the ocean and our world
darkens, and the cold moon rises from the lowest heaven to silver the
high mountains, the good shepherd leaves the bright spring and gathers
his flock at its fold, and the weary pilgrim draws together his wearied
forces, barely obedient to his will; and I who see the night approaching
and the hours and days flying and the years and the decades, and who
now turn my back on the first half of my third—I hasten my steps, and,
before night can fall, muster the horde of my scattered thoughts, that
they may gleam eternally in heaven.

Sonnet ABBA ABBA CDE CED. Battiferri 1560, 28. Battiferri's *Primo libro delle opere
toscane* contains several birthday meditations, reflecting on time and mortality (for
another example, see no. 92). Her models are Petrarch's anniversary poems, typi-
cally penitential in character and marking the anniversaries of his falling in love
with Laura. This sonnet, one of Battiferri's loveliest, is dated in l. 11 to her twenty-
fifth birthday (*lustri*, in l. 10, translated "decades," in fact means "lustrums," or five-
year periods, and Battiferri speaks of her fifth lustrum having passed). Battiferri
abandons her usual complex syntax in this poem for a simpler, more fluid, *paratac-
tic style, underlined by the use of *polysyndeton (the conjunction *e*, introducing
clauses, occurs eight times). The theme of time fleeing is characteristic of Petrarch,
as is the metaphor of "scattering" in l. 13 (for *pensier sparsi*, see his sonnet 298, l. 2).
The tercets feature two inclusive rhymes, *notte/s'annotte* and *lustri/illustri*.

199

Pria che la chioma che mi die' natura,
e quel vigor ch'ancor riserbo intero
si cangi e scemi al trapassar leggero
di lui che 'l men ne lascia e 'l più ne fura,   4
spero quest'acqua e sì chiara e sì pura
e quest'ombrosa valle e questo altero
monte tanto cantar, quanto il pensiero
per lor posto ha in non cale ogni altra cura;   8
s'altrui volere e cruda invida stella,
usi a giusti desii far danno e scorno,
non mi vietin fornire opra sì bella.   11
Apollo, tu che a queste piaggie intorno
sai ch'ombreggia la fronde tua novella,
scendi talor nel dolce mio soggiorno.   14

Before the tresses Nature gave me and the vigor I still command are greyed and dwindle with the light passing of him who steals the most from us and leaves us with the least, I hope to hymn this shady vale and this proud peak in such a manner as befits the way they have taken possession of my every thought, if the will of others and my cruel, grudging star, accustomed to thwarting just desires, do not prevent me from perfecting this fair work. Apollo, you know your fresh leaves shadow these slopes; descend sometimes into my sweet abode.

Sonnet ABBA ABBA CDC DCD. Battiferri 1560, 37. Battiferri's syntax is notably sinuous in this *enjambment-rich sonnet, expressing her poetic ambitions. The mountain and valley she aspires to praise are Mount Ceceri (cf. no. 197) and the Mensola valley near Maiano, where she and her husband had a country house. The opening lines offer an instance of *rapportatio, with the verbs "grey" (lit. "change") and "dwindle" (3) referring, respectively, to the "tresses" and "vigor" of ll. 1–2. Further ornament is offered by the *polysyndeton of ll. 5–6, the insistent sound repetitions of ll. 7–8, and l. 4's *periphrasis for Time ("him who steals . . ."). After the intricacies of the first eleven lines, the simple and beautiful ll. 12–14 have particular impact. Apollo was god of poetry; his "frond," the laurel tree, which was also the poet's *senhal (see nos. 93 and 138–39). The imagery recalls Petrarch's 188, also addressed to Apollo and using *soggiorno/intorno* in rhyme, while l. 10 echoes a line of Bembo's opening sonnet (6).

Lucchesia Sbarra (1610)

200

Vent'anni vissi in libertade e in pace,
piena sol d'un desio ch'a nulla pensa,
né turbommi rea sorte o nube densa
d'ambizïon, né mai d'Amor la face.   4
E solo chi cantò Turno e Aiace
cara mia cura agli occhi miei dispensa,
cibo soave e delicata mensa,
quando è il ciel cheto e l'aura e l'euro tace.   8
Allor vissi, allor seppi d'esser viva!
La faccia allor, ch'or pallida e smarrita,
e di rose e di gigli si copriva.   11
O cara, o dolce, anzi o beata vita:
o stelle, o sorte rea, chi me ne priva,
e a chi non m'ode fa ch'io chieda aita?   14

Twenty years I lived in freedom and in peace, filled solely with one carefree desire. Ill fortune never disturbed me, nor ambition's dense cloud, nor ever Love's fierce brand. Only those who sang of Turnus and Ajax dispensed a cherished care to my eyes: sweet nourishment and a delicate repast, when the heavens are quiet and the least breeze does not breathe. Then I lived, then I knew I was alive. My face, now so pale and lost, then bloomed with roses and lilies. O beloved, o sweet, indeed o blessed life! O stars, o cruel fate, who has deprived me of it, leaving me to ask help of one who will not hear?

Sonnet ABBA ABBA CDC DCD. Sbarra 1610, A9r (unnumbered). Thematically, this poem describing the poet's early life is extremely unusual: of female poets, only Francesca Turina (nos. 202–5) engaged with this theme. The last line of Sbarra's sonnet probably indicates that it was written as part of a sequence of love poems, addressed to a stereotypical unresponsive lover, although in her 1610 *Rime* it forms part of a sequence mainly focused on her son's brief life and death (nos. 179, 184–85). Sbarra portrays her youth as a time of freedom and scholarly leisure ("those who sang of Turnus and Ajax" are Virgil and Homer). Stylistically, the poem is relatively simple and unshowy for Sbarra, perhaps suggesting that it was an early composition, though the sound effects of ll. 8 ("l'aura e l'euro") and 10 ("allor, ch'or") anticipate her later taste for wordplay. The end of l. 8 literally means "when the breeze and Eurus [the god of the east wind] are silent."

201

O quante volte i limpidi ruscelli,
per cristallo servito han questa chioma;
o quante volte ai fior vari novelli
furo le membra mie gravosa soma;   4
o quante volte ad emular gli augelli
ornai la lingua mia d'altro idioma.
Ahi, di man non m'avea tratto i capelli
Fortuna ancor, né la mia forza doma!   8
Allor, s'avena o pastorale flauto
l'orecchio in qualche bosco mi feriva,
giva coll'occhio ad incontrarlo cauto.   11
Or godea di veder sopra una riva
farsi ninfe e pastor un cibo lauto
d'erbe, e un dolce vin d'un'acqua viva.   14

O, how many times have the limpid streams served as mirror for these locks; how many times did I rest my limbs on the mingled, new-sprung flowers; how many times to vie with the birds did I adorn my voice with a different tongue. Alas, Fortune had not yet wrenched her hair from my hand, nor worn down my strength! When, in some wood, the sound of the pipes or a pastoral flute struck my ear, I would wander to find it with a cautious eye. Other times, I loved to watch nymphs and shepherds on some riverbank making a fine banquet of herbs and a sweet wine of bright water.

Sonnet ABAB ABAB CDC DCD. Sbarra 1610, A9v (unnumbered). Like Turina (nos. 203, 205), Sbarra here figures her youth using the language of pastoral poetry: an appropriate choice, given that the pastoral world of Arcadia represented a moment of dawnlike innocence in the world. The nymph using a stream or pond as a mirror (1–2) is a familiar motif in pastoral drama. The first tercet, using *avena*, in the unusual sense of "pipes," probably alludes to a famous pastoral scene in Tasso's *GL* 7.6. An effective formal feature of the sonnet is the *anaphora of ll. 1, 3, and 5 ("O quante volte"), a sequence broken by the *Ahi* of l. 7. The reference to Fortune's hair (7–8) is to traditional representations of Fortune or Opportunity as bald at the back of her head, with a lock of hair in front that must be grasped to possess her. The simplicity of the Arcadian diet, alluded to in the last lines, was a pastoral *topos, expressing by synecdoche the purity of the age.

Francesca Turina (1628)

202

Di dominio, di aver, d'opre, di onore
era nel colmo il mio paterno nido,
quando misera apersi in questo infido
mondo gli occhi a le lacrime, al dolore;   4
ché tosto priva fui del genitore,
onde poscia cangiai fortuna e lido
con la mia madre, e de l'amato e fido
albergo uscimmo lagrimando fuore.   8
Né qui fermò, ché la mia sorte ingrata
nel maggior uopo ancor mi tolse lei,
onde fui in tutto dei parenti orbata.   11
Nel libero Catai crebbi, ed amata
fui dal materno zio, ch'a' danni miei
pianse pietoso, sol per pianger nata.   14

Power, wealth, achievements, honor abounded in my paternal nest
when I wretchedly opened my eyes in this treacherous world to tears
and pain; for soon I was deprived of my father, so that I was forced
to change fortune and shore with my mother, and we issued forth
weeping from our beloved and trusted home. Nor did it stop here, for
my thankless fate deprived me of her also at the time of my greatest
need, so that I was quite bereft of my parents. In free Gattara I grew,
beloved of my maternal uncle, who wept pityingly at the troubles of
one born only to weep.

Sonnet ABBA ABBA CDC CDC. Turina 1628, 117. This sonnet opens a remarkable
autobiographical sequence by Turina recounting her life from the time of her birth.
The proemial sonnet recounts the poet's early orphanhood, establishing her as a
tragic heroine, fated from birth to a world of tears (3–4, 14). The narrative corre-
sponds to the facts of Turina's life, but the trajectory from plenitude to expulsion
also recalls the archetype of the Fall, giving her poet figure a paradigmatic status.
After *apersi* (3), the poet is the subject mainly of passive constructions (5, 11, 12–13),
in a manner that emphasizes her powerlessness, the antithesis of *dominio* (1). The
language of the poem is mainly simple, in keeping with the sonnet's narrative char-
acter, though note the *assonance across the break of ll. 1–2, and the *alliteration of
the last line. The description of Gattara, seat of Turina's maternal family, as "free"
refers to its formal independence from papal or imperial rule.

203

Per trapassare i dì noiosi e gravi
in cara solitudine romita,
or l'anima con Dio tenni rapita,
or con suoni accordai voci söavi;   4
ed or mi rispondea da' sassi cavi
Eco, che in quelle grotte ha spirto e vita,
che m'era via più dolce e più gradita,
che le canne di Cipro o d'Ibla i favi.   8
E per quei boschi salutare il giorno
udia gli augelli, e rimirava l'onde
chiare irrigar quelle campagne intorno.   11
Trassi talor su le fiorite sponde
con le mie muse un placido soggiorno,
io di lor vaga, ed esse a me seconde.   14

To pass my weary, burdensome days in a dear hermit solitude I would
sometimes spend my time rapt in conversation with God; other times,
I would harmonize sweet voices with notes, and sometimes, from the
hollow rocks, Echo would respond to me, who has her spirit and life in
those caves—a sound more sweet and welcome by far to me than the
reeds of Cyprus or the honeycombs of Hybla. I would hear the birds
saluting the dawn in those woods, and watch the clear streams
watering the fields all around. Sometimes I would enjoy a peaceful
sojourn on their flowery banks with my muses, I enchanted with them,
they gracious to me.

Sonnet ABBA ABBA CDC DCD. Turina 1628, 120. Although she was in fact raised
with a large family of cousins, Turina's mythologized account of her youth shows
her largely in solitude, as here, or accompanied by local shepherdesses (see no. 205).
As in Lucchesia Sbarra's nos. 200–201, pastoral literature supplies a descriptive lan-
guage for an idealized rural youth, although Turina's lyrics combine nostalgia with
a vein of melancholy relating to her orphaned state (the "dì noiosi e gravi" of l. 1).
Echo, a nymph who pined away for love, remaining solely as an echoing voice, is
frequently cited in pastoral literature. Her trapped voice is contrasted here with the
poet's freer voice, implicitly associated with birdsong and running water in the lyri-
cal first tercet. Line 8 echoes a line in Battista Guarini's pastoral *Il pastor fido* (2.1,
l. 185), similarly using Cyprus's sugarcanes and the honey of Mount Hybla, in Sicily,
as paradigmatic of sweetness.

204

Talor per dare al mio dolor soccorso
e serenare il torbido pensiero
a un agile destrier premeva il dorso,
che la mano obedia presto e leggiero;   4
e prendendo il più facile sentiero,
or di galoppo, or lo stendea al corso,
ché bench'egli sen gisse ardito e fiero,
resil, volendo, obedïente al morso;   8
ed or da la sinistra, or da la destra,
raddoppiar li facea angusti giri,
come mi suggeriva arte mäestra,   11
ed or dovunque il fiumicel si aggiri,
saltando, or su per una rupe alpestra,
ché il periglio il piacer fa che non miri.   14

Sometimes to relieve my suffering and soothe my turbulent thoughts, I would burden the back of an agile steed, who obeyed my hand swift and light; and, taking the easiest path, I would gallop or run with him, for, however bold and proud he was, I rendered him obedient to the bit through my will. Now to the left, now to the right, I would make him double in narrow turns, as the master art suggested to me; now wherever the stream twisted in its path, leaping, now up onto some mountain crag, for pleasure makes you careless of danger.

Sonnet ABAB BABA CDC DCD. Turina 1628, 126. This first-person portrait of the author as dashing horsewoman is thematically unique, although Baroque love lyric often portrays the beloved in action (cf. no. 72). The poem is one of Turina's most striking and vivid. Interesting in view of the thematics of the sequence as a whole is the emphasis on mastery and dominance, as in l. 8, where the power of the poet's will is foregrounded through the intrusion of *volendo* between *resil* (= *resilo*, or *lo resi*) and *obediente*. The reference to the "master art" (11) is to the formalized art of equitation, centered on dressage, which grew up in the sixteenth century. The simplified, sequential rhyme scheme, reminiscent of ottava rima, is characteristic of Turina's autobiographical verse (see appendix C).

205

Or Camilla la volsca imitar volsi,
che nel correr le piante ebbe sì snelle
ed al corso sfidai le pastorelle,
e del mio fatigar frutto raccolsi,   4
ché con le più veloci il passo sciolsi,
e vincente restai spesso di quelle,
tant'ebbi favorevoli le stelle,
e a tutte l'altre il plauso e 'l premio tolsi.   8
Ond'or di ghirlandette il crin mi ornaro,
ed or d'un pastoral mirto nodoso
con ferro in punta la mia destra armaro;   11
ed or di lauro un ramoscel frondoso,
don più d'ogni altro prezïoso e caro,
di cui più che d'ogni altro è il cor bramoso.   14

Sometimes I wished to imitate the Volscian Camilla, whose feet were
so swift in running, and I challenged the shepherdesses to races and
received fruit for my labors, for my paces flew freely with the fleetest.
Often I remained the victor, so favorable to me were the stars, and I
snatched the applause and the prize from all the rest. Sometimes they
would crown my locks with pretty garlands, sometimes arm my right
hand with a knotty, iron-tipped pastoral myrtle. Sometimes they would
hand me a little branch of leafy laurel—that gift more dear and precious
than any other and for which the heart most yearns.

Sonnet ABBA ABBA CDC DCD. Turina 1628, 127. As in no. 204, Turina portrays her-
self here as an action heroine, somewhere between the worlds of epic and pastoral.
The Volscian princess Camilla, a skilled archeress, features in Virgil's *Aeneid*. The
name had special meaning for Turina as her mother's name; she also gave it to her
daughter. Since the poem is describing a recurrent activity, one would expect the
verbs to be in the imperfect tense rather than the past definite, but the phonetically
emphatic sequence of first-person verbs in rhyme (*volsi/raccolsi/sciolsi/tolsi*) is effec-
tive in underlining the poet's agency and will. Garlands and sticks, often lovingly
described, are staple gifts and prizes in pastoral literature, which frequently por-
trays sports, including foot races. The association of the laurel with poetic triumph
is obviously relevant to l. 14's description of it as the ultimate object of desire. The
pairing of the diminutive *ramoscel* with *lauro* derives from Petrarch's canzone 359
(7–8).

206

Stanza, dove le luci apersi al pianto
il dì dell'infelice nascer mio,
se ben per breve spazio il fato rio
mi ti concesse ai genitor accanto,   4
ché ti lasciai rivolta in negro manto,
a rivederti spingemi il desio,
ancor ch'io pensi a la cagion perch'io
fui da te lungi, ne sospiro intanto;   8
e ben riveggio voi, mura dilette,
ma non in voi le glorie e gli splendori
che ti aportava il padre e i frati miei.   11
E pur un non so che vien che mi alette
a rimembrar coi vostri antichi odori
quel sospirato ben ch'io non godei.   14

Room, where I opened my eyes to grief on the day of my unhappy
birth, even though cruel fate only allowed me to inhabit you for a brief
space of time at my parents' side, before I left you wrapped in a black
mantle—desire urges me to see you once again, even though it makes
me sigh when I think of the reason why I was distant from you. I do
indeed see you again, beloved walls, but nothing in you of the glories
and splendors my father and brothers brought you. Yet something—I
know not what—entices me to remember, with your smell of times
long past, that sighed-for good I never enjoyed.

Sonnet ABBA ABBA CDE CDE. Turina 1628, 197. Place is a strong organizing prin-
ciple in Turina's autobiographical verse, with the poet often revisiting sites of emo-
tional significance (cf. nos. 57, 126). Here, she visits her birthplace in Città di Cas-
tello, which she left as an infant after her father's death. Formally, the poem is
uneven: the quatrains are laxly composed and syntactically awkward at one point
(7–8), but the sonnet is redeemed by its beautifully calibrated final tercet, which
transfers the Petrarchan themes of memory, desire, and the passage of time into a
narrative situation more characteristic of a modern novel than an early modern
lyric. "Non so che" (12) is a phrase especially associated with the Tasso of *Gerusa-
lemme liberata* (see, for example, GL 2.37, l. 3; 12.66, l. 6). The *-ei* nexus in the rhymes
miei and *godei* in the tercets should be read as bisyllabic (*diaeresis).

Silvestra Collalto (1646)

207

Con il dito alle labbra a me rivolto,
Arpocrate il silenzio mi commisse;
né le stridule canne mi permisse
toccar del dio silvan poco né molto,   4
onde la musa mia con mesto volto,
volendosi sottrar da oltraggi e risse,
entro l'opache selve il piè rimisse,
ove il suo antico ovil giace sepolto;   8
e l'alme Tespie unite a danno mio
rinchiuse han tutte l'apollinee balze
che guidan di Parnaso al Campidoglio,   11
e la famosa tua diletta Clio
sommerso ha in Lete del mio nome il foglio,
perché il crin cinto ho sol di smorto salze.   14

Turning to me with a finger on his lips, Harpocrates bid me to silence, nor would he let me touch the strident reeds of the sylvan god, little or much; so my Muse, with sorrowing face, wishing to screen herself from insult and affray, turned her steps once more to the dark woods where her ancient lair lurks. The bountiful Thespian muses, united against me, have sealed off the Apollonian slopes that lead from Parnassus to the Capitol, and your famous beloved Clio has submerged my name's page in Lethe, so my locks are crowned solely with dull flint.

Sonnet ABBA ABBA CDE CED. Bergalli 1726, 2:145 (*apollinee* in l. 10 corrected from *appollinee*). Luisa Bergalli's 1726 anthology of women's verse includes five poems by Silvestra Collalto, taken from a manuscript Bergalli dates to 1646. Three of the poems have a shared theme of poetic renunciation, echoing Lucchesia Sbarra's no. 185 (Sbarra was Collalto's maternal aunt). Harpocrates (2) is the Greek god of silence. The "sylvan god" (4) is probably Pan, associated with pastoral poetry. Thespiae (9) was a town near Mount Helicon, home to the Muses. For Parnassus (11), see no. 58. The Capitol, in Rome, was where poet laureates were crowned. Lethe (13) was one of the rivers of Hades, causing oblivion in all who drank from it, while Clio (12) was the muse of history. *Smorto salze* (14) quotes from a sonnet of Lucchesia Sbarra's to her sister Lodovica, Collalto's mother, where it is similarly contrasted with the poetic laurel (Sbarra 1610, F3v). *Ovile* (8), translated "lair," means literally "sheepfold," an appropriate dwelling for a pastoral muse.

Comic
& Dialect Verse

Girolama Corsi (before 1509)
208

Io son fatta villanela
per la mia mala ventura
posta a forza in questa obscura
picoleta capanella.

[1] I', s' 'l dico al mio marito,
ch'i' nol posso comportare,
che di me pigli partito,
lui mi viene a lusengare: 4
—Alma mia, che vuo' tu fare?
stiàno in questo loco ameno
che di fiori e frutti è pieno
e d'erbeta tenerella—. *Io son fata vilanella . . .*   8

[2] I' gli mostro el petto e 'l viso
ch'era biancho e delichato;
lu' me mira e sta' conquiso,
ché sì negro è diventato;   12
po' me dice:—Te harò insegnato
a lavarti ogni matina
con una acqua chiara e fina,
ché serai, com'eri, bella—. *Io son fatta villanela . . .*   16

[3] E gli dico:—Chome faron,
se da Pava mi menate,
che dirò: 'su andagòn'
a le mie compagne ornate—.   20
—Lasserai queste brigate;
state mecho a solazare,
e già mai potrai imparare
la sua roza e mal favella—. *Io son facta vilanella . . .*   24

[4] I' gli dico:—Hor non vedete
che di tella i' von vestita.
Forsi poi, quando vorete,
non saprò andar polita—.   28
—Ti farò, dolce mia vita,
una veste sì lezadra,
che per chiesia e per istrada
se dirà cossa novella—. *Io son fatta villanella . . .*   32

[5] —Oimè, che le matine,
quando i' debbo riposare,
porzi, chani, galli e galine
dispetosa mi fa levare—.   36
—Figlia, non ti lamentare,
ché levar presto del letto
sì t'ha fatto un vago aspetto
e tondeta qual tortorella—. *Io son fata vilanella . . .*   40

[6] —Che vi par ch'io non possa
udir messa, né matino;
anderone in charne e in ossa
giò in Inferno a capo chino—.   44
—Nol pensar, che Dio divino
non vol altro ch'el bon core;
basta dirgli: "Oimè, Signore,
miserere a st'alma fella"—. *Io son facta vilanella . . .*   48

[7] E non n'o tanti argumenti
quanti gli ha contraditioni,
e vol pur che i mie' tormenti
mi sia giocho e sia cancione.   52
Cussì, persa ogni ragione,
mi rimango in questa grotta.
Fossi stata presa o morta
quando vini in capanella! *Io son fatta vilanella . . .*   56

I am made a country maid, through my ill fate, stuck in this little dark hut.

[1] If I tell my husband I won't be pushed around, he tries to win me over, saying: "Darling, what more could you want? Let's stay in this lovely spot, full of flowers and fruit and fresh spring grass." *I am made a country maid . . .*

[2] I show him my breast and my face, which used to be white and refined. He looks and is vanquished, seeing how dark I have turned; then he says, "I'll teach you to wash yourself every morning with a fine, clear water. You'll soon be as lovely as you were." *I am made a country maid . . .*

[3] I say to him, "Well, and what'll *us* do if you take me away from *Pava*? Shall I say to my charming friends here, *We'm gwain?*" "Don't worry about those women. Stay with me, and let's be happy together. You'll

never have to pick up their horrible speech." *I am made a country maid . . .*

[4] I say to him, "Don't you see I'm going around dressed in a sack? Maybe later, when you want me to dress nicely, I'll have forgotten how." "My sweet, I'll have such a charming dress made for you that people will be pointing it out as a marvel at church and in the streets." *I am made a country maid . . .*

[5] "Alas! In the morning, when I need to rest, pigs, dogs, roosters, and hens drive me from my bed in a vile mood." "Dearest, don't complain. All these early mornings have done wonders for your looks—you're round as a little turtle dove." *I am made a country maid . . .*

[6] "What about the fact that I can't hear mass here or matins? I'll go straight to hell in flesh and blood without being able to lift a finger to stop it." "Don't worry, for God in heaven wants nothing from us but a good heart. All you need to do is say to Him, 'Alas, Lord, take pity on this wicked soul.'" *I am made a country maid . . .*

[7] I don't have as many arguments as he has contradictions. He even wants my torments to be turned into a joke and a song. So, having lost my cause, I remain in this cave. Would that I had been waylaid or murdered the first time I was coming to this hut! *I am made a country maid . . .*

Barzelletta xyyx + ababbccx. Venice, Biblioteca Marciana, MS IX, 270 [6367], 21v–23v. Although Girolama Corsi's poetic corpus mainly takes the form of sonnets, two strophic poems by her with refrains are contained in the manuscript of her verse collected by Marin Sanudo in 1509. Sanudo refers to them in his prefatory letter as *canzonette*. The second of the two, "Quel che 'l cielo mi dà per sorte" (24r–25v) is a love poem, written within Corsi's usual, serious, Petrarchan register. "Io son fatta vilanella," by contrast, is a comic dialogue, unique in tone within Corsi's surviving output and, indeed, without any real parallel in the entire female-authored poetic tradition of the age.

Corsi's poem is structured as a dialogue between a bored urban wife forced to live or vacation in the country and her doting but determined husband, who counters her increasingly desperate pleas for escape. We do not know enough about Corsi's life to ascertain whether the poem voices a fictional figure's dilemma or humorously reflects on Corsi's own situation, though the remark in the last stanza that her husband wants her travails to be turned into "a song and a joke" suggests the latter. The *barzelletta* was a metrical form essentially framed for musical setting, and it is likely that this was intended as a performance piece.

The poem reflects the growing fashion among Venetian aristocrats to retreat to their country estates in summer; it also demonstrates the deep-rooted urban bias of Italian society, which, ever since the later middle ages, had increasingly tended to associate city dwelling with the cultural value of "urbanity" and country life with rusticity and crudeness. This negative vision of the country was in tension with the idealizing, pastoral strain within Italian literature, which delighted in exquisite, stylized descriptions of natural beauty (see, for example, nos. 6, 193). Corsi plays the two traditions off against each other wittily in this poem, especially in the first stanza, where the husband's poetically tinged vision of the landscape stands in stark contrast with his wife's revulsion at all the countryside represents (*loco ameno* [6] echoes the Latin *locus amoenus*, a general term for an idyllic landscape, while diminutives such as *erbetta* and *tenerella* [8] were a frequent feature of poetic descriptions of landscapes). The second stanza reflects the social preference for white skin, prized as a token of aristocracy and a means of differentiating elite women and men from those who engaged in physical, outdoor labor. The "clear water" the husband offers will be some kind of cosmetic preparation for whitening the skin, for which many recipes circulated at the time. The argument between husband and wife concerning church attendance in the sixth stanza is interesting in a poem written no more than a couple of decades before the beginning of the Reformation. The husband's argument that attendance of mass is irrelevant and that salvation is possible through a direct, unmediated relationship between the worshipper and God was one that would characterize the Reformist position.

Corsi was Tuscan by birth, and the poem is mainly written in a colloquially inflected literary Tuscan, without differentiation between the voices of wife and husband (the frequent, though inconsistent, use of single consonants where double would be expected in Tuscan presumably reflects the Venetian literary background of Sanudo's scribe). An interesting sociolinguistic feature is that the wife is portrayed as addressing her husband with the more honorific *voi* form, while he addresses her more familiarly as *tu*. In the third stanza, where the wife pours scorn on the local women's rustic speech, *Pava* for *Padova* and the first-person plural verb ending *-on* (*faron, andragòn*) are dialect features. I have picked out these terms in italics in the translation, and rendered them in a rural dialect of English with which I am familiar that has a similarly distinctive treatment of the first-person plural (West Country British English).

Issicratea Monte (1580)

209

Magagnò, el versurare è 'na nöela
ch'a ve' sè dir ch'a puochi se conven.
El no basta haër sletra solamen
se 'l non ne piove in cao 'na bona stela.   4
El bognerave haër la zaramela
de quel Pre Cecco, che contugnamen
portè tanti agni un bel'oraro in sen
senza mè dezularse la gonela;   8
perqué, secondo ch'ello in sul Pavan
pianzé qui suò biè rami in muò ch'a' sento
stopirse agno poleta, agno sletran.   11
An mi, se ben a non gh'ho quel scaltrimento,
a vorae far la sera e la doman
pianzere el bon Pallabio a pì de cento,   14
de muò che inchina el vento
fuorsi s'artegneräe e harae deleto
sentir laldarlo in t'un me sonaggieto.   17
Perqué l'iera in affeto
la gluoria de Vicenza, e Pava zura
ch'esserghe mare e haërlo in sopoltura   20
l'harae per pì ventura
ch'haër habbìo quel gran Piero da i Bagni
e 'l stuorico sì bon de i Livïagni.   23
Tonca sti nuostri lagni
se derae stramuär sempre in laldare
quel glorïoso e santo Gieson Pare   26
che l'ha vogiù cavare
de sto mal mondo e tirarlo su in quela
paltria per farla fuorsi anche pì bela.   29

Magagnò, scribbling verse is the kind of thing, to tell the truth, that few should set their hand to. It's no good just being well lettered: the right star has to rain down on your head. You'd have to have the pipes of that *pre* Cecco, who carried a pretty laurel round in his breast all those years without ever messing up his cassock and wept away in our Paduan countryside over those pretty branches of his so well that all the poets and lettered men are amazed. I may not be as clever as him, but I'd like to make a hundred folk cry over good old Pallabio night and day, so that even the wind might calm down for a minute and listen with pleasure to my sonnet. Because it's true that he was the glory of Vicenza, and

Padua swears she'd be happier to be his mother and have his tomb than to boast of the great Peter of the Baths or that great historian born of the Liviagni. But enough of this whining: we should devote ourselves to praising that glorious and holy Father Jesus, who took him out of this horrible world and took him up to that fatherland in the sky, perhaps to make it even prettier than it is.

Sonetto caudato ABBA ABBA CDC DCD + dEE eFF fGG gHH hII. Maganza, Rava, and Thiene [?1583], 81r–v (with double consonants likely to have been introduced by printers simplified: see Pasqualigo 1908, 65; straight transcription in Cenini 2009, 485–86). The world of dialect poetry, which flourished especially in the sixteenth century in Venice, Genoa, and the Venetian mainland (especially Padua, Vicenza, and Rovigo) was for the most part exclusively masculine. An exception occurred within the mainland Veneto tradition in the early 1580s, when we see four female poets figuring as published authors of texts in the rustic Paduan dialect *pavan*. This *sonetto caudato* by Issicratea Monte was the first, datable to some time after August 19, 1580, when the great architect Andrea Palladio died in Vicenza. The Vicentine poet and painter Giovanni Battista Maganza, in his comic peasant-persona Magagnò, wrote a *sonetto caudato* to Monte's father asking him to persuade his daughter to contribute a lyric mourning Palladio's death, either in dialect (*'l nostro cantare*) or in Neapolitan (*pulitan*)—Magagnò's approximative identification of the language of Monte's usual poetry: in fact, literary Tuscan. Monte not only contributed a dialect poem but also crafted it as a *risposta*, using the same metrical form and rhymes as his original—a considerable tour de force for a poet new to this language. The novelty for contemporaries of seeing a female poet participate in this deliberately indecorous tradition of verse is well conveyed by Monte's correspondent, the poet and dramatist Luigi Groto ("Cieco d'Adria"), who wrote of a later dialect sonnet of hers that he could not contain his wonderment at seeing this "wild language" (*salvatica lingua*) in her "learned, sweet, refined, urbane mouth" (Milani 1983, 398).

Monte's poem, while following the conventions of "straight" funerary verse in praising the dead and belittling her own poetic capacity, is full of the mock naïveté characteristic of the verse of the *pavan* tradition. *Pre Cecco* (6)—*pre* means "priest," while Cecco is a contraction of Francesco—is an allusion to Petrarch, claimed here as a local since he spent the latter years of his life near Padua, at Arquà. The instrument Monte attributes to Petrarch is a *ciaramella*, a double reed pipe similar to an oboe, normally played with the bagpipe (*zampogna*), which is more commonly used as a metonym for poetic activity. "Pier da i Bagni" (22) is the medieval philosopher and astrologer Pietro d'Abano, whose birthplace, Abano, was the site of a famous spa. The "stuorico de i Liviagni" is the Roman historian Livy (Titus Livius), who was born in Padua. Palladio was also a native of Padua but made his career in Vicenza; hence the reference to the ownership dispute in ll. 18–20 (in fact, he was buried in the church of Santa Corona in Vicenza). The last line may be taken either as conventional funerary hyperbole (the addition of a beautiful soul makes Paradise more beautiful) or as a suggestion that as an architect, Palladio might beautify heaven as he had Vicenza.

Maddalena Campiglia (1583)

210

Cenzo, le nuove Tose de Sgnicona
pò ben sgnicare e n'ha 'na gran cason,
das ché 'l so dolce e 'l so caro Menon
el monte, i buschi e 'l so fime arbandona.   4
No pense zà la ria Morte poltrona
ch'ancuò mil'agni in la bocca d'agnon
el no sea vivo per le suò canzon,
ché in t'agno vila le se canta e sona.   8
Mi per qui maregale che 'l m'ha fati
son ubigà a quest'anema beneta
né no gh'è muo' ch'a mi'n possa dar pati.   11
Mo non bastava a la Morte maleta
co 'l tuor 'na Lanza portarme via el bati
senza darme per elo an sì gran streta?   14

Cenzo, the nine Wenches of Weepicon may well weep their hearts
out; they have good cause to because their dear sweet old Menon has
abandoned their hill, woods, and river. That old fool Death hasn't
reckoned that, a thousand years on, he will still be in everyone's mouths
through the power of his songs, which are sung and played in every
town. I am indebted to that blessed soul for the madrigals he wrote to
me. I can't reconcile myself to his death. Why wasn't it enough for that
cursed Death, carrying off a Lance, to take away my support, without
giving me such a horrible wrench through him?

Sonnet ABBA ABBA CDC DCD. Maganza, Rava, and Thiene [?1583], 128v (with *h*
deleted in *Snichona/snichare* (1–2) and double consonants simplified throughout: see
Pasqualigo 1908, 65; straight transcription in Cenini 2009, 554–55). Like Issicratea
Monte (no. 209), Campiglia here responds *per le rime* to a *proposta* eliciting a sonnet
to mourn a prominent local figure: here "Menon" (Agostino Rava), a dialect poet
with whom Campiglia had previously corresponded in the madrigals referred to in
l. 9 (Milani 1983, 388). The *proposta* was from "Cenzon," or Vincenzo del Bianco, the
nephew of Monte's correspondent Magagnò. Cenzon's sonnet ends with the line
"negun v'alde a snicarlo e agn'un v'aspetta" (No one hears you mourning him; ev-
eryone is waiting), and Campiglia picks up the motif of *snicare* in ll. 1–2, using it for
her "rustic" distortion of Elicona, or Mt Helicon, dwelling place of the Nine Wenches
of l. 1, the Nine Muses). Lanza (13) is probably Aquilia Lanza, subject of an elegiac
sonnet addressed to Campiglia in the same volume (114v–15r).

Francesca Turina (?1630s)

211

Zuppa, fichi, bostrengo e pan bollito
son propria provision per li miei denti,
ma, invece di goder, faran ch'io stenti,
sì scarso al mio bisogno è tal convito;
né posso mai cavarmi l'appetito,   5
e qual mummia sarà ch'io ne diventi,
se non mi giova aver fiorita carne,
né pollami né starne;
perché se masticare io non le possa,
gettinsi pur per me le carni e l'ossa.   10

Soup, figs, *bostrengo*, and boiled bread are provisions fit for my teeth, but, instead of pleasure, they only bring hardship: no meal of that kind can give me what I need or satisfy my cravings. I will soon be a mummy if I can make no use of good, healthy flesh, chickens and partridges. So, if I can't chew them, just throw them all away, flesh and bones.

Madrigal ABBAABCcDD. San Giustino, Archivio Bufalini, Inventario Azzi MS 185, sez. IV, c. 4 (*sì*, in l. 4, amended from *se*). Among Turina's unpublished verses are a few comic madrigals, such as this one, recounting her frustration in old age—she lived into her late eighties—at no longer being about to eat solid food, and especially meat. The theme of aging is also found in her serious verse (see Turina 2010, 239 [no. 233]) for a sonnet on the loss of a tooth). *Bostrengo* is a sweet dish, rather like a rice pudding, of grains or rice cooked with milk and flavored with honey. *Perché* (9) is meant in the sense of *perciò* ("so," "therefore").

Notes on Authors

The following notes provide basic details of the life and works of the authors included in this anthology, along with a minimal bibliography, limited to key modern sources, in English where available. Further bibliographical information is available in Cox 2008 and 2011. Writers with an entry in the *Dizionario biografico degli italiani* (down to vol. 73: Meda–Messaglia) are marked with the abbreviation *DBI*. Writers with an entry in the appendix to Cox 2011 are marked *PM*.

Aleardi, Amedea degli (fl. 1405)

Based in Verona. Little is known of her life. Pacchioni 1907.

Andreini, Isabella (1562–1604)

Born in Padua (probably as Isabella Canali). Married Francesco Cerracchi (Andreini was their professional name) and joined acting company I Gelosi c. 1578. Seven children, including actor and dramatist Giovanni Battista Andreini (c. 1579–1654). Died in childbirth in Lyons, following acting tour in France. Member of Accademia degli Intenti, Pavia, from 1601. Published pastoral drama *Mirtilla* (1588), much reprinted and twice translated into French; *Rime* (1601). Francesco Andreini published several other volumes of Isabella's writings posthumously, notably another volume of *Rime* (1605) and one of *Lettere* (1607). MacNeil 2005; *DBI* (under "Canali, Isabella"); *PM*.

Armani, Vincenza (d. 1569)

One of the earliest Italian actresses known to us by name. Performed to great acclaim in Mantua in 1566–67; murdered in 1569, perhaps by a jealous admirer. Object of a tribute by her fellow actor Adriano Valerini praising her for her learning, grace, and exceptional performance skills. Henke 2002, 85–100; *DBI*; *PM*.

Battiferri, Laura (1523–89)

Born in Urbino. Illegitimate daughter of nobleman and prelate Giovanni Antonio Battiferri and Maddalena Coccapani. Married (1) Vittorio Sereni, musician (d. 1549); (2) Bartolomeo degli Ammannati (1511–92), sculptor and architect. Lived in Urbino, Rome, and, following her second marriage, Florence. Published *Primo libro delle opere toscane* (1560); *Sette salmi penitenziali* (1564). A manuscript in the Biblioteca Casanatense, Rome (3229) contains much late unpublished verse by her. Battiferri 2006; *DBI*; *PM*.

Bembo, Pietro (1470–1547)

Born into a distinguished Venetian patrician family; son of diplomat Bernardo Bembo. Attached to various courts, including, most famously, Urbino. Based in Rome as secretary to Pope Leo X, 1513–21; from 1521 in Padua and Venice, where he was appointed official historian to the Republic in 1529; from 1539 in Rome, after his appointment as cardinal by Pope Paul III. Influential as poet and literary and linguistic theorist. Published works include *Gli Asolani* (1505), a dialogue on love; *Prose della volgar lingua* (1525), a treatise on literary language and style; *Rime* (1530, 1535, 1548); *Lettere* (1548). DBI.

Bernardi, Leonora (1559–1616)

Born in Lucca; noblewoman. Married Vicenzo Belatti of Garfagnana, with whom she spent some years at the Este court at Ferrara in 1580s–90s. At least one son, Pietro Paolo. Noted as musical performer. Went blind around 1611. Besides a few lyrics published in anthologies, she wrote a pastoral drama (probably the anonymous *Tragicomedia pastorale* found in Venice, Biblioteca Marciana, It. 9. 239 [6999], 1r–66r) and a lost religious narrative poem. PM.

Bragadin, Veneranda (c. 1566/67–post 1619)

Born in Venice; daughter of Venetian Giovanni Antonio Bragadin; married Ottavio Cavalli of Verona (1560–1618). Mother of poet Francesco Cavalli. Published three volumes of verse between 1613 and 1619. Cox 2012; PM.

Bronzino, Agnolo (1503–72)

Born in Florence; son of a butcher; trained as a painter with Jacopo Pontormo; worked in Urbino in 1530s before returned to Florence, where he became court painter to Cosimo de' Medici and Eleonora of Toledo. Parker 2000.

Campiglia, Maddalena (1553–95)

Born in Vicenza; noblewoman. Born illegitimately to Carlo Campiglia (d. 1571) and Polissena Verlato (d. 1572), the illegitimate daughter of a Vicentine nobleman; legitimized 1565. Married Dionisio Colzè in 1576; separated from him before 1577 and lived as a single woman after that time. Author of a *Discorso sopra l'Annonciatione* (Discourse on the Annunciation) (1585); a pastoral drama, *Flori* (1588); an eclogue, *Calisa* (1589); and a lost work, probably a tragedy, on St. Barbara. Campiglia 2004; DBI; PM.

Cappello, Laura Beatrice (c. 1540–1617)

Born to a father from Venetian patrician family of Cappello; mother from noble Brescian family of Martinengo. Brought up in Pavia by maternal aunt Lucrezia Martinengo; tutored by poet Filippo Binaschi (d. 1589). Became nun at the Augustinian convent of Santa Maria Teodote; professed 1561; prioress from 1581. PM.

Castagna, Girolama (fl. c. 1600–1607)

Nothing is known of this poet, other than her married name, Malatesta, given in the anthology containing her one surviving poem (no. 121).

Castellani, Girolama (fl. 1551)

From a Bolognese patrician family. Niece of the poet Tommaso Castellani; nun in Dominican convent of San Giovanni Battista. Verse by her was published in two anthologies of the 1550s, including encomiastic poems to the reform-minded Renata di Francia (1510–75), duchess of Ferrara, and to the Portuguese female humanist Luisa Sigea (1522–60). Graziosi 2009.

Cavaletti (or Cavalletti), Orsina (1531–92)
Born in Ferrara; daughter of an intellectual, Camillo Bertolai; married poet Ercole
Cavaletti (1553–89); their daughter Barbara was also a poet. Aquaintance of Torquato
Tasso, who portrayed Ercole and Orsina in conversation with him in his dialogue on
lyric poetry, *La Cavaletta, overo de la poesia toscana*. A selection of twenty-eight son-
nets and madrigals by her was published in *Rime 1587*. DBI (under Bertolai, Orsola);
PM.

Cervoni, Isabella (c. 1576–post 1600)
From Colle di Val d'Elsa, near Siena; later lived in Pisa. Daughter of poet Giovanni
Cervoni (fl. 1574–post 1607). Member of Accademia degli Affidati, Pavia, probably
from around 1598. Published encomiastic verse, mainly dedicated to the Medici,
between 1592 and 1600; also an oration addressed to Pope Clement VIII (1598). PM.

Colao, Lucia (fl. 1578–87)
Born in Venice; later lived in Oderzo, near Treviso. Appears to have been blind or
partially sighted. Wrote collection of religious *contrafacta* of Petrarch's sonnets,
dedicated to Francesco de' Medici and Bianca Cappello, partially published in
Bergalli 1726; working manuscript survives in Treviso, Biblioteca Comunale (MS
3215). PM.

Collalto, Silvestra (1610–74)
Born in Conegliano. Daughter of Lodovica Sbarra and Giulio Collalto; niece of
Lucchesia Sbarra. Married Giovanni Sebanelli. Poems of hers are included in Ber-
galli 1726.

Colonna, Vittoria (1490/92–1547)
Born in Marino, near Rome. Daughter of *condottiere* Fabrizio Colonna (c. 1450–1520)
and Agnese da Montefeltro, daughter of Federico da Montefeltro, duke of Urbino
(1422–82). Descended through her mother from the fifteenth-century female erudites
Battista da Montefeltro, Costanza Varano, and Battista Sforza. Married Spanish-
Neapolitan *condottiere* Ferrante Francesco d'Avalos, 1509; widowed, 1525. No chil-
dren. Resisted remarriage. Famed in later life for involvement with the Italian re-
form movement; close friend of Reginald Pole (see no. 175) and of Michelangelo.
Printed editions of her verse were published from 1538 onward, all unsanctioned: her
preference was for manuscript circulation. Colonna 2005; Brundin 2008; DBI.

Copio, Sarra (c. 1600–41)
Lived in Venice; daughter of Jewish merchant Simone Copio (d. 1606) and Ricca de'
Grassini (d. 1642). Married Jacob Sullam c. 1614; one daughter (d. 1615). Noted as a
singer. Became famous through a literary correspondence with the Genoese poet
Ansaldo Cebà (published 1623) and a polemic with Baldassare Bonifaccio (see no. 174).
Retreated from public life after a further controversy in which she was accused of
plagiarism. Copio 2009; DBI; PM.

Corsi, Girolama (fl. 1490–1509)
Tuscan in origin, Corsi seems to have lived most of her adult life in Padua, where she
probably accompanied her brother Jacopo Corsi, also a poet (d. 1493). Her married
name was Ramos, but the date of her marriage and the identity of her husband, prob-
ably Spanish in origin, are unknown. A manuscript in the Biblioteca Marciana, Ven-
ice (It. IX, 270 [6367]) contains a substantial verse collection by her, compiled by the
diarist Marin Sanudo. Rossi 1890; DBI.

d'Aragona, Tullia (c. 1510–56)

Born and raised probably in Rome or Siena. Her mother, courtesan Giulia Campana. D'Aragona claimed as her father Cardinal Luigi d'Aragona (1474–1519), of the former ruling house of Naples, although it has also been argued that she was the daughter of a servant of the Aragona, Costanzo Palmieri d'Aragona. Around 1531, d'Aragona moved with her mother to Adria, near Ferrara, her mother's birthplace, and later in the 1530s spent time in Venice and Ferrara. She moved to Siena in 1543, where she contracted a marriage of convenience; then spent 1545–48 in Florence, where she published her *Rime* and *Dialogo dell'infinità d'amore* (Dialogue on the Infinity of Love), both dedicated to the Medici. She spent her last years in Rome. A chivalric romance, *Il Meschino*, was published in Venice after her death in 1560 with an attribution to her, though critics are divided on the question of its authorship. Jones 1990, 103–17; Basile 2001; Hairston 2003.

d'Avalos, Costanza (before 1504–c. 1575)

Daughter of the Spanish-Neapolitan aristocrat Iñigo d'Avalos, Marquis of Vasto, and Laura Sanseverino; cousin of Vittoria Colonna's husband, Ferrante Francesco d'Avalos; sister of the imperial general Alfonso d'Avalos (1502–46). Married Alfonso Piccolomini, Duke of Amalfi (d. c. 1564/65); seven children. Became Clarissan nun in Naples at the end of her life. *DBI.*

della Rovere, Claudia

Daughter of Filippo Valperga, lord of Villars, in Savoy (d. 1530) and Carlotta Vagnone; married (1) Filiberto Bolleri; (2) Stefano della Rovere, lord of Vinovo, in 1534. Verse by her is found in Domenichi 1559 and Ranza 1769, 11–18.

della Valle, Lucrezia (d. 1622)

From Cosenza, Calabria; noblewoman. Daughter of Sebastiano della Valle and Giulia Quattromani; niece of *letterato* Sertorio Quattromani (1541–1603); sister of poet Fabrizio della Valle. Married Giovanni Battista Sambiasi. Author of a love *canzoniere* composed of fifty-three poems, surviving into the eighteenth century. Spiriti 1750; *PM.*

Fonte, Moderata (Modesta Pozzo) (1555–92)

Born in Venice; of *cittadino originario* class (an elite class, unique to Venice, immediately below the ruling patriciate). Daughter of lawyer Girolamo Pozzo and Marietta dal Moro; orphaned in infancy. Married *cittadino* and lawyer Filippo Zorzi (1558–98). Four children; died following birth of the fourth. Published chivalric romance *Il Floridoro* (1581); drama *Le feste* (1582); two religious narrative works on the passion and resurrection of Christ (1582 and 1592); and a dialogue *Il merito delle donne* (*The Worth of Women*, posthumously published in 1600). Fonte 1997; Fonte 2006; *PM.*

Forteguerri, Laodomia (1515–?post 1572)

Born in Siena; noblewoman. Daughter of Alessandro Forteguerri and Virginia Pecci. Married (1) Giulio Cesare Colombini (1507–42), probably c. 1531/2; three children; (2) Petruccio Petrucci (1513–92), in 1543. A will made by her second husband in August 1572 shows her still to have been alive at that time. Friend and muse of the poet and dramatist Alessandro Piccolomini, who praised her for the breadth of her intellectual interests, for example, in astronomy. She was reputed to have participated in the War of Siena in the 1550s. Six sonnets survive by her. Eisenbichler 2012b, 101–63; *DBI;* additional archival information courtesy of Philippa Jackson (private communication).

Franco, Veronica (1546–91)
Born in Venice. Daughter of Francesco Franco and Paola Fracassa. Married Paolo Panizza; separated by 1564. Courtesan. Six children, three of whom died in infancy (Rosenthal 1992, 66). Published collection of terza rima poems (1575) and collection of letters (1580); both published in a semiclandestine manner, without publisher's name or official permission. Rosenthal 1992; *DBI*; *PM*.

Gambara, Veronica (1485–1550)
Born in Pralboino, near Brescia. Daughter of *condottiere* Giovanni Francesco Gambara and Alda Pio, sister of the Emilia Pio of Castiglione's *Book of the Courtier.* Her paternal grandmother was Ginevra Nogarola, sister of the humanist Isotta. Married Giberto X da Correggio, count of Correggio, 1509; two sons, Ippolito and Girolamo; widowed 1518. Ruled Correggio as regent until her elder son Ippolito's majority, then as proxy during his absence at war. Gambara forthcoming; *DBI*.

Gonzaga, Curzio (1536–99)
Born into minor branch of ruling family of Mantua. Based in Rome, 1559–75; then retired to Mantua. Published *Rime* (1585; 1591); chivalric romance *Il Fidamante* (The Faithful Lover) (1582; 1591); comedy *Gli inganni* (Deceptions) (1592). He seems to have entrusted Maddalena Campiglia with control of his literary manuscripts in the late 1580s and 1590s; she contributed editorial material to *Il Fidamante* and the dedicatory letter to *Gli inganni. DBI.*

Grillo, Angelo [born Vincenzo] (1557–1629)
Born in Genoa, into a noble family; his mother was from another prominent noble family, the Spinola. Orphaned young; entered Benedictine order in 1572. Published love poetry in the 1580s under the pseudonym Livio Celiano; gained increasing fame from the 1590s as a religious poet; seen as a key forerunner of the Baroque style. Author of an important letter collection, published from 1612. Notable for the extent of his relations with female poets and artists (see Cox 2011, 24). Durante and Martellotti 1989; *DBI*.

Ingegneri, Angelo (c. 1550–1613)
Born in Venice. Dramatist; dramatic theorist; translator of Ovid. Worked at the Farnese court of Parma in the 1580s and in Rome in the 1590s for Cardinal Cinzio Aldobrandini (1551–1610). Associated with the drama-oriented academies of the Olimpici (Vicenza) and the Innominati (Parma). *DBI*.

Malipiero, Olimpia (after 1523–69)
Daughter of a Venetian patrician, Leonardo Malipiero, and a lady from the patrician Pisani family. Her verse indicates that she lived in Florence for some time, probably in the 1550s, but she appears to have returned to Venice, since she is recorded as having died in the family villa in 1569. Verse published in several anthologies, 1559–68. Cicogna 1824–53, 5:57–59.

Marchesi, Catella (c. 1585–after 1623)
Daughter of a wealthy, though nonnoble, couple, Antonio Marchesi and Livia Sasso. Grew up in Udine, in Friuli; educated in Latin and vernacular literature by a private tutor, the poet Giovanni Bratteolo, who published some of her verse in a collection of 1597. Married Count Giulio della Torre, c. 1600; three children. Widowed 1623. Cox 2011, 13–14; *PM*.

Marinella, Lucrezia (1571 or 1579–1653)

Daughter of medic and writer Giovanni Marinelli (d. before 1593), originally from Modena, but based in Venice; sister of medic and writer Curzio Marinelli (d. 1624). Married Girolamo Vacca (c. 1559–1629), Paduan medic, in 1607; two children, Antonio (d. 1662) and Paolina. Lucrezia seems to have lived between Padua and Venice after her marriage. Far the most prolific female author of her day. Published numerous hagiographic works in verse and prose, a pastoral romance, *Arcadia felice* (Happy Arcadia, 1605), a mythological poem, *Amore innamorato e impazzato* (Love Enamored and Driven Mad, 1618), a patriotic epic, *Enrico overo Bisantio Acquistato* (Enrico, or Byzantium Acquired, 1635), and a polemical treatise, *La nobiltà et l'eccellenza delle donne* (The Nobility and Excellence of Women, 1600). Marinella 1999; 2009; *DBI*; *PM*.

Matraini, Chiara (1515–1604)

Born in Lucca; from nonnoble, mercantile background. Daughter of Benedetto Matraini and Agata or Agnese Serantoni. Married Vincenzo Cantarini in 1530; one son. Her paternal family were involved in an insurrection in 1531, following which one of her brothers was executed; another died in prison in 1535. Widowed 1542. Rumored to have had an affair c. 1547 with the married Bartolomeo Graziani, who was murdered in obscure circumstances. Critics generally take Graziani to be the beloved of Matraini's *Rime*, relying on allusions to his violent death in some poems, although wordplay in the initial sonnet seems to suggest that her husband was the addressee at least of some of her poems. Matraini's verse was published in 1555 and 1556 (the second time in Dolce 1556); then, in a revised and probably unauthorized version, in 1595, and in an authorially sanctioned revised version in 1597. Matraini 2007; *DBI*; *PM*.

Miani, Valeria (d. after 1620)

Lived in Padua. Daughter of lawyer Vidal Miani (d. before 1615). Married Domenico Negri of Venice (d. 1612–14) in 1593; at least one daughter (d. 1618) and four other children or stepchildren. Published pastoral drama *Amorosa speranza* (Amorous Hope) in 1604 and tragedy *Celinda* in 1611, the first secular published tragedy by an Italian woman. Miani 2010; *PM*.

Molza, Tarquinia (1542–1617)

Born in Modena; granddaughter of poet Francesco Maria Molza (1489–1544). Received full humanistic education, including Greek, Hebrew, and Latin. Married Pietro Porrino (1535–79) in 1560; her studies continued after her marriage. Famous as a singer already in the years of her marriage, she moved to Ferrara in 1583, four years after her husband's death, and joined Duke Alfonso II d'Este's famous female vocal consort, the Concerto delle Donne. Left court in 1589, reputedly as a result of a scandal involving an affair with the composer Jacques de Wert, and returned to Modena. Elected to Accademia degli Innominati, Parma, by 1581; made honorary citizen of Rome in 1600. Riley 1986; *DBI*; *PM*.

Monte, Issicratea (1564–84/85)

Born in Rovigo. Daughter of lawyer *Gio*vanni Monte of Vicenza; descendent, through her mother, of humanist Celio Rodi*gino* (Lodovico Ricchieri) (1469–1525). Marriage arranged in 1582 with Giulio Mainente; fell through as a result of dowry issues. Published a series of orations (1578–81) and occasio*nal* poems in anthologies. De Vit 1883; *PM*.

Morata, Olimpia (1526–55)

Born in Ferrara. Daughter of humanist Fulvio Pellegrino Morato (1483–c. 1548). Educated in Vicenza and Ferrara. Developed reformist sympathies, partly under the influence of the duchess of Ferrara, Renata da Francia, and the reformist intellectual Celio Secondo Curione (1503–69), a contact of her father's. Married German medic Andreas Grundler 1550; left with him for Germany. Most of her works were lost when the couple had to flee Schweinfurt, Grundler's birthplace, in 1554. Curione posthumously edited a volume of her remaining Latin and Greek works, including letters, dialogues, and verse. Morata 2003; *DBI*.

Morra, Isabella (c. 1516–45/46)

Daughter of Giovanni Michele da Morra, lord of Favale (in exile in France from 1528), and Luisa Brancaccio. Murdered by her brothers, apparently on suspicion of a relationship with a local Spanish nobleman and poet, Diego Sandoval de Castro, whom Morra's brothers also killed. Political antagonisms may have underpinned the murder. Morra's surviving verse, seemingly unearthed during investigations following her murder, was published in anthologies from 1552. Schiesari 1994.

Muzio, Girolamo (1496–1576)

Born in Padua, but identified with his paternal homeland of Capodistria. Led peripatetic life as courtier and writer, working at Ferrara, Pesaro, and Urbino. Published prolifically in his later career including works on poetic theory and religious polemic, and a popular work on the etiquette of the duel (1550).

Nogarola, Isotta (1418–66)

Born in Verona; noblewoman. Daughter of Leonardo Nogarola and Bianca Borromeo; niece of poet Angela Nogarola (d. 1436). Became famous as a Latinist, along with her sister Ginevra. Wrote an important letter collection, also several orations and an epistolary dialogue, *On Whether Adam or Eve's Sin Was the Greater*. Remained single by choice without entering a convent, an exceptional choice for the period. Nogarola 2004.

Petrucci, Aurelia (1511–42)

Born in Siena. Daughter of Borghese Petrucci (1490–1526), ruler of Siena from 1512, and Vittoria Todeschini Piccolomini, great-niece of the humanist pope Pius II. Borghese Petrucci was overthrown in a coup in 1516 and exiled. Aurelia was raised under the protection of her uncles Giovanni and Alessandro Todeschini Piccolomini. Married (1) Giovanfrancesco di Iacopo Petrucci, a second cousin, exiled after the expulsion of Aurelia's uncle and his cousin, Fabio Petrucci, in 1523; (2) Camillo Venturi (probably c. 1531). Two children from each marriage. Aurelia was the dedicatee of various literary works, including the first edition of Leone Ebreo's *Dialoghi d'amore* (1535). The writer Alessandro Piccolomini commemorated her death with a funeral oration that constructs her as a heroic feminine ideal. Eisenbichler 2012b, 59–99; additional archival information courtesy of Philippa Jackson (private communication).

Piccolomini, Agnese (fl. 1596)

Presumably from a branch of the famous Sienese patrician family. Probable author of two sonnets published under the initials A.P. in *Poesie* 1596. *PM*.

Pii, Livia (fl. 1559; d. before 1588)
Bolognese noblewoman, married to a soldier in the service of the Venetian republic, Alessandro Poeti. Fantuzzi 1781–94, 7:41.

Poggi, Semidea (died after 1637)
Bolognese noblewoman; daughter of Cristoforo Poggi and Lodovica Pepoli. Became a Lateran Canoness: entered convent of San Lorenzo, late 1570s or early 1580s. Some of her verse hints intriguingly at periods of depression or spiritual crisis. Published volume of verse, *La Calliope religiosa* (The Religious Calliope) in 1623; a second collection *Desideri di Parnaso* (Yearnings for Parnassus) is also recorded. *PM.*

Salutati, Barbara (fl. 1520s)
Probably born in Florence. Her natal surname was Raffacani; Salutati presumably was the name of a husband. Musical virtuosa and probably a courtesan, mainly known through her amorous and artistic association with Niccolò Machiavelli in the 1520s and, especially, her collaboration with the French composer Philippe Verdelot on the music for a performance of Machiavelli's comedy *Clizia* in 1525. Giorgio Vasari mentions a portrait of her by Domenico Puligo (1492–1527), which has recently been identified in a private collection. Rogers 2000.

Salvetti, Maddalena (1557–1610)
Born in Florence. Daughter of patrician Salvetto Salvetti. Married patrician Zanobi Accaiuoli (1548–1613) in 1572; at least one son, Mario (1583–1651). Published *Rime toscane*, 1590. Her husband published her unfinished works posthumously (the beginnings of an epic and a volume of spiritual verse). Cox 2011, 85–86, 157–63.

Salvi, Virginia (c. 1510–13–post 1571)
Sienese; daughter of a lawyer, Giovanni Battista Casolani. She is sometimes referred to as Virginia Martini; her full natal name is Virginia Martini Casolani. Married Matteo Salvi, c. 1535; at least one daughter, Beatrice Salvi, also a poet. Salvi attained fame as a poet in the 1540s and was briefly in trouble with the law, for political reasons, in the same decade. Pro-French in her sympathies, she fled to Rome after Siena's accession by the pro-imperial Medicean duchy of Tuscany in 1555. Salvi remained in Rome for the remainder of her life but was elected to the Sienese Accademia dei Travagliati in 1560. She was widely published in anthologies; Domenichi 1559 has forty-five poems by her, far more than any other poet. Eisenbichler 2012b, 165–14; *DBI* (under "Martini, Virginia").

Sanseverino, Dianora [Leonora] (c. 1522/24–d. 1581)
Naples. Daughter of Pietro Antonio Sanseverino (d. 1559), prince of Bisignano, and Giulia Orsini (d. before 1539), granddaughter of Pope Julius II through his daughter Felice della Rovere. Married Fernando de Mendoza y Alarcon, marquis of Valle Siciliana, in 1543. Friend and patron of Laura Terracina. Very little survives by her.

Sbarra, Lucchesia (1576–?1662)
Born into local nobility of Conegliano, north of Venice. Daughter of Pietro Sbarra and Tranquilla da Colle; sister of academician and literary patron Pulzio Sbarra. Married (1) Monfiorito Coderta (d. pre-1607); (2) Giovanni Battista Rota, after 1615; at least one child from her first marriage, Giovanni Battista Coderta (d. pre-1607). Published *Rime* (1610); also possible previous volume of *Rime* and ottava rima poem, both lost. Cox 2011, 78–80; *PM.*

Scarampa, Camilla (1476–1520)

Born in Asti (Piedmont) to a Milanese aristocratic family. At court of Lodovico Sforza in Milan from 1491, in the entourage of Duchess Beatrice d'Este (d. 1497). Married c. 1502–3 to Ambrogio Guidobono, lord of Momperone and Brignano, near Tortona; four children. The first nationally famed female lyric poet in Italy, praised by Matteo Bandello, along with Cecilia Gallerani, as a "great light of the Italian tongue." Subject of Luca Valenziano's epyllion *Il Camilcleo* (1513). Leone 1962; Rozzo 1982.

Soderini, Fiammetta

From a prominent Florentine patrician family. Married Alessandro Soderini (d. 1573). Celebrated as a poet in her lifetime and said to have translated a comedy by Terence, although very little survives by her. Appears as a speaker in Silvano Razzi's *Dell'economia cristiana e civile* (1568).

Spinola, Livia (fl. 1587–91)

Born in Genoa, into the noble Spinola family. Married another Spinola, Alessandro, solider and poet. Cousin by marriage of the poet Angelo Grillo, with whom she corresponded. A handful of sonnets by her survive, mainly in anthologies. *PM*.

Spolverini, Ersilia (1571–97)

Born in Verona. Daughter of silk merchant Giovanni Girolamo Sebastiani and Lavinia Verità, illegitimate daughter of Count Michele Verità, from one of the leading families of the city. Married Licurgo Spolverini, nobleman and lawyer; at least one child, Adria, b. 1591. Her only extant works are the group of poems and the oration published in 1596 for Chiara Dolfin Cornaro (see no. 154). Smith 2009; *PM*.

Stampa, Gaspara (c. 1525–54)

Born in Padua, a jeweller's daughter. Following her father's death, Stampa's mother moved with her family to Venice, where Gaspara's brother, Baldassare (d. 1544), a poet, introduced her to literary and musical circles. Both she and her sister Cassandra were noted singers, performing at elite social gatherings. Stampa's verse, which she probably performed to music, as well as circulating it in manuscript, mainly celebrates her love for the nobleman, soldier, and literary patron Collaltino da Collalto (1523–69). It was published after her premature death by her sister. Stampa 2010.

Strozzi, Lorenza [born Francesca] (1514–91)

From Florentine patrician family. Sister of humanist and Greek scholar Ciriaco Strozzi (1504–65). Nun in Dominican convent of St. Niccolò, Prato. Published collection of Latin hymns, 1588. Stevenson 2002.

Terracina, Laura (1519–?77)

Born in Naples or nearby Piaggia di Chiaia; a noblewoman, though not of the leading nobility of the city. Terracina seems to have lived in reduced circumstances and to have written partly for financial reasons. Member of Accademia degli Incogniti, 1545–47, one of the earliest women to be admitted to a literary academy. Married relatively late, to a relative, Polidoro Terracina. Spent 1570–72 in Rome, writing verse to cardinals gathered for the conclave that elected Gregory XIII. Published eight books of verse, the last of which remained unpublished at her death, including an extremely popular volume of reworkings of the initial stanzas of each canto of Ariosto's *Orlando Furioso*. Shemek 1998, 126–57; Milligan 2010.

Tornabuoni, Lucrezia (1425–82)

Born in Florence. Daughter of patricians Francesco Tornabuoni and Nanna Guicciardini. In 1444 married Piero di Cosimo de' Medici (1416–69), effective ruler of Florence after his father's death in 1464; widowed in 1469. Four children, including Lorenzo de' Medici (1449–92), poet and ruler of Florence, and Giuliano de' Medici (1453–78), murdered in the Pazzi conspiracy. Wrote ottava rima sacred narratives on Esther, Susanna, Tobias, Judith, and John the Baptist, as well as religious verse (*laude*). Tornabuoni 2001.

Turina, Francesca (1553–1641)

Born in Città di Castello; noblewoman. Daughter of soldier Giovanni Turrini (d. 1554) and Camilla di Carpegna; orphaned as a child and brought up by Count Pietro di Carpegna (1514–86). Married Giulio Bufalini (1504–83) in c. 1573; three children, Giulio (1576–1642), Camilla (b. 1579), and Ottavio (1582–1623). Lived for a while after her widowhood with the Colonna family of Paliano; her *Rime* of 1628 is dedicated to Anna Colonna, who married into the papal Barberini family. Published *Rime spirituali* 1595 (a religious narrative verse sequence, dedicated to Pope Clement VIII) and *Rime* 1628 (the volume containing her autobiographical verse). Many works by her, including lyric verse and an ottava rima romance, *Il Florio*, based on Boccaccio's *Filocolo*, remain in manuscript in her marital home of San Giustino, near Sansepolcro. Turina 2009; *PM*.

Vernazza, Battista [born Tommasina] (1497–1587)

Born in Genoa. Daughter of patrician Ettore Vernazza (d. 1524), founder of the Oratory of Divine Love, a religious movement, and Bartolomea Rizzo. Goddaughter of St. Catherine of Genoa (Caterina Fieschi Adorno, 1447–1510). Spent her life as Lateran Canoness in convent of Santa Maria delle Grazie. Her collected *Opere*, four volumes of devotional and mystical writings, including numerous poems in terza rima, appeared posthumously, in 1588 and 1602. A slim collection of sonnets was published in the nineteenth century. Parisotto 2009; *PM*.

Appendix A POEMS BY AUTHOR

Poets are listed here in chronological order (by date of birth, where known; otherwise by date of activity). The poems are listed under each author's name in the order they occur in the anthology. This list is intended to be complementary to the index, which allows for alphabetically ordered searches by author's name if preferred.

Amedea degli Aleardi
1 / *Deh, non esser Iason, s'io son Medea*

Isotta Nogarola
192 / *salvete, o Cyani fontes dulcesque recessus*

Lucrezia Tornabuoni
73 / *Echo el Re forte*

Girolama Corsi
2 / *Io me ne vo, non già del tutto esciolta*
156 / *Nel bel paese mio toscho gentile*
208 / *Io son fatta villanela*

Camilla Scarampa
3 / *Chiaro conosco vostra fiera voglia*
157 / *Misera Italia, il ciel pur te minaccia*
166 / *Biasimi pur chi vuol la mia durezza*
167 / *Amor, tu vien ver me sì pien d'orgoglio*

Veronica Gambara
4 / *Quando sarà ch'io mora*
5 / *Occhi lucenti e belli*
6 / *Ombroso colle, amene e verdi piante*
40 / *Quel nodo in cui la mia beata sorte*
85 / *O gran misterio e sol per fede inteso!*
86 / *Oggi per mezzo tuo, Vergine pura*
132 / *A l'ardente desio ch'ognior m'accende*
134 / *O de la nostra etade unica gloria*
158 / *Vinca gli sdegni e l'odio vostro antico*
159 / *Mira, Signor, la stanca navicella*
193 / *Con quel caldo desio che nascer suole*
194 / *Tu che mostrasti al rozzo mondo prima*

Vittoria Colonna

7 / *Eccelso mio Signor, questa ti scrivo*
41 / *Scrivo sol per sfogar l'interna doglia*
42 / *A le vittorie tue, mio lume eterno*
43 / *Quand'io dal caro scoglio miro intorno*
44 / *Questo sol ch'oggi agli occhi nostri splende*
45 / *Nodriva il cor d'una speranza viva*
46 / *Qual tigre dietro a chi le invola e toglie*
47 / *Tralucer dentro al mortal vel cosparte*
48 / *Mentre la nave mia, longe dal porto*
49 / *Sogno felice e man santa che sciolse*
50 / *Occhi, piangeno tanto*
74 / *Poi che 'l mio casto amor gran tempo tenne*
75 / *Spiego ver voi, Signor, indarno l'ale*
76 / *Se 'l breve suon che sol quest'aer frale*
77 / *Vorrei l'orecchia aver qui chiusa e sorda*
78 / *Qual digiuno augellin, che vede ed ode*
79 / *Vorrei che 'l vero Sol, cui sempre invoco*
80 / *In forma di musaico un alto muro*
81 / *Se per serbar la notte il vivo ardore*
82 / *Eterna luna, alor che fra 'l Sol vero*
83 / *Vergine pura, che dai raggi ardenti*
84 / *Donna accesa animosa, e da l'errante*
130 / *Ahi quanto fu al mio Sol contrario il fato*
135 / *Di novo il cielo de l'antica gloria*
160 / *Prego il Padre divin che tanta fiamma*
175 / *Figlio e signor, se la tua prima e vera*

Battista Vernazza

101 / *È questo il dì cui nel bell'orto nacque*

Costanza d'Avalos

89 / *Se 'l vero Sol coverto d'uman velo*

Barbara Salutati

8 / *Ardeva il petto mio, ardeva l'alma*

Dianora Sanseverino

60 / *La bella Bradamante che sé stessa*

Tullia d'Aragona

9 / *Qual vaga Filomela che fuggita*
10 / *Se forse per pietà del mio languire*
136 / *Fiamma gentil che da gl'interni lumi*
146 / *Se gli antichi pastor di rose e fiori*
168 / *Bernardo, ben potea bastarvi averne*
169 / *Poiché mi die' natura a voi simile*

Aurelia Petrucci

161 / *Dove sta il tuo valor, patria mia cara*

198 / *Quando nell'ocean l'altera fronte*
199 / *Pria che la chioma che mi die' natura*

Olimpia Morata

170 / οὔποτε μὲν ξυμπᾶσιν ἐνὶ φρεσὶν ἥνδανε ταὐτὸ

Gaspara Stampa

13 / *Voi ch'ascoltate in queste meste rime*
14 / *Chi vuol conoscer, donne, il mio signore*
15 / *Se così come sono abietta e vile*
16 / *Altri mai foco, stral, prigione o nodo*
17 / *Dura è la stella mia, maggior durezza*
18 / *Piangete, donne, e poiché la mia morte*
19 / *Novo e raro miracol di Natura*
20 / *A che, Conte, assalir chi non repugna?*
21 / *Con quai degne accoglienze o quai parole*
22 / *O notte, a me più chiara e più beata*
23 / *Signor, io so che 'n me non son più viva*
24 / *Or sopra il forte e veloce destriero*
25 / *Amor m'ha fatto tal ch'io vivo in foco*
26 / *A mezo il mare ch'io varcai tre anni*
27 / *Dimmi per la tua face*
28 / *Il cor verrebbe teco*
88 / *Mesta e pentita de' miei gravi errori*

Livia Pii

181 / *Alma beata, che già al mondo involta*

Olimpia Malipiero

91 / *Oggi 'l celeste pelicano il petto*
176 / *Privo di stelle 'l cielo e del mar l'onde*

"Gentildonna palermitana"

189 / *Scemo di Laura il capo, al empio caso*

Fiammetta Soderini

62 / *Febo nell'ocëan tuffato avendo*

Vincenza Armani

61 / *Notte felice e lieta*

Laura Beatrice Cappello

177 / *Questo ramo d'alloro*
178 / *Questo crin, ch'io disposi*

Tarquinia Molza

112 / *Felsina clara virum ingeniis, et clarior almae*

Veronica Franco

34 / *Non più parole: ai fatti, in campo, a l'armi*
35 / *Quel che ascoso nel cor tenni gran tempo*

Semidea Poggi
124 / *Qual sole, o pellegrin, da l'orïente*
125 / *Da le vene del Cielo*

Livia Spinola
54 / *Qual vite che dell'orno è sciolta unquanco*
110 / *Chi del barbaro fin l'acerba sorte*

Agnese Piccolomini
183 / *Già non si deve a te doglia né pianto*

Leonora Bernardi
111 / *Se pur fin su negli stellanti chiostri*
141 / *Se le mie preci ed umili e devote*

Isabella Andreini
65 / *S'alcun fia mai che i versi miei negletti*
66 / *Sdegno, campione audace*
67 / *Qualor, candida e vaga*
68 / *Tu m'uccidesti e già son fatta polve*
69 / *Deh girate*
70 / *Movea dolce un zefiretto*
145 / *Un bel sembiante in abito negletto*

Issicratea Monte
209 / *Magagnò, el versurare è 'na nöela*

Veneranda Bragadin
173 / *Se i bassi merti tuoi forse ti fero*
186 / *So ch'in ciel vivi, o mia diletta e cara*

Ersilia Spolverini
154 / *Naïadum vos pulchra manus, vos humida aquarum*

Lucchesia Sbarra
71 / *Fattosi in Tiro toro il gran tonante*
72 / *A che, bella e crudel, tender le reti*
179 / *In molte cose il ciel mi fu cortese*
184 / *Prestami i draghi, o Dea, prestami i pini*
185 / *Anch'io, folle, pensai di secco salce*
200 / *Vent'anni vissi in libertade e in pace*
201 / *O quante volte i limpidi ruscelli*

Valeria Miani
122 / *Carca di quel languir di cui maggiore*

Isabella Cervoni
155 / *Donna real, che, dentro a nobil velo*
165 / *Divino Atlante, a cui commesso ha 'l pondo*

Lucrezia Marinella
113 / *Tremò la terra e 'l mar, pianse lo 'nferno*
114 / *Di glorie oggi, di gemme e di splendori*
115 / *Ardi in giel d'onestade, ardi d'amore*

Appendix B POEMS BY METER

ballata

barzelletta

canzone

capitolo

elegaic distichs

hexameters

madrigal

ottava rima. See *stanze*

sapphics

scherzo

sesta rima

sestina

sonetto caudatio

sonetto continuo

sonetto ritornellato

sonnet

31 / *Alti son questi monti ed alti sono*
16 / *Altri mai foco, stral, prigione o nodo*
26 / *A mezo il mare ch'io varcai tre anni*
25 / *Amor m'ha fatto tal ch'io vivo in foco*
167 / *Amor, tu vien ver me sì pien d'orgoglio*
185 / *Anch'io, folle, pensai di secco salce*
115 / *Ardi in giel d'onestade, ardi d'amore*
168 / *Bernardo, ben potea bastarvi averne*
166 / *Biasimi pur chi vuol la mia durezza*
210 / *Cenzo, le nuove Tose de Sgnicona*
3 / *Chiaro conosco vostra fiera voglia*
110 / *Chi del barbaro fin l'acerba sorte*
128 / *Chi non saria, Gesù, preso e conquiso*
14 / *Chi vuol conoscer, donne, il mio signore*
94 / *Come padre pietoso, che l'amato*
207 / *Con il dito alle labbra a me rivolto*
174 / *Con la tua scorta, ecco, Signor, m'accingo*
21 / *Con quai degne accoglienze o quai parole*
142 / *Curzio, impiumando al mio pensier sovente*
202 / *Di dominio, di aver, d'opre, di onore*
114 / *Di glorie oggi, di gemme e di splendori*
59 / *Diletto mio, che 'l sol mi rassomigli*
135 / *Di novo il cielo de l'antica gloria*
84 / *Donna accesa animosa, e da l'errante*
161 / *Dove sta il tuo valor, patria mia cara*
17 / *Dura è la stella mia, maggior durezza*
196 / *Ecco ch'un'altra volta, o valle inferna*
106 / *Ecco la Maddalena ai piedi santi*
101 / *È questo il dì cui nel bell'orto nacque*
82 / *Eterna luna, alor che fra 'l Sol vero*
71 / *Fattosi in Tiro toro il gran tonante*
148 / *Felicissima donna, a cui s'inchina*
30 / *Fera son io di quest'ombroso loco*
136 / *Fiamma gentil che da gl'interni lumi*
175 / *Figlio e signor, se la tua prima e vera*
149 / *Folta, frondosa e verdeggiante selva*
116 / *Fra 'l candor di ligustri ardente rosa*
183 / *Già non si deve a te doglia né pianto*
190 / *Hai pur disciolto, o dispietata Morte*
80 / *In forma di musaico un alto muro*
179 / *In molte cose il ciel mi fu cortese*
99 / *Io amo sì di quel lume l'assalto* (contrafactum)
2 / *Io me ne vo, non già del tutto esciolta*
129 / *Io non già da vil fango ebbi i natali*
188 / *Lassa, nel tuo partire, ahi lassa, in quante*
171 / *Libero cor nel mio petto soggiorna*
38 / *Mentre del Tebro i liquefatti argenti*

163 / *Qui dove noi viviam franchi e securi*

65 / *S'alcun fia mai che i versi miei negletti*

189 / *Scemo di Laura il capo, al empio caso*

41 / *Scrivo sol per sfogar l'interna doglia*

15 / *Se così come sono abietta e vile*

10 / *Se forse per pietà del mio languire*

146 / *Se gli antichi pastor di rose e fiori*

173 / *Se i bassi merti tuoi forse ti fero*

76 / *Se 'l breve suon che sol quest'aer frale*

141 / *Se le mie preci ed umili e devote*

89 / *Se 'l vero Sol coverto d'uman velo*

151 / *Se nel bel colle Ideo vostra bellezza*

36 / *Se penato hai fuor del paterno tetto*

81 / *Se per serbar la notte il vivo ardore*

12 / *Se quel ch'amo di voi non è mortale*

92 / *Servo fedel, che in alta croce affisso*

139 / *Sì come al fonte ebb'io larghe e seconde*

23 / *Signor, io so che 'n me non son più viva*

105 / *Signor, se per amor, per pianger molto*

191 / *S'io 'l feci mai, ch'io venga in odio al cielo*

186 / *So ch'in ciel vivi, o mia diletta e cara*

49 / *Sogno felice e man santa che sciolse*

100 / *Solo sperando, i suoi fecondi campi* (contrafactum)

152 / *Son questi que' crin d'oro al mondo soli*

108 / *Speme del sommo ben, che 'l dolce e chiaro*

75 / *Spiego ver voi, Signor, indarno l'ale*

57 / *Spinta talor d'ardente alto desio*

206 / *Stanza, dove le luci apersi al pianto*

204 / *Talor per dare al mio dolor soccorso*

195 / *Torbido Siri, del mio mal superbo*

47 / *Tralucer dentro al mortal vel cosparte*

113 / *Tremò la terra e 'l mar, pianse lo 'nferno*

194 / *Tu che mostrasti al rozzo mondo prima*

117 / *Tu che 'n vil specchio già di vetro privo*

145 / *Un bel sembiante in abito negletto*

37 / *Vago augellin, che per quei rami ombrosi*

200 / *Vent'anni vissi in libertade e in pace*

93 / *Verace Apollo, a cui ben vero amore*

83 / *Vergine pura, che dai raggi ardenti*

158 / *Vinca gli sdegni e l'odio vostro antico*

180 / *Viscere del mio sen, cara pupilla*

187 / *Viscere del mio sen, figlio diletto*

32 / *Viva mia bella e dolce calamita*

51 / *Vivo mio foco, ond'io solea aver vita*

13 / *Voi ch'ascoltate in queste meste rime*

79 / *Vorrei che 'l vero Sol, cui sempre invoco*

77 / *Vorrei l'orecchia aver qui chiusa e sorda*

stanze

    193 / *Con quel caldo desio che nascer suole*

    62 / *Febo nell'ocean tuffato avendo*

    60 / *La bella Bradamante che sé stessa* (tramutazione)

    162 / *Valoroso Signor, nella cui mente*

terza rima. See *capitolo*

Appendix C   METRICAL ANALYSIS

This anthology contains 151 sonnets in total, excluding poems with more than fourteen lines (the two *sonetti caudati* and the *sonetto ritornellato*). If we further exclude six poems where the poet's choice of rhyme scheme was constrained (three risposta poems using the same rhyme scheme as the *proposta* and Lucia Colao's three metrically faithful reworkings of Petrarchan sonnets), we are left with a sample of 145. The number is sufficient to permit a reasonably well grounded statistical analysis of female poets' metrical choices in this most common of Italian poetic forms.

The first percentage in parentheses following each scheme relates to the frequency of occurrence of the scheme within the 317 sonnets of Petrarch's *RVF*. The second percentage relates to the frequency of occurrence of the scheme on the Web site ALI RASTA (*Antologie della lirica italiana, raccolte a stampa*, http://rasta.unipv.it/), consulted on March 16, 2012. This database collates material from nineteen lyric anthologies published in Italy between 1545 and 1586 and contains 6,145 sonnets in total. The number and percentage after each scheme relate to the number of occurrences of that scheme among the 145 qualifying sonnets in this anthology. All percentages have been rounded to two decimal points.

Two-Rhyme Schemes
ABAB ABAB ABA BAB: 1 (0.69%) (RVF 0, 0.00%; AL 1, 0.02%)

Four-Rhyme Schemes (divided by quatrain scheme)
ABAB ABAB CDC DCD: 1 (0.69%) (RVF 3, 0.95%; AL 24, 0.39%)
ABAB BAAB CDC DCD: 1 (0.69%) (RVF 1, 0.31%; AL 1, 0.02%)
ABAB BABA CDB DCB: 1 (0.69%) (RVF 0, 0.00%; AL 0, 0.00%)
ABAB BABA CDC DCD: 3 (2.07%) (RVF 1, 0.31%; AL 13, 0.21%)
ABBA ABBA CDC CDC: 3 (2.07%) (RVF 7, 2.21%; AL 62, 1.00%)
ABBA ABBA CDC DCD: 43 (29.66%) (RVF 109, 34.38%; AL 1,657, 26.97%)

Five-Rhyme Schemes (divided by quatrain scheme)
ABAB ABAB CDE DEC: 1 (0.69%) (RVF 1, 0.31%; AL 10, 0.16%)
ABAB BAAB CDE CDE: 1 (0.69%) (RVF 1, 0.31%; AL 6, 0.10%)
ABAB BABA CDE EDC: 1 (0.69%) (RVF 0, 0.00%; AL 2, 0.03%)
ABBA ABBA CDC EDE: 2 (1.38%) (RVF 0, 0.00%; AL 83, 1.35%)
ABBA ABBA CDE CDE: 47 (32.41%) (RVF 116, 36.60%; AL 2,064, 33.58%)
ABBA ABBA CDE CED: 12 (8.28%) (RVF 0, 0.00%; AL 427, 6.90%)

ABBA ABBA CDE DCE: 14 (9.66%) (RVF 65, 20.50%; AL 689, 11.21%)
ABBA ABBA CDE DEC: 4 (2.76%) (RVF 1, 0.31%; AL 356, 5.79%)
ABBA ABBA CDE ECD: 3 (2.07%) (RVF 0, 0.00%; AL 203, 3.30%)
ABBA ABBA CDE EDC: 7 (4.83%) (RVF 1, 0.31%; AL 320, 5.20%)

The correlation between the percentages yielded by the ALI RASTA database and
the anthology is strong. In the ALI RASTA database, approximately 63% of sonnets
employ the two most frequent tercet schemes, CDC DCD and CDE CDE, with a
further 32% using the schemes CDE CED, CDE DCE, CDE DEC, CDE ECD and CDE
EDC (always with the standard octave scheme ABBA ABBA). In this anthology, around
62% of sonnets use the two most popular schemes, and around 27% employ the other
five schemes listed above. There is a higher incidence of rarer metrical schemes in the
anthology sample (the seven recognized schemes in the anthology that use an octave
scheme different from ABBA ABBA together make up around 6% of the sample,
compared to the ALI RASTA sample, where the same seven schemes make up around
1%).[1] This is probably due to the fact that the anthology sample contains more
late-sixteenth-century material, dating from a time when metrical experimentation
had become more common (eighteen of the nineteen anthologies sampled for the
ALIRASTA database were published in or before 1560).

The increased tendency toward metrical experimentation in the later sixteenth
century is illustrated very clearly if we look at a breakdown of metrical schemes by
author, with the authors placed in the approximate chronological order developed
for Appendix A. The metrical schemes each author uses are listed after her name in
descending order of frequency of use. Rarer metrical schemes (those with fewer than
100 occurrences in the ALI RASTA sample) are highlighted for ease of identification.

Corsi (1): ABBA ABBA CDC DCD (×1)
Scarampa (4): ABBA ABBA CDC DCD (×3); ABBA ABBA CDE DCE (×1)
Gambara (9): ABBA ABBA CDE CDE (×7); ABBA ABBA CDC DCD (×1); ABBA
ABBA CDE CED (×1)
Colonna (22): ABBA ABBA CDE CDE (×9); ABBA ABBA CDE DCE (×5); ABBA
ABBA CDE CED (×3); ABBA ABBA CDC DCD (×2); ABBA ABBA CDE DEC (×2);
ABBA ABBA CDC CDC (×1)
Vernazza (1): ABBA ABBA CDC DCD (×1)
d'Avalos (1): ABBA ABBA CDC DCD (×1)
d'Aragona (6): ABBA ABBA CDE CDE (×3); ABBA ABBA CDC DCD (×2); ABBA
ABBA CDE DCE (×1)
Petrucci (1): ABBA ABBA CDE CDE (×1)
Salvi (3): ABBA ABBA CDC DCD (×1); ABBA ABBA CDE CDE (×1); ABBA ABBA
CDE EDC (×1)
Matraini (9): ABBA ABBA CDE CDE (×7); ABBA ABBA CDC DCD (×1); ABBA
ABBA CDE CED (×1)
Forteguerri (1): ABBA ABBA CDC DCD (×1)
Morra (2): ABBA ABBA CDC DCD (×2)

---

[1] I have omitted the anomalous scheme of no. 187 (ABAB BABA CDB DCB) from this calculation. I
should like to thank Anna Wainwright and Veronica Andreani for their help in coordinating the
metrical calculations given here.

Castellani (1): ABBA ABBA CDE EDC (×1)

Della Rovere (1): ABBA ABBA CDE CED (×1)

Battiferri (11): ABBA ABBA CDE CED (×5); ABBA ABBA CDE DCE (×2); **ABAB ABAB ABA BAB** (×1); ABBA ABBA CDC DCD (×1); ABBA ABBA CDE CDE (×1); ABBA ABBA CDE DEC (×1)

Stampa (15): ABBA ABBA CDC DCD (×14); ABBA ABBA CDE CDE (×1)

Pii (1): ABBA ABBA CDE EDC (×1)

Malipiero (2): ABBA ABBA CDE CDE (×1); ABBA ABBA CDE ECD (×1)

"Gentildonna" (1): ABBA ABBA CDE EDC (×1)

Cavaletti (1): ABBA ABBA CDE ECD (×1)

Campiglia (4): **ABAB ABAB CDE DEC** (×1); **ABAB BABA CDE EDC** (×1); ABBA ABBA CDC DCD (×1); ABBA ABBA CDE EDC (×1)

Turina (18): ABBA ABBA CDC DCD (×8); ABBA ABBA CDE CDE (×4); **ABAB BABA CDC DCD** (×3); **ABBA ABBA CDC CDC** (×2); **ABAB BABA CDB CDB** (×1)

Fonte (2): ABBA ABBA CDC DCD (×1); ABBA ABBA CDE DCE (×1)

Salvetti (4): **ABAB BAAB CDC DCD** (×1); **ABAB BAAB CDE CDE** (×1); ABBA ABBA CDE DEC (×1); **ABBA ABBA CDC EDE** (×1)

Poggi (1): ABBA ABBA CDE CDE (×1)

Spinola (2): ABBA ABBA CDE CDE (×1); ABBA ABBA CDE DCE (×1)

Piccolomini (1): ABBA ABBA CDC DCD (×1)

Andreini (2): ABBA ABBA CDE CDE (×1); ABBA ABBA CDE DCE (×1)

Bragadin (2): ABBA ABBA CDE EDC (×2)

Sbarra (7): **ABAB ABAB CDC DCD** (×1); ABBA ABBA CDE CDE (×3); ABBA ABBA CDC DCD (×1); ABBA ABBA CDE DCE (×2)

Marinella (5): ABBA ABBA CDE CDE (×5)

Marchesi (1): **ABBA ABBA CDC EDE** (×1)

della Valle (1): ABBA ABBA CDE CDE (×1)

Copio (1): ABBA ABBA CDE ECD (×1)

Collalto (1): ABBA ABBA CDE CED (×1)

Of the fifteen instances of rarer rhyme schemes in the collection, fourteen were composed after 1560. The sole instance of a two-rhyme scheme (Laura Battiferri's *sonetto continuo*, no. 97) dates from this period, as do all nine of the other sonnets in this anthology with quatrain rhyme schemes other than ABBA ABBA. This fully bears out the point made in the introduction concerning the relative metrical freedom of later-sixteenth-century lyric. Of the 143 sonnets in this collection that can be dated with reasonable certainty, only one out of eighty written before 1560 (1.25%) departs from the seven most common Petrarchist metrical schemes. Of the sixty-three poems written after 1560, fourteen are written using less common meters (around 22%).

Two of the poets who feature most saliently in this anthology, Gaspara Stampa and Francesca Turina, are among the most metrically divergent. Stampa's sonnets are noteworthy on account of their relative metrical monotony. The fifteen sonnets of Stampa's featured in this anthology do not venture beyond the two most common Petrarchan schemes, ABBA ABBA CDC DCD and ABBA ABBA CDE CDE. The first is hugely dominant, appearing in fourteen of the fifteen. Overall, of the 280 sonnets in Stampa's 1554 *Rime*, 273 adhere to these two schemes (around 98%), with 251 sonnets (around 90%) following the CDC DCD tercet scheme. This differentiates Stampa quite sharply from contemporaries such as Colonna, Battiferri, d'Aragona, and Matraini, who strove for greater metrical variety in their verse, following Petrarch's example. In Colonna, for example, while the CDE CDE tercet scheme is dominant, occurring in around 35% of her sonnets, four other schemes break the 10% mark (CDC DCD, CDE DEC, CDE DCE, and the non-Petrarchan CDE CED).[2]

Francesca Turina shares with Stampa a marked preference for the ABBA ABBA CDC DCD scheme, which dominates her 1628 *Rime* (196 of the 261 sonnets in total, amounting to 75% of the whole). What distinguishes Turina's practice from Stampa's, as well as from that of Petrarchist poets generally, however, is her liking for alternating rhyme schemes in the quatrains of the sonnet. The third most frequent rhyme scheme deployed in the *Rime*, with 14 sonnets (5.36% of the total), is ABAB BABA CDC DCD, which occurs only once in Petrarch (sonnet 279) and thirteen times on the ALI RASTA database, among 6,145 sonnets (0.21%).[3] Turina first began to employ alternating rhyme schemes of this kind in her *Rime spirituali sopra il santissimo rosario* of 1595, where, unusually, she deploys the sonnet sequence as a vehicle for sacred narrative, and it may be that we should see her preference for alternating metrical schemes in her sonnets as reflecting the unusually high narrative content of her verse.[4] In the 1628 *Rime*, nine of the fifteen occurrences of the ABAB BABA CDC DCD rhyme scheme are found in the long autobiographical sequence that lies at the core of the work (nos. 108–221 in the modern edition, Turina 2010), while one of the remaining six (no. 69) falls in an autobiographical interlude in the opening, mainly encomiastic, sequence.

A final metrical eccentricity in Turina is her willingness, on one occasion at least (no. 180), to break the rules of sonnet construction entirely, experimenting with a scheme that has a rhyme migrate from octave to sestet, ABAB BABA CDB CDB. While this may be due to an oversight, it is also possible that we should see it as intentional, considering Turina's generally unorthodox attitude to meter.

---

[2] For details of the basis of this analysis, see n. 78 to the introduction. The dominance of five-rhyme schemes in Colonna is striking, by contrast with Stampa: between them, the tercet schemes CDE CDE, CDE DCE, CDE DEC, and CDE CED make up around 80% of her output. A comparative analysis of the metrical practices of the principal Petrarchist poets (including Colonna and Stampa) may be found in Afribo 2001, 146–50.

[3] The sonnets are the following (numbering from 2010 edition): 40, 45, 52, 69, 109, 117, 124, 131, 134, 144, 193, 197, 203, 230. Another sonnet (153) takes the fully alternating scheme ABAB ABAB CDC DCD. The second most frequent scheme in Turina's collection is ABBA ABBA CDE CDE, with 24 occurrences, around 9%.

[4] On meter in Turina 1595, see Cox 2011, 139 and 330, n. 47.

Appendix D   CITATIONS AND SOURCES

All references are to citations, allusions, or imitations mentioned or discussed in the commentaries to the poems. The numbers in each case are poem numbers, not page numbers. Only poems by female authors have been included in this index, not the correspondence sonnets by male authors.

Numbers following authors' names, rather than following the titles of their works, refer to poems that name or allude to these authors explicitly. Numbers of poems that constitute overt tributes to the work of a given author (*contrafacta*, centos, *trasmutzioni*, appreciations) are in bold type.

Alighieri, Dante 139
> *Inferno* 35, 48, 49, 73, 94, 101, 111
> *Paradiso* 33, 78, 83, 153
> *Purgatorio* 33, 59, 78, 159, 160
> *Rime* 51

Ariosto, Lodovico
> *Orlando furioso* 58, **60**, 98, 151, 165, 171, 173, 185

Battiferri, Laura
> *Rime* 153

Bembo, Pietro
> *Rime* 13, 44, 46, 65, 93, 150, 151, 152, 179, 199

Bible
> New Testament 73, 74, 96, 98, 102, 103, 104, 105, 112, 120, 121, 122, 125, 127, 128, 160
> Old Testament (and apocrypha) 73, 74, 85, 96, 123, 174, 182

Boccaccio, Giovanni
> *Decameron* 35

Carafa, Ferrante
> *L'Austria* 97

Catherine of Siena (Caterina Benincasa)
> *Letters* 165

Catullus (Gaius Valerius Catullus)
> *Poems* 192, 193

Metamorphoses 154, 188, 192, 193
Tristia 176

Petrarca, Francesco 139

RVF 93; (no. 1) 13, 45, 65, 78, 88; (no. 18) **52**; (no. 23) 39; (no. 28) 48, 116; (no. 35) **100**; (no. 39) **99**; (no. 61) 8; (no. 72) 132; (no. 77) 54; (no. 90) 35; (no. 91) **52**; (no. 95) 132; (no. 105) 111; (no. 107) 155; (no. 125) 78, 111; (no. 126) 87, 114; (no. 128) 157, 165, 193; (no. 132) 111; (no. 135) 32; (no. 136) 162; (no. 139) **182**; (no. 142) 42, 74; (no. 146) 84; (no. 164) 150; (no. 167) 134; (no. 180) 168; (no. 188) 199; (no. 191) 35, 51; (no. 198) 87; (no. 206) 159, 191; (no. 207) 17, 25, **52**, 142; (no. 208) 92; (no. 210) 173; (no. 219) 38, 44; (no. 224) 21; (no. 233) **52**; (no. 235) 159; (no. 243) 33; (no. 248) 14; (no. 260) 180; (no. 263) 166; (no. 267) **52**; (no. 270) 160; (no. 275) 52; (no. 276): 41; (no. 278) 52; (no. 279) 30; (no. 289) 40; (no. 292) 51, **52**, 184; (no. 293) 41; (no. 298) 198; (no. 302) 49; (no. 303) 98; (no. 321) 109; (no. 324) 52; (no. 327) **52**, 55; (no. 331) **52**, 175; (no. 332) **52**; (no. 359) 132, 205; (no. 366) 83, 87, 101, 175
Trionfi 7, 19, 35, 111, 167, 184

Poliziano, Angelo
Stanze per la giostra 8, 149

Propertius (Sextus Propertius)
Elegies 22

Sannazaro, Iacopo
Arcadia 196
Rime disperse 196
Sonetti e canzoni 6, 48

Sbarra, Lucchesia
Rime 207

Tasso, Torquato
Gerusalemme liberata 54, 72, 111, 114, 190, 201, 206
Rime 65, 111, 150

Tebaldeo, Antonio
Rime 167

Uberti, Fazio degli
Rime 46

Venier, Domenico
Rime 16

Virgil (Publius Vergilius Maro) 163, 200
Aeneid 30, 192, 205
Eclogues 193
Georgics 193, 194

Glossary

For names of metrical forms, see Note on Meter, Rhythm, and Rhyme.

adynaton (pl. adynata) The citation of an impossible thing, usually as a form of hyperbolic comparison ("pigs might fly").

alliteration Repetition of consonants in close succession at the beginning of words (a special case of *consonance).

anacoluthon A shift of grammatical structure within a sentence so that the initial clause remains grammatically incomplete.

anadiplosis The repetition of the last word of one sentence or clause at the beginning of the next.

anaphora The repetition of the same word or words at the beginning of a series of sentences or clauses.

antithesis The juxtaposition of contrasting words or ideas, often underlined by structural *parallelism.

assonance Repetition of similar vowel sounds in words in close succession.

captatio benevolentiae A passage at the beginning of a speech or written argument intended to capture the audience's attention and goodwill.

chiasmus (adj. chiastic) *Parallelism involving two grammatical elements repeated but with their order reversed so that they form the pattern ABBA ("fair is foul and foul is fair").

conceit A poetic metaphor, especially an ingenious, improbable or extreme one. The conceit was especially valued in Baroque verse, in reaction to the generally restrained metaphorical language of Petrarchism.

concorso di vocali A term used in sixteenth-century poetics denoting the juxtaposition of vowels, especially the same vowel, in successive words. Tasso considered this to add gravity and grandeur to style, citing the "fiamma amorosa arse" of Petrarch's sonnet 304 as an example (see Afribo 2001, 87–89).

congedo The last, truncated stanza of a canzone, in which the poet takes her leave (lit. "farewell").

consonance Repetition of similar consonant sounds in words in close succession.

contrafactum (pl. contrafacta) A reworking of a poem, retaining a close connection with the original (used especially of religious reworkings of originally secular texts). Also used in music for religious appropriations of secular songs.

diaeresis The pronunciation as separate of two vowels that are normally fused, common in poetry to facilitate scansion.

ekphrasis (adj. ekphrastic) A verbal evocation of a work of art, typically attempting to rival the painted or sculpted source through graphic and vivid description.

enargeia A mode of description capable of evoking lived, sensory experience with such vividness that it seems "placed before the eyes."

end-stopped (adj.) Verse in which line breaks coincide with the closure of syntactic units, by contrast with *enjambment.

enjambment A term from the French, literally meaning "straddling," signifying the continuation of a syntactic unit, such as a phrase or clause, across a line break in a poem. It may be contrasted with the term *end-stopped.

epistrophe The repetition of the same word or phrase at the end of successive clauses; the opposite of *anaphora.

exemplum (pl. exempla) A paragon or exemplary figure, embodying a particular vice or virtue to a remarkable degree.

hypotaxis (adj. hypotactic) The organization of phrases and clauses in a sentence in hierarchic relationships of subordination and dependency; compare with *parataxis.

ineffability topos A statement of the impossibility of doing justice in words to what is being described, used to emphasize the wondrousness of the poet's subject matter and, sometimes, implicitly to call attention to her skill.

isocolon Parallelism consisting of two or more structurally similar or identical clauses.

oxymoron The juxtaposition of antithetical terms ("living death," "icy fire"), a rhetorical device much favored in Petrarchan lyric.

parallelism Similarity of structure in a pair or series of related words, phrases, or clauses.

parataxis (adj. paratactic) The organization of phrases and clauses in a sentence in nonhierarchic relationships, connected either with no conjunctions ("I came, I saw, I conquered") or with simple coordinating conjunctions such as *and, but,* and *or.* Compare with *hypotaxis.

pathetic fallacy The empathetic projection of emotion or passion (Gk. *pathos*) onto inanimate objects or landscapes. Coined by John Ruskin as a pejorative term, it is now used as a neutral description.

polyptoton (pl. polyptota) Repetition in close succession of words deriving from the same root, often nominative and verbal forms.

polysyndeton The repetition of conjunctions in close succession, especially when they could be omitted.

proposta A correspondence sonnet sent to another poet with the hope of eliciting a reply (*risposta).

prosopopoeia The dramatic reconstruction of direct discourse, generally by a fictional or historic character or an abstraction.

rapportatio A reordering of two or more parallel sentences juxtaposing the cognate grammatical elements (subjects, verbs, objects, etc.). A famous example is Domenico Venier's sonnet "Non punse, arse, o legò stral, fiamma, o laccio" (No arrow, flame, or rope ever pierced, burned, or bound).

rima equivoca Rhyme of two or more homonymous words with different meanings. See Note on Meter, Rhythm, and Rhyme for further discussion of complex rhymes.

risposta A reply sonnet constructed in response to a specific *proposta* from another poet. *Risposte* typically used the rhymes of the *proposta* (in a practice termed replying *per le rime*) and sometimes the actual rhyme words, making them an exercise requiring much skill. Replying using the same rhyme words in the same order was termed replying *per le desinenze*, while replying using the same rhyme words in a different order was known as replying *per le confuse*.

senhal A poetic name used for the beloved and encapsulating her identity or some quality in her. The term first evolved in medieval Provençal poetry. The most famous examples in Italian are Dante's Beatrice ("bringer of blessings") and Petrarch's Laura ("laurel").

syllepsis A subspecies of *zeugma in which the verb changes meaning with respect to the nouns to which it relates.

synecdoche The use of a part of something to refer to the whole.

synonymous doublet The pairing of two synonymous words (e.g., "brevi e corti," no. 40), the simplest form of the rhetorical device of synonymia.

topos A poetic commonplace, such as the metaphor of love as fire, or the notion that love refines the soul. Literally a "place" where the poet may go for (ready-made) inspiration.

type In Christian biblical hermeneutics, a figure or episode in the Old Testament considered to prefigure one in the New Testament.

zeugma A construction in which two or more parts of a sentence, presented in parallel, depend on a single common verb (usually) or noun.

Bibliography

Primary Sources

Manuscripts

Battiferri, Laura. "Rime." MS 3229. Biblioteca Casanatense, Rome.

Colao, Lucia. "Rime." MS 3125. Biblioteca Comunale, Treviso.

Colonna, Vittoria. "Rime." MS II. IX. 30. Biblioteca Nazionale Centrale, Florence.

Corsi, Girolama. "Rime." MS It. IX 270 (6367). Biblioteca Marciana, Venice.

"Raccolta di poesie." MS Fondo Antinori 161. Biblioteca Medicea-Laurenziana, Florence.

"Raccolta di rime di varii rimatori del '500." MS 828 (1250). Biblioteca Universitaria, Bologna.

"Rime di diversi autori." MS α N. 7. 28. Biblioteca Estense, Modena.

"Rime di diversi autori." MS Palatino 221. Biblioteca Nazionale Centrale, Florence.

Turina, Francesca. "Poesie di Francesca Turina Bufalini in parte autografe, e di vari a lei." Inventario Azzi, busta 185, sec. 4. Archivio Bufalini, San Giustino.

Printed works

Alighieri, Dante. 2001. *Comedia*. Edited by Federico Sanguineti. 3 vols. Florence: Edizioni del Galluzzo.

Andreini, Isabella. 1601. *Rime*. Milan: Girolamo Bordone and Pietromartire Locarni.

———. 1605. *Rime*. Milan: Girolamo Bordone and Pietromartire Locarni.

———. 2005. *Selected Poems of Isabella Andreini*. Edited by Anne MacNeil. Translated by James Wyatt Cook. Lanham, MD: Scarecrow.

Anselmi, Gian Mario, Keir Elam, Giorgio Forni, and Davide Monda, eds. 2004. *Lirici europei del Cinquecento: Ripensando la lirica del Petrarca*. With contributions from Roberto Roversi and Martin Rueff. Milan: Rizzoli.

Ariosto, Lodovico. 1976. *Orlando furioso*. Edited by Cesare Segre. 2nd ed. Milan: Mondadori.

Arslan, Antonia, Adriana Chemello, and Gilberto Pizzamiglio, eds. 1991. *Le stanze ritrovate. Antologia di scrittrici venete dal Quattrocento al Novecento*. Mirano-Venice: Eidos.

Atanagi, Dionigi, ed. 1565. *De le rime di diversi nobili poeti toscani . . . libro primo*. Venice: Lodovico Avanzo.

Baldacci, Luigi, ed. 1975. *Lirici del Cinquecento*. 2nd ed. Milan: Longanesi.

Bandello, Matteo. 1992–96. *La prima-quarta parte de le novelle*. Edited by Delmo Maestri. 4 vols. Alessandria: Edizioni dell'Orso.

Baruffaldi, Girolamo, ed. 1713. *Rime scelte de' poeti ferraresi antichi e moderni*. Ferrara: Heirs of Bernardino Pomatelli.

Battiferri, Laura. 1560. *Il primo libro dell'opere toscane*. Florence: Giunti.

————. 1564. *I sette salmi penitentiali del santissimo profeta Davit, tradotti in lingua toscana . . . insieme con alcuni . . . sonetti spirituali*. Florence: Giunti.

————. 2005. *I sette salmi penitenziali di David con alcuni sonetti spirituali*. Edited by Enrico Maria Guidi. Urbino: Accademia Raffaello.

————. 2006. *Laura Battiferra and Her Literary Circle*. Edited and translated by Victoria Kirkham. Chicago: University of Chicago Press.

Bembo, Pietro. 1535. *Delle rime*. Venice: Giovanni Antonio Nicolini da Sabbio.

————. 1960. *Prose e rime*. Edited by Carlo Dionisotti. Turin: UTET.

Bergalli, Luisa, ed. 1726. *Componimenti poetici delle più illustri rimatrici d'ogni secolo. Parte prima-seconda*. Venice: Antonio Mora.

Bozi, Paolo, ed. 1614. *Vita, attioni, miracoli, morte, resurrettione, et ascensione di Dio humanato, raccolti dal Clariss[imo] Sig[nor] Leonardo Sanudo in versi lirici da' più famosi Autori di questo secolo*. Venice: Santo Grillo and Fratelli.

Bragadin, Veneranda. 1619. *Rime*. Verona: Angelo Tamo.

Bratteolo, Giacomo, ed. 1597. *Rime di diversi elevati ingegni de la città di Udine*. Udine: Giovanni Battista Natolini.

Buonarroti, Michelangelo. 1991. *The Poetry of Michelangelo*. Edited and translated by James A. Saslow. New Haven, CT: Yale University Press.

Calderari, Cesare. 1588. *Il trofeo della croce di n[ostro] sig[nor] Giesu Christo*. Vicenza: Agostino dalla Noce.

Campiglia, Maddalena. 1585. *Discorso . . . sopra l'annonciatione della beata Vergine, et la incarnatione del s[ignor] n[ostro] Giesu Christo*. Vicenza: Perin Libraro and Giorgio Greco.

————. 2004. *Flori: A Pastoral Drama*. Edited with an introduction and notes by Virginia Cox and Lisa Sampson. Translated by Virginia Cox. Chicago: University of Chicago Press.

Carafa, Ferrante. 1573. *Dell'Austria . . . dove si contiene la vittoria della santa lega all'Echinadi, divisa in cinque parti*. Naples: Giuseppe Cacchi dell'Aquila.

Castiglione, Baldassare. 2002. *The Book of the Courtier*. Edited by Daniel Javitch. Translated by Charles Singleton. New York: Norton.

Catullus, Gaius Valerius. 1962. *Poems*. In *Catullus, Tibullus, Pervigilium Veneris*, translated by F. W. Cornish, J. W. Mackail, and J. P. Postgate; 2nd ed., revised by G. P. Goold. Cambridge, MA: Harvard University Press.

Cervoni, Isabella. 1598. *Orazione . . . al santissimo e beatissimo padre e signor nostro papa Clemente ottavo sopra l'impresa di Ferrara. Con una canzone . . . a' prencipi christiani*. Bologna: Giovanni Battista Bellagamba.

————. 1600. *Tre canzoni . . . in laude de' christianiss[imi] re, e regina di Francia e di Navarra, Enrico quarto, e madama Maria de' Medici*. Florence: Giorgio Marescotti.

Colonna, Vittoria. 1546. *Le rime spirituali*. Venice: Vincenzo Valgrisi.

————. 1548. *Le rime spirituali . . . alle quali di nuovo sono stati aggiunti . . . più di trenta, ò trentatre sonetti, non mai più altrove stampati*. Venice: Vincenzo Valgrisi.

————. 1558. *Tutte le rime . . . Con l'espositione del signor Rinaldo Corso*. Edited by Girolamo Ruscelli. Venice: Giovanni Battista e Melchiorre Sessa.

————. 1560. *Rime . . . con l'aggiunta delle rime spirituali*. Edited by Lodovico Dolce. Venice: Gabriele Giolito.

————. 1840. *Le rime*. Edited by Pietro Ercole Visconti. Rome: Salviucci.

————. 1982. *Rime*. Edited by Alan Bullock. Bari: Laterza.

————. 1998. *Sonetti in morte di Francesco Ferrante d'Avalos marchese di Pescara: Edizione del ms. XIII. G. 43 della Biblioteca Nazionale di Napoli*. Edited by Tobia R. Toscano. Milan: Mondadori.

————. 2005. *Sonnets for Michelangelo*. Edited and translated by Abigail Brundin. Chicago: University of Chicago Press.

Colonna, Vittoria, Chiara Matraini, and Lucrezia Marinella. 2008. *Who Is Mary? Three Early Modern Women on the Idea of the Virgin Mary*. Edited and translated by Susan Haskins. Chicago: University of Chicago Press.

Contini, Gianfranco, ed. 1960. *Poeti del Duecento*. 2 vols. Milan: Ricciardi.

————. 1970. "Preliminari sulla lingua del Petrarca." In *Varianti e altra linguistica: una raccolta di saggi (1938–68)*, 169–92. Turin: Einaudi.

Copio, Sarra. 1621. *Manifesto . . . nel quale è da lei riprovata e detestata l'opinione negante l'immortalità dell'anima, falsamente attribuitale dal sig[nor] Baldassare Bonifaccio*. Venezia: Giovanni Alberti.

————. 2009. *Jewish Poet and Intellectual in Seventeenth-Century Venice: The Works of Sarra Copia Sullam, along with Writings of her Contemporaries in her Praise, Condemnation, or Defense*. Edited and translated by Don Harran. Chicago: University of Chicago Press.

d'Aragona, Tullia. 1547. *Rime della signora Tullia d'Aragona et di diversi a lei*. Venice: Gabriele Giolito.

————. 1891. *Le rime di Tullia d'Aragona, cortigiana del secolo XVI*. Edited by Enrico Celani. Bologna: Romagnoli Dall'Acqua.

Della Casa, Giovanni. 2001. *Rime*. Edited by Giuliano Tarturli. Parma: Guanda.

Della Chiesa, Francesco Agostino. 1620. *Theatro delle donne letterate con un breve discorso della preminenza e perfettione del sesso donnesco*. Mondovì: Giovanni Gislandi and Giovanni Tommaso Rossi.

Dolce, Lodovico, ed. 1555. *Libro quinto delle rime di diversi illustri signori napoletani, e d'altri nobilissimi ingegni*. Venice: Giolito.

————, ed. 1556. *Rime di diversi signori napoletani, e d'altri. Libro settimo*. Venice: Gabriele Giolito.

Domenichi, Lodovico, ed. 1549. *Rime diverse di molti eccellentiss[imi] auttori nuovamente raccolte. Libro primo con nuova additione ristampato*. Venice: Giolito.

————, ed. 1559. *Rime diverse d'alcune nobilissime et virtuosissime donne*. Lucca: Vincenzo Busdraghi.

Ducchi, Gregorio. 1607. *Il giuoco de gli scacchi, ridotto in poema eroico sotto prosopopea di due potenti re, e de gli eserciti loro*. Vicenza: Perin Libraro and Giorgio Greco.

Ferentilli, Agostino, ed. 1571. *Primo volume della scielta di stanze di diversi autori toscani*. Venice: Heirs of Melchiorre Sessa.

Flora, Francesco, ed. 1962. *Gaspara Stampa e altre poetesse del '500*. Milan: Nuova Accademia.

Fonte, Moderata. 1581. *Tredici canti del Floridoro*. Venice: Heirs of Francesco Rampazetto.

————. 1582. *La passione di Christo descritta in ottava rima . . . Con una canzone nell'istesso soggetto*. Venice: Domenico and Giovanni Battista Guerra.

————. 1997. *The Worth of Women*. Edited and translated by Virginia Cox. Chicago: University of Chicago Press.

————. 2006. *Floridoro: A Chivalric Romance*. Edited by Valeria Finucci and Julia Kisacky. Introduction by Valeria Finucci. Translated by Julia Kisacky. Chicago: University of Chicago Press.

Franco, Veronica. 1999. *Poems and Selected Letters.* Edited and translated by Ann Rosalind Jones and Margaret F. Rosenthal. Chicago: University of Chicago Press.

Franco, Veronica, and Gaspara Stampa. 1913. *Rime.* Edited by Abdelkader Salza. Bari: Laterza.

Gambara, Veronica. 1759. *Rime e lettere.* Edited by Felice Rizzardi. Brescia: Giovanni Maria Rizzardi.

———. 1879. *Rime e lettere.* Edited by Pia Mestica Chiappetti. Florence: G. Barbera.

———. 1890. *Sonetti amorosi inediti o rari.* Edited by Emilio Costa. Parma: Luigi Battei.

———. 1995. *Rime.* Edited by Alan Bullock. Florence: Olschki.

———. Forthcoming. *Complete Verse.* Edited and translated by Paola Ugolini and Molly Martin. Introduction by Molly Martin. Toronto: Centre for Reformation and Renaissance Studies.

Gigliucci, Roberto, ed. 2000. *La lirica rinascimentale.* Selection and introduction by Jacqueline Risset. Rome: Istituto Poligrafico e Zecca dello Stato.

Giustinian, Orsatto. 2001. *Sonetti alla moglie.* Edited by Simona Mammana. Florence: Le Cáriti.

Giustinian, Orsatto, and Celio Magno. 1600. *Rime.* Venice: Andrea Muschio.

Gonzaga, Curzio. 1591. *Rime.* Venice: Heirs of Curzio Troiano Navò [al segno del Leone].

Grillo, Angelo, 1589. *Parte prima [-seconda] delle rime.* Bergamo: Comino Ventura.

Groto, Luigi. 2007. *Le famigliari del Cieco d'Adria.* Edited by Marco de Poli, Luisa Servadei, and Antonella Turri. Introductory essay by Mario Nanni. Treviso: Antilia.

Guaccimani, Giacomo, ed. 1623. *Raccolta di sonetti d'autori diversi, et eccellenti dell'età nostra.* Ravenna: Pietro de' Paoli and Giovanni Battista Giovannelli.

Guerrini, Olindo, ed. 1882. *Rime di tre gentildonne del secolo XVI.* Milan: Edoardo Sonzogno.

Laude facte e composte da piu persone spirituali a honore dello omnipotente idio e della gloriosa vergine Madonna Sancta Maria e di molti altri sancti e sancte. 1485. Florence: Francesco Bonaccorsi.

Luna, Fabrizio. 1536. *Vocabulario di cinquemila vocabuli toschi non men oscuri che utili e necessarij del Furioso, Bocaccio, Petrarcha e Dante novamente dechiarati e raccolti.* Naples: Giovanni Sultzbach.

Maganza, Giovanni Battista, Agostino Rava, and Marco Thiene. [1583?]. *La quarta parte delle rime alla rustica di Menon, Magagnò, e Begotto.* Venice: Giorgio Angelieri.

Marchetti, Salvestro, ed. 1596. *Poesie toscane e latine da diversi autori composte nell'essequie dell'illustre Sig[nora] Isabella Marescotti de' Ballati, gentildonna sanese.* Siena: Bonetti.

Marinella, Lucrezia. 1597. *Vita del serafico, et glorioso S[an] Francesco . . . Con un discorso del rivolgimento amoroso, verso la somma bellezza.* Venice: Pietro Maria Bertano and Brothers.

———. 1603. *Rime sacre.* Venice: ad istanza del Collosini.

———. 1643. *Le vittorie di Francesco il serafico. Li passi gloriosi della diva Chiara.* Padua: Giulio Crivellari.

———. 1999. *The Nobility and Excellence of Women and the Defects and Vices of Men.* Edited and translated by Anne Dunhill. Introduction by Letizia Panizza. Chicago: University of Chicago Press.

———. 2009. *Enrico, or Byzantium Conquered: A Heroic Poem.* Edited and translated by Maria Galli Stampino. Chicago: University of Chicago Press.

Matraini, Chiara. 1555. *Rime et prose.* Lucca: Vincenzo Busdraghi.

———. 1590. *Breve discorso sopra la vita e laude della beatissima vergine e madre del figliuol di Dio.* Lucca: Vincenzo Busdraghi.

———. 1597. *Lettere . . . con la prima e seconda parte delle sue Rime. Con una lettera in difesa delle lettere, e delle arme.* Venice: Nicolò Moretti.

———. 1989. *Rime e lettere.* Edited by Giovanna Rabitti. Bologna: Commissione per i Testi di Lingua.

———. 2007. *Selected Poetry and Prose.* Edited and translated by Eleanor Maclachlan. Introduction by Giovanna Rabitti. Chicago: University of Chicago Press.

Medici, Lorenzo de'. 1992. *Tutte le opere.* Edited by Paolo Orvieto. 2 vols. Rome: Salerno.

Miani, Valeria. 2010. *Celinda: A Tragedy.* Edited by Valeria Finucci. Translated by Julie Kisacky. Toronto: Centre for Reformation and Renaissance Studies.

Morandini, Giuliana. 2001. *Sospiri e palpiti: Scrittrici italiane del Seicento.* Genova: Marietti.

Morata, Olimpia. 2003. *The Complete Writings of an Italian Heretic.* Edited and translated by Holt N. Parker. Chicago: University of Chicago Press.

Morra, Isabella. 2000. *Rime.* Edited by Maria Antonietta Grignani. Rome: Salerno.

Nogarola, Isotta. 1886. *Opera quae supersunt omnia Isotae Nogarolae veronensis; accedunt Angelae et Zenevrae Nogarolae epistolae et carmina.* 2 vols. Edited by Eugenius Abel. Vienna: Gerold; Budapest: Kilian.

Ossola, Carlo, and Cesare Segre, eds. 1997. *Antologia della poesia italiana: Cinquecento.* Turin: Einaudi.

Ovid. 1984. *Metamorphoses.* Edited by G. P. Goold. Translated by Frank Justus Miller. 3rd ed. 2 vols. Cambridge, MA: Harvard University Press.

Palermo, Policarpo, ed. 1596. *Varie compositioni scritte in lode dell'Ill[ustrissi]mo signor Giovanni Cornaro, capitanio di Verona, et de l'Ill[ustrissi]ma signora Chiara Delfina sua consorte.* Verona: Girolamo Discepolo.

Petrarca, Francesco. 1976. *Petrarch's Lyric Poems.* Edited and translated by Robert M. Durling. Cambridge, MA: Harvard University Press.

———. 1996a. *Canzoniere.* Edited by Marco Santagata. Milan: Mondadori.

———. 1996b. *Trionfi, rime estravaganti, codice degli abbozzi.* Edited by Vinicio Pacca and Laura Paolino. Introduction by Marco Santagata. Milan: Mondadori.

Piccolomini, Alessandro. 1541. *Lettura . . . fatta nell'Accademia degli Infiammati.* Bologna: Bartholomeo Bonardo and Marcantonio da Carpi.

Poesie toscane, et latine di diversi eccel[lenti] ingegni, nella morte del s[ignor] d[on] Giovanni cardinale, del sig[nor] don Grazia [sic] de' Medici, & della s[ignora] donna Leonora di Toledo de' Medici duchessa di Fiorenza, et di Siena. 1563. Florence: Torrentino.

Poggi, Semidea. 1623. *La Calliope religiosa.* Vicenza: Francesco Grossi.

Poliziano, Angelo. 1993. *The Stanze of Angelo Poliziano.* Edited and translated by David Quint. University Park: Pennsylvania State University Press.

Ponchiroli, Daniele, and Guido Davico Bonino, eds. 1968. *Lirici del Cinquecento.* 2nd ed. Turin: UTET.

Querini, Carlo. 1597. *Orazione in laude della mag[nifica] città di Verona.* Verona: Girolamo Discepolo.

Ranza, Giovanni Antonio. 1769. *Poesie e memorie di donne letterate che fiorirono negli stati di S[ua] S[acra] R[eale] M[aestà] il re di Sardegna . . . con alcune antiche e moderne poetiche iscrizioni di nobili donne vercellesi, non più pubblicate.* Vercelli: Giuseppe Panialis.

Rime delle signore Lucrezia Marinella, Veronica Gambara, ed Isabella Della Morra . . . con giunta di quelle fin'ora raccolte della signora Maria Selvaggia Borghini. 1693. Naples: Antonio Bulifon.

Rime di diversi belli spiriti della città di Palermo nella morte della signora Laura Serra et Frias. 1572. Palermo: Giovanni Matteo Mayda.

Rime di diversi celebri poeti dell'età nostra, nuovamente raccolte e poste in luce. 1587. Bergamo: Comino Ventura.

Rossi, Armonio, ed. 1587. "Diverse compositioni di poesia toscane e latine." In Gherardo Bellinzona, *Oratione funerale . . . in morte del reverendissimo p[adre] maestro Spirito Pelo Angusciola.* Vicenza: Agostino dalla Noce.

Ruscelli, Girolamo, ed. 1553a. *Rime di diversi eccellentissimi autori bresciani.* Venice: Plinio Pietrasanta.

———, ed. 1553b. *Il sesto libro delle rime di diversi eccellenti autori.* Venice: Giovanni Maria Bonelli (al segno del Pozzo).

———. 1559. *Del modo di comporre in versi nella lingua italiana.* Venice: Giovanni Battista and Melchiorre Sessa.

Salvetti, Maddalena. 1590. *Rime toscane . . . in lode della serenissima signora Cristina di Loreno gran duchessa di Toscana.* Florence: Francesco Tosi.

———. 1611. *Il David perseguitato o vero fuggitivo, poema eroico.* Florence: Giovanni Antonio Caneo.

Sannazaro, Iacopo. 1990. *Arcadia.* Edited by Francesco Erspamer. Milan: Mursia

Sbarra, Lucchesia. 1610. *Rime.* Conegliano: Marco Claseri.

Scelta di rime di diversi moderni autori non più stampate, parte prima-seconda. 1591. Genoa: heirs of Girolamo Bartoli.

Segni, Giulio, ed. 1601. *Componimenti poetici volgari, latini, e greci di diversi sopra la s[anta] imagine della beata Vergine dipinta da san Luca la quale si serba nel monte della Guardia presso Bologna, con la sua historia in dette tre lingue scritta da Ascanio Persij.* Bologna: Vittorio Benacci.

Sonetti e canzoni di diversi antichi autori toscani in dieci libri raccolte. 1527. Florence: Heirs of Filippo Giuntii.

Stampa, Gaspara. 1554. *Rime.* Venice: Plinio Pietrasanta.

———. 1738. *Rime di Madonna Gaspara Stampa, con alcune altre di Collaltino, e di Vinciguerra, conti di Collalto, e di Baldassare Stampa.* Edited by Luisa Bergalli. Venice: Francesco Piacentini.

———. 1877. *Rime.* Edited by Pia Mestica Chiappetti. Florence: G. Barbera.

———. 2010. *The Complete Poems: The 1554 Edition of the "Rime," a Bilingual Edition.* Edited by Jane Tylus and Troy Tower. Translated with an introduction by Jane Tylus. Chicago: University of Chicago Press.

Stortoni, Laura Anna, ed. 1997. *Women Poets of the Italian Renaissance: Courtly Ladies and Courtesans.* Edited by Laura Anna Stortoni. Translated by Laura Anna Stortoni and Mary Prentice Lillie. New York: Italica Press.

Strozzi, Lorenza, 1588. *In singula totius anni solemnia hymni.* Florence: Filippo Giunta.

———. 1601. *In singula totius anni solemnia hymni.* 2nd ed. Paris: Denis Binet.

Tasso, Torquato. 1875. *Lezione sopra il sonetto di Monsignor della Casa, "Questa vita mortal."* In *Prose diverse,* edited by Cesare Guasti, 2 vols. Florence: Heirs of Le Monnier.

———. 1980. *Gerusalemme liberata.* 2nd ed. Edited by Lanfranco Caretti. Turin: Einaudi.

———. 1994. *Rime.* Edited by Bruno Basile. 2 vols. Rome: Salerno.

Terracina, Laura. 1548. *Rime.* Venice: Gabriele Giolito.

———. 1549. *Rime seconde della Signora Laura Terracina di Napoli et di diversi a lei.* Florence: Lorenzo Torrentino.

Tomasi, Franco, and Paolo Zaja, eds. 2001. *Rime diverse di molti eccellentissimi autori* [1545]. San Mauro Torinese: RES.

Torelli, Barbara. Forthcoming. *Partenia: A Pastoral Play*. Edited and translated by Barbara Burgess-Van Aken and Lisa Sampson. Toronto: Centre for Reformation and Renaissance Studies.

Tornabuoni, Lucrezia. 1900. *Le laudi*. Edited by Guglielmo Volpi. Pistoia: Flori.

———. 2001. *Sacred Narratives*. Edited and translated by Jane Tylus. Chicago: University of Chicago Press.

Turina, Francesca. 1595. *Rime spirituali sopra i misterii del santissimo rosario*. Rome: Domenico Gigliotti.

———. 1628. *Rime*. Città di Castello: Santi Molinelli.

———. 2005. *Rime spirituali sopra i misteri del Santissimo Rosario*. Edited by Paolo Bà. In *Letteratura italiana antica*, 6:147–223.

———. 2009. *Autobiographical Poems: A Bilingual Selection*. Edited by Natalia Costa-Zalessow. Translated by Joan E. Borelli with Natalia Costa-Zalessow. New York: Bordighiera.

———. 2010. *Le rime*. Edited by Paolo Bà. In *Letteratura italiana antica*, 11:141–276.

Valenziano, Luca. 1984. *Opere volgari*. Edited by Maria Pia Mussini Sacchi. Introduction by Ugo Rozzo. Tortona: Centro Studi Matteo Bandello.

Valerini, Adriano. 1570. *Oratione . . . in morte della divina signora Vincenza Armani, comica eccellentissima . . . con alquante leggiadre e belle compositioni di detta signora Vincenza*. Verona: Bastiano dalle Donne e Giovanni Fratelli.

Varchi, Benedetto. 1555. *De' sonetti . . . parte prima*. Florence: Lorenzo Torrentino.

Vernazza, Battista. 1819. *Sonetti inediti*. 2nd ed. Edited by Giuseppe Ronco. Genoa: Stamperia Pagano.

Zarrabini, Onofrio. 1586. *Rime di Onofrio Zarrabini . . . e d'altri huomini illustri*. Edited by Giulio Morigi. Venice: Niccolò Moretti.

Secondary Sources

Afribo, Andrea. 2001. *Teoria e prassi della gravitas nel Cinquecento*. Introduction by Pier Vincenzo Mengaldo. 2 vols. Florence: Franco Cesati.

———. 2009. *Petrarca e petrarchismo. Capitoli di lingua, stile e metrica*. Rome: Carocci.

Agnelli, Giuseppe, and Giuseppe Ravegnani. 1933. *Annali delle edizioni ariostee*. Bologna: N. Zanichelli.

Allen, Prudence, R. S. M. 2002. *The Concept of Woman*. Vol. 2, *The Early Humanist Reformation, 1250–1500*. Grand Rapids, MI: W. B. Eerdmans.

Ambrosini, Federica. 2000. "Toward a Social History of Women in Venice: From the Renaissance to the Enlightenment." In Martin and Romano 2000, 420–53.

Andrews, Richard. 2000. "Isabella Andreini and Others: Women on Stage in the Late Cinquecento." In Panizza 2000, 316–33.

Bà, Paolo. 2009. "Alcuni sonetti inediti di Francesca Turina Bufalini." In *Annali. Dalla ricerca alla sperimentazione*, edited by Filippo Pettinari, 117–33. Città di Castello: Liceo Classico "Plinio il Giovane."

Balsano, Maria Antonella. 1988. Introduction to Giandomenico Martoretta, *Il secondo libro di madrigali cromatici a quattro voci (1552)*, edited by Maria Antonella Balsano, i–xxii. Florence: Olschki.

Barezzani, Maria Teresa Rosa. 1989. "Intonazioni musicali sui testi di Veronica Gambara." In Bozzetti, Gibellini, and Sandal 1989, 125–42.

Basile, Deanna. 2001. *"Fasseli gratia per poetessa:* Duke Cosimo I de' Medici's Role in the Florentine Literary Circles of Tullia d'Aragona." In *The Cultural Politics of Duke Cosimo I de' Medici,* edited by Konrad Eisenbichler, 135–47. Aldershot, UK: Ashgate.

Bausi, Francesco. 1993. " 'Con agra zampogna.' Tullia d'Aragona a Firenze (1545–48)." *Schede umanistiche* n.s. 2:61–91.

Belloni, Antonio. 1893. *Gli epigoni della "Gerusalemme liberata," con un'appendice bibliografica.* Padua: Angelo Draghi.

Beltrami, Pietro. 1991. *La metrica italiana.* Bologna: Il Mulino.

Benson, Pamela Joseph, and Victoria Kirkham, eds. 2005. *Strong Voices, Weak History: Early Modern Women Writers and Canons in England, France, and Italy.* Ann Arbor: University of Michigan Press.

Besomi, Ottavio. 1969. *Ricerche intorno alla "Lira" di G. B. Marino.* Padua: Antenore.

Bireley, Robert. 1999. *The Refashioning of Catholicism, 1450–1700: A Reassessment of the Counter Reformation.* Washington, DC: Catholic University of America Press.

Bolzoni, Lina. 2008. *Poesia e ritratto nel Rinascimento.* Texts edited by Federica Pich. Bari: Laterza.

———. 2010. *Il cuore di cristallo: ragionamenti d'amore, poesia e ritratto nel Rinascimento.* Turin: Einaudi.

Bowers, Jane. 1986. "The Emergence of Women Composers in Italy, 1566–1700." In Bowers and Tick 1986, 116–67.

Bowers, Jane, and Judith Tick, eds. 1986. *Women Making Music: The Western Art Tradition, 1150–1950.* Urbana: University of Illinois Press.

Bozzetti, Cesare, Pietro Gibellini, and Ennio Sandal, eds. 1989. *Veronica Gambara e la poesia del suo tempo nell'Italia settentrionale: atti del convegno (Brescia-Correggio, 17–19 ottobre 1985).* Florence: Olschki.

Brown, Phyllis R., Laurie J. Churchill, and Jane E. Jeffrey, eds. 2002. *Women Writing Latin: From Roman Antiquity to Early Modern Europe.* 3 vols. New York: Routledge.

Brundin, Abigail. 2001. "Vittoria Colonna and the Virgin Mary." *Modern Language Review* 96 (1):61–81.

———. 2008. *Vittoria Colonna and the Spiritual Poetics of the Italian Reformation.* Aldershot, UK: Ashgate.

Bruscagli, Riccardo. 2007. "La preponderanza petrarcesca." In *Storia letteraria d'Italia— Il Cinquecento,* vol. 3, *La letteratura tra l'eroico e il quotidiano. La nuova religione dell'utopia e della scienza (1573–1600),* edited by Giovanni Da Pozzo, 1559–615. Padua: Piccin–Nuova Vallardi.

Bullock, Alan. 1971. "Un sonetto inedito di Vittoria Colonna." *Studi e problemi critica testuale* 2:229–35.

———. 1973. "Veronica o Vittoria? Problemi di attribuzione per alcuni sonetti del Cinquecento." *Studi e problemi di critica testuale* 6:115–31.

———. 1977. "Vittoria Colonna and Francesco Maria Molza: Conflict in Communication." *Italian Studies* 32:41–51.

Calitti, Floriana. 2004. *Fra lirica e narrativa: storia dell'ottava rima nel Rinascimento.* Florence: Le Cáriti.

Callegari, Danielle, and Shannon McHugh. 2011. " 'Se fossimo tante meretrici': The Rhetoric of Resistance in Diodata Malvasia's Convent Narrative." *Italian Studies* 66 (1): 21–39.

Carter, Tim. 1999. "Finding a Voice: Vittoria Archilei and the Florentine 'New Music.'" In *Feminism and Renaissance Studies*, edited by Lorna Hutson, 450–67. Oxford: Oxford University Press.

Casapullo, Rosa. 1998. "Contatti metrici fra Spagna e Italia: Laura Terracina e la tecnica della glosa." In *Atti del XXI Congresso Internazionale di Linguistica e Filologia Romanza*, edited by Giovanni Ruffino, 4:361–89. Tübingen: Max Niemeyer.

Cenini, Carlo. 2009. "*Le rime in lingua rustica padovana di Magagnò, Menon, e Begotto*: testo critico e commento." Ph.D. dissertation, Università degli Studi di Padova.

Chemello, Adriana. 2000. "Le ricerche erudite di Luisa Bergalli." In *Geografie e genealogie letterarie: erudite, croniste, narratrici, "épistolières," utopiste tra Settecento e Ottocento*, edited by Adriana Chemello and Luisa Ricaldone, 49–88. Padua: Il Poligrafo.

Cicogna, Emmanuele Antonio. 1824–53. *Delle inscrizioni veneziane*. 6 vols. Venice: Giuseppe Orlandelli and Giuseppe Picotti.

Clubb, Louise George, and William G. Clubb. 1991. "Building a Lyric Canon: Gabriel Giolito and the Rival Anthologists, 1545–1590." *Italica* 68 (3): 332–44.

Coppens, Christian, and Angela Nuovo. 2005. *I Giolito e la stampa nell'Italia del XVI secolo*. Geneva: Droz.

Costa-Zalessow, Natalia. 1982. *Scrittrici italiane dal XIII al XX secolo. Testi e critica*. Ravenna: Longo.

Cox, Virginia. 1995. "The Single Self: Feminist Thought and the Marriage Market in Early Modern Venice." *Renaissance Quarterly* 48 (3): 513–81.

———. 2005. "Sixteenth-Century Women Petrarchists and the Legacy of Laura." *Journal of Medieval and Early Modern Studies* 35 (3): 583–606.

———. 2008. *Women's Writing in Italy, 1400–1650*. Baltimore: Johns Hopkins University Press.

———. 2009a. "Gender and Eloquence in Ercole de' Roberti's *Portia and Brutus*." *Renaissance Quarterly* 62 (1): 61–101.

———. 2009b. "Leonardo Bruni on Women and Rhetoric: *De studiis et litteris* revisited." *Rhetorica* 27 (1): 47–75.

———. 2011. *The Prodigious Muse: Women's Writing in Counter-Reformation Italy*. Baltimore: Johns Hopkins University Press.

———. 2012. "Una scrittrice femminista del Seicento: Veneranda Bragadin Cavalli." In *Verona al femminile: una storia della città dal medioevo a oggi*, edited by Paola Lanaro and Alison Smith, 163–77. Verona: Cierre.

Curran, Stuart. 2005. "Recollecting the Renaissance: Luisa Bergalli's *Componimenti Poetici* (1726)." In Benson and Kirkham 2005, 263–86.

Cusick, Suzanne G. 2005. "Epilogue: Francesca among Women, a '600 Gynecentric View." In *Musical Voices of Early Modern Women: Many-Headed Melodies*, edited by Thomasin LaMay, 425–43. Aldershot, UK: Ashgate.

———. 2009. *Francesca Caccini at the Medici Court: Music and the Circulation of Power*. Chicago: University of Chicago Press.

Debby, Nirit Ben-Ayreh. 2003. "Vittoria Colonna and Titian's *Pitti Magdalene*." *Women's Art Journal* 24 (1): 29–33.

D'Elia, Una Roman. 2006. "Drawing Christ's Blood: Michelangelo, Vittoria Colonna, and the Aesthetics of Reform." *Renaissance Quarterly* 59 (1): 90–129.

Demetz, Peter. 1958. "The Elm and The Vine: Notes Towards the History of a Marriage Topos." *PMLA* 73 (5), part 1: 521–32.

De Vit, Vincenzo. 1883. "Dell'illustre donzella Issicratea Monti." In *Opuscoli letterari editi e inediti*, 7–25. Milan: Borniardi-Pogliani.

Dionisotti, Carlo. 1999. *Geografia e storia della letteratura italiana*. 2nd ed. Turin: Einaudi.

———. 2002. "Appunti sul Bembo e su Vittoria Colonna." In *Scritti sul Bembo*, edited by Claudio Vela, 115–40. Turin: Einaudi.

Ditchfield, Simon. 2004. "Of Dancing Cardinals and Mestizo Madonnas: Reconfiguring the History of Roman Catholicism in the Early Modern Period." *Journal of Early Modern History* 8 (3–4): 386–408.

Durante, Elio, and Anna Martellotti. 1989a. *Cronistoria del concerto delle dame principalissime di Margherita Gonzaga d'Este*. 2nd ed. Florence: S.P.E.S. (Studio per Edizioni Scelte).

———. 1989b. *Don Angelo Grillo, O.S.B. alias Livio Celiano, poeta per musica del secolo decimosesto*. Florence: S.P.E.S. (Studio per Edizioni Scelte).

Durling, Robert M. 1971. "Petrarch's 'Giovane donna sotto un verde lauro.'" *MLN* 86 (1): 1–20.

Eisenbichler, Konrad. 2003. "'Un chant à l'honneur de France': Women's Voices at the End of the Republic of Siena." *Renaissance and Reformation* 27 (2): 87–99.

———. 2012a. *L'opera poetica di Virginia Martini Salvi (Siena, c. 1510–Roma, post 1571)*. Siena: Accademia degli Intronati.

———. 2012b. *The Sword and the Pen: Women, Politics, and Poetry in Sixteenth-Century Siena*. Notre Dame, IN: University of Notre Dame Press.

Erdmann, Axel. 1999. *My Gracious Silence: Women in the Mirror of Sixteenth-Century Printing in Western Europe*. Luzern: Gilhofer & Ranschburg.

Eschrich, Gabriella Scarlatta. 2009. "Women Writing Women in Lodovico Domenichi's Anthology of 1559." *Quaderni d'italianistica* 30 (2): 67–85.

Fantuzzi, Giovanni. 1781–94. *Notizie degli scrittori bolognesi*. 9 vols. Bologna: Stamperia di San Tommaso d'Aquino.

Fatini, Giuseppe. 1910. "Curiosità ariostesche: intorno a un'elegia dell'Ariosto e a un brano del *Furioso*." *Giornale storico della letteratura italiana* 55:77–98.

Fedi, Roberto. 1996. "From the 'Auctor' to the Authors: Writing Lyrics in the Italian Renaissance." *Quaderni d'Italianistica* 17 (2): 61–74.

Feldman, Martha. 1995. *City Culture and the Madrigal at Venice*. Berkeley: University of California Press.

Feldman, Martha, and Bonnie Gordon, eds. 2006. *The Courtesan's Arts: Cross-Cultural Perspectives*. Oxford: Oxford University Press.

Forni, Giorgio. 2006. "'L'orecchie mi tirò ne l'ore prime.' Nota su Giovanni Della Casa e Gaspara Stampa." In *Giovanni della Casa: Un seminario per il centenario*, edited by Amedeo Quondam, 289–99. Rome: Bulzoni.

Fortini Brown, Patricia. 2004. *Private Lives in Renaissance Venice: Art, Architecture, and the Family*. New Haven, CT: Yale University Press.

Garrard, Mary D. 1989. *Artemisia Gentileschi: The Image of the Female Hero in Italian Baroque Art*. Princeton, NJ: Princeton University Press.

———. 1994. "Here's Looking at Me: Sofonisba Anguissola and the Problem of the Woman Artist." *Renaissance Quarterly* 47 (3): 556–622.

Gerbino, Giuseppe. 2009. *Music and the Myth of Arcadia in Renaissance Italy*. Cambridge: Cambridge University Press.

Ginzberg, Louis. 2003. *The Legends of the Jews*. Translated by Henrietta Szold and Paul Radin. 2nd ed. 2 vols. Philadelphia: Jewish Publication Society.

Goffman, Daniel. 2002. *The Ottoman Empire and Early Modern Europe.* Cambridge: Cambridge University Press.

Grayson, Cecil. 1971. "Four Love Letters Attributed to Alberti." In *Collected Essays on Italian Language and Literature Presented to Kathleen Speight,* edited by Giovanni Aquilecchia, Stephen N. Cristea, and Sheila Ralphs, 29–44. Manchester: Machester University Press.

Graziosi, Elisabetta. 2009. "Due monache domenicane poetesse: una nota, una ignota, e molte sullo sfondo." In *Il velo, la penna, e la parola. Le domenicane: storia, istituzioni, e scritture,* edited by Gabriella Zarri and Gianni Festa, 163–76. Florence: Nerbini.

Grubb, James S. 2000. "Elite Citizens." In Martin and Romano 2000, 339–64.

Hairston, Julia L. 2003. "Out of the Archive: Four Newly-Identified Figures in Tullia d'Aragona's *Rime della Signora Tullia di Aragona et di diversi a lei (1547)." MLN* 118 (1): 257–63.

Hanlon, Gregory. 2000. *Early Modern Italy, 1550–1800: Three Seasons in European History.* London: Palgrave.

Harness, Kelley. 2006. *Echoes of Women's Voices: Music, Art, and Female Patronage in Early Modern Florence.* Chicago: University of Chicago Press.

Harrán, Don. 2009. Introduction. In Copio 2009, 1–90.

Haskins, Susan. 1993. *Mary Magdalen: Myth and Metaphor.* London: Harper Collins.

———. 2008. Introduction. In Colonna, Matraini, and Marinella 2008, 1–42.

Hay, Denys, and John E. Law. 1989. *Italy in the Age of the Renaissance, 1380–1530.* New York: Longman.

Henke, Robert. 2002. *Performance and Literature in the Commedia dell'Arte.* Cambridge: Cambridge University Press.

Insana, Lina. 2005. "Fascist Appropriations: The Case of Jolanda de Blasi's *Le scrittrici italiane.*" In Benson and Kirkham 2005, 314–40.

Jacobs, Frederika H. 1997. *Defining the Renaissance "Virtuosa": Women Artists and the Language of Art History and Criticism.* Cambridge: Cambridge University Press.

James, Sharon L. 2003. *Learned Girls and Male Persuasion: Gender and Reading in Roman Love Elegy.* Berkeley: University of California Press.

Jones, Ann Rosalind. 1990. *The Currency of Eros: Women's Love Lyric in Europe, 1540–1620.* Bloomington: Indiana University Press.

———. 2005. "Bad Press: Modern Editors versus Early Modern Women Poets (Tullia d'Aragona, Gaspara Stampa, Veronica Franco)." In Benson and Kirkham 2005, 287–313.

Jordan, Constance. 1990. *Renaissance Feminism. Literary Texts and Political Models.* Ithaca, NY: Cornell University Press.

Kirkham, Victoria. 1996. "Laura Battiferri's *First Book* of Poetry: A Renaissance Holograph Comes Out of Hiding." *Rinascimento* 36:351–91.

———. 1998. "Dante's Phantom, Petrarch's Specter: Bronzino's Portrait of the Poet Laura Battiferra." In *Visibile Parlare: Dante and the Art of the Italian Renaissance,* edited by Deborah Parker; special issue of *Lectura Dantis* 22–23: 63–139.

———. 2005. "Sappho on the Arno: The Brief Fame of Laura Battiferra." In Benson and Kirkham 2005, 176–98.

Laven, Mary. 2006. "Encountering the Counter-Reformation." *Renaissance Quarterly* 59 (3): 706–20.

Leone, Giuseppe. 1962. "Per lo studio della letteratura femminile del Cinquecento." *Convivium* n.s. 30:293–300.

Lowe, K. J. P. 2003. *Nuns' Chronicles and Convent Culture in Renaissance and Counter-Reformation Italy*. Cambridge: Cambridge University Press.

Maclean, Ian. 1980. *The Renaissance Notion of Woman: A Study in the Fortunes of Scholasticism and Medical Science in European Intellectual Life*. Cambridge: Cambridge University Press.

MacNeil, Anne. 2003. *Music and Women of the Commedia dell'arte*. Oxford: Oxford University Press.

————. 2005. Introduction. In Andreini 2005, 1–21.

Maggi, Armando. 2008. "Francesco d'Assisi e le stimmate alla luce del Barocco: *Sette canzoni di sette famosi autori* (1606) e *Rime spirituali di diversi autori* (1606) raccolte da F. Silvestro da Poppi minore osservante." *Studi secenteschi* 49:79–130.

Maroi, Lina. 1913. *Laura Terracina: poetessa napoletana del secolo XVI*. Naples: Francesco Perrella.

Martin, John Jeffries, and Dennis Romano, eds. 2000. *Venice Reconsidered: The History and Civilization of an Italian City State, 1297–1797*. Baltimore: Johns Hopkins University Press.

Milani, Marisa, ed. 1983. "Quattro donne fra i pavani." *Museum patavinum* 1 (2): 387–412.

Milligan, Gerry. 2010. "Proving Masculinity before God and Women: Laura Terracina and Chiara Matraini Writing War in the Renaissance." In *The Poetics of Masculinity in Early Modern Italy and Spain*, edited by Gerry Milligan and Jane Tylus, 185–212. Toronto: Center for Reformation and Renaissance Studies.

Monson, Craig. 1995. *Disembodied Voices: Music and Culture in an Early Modern Italian Convent*. Berkeley: University of California Press.

Morsolin, Bernardo. 1882. *Maddalena Campiglia, poetessa vicentina: episodio biografico*. Vicenza: Paroni.

Moss, Ann. 1986. "The Counter-Reformation Latin Hymn." *Acta conventus neo-latini sanctandreani* 38:371–78.

Mullett, Michael A. 1999. *The Catholic Reformation*. London: Routledge.

Nelson, Jonathan K., ed. 2008. *Plautilla Nelli (1524–88): The Painter-Prioress of Renaissance Florence*. Florence: Syracuse University Press.

Newcomb, Anthony. 1986. "Courtesans, Muses, or Musicians? Professional Women Musicians in Sixteenth-Century Italy." In Bowers and Tick 1986, 90–115.

Nicholson, Eric. 1999. "Romance as Role Model: Early Female Performances of *Orlando Furioso* and *Gerusalemme Liberata*." In *Renaissance Transactions: Ariosto and Tasso*, edited by Valeria Finucci, 246–69. Durham, NC: Duke University Press.

Østermark-Johansen, Lene. 1999. "The Matchless Beauty of Widowhood: Vittoria Colonna's Reputation in Nineteenth-Century England." *Art History* 22 (2): 270–94.

Pacchioni, Guglielmo. 1907. *Un codice inedito della Biblioteca Estense: un poeta ed una poetessa petrarchisti del secolo XV (complemento ad una notizia incerta data dal Tiraboschi)*. Modena: Cooperativa Tipografica.

Panizza, Letizia, ed. 2000. *Women in Italian Renaissance Culture and Society*. Oxford: European Humanities Research Centre.

Parisotto, Edoardo. 2009. *La venerabile Battista Vernazza*. Genova: De Ferrari.

Parker, Deborah. 2000. *Bronzino: Renaissance Painter as Poet*. Cambridge: Cambridge University Press.

Parker, Holt. 2002. "Angela Nogarola (c. 1400) and Isotta Nogarola (1418–66): Thieves of Language." In Brown, Churchill, and Jeffrey 2002, 11–30.

Pasqualigo, Cristoforo. 1908. *La lingua rustica padovana nei due poeti G. B. Maganza e Domenico Pittarini: con cenni su alcuni dialetti morti e vivi e proverbi veneti*. Verona: Libreria Dante di R. Cabianca.

Pelikan, Jaroslav. 1996. *Mary through the Centuries: Her Place in the History of Culture*. New Haven, CT: Yale University Press.

Phillippy, Patricia. 1992. "'Altera Dido': The Model of Ovid's *Heroides* in the Poems of Gaspara Stampa and Veronica Franco." *Italica* 69 (1): 1–18.

Piastra, Clelia Maria, ed. 2002. *La poesia mariologica dell'umanesimo latino: testi e versione italiana a fronte*. Preface by Claudio Leonardi. Tavernuzze, Florence: Edizioni del Galluzzo.

Piatti, Angelo Alberto. 2007. "'E l'uom pietà da Dio, piangendo, impari.' Lacrime e pianto nelle rime sacre nell'età del Tasso." In *Rime sacre tra Cinquecento e Seicento*, edited by Maria Luisa Doglio and Carlo Delcorno, 53–106. Bologna: Il Mulino.

Piéjus, Marie-Françoise. 1982. "La première anthologie de poèmes féminins: l'écriture filtrée et orientée." In *Le pouvoir et la plume: Incitation, controle, et répression dans l'Italie du XVIe siècle*, 193–213. Paris: Centre Interuniversitaire de Recherche sur la Renaissance Italienne.

Piscini, Angela. 1991. "Domenichi, Ludovico." *Dizionario biografico degli italiani* 40: 595–600.

Plazzotta, Carol. 1998. "Bronzino's Laura." *Burlington Magazine* 140–41: 251–63.

Pomata, Gianna, and Gabriella Zarri, eds. 2005. *I monasteri femminili come centri di cultura fra Rinascimento e Barocco*. Rome: Edizioni di Storia e Letteratura.

Quondam, Amedeo. 1974. *Petrarchismo mediato: per una critica della forma "antologia."* Rome: Bulzoni.

Rabitti, Giovanna. 1985. "Inediti vaticani di Chiara Matraini". In *Studi di filologia e critica offerti dagli allievi a Lanfranco Caretti*, 1:225–50. Rome: Salerno.

Ravasini, Ines. 2003. "Las *Stancias de Rugier nuevamente glosadas* de Alonso Nuñez de Reinoso: una glosa ariostesca de origen italiano." *Rivista di Filologia e Letterature Ispaniche* 6:65–86.

Ray, Meredith, and Lynn Westwater. 2005. "Introduzione." In Arcangela Tarabotti, *Lettere familiari e di complimento*, edited by Meredith Ray and Lynn Westwater, introduction by Gabrielle Zarri, 25–39. Turin: Rosenberg & Sellier.

Re, Lucia. 2000. "Futurism and Fascism, 1914–1945". In *A History of Women's Writing in Italy*, edited by Letizia Panizza and Sharon Wood, 190–204. Cambridge: Cambridge University Press.

Rebhorn, Wayne A. 1978. *Courtly Performances: Masking and Festivity in Castiglione's "Book of the Courtier."* Detroit: Wayne State University Press.

Richardson, Brian. 2009. *Manuscript Culture in Renaissance Italy*. Cambridge: Cambridge University Press.

Riley, Joanne Marie. 1988. "Tarquinia Molza (1542–1617): A Case Study of Women, Music, and Society in the Renaissance." In *The Musical Woman: An International Perspective*, edited by Judith Lang Zaimont, 470–93. New York: Greenwood Press.

Robin, Diana. 2007. *Publishing Women: Salons, the Presses, and the Counter-Reformation in Sixteenth-Century Italy*. Chicago: University of Chicago Press.

Rogers, Mary. 2000. "Fashioning Identities for the Renaissance Courtesan." In *Fashioning Identities in Renaissance Art*, edited by Mary Rogers, 91–105. Aldershot, UK: Ashgate.

Rosenthal, Margaret F. 1992. *The Honest Courtesan: Veronica Franco, Citizen and Writer in Sixteenth-Century Venice*. Chicago: University of Chicago Press.

Ross, Sarah Gwyneth. 2009. *The Birth of Feminism: Woman as Intellect in Renaissance Italy and England.* Cambridge, MA: Harvard University Press.

Rossi, Vittorio. 1890. "Di una rimatrice e di un rimatore del secolo XV: Girolama Corsi Ramos e Jacopo Corsi." *Giornale storico della letteratura italiana* 15:183–215.

Rozzo, Ugo. 1982. "Un personaggio bandelliano: la poetessa Camilla Scarampa." In *Matteo Bandello, novelliere europeo,* edited by Ugo Rozzo, 419–37. Tortona: Cassa di Risparmio di Tortona.

Russell, Rinaldina. 2000. "Vittoria Colonna's Sonnets on the Virgin Mary." In *Maria Vergine nella letteratura italiana,* edited by Florinda M. Iannace, 125–37. Stony Brook, NY: Forum Italicum.

Sabbadini, Remigio. 1911. "Versi latini di Gian Nicola Salerno." *Giornale storico della letteratura italiana* 58: 358–66.

Saccone, Eduardo. 1983. "*Grazia, sprezzatura, affettazione* in the *Courtier.*" In *Castiglione: The Real and the Ideal in Renaissance Culture,* edited by Robert W. Hanning and David Rosand, 45–67. New Haven, CT: Yale University Press.

Salzberg, Rosa. 2010. "In the Mouth of Charlatans: Street Performers and the Dissemination of Pamphlets in Renaissance Italy." *Renaissance Studies* 24 (5): 638–53.

Sampson, Lisa. 2006. *Pastoral Drama in Early Modern Italy: The Making of a New Genre.* Oxford: Legenda.

Santore, Cathy. 1988. "Julia Lombardo, 'Somtuosa Meretrize': A Portrait by Property." *Renaissance Quarterly* 41 (1): 44–83.

Schiesari, Juliana. 1994. "Isabella di Morra (c. 1520–1545)." In *Italian Women Writers: A Bio-bibliographical Sourcebook,* edited by Rinaldina Russell, 279–85. Westport, CT: Greenwood Press, 1994.

Shemek, Deanna. 1998. *Ladies Errant: Wayward Women and Social Order in Early Modern Italy.* Durham, NC: Duke University Press.

———. 2005. "The Collector's Cabinet: Lodovico Domenichi's Gallery of Women." In Benson and Kirkham 2005, 239–62.

Smarr, Janet Levarie. 1991. "Gaspara Stampa's Poetry for Performance." *Journal of the Rocky Mountain Medieval and Renaissance Association* 12: 61–84.

Smith, Alison A. 2008. "Women and Political Sociability in Late Renaissance Verona: Ersilia Spolverini's *Elogio* of Chiara Cornaro." In *Donne di potere del Rinascimento,* edited by Letizia Arcangeli and Susanna Peyronel, 405–15. Rome: Viella.

Spiriti, Salvatore. 1750. *Memorie degli scrittori cosentini.* Naples: Stamperia de' Muzi.

Stampino, Maria Galli. 2009. "A Singular Venetian Epic Poem." In Marinella 2009, 1–66.

Stevenson, Jane. 2002. "Conventual Life in Renaissance Italy: The Latin Poetry of Suor Laurentia Strozzi (1514–1591)." In Brown, Churchill, and Jeffrey 2002, 3:109–31.

———. 2005. *Women Latin Poets: Language, Gender, and Authority, from Antiquity to the Eighteenth Century.* Oxford: Oxford University Press.

Torrioli, Igea. 1940. "Francesca Turina Bufalini e la società colta tifernate nel sec. XVI." *L'Alta Valle del Tevere* 8:1–36.

Toscano, Tobia R. 2000. *Letterati corti accademie. La letteratura a Napoli nella prima metà del Cinquecento.* Naples: Loffredo.

Tylus, Jane. 2010. Introduction to Stampa 2010, 1–45.

Vecce, Carlo. 1993. "Vittoria Colonna: il codice epistolare della poesia femminile." *Critica letteraria* 21 (78): 3–34.

Vela, Claudio. 1989. "Poesia in musica: rime della Gambara e di altri poeti settentrionali in tradizione musicale." In Bozzetti, Gibellini, and Sandal 1989, 399–414.

Verdile, Nadia. 1989–90. "Contributi alla biografia di Margherita Sarrocchi." *Rendiconti dell'Accademia di Archeologia, Lettere e Belle Arti di Napoli* 61:165–206.

Volpi, Mirko. 2005. "Bernardino Baldi lirico." In *Bernardino Baldi (1553–1617), studioso rinascimentale: poesia, storia, linguistica, meccanica, architettura*, edited by Elio Nenci, 25–53. Milan: Franco Angeli.

Warner, Marina. 1976. *Alone of All Her Sex: The Myth and the Cult of the Virgin Mary*. London: Weidenfeld & Nicolson.

Weaver, Elissa B. 2002. *Convent Theater in Early Modern Italy: Spiritual Fun and Learning for Women*. Cambridge: Cambridge University Press.

———, ed. 2009. *Scenes from Italian Convent Life: An Anthology of Convent Theatrical Texts and Contexts*. Ravenna: Longo.

Wiesner, Merry. 2008. *Women and Gender in Early Modern Europe*. 3rd ed. Cambridge: Cambridge University Press.

Woodhouse, John R. 1978. *Baldesar Castiglione: A Reassessment of "The Courtier."* Edinburgh: Edinburgh University Press.

Zaja, Paolo. 2009. "'Perch'arda meco del tuo amore il mondo': Lettura delle *Rime spirituali* di Gabriele Fiamma." In *Poetica e retorica del sacro tra Cinque e Seicento*, edited by Erminia Ardissino and Elisabetta Selmi, 235–92. Alessandria: Edizioni dell'Orso.

Zancan, Marina. 2012. "Quadri rinascimentali. Interferenze delle prospettive di genere nella tradizione storico-letteraria." In *Verso una storia di genere della letteratura italiana. Percorsi critici e gender studies*, edited by Virginia Cox and Chiara Ferrari, 103–19. Bologna: Il Mulino.

Index

Cicero, 19, 341

Ciceronianism, 19

Cino da Pistoia, 20

circumcision of Christ, 229–31

Città di Castello, 380, 400

classical language and imagery, use of, in
Christian contexts, 214, 217, 230, 233, 237

classical mythology. *See individual
classical figures*

Claudian (Claudius Claudianus), 363

Clement VIII (pope; Ippolito Aldobran-
dini), 324–25, 400

Clio (mythological figure), 184, 381

Clothilde (queen of the Franks), 302

Clovis I (king of the Franks), 302

Coccapanni, Cesare, 335

Coderta, Giovanni Battista, 344, 350–51, 398

Cognati, Imperia, 14

Colao, Lucia, 39, 44, 66n106, 393; poems
by, 226–27, 348

Collalto, Antonio Rambaldo da, 40

Collalto, Collaltino da, 33–34, 40, 92–107,
399

Collalto, Silvestra, 36, 393; poem by, 381

Colle di Val d'Elsa, 325

Colonna, Ascanio, 310

Colonna, Fabrizio, 77, 393

Colonna, Vittoria, 6, 23–25, 46–47, 152–53,
210–11; and *capitolo* form, 17, 80, 87;
family background and social status of,
12, 393; as love poet, 32–33, 134–47, 150,
155; metrical choices of, 17, 30, 415, 417;
as model for imitation, 32, 114, 419;
poems by, 77–82, 134–47, 192–202, 268–70,
273–74, 310, 340; reception / critical
fortunes of, 24, 31, 38–44, 66n124,
67nn127–28; as religious poet, 8, 10,
30–31, 192–202; and religious reform, 8,
22, 193; stylistic qualities of, 27–28, 155,
194; textual issues connected with,
56–58, 67n139, 145, 308; tributes to, 150,
155, 268–70, 273–74

Colonna family, 155, 400

comic verse, 37–38, 49, 51, 383–90

Commedia (Alighieri), 23, 49, 261;
imitations of, listed, 418

composers, 75, 108, 161, 172, 201, 396;
female, 4–5

concatenatio, 48

conceits (literary term), 29, 64n76;
examples of, 137, 151, 213, 262, 343; in
Fonte, 173, 290; in Sbarra, 185–86

concorso di vocali, 97, 110, 175, 177, 289, 325;
in Colonna, 140, 192; defined, 421

Conegliano, 393, 398

congedo (poetic term), 48, 50–51, 135, 192,
280; defined, 421; examples of, 114–15,
224, 247–48, 303, 325

consonance, 421; examples of, 73, 241, 276,
278, 285, 325, 328

Constantine (Roman emperor), 326

Contini, Gianfranco, 23

contrafacta, 46, 190, 393, 421; examples of,
226–27, 241, 348

convents, 9, 11. *See also* nuns

Copio, Sarra, 5, 15, 36, 44, 63n43, 393; poem
by, 337

Coreglia, Isabetta, 36

Cornaro, Giovanni, 297

Cornaro, Luigi, 297–98

Cornelia, wife of Pompey, 82

Correggio, 6, 368, 395

correspondence verse, 22, 25–26, 45,
268–85; rhyme in, 54, 269, 274, 280, 285,
422–23. *See also* epistolary verse

Corsi, Girolama, 6, 16–17, 38, 60, 393;
poems by, 72, 305–6, 383–86

Cosenza, 394

Cossé, Charles de, 317

Costa, Margherita, 36

Counter-Reformation, 7–9, 14–15, 217;
cultural/literary influences of, 8, 27,
30–32, 119, 196, 243, 280

court, papal, 13, 18, 316

courtesans, 13–15, 24, 41. *See also*
d'Aragona, Tullia; Franco, Veronica;
Salutati, Barbara

courts, princely, 11–12, 16, 20–23. *See also*
Ferrara; Mantua; Urbino

critical history. *See* reception and critical
history

Croce, Benedetto, 41, 66n117

crucifixion. *See* Passion of Christ

crusade, as theme, 7, 308, 319–26

Cupid (or Eros), god of Love, 106, 175, 184,
227, 278, 329